The Valley
of the
Shadow of Death

by

J. Alwyn Phillips. DFM

Air Research Publications

First published 1992 by
Air Research Publications
34 Elm Road, New Malden,
Surrey, KT3 3HD,
England.

Printed in Great Britain by
Antony Rowe Ltd,
Chippenham, Wiltshire.

ISBN 1 871187 13 3

The Valley
of the
Shadow of Death

An account of the Royal Air Force Bomber Command
night bombing and minelaying operations including
'The Battle of the Ruhr'
March 5th/6th to July 18th/19th, 1943.

By

J. Alwyn Phillips
DFM

Ex Flight Lieutenant Royal Air Force No. 405 (RCAF) Squadron,
Pathfinder Force 78 Squadron, 4 Group

Dedication

All Bomber Aircrew who survived one or more operational flying tours in World War II have some extraordinary story of luck, fate or chance to relate. These experiences are mostly known to only a few, for they have never been written down, as many aircrew tend to keep these experiences to themselves. But now as forty or more years have elapsed since the end of World War II, there is a growing awareness that unless these stories are recorded the sands of time will run out and these reminiscences will be lost forever.

The following is an account of Bomber Command's battle over targets in the Ruhr and other targets in Germany and the Occupied Countries from March 5th to July 19th, 1943. It is an attempt to record operations and the successes and failures encountered by the many aircrew who took part in these raids.

This book is dedicated to the memory of those aircrew who never made it back to their home bases.

Night Bombers

Eastwards they climb
Black shapes against the grey of falling dusk,
Gone from the nodding day
From English fields,
Not theirs the sudden glow of triumph
That their fighter brothers knew,
Only to fly through cloud
Through storm, through night
Unerring, to keep
Their purposes bright,
Nor turn until
Their dreadful duty done,
Westward they fly
To race the awakened sun.

Anonymous.

Acknowledgements

My sincere thanks to the following who were extremely helpful in answering my queries.

Bent Anthonisen (Denmark). Joe Ayres (Leeds). George Barclay (Edinburgh). H.E.Batchelder DFM (Olney). F.C.Blair DFM (Southwaite). Mrs.S.Boyle (Canterbury). Fred Brown (Watford). Fred Brown (Australia). Jim Carrie (Penrith). Peter Celis (Belgium). L.Chick (Australia). Roy Child (Meifiod,Powys). Bill Chorley (Salisbury). G.E.Clay (Poynton). Jacques De Vos (Belgium). Bernard Dolny (Peterborough). H.Elford (Chandlers Ford). Vince Elmer (Canada). Alex Flett (Norwich). W.G.Horner (Bedford). Hughie Huston (Canada). Mrs.B.Jones (Hirwaun). Bert Lancashire (Darwen). Harry Learey (Hull). S/Ldr D.Leicester DFC* (Australia). Neil Lindsay (Australia). Jim McDonald (Hanworth). Norman Mackie (Oxted). Arthur Minnitt (Nottingham). Peter Monasso (Holland). Reg Newdick (Bexhill). Hans Onderwater (Holland). Carsten Petersen (Holland). Stan Reed (Birchington). Jean Louis Roba (Belgium). Eileen Robinson (Caterpillar Club). J.A.Rossbottom (Heswall). A.Simpson (Ruislip). Dr.H.Stapert (Holland). Peter Stead DFC (Ellesmere). George Stewart (Birkenhead). Geoff Thompson (Wolverhampton). A.R.Tod (Canada). Ron Waite (Weymouth). Roy Wilkinson (Bury). Dave Williams (St Leonards). Eric Wright (Leicester).

To the following for their valuable help in allowing me the use of their records and reference facilities. Staff of the Public Record Office (Kew). Staff of the Air Historical Branch, Ministry of Defence (London). Staff of the Kingston upon Hull Reference Library. Staff of the Sikorski Museum and Polish Institute (London). Commonwealth War Graves Commission (Maidenhead).

Last but not least to my wife, Mabel, for being so patient in putting up with many years of my burning the midnight oil when researching this book.

Bibliography

THE STIRLING BOMBER - BOWYER M.J.F. Faber & Faber
PATHFINDERS AT WAR - BOWYER CHAZ Ian Allan
HALIFAX - MERRICK K.A. Ian Allan
THE HALIFAX FILE - ROBERTS R.N. Air Britain
MOST SECRET WAR - JONES R.V. Hamish Hamilton
LANCASTER - STORY OF A FAMOUS BOMBER - ROBERT-
SON Harleyford
CONFOUND AND DESTROY - STREETLY M. Macdonald &
Janes
No.5 BOMBER GROUP R.A.F. - LAWERENCE W.J. Faber &
Faber
No. 2 GROUP - BOWYER M.J.F. Faber & Faber
PATHFINDER FORCE - MUSGROVE G. Macdonald & Jane
44 (RHODESIA) SQUADRON - WHITE A.N. White
THE BOMBER OFFENSIVE AGAINST GERMANY - FRANK-
LAND N. Faber & Faber
THE STIRLING FILE - GOMERSALL B. Air Britain
MOSQUITO - BOWYER & SHARP Faber & Faber
THE LUFTWAFFE WAR DIARIES - BEKKER C. Macdonald
BATTLE OVER THE REICH - PRICE A. Macdonald
THE STRATEGIC AIR OFFENSIVE AGAINST GERMANY
(1939/45) - WEBSTER & FRANKLAND H.M.S.O.
THE LOST COMMAND - REVIE A. Military Book Society
BOMBER COMMAND WAR DIARIES - MIDDLEBROOK M.
Penguin

Contents

Bomber Command
Order of Battle

On March 5th/6th, 1943
Commander in Chief :- Air Chief Marshal Sir Arthur Harris.
Deputy Commander :- Air Marshal Sir Robert Saundby.

No.1 Group :- Air Vice Marshal E. A. B. Rice.
Headquarters :- Bawtry Hall, Bawtry, Yorkshire

Sqn.	Airfield	Aircraft	Strength
12	Wickenby	Lancaster	19
100	Grimsby(Waltham)	Lancaster	19
101	Holme on Spalding Moor	Lancaster	20
103	Elsham Wolds	Lancaster	18
460 (R.A.A.F.)	Breighton	Lancaster	18
166	Kirmington	Wellington	22
199	Ingham	Wellington	12
300 (Polish)	Hemswell	Wellington	14
301 (Polish)	Hemswell	Wellington	12
305 (Polish)	Hemswell	Wellington	11

No.2 Group :- Air Vice Marshal J. H. D'Albiac.
Headquarters :- Castelwood House, Huntington, Huntington-shire.

Sqn.	Airfield	Aircraft	Strength
88	Oulton	Boston	14
107	Great Massingham	Boston	5
226	Swanton Morley	Boston	14
105	Marham	Mosquito	16
139	Marham	Mosquito	19
		Blenheim	4
21	Methwold	Ventura	19
464 (R.A.A.F.)	Feltwell	Ventura	18
487 (R.N.Z.A.F)	Feltwell	Ventura	17
98	Foulsham	Mitchell	19
180	Foulsham	Mitchell	19

No.3 Group :- Air Vice Marshal R. Harrison.

Headquarters :- Exning, Suffolk.

Sqn.	Airfield	Aircraft	Strength
15	Bourn	Stirling	19
75	Newmarket	Stirling	19
90	Ridgewell	Stirling	19
149	Lakenheath	Stirling	19
214	Chedbergh	Stirling	19
218	Downham Market	Stirling	19
115	East Wretham	Lancaster	19
		Wellington	1
138 (Special Duty)Tempsford		Halifax	13
161 (Special Duty)Tempsford		Halifax	5
		Lysander	8
		Havoc	2
		Albermarle	2
192 (Special Duty)			
	Gransden Lodge	Halifax	2
		Wellington	10
		Mosquito	4

No.4 Group :- Air Vice Marshal C. R. Carr.

Headquarters :- Heslington Hall, York, Yorkshire.

Sqn.	Airfield	Aircraft	Strength
10	Melbourne	Halifax	22
51	Snaith	Halifax	22
76	Linton upon Ouse	Halifax	17
77	Elvington	Halifax	18
78	Linton upon Ouse	Halifax	18
102	Pocklington	Halifax	18
158	Rufforth	Halifax	23
196	Leconfield	Wellington	17
429 (R.C.A.F.)East Moor		Wellington	14
431 (R.C.A.F.)Burn		Wellington	20
466 (R.A.A.F.)Leconfield		Wellington	20

11

No.5 Group :- Air Vice Marshal The Hon. R. C. Cochrane.
Headquarters :-'St.Vincents', Grantham, Lincolnshire.

Sqn.	Airfield	Aircraft	Strength
9	Waddington	Lancaster	19
44	Waddington	Lancaster	17
49	Fiskerton	Lancaster	18
50	Skellingthorpe	Lancaster	16
57	Scampton	Lancaster	17
61	Syerston	Lancaster	18
97	Woodhall Spa	Lancaster	20
106	Syerston	Lancaster	17
207	Langer	Lancaster	18
467 (R.A.A.F.)	Bottesford	Lancaster	18

No.6 Group :- Air Vice Marshal G. E. Brookes.
Headquarters :- Allerton Park, Allerton, Yorkshire.

Sqn.	Airfield	Aircraft	Strength
405 (R.C.A.F.)	Topcliffe	Halifax	21
408 (R.C.A.F.)	Leeming	Halifax	18
419 (R.C.A.F.)	Middleton St.Gge	Halifax	18
420 (R.C.A.F.)	Middleton St.Gge	Wellington	18
424 (R.C.A.F.)	Topcliffe	Wellington	18
425 (R.C.A.F.)	Dishforth	Wellington	17
426 (R.C.A.F.)	Dishforth	Wellington	19
427 (R.C.A.F.)	Croft	Wellington	15
428 (R.C.A.F.)	Dalton	Wellington	18

No.8 Group :- Air Commodore D. C. T. Bennett.
Headquarters :-Wyton, Huntingtonshire.

Sqn.	Airfield	Aircraft	Strength
7	Oakington	Stirling	23
35	Graveley	Halifax	24
83	Wyton	Lancaster	18
156	Warboys	Lancaster	18
109	Wyton	Mosquito	22

Battle of the Ruhr

Bomber Command squadrons on night operations
(March 5th/6th to July 18th/19th, 1943)

Squadron	Letter	Group	Base	Aircraft
7	MG	8	Oakington	Stirling
9	WS	5	Waddington	Lancaster
	wef April 43		Bardney	
10	ZA	4	Melbourne	Halifax
12	PH	1	Wickenby	Lancaster
15	LS	3	Bourn	Stirling
	wef 14/4/43		Mildenhall	
35	TL	8	Graveley	Halifax
(Madras Presidency)				
44	KM	5	Waddington	Lancaster
(Rhodesia) wef May 43			Dunholm Lodge	
49	EA	5	Fiskerton	Lancaster
50	VN	5	Skellingthorpe	Lancaster
51	MH	4	Snaith	Halifax
57	DX	5	Scampton	Lancaster
61	QR	5	Syerston	Lancaster
75	AA	3	Newmarket	Stirling
(New Zealand) wef 29/6/43			Mepal	
76	MP	4	Linton upon Ouse	Halifax
	wef June 43		Holme on Spalding Moor	
77	KN	4	Elvington	Halifax
78	EY	4	Linton upon Ouse	Halifax
	wef 16/6/43		Breighton	
83	OL	8	Wyton	Lancaster
90	WP	3	Ridgewell	Stirling
	wef 31/5/43		West Wickham	
97	OF	5	Woodhall Spa	Lancaster
(Straits Settlement) wef April 43 Bourn				
100	HW	1	Grimsby (Waltham)	Lancaster
101	SR	1	Holme on Spalding Moor	Lancaster
	wef June 43		Ludford Magna	
102	DY	4	Pocklington	Halifax
(Ceylon)				
103	PM	1	Elsham Wolds	Lancaster
105	GB	8	Marham	Mosquito
106	ZN	5	Syerston	Lancaster
109	HS	8	Wyton	Mosquito
115	KO	3	East Wretham	Lancaster
138	NF	3	Tempsford	Various (Special Duties)

13

139	XD	2	Marham	Mosquito
(Jamaica)		8-wefJune43		
149	OJ	3	Lakenheath	Stirling
156	GT	8	Warboys	Lancaster
158	NP	4	Lissett	Halifax
166	AS	1	Kirmington	Wellington
196	ZO	4	Leconfield	Wellington
wefJuly43		3	Witchford	Stirling
199	EX	1	Ingham	Wellington
wefJune43		3	Lakenheath	Stirling
207	EM	5	Langar	Lancaster
214	BU	3	Chedburgh	Stirling
(FederatedMalayStates)				
218	HA	3	DownhamMkt	Stirling
(GoldmCoast)				
300(Polish)BH		1	Hemswell	Wellington
(Masovian)WefJune43			Ingham	
301(Polish)GR		1	Hemswell	Wellington
(Pomeranian)				
305(Polish)SM		1	Hemswell	Wellington
(ZiemaWielkoplska)				
wefJune43			Ingham	
405(R.C.A.F)LQ		6	Leeming	Halifax
(Vancouver)				
wef17/4/43		8	GransdenLge	Halifax
408(R.C.A.F)EQ		6	Leeming	Halifax
(Goose)				
419(R.C.A.F)VR		6	MiddletonStGge	Halifax
(Moose)				
420(R.C.A.F)PT		6	MiddletonStGg	Wellington
(SnowyOwl)				
424(R.C.A.F)QB		6	Topcliffe	Wellington
(Tiger)	wefApril43		Leeming	
	wefMay43		Dalton	
425(R.C.A.F)KW		6	Dishforth	Wellington
(Alouette)				
426(R.C.A.F)KW		6	Dishforth	Wellington
(Thunderbird)				
wefJune43			LintononOuse	Lancaster
427(R.C.A.F)ZL		6	Croft	Wellington
(Lion)	wefJune43		Leeming	Halifax
428(R.C.A.F)NA		6	Dalton	Wellington
(Ghost)	wefJune43		MiddletonStG	Halifax
429(R.C.A.F)AL		4	EastMoor	Wellington
(Bison)		6-wefApril43		
431(R.C.A.F)SE		6	Burn	Wellington
(Iroquois)	wef14/7/43		Tholthorpe	Halifax

432(R.C.A.F)QO	6	Skipton on Swale	Wellington
(Leaside)			
434(R.C.A.F)IP	6	Tholthorpe	Halifax
(Bluenose)			
460(R.A.A.F.)UV	1	Breighton	Lancaster
wef 14/5/43		Binbrook	
466(RAAF)HD	4	Leconfield	Wellington
467(RAAF)PO	5	Bottesford	Lancaster
617 AJ			
wef May 43	5	Scampton	Lancaster
619 PG			
wef 18/4/43	5	Woodhall Spa	Lancaster
620 QS			
wef 17/5/43	3	Chedburgh	Stirling

Introduction

During the period from March 5th to July 19th, 1943, fifty-one major raids were mounted by RAF Bomber Command. Thirty-one of these were on the Ruhr and the remainder spread from Stettin in the North bordering the Baltic Sea, south to Munich in the Southern Bavaria area of Germany, Turin in Northern Italy and East as far as Pilsen in Czechoslovakia. Bomber Command never concentrated on one region, although the bombing concept developed at this time was one of concentration. To bomb one target until it was completely destroyed by the bombers would allow the German defences to focus their fighters and *Flak* guns in that one area and so minimise the number of bombers getting through to their target.

Flexibility of target selection was essential. Sir Arthur Harris, Commander in Chief of Bomber Command had nurtured his bombing force up to this time, slowly building up its striking power. He had at his disposal in March 1943 an effective operational strength of 37 heavy four engined bomber squadrons and 16 twin engined bomber squadrons giving an approximate first line strength of 690 heavy and 250 medium aircraft. As he stated at that time and with the new RDF aids, "At long last we are ready and equipped. Bomber Command's main offensive and task is to destroy the main cities of the Ruhr." By May 1943, at the height of the Ruhr Battle, this squadron strength had increased to over 1,000 aircraft,the majority being four engined aircraft. This certainly showed the great efforts that were made in Britain's wartime aircraft industry in building up such large numbers of aircraft in the production lines and was a significant difference to May, 1942, when the first 1,000 bomber force was formed to bomb Cologne. In this raid the majority of aircraft were twin engined Wellington bombers and some of the aircraft in that force were training bombers crewed by men from Operational Training Units and not by front line experienced operational squadrons' crews.

On January 21st, 1943, the Casablanca directive for the Bomber Offensive from the United Kingdom was drawn up by the Combined Chiefs of Staff and approved by Churchill and Roosevelt. The directive was addressed to the British and U.S.

Army Air Force Commanders, Harris and General Ira C. Eaker. It was classed as the most important Allied Air Order of the War. It stated :

"Your Primary object will be the progressive destruction and dislocation of the German military, industrial and economic system and the undermining of the morale of the German people to the point where their capacity for armed resistance is fatally weakened. Within that general concept your primary objective, subject to the exigencies of weather and of tactical feasibility will for the present be in the following order.

a. German Submarine construction yards.

b. German aircraft industries.

c. Transportation.

d. Oil Plants.

e. Other targets in the enemy war industry.

The above order of priority may be varied from time to time according to developments in the strategic situation. Moreover other objectives of great importance either from the political or military point of view must be attacked."

This directive was very much to Harris's liking and reflected many of the recommendations that he had made to the Chief of the Air Staff in 1942, when he had fought to expand Bomber Command to a strength that could be decisive in the War. He felt, however, that the directive was more a statement of policy than of an actual detailed direction of the way that the bomber force should be used. He felt it was open to a certain amount of interpretation, and this is how he fought the Battle of the Ruhr. In early 1943 the military situation for Germany was beginning to worsen, with reverses in North Africa and the Western Desert, defeat in Stalingrad and the beginning of the Soviet Offensives. The time had come for a major bomber offensive, which would help to stop Germany renewing its onslaught by seriously weakening its industrial capacity.

17

Pathfinder Force

During the build up of the bomber strength in the squadrons, Harris had also experimented with new tactics such as the introduction of a Pathfinding Force. On August 15th, 1942, the PFF was established with its headquarters initially at RAF Wyton in Huntingtonshire and comprised of four units. These were 7 Squadron, formerly with 3 Group flying Stirling aircraft and based at Oakington, 35 Squadron flying Halifaxes at Graveley and formerly attached to 4 Group, 83 Squadron flying Lancasters at Wyton and formerly from Scampton in 5 Group and 156 Squadron at Warboys equipped with Wellington aircraft, later equipped with Lancasters. A fifth unit on temporary loan from 2 Group was 109 Squadron with Mosquito aircraft and they were also based at the Wyton HQ. At its initial conception PFF (Pathfinder Force) came under the aegis of No.3 Group Bomber Command for all its administrative needs but it was directly answerable to AOC-in-C Harris. This new force was led by a comparatively young Wing Commander, aged 32, who even at this time was well qualified for the important rôle having had experience as an operational bomber pilot. He had previously been in command of two operational bomber squadrons, No. 77 and No. 10 Squadrons, and was also a navigation expert with pre-war flying experience with BOAC flying boats. In picking the Australian Wing Commander Donald Bennett, who was later promoted to Group Captain on being appointed leader of the new force, Harris could not have made a wiser choice. In August 1942, Harris was not totally enthusiastic about the formation of an elite force of bomber crews. He would have preferred to have specific squadrons formed inside each bomber group to act as raid leaders, but at that time he was overruled by the Chief of Air Staff.

Accepting the inevitable at that time, Harris then strived to get the best deal for this new force. He pressed and succeeded in getting a unique emblem for the crews of an RAF eagle in gilt, to be worn under the medal ribbons. He also won the right for special promotion for members of the new force in view of the fact they would have to do a tour of 45 operations, as opposed to the normal tour of 30 by Main Force crews. On January 8th,

1943, the PFF was elevated to group status as No. 8 Group (PFF). Bennett was further promoted to Air Commodore and eventually to Air Vice Marshal.The four initial squadrons, each with their different types of aircraft and with different operational capacities, were joined during the Battle of the Ruhr period (April 1943) by two other squadrons. No. 405 (RCAF) Squadron came from the newly formed 6 Group, the only Canadian squadron to serve with the PFF, and they were stationed at Gransden Lodge, flying Halifaxes. The other newcomer was 97 Squadron, based at Bourn and flying Lancasters. In early June 1943, two Mosquito units joined 109 Squadron in the *Oboe* aspect of PFF operations, these being 105 and 139 Squadrons based at Marham. Further additions were later made to the strength of the Pathfinder Force, but for the period of the Battle of the Ruhr it consisted of nine squadrons, three being Mosquito *Oboe* equipped.

Initially the Pathfinder squadron crews consisted of volunteers but, owing to the demand made and sometimes the high losses sustained, some crews were posted to the Pathfinder units from their heavy bomber conversion units or from regular front line squadrons who were visited by a pathfinder wing commander who 'poached' likely looking crews. These new crews then went through a period of training at a special Navigational Training Unit based initially at Gransden Lodge and later at Warboys, where instructors who had already finished their pathfinder tours instructed the new crews on special equipment and a high standard of navigational flight training was undertaken. Before the crews were accepted on the pathfinder squadrons each member of a crew had to pass a special examination to show that they were proficient in their own trade as well as that of another member of the crew. They also had to be consistent in keeping to an extra tight time schedule in all their training navigation flights.

The tactics of the pathfinders were constantly changing, but always they had to keep to an exact time and position schedule along the route that they had been briefed to take. Any attack was then compressed into the minimum amount of time and main line bombers were kept on the scheduled flight path. Markers were dropped by pathfinder crews as navigational aids for other aircraft on route and over the target itself so that accurate bombing could take place. Three types of markers were adopted.

1. Route ground markers *Paramatta*.
Different colours (Red, green, yellow or red and yellow) were used for turning points on the way to and from the target. Specific colour details were given for each attack in bomber crew briefings. Ground markers were also dropped in the target area, this was very much dependent on prevailing weather and cloud conditions.

2. Sky markers *Wanganui*.
Normally used for target and route markings in very cloudy conditions.

3. Ground flares *Newhaven*.
White and yellow flares which were used to illuminate targets.

If a combination of ground and sky markers was used the prefix *Musical* was added to the particular code, depending on the majority of any particular type of markers involved. As pathfinder techniques developed other forms of markers were used in a variety of pyrotechnical displays. Pathfinder crews were usually divided up into the following categories.

a. Blind Markers:- Usually performed by very experienced Pathfinder crews who were first in the target area, setting down either ground or sky markers.

b. Blind Backers Up:- Similar duties as Blind Markers except that they usually flew in the main bomber stream on an exact time table throughout the raid period.

c. Visual Backers Up:- New crews were given target identifying experience by performing this function.

d. Visual Markers:- Used when a small and specific target needed marking.

e. Supporters:- New crews in pathfinders, who carried a normal bomb load, but went to attack on zero hour to create ideal conditions for main force bombers carrying incendiaries.

Later in 1943 the technique of the Master Bomber was established which allowed very experienced squadron commanders to control the attacks by radio communication.

Oboe

Oboe was a piece of radar equipment which used radar pulses from two UK stations and basic geometry. One of the stations was at Trimingham, Norfolk and the other at Walmer in Kent, they were called Cat and Mouse stations. By using the known distance to any selected target in Germany as the radii of two separate arcs of a circle, each measured independently from each station, with one station acting as constant tracker of the bomber, the intersection of the two arcs became the accurate bombing release point. At briefing, the Mosquito bomber crew were given the target and a latitude and longitude point which was ten minutes flying time from the target. This point was known as the switching on point. Crews were given a time to be at this point and began a listening watch some five minutes before it. Each aircraft had a two letter code and once this was heard the transmitter was switched on. The procedure then took an imaginary beam running from the switch on point to the target, location of the aircraft at this time in relation to the beam being indicated to the pilot by whether he heard dots or dashes in his headset (Left or right of the beam, similar to that of the Blind Approach installations at many airfields). On beam was indicated by a steady note in the pilot's ear, from which sound, similar to a note of the musical instrument the *Oboe*, the system was named. The exact position was not known until the crew heard the first letter on the beam; thus with the switch on point as the letter 'D', then quarter of the way to the target was 'C'; half way 'B' was given; three quarters of the way 'A'. It was essential therefore that the aircraft's position was never nearer than point 'C' when initially switched on, otherwise the pilot had no time to get settled and maintain a set airspeed of 260 knots and a set height of 28,000 feet on the beam. The release bombs point was signified after the pilot reached point 'A' by listening to the steady note and releasing his load of target indicators or bombs when this cut out occurred. Once his load was dropped it was very important for the pilot to switch off the transmitter to avoid blanketing the ground station, and thereby prevent it calling in any following aircraft.

Oboe had been tested twice, once in bombing over Lorient and St Nazaire in December 1942, when it proved accurate to 600 yards of an aiming point, and the second time was on a raid to Florennes in Belgium, also in December 1942. It was planned on that particular raid that the Belgian underground would be informed of the target and the date and time of the raid beforehand, obviously a very risky proceedure. This was done so that reports made by the underground agents of the raid's accuracy could be assessed in greater detail. Within a few days following the actual raid, reports were received from Belgium which gave an unqualified success to this test raid. The reports gave distances in yards from the planned aiming point and to everyone's delight that one of the bombs had hit a nightfighter headquarters building. The important work of the members of the underground movements in Belgium, Holland, Denmark and France cannot be too highly praised for not only did they risk their lives in helping aircrew in escaping or evading capture they kept sending back to London vital information. Photographs and the location of the German Air Defences, Radar, Search-light, and *Flak* sites as well as Fighter control buildings helped the Royal Air Force in the constantly changing tactical counter measures being undertaken to minimise bomber losses. A special Group (No. 100) in Bomber Command was formed later in 1943 for such radio and radar counter measures.

There were, however, some drawbacks to the use of *Oboe*. One was that it had a limited range from the English ground stations due to the curvature of the Earth's surface. Secondly Bomber Command only had two ground stations operating, so they could only control twelve aircraft fitted with *Oboe* for any hour over the target. This disadvantage was not serious in that only a few *Oboe* aircraft would be needed to drop initial markers for the Main Force. Another drawback was that the Oboe aircraft had to transmit a signal which might be homed upon by an enemy night fighter, but this caused no real threat in practice as the *Oboe* sets were used in the main by Mosquito aircraft which were too fast for the enemy night fighters. The contribution that the high flying and fast Mosquito made was considerable, especially in dropping the primary markers on the target aiming point. The Mosquito's *Oboe* efforts were normally complemented by the heavy bombers from the new pathfinding force which backed up the primary markers with different colours and so maintained a coloured aiming point during the period of the Main Force attack. In the regions where the *Oboe* equipped Mosquitoes were ineffective, the other heavy Pathfinder squadrons did the main target marking as well as doing the backing up procedure throughout the course of the raid. They were normally first in and last out of the target area.

The Ruhr was selected as the area for this first main offensive for the bomber force, because the whole area was Europe's principal producing area for coal, coke, iron and steel. It was the home of vast metallurgical and chemical industries and above all it was the centre of Krupps, Germany's vitally important armaments industrial complex. In fact the whole area was one on which many other German industries were dependent for raw materials, especially those connected with war production and to the general German war effort. It was well within the range of *Oboe*, the new blind marking device, and it was also the logical area for targets that could be reached by the bombers during the much shorter nights in the Spring and Summer of 1943.

Luftwaffe Night Defences

To appreciate what air defences the crews of bombers encountered during their operations over Germany and the Occupied countries during this period of the bombing campaign, it is important to go back to the beginning of World War Two. Germany at that time possessed a fairly adequate night fighter defence system, but this was not brought into much action for in the early war period the Royal Air Force's Bomber Command policy was mainly to undertake daylight operations. Even so the German night defence system was prepared should the threat of night bombing be envisaged in a change of RAF policy.

Early in the war the *Luftwaffe* had under its control 31 *Flak* regiments equipped with 88 mm guns, which proved to be the best anti aircraft gun used in the war. The *Flak* (*Fliegerab-*

wehrkanonen) regiments were backed up by a very efficent searchlight organisation.

By 1940, however, Bomber Command realised that they were unable to pursue a daylight offensive in the face of the *Luftwaffe* day fighters' successes and changed their policy to that of night bombing. In hindsight, the early Bomber Command night bombing was a fruitless exercise, and caused little damage to Germany or its industries, except perhaps in sowing the first seeds of disquiet and doubts in the minds of the *Luftwaffe* as to the efficency of their defence system. A comparatively small number of bombers would set out on their own individual courses to Germany to attack various targets, only a few, of those who initially took off would reach their designated target. The courage and tenacity of these early bomber crews is not in question, for they battled in appalling weather conditions struggling to reach their target. It was mainly by luck that they got anywhere near the target to drop their bombs for poor navigational aids, bad weather forecasts for wind information, poor bombsights, inadequate aircraft to meet such operational flights and in many cases poor bombs, which did not explode, limited any degree of success.

These nightly attacks by the RAF did, however, prompt the Germans to reassess their defence systems and it was mainly due to the efforts of *Generalmajor* Josef Kammhuber, who had been released by the French after being taken prisoner early in the war, that the German modern night fighter force was developed. The choice of this General was rather odd, for he had little knowledge of radar (*Funkortung*) or any fighter interception work. He did compensate this deficency, however, by good organisational qualities and tremendous drive and energy for the task ahead. Firstly he expanded the aircraft strength under his control and then repositioned the existing searchlight and sound detectors into three areas, the Zuider Zee, the Rhine Estuary and the Ruhr Valley. These were the main routes used by Bomber Command into Germany, stretching for more than 650 miles.

Each of these zones was further divided into boxes, each box measuring 27 miles on the seaward side and approximately 13 miles deep inland. The coastal side was occupied by the sound locators to give early warning of the direction of the bombers. Behind these and deeper into each box were the searchlight batteries, then finally a light and radio beacon. A night fighter was allocated to each box or zone and would orbit the beacon at the back of each box until a bomber crossed into the area of searchlight batteries. Once the unfortunate bomber was caught in the beams, the fighter would then go from his beacon to attack. When a bomber had been shot down or contact had been lost, the fighter would fly back to the beacon and await his next victim. This system was called *Helle Nachtjagd* (illuminated night fighting) and although an improvement, it was far from ideal for it had serious drawbacks. Firstly the searchlights could only operate effectively in clear weather and even in good weather they had problems of locating an area of sky relative to the bomber's speed and track. Such information would have been given to the searchlight batteries by the sound locators, but these were the Achilles heel of the system for their information was very unreliable.

In those early days the German night fighters found little success in their interceptions and there were many accidents due to lack of blind flying radio aids. Often German fighters fired on each other in error. Morale amongst the pilots became low and was made even worse by the fact that their daylight counterparts were more successful, especially at this period of the war when the Reich was more on the offensive than the defensive.

From 1940 onwards intruder operations to English bomber stations had taken place with varying degrees of success. Kammhuber was a firm advocate of intruder operations as part of the German defence system and the curtailment of these operations on Hitler's orders was described by *Luftwaffe* senior officers at the time as one of Germany's most serious errors of judgement in the air war. Some evidence from German sources after the war showed that these curtailment orders were not completely obeyed and small scale intruder raids continued with some successes. However, they did not capitalise on this aspect of air warfare, which could have been a potent weapon in their arsenal. Apart from the damage they could have caused, the panic and confusion would have been greater, for the thought of being intercepted before crossing the enemy coast and then not being safe from attack on returning from operations would have been nerve wracking for the bomber crews. The possibility of an intruder being in the circuit, which sometimes happened although fortunately not that often, was a nightmare situation. Bombers milling around, often very low down on fuel and anxiously awaiting their turn to land lead to several accidents.

The solution to some of the problems in the German Night Fighter defence system came with the introduction of the *Würzburg* radar set. The early *Freya* radar set was only available in limited numbers and it really was an early warning set lacking precision, just giving a general picture of the air space situation. The introduction of *Würzburg* was a major improvement. It was a gun laying radar set able to supply searchlight batteries with data on the speed and track of the incoming bombers, which would then allow time to illuminate the target for a much longer period. Kammhuber was able to replace the sound locators with *Würzburgs*, which he still located in the forward field of each box in the *Helle Nachtjagd* system, but he moved the radio beacon, *Kleine Schraube* (Little Screw) right into the centre of the searchlight belt so that orbiting fighters could have more time to concentrate more fully on interceptions. The increased efficency of this system enabled the German defence to shoot down more British bombers, and the morale of the German fighter pilots and searchlight battery crews increased correspondingly. The only serious problem remaining was that the searchlights were very dependent on reasonable weather conditions. This was a problem with the climate in Northern Europe and better ways of tracking the bombers had to be found. The organisation of the searchlight system was based on three lights to a *Zug* (Squad), each *Zug* covered an area approximately 5 Kms by 3 Kms, three *Zugs* to a *Batterie*, (Battery), one behind each other. Three Batteries to an *Abteilung*, (Battalion) which were alongside each other and three *Abteilungen* to a Regiment. Each *Abteilung* covered a front of 30 Kms.

Kammhuber worked quickly to find a solution to this problem and he and his team created a fully radar dependent interception system code named *Himmelbett* (heavenly or four poster bed), which retained the box concept from *Helle Nachtjagd*, but replaced the searchlights with radar. Under this new system each box contained two *Würtburg* sets, a *Freya* set, a light and radio beacon for orbiting and a control room. The *Freya* still continued to give a long range picture of the air situation, picking up incoming bombers and directing a *Wurtzburg* on to them. The *Würzburg* would direct the three surrounding searchlights towards the bomber. If the searchlights succeeded in illuminating the plane, it would then be visible to a battalion of searchlights behind, which would light up and try and hold the bomber in view as it crossed the belt so that a night fighter could attack. The *Würtburgs* gave a shorter and more accurate picture for interception purposes. The sets were coded Red for the target tracking and Blue for intercepter fighter tracking. These two sets were linked by a land line to a two storied control post, where the plots were displayed on a frosted glass screen which was gridded to correspond to the standard *Luftwaffe* map of the area covered by the box. On the first floor level of the control room and beneath the screen sat two operators who were equipped with pencil lights and they plotted the respective Red and Blue plots on to the under side of the screen. On the first floor level and above the screen a plotter marked in the traces with a wax crayon pencil and then a controller, from the information displayed, directed the fighters by radio into an interception position.

By the end of 1941 six of these defence boxes were in position and overlapping from the estuary of the Rhine to the Danish Border. Each box was code named with the name of an animal, the first letter of the animal being the same as that of the nearest village or town such as *Hamster* for Hamstede, *Tiger* for Terschelling, *Languste* for Langeoog etc. The RAF gathered information as to the location of these zones and of night fighter stations from the excellent work done by the resistance movements and also decoded from the *Enigma* code machine.

As a second line of defence an additional *Helle Nachtjagd* system was postioned behind the first and stretched from Kiel in the north to way past the Ruhr in the south. Important target areas were also further defended by a combined force of *Himmelbett*, *Nachtjagd* and *Flak* defences, these areas were code named, *Kiebitz* for the area around Kiel, *Hummel* for the

Hamburg area, *Roland* for the Bremen area, *Drossel* and *Kolibri* overlapping the two vital areas from Düsseldorf to Cologne and *Bär* for the Berlin area. Finally a further *Himmelbett* box covered the southern end of the Ruhr with a combined code name of *Kranich* and *Dachs*. This whole defence system was further expanded by the end of 1942 when the *Himmelbett* boxes along the coast had expanded from six to eleven and increased in diameter to 35 miles by the new giant *Würzburg-Reise* radar sets. Also the *Helle Nachtjagd* zones had been extended as far south as Luxembourg. Further backing was given to all this by the creation of Dark Night Fighting Zones called *Dunkel Nachtjagd*. This system provided powerful radar directed searchlights in front and behind each *Helle Nachtjagd* box so that in adverse weather the precise position of a bomber could be indicated to the fighter interceptor, if only by a glow on the cloud base.

Airborne radar had also been introduced, but this had met with strong opposition and slow acceptance into the system from the pilots who believed that the aerial array caused too much drag and slowed their planes. Fortunately for Bomber Command, airborne radar had come too late to help the *Luftwaffe*. The RAF had also been watching closely the development of Germany's night defences and had realised its vulnerability. Firstly it was geared to the interception of one bomber at a time in each box and the average time for each interception was about 10 minutes. This might have been sufficient during the early phases of the bomber offensive, when pilots picked their own routes to targets and entered German air space at widely scattered points, but from 1942 onwards the mass bomber stream overwhelmed the fighter control centres. For every bomber that was intercepted and either damaged or shot down, 20 more safely penetrated the Kammhuber Line.

Another side to the battle revolved around radio and radar. Jamming systems devised by the boffins in England also tampered with the German night fighter control, for British scientists matched every technological advance with a better one of their own. By mid 1943 the Kammhuber Line was a gigantic battlefield. The bomber pilots were trying to get their bomb loads through to their targets fighting the German controllers, searchlights, radar directed fighters and radar controlled *Flak* batteries. Bomber losses, with some exceptions, were maintained at an 'acceptable level' with the aircraft industry being able to keep up production of bombers to balance the losses. RAF Training Command was able to keep up the supply of well qualified air crew.

The Introduction of *Window*

It was after the end of the Ruhr Battle, with the introduction of *Window* by the British bombers, that the downfall of Kammhuber's carefully constructed system came with incredible swiftness. *Window* was a very simple idea. Strips of metallised paper which, when dropped from an aircraft, would swamp the ground radar with false echoes. Each bomber carried packs of these strips, about 2,200 per bundle. Each strip measured 27 centimetres long and 2 centimetres wide, black paper on one side with aluminium foil on the other side. Its use earlier in the air war had been forbidden, lest the Germans should use a similar tactic in the raids against England. The idea was not particularly new, the Japanese had used a similar paper with success against American radar in the Pacific. The Germans also had discovered its potential very early on and code named it *Düppel*, but they realised its devastating effect on existing radar and they too had forbidden its use.

It was on the night of July 25th/26th, 1943, on the Hamburg raid that the previous three years work of the German air defences was destroyed, the *Würzburg-Reise* sets became unusable and the airborne sets had similar problems. In spite of the heavy bombing meted out to Germany in 1943, it was at the insistence of Hitler and Goering that the *Luftwaffe* was primarily an offensive weapon. The Fuhrer's orders that aircraft factories should concentrate only on producing bombers rather than fightersbecame the greatest barrier to an adequate defence of the Reich and therefore the German High Command showed this in their lack of enthusiasm for night fighting. The night fighter force at the beginning of 1943 was made up of 390 aircraft, mostly twin engined Me 110s, with which to fend off the bomber force which was often twice as large. It was entirely due to Kammhuber's drive and forceful personality that the Reich had any night air defence at all, but his reluctance to change his form of defence structure, even though tactical conditions demanded such change, was his undoing. His proposals to massively increase the numbers of fighters to 18 night fighter Geschwadern (Wings) covering the whole of Germany and to put Window proof radar sets into his existing system were rejected out of hand by Goering and Hitler. They dismissed and ridiculed Kammhuber's proposals when he began his report by stressing that American aircraft production was reaching 5,000 combat aircraft every month and that a large quantity of these were destined to reach the European theatre of war. The result was that the entire night fighter force was reorganised and Kammhuber posted to the Norwegian Air Command. Towards the last few months of 1943, as the bombing raids both by night and day increased in frequency and effectiveness, some anxiety began to mount among senior *Luftwaffe* officers. Goering, under great pressure, decided on a dramatic turn about of policy in that the *Luftwaffe* should go on the defensive. Once again Hitler would not hear about defence, his motto was always attack. Although he never really brought his image of the Luftwaffe as an offensive weapon into line with the changing reality of the war, the pressure of necessity ultimately transformed the German Air Force into a defensive arm. By late 1943 more than 80% of the *Luftwaffe's* strength was devoted to the defence of the Reich from British and American bombers.

New Night Fighter Tactics

In the void left by the destruction of the *Himmelbett* system, two new tactical plans appeared in the air defence of Germany. The first was introduced late in the Battle of the Ruhr on the night of 3rd/4th July, during Bomber Command's attack on Cologne. This new tactical innnovation was the brain child of a *Major* Hajo Hermann, a very experienced bomber pilot who had been the hero of the raid on the Greek port of Piraeus in April 1941 and who was now assigned to the *Luftwaffe* Staff College. He argued that night fighters could overcome British electronic trickery if they did not depend on radar or radios for guidance, but rather stalked the bombers in a free chase. He reasoned that the amount of light available over one of Bomber Command's targets from pathfinder markers, ground fires and searchlights should be enough for an experienced pilot to be able to intercept visually without the use of any radar aids. This was not an unrealistic assumption to make, for bomber crews often saw other bombers over the illuminated targets, silhouetted against infernos on the ground. They were seen even more clearly against the background of cloud which often covered target aiming points. Hermann's type of attack also proposed the use of single engined day fighters and the daytime fighter control system to direct the *Wilde Sau* (Wild Boar), to the target under attack by means of a running commmentary on the bomber's course, altitude and likely destination. High flying planes were also to drop lanes of flares well above the bomber stream so that the fighters would have further help to home in on their prey. Hermann's plan did not meet with the approval of the Commander of the *Fliegerkorps, Generalleutnant* Kammhuber, who thought it was a backward step from his sophisticated radar control system. However, Hermann persisted with his idea and went over Kammhuber's head to his superior *Generaloberst* Weise, who gave approval for a trial period. *Flak* defences over the Ruhr were even limited to a maximum ceiling of fire of 15,000 feet to allow the fighters to operate without hindrance from the ground defences. After the summer and autumn of 1943, when the German fighters began to suffer heavy losses due to accidents in bad weather conditions and more and more pilots baled out, rather than attempt to land, the scheme was dropped. Although only a stop gap, *Wilde Sau* did provoke questions about the whole issue of tactics in night air defence.

In the Luftwaffe's Berlin Staff College, *Oberst* von Lossberg produced a follow up tactic to *Wilde Sau*. It was *Zahme Sau* (Tame Boar) which, when implemented, brought the night fighters their greatest success. The main idea of *Zahme Sau* was to get the night fighters into the bomber stream early and then to keep them there as long as possible. Part of the *Himmelbett* system was retained, that of the radar which was now used solely for early warning rather than interception. From the end of 1943 to the end of the war the following approach was made by the Germans in the night defence of the Reich.

During daylight hours the listening service operated by the *Luftwaffe* kept a watch for test transmissions on radio or radar emanating from England. If these were heard in any great numbers a raid of some sort could be anticipated. It is worth mentioning at this point the general lack of radio discipline exercised by bomber stations during daylight hours. Aircraft air tests were carried out before raids and the amount of radio transmissions was a real give away to the *Luftwaffe* listeners. In hindsight it is rather odd that this was allowed to continue without any form of restriction. These radio transmissions plus weather conditions allowed the German controllers to make a calculated projection as to the most likely area that would be penetrated that night. The night fighter stations would be informed of this decision and would begin to make their preparations for the night. Early warning radar along the coast would be put on the alert and those radar sites in the most likely area of penetration would become operational very early indeed. As soon as the bombers were picked up on radar the nearest control centre (there were five of these at Döberitz, Stade, Arnhem/Deelen, Metz and Schleissheim) would take control and then direct operations.

The first action by the control centre would be to send out a reconnaissance plane to monitor the bomber stream sometimes meeting the stream half way across the North Sea. This plane would then report the general course, strength and altitude of the bomber force and attempt to keep in touch with it. It was then the controller's task to attempt to establish the most likely target and prepare his fighter defence accordingly. At the best of times this was difficult, but it became increasingly hard as 100 Group attempted to lessen the staggering losses of Bomber Command. The controller had three types of interceptions available to him, *Himmelbett*, *Zahme Sau* and *Wilde Sau* and he allocated aircraft according to the suitability of interception. The *Zahme Sau* aircraft were controlled by means of a running commentary over the Y system, giving the fighters details of the bomber stream's composition, altitude and heading. Aircraft from all over Europe were scrambled and navigated by means of radio beacons to a designated stacking beacon where they would orbit at different heights. As many as 50 fighters would sometimes be orbiting awaiting their individual call to leave the stack and make off with current information into the bomber stream. If or when the fighter made visual or radar contact with a bomber the pilot would radio back the exact position of the stream, before going into the attack. If the bomber stream changed course and went into another control centre area the new controller would take over. This happened from control to control until the bomber stream finally left Germany.

Throughout the night battles that were waged over Germany in 1943, two aircraft types formed the backbone of the *Luftwaffe's* night fighter defence force. These were the Junkers Ju88 and the Messerschmitt Bf110. In the first half of 1943 *Generalleutnant* Kammhuber pressed strongly for a greater production of a twin engined night fighter, the Heinkel He219 Uhu (Owl). It was a formidably armed fighter with six 30 mm cannon and equipped with the latest A.I. radar. Only about 300 were produced in spite of Kammhuber's target of 2,000. If that target had been achieved the He219 would have undoubtedly caused greater losses in the squadrons of Bomber Command. The single seater fighters, such as the Messerschmitt Bf109 and the Focke-Wulf FW 190 were also brought into service from day to night fighter defence rôles in *Wilde Sau* attacks in July 1943. The Dornier Do217 was also adapted for a night fighter rôle and was equipped with four 20mm cannon and four 7.9 mm machine guns in a converted nose cone.

In the latter half of 1943 a most ingenious gun mounting was introduced in the Messerschmitt Bf110. It was a mounting of two 20 mm cannon placed in the top of the fighter's fuselage with their muzzles pointing upwards at a fixed angle. The guns were fired by the pilot with the aid of a reflector sight mounted in the cockpit roof. This enabled the pilot to take advantage of a bomber's blind spot under the main fuselage and where the bomber's large wings, which contained the fuel tanks, were extremely vulnerable to attack. The gun mounting was known as the *Schräge Musik* (Jazz Music) and was responsible for many a bomber's fate.

The Bomber Crews

The crew of a four engined bomber normally consisted of seven airmen; the pilot, navigator, bomb aimer, wireless operator, flight engineer, mid upper gunner and rear gunner. The only twin engined bomber, the Wellington had the same crew except for the flight engineer and mid upper gunner. They were either all non commissioned rank or a mixture of non commissioned and officer rank, rarely was there an all officer crew. The pilot, regardless of rank, was normally classed as the captain or skipper and he had full responsibility for all the crew as well as flying the aircraft. The navigator had the responsibility of working out the route and any alterations caused by change of wind etc. to and from the target. He was also responsible for operating all the radar navigational aids. The bomb aimer, apart from his rôle of dropping the bombs, controlled the bomb run by verbal commands to the pilot and also acted as an additional map reader. The wireless operator was in charge of receiving and transmitting radio messages, although for many operations radio silence was kept. He also had to get radio fixes to help the navigator plot his positions. The flight engineer was responsible for proper fuel control and consumption and had to keep a careful watch on the engine controls and temperatures. His running log was an important document for the ground crew who looked after the aircraft and kept it in first class condition. The gunners were the eyes of the aircraft and their careful watch for enemy fighters ensured that the pilot was able to take the necessary emergency manoeuvres. In good crews, members trained each other to be interchangeable so that in an emergency appropriate measures could be taken. For example the bomb aimer could also be a competent navigator, the flight engineer able to handle the aircraft controls as well as take astro shots with a sextant from the astrodome above his position. The wireless operator may be able to use the Browning machine guns, while the navigator could take over the bomb aiming.

Many of the aircrew, especially the pilots and navigators, were trained abroad in Rhodesia, South Africa or Canada under the Empire Air Training Scheme. In the USA there were the British Flying Schools and the Arnold Training Scheme. All these countries had a climate which was usually more suitable for flying than that of Britain. The failure rate in the pilot's courses was fairly high and those who dropped out were usually sent on to navigator training schools or remustered into another aircrew category. The pilots were trained mainly on single engined aircraft, and many had aspirations of being fighter pilots. They had rude awakenings when they found themselves posted on return to the United Kingdom to twin engined Advanced Training Schools to learn to fly Oxfords and Ansons before being posted to an Operational Training Unit to fly Whitley or Wellington bombers.

It was at the OTU that the nucleus of the crew was formed which would normally stay together throughout their operational tour. The OTU aircraft only required five aircrew so, at this stage, the mid upper gunner and the flight engineer were not in the crew. After many months of intensive training as individuals in their respective aircrew categories, for the pilots over a year's training, they were all brought together in a large briefing room to get crewed up. Not only English, Scottish, Irish and Welsh accents could be heard, but those of Canada, Australia and New Zealand added to the assembly of aircrew. At the start, standing in groups, only their respective flying badges distinguishing one group from another. After the initial welcoming speech by the Wing Commander in charge of training there was a milling mass of aircrew left to make up a crew by natural selection. It seemed a rather odd way of going about it, especially as the Air Force had done a great deal of assessment and training in the selection for each particular aircrew category. In retrospect, however, it seemed to work for within about half an hour, from the somewhat self conscious airmen who might have wondered if a pilot was any good, whether a navigator could find his way about the skies or a rear gunner was eagle eyed enough to spot an enemy fighter, a newly formed crew would emerge. Once the ice had been broken crew members got to know each other better. The barriers of rank were purely artificial and were not apparent at all in the air. Even on the ground the only difference appeared to be in quarters and messing facilities. Training soon began in earnest, ground school training as well as the important air training. The majority of the instructors were tour expired aircrew who had been posted to training commands as a rest from operations. Under difficult weather conditions and flying tired and battle weary aircraft, Wellingtons or Whitleys which had been passed down from front line operational squadrons, these instructors certainly did not have a restful time. In fact many thought it was more dangerous to be screened than do a tour of ops. The accident rate in OTUs was very high indeed. In months from their initial meeting at the OTU's briefing room, the crew would be ready to do their final part of training in either a *Bullseye* exercise, which would involve crossing the enemy coast and dropping leaflets, or make a diversionary raid to help the main force of bombers on a particular operation.

Although still a sprog (new) crew, the next posting for some of the crews destined for heavy bombers would be to a Heavy Conversion Unit, which was normally equipped with battle weary Halifaxes or Stirlings from squadrons or maintenance units following repair work. The Lancasters were in such a demand that it was not until late 1943 that they were brought into use with HCUs. The Heavy Conversion Units normally served a particular group in Bomber Command and crews would usually be posted to a squadron on that group which needed crew replacements.

The HCU course was again a mixture of ground and air training, but with a little more emphasis on crew training in the air. Take offs and landings, or circuits and bumps as sometimes the crew would affectionately call them, were the main part of both day and night familiarisation to the heavy four engined bomber. Three engined practice landings and emergency feathering proceedures for the pilot, who perhaps six months earlier had been throwing his single engined aircraft around the sky in aerobatics, were essential. Two more members were added to the crew, the mid upper gunner and flight engineer. These important crew members made up the seven and for the majority of the conversion course they would work together as a team. Training progressed from local bombing practice, cross country flights, fighter affiliation exercises and air to sea gunnery practices to long night flying exercises, called *Bullseyes* and sometimes leaflet dropping trips over Occupied France called

Nickeling. Apart from this flying training, ground drills for dinghy training and emergency escape procedure went along at the same time, the crew gaining more experience and confidence in each other. They came to realise that it was important to do their tasks efficently, not only for self satisfaction, but for the benefit of each crew member for they had each others lives in their hands.

Soon the day would arrive for that long awaited posting to a front line squadron. The pilot was often given a few trips as a second pilot (second dickie), but this depended very much on the pressure the squadron was under at the time. If there had been many crew losses there was not much time to be wasted and the crew would often be put on operations straight away, but even then squadron commanders would try and wean them in gently, giving them a relatively easy trip, though operations on even lightly defended targets were not that easy. Pilots who did go on second pilot trips usually went with an experienced captain and crew, but even then many new crews found themselves minus their pilot without even going on operations. The remainder of the crew had to then fill in as spare bods on the squadron or be sent back to an OTU or HCU to be crewed up again. Bomber front line operational squadrons were based on a variety of sites ranging from the peace time RAF stations, such as Scampton with their creature comforts, to the new stations which had been built by 'Works and Bricks' at lonely country places away from towns. Here aircrews were often billeted in Nissen huts, which roasted one on a hot summer's day or froze you in winter. They also dripped water from condensation on their curved tin roofs in the cold damp lowland areas which were where new airfields were usually built.

Normally a station housed only one squadron, but there were many cases where two squadrons were based on one drome. Squadrons were hives of activity for 24 hours a day and 7 days a week throughout the year, shift working being the normal rule for ground crews who serviced the bombers. It is important to state that these ground staff have been seriously underrated in many past accounts of the RAF, for they were the unsung heroes. Working sometimes in terrible conditions, out of doors in all types of weather, changing aircraft engines in record times and doing the servicing so vital to the safety of bomber crews, they kept Bomber Command in the air. The pride these ground crews took in the planes for which they were responsible was immense and quite often there was a strong personal bond between a bomber's air and ground crew. Other ground crew on the station were also essential personnel, for without the parachute packers, instrument and radio repairers, armourers, drivers, clerks etc. the bomber crews could not have flown on operations. Special mention must also be made about the women who served in the Women's Royal Air Force, who performed such outstanding work in keeping the bombers flying. A good station was easily spotted, the morale was high and a great pride was taken by all personnel of the squadron in which they served.

A Day in the Life of a Bomber Crew

Normally crew members reported to their respective flight offices in the morning and were told whether or not there would be a stand down for that night or that operations were probable. If there was a stand down, crew training was laid on, either practice bombing, fighter affiliation exercises or cross country flights for practice in operating new navigational aids. If no flying was involved, lectures would be arranged by the intelligence section, dinghy drills would be practised or aircraft compass swinging would take place. If operations were probable the crew would normally go to their respective aircraft to check on its serviceability and maybe do an air test on the plane to check some work that had just been completed. The bombers were widely dispersed around the airfield and getting to an aircraft's hard standing would mean either cadging a lift on a lorry or cycling around the perimeter track. Bicycles were the most common form of transport for the majority of aircrew. The dispersal points were a hive of activity if ops were on. Petrol bowsers pumped the ordered number of gallons into the aircraft's tanks and various section vans buzzed around checking the radio and instruments in each plane. Tractors pulled along the bomb dollies, just like miniature railway trains, to and from the far distant bomb dumps where the bombs were being fused and armed for that night's operation.

After a brief chat with the plane's flight sergeant in charge of the ground crew, the pilot would have a quick look around while the gunners would check their guns and see that the perspex surrounding their turrets was gleaming clean. Lunch was taken in their respective messes before the strident notes of the Tannoy announced to all the time for flying meals and briefing. By this time, for security reasons, all commmunications to the outside world would be cut off from the camp. Only essential operational communications continued.

Crews would gather outside the large briefing room before finally going in, sitting together on the hard wooden forms which lined the room facing the end wall. The wall was dominated by a large map of northern Europe, normally covered by a dark curtain. When all designated for that night's operations had assembled, a roll call was made by the pilot's name being called. The whole assembly would smartly rise to attention on the entrance of the Station Commander, normally a Group Captain, the squadron Commanding Officer, usually a Wing Commander and his senior flight commanders. After the briefing room doors were closed by an RAF policeman, who then stood outside on guard, the curtains would be drawn back to reveal the target for that night. The route to be taken would be taped in red. Also displayed on the map would be the cross hatched red celluloid areas which showed known *Flak* positions and the green celluloid areas for known search light belts. Other coloured pins showed essential information. The most important thing, however, to all the assembled aircrew at that time would be where the red tape ended, the target itself. First on the rostrum would be the Senior Intelligence Officer who would explain the nature of the target, its importance and any special information necessary for that operation. In succession the various leaders, signals, bombing and navigation would give their gen, usually routine stuff. Then came the Flying Control Officer who would explain the marshalling times, engine starting up times and the probable runway to be used that evening. Next the Met Officer would show his charts with wind speeds and cloud heights, probable weather over the target and the forecast of what the weather would be like on return to base. Lastly the Squadron Wing Commander would add his views about the particular operation in such detail that the final remark of any questions would often be met with complete silence. The Group Captain would wish everyone good luck and after being dismissed the pilots and navigators would obtain the specific maps required and draw up the intended routes and times. The wireless operators would get their flimsies (sheets of rice paper which could easily be disposed of) on which were printed the relevant frequencies to be used and the current colours of the day.

Flying meal times varied quite often, before or after briefing, when crew members would go to their respective messes to have their bacon and egg suppers. First a visit to the parachute section to collect the all important 'chute and Mae West. Then on to the crew rooms where all pockets were emptied of any personal possessions and information which could prove of value to the Germans if one was captured. The odd stub of a ticket from a cinema visit or receipt could be of immense value to German interrogators. Into one of the empty blouse pockets of the light blue battle dress would go the plastic escape box which mainly contained a silk map, Horlicks tablets, chewing gum, rubber water bottle, benzedrine and water purifying tablets, small compass, needle and thread and a small amount of French and Dutch money. Gunners were the ones who took a long time to don their equipment for they wore Long John underwear beneath their battle dress over which they wore electrically heated fleecy lined leather trousers and jackets.

When all the members of a crew were ready they would make their way to the distant dispersal pads around the airfield, either by crew bus or open lorry driven by the usually cheerful WAAF drivers. On summer nights, when the dying rays of the sun would make the English landscape look so peaceful, the irony of their situation came home to the bomber crews, for in a few hours they would be going through intense anti aircraft fire and fighter attacks, getting hell, but also giving sheer hell to the inhabitants of some distant German city or town.

The waiting on dispersals was often a nervy, gut tightening time when most crews would be anxious to see the green Verey light arc in the darkening sky above the control tower, the signal to start engines. Often operations were scrubbed even at this late hour. This was certainly not the most popular time for a reprieve, for most crews had geared themselves up to go and knew that it was only a temporary reprieve, for they would have to go again, either the next day or the night after. If the operation was cancelled it would often be too late to go out for the night to the nearest town.

Once aboard the aircraft all crew would go to their respective positions and the pilot would give the thumbs up signal to the ground crew on the battery cart that he was ready to start up engines. Soon the puff of smoke tinged with flame would come from each engine as the pilot pressed each starter button in turn before the engines coughed and roared into ear splitting life. Oil pressures and magneto drops were checked by the engineer as the pilot tested each engine in turn before signing Form 700 and handing it back to the Sergeant in charge of the plane's ground crew. The intercom was checked to all positions, especially the tail gunner who by now was tightly wedged in his lonely turret where he would be isolated from the rest of the crew for the duration of the trip. The rear hatch door was checked and the chocks were waved away to allow the heavily laden bomber to trundle on to the perimeter track and join the procession of bombers awaiting their turn to get on to the runway. Once the green Aldis light was flashed from the airfield control caravan at the end of the runway the bomber would swing into position and line up. Final checks were made and the thumbs up sign was given to the assembled group of WAAFS, ground crews and other senior officers who lined the top of the runway to wave the bombers on their way. The brakes were held on and the throttles were pushed forward by the pilot with the engineer following through with his hands to lock them when fully open. Straining against the leash, the brakes were released and slowly the bomber would begin to roll forward, clumsily at first but slowly gaining speed. The tail came up and then the bomber accelerated down the full length of the runaway before the wheels left the ground and the bomber became airborne. Each plane's take off time was recorded on a blackboard in the control tower. Usually bombers would take off every 45 to 60 seconds until the last droning bomber would leave the station in peace.

An Operational Sortie

As soon as the bomber was airborne the pilot would slowly climb his heavily laden bomber to the group's assembly point on the English coast. Inside the aircraft the navigator in his dimly lit compartment would begin to adjust the brilliance knob on his *Gee* radio navigational aid. Its effectiveness could only be relied upon within a short distance of the English coastline as the Germans normally jammed the signals before the bombers crossed the enemy coast. Main force bomber navigators had to rely solely on dead reckoning navigation and in clear conditions on astro navigation. Some bombers during the middle of 1943 had H^2S sets on board, but these were only truly effective when there was some water about and were only switched on when crossing the enemy coast to check for an accurate landfall. The H^2S set unfortunately acted as a homing device for enemy fighters which were equipped to pick up H^2S signals.

After crossing the English coast (Cromer for groups below the River Humber and for those north of the Humber usually Flamborough Head or Spurn Point) captains would allow their gunners to test their guns in short bursts. The chattering hammer sound and smell of cordite were a reassuring sound and smell to the crew. Steadily climbing to gain the briefed height at the enemy coast, the captain would order his crew to switch on their oxygen supply at 5,000 feet. Intercom talk would be kept to the minimum, although the gunners appreciated the odd check by the captain to reassure them and relieve the claustrophobic effects of their tiny and uncomfortable turrets. The gunners constantly swung their four Browning guns from port to starboard and adjusted the garticule light above the guns, for it was easier to focus with a minimum of glare. Many rear gunners would close their eyes periodically, for staring into the inky darkness could make them imagine that a tiny speck of dirt on the turret perspex was a fighter coming in on the attack. Although the rear turret was a bitterly cold position, and sometimes the electrically heated flying suits failed to supply sufficient heat, some gunners had the perspex panels above the guns removed so that they had a clearer view, putting up with the extreme cold which resulted.

Behind the pilot, the flight engineer would be carefully monitoring the luminous dials on his panel and switching petrol cocks from one tank to another whilst listening to the steady throb of the four engines. In many crews the engineer was trained to take the occasional star fix from the perspex astro dome above his position, handing his time and fix to the navigator to double check the bomber's position. The wireless operator in his small cubby hole under the pilot's feet would be tuning his set to find the wave length which he had been given at briefing and listening out for the broadcast winds which came through at prearranged times. These were a mean average worked out in England after information had been received from selected bombers which were on the raid. These wind directions and speeds were given so that all the bombers on the operation could navigate on the same wind and so maintain a degree of concentration. Often they confirmed the winds that the navigator had been using, which was very reassuring. In the nose of the bomber, lying flat on his stomach, the bomb aimer would be anxiously peering ahead to catch the first glimpses of gunfire which more often than not signalled the enemy coast ahead and that the coastal batteries were opening up against the bombers already crossing the coast.

Although weather conditions could vary quite a lot there was always doubts about the weather forecast given by the Met Officer at briefing. In fairness to the Met man, it was a difficult task to accurately forecast weather along the route and over the target. It is a chancy business, even in peacetime with the benefit of reports from around the world, but in wartime it was a hit or miss affair, even with the observations from the high flying Met Flight Spitfires. There was strict radio silence from shipping and the German occupied territories were just uncharted areas. Clear weather conditions were not very welcome by crews, especially if there was a moon. This is sometimes inaptly called a Bombers's Moon, but in reality it was a Fighter's Moon, when bombers could be easily picked out over the target area silhouetted against the fiery inferno below. Cumulus cloud conditions suited the bombers best, but the dreaded nimbus clouds with their often icy conditions were the worst. Heavily laden bombers had to struggle through with chunks of ice from propellers smashing against the side of the fuselage and the invisible icy sheen gathering on the leading edges of the wings. This would ultimately stop a sluggish bomber from climbing any more and even cause it to stall and slip into a spin.

Changing course after crossing the enemy coast, quite often around Egmond in Holland, the navigator would inform the pilot of a new course to their target in the Ruhr with an estimated time of arrival. The pilot would be weaving the bomber along this track, changing height and direction continually in an attempt to fool the enemy radar. Pilots differed in their tactics, some even flew on straight and level relying on their gunners having a first glimpse of an approaching fighter before they would go into a corkscrew to outwit the attacker or searchlight beams, a stomach churning manoeuvre.

Flying time was just 30 to 40 minutes to the Ruhr from the Dutch coast, but for bomber crews it felt like eternity. Ahead of the main stream, the first bombers would be meeting the full weight of the intense box barrage of anti aircraft fire from the ground *Flak* gunners, who had ample practice every night to reach perfection. At first the pencil slim searchlights would appear to be weaving aimlessly in the sky until, suddenly, one master blue light would pick up a stray bomber in its beam. Instantly twenty to thirty other lights would latch on to it, holding it like a moth in a flame. The *Flak* would converge and the shells would soon erupt in the centre of the apex of lights. However much the bomber twisted and turned the lights were locked on to it and more often than not a small red glow of light would appear and soon explode and fall slowly to earth. Another bomber and its crew would not return to their base that night.

As the bombers neared the target the bomb aimer would be on the look out for the yellow datum flares dropped by the pathfinders, giving a time and distance run to the actual target aiming point. The bomb doors open signal would be given and any corkscrew would be modified as a violent manoeuvre would often result in a mid air collision with another bomber intent on the run in to the target. The scene below can only be described as horrific. A Dante's Inferno with great outbursts of flame and smoke rising up, flashes from the anti-aircraft guns and bomb bursts as well as the myriad of twinkling lights where tons of incendiaries had fallen. Photo flashes burst right in the centre of this holocaust, the red and green markers cascading down in fiery waterfalls of liquid colour above the aiming point awaiting another bomber's load of bombs. A giant colourful scene as if made by a wild and mad painter with a palette full of brilliant red, orange, green and blue colours.

Straight and level flying was now the order, the climax of every operation, hoping that another bomber was not directly above also on its bomb run for many bombers had bombs and incendiaries dropped on them during this crucial time. Now with the bomb aimer's voice gave the orders, 'Left, left, steady. Hold it. Right a little, Steady'. Tension was high, for there was no way to take any evasive action now. Then that wonderful shout of bombs gone. For thirty seconds the same course had to be held to allow the photo flash to fall from the bomber and explode with tremendous light so that the aircraft's camera could record that important picture of the aiming point. Without the photo the trip would not count as part of the tour of thirty operational trips. Those seconds after the bombs had gone, when one's instinct was to turn and dive away from the intense gunfire and tracer, seemed never ending and were quite nerve racking. The bomb aimer would check that all the bombs had gone and that there were no hang ups which would have meant going around and making another run in to the target, not the most welcome decision for any pilot to tell his crew.

Now back on the homeward leg, often the most dangerous, for if one had missed the fighters on the way in it was more or less certain that they would be waiting around the Dutch or Belgian coast for any bomber off track or which was damaged by *Flak* and limping on its way home. Vigilance was the watch word for all the crew and weary eyes would be strained in the darkness to forewarn of any fighter approaching. The wireless operator would be busy tuning his transmitter onto a given German waveband to listen for a German woman fighter controller's message to the night fighters. Although unable to understand German, he would quickly clamp down his morse key to produce ear shattering blasts through the microphone which was placed in the port inner engine, so making communication extremely difficult from ground control to the night fighters.

45

Flight engineers juggled with the fuel in the tanks, computing consumption on all engines so that there was sufficient fuel to get back to base. Flying rations would be handed round after reaching the comparative safety of the North Sea, but those crews who came back unscathed realised that to remain alive they could not relax their constant vigilance until they were well and truly on the ground. Many a bomber was shot down by German intruder aircraft even in the circuit over their English bomber base. The lucky crews who came back relatively untouched would pass their comrades struggling along. Battle damaged, on two or three engines, even with undercarriages hanging loosely down, bomb doors open and flaps down, the invalids tried to keep airborne to reach the extra long emergency landing strips at Woodbridge, Manston or Carnaby.

On crossing the English coast all eyes would be searching for the white beacon which blinked out in Morse the code sign for home base, then a quick call on the TR9 radio set to the control tower for permission to land. If one was unlucky, a bomber with an injured man, lack of fuel or damaged controls would be given a priority. It would then mean being stacked up circling the airfield, not a healthy occupation when landing circuits of two neighbouring stations merged. You waited your turn before coming in on final approach and hearing the reassuring thump of the undercarriage locking down safely before the tired pilot would make a landing on the black tyre streaked runway. Often a bomber would unknowingly have a tyre which had been struck by stray *Flak* shrapnel and burst. Then the pilot's skill would be put to the test to steer his plane off the runway and on to the grass so that following bombers would at least be able to get down. If the aircraft was comparatively undamaged the pilot would taxi back to the dispersal before switching off all engines. The tired crew would then wearily emerge from the bomber, with oxygen mask marked, strained faces and red rimmed eyes, inhaling the sweet fresh air, but still hearing the heavy throb ringing in their ears. Work was not yet over for it was back by crew bus to the interrogation room, where busy WAAF and RAF intelligence officers would scribble down the notes about each crew's operation. Bedraggled looking aircrew would gulp the welcoming cup of coffee which was usually laced with rum and smoke that welcome cigarette, so kindly provided by the station Padre. Anxious eyes would scan the operational blackboard to see the aircraft landing times and so note those crews who had not made it back this time or who might have diverted to another airfield. For the crew it would be back to the billet for much needed sleep befor the next night's operation, perhaps for another trip to the same place.

March 1943
Essen

March 5th/6th, 1943

The assault on the Ruhr, Bomber Command's 100,000th sortie of the war, started at 21.00 hours on the moonless night of Friday the 5th March, 1943, when a single Pathfinder Mosquito, equipped with *Oboe*, dropped its red coloured primary markers perfectly on the centre of Essen. This was followed by a salvo of green target indicators (TIs) dropped by a Pathfinder Lancaster at 21.03 hours, as recorded on a clock in the aircraft's bomb bay. A second Mosquito dropped its red TIs in the centre of the Krupps' works and throughout the raid at three minute intervals 22 heavy bombers from the Pathfinder force backed up the aiming point with green TIs exactly as planned. Altogether a total of forty-five 250 pound coloured target indicators were dropped. There was a ground industrial haze over the city, as nearly always over the Ruhr industrial area, a constant problem to the bomber force in its effort to accurately identify the target aiming point. With the blind marking by *Oboe*, this caused no visual identification problems on that night.

The total force of 442 aircraft consisted of 407 main force aircraft - 138 Lancasters, 88 Halifaxes, 50 Stirlings and 131 Wellingtons. The 35 Pathfinder aircraft comprised of 19 Lancasters, 6 Halifaxes, 2 Stirlings and 8 Mosquitoes. At the outset there was a serious tactical setback to this raid for 71 aircraft turned back early for technical and other reasons. Five of these returning aircraft were Pathfinders, unfortunately three were the important *Oboe* equipped Mosquitoes. This represented an overall early return rate of 16.3%.

One Wellington from 429 Squadron, piloted by R/55965 Flight Sergeant R. F. Conroy, crashed on take off with a full load of bombs. Only one member of the crew, the navigator R/79393 Flight Sergeant E. M. Bell, was killed, the remainder having a miraculous escape. Flight Sergeant Conroy must have had a guardian angel for later he was the sole survivor of Wellington HE593 which crashed south-east of Eindhoven after the Düsseldorf raid on June 11th, 1943. Not only did he bale out on

48

that occasion, but also evaded capture and returned to England as well.

Weather conditions for the bombers en route to the target were relatively good with 4/10ths to 7/10ths layer cloud with a base of 4,000 to 5,000 feet over the sea as far as the Dutch coast. From there to the target the cloud cleared up. There was also a tail wind of 40 mph at 15,000 feet on the outward leg.

The raid was planned as a *Musical Paramatta*, (ground markers) with yellow TIs also being dropped by the backers up on track, finishing 15 miles away from the target. These were used as a datum point to assist accurate timing and navigation. The Halifaxes and Wellingtons of 1, 4 and 6 Group in the main force were the first wave to attack, bombing from Zero Hour +2 to Z+20. They soon had big fires going. 3 Group Stirlings came next from Z+15 to Z+25, bombing the red TIs which fell plumb centre of the inferno below. In the third and final wave the Lancasters of 1 and 5 Group bombed from Z+20 to Z+40 and kept the fires well stoked up. Each wave of bombers overlapped throughout the 40 minute raid. 356 crews reported to have dropped their bombs on the coloured markers. 219,393 incendiaries, a total of 511.9 tons, were dropped along with 467.7 tons of instantaneous and long delay high explosive bombs. An overall bomb total of 979.6 tons of bombs were dropped.

Aerial reconnaissance the following day showed an area of 160 acres destroyed with 53 buildings in the Krupps armament complex destroyed. The Goldschmidt Works, Maschinbeau Union Works, the Main Power Station and Gas Works were also badly damaged. After the raid the head of the Krupp family, Gustav Krupp von Bohlen und Halbach viewed the Krupps works wreckage and was so shocked that he suffered a major stroke from which he never recovered. German reports record that in this raid 3,018 houses were destroyed and 2,166 seriously damaged making 30,000 people, mostly Krupp workers, homeless. 482 people were killed.

There was a loss of 14 aircraft on this operation, 3.9% of the attacking force. Seven of the aircraft were shot down over the target area and possibly the remainder on the homeward leg when many fighters were encountered over the Amsterdam area.

From the 14 aircraft lost, manned by 92 aircrew, 37 were killed, 37 were posted missing, 17 became prisoners of war, 1 evaded capture and one was killed in a take off crash.

A Lucky Crew

One PFF Lancaster from 83 Squadron based at Wyton and piloted by Flying Officer Garvey had a cine colour camera on board and the 'intrepid' pilot decided to go round on a second run across the target to have a better picture of the 4,000 lb 'Cookie' bomb falling. Unfortunately as soon as the bomb was released it received a direct hit from *Flak* and exploded, blowing the Lancaster vertically upwards. The whole aircraft was riddled with shell splinters and bomb casing and the plane was set on fire. Luckily the crew remained calm, the fire was soon extinguished, and the plane returned to base. On examining the plane next day the crew realised what a very lucky escape they had had, and all for the sake of a picture. Lodged in many parts of the plane were pieces of the 4,000 lb bomb, the bomb's arming pistol was even found lodged in one engine nacelle.

Uneventful Trip

Although 214 Squadron lost one Stirling on this first raid another aircraft from the same squadron, EF331 (BU/A) captained by Canadian Flight Sergeant Miller, reported a relatively uneventful trip of 4 hours and 20 minutes with only a minor problem reported back at base - slight overheating of the starboard inner engine. Stirling EF331, however, had only a short life span left for on the night of April 14th/15th, on the Stuttgart raid, it failed to return. Flight Sergeant Miller had taken over another aircraft by this time.

Sergeant Alvin Turner's Evasion

Canadian Sergeant R/62322 Alvin C. Turner of 419 Halifax Squadron was the only airman who managed to evade capture after this operation. He was a flight engineer on Halifax DT646, captained by 141771 Flight Lieutenant L. Bakewell, who encountered starboard inner engine problems over the English Channel while outbound to the target. By adding extra boost to the starboard outer engine the pilot was able to maintain a height of approximately 17,000 feet, but when intense and accurate *Flak* was encountered on the target approache he had to dive his Halifax to 14,000 feet and then further down to 11,000 feet, from which height the target was bombed.

Shortly after the bombs were released, the starboard inner engine lost its power completely and the bomber lost further height. It then was almost immediately picked up by searchlights and engaged by *Flak*. In an effort to evade the *Flak* trap, Sergeant Bakewell had to dive his Halifax down to 4,500 feet and make a starboard turn out of the target instead of the planned port turn. Before he managed to escape the *Flak*, he was well south of track.

Free of its heavy bomb load the captain coaxed his bomber slowly back to 12,000 feet to get into the prescribed bomber stream and relative safety. Over the Zuider Zee the tail gunner, Flight Sergeant J. R. Couper, reported that enemy fighters were approaching and that his rear turret would not rotate. His guns were also jammed. Since this Halifax was not fitted with a mid upper turret and the other gunner only manned a front turret with two guns which could rarely be brought into play in a fighter attack the bomber by now was practically defenceless. To add to the problems the Halifax engines were not fitted with exhaust shrouds, this meant that any fighter could easily maintain contact with the bomber by the give away flames from the engine exhausts. Although unable to use the turret, Couper gave a running commentary on the fighter's approach and directed his pilot into evasive corkscrew actions. The first pass and opening fire from the Ju88 was therefore wide of the mark. By now the crew realised that they had met a formation of fighters working as a team, for two other Ju88s came in on the attack from the rear. Still evading their attacks by evasive action, the bomber continued on its struggle back to base. Under the circumstances, it was only a matter of time before the attacks took their toll. Tracers found the starboard wing and engines and soon the wing caught fire. Realising that the fire had a firm hold the captain gave the bale out order and all the crew, except the rear gunner managed to get out. He was the only fatal casualty. It can only be speculated that either he was fatally wounded in the fighter attack or failed to make the bale out.

Sergeant Turner remembers little of his bale out, for he thinks he must have been knocked out as he got out of the aircraft. His first recall after hearing the bale out order was lying in a grass field. His landing place was believed to be near Buiksloot, two miles north of Amsterdam. Blood was flowing rather freely from a wound near his eyes and his parachute was well blood stained. By tearing a clean piece of silk from his 'chute he managed to staunch the flow of blood. Then he tore away his flying badge, but in the process ripped off his left hand tunic pocket.Preparing for a long walk he rolled his trousers down over his extra large flying boots, under which he wore ordinary shoes. Unwittingly he forgot to remove his sergeant's stripes and the 'Canada' badges on his shoulders. Still more puzzling he forgot to take off the more obvious leather flying helmet which later almost spoilt his chance of successful evasion. After going through the trauma of persistent fighter attacks and a sudden bale out a kind of after shock must have set in. Coupled with the fact that he was knocked unconscious he was not thinking clearly at this time, in fact his evasion methods were quite a mixture of rights and wrongs, but his luck was in and he was to get away with all the wrongs.

At 03.00 hours, guided by his escape compass, he began walking in a southerly direction and very soon reached the Noordzee Canal, the other side of which lay a large city. It was Amsterdam, although at the time Turner was unaware of this, or even the name of the canal. Shortly afterwards he came upon three German E boats which were moored along the canal bank. From the boats came sounds of laughter and singing, it was obvious that on one of the boats there was a party in full swing. Deciding to capitalise on the E Boat crews' revelry, he found a nearby rowing boat and pushed it quietly into mid stream, before using the oars and rowing to the other side. Once there he pushed the boat back into the canal in an effort to hide his tracks. Climbing a nearby wall he again started walking southwards, keeping to the shadows and hiding momentarily in doorways when he thought he heard anyone approaching. He moved on steadily for about two hours and by daybreak found himself well clear of the city. For the rest of the day he hid himself in a small wood north west of Diemerourg and treated himself to one Horlicks tablet from his escape kit. After studying his silk escape maps, at about eight o'clock the next evening, March 6th, he set out again walking on a bicycle track which ran south east parallel to a railway line which unknown to Turner was the main line between Amsterdam and Hilversum. Avoiding several German patrols he kept going until dawn when he refilled his rubber water bottle from a nearby stream before hiding in a haystack. He treated himself to another Horlicks tablet before consulting his map once again. He resumed his walk and by midnight reached the outskirts of Utrecht. Very early the next morning he had to make a rather quick getaway to avoid a large group of about 200 German soldiers who were marching down the road. Soon he reached a well guarded railway crossing where he was stopped by a German guard who shone a torch on him and asked him something in German. Turner was still wearing his flying helmet, his chevrons and his Canada badges were clearly showing at the top of his tunic sleeves. The guard must not have seen these obvious signs of an RAF airman for he continued to talk in German and Turner, unable to speak German, just replied with guttural sounds. Finally the guard pointed to something down the railway line and Turner walked in the direction given before quickly turning away from the railway when the guard was out of sight. Turner kept running for about an hour afterwards to make sure he was well away before, exhausted, he burrowed into a nearby haystack, realising how lucky he had been to escape.

At dusk he continued to walk, following the rail line from Utrecht to s'Hertogenbosch, reaching another canal near Culemborg where he removed all his outer clothing and flying boots and swam across the bitterly cold water with the clothing bundle on his back. Once on the other bank, he dressed and walked through Culemborg. At daybreak he hid out in a haystack and put his very wet clothes to dry out in the sun. After dark on the night of March 9th, he broke into a chicken shed and took two fresh eggs, his first real meal since baling out. Refreshed by the food and rest he pressed on and reached Utrecht where he decided to board a goods train. By this time he was having some pain from his right shoulder which he must have injured in the bale out. He was now unable to lift his arm at all.

At midnight he boarded an empty goods wagon of a train which soon began to move off in a southerly direction. The train stopped several times and on one occasion Turner had to get under the wagon when he heard a guard approaching. He remained on the train until 4.30 on the morning of March 11th, when he noticed that the train was moving in a more south easterly direction towards Germany. He got off rather smartly the next time the train stopped at a signal. Turner later found out that he had jumped off the train somewhere between Wijk and Aachen. After walking away from the railway he soon found the pain in his shoulder was becoming unbearable, so he decided to take his chances and ask for help at the next farmhouse he came upon. The first farmer was not very helpful and pointed out that he should keep on walking. After another further three miles he approached an isolated house, but by now he was completely exhausted. This time he was fortunately welcomed into the house. One of the first things the people inside the house did was to hold up a mirror for him to see himself. He was still wearing his flying helmet, he had a heavy growth of beard and his face was covered with blood. His uniform was covered with blood stains and he must have looked a truly frightening sight. He then realised why he had perhaps been rebuffed by the farmer he had met earlier. Only when he saw himself in the mirror did Turner realise with horror that he was still wearing the helmet, the chevron stripes and Canada badges. He certainly had a very lucky escape from his encounter with the German sentry, who must have been half witted or half asleep, for Turner must have looked quite conspicuous in the light of a torch. He was given some food and while he was sitting down at his meal he saw one of the men from the house leave quietly. He thought that he was going to be betrayed to the Germans, but his worry was needless for the man returned in a few minutes with an English speaking neighbour who questioned Turner quite extensively as to whether he had escaped from German hands and whether he was being pursued by them. Apparently satisfied with the answers given, Turner was supplied with an old raincoat to cover his uniform and a hat, then he was taken to the English speaking Dutchman's house. There he had a most welcome hot bath and shave, after which he was given a complete set of civilian clothes. It was shortly after this that Turner heard that the Gestapo had arrived in a nearby village, on the look out for any aircrew. His new Dutch friends were quite scared and Turner was taken by car and hidden in a haystack, way out in the countryside, where he remained until March 12th, when at dusk the English speaking Dutchman picked him up and drove him to within a mile of the Dutch-Belgian border. Here he was pointed out an electric power line and told to follow it to Liége. Now loaded with an attaché case full of food which he had been given, Turner set out again walking. His shoulder was still painful, but he stuck at walking for the next seven hours, still following the power lines, until he crept into a haystack to rest. He was abruptly awoken after a few hours by the prod from a pitchfork wielded by a Belgian farmer, who proved to be very unhelpful.

Continuing his walk he came upon two women working in a field, who directed him to the village of Barchon, from where he boarded a tram to Liége, reaching the city centre about mid day on March 12th. After walking around the city centre for a few hours he set off in the direction of Mons where, to his astonishment, he came to a small café in whose window was a small sign saying 'English spoken here'. He could hardly believe his eyes and his good fortune. Entering the café he asked for a cup of tea, hoping that by this request he would arouse the café owner's curiosity. He was certainly successful, for when he wrote on a piece of paper supplied by the owner 'Parlez Anglais', an English speaking Belgian quickly appeared and took Turner back to his home. From that point the remainder of Turner's journey was safely arranged for him by the underground escape movement and he arrived back in England via Gibraltar before the end of June 1943.

Headquarter's Reflection on the Essen Raid

When Bomber Command's first major raid on the Ruhr using the blind marking system had ended, reports began flooding in to Command Headquarters at High Wycombe in Buckinghamshire from the airfields with debriefing comments of large explosions and of raging fires. The final report from the last returning Lancaster stated that the target area was covered by a pall of smoke. In the minds of Headquarter Staff the raid was considered an extraordinary success in its accuracy and resultant devastation. After the war Goebbel's war diary was seen and an extract from it stated.

> During the night Essen suffered an exceptionally severe raid. The city (sic) of Krupps has been hard hit. The number of deaths has been considerable. If the English continue their raids on this scale, they will make things exceedingly difficult for us. Our anti aircraft guns are inadequate. The success of our night fighters though notable are not sufficent to compel the English to desist from their night attacks.

The raid certainly didn't help the morale of German soldiers fighting on the Eastern Russian Front either. An extract from a letter found on the body of a German soldier killed there told of the civilian morale situation in the Ruhr area at this time. It referred to the Essen raid of March 5th/6th, 1943.

> It was an inferno. Bomb followed bomb, streams of phosphorus flowed from above and incendiary bombs fell without interruption. It is a miracle we are still alive. Our district is completely in ruins and only the western parts of Essen remain standing. It is difficult to visualise what everything looks like now. Thousands of people have been left without a house. We are completely worn out, only ruins are to be seen everywhere one looks. If everything is going to be destroyed including our home, it would be better for you not to come back here. I shall not be able to stick it. Approach of darkness always makes me shiver in anticipation of air raids.

> Your wife and son

Casualties March 5th/6th, 1943. Target Essen

83 Squadron 8 Group Lancaster W4847 OL/V
Pilot. J16966 P/O H.L.Partridge Missing, Runnymede Memorial 177
Nav. 116671 F/O L.W.Sprackling Killed Workum (Spoordyk), Holland. D-1-1
B/A. R87122 Sgt R.O.Fulton Killed Hindeloopen, Holland. D-1-6 Washed ashore at Island of Scharhorn (2/5/43)
W/OP. 1376200 Sgt J.M.Freshwater Missing, Runnymede Memorial 150
F/E. 541922 Sgt J.L.Organ Killed Hindloopen, Holland. D-1-5
A/G. 1379924 Sgt H.Fell Missing, Runnymede Memorial 149
A/G. 1337405 Sgt A.D.Dinnis Killed Wonseradee (Makkum), Holland. M-34

156 Squadron 8 Group Lancaster LM304 GT/ Pilot. 84339
W/Cdr S.G.Hookway DFC Killed Rheinberg, Germany. 2-D-3
Nav. 143869 P/O F.W.Hart DFM Killed Rheinberg, Germany. JG 2-D-8/9
B/A. 1186313 F/O R.D.Turk Killed Rheinberg, Germany. 2-D-4
W/OP. 47914 F/O E.Luff Killed Rheinberg, Germany. 2-D-6
F/E. 1020978 Sgt E.B.Alsop Killed Rheinberg, Germany. 2-D-5
A/G. 947067 Sgt D.Heap DFM Killed Rheinberg, Germany. 2-D-7
A/G. 636060 Sgt W.H.Clark Killed Rheinberg, Germany. JG 2-D-8/9

300 Squadron 1 Group Wellington BK150 BH/Q
Pilot. P0882 F/Lt K.Romaniszyn PoW. Stalag Luft 3, Sagan. 42764
Nav. P0053 S/Ldr J.Jankowski Killed Rheinberg, Germany. 2-D-10
B/A. P794357 Sgt M.Wozniak PoW. Stalag 357, Kopernikus. 27671
W/OP. P794398 Sgt Z.Abramik PoW. Stalag 357, Kopernikus. 27627
A/G. P782047 Sgt C.Zaleski PoW. Stalag 357, Kopernikus. 27670

90 Squadron 3 Group Stirling R9271 WP/Q
Aircraft crashed at St.Peter, Germany.
Pilot. 110139 F/O W.A.Fowlie M Runnymede Memorial 124
Nav. 655901 W/O M.Renaut PoW. Stalag 344, Lamsdorf. 27652
B/A. 931658 F/Sgt W.M.Werkendam PoW. Stalag 344, Lamsdorf. 27666
W/OP. 1176593 W/O J.Eccles PoW. Stalag 344, Lamsdorf. 27638
F/E. 1107377 Sgt A.M.Mollison Missing, Runnymede Memorial 175
A/G. J/16713 P/O J.B.Courtney Missing, Runnymede Memorial 175
A/G. 1266969 F/Sgt E.E.Garnett PoW. Stalag 344, Lamsdorf. 27641

214 Squadron 3 Group Stirling BK662 BU/K
Aircraft crashed in North Sea west of Texel, Holland.
Pilot. 657240 Sgt H.Baldock Missing, Runnymede Memorial 141
Nav. 1336307 Sgt P.R.Kimber Missing, Runnymede Memorial 155
B/A. 526692 Sgt E.A.Wright Missing, Runnymede Memorial 170
W/OP. 1458100 Sgt W.Taylor Missing, Runnymede Memorial 166
F/E. 129058 F/O H.T.Etienne Missing, Runnymede Memorial 124
A/G. 1128255 Sgt W.H.Trotter Killed Texel, Holland. Killed-2-40
A/G. R/88416 Sgt A.B.Amirault Missing, Runnymede Memorial 181

218 Squadron 3 Group Stirling R9333 HA/Y
Aircraft crashed at Essen, Germany.
Pilot. 138648 P/O G.A.Ratcliffe Killed Reichswald Forest. CG 10-6-6/11
Nav. A/400612 F/Sgt K.R.Heming Killed Reichswald Forest. CG 10-6-6/11
B/A. 1322282 Sgt D.H.Melville Killed Reichswald Forest. CG 10-6-6/11
W/OP. 1380140 Sgt W.E.Waddington Killed Reichswald Forest. 10-B-4
F/E. 614960 Sgt J.Turner Killed Reichswald Forest, Germany. CG 10-6-6/11
A/G. 621023 Sgt J.T.Charlton Killed Reichswald Forest. CG 10-6-6/11
A/G. 657140 Sgt W.T.Hurl Killed Reichswald Forest, Germany. CG 10-6-6/11

76 Squadron 4 Group Halifax BB282 MP/R
Pilot. R/92878 W/O C.A.Milan Missing, Runnymede Memorial 180
Nav. J/49032 F/O C.G.Hitt Missing, Runnymede Memorial 125
B/A. J/16944 P/O E.J.Fry Missing, Runnymede Memorial 175
W/OP. 1286321 Sgt H.W.Edwards Missing, Runnymede Memorial 148
F/E. 1094818 Sgt O.J.Trainor Missing, Runnymede Memorial 167
A/G. 1321550 Sgt H.C.Cope Missing, Runnymede Memorial 146
A/G. R/109924 W/O R.B.Van Buren Missing, Runnymede Memorial 180

78 Squadron 4 Group Halifax HR687 EY/
Pilot. 141457 P/O J.R.Thompson Killed Staphorst (Rouven), Holland. 4
Nav. 1128120 F/Sgt K.W.Mercer PoW. Stalag 344, Lamsdorf. 27727
B/A. 143493 F/O A.C.Loveland PoW. Stalag Luft 3, Sagan. 27725
W/OP. 1377328 F/Sgt A.E.Blackwell Killed Staphorst (Rouven), Holland. 3
F/E. 1060706 F/Sgt O.V.Proctor PoW. Stalag 344, Lamsdorf. 27732
A/G. 1337753 Sgt E.C.B.Williams Killed Staphorst (Rouven), Holland. 2
A/G. R/12280 W/O D.R.Chiswell PoW. Stalag 344, Lamsdorf. 27702

466 Squadron 4 Group Wellington HE270 HD/Q
Pilot. 1126332 F/Sgt A.C.Yielder Missing, Runnymede Memorial 140
Nav. 1335889 Sgt C.J.H.Smith Missing, Runnymede Memorial 165
B/A. 1318696 Sgt R.D.Baker Missing, Runnymede Memorial 141
W/OP. 1262308 Sgt J.W.Gould Killed Reichswald Forest, Germany. 8-D-18
A/G. 946593 Sgt J.Linacre Missing, Runnymede Memorial 157

49 Squadron 5 Group Lancaster ED431 EA/
Pilot. 1368871 Sgt J.M.Thom Missing, Runnymede Memorial 167
Nav. 632330 Sgt D.G.Fairlie Missing, Runnymede Memorial 149
B/A. 1375981 F/Sgt J.H.Prior Missing, Runnymede Memorial 138
W/OP. 989205 F/Sgt K.Bolton Missing, Runnymede Memorial 135
F/E. 1546821 Sgt D.S.Bratt Missing, Runnymede Memorial 143
A/G. R/76770 W/O A.M.Horne DFM Missing, Runnymede Memorial 180
A/G. 1316193 Sgt F.L.H.Vines Missing, Runnymede Memorial 168

106 Squadron 5 Group Lancaster W4918 ZN/
Pilot. 80222 F/Lt W.J.Picken DFC Killed Reichswald Forest, Germany. 8-G-17
Nav. 1268207 F/Sgt L.G.Hudson Killed Reichswald Forest, Germany. 8-D-16
B/A. 657619 Sgt J.E.Bonson Killed Reichswald Forest, Germany. 8-D-17
W/OP. R/79066 W/O J.C.E.Dellar Killed Reichswald Forest, Germany. 8-G-16
F/E. 612661 Sgt J.F.L.Wilson Killed Reichswald Forest, Germany. 10-B-3
A/G. 625778 Sgt L.A.Leadbitter Killed Reichswald Forest, Germany. 8-G-18
A/G. 1338127 Sgt G.J.Powell Killed Reichswald Forest, Germany. 8-D-15

419 Squadron 6 Group Halifax DT646 VR/
Crashed north of Amsterdam, Holland after fighter attack.
Pilot. 141771 F/Lt L.Bakewell PoW. Stalag 344, Lamsdorf. 27630
Nav. R/87500 W/O D.D.Scowen PoW. Stalag 344, Lamsdorf. 27657
B/A. J/16940 F/O J.E.Marvel PoW. Stalag Luft 3, Sagan. 27751
W/OP. R/77405 W/O J.A.Bennett PoW. Stalag 344, Lamsdorf. 27676
F/E. R/62322 Sgt A.C.Turner Evaded Capture
A/G. R/92367 W/O W.J.Clark PoW. Stalag 344, Lamsdorf. 27703
A/G. 1126438 F/Sgt J.R.Couper Missing, Runnymede Memorial 135

420 Squadron 6 Group Wellington HE280 PT/
Pilot. J/16414 P/O R.Graham Killed Reichswald Forest, Germany. 3-C-2
2/Pilot. J/13076 F/O J.K.Macdonald Killed Reichswald Forest, Germany. 3-C-1
Nav. 127921 P/O W.G.Lee Killed Reichswald Forest, Germany. 3-B-18
B/A. J/12978 P/O D.E.Bennett Killed Reichswald Forest, Germany. 3-C-8
W/OP. R/101307 F/Sgt H.T.Lawson Killed Reichswald Forest, Germany. 3-C-7
A/G. R/84400 W/O D.G.Culver Killed Reichswald Forest, Germany. 3-C-9

426 Squadron 6 Group Wellington BK401 KW/
Pilot. J/16651 P/O C.R.Trask Missing, Runnymede Memorial 281
Nav. 128617 F/O C.E.Chapman Missing, Runnymede Memorial 123
B/A. R/104057 F/Sgt W.J.R.Davies Missing, Runnymede Memorial 181
W/OP. R/111185 F/Sgt N.F.Paterson Missing, Runnymede Memorial 185
2/WOP. R/107124 F/Sgt G.Walen Missing, Runnymede Memorial 186
A/G. R/137111 Sgt R.E.Williams Missing, Runnymede Memorial 186

429 Squadron 6 Group Wellington BJ755 AL/
Crashed after take off from Eastmoor for Essen
Pilot. R/55965 F/Sgt R.F.Conroy Inj
Nav. R/79393 F/Sgt E.M.Bell Killed Sutton Forest, Yorkshire. E-1
B/A. R/1044206 Sgt G.R.Desmore Inj
W/OP. 353790 Sgt J.Bates Inj
A/G. R/144158 Sgt J.Burns Inj

Minelaying

On the same night as the first Essen raid, March 5th/6th, a
small force of seven aircraft, three Halifaxes and four Wellingtons from 4 Group, set out to lay mines around the Frisian
Islands. Two of the Wellington crews aborted their mission, but
the remaining aircraft dropped 14 mines without suffering any
losses.

The following evening, March 7th/8th, the Frisians were again
the area for continued minelaying by a force of six Halifaxes and
14 Wellingtons also from 4 Group. There was a cloudless sky,
but no moon. Visibility was generally poor and seven crews did
not drop their mines as they were unable to get that important
positional fix, so essential in minelaying operations. The
remaining aircraft dropped 30 mines. Two aircraft failed to
return from this operation, one being shot down by a night
fighter north-west of Vlieland and the other was possibly a
victim of the *Flak* at Schiermonnikoog.

Casualties March 7th/8th, 1943. Minelaying (Frisians)

51 Squadron 4 Group Halifax DT567 MH/
Pilot. 126601 F/O A.L.Holmes Killed Sage, Germany.(Buried 29/4/43) 7-F-5
Nav. 1149217 Sgt J.G.Ramshaw Killed Ameland (Nes), Holland. D-13-14
B/A. 131775 P/O J.E.Ulrich Missing, Runnymede Memorial 133
W/OP. 551841 F/Sgt R.E.Dormon Missing, Runnymede Memorial 136
F/E. 577306 Sgt A.R.Harding Missing, Runnymede Memorial 152
A/G. 1294414 Sgt P.McAleese Killed Kiel, Germany. 3-E-6
A/G. 1037931 Sgt G.Tombe Killed Sage, Germany.(Buried 21/5/43) 3-F-8

431 Squadron 4 Group Wellington HE202 SE/Z
Shot down by fighter N.W. of Vlieland, Holland.
Pilot. NZ/413470 W/O D.C.Pitts PoW. Stalag 344, Lamsdorf. 27655
Nav. 1147399 F/Sgt R.McHugh PoW. Stalag 344, Lamsdorf. 27649
B/A. 120888 F/Lt K.D.Tutton PoW. Stalag Luft 3, Sagan. 262
W/OP. 1379087 F/Sgt B.G.Peart PoW. Stalag 344, Lamsdorf. 27650
A/G. 1288756 F/Sgt D.E.H Dyer PoW. Stalag 344, Lamsdorf. 27635

Minelaying

The primary purpose of minelaying operations was to lay mines
in the enemy swept channels and waterways which were very

narrow, ranging from half a mile to a mile wide. Successful minelaying depended on very accurate navigation as mines which were dropped outside swept channels were practically useless. It was desirable that the mines were dropped from as low an altitude as possible, not above 1,500 feet. A minimum height of 1,000 feet was laid down to cover misjudgement in height or loss of altitude when turning. Later in the campaign of mining operations, from August 1944, the minimum height for dropping mines was raised to 6,000 feet for aircraft with H^2S sets which were particularly effective on coast lines and allowed freedom from having to identify a landmark visually.

From a visual pin point, either a point on the coast or landmark, the mining aircraft had to make a timed run of about 12 miles on a steady course with a ground speed of between 180 and 200 mph otherwise the parachute attached to the mine could be pulled away. A steady course had also to be maintained for at least 2 to 3 minutes after the mines had been dropped, this was an attempt to deceive the enemy as to the exact dropping position. Mines were dropped in 3.5 second intervals from four engined bombers and in 5 second intervals from the twin engined Wellington bombers. If for some reason the mines were not dropped, they were brought back to base. There were no particular dangers in doing this, for the method of arming aircraft mines was fairly foolproof. They had three safety devices, firstly the ordinary safety switch inside the aircraft, secondly the mine had a soluble plug which would take 40 minutes to dissolve in sea water and lastly the mine had a hydrostatic switch which operated only when the water pressure was high enough, in excess of five fathoms. It was therefore almost impossible for a mine to detonate, even in a crash landing. In the event of such a situation arising where a mine did have to be jettisoned, there were carefully laid out procedures for where they should, if possible, be dropped and their position carefully plotted.

A four engined aircraft normally carried six mines and the two engined Wellington usually carried two mines. The aircraft mine weighed 1,500 pounds and differed from the sea mine for it did not float in the water, nor was it moored, and it had no contact horns. It was cylindrical in shape with a wooden fairing at one end to allow its easy entry into the water. At the other end a small parachute was placed to ensure that the mine dropped vertically and that the impact into the water was softened. Aircraft mines were either magnetic or acoustic, or even a mixture of both, and as they remained on the sea bed the water depth had to be relatively shallow for them to be effective.

Minelaying was nicknamed 'Gardening' by bomber crews as the code names used by intelligence for the mining areas around the German and French coasts had names such as 'Forget me Nots', 'Daffodils', 'Nectarines', 'Artichokes'. The mines were often called seeds to be planted. Some RAF/Navy planners must have been keen gardeners to concoct some of these names, unless the RAF slang term of 'Gardening' had given them the idea. Naval officers were always attached to bomber stations to act as liaison officers for minelaying and also for the issue of Allied convoy information. This was important to aircrews returning from raids, especially if they were in damaged aircraft which might have diverted from the original return route. Allied convoys were prone to fire their anti-aircraft guns first and question colours of the day after.

'Gardening' sorties were not the most popular operations with the bomber crews. They were no sinecure for they took their toll of many brave crews. The low dropping height made a bomber especially vulnerable to light *Flak* from the many *Flak* ships carefully positioned in the main shipping lanes for the Germans were quick to realise the problems that mining caused to shipping. The long timed run from a visual pin point and the necessity of holding a steady course for such a long time, even after the mines were released, made the bombers fairly easy to pick up on radar and gave the *Flak* ample time to get the range. Overall losses, however, were low compared with bombing operations over Germany. There were exceptions, especially when a large minelaying force was used or when the route had to cross areas such as Denmark which were heavily defended by night fighters and *Flak* positions. The damage caused to enemy shipping by mining operations was rarely known for some time after the operation, but they were found to be highly profitable in the number of sinkings and the number of ships damaged. A large German naval force was also kept fully occupied, constantly having to sweep the areas around the German and French coasts so that shipping moving vital war equipment and materials was not sunk or seriously delayed.

Nuremburg

March 8th/9th, 1943

Before the next big raid to the Ruhr, Bomber Command mounted major attacks on two important German cities. The targets were well outside the *Oboe* ground station range. The first raid was to Nuremburg on the night of Monday 8th March, when 335 aircraft left their English bases at approximately 19.00 hours. 170 Lancasters, 103 Halifaxes and 62 Stirlings, took off for a round trip of eight hours. 43 of the bombers returned early to their bases for a variety of reasons, leaving only 285 aircraft to attack Nuremburg. The Pathfinders on this raid were Lancasters, Halifaxes and Stirlings equipped with H²S sets and they were using the *Newhaven* (Ground Marking) method of marking the target with TIs.

Fourteen heavy Pathfinder crews planned to use their *H²S* sets plus visual identification to mark the Nuremburg target area. Although there was no cloud, they had no moon either to help in their visual marking and they were also hampered by haze over the city making accurate marking impossible. Nine of the pathfinders marked blindly using their *H²S* sets and the remaining five marked visually, because their sets were unserviceable. As in the Essen raid, the main force of bombers went in in three waves, Zero Hour being 23.14 hours. The Halifaxes went in from $Z + 4$ to $Z + 20$, the Stirlings in the second wave from $Z + 10$ to $Z + 20$, and finally the Lancasters from $Z + 15$ to $Z + 30$. The bombing was very scattered. Photographs taken by a reconnaisance plane the next day showed that the attack stretched along a line 7 miles south to 2 miles north-west of the planned aiming point. A total of forty-four 250 lbs target indicators and 189 flares had been dropped by the Pathfinders and 358.6 tons of high explosive bombs along with 176,924 incendiaries (412 tons) by the main force. The total bomb tonnage for this raid was 775.5 tons. The Siemens Schuckert factory, which made diesel engines for the U-Boats, was heavily damaged as well as the industrial southern area of the city. Damage was also extensive to houses as well as industrial premises. People were told to repair their own homes as best they could and also help their neighbours. On the Saturday and Sunday following the raid all the people in the city had to 'volunteer' to clean up the debris in the city centre. Seven bombers were lost on the raid and one ditched in the Channnel, three were from the Pathfinder force. There was a loss rate of 2.4% of the attacking aircraft. From the 56 aircrew manning the lost aircraft 34 were killed, nine missing, nine became prisoners of war, three evaded capture and one was rescued from the ditched aircraft.

H^2S Navigation Set

H^2S was the first airborne radar set that could paint a shadowy image of the ground below on a cathode ray tube in an aircraft above. First use of H^2S, the new RDF navigational aid, had taken place against Hamburg on the night of 30th/31st January, 1943, when a small force of 148 aircraft were led by heavy Pathfinder bombers equipped with H^2S. This had been in the nature of an operational trial and one which was successful enough to indicate the future promise of the device. Whilst Oboe was available to ensure the good marking for bombers of the main force to destroy the Ruhr, H^2S was the means of striking deep into Germany with terrifying effect. This new navigational aid undoubtedly revolutionised the tactics of night bombing. It enabled the bomber force to operate outside the *Oboe* range with good accuracy and made the bombers largely independent of weather conditions en route to and over the target area. Attacks could be successfully made in no moon periods and under conditions which were not favourable for the German night fighters to operate. The H^2S had a 360 degree scanner which was housed in a black plastic dome (radome) underneath the main fuselage of an aircraft. The sets suffered many early teething troubles and required constant maintenance, especially the sets which were issued initially only to Pathfinder aircraft. The sets always performed best in the vicinity of bodies of water, which showed up clearly on the cathode ray screen. Bomb aimers often operated the sets, although in many crews this task was carried out by the navigator. H^2S sets operated on a 10cm waveband that could not be jammed by the Germans.

One of the first H^2S sets fitted to a bomber was captured by the Germans when Stirling R9253 (MG/L) from 7 (PFF) Squadron crashed at Hendrik-Ido-Ambacht, near Rotterdam on a raid to Cologne on the night of 2nd/3rd February, 1943. The crew were injured and unable to destroy their valuable equipment. Later sets were fitted with self destruct devices. The Germans were extremely impressed, if not awed, after they had examined the captured H^2S set and the cavity magnetron that it contained. After understanding the general principle upon which the H^2S worked they went to great trouble to alter the H^2S silhouette of the countryside around some key targets and towns, especially in Hamburg Docks and the lakes around Berlin, where they built huge rafts of metal strips to float on the water. Later they also devised a radar to fit to their night fighters, code named *Naxos*, which could home in on an H²S transmission from a bomber. The emissions from the set were like a lighthouse to patrolling *Luftwaffe* night fighters. *Naxos* was so successful that Bomber Command went to the extent of issuing an order that the H^2S sets should only be switched on for short intervals over enemy territory.

Left all alone

A mid upper gunner, Sergeant D. R. Spanton, in Stirling BK592 of 7 Squadron had a remarkable escape. As the plane was on its return flight over the Channel, the gunner realised that he was the only one left on the plane. The rest of the crew, who were new to the Pathfinder squadron, had baled out earlier. For some reason Sergeant Spanton had not heard the bale out order and was not unduly concerned on the return flight because they had not been attacked by a fighter or hit by *Flak*. The bale out order must have been given for some engine fault or fuel problem which had later rectified itself. Luckily the mid upper gunner discovered his predicament when the Stirling had crossed the English coast, still flying on 'George', the automatic pilot. He baled out rather smartly when he realised his plight and landed safely in Kent. The plane eventually crashed in the sea off Dungeness. The remainder of the crew were never found and it was presumed that they baled out over the Channel, perhaps believing they were over northern France. Sergeant Spanton's luck held out a little longer, but he and his new crew went missing too, on a raid to Wuppertal in Stirling EF392 (MG/Z) on the night of 24th/25th June, 1943. They were never found.

Flight Sergeant Sibbald's Evasion

Another of the Pathfinders which went missing on the Nuremburg raid was Halifax W7851 (TL/Y) of 35 Squadron captained by Flying Officer Brown. About 01.00 hours on their return flight the aircraft was caught unawares by an enemy night fighter and the bomber quickly set on fire. The flight engineer, Sergeant Tacey, was badly wounded along with the pilot when ammunition inside the plane exploded. All the crew managed to bale out, in spite of their injuries, from a height of 12,000 feet north-east of Avesnes. Only one of the crew, New Zealander Flight Sergeant D. A. Sibbald, was fortunate enough to evade capture with the help of the French underground. He landed in a tree uninjured and after hiding his parachute and Mae West in a hollow tree, made off rather quickly in a south westerly direction.

Early on the morning of 9th March he came to a dense wood which was an ideal place to lay up for the day. He spent his time studying his map and eating some of the delicious chocolate in his escape box. Unable to rip off his heavily sewn on badges, he smeared them thickly with mud to make them less conspicious. As it was getting dark at around 19.00 hours, he decided to walk on.

After walking most of the night, at dawn on 10th March, he came to the village of Cartignies where he crawled into an old wood shed. About two hours later, as he was getting hungry, he decided to knock at the door of a nearby farmhouse. He could not speak French so he used sign language to the woman who answered his knocking, to ask for food. She motioned that he should go around to the back door, where he was taken in and given a meal. The woman also brought a young girl who produced a French / English dictionary and with the aid of this Sibbald was able to explain who he was and that he required help. Later a number of other French people came to the house to see him. His new found hosts took him into a hay loft where he was able to sleep until late that afternoon. At around 16.00 hours an elderly Englishman called Mr. Bamford arrived and explained that he was a civilian internee. He suggested that Sibbald should walk along the road and give himself up to the Germans. The young girl also explained that the people in the house would prefer that he surrender himself. After some discussion the people eventually agreed that they would keep him for another two nights, during which time he was given civilian clothes, a pair of boots and adequately fed.

On March 12th a man came along and took Sibbald on a bicycle from Cartignies to Avesnes, where he stayed for another five days in a Frenchman's house. During his stay here he was visited by yet another Frenchman who asked him details of other members of his crew. The wounded Sergeant Tacey, the flight engineer, had been captured and was a prisoner in a German controlled hospital at Maubeuge. Tacey had asked a French member of the hospital staff to help him escape, but he had been advised that his injuries were too severe for this to be attempted. The pilot, Flying Officer Brown, who had also been wounded aboard the plane, had been captured and was being treated in a smaller hospital at Avesnes. Sibbald was able to send a message via his helpers to let both of the wounded crew know that he was safe.

Sibbald was again on the move to another house on the outskirts of Avesnes on the 17th and on the 20th a French underground member who spoke good English took him along by bicycle to Semeries where he stayed for ten days. It was here that one of the helpers had let slip in the course of conversation that he was helping an English airman escape and Sibbald was taken rather quickly out of the way by bicycle to a safer house in the village of Felleries. Here he remained until April 17th, when he was taken by car back to Avesnes, from where his final journey back to England was arranged for him.

Two Evaders Captured

While Halifax JB840 from 102 Squadron was on its way to Nuremburg it was attacked by a night fighter at 22.43 hours west of Verdun, France. It was so badly damaged that there was no alternative but for a bale out order to be given by the captain, Sergeant R. C. Hibben. All the crew safely baled out and the bomb aimer, Sergeant A. R. Mansford, with the flight engineer, Sergeant W. Hughes, were fortunate in avoiding capture and finally getting back to the UK. One of the gunners, Sergeant R. Atkinson, was able to get away from the bale out site, but was unlucky to be captured in a Police check on a Lyons bound train. He ended the war at Barth Vogelsang Camp as Prisoner of War 996. The navigator, Sergeant Slocombe, travelled even further in his evasion attempt before he was captured by German guards as he was crossing the Pyrenees on his way into Spain. He ended the war at Stalag 357, Kopernikus as Prisoner 1036.

Casualties March 8th/9th, 1943. Target Nuremburg

156 Squadron 8 Group Lancaster W4896 GT/
Pilot. J/17541 P/O M.E.White DFM Killed Durnbach, Germany. 8-D-15
Nav. R/86739 W/O R.H.Ward Killed Durnbach, Germany. 8-D-16
B/A. R/102783 W/O R.D.Strong Killed Durnbach, Germany. 8-D-18
W/OP. J/18155 P/O W.R.Affleck Killed Durnbach, Germany. 8-D-17
F/E. 1240819 Sgt C.R.Swift Killed Durnbach, Germany. 8-D-19
A/G. 1621821 Sgt J.Neale Killed Durnbach, Germany. 8-D-20
A/G. 529468 F/Sgt J.W.A.Dorsett Killed Durnbach, Germany. JG 8-D-13/14

35 Squadron 8 Group Halifax W7851 TL/Y
Aircraft crashed Avesnes, France after fighter attack.
Pilot. 10928 F/O J.H.Brown Killed Cambrai, France. 1-B-1
Nav. 77214 S/Ldr G.D.Waterer PoW. Stalag Luft 3, Sagan. 937
B/A. NZ/404900 F/Sgt A.G.M.Coulam PoW. Stalag 357, Kopernikus. 42719
W/OP. NZ/411102 F/Sgt D.A.Sibbald Evaded capture
F/E. 1057600 W/O A.Tacey PoW. Stalag 344, Lamsdorf. 27744
A/G. 1174414 F/Sgt P.Flynn Killed Cambrai, France. 1-B-2
A/G. NZ/413286 F/Sgt S.S.Vinicombe Killed Cambrai, France. 1-B-3

7 Squadron 8 Group Stirling R9270 MG/Q
Aircraft crashed at Les Souhesmes, France.
Pilot. 68742 F/Lt J.P.Trench DSO Killed Les Souhesmes, France. CG 6/7
Nav. 109922 F/Lt C.L.Selman DFC Killed Les Souhesmes, France. CG 6/7
B/A. A/402985 P/O L.G.Gosper DFC Killed Les Souhesmes, France. CG 6/7
W/OP. 142910 P/O H.Harwood DFM Killed Les Souhesmes, France. CG 6/7
F/E. 616283 F/Sgt F.W.R.Cole DFM Killed Les Souhesmes, France. CG 6/7

A/G. 1277051 Sgt E.T.Beney Killed Les Souhesmes, France. CG 6/7
A/G. 1378108 F/Sgt W.P.Hudson Killed Les Souhesmes, France. CG 6/7

7 Squadron 8 Group Stirling BK592 MG/P
Aircraft ditched off Dungeness.
Pilot. J/17295 P/O L.L.V.Toupin Missing, Runnymede Memorial 178
Nav. 1030197 Sgt J.Goddard Missing, Runnymede Memorial 150
B/A. 1266197 F/Sgt R.G.Thorne Missing, Runnymede Memorial 139
W/OP. 1380825 Sgt H.Kilvington Killed Cardiff Western F-959 Body
recovered at Newhaven
F/E. 966932 Sgt G.Bell Killed Abbeville, France. 7-B-1
A/G. 1323191 Sgt D.R.Spanton Rescued
A/G. R/61217 W/O W.W.Freeland Missing, Runnymede Memorial 180

15 Squadron 3 Group Stirling BK697 LS/P
Aircraft crashed at Campneuville, France.
Pilot. J/16519 P/O J.G.Ripley Killed Verdun-sur-Meuse, France. 3
Nav. R/106054 F/Sgt A.J.Bagg Killed Verdun-sur-Meuse, France. 5
B/A. R/93534 W/O A.M.Reid PoW. Stalag 344, Lamsdorf. 27735
W/OP. 1109609 F/Sgt C.Burkhill Killed Verdun-sur-Meuse, France. 4
F/E. 653824 Sgt J.F.Farrelly Killed Verdun-sur Meuse, France. 6
A/G. R/103796 F/Sgt E.K.Matlock Killed Verdun-sur-Meuse, France. 1
A/G. J/11120 F/O L.M.Wadman Killed Verdun-sur-Meuse, France. 2

75 Squadron 3 Group Stirling BF437 AA/L
Aircraft crashed at Huttenheim, Germany.
Pilot. NZ/419937 Sgt C.R.Davey Killed Durnbach, Germany. 2-G-11
Nav. R/84152 W/O A.Arlen Missing, Runnymede Memorial 179
B/A. 149883 P/O I.J.D.Brodie Killed Durnbach, Germany. 2-G-12
W/OP. 1313099 Sgt L.M.Stone Missing, Runnymede Memorial 166
F/E. 528778 Sgt A.E.Howlett Missing, Runnymede Memorial 154
A/G. 632983 Sgt A.J.Feenan Missing, Runnymede Memorial 149
A/G. 1450019 Sgt A.B.Tarrant Missing, Runnymede Memorial 166

102 Squadron 4 Group Halifax JB840 DY/
Pilot. 1331873 W/O R.C.F.Hibben PoW. Stalag 357, Kopernikus. 42717
Nav. 1380460 W/O F.R.Slocombe PoW. Stalag 357, Kopernikus. 1036
B/A. 1393137 Sgt A.R.Mansford Evaded capture
W/OP. 115659 F/Sgt H.M.Simpson PoW. Stalag 344, Lamsdorf. 27743
F/E. 1074684 Sgt W.Hughes DFM Evaded capture
A/G. 970286 W/O R.Atkinson PoW. Stalag Luft 1, Barth Vogelsang. 996
A/G. 1332196 F/Sgt E.G.Sawkins PoW, Stalag 344, Lamsdorf. 27742

61 Squadron 5 Group Lancaster W4903 QR/
Pilot. A/402334 F/Lt C.A.Giles DFC Killed Durnbach, Germany. 8-D-7
Nav. 50038 P/O K.D.Babington-Browne Killed Durnbach, Germany. 8-D-9
B/A. 131992 P/O B.J.Gunter Killed Durnbach, Germany. 8-D-10
W/OP. 616838 F/Sgt G.Mitchell Killed Durnbach, Germany. 8-D-11
F/E. 106862 F/O F.Richards Killed Durnbach, Germany. 8-D-8
A/G. 998856 Sgt E.Carr Killed Durnbach, Germany. 8-D-12
A/G. 973384 F/Sgt D.Forbes Killed Durnbach, Germany. JG 8-D-13/14

Minelaying

March 8th/9th, 1943

Sixteen Wellingtons from the Canadian 6 Group continued minelaying along the Frisian Islands. Five of them failed to get an accurate fix for dropping the mines and returned with them to base. The remaining aircraft dropped 22 mines in the correct areas. No losses were incurred in these minelaying sorties.

Minor Raids by Mosquitos

Three Mosquitoes made nuisance raids on the three Ruhr towns of Cologne, Essen and Hagen, dropping a total of of 2.1 tons of high explosive bombs. There were no losses from these minor operations.

Munich

March 9th/10th, 1943

264 aircraft made up of 142 Lancasters, 81 Halifaxes and 41 Stirlings set off from their bases at around 19.00 hours. Again there was a high percentage of aborted flights, 47 bombers making an early return to their bases. The attack opened at two minutes before midnight, the Pathfinders easily identifying their aiming point in the cloud free target. This was a fairly successful raid in spite of a wrongly forecast wind which resulted in the attack concentrating on the western half of the city, instead of dead centre. Route marking by Pathfinders at Metz served to pull the main force bombers back on to track and other markers at Ammer See gave all aircraft an accurate dead reckoning point for the run in to Munich, which later became shrouded by haze. *Flak* was experienced in various intensities, but nowhere very accurate. Night fighters were very active on the return leg, especially around Rheims.

According to German post war records heavy damage in Munich as a result of this particular raid was as follows; 291 buildings destroyed, 660 very severely damaged and 2134 damaged. These buildings included 11 hospitals, a cathedral and 14 churches. 294 military buildings were also hit and the biggest industrial damage was caused to the BMW aero engine works. 281.1 tons of HE and 265 tons of incendiaries along with thirty three 250 lb TIs and 232 flares were dropped, a total of 549.8 tons. Eight aircraft were lost and of the 56 aircrew manning these bombers 33 were killed, six were missing, nine men became prisoners of war. The high total of eight men managed to evade capture, having baled out in the north-east area of France where helpers in the escape organisation were more active.

J for Johnny's Lucky Crew

Halifax DT734, J for Johnny of 77 Squadron from 4 Group, piloted by 39342 Squadron Leader R. J. Sage AFC, was shot down by *Flak* at 02.00 hours on 10th March over Boussu-lez-Mons, Belgium. Three of the crew evaded capture. The flight engineer, 950785 Sergeant B. J. I. Walker DFM, and the navigator, 129452 Flight Lieutenant B. D. Barker, returned through Spain. The bomb aimer, Sergeant M. Crabtree, got back via neutral Switzerland. The air gunner, Sergeant D. L. Morris, although having the help of the resistance movement was not so fortunate in evading capture. He was eventually taken to Brussels where he was accommmodated for nearly two months at 21 Quai de Commerce. During this time he met the infamous 'Captain', a man who was involved in arranging many evaders' journeys when in the Belgian capital. He was responsible for many aircrew being arrested by the Gestapo, either in a Brussels hotel or afterwards on their train journey to Bordeaux from Brussels.

Sergeant Morris, in company with some other aircrew, was taken to Bordeaux by train in a party which was in the charge of a guide called Marcel. When the airmen reached Bordeaux they were taken to an hotel on May 20th, but next day were arrested by the Gestapo. It was a story of betrayal which became all too familiar in aircrew's stories who were finally captured after varying periods of time on the loose.

Sergeant Walkers's account illustrates the courage, tenacity, perseverance and often the good luck that was so essential in making a successful evasion. The Halifax had developed engine trouble on the way to the target and when about five miles short of the target itself the pilot had to jettison the bomb load and turn back to base. On the return flight the aircraft encountered some heavy *Flak* over Belgium and was badly hit in the port wing which resulted in the aircraft's petrol tanks catching fire and the bale out order being given. Sergeant Walker was the last but one to leave the aircraft, after he had performed his last duty of removing the pilot's Sutton safety harness and clamping a 'chute on the pilot's chest.

He landed in a grass field at about 02.00 hours somewhere between Mons and the French frontier. His first task was to get rid of his 'chute and Mae West, which he did by hiding them in some reeds in a dyke, before he started walking south-south-west guided by the stars. He trudged across country until dawn when he decided to lay up in a stack of wood about half a mile from a lonely farm. He stayed there all day without seeing anyone. At dusk, after his brief rest, he began walking once again. He was fortunate in that he was wearing ordinary shoes instead of flying boots which made his walking easier.

That night he guessed he had crossed the frontier into France and as he was travelling along a canal bank he came upon some lock gates where, much to his dismay, he saw a group of German soldiers examining people's papers as they went across a bridge over the canal. To avoid this patrol he quickly left the path and trudged through some very marshy ground skirting the lock gates to rejoin the canal path further west and most probably crossing the frontier again en route. Still in his uniform he thought that it would be wise to tear off his badges of rank and flying brevet to make himself less conspicuous.

Now using the escape compass, he continued on his way until coming to the town of Conde. It was here that he had his first stroke of good luck, for a passing German soldier shone a torch into his face, but fortunately did not stop or question him. At Conde he managed to cross over the canal by a railway bridge and kept walking all night following the railway line in a south westerly direction. By dawn he had arrived somewhere between Douai and Denain. At 06.00 hours on March 11th, tired out, he decided to go to a small farm on the town outskirts. As he could not speak French he explained by signs as best he could who he was and asked for food. Luckily he was given some breakfast by the occupants and allowed to sleep in the barn until 14.00 hours when he was awoken and given a civilian jacket, scarf, beret and advised to try and get to Douai.

After leaving the farm, Sergeant Walker struck out south-west again across country and joined the Douai to Cambrai road at a village he believes was called Brunemont, about 12 kms from Cambrai. From this village he continued down the main road until to his surprise he came to a part of the road which appeared to run through a German airfield near Epinoy. There was a pole barrier across the road, so to avoid this he cut south across fields until he reached another main road, the Arras to Cambrai road. Crossing this he continued until he came to the village of Fontaine. By this time in spite of his civilian shoes his feet had developed large blisters and they felt in a bad state. At about 16.00 hours he realised he could not walk much further, but then he saw an opportunity to steal a bicycle which was left standing outside a shop. Grateful for the fact that road signposts, unlike England, were still around in France, he cycled away following the signs to Peronne then on to Roye and Cuvilly, which was about 7 miles north west of Compiegne. When he reached the outskirts of the village he was feeling very hungry so he decided to ask for food at a farm. Again he was fortunate that the French farmers were sympathetic, for he was given food and allowed to spend the night in the barn.

Next morning, March 12th, off he went again cycling through Senlis until he came to the village of Meaux where he thought his luck had run out, for he was stopped by two gendarmes because he had no licence plate on his bicycle. Fortunately one of them spoke a little English and after he explained who he was he was allowed to go on, but not before one of them marked his map with a route to Spain and suggested that St. Girons would be a suitable place from which to try to cross the Pyrenees. Elated with his good luck he cycled on until he came to the village of Neufmeutiers at about 22.00 hours, where again a sympathetic French farmer gave him shelter for the night. On the following morning the farmer turned out to be very pro British and suggested that his son should accompany Sergeant Walker on his way back, for the son was anxious to join the Free

French forces in England and would be of some help in any language problems which would arise on their journey back.

On the morning of March 13th the farmer, his son and Sergeant Walker travelled by train to Paris, taking their bicycles along with them. The rail ticket was bought from the money in the Sergeant's escape kit. They changed stations in Paris and caught the Tours train, arriving there at about 15.00 hours. From Tours they all cycled to Cormey, where they stayed with another Frenchman who had been a fellow prisoner of war with the farmer. The next morning, March 14th, was another day for a piece of good luck to come Sergeant Walker's way. The Frenchman obtained an identity card for him from the Police Prefecture using one of the civilian escape photographs that Walker had in his pocket. A timely piece of good preparatory intelligence work that had been done on his squadron. The card he obtained showed that the bearer was deaf and dumb.

Leaving their kind benefactor early next day they continued cycling until they arrived at Loches, where good fortune smiled on them for they found that the barrier along the main road which marked the Line of Demarcation was raised and unguarded. There appeared to be a German guardroom on the side, but there didn't seem to be anybody about. Crossing quickly they got into Loches and into the railway station, boarding a train along with their bicycles to Toulouse, changing at Chateauroux. They were making for Bayonne, but the French farmer had decided that it would be better to travel via Toulouse to avoid the coastal strip which would have more German troops about.

After spending a night at an hotel, on March 16th, they took the train to Bayonne. At the small town of Orthes the train was stopped for half an hour by German patrol guards so that identity cards could be checked. As Sergeant Walker's card was genuine, he kept mum and the guards didn't give him a second look after examining his card. The farmer was more unfortunate for he had to hide in the train toilet, as his card was only valid in northern France. On March 17th they arrived at Boussens which had a good bus service to various places around the district. After travelling by bus to St Girons, which was as far south as one could go without entering the prohibited zone, they stayed at an hotel. The farmer visited a local priest to ask for a guide to take them over the Pyrenees. Unfortunately the priest could offer no help, so reluctantly the disillusioned farmer and his son decided to give up and return home. The three returned to Boussens where Sergeant Walker parted company with them.

Now on his own he returned to the Boussens left luggage office to collect his bike and then decided to try and canvass the help of a local priest in a neighbouring village. Luck was again on the Sergeant's side for this priest spoke a little English and took him to some neighbours who were more fluent in English. Sergeant Walker asked them if they could help him in any way to get into Spain. He was taken to a family in neighbouring Mazeres, but the Pyrenees were impassable at this time of year due to snow. He spent a few days with them before he was moved to yet another family home in Belbeze-Escoulis, spending ten days with them before being again transferred to a workman's house in Mazeres for another ten days.

Once news came through that the mountains were clear of snow he was taken to St Girons to join a party of about 20 Frenchmen and two guides. Starting off the same night they made their way through the woods to the frontier and then across Mount Valliez into Spain, the whole journey taking two and half days. Arriving in Alos in Spain, the Frenchmen decided to give themselves up to the authorities. Sergeant Walker, however, wanted to go on alone and he tried to walk around Alos on the high ground. He was arrested by volunteer frontier guards who were out shooting on their day off and taken back to Alos to join the rest of the original party in gaol. They were all detained for one night before being moved on to Sort, where at least they stayed in an hotel before being taken to the political prison at Lerida. After fourteen days there, Sergeant Walker was taken by some Spanish Air Force men to Alhama De Aragon and put into an hotel for five days. Finally he was sent on to Madrid and eventually to Gibraltar, arriving there on May 8th, 1943, before being flown back to England.

More Munich Evaders

Three other evaders from the Munich raid were from Stirling R9149, of 7 Squadron, piloted by J/16659 Pilot Officer F. M. Tomlinson, who was unfortunately killed. The aircraft en route to the target was attacked head on by a night fighter west of Luxembourg. The plane was badly damaged and lost height rapidly, so the bale out order was given at Elan, south of Charleville. The three lucky evaders were the navigator, R/104339 Sergeant D. M. Cox, bomb aimer, 655165 Sergeant G. R. Howard, and flight engineer, 96874 Sergeant L. Marsh.

Sergeant Marsh's evasion account shows not only what good luck he had after his bale out but his determination afterwards in not being a guest of the Third Reich for the rest of the war.

After landing in a ploughed field at 22.30 hours about 2 kms from Elan, he quickly buried his flying gear in a forest and started to walk in a south-westerly direction. Unsure of his exact location he decided to call at a house around 01.30 hours. Fortunately he was asked in and after he was given a meal he stayed there resting for about four hours before the owner pointed out to him the direction of the road for Reims.

Heading west he observed a German foot patrol and then two Storch observation planes out searching, so he decided to return to the forest where there was more cover. Later he continued walking to reach Poix-Terrow where he met a farmer who took him into his house and gave him a suit of civilian clothes, although he could not find any shoes to fit Marsh's big feet. The farmer also brought a girl and her father to see Marsh and they said that they knew someone who could help in his escape. Later they took him along to see this person who from that point arrranged his journey for him.

On September 22nd, after a long stay with his helpers, Marsh cycled to Ville-sur-Retourne to get some clothes and while returning on September 24th stopped to have a drink at a bar at Heutregville. Afterwards he went into the back yard of the estaminet to find a toilet. There in the yard were two German officers and a sergeant supervising the distribution of meat to the local villagers. One of the officers stopped Marsh and asked him who he was and what he was doing there. Although he showed them his identity card which had been provided by the escape organisation, the officer was not satisfied because Marsh did not have the necessary Labour Card as well. He was arrested and then had no option but to admit that he was a member of the RAF. The officer, however, did not record the name, rank and number which Marsh gave him and he was taken under guard to Reims.

The next day, still under guard, he was taken to the railway station to await a train for Chalons. At the station Marsh asked his guards if he could go to the toilet, permission was granted and the sergeant from the escort stayed outside the toilet building while the corporal stayed outside the toilet door. Once inside Marsh saw that it was easy to climb over the partition into the women's toilet next door without arousing the German corporal's attention. He emerged on the other side, fortunately on to a different platform, where he found an unattended bicycle on which he cycled quickly away in the direction of Chalons. About 10 kms outside Reims he abandoned the bicycle and made his way back to Beime, reaching there on September 25th, wondering how his escort had explained how they lost a prisoner. From there his interrupted journey to freedom was arranged for him again by the escape organisation.

Other Lucky Evaders

Some aircrew from a Lancaster from 207 Squadron, captained by 1255050 Flight Sergeant I. Wood, were also fortunate to evade capture after being brought down on the Munich raid. They were the flight engineer Sergeant G. Brownhill and Sergeant R. Brown, the navigator. The rest of the crew, except for the wireless operator, Sergeant Lishman who became a prisoner, were all killed. Sergeant Brown relates his account of that night and his subsequent evasion story.

Their plane was shot down by a fighter 30 miles north-east of Reims at 03.00 hours while on their way to the target. The Lancaster was quickly on fire after the first burst from the fighter caught one of the inner engines. The bale out order, although quickly given, only allowed time for three members of crew to get out safely. Sergeant Brown landed in some woods near Avancon, where he hid his flying gear and started walking quickly away from the crash site. On reaching the village of Bazancourt he spotted and avoided a passing German motor cycle patrol, probably looking for survivors from his crashed plane. By this time it was beginning to get light and he approached a young Frenchman on the road. As Brown could speak a little French he told the man his identity and asked for help. The Frenchman took him to his home, supplied him with some food and, taking a big chance, allowed him to stay there for the rest of the day. At night Brown was given an old coat to cover his uniform and after thanking the Frenchman for his help set out walking south in the darkness. At Beaumont-sur-Vesle, Brown had another stroke of good luck for another Frenchman took him to his sister-in-law's house and allowed him to rest. After a few hours he was given a packet of food and he continued walking, then concealing himself near Conde-sur-Marne during the day. At dusk he crossed an unguarded bridge across the River Marne and after passing through a few villages he reached Plancy at 01.00 hours on March 12th, where he spent the rest of the night in an open field, sleeping in some hay. On the morning of the 12th he walked to Mer-sur-Seine, where he received some help again in the form of food and shelter and, more importantly was given a suit of civilian clothes. The helper then accompanied him to Troyes, where he left after giving directions to Maiche and an address where further help could be received.

From Troyes, Brown boarded the Paris / Cologne express train. He had to change at Belfort, where he got lost on the station and had to go to the inquiry office and ask a German booking clerk from which platform he could catch a train for Baumes-les-Dames. His helper at Troyes had told Brown to travel at this time of night when he guessed that controls would be very slack.

He reached Baumes-les-Dames safely at 07.00 hours and walked from there to Maiche, arriving there at 22.00 hours, feeling very tired and footsore. Unable to find the address he had been given at that time of night, Brown spent the night sleeping in the back of a truck parked near a garage. At dawn he went into the nearby woods and remained there until 08.00 hours before going back into the village where he located the address he had been given. He was welcomed and spent two days resting.

On the third day his new helper and a friend of his agreed to take Brown almost into Switzerland. The three travelled by car to Trevillers, about 7 kms north-east of Maiche. There the helper left them and the friend, along with Brown, walked to a village nearby where the unknown friend attended to some business during the day and returned at 18.00 hours to Brown who was hiding. From his hiding place, Brown watched a German patrol of two men and dogs pass at irregular intervals along a piece of ground about 3 kms behind the frontier.

When the friend returned he took Brown into some woods south of Fuesse and after giving him directions of how to cross the frontier, left him. Wasting no time, Brown continued eastwards running and sometimes crawling until he could see 30 feet below him the Swiss frontier post.

The first town he reached in Switzerland was Soubey and as he was sitting by the roadside regaining his breath after the mad dash across the frontier, he was overtaken by a Swiss policeman who took him back to the frontier post at Clairble. After questioning he was given a meal and taken into the town of Soubey, where he was thoroughly searched and his maps and compass confiscated. He slept that night in a hut with some Swiss soldiers and the next morning was taken by a policeman to Saignelegeir, where he was treated as a civilian refugee and put in gaol for seven days. On March 26th, he was taken to Neuchatel and spent another four days in prison there before being taken to Berne on March 30th. At Berne he was taken to see a Swiss Colonel who interrogated him on service matters, the questions mainly being about navigational aids. Beyond stating that the RAF used maps and stars to navigate by, Brown gave no further information. He was also asked questions about the German defences and the reasons why the RAF had changed from the Manchester to the Lancaster. Later he was taken to the local internment camp before a British officer, Major Fryer, took him to see the Air and Military Attaches. Brown remained in the Internment Camp in Switzerland before returning to the UK on Saturday, January 8th, 1944.

Casualties March 9th/10th, 1943. Target Munich

156 Squadron 8 Group Lancaster W4856 GT/
Pilot. 126584 F/Lt L.G.Goodley DFC Killed Rheinberg, Germany. 18-C-5
Nav. 39786 S/Ldr W.A.C.Ball DFC Killed Rheinberg, Germany. 18-C-1
B/A. 143217 P/O J.B.Thompson Killed Rheinberg, Germany. 18-C-3
W/OP. 49839 P/O L.Jones PoW. Stalag Luft 3, Sagan. 248
F/E. 1185099 Sgt R.G.Riley Killed Rheinberg, Germany. 18-C-2
A/G. 144692 P/O G.Percy Killed Rheinberg, Germany. 18-C-6
A/G. 74331 F/Lt C.D.Gilliat Killed Rheinberg, Germany. 18-C-4

7 Squadron 8 Group Stirling R9149 MG/B
Aircraft attacked by fighter and crashed at Elan, France.
Pilot. J/16659 P/O F.M.Tomlinson Killed Elan (Mezieres), France. No number
Nav. R/104339 Sgt D.M.Cox Evaded capture
B/A. 655165 Sgt G.R.Howard Evaded capture
W/OP. 1112746 W/O C.Davies PoW, Stalag Luft 6, Heydekrug. 988
F/E. 968474 Sgt L.Marsh Evaded capture
A/G. 976466 Sgt J.Jennings PoW. Stalag 357, Kopernikus. 1008
A/G. R/126002 W/O V.A.Fox PoW. Died 19-4-45 Berlin. 6-B-6

100 Squadron 1 Group Lancaster ED587 HW/V
Pilot. 40070 S/Ldr D.M.Barker Killed Maubeuge, France. B-21
Nav. 658252 Sgt R.W.Walker Killed Maubeuge, France. B-18
B/A. 658473 Sgt J.Morgan Killed Maubeuge, France. B-23
W/OP. 1207000 Sgt H.Brock Killed Maubeuge, France. B-20
F/E. 1219680 Sgt F.G.G.Edwards Killed Maubeuge, France. B-19
A/G. 1560123 Sgt T.F.Millar Killed Maubeuge, France. B-17
A/G. 1125185 F/Sgt F.Salvage Killed Maubeuge, France. B-22

103 Squadron 1 Group Lancaster W4860 PM/
Pilot. 1185420 F/Sgt J.V.Roper Killed Lavannes, France. 3
Nav. 142321 P/O J.M Curnow PoW. Stalag 357, Kopernikus. 1006
B/A. 1254715 Sgt J.A.Todd Killed Lavannes, France. 5
W/OP. 979710 Sgt J.S.Dobie Killed Lavannes, France. 1
F/E. 1150866 Sgt S.J.Rose Killed Lavannes, France. 6
A/G. 1534965 Sgt J.Smith Killed Lavannes, France. 2
A/G. 519643 Sgt E.S.Waghorn Killed Lavannes, France. 4

77 Squadron 4 Group Halifax JB795 KN/H
Pilot. 131487 F/O J.B.O.Huggard Missing, Runnymede Memorial 125
Nav. 1177722 F/Sgt C.Hanstock Missing, Runnymede Memorial 136
B/A. 1251519 F/O E.G.Shreeves Missing, Runnymede Memorial 129
W/OP. 1253915 F/Sgt M.L.Durling Missing, Runnymede Memorial 136
F/E. 1229956 Sgt T.E.Edwards Missing, Runnymede Memorial 148
A/G. 1381323 F/Sgt J.H.Hughes Killed Durnbach, Germany. 4-C-27
A/G. 136048 P/O L.M.Bridger Missing, Runnymede Memorial 130

77 Squadron 4 Group Halifax DT734 KN/J
Shot down at 0215 hrs at Boussu-lez-Mons, Belgium. Crashed at St.Ghislain.
Pilot. 39342 S/Ldr P.J.Sage AFC PoW. Stalag Luft 3, Sagan. 258
Nav. 129452 F/Lt B.D.Barker Evaded capture
B/A. 139205 F/O D.W.Bateman PoW. Stalag Luft 3, Sagan. 242
W/OP. 1206747 Sgt M.Crabtree Evaded capture
F/E. 950785 Sgt B.J.T.Walker DFM Evaded capture
A/G. 1476160 W/O D.L.Morris PoW. Stalag 4B, Muhlberg(Elbe). 222747
A/G. 124637 F/O K.A.Adam Killed Chievres, Belgium. 8

61 Squadron 5 Group Lancaster ED703 QR/
Pilot. 1253897 Sgt F.L.Walters Killed Durnbach, Germany. 6-G-21
Nav. 1079010 Sgt A.R.Spencer Killed Durnbach, Germany. 6-G-22
B/A. 1245321 Sgt F.Bestwick Killed Durnbach, Germany. 6-G-20
W/OP. J/19577 P/O G.A.Young Killed Durnbach, Germany. 6-G-19
F/E. 645957 Sgt H.McCullough Killed Durnbach, Germany. 6-G-23
A/G. 1546261 Sgt A.Briggs Killed Durnbach, Germany. 6-G-17
A/G. R/126429 W/O C.F.Daley Killed Durnbach, Germany. 6-G-18

207 Squadron 5 Group Lancaster W4172 EM/
Shot down by fighter 30 miles NE of Reims, France
Pilot. 1255050 F/Sgt I.Wood Killed Lavannes, France. CG-7
Nav. 1046183 Sgt R.Brown Evaded capture
B/A. 842606 Sgt R.H.Warren Killed Lavannes, France. CG-7
W/OP. R/106427 W/O R.G Lishman PoW. Stalag 344, Lamsdorf. 27720
F/E. 649093 Sgt G.Brownhill Evaded capture
A/G. 1336916 Sgt G.S.Margetson Killed Lavannes, France. CG-7
A/G. 1392722 Sgt G.Mortimore Killed Lavannes, France. CG-7

Minelaying

March 9th/10th, 1943

Minelaying continued on the same night as the Munich raid, when 50 Wellingtons from 1, 4 and 6 Groups with eight Stirlings from 3 Group and four Lancasters from 5 Group, went to the Kiel bay area laying 113 mines. Fourteen of the aircraft failed to drop their mines in the designated area and aborted their missions. Three Wellingtons failed to return from this minelaying operation. From the 15 airmen lost, only one survived to become a prisoner, the remainder were killed or missing.

Search Patrol for a Missing Aircraft

When one of the returning Wellingtons arrived at its base at Dishforth, the pilot reported at his debriefing that he had seen a light flashing SOS from the sea at a position 5455N 0030E. The staff at 6 Group Headquarters felt that there was a possibility that this distress signal could have come from one of the missing bombers, so a search aircraft was despatched at 07.30 hours. The search aircraft returned to base at 12.00 hours with a report that a red Verey cartridge flare had been sighted at 5505N 0120E, but on further investigation nothing had been sighted. As a result of this further sighting of a distress signal, six more Wellingtons were sent on a sea search of the area at 15.00 hours, but all had returned by 19.00 hours after a fruitless search. Due to the lack of further sightings the search was reluctantly abandoned.

Casualties March 9th/10th, 1943. Minelaying

166 Squadron 1 Group Wellington BK368 AS/P
Aircraft shot down by Naval and *Luftwaffe Flak* at 2158 hrs.and crashed at Filskor - Grinsted, Denmark.
Pilot. J/17135 P/O J.P.Kavanagh Killed Esbjerg (Fourfelt), Denmark. AIII-7-5
Nav. 126040 F/O D.G.Denslow Killed Esbjerg (Fourfelt), Denmark. AIII-7-4
B/A. 1057969 W/O J.Sandilands PoW. Stalag 357, Kopernikus.. 1035
W/OP. J/17138 P/O A.L.Weller Killed Esbjerg (Fourfelt), Denmark. AIII-7-6
A/G. 98336 Sgt W.Bullen Killed Esbjerg (Fourfelt), Denmark. AII1-7-7

429 Squadron 4 Group Wellington BK429 AL/
Pilot. 1387215 Sgt K.A.Holbeach Missing, Runnymede Memorial 153
Nav. 1501195 Sgt R.R.Parry Missing, Runnymede Memorial 161
B/A. 124313 F/O D.L.Cartwright Missing, Runnymede Memorial 123
W/OP. 1292990 Sgt J.E.W.Heydon Missing, Runnymede Memorial 153
A/G. R/117594 F/Sgt J.N.A.Tremblay Missing, Runnymede Memorial 186

426 Squadron 6 Group Wellington X3284 KW/
Pilot. J/16767 P/O G.R.Baker Missing, Runnymede Memorial 175
Nav. R/92573 F/Sgt D.B.Coons Missing, Runnymede Memorial 181
B/A. R/111112 F/Sgt M.Zeavin Missing, Runnymede Memorial 186
W/OP. R/76910 W/O L.Murphy Missing, Runnymede Memorial 180
A/G. R/149418 Sgt L.J.Baribeau Missing, Runnymede Memorial 186
A/G. R/97436 W/O D.P.McLachlan Missing, Runnymede Memorial 180

Seven Nuisance Raids

March 9th/10th, 1943
Mosquitoes also kept up their nuisance raids on the Ruhr, with attacks spread throughout the night. Seven of them attacked the following locations; Rheinhausen, at 23.06 hours, Ruhrort at 00.51 hours, Bochum, at 01.30 hours, Essen at 02.06 hours, Hamborn at 03.01 hours, Mulheim at 04.17 hours and finally at first light, 05.05 hours, Duisburg was awakened by air raid sirens.

Plans for more incendiaries

After analysing the raid reports on the last two major operations, Headquarters Staff at Bomber Command were able to conclude that more widespread damage could be caused by an even greater concentration of incendiaries in bomb loads. City centres were more vulnerable to fire damage than the surrounding suburbs. These conclusions were soon put into practice in planning future operational bomb loads.

Gardening Continues

March 10th/11th, 1943
A mixed force of 20 Lancasters and 15 Stirlings went to two areas, the Bay of Biscay and the Baltic sea, to lay mines. Five of the Lancasters brought their mines back as they were unable to get an accurate identification of the mining area. A total of 115 mines were laid on these two operations. Two of the Lancasters failed to return to their bases.

Casualties March 10th/11th, 1943. Minelaying

44 Squadron 5 Group Lancaster W4841 KM/W
Pilot. 1270591 Sgt J.D.Gayton Killed Berlin, Germany. 2-G-3
Nav. 1331062 Sgt W.C.Burgess Killed Berlin, Germany. 2-G-2
B/A. 1322348 Sgt L.A.Quick Killed Berlin, Germany. JG 2-G-6/7
W/OP. R/69640 W/O D.H.Miller Killed Berlin, Germany. JG 2-G-6/7
F/E. 990083 Sgt R.D.Kirkup Killed Berlin, Germany. 2-G-1
A/G. 1030279 Sgt G.Allen Killed Berlin, Germany. JG 2-G-4/5
A/G. 1333164 Sgt A.J.Taylor Killed Berlin, Germany. JG 2-G-4/5

44 Squadron 5 Group Lancaster ED305 KM/S
Shot down by fighter at 22.15 hours at Statznitz, Denmark
Pilot. 1331504 Sgt B.T.C.Smith Missing, Runnymede Memorial 165
Nav. 127260 F/O R.H.Carr Missing, Runnymede Memorial 123
B/A. 1387411 Sgt C.H.D.Cook Missing, Runnymede Memorial 146
W/OP. 1290988 Sgt G.S.Love Missing, Runnymede Memorial 157
F/E. R/75540 Sgt G.R.Black Missing, Runnymede Memorial 186
A/G. 1192773 F/Sgt C.V.Brown Missing, Runnymede Memorial 143
A/G. 1130063 Sgt A.Healey Missing, Runnymede Memorial 142

Mosquitoes keep the Ruhr on the Alert

Two Mosquitoes kept the Ruhr area sirens going when they visited Essen and Mulheim on March 10th/11th, dropping their bombs by *Oboe* navigational aid. These high flying and fast aircraft kept the German defences guessing and wondering if a full major raid would develop.

Stuttgart

March 11th/12th, 1943

Stuttgart was the name chalked on the target boards of many bomber stations for 314 aircraft consisting of 152 Lancasters, 109 Halifaxes and 53 Stirlings sent out to attack this German city on Thursday night, March 11th, 1943. Weather conditions were reasonably good with 2/10ths-5/10ths thin, medium cloud at about 18,000 feet on route and over the target, although there was some industrial haze at the aiming point. For various technical reasons 36 aircraft failed to reach the target and returned early to their bases. It was on this raid that the Germans started to drop dummy Pathfinder markers in an attempt to confuse the bombers and they certainly fulfilled their purpose on this occasion. The Pathfinders claimed to have marked their aiming point accurately and also dropped incendiaries on Baden-Baden as route markers to provide a beacon for crews to prevent them straying into the defences of Karlsruhe and Strasbourg. The main force was reported late in arriving and some crews were confused by the double markers to such an extent that most of the bombs (373.7 tons of high explosive and 386.6 tons of incendiaries) fell in open and wooded countryside in the south western suburbs of the city. 112 people were killed and 386 injured in this raid, which caused comparatively minor damage to buildings. A total of eleven aircraft; two Lancasters, three Stirlings and six Halifaxes, failed to return from this raid, 4% of the attacking force. From the missing 80 aircrew 42 were killed, 24 made prisoners of war and 14 successfully evaded capture.

Halifax Returns on Two Engines

Flight Sergeant Tom Gallantry was the pilot and captain of Halifax II MP/H DT492 which set off from its home base station of Linton upon Ouse in Yorkshire at 18.00 hours on 11th March. 76 Squadron were losing a steady one or two aircraft a night and Tom and his crew, who were on their 25th operation, were classed as fairly experienced for they had been lucky and skilful enough to survive the first twenty trips. Tom's crew were in a group of only five crews on the squadron at that time who were classed in this category.

The flight out to the target was relatively uneventful as the weather was good and sky clear. Under the watchful eye of Sergeant Len Exton, the navigator, the Halifax arrived spot on time over the target at a height of 15,000 feet. Heavy *Flak* was very intense at this height and Tom, the captain, calculated that the light *Flak* appeared to be bursting quite a lot lower at approximately 10,000 feet. At this period of the bombing offensive captains had a certain degree of latitude with their bombing height, so he decided that it would be a wise decision to let down and come in on his bombing run at 12,000 feet. As soon as Tom had settled his aircraft on the bombing run his Canadian bomb aimer, Sergeant Higgins, began giving him his instructions and finally the bombs gone signal. Suddenly the aircraft received a direct hit from *Flak*, which obviously had been tracking them in spite of their change of bombing heights. There was an enormous flash and the plane bounced around like a cork. Tom's first concern was to regain control of his aircraft, although he recalls that at that time he was not sure whether he was upside down or what, for the pilot's blind flying panel had gone beserk and the instruments were spinning wildly about. There were seconds of disorientation before he eventually brought the plane back to a relatively straight and level attitude. Assessment of the damage was quickly made. The port outer engine was windmilling badly and causing very heavy vibrations in the port wing. Coupled with this, the aircraft was still in the midst of the predicted *Flak* being thrown about them. The elevators were found to be damaged for Tom had a lot of trouble in pushing the controls forward to increase his speed to get away from the now heavy *Flak* bursting all around. Further problems with his rudder controls would only allow him to do gentle turns, instead of the violent evasion action which was called for at that time. The bomb doors were stuck in the open position which caused further drag especially with only three good engines.

It was obvious to the crew that it would be touch and go whether they would make it back to England. Luck as well as skill would have to be very much on their side if they were going to make it. Losing height steadily on the homeward leg, the descent of the aircraft being controlled only by manipulating the throttles instead of elevators, Halifax H for Harry was now a sitting target for the night fighters. The hydraulics were found to be unserviceable and the two gunners could only keep a keen eye out for fighters, knowing that their turrets could only be cranked around by hand and that any return fire from their Browning machine guns would be practically useless.

At 40 to 50 miles from the French coast the temperatures of the remaining three engines began rocketing up the gauges in spite of them being nursed by flight engineer, Sergeant Middleton. The starboard outer engine finally packed up and was feathered before it caught fire. The odds now appeared to be heavily stacked against the bomber, now flying only on its two inner engines, of reaching the English coast. The wireless operator, Canadian Flying Officer McClure, started to send out an SOS on the *Darkie* system when the plane was over the Channel and to Tom's relief he saw in the distance the very welcoming sight of two searchlights coned. This was the answer to their call for assistance. Unfortunately the lights were from a fighter aerodrome at Redhill, Surrey, and the small airfield was not big enough for landing a serviceable bomber, let alone a crippled bomber on two engines with full flaps down, no undercarriage and bomb doors fully open. Even on a bomber aerodrome a landing would have been extremely hazardous, so Tom decided that discretion was the better part of valour and gave the order for a controlled bale out through the front escape hatch. He could make a head count to see that his crew had all safely left before he skidded the aircraft around to head out to the Channel before he left the controls. Tom recalls looking out into the inky darkness and wondering whether he ought to get back into the driver's seat and have a go at landing the plane, however he finally jumped and saw the massive Halifax tail plane whizz over his head.

It was exactly nine hours after take off from Yorkshire that Tom and his crew were back in England after baling out by parachute near Hand Cross, Sussex. All were quickly reunited on the ground minus their plane. After travelling back to base Tom and his crew continued to be fortunate for they carried on with operations and successfully completed their tour, with Tom being commissioned and being finally awarded the Distinguished Flying Cross.

Evasion on his First Operation

A Lancaster from 83 Squadron (8 Group Pathfinders) was another of the aircraft that did not return to its base from the Stuttgart raid. It was piloted by Flight Lieutenant Mackie who had on board that night 1291378 Sergeant Ralph Henderson for his first operation acting as a second pilot to get first hand experience,. He had been detailed at such short notice for the operation that he didn't even know all the crew's names. When the Lancaster was on its return flight it was attacked by night fighters at about 04.00 hours and the aircraft was so badly damaged that it went out of control. The captain ordered an immediate bale out. Sergeant Henderson was the first to go out and he landed in a tree, his 'chute became so entangled in the branches that he had a great deal of difficulty in extricating himself. After he finally dropped to the ground, he managed to drag the billowing silk from the branches and buried it along with its harness and Mae West in a nearby swamp. He was quite unsure of where he was not having been involved in the navigation.

After walking some distance he came upon a road sign post which showed that he was in France and he calculated that he was east of Possesse, which is about 18 miles north-west of St Dizier. His first job was to cut off his sergeant stripes and his flying brevet and he opened his escape box and put the contents in his pockets. The clear plastic box was a dead give away that he was an airman, so he buried it. It is interesting to note that the intelligence authorities who so carefully compilied the essential items which were found so necessary in helping evaders never really considered the fact that many of the items were wrapped with paper which bore English printing, as some airmen found to their cost when they were apprehended.

After walking a while he came to the to the village of Lisse on the outskirts of Lille. As he had been a school master before joining the RAF and could speak a little French, he approached the occupants of a house, declared who he was, and asked for help. Fortunately for him the occupants took him in, but they could not understand him. Ralph asked them if there was a local priest living nearby, thinking that he might speak some English. After being directed to the priest's house Ralph found that he too could not understand English and had great difficulty even in understanding Ralph's rusty French questions. He was, however, able to make out from the conversation that there were many German troops in the neighbouring town of Chalons-sur-Marne, which he should avoid.

An important acquistion from his visit were some maps of the local district. Armed with these he set off and reached St Amand at 08.30 hours on March 12th, where he stopped at a shoemaker's shop to try and exchange his cumbersome flying boots for a pair of civilian shoes, but he was unsuccessful. Continuing on walking he had nearly reached Aulnay-l'Aitre when he stopped at a house. It was here that he had his first stroke of luck, for the people living there were prepared to exchange his uniform for a civilian suit, a beret and a pair of brown walking shoes. Considering the possibility, now that he was not so conspicious, of going on to Toulouse, Sergeant Henderson walked to Vitry-le-Francois to try to catch a train. On nearing the railway station he saw that there were so many Germans about that an attempt to travel by train without some sort of help and identity card would be nigh impossible. He decided to carry on walking and reached Blaise-sous-Arzillieres at about 20.00 hours. Outside one house on the outskirts he saw a youth standing, so he approached him and tried to tell him that he was English and wished for some sort of shelter for the night. The youth quickly took him inside and half an hour later 120865 Flight Lieutenant Ogilvie DFC and Bar, the navigator from Ralph's aircraft, was brought to the same house. From there the two aircrew's subsequent journey was all arranged for them by the underground movement. Both finally reached Gibraltar on May 24th and flew back to England.

88410 Flight Lieutenant N. A. Mackie DFC, the pilot of the plane, also baled out near St Dizier. After burying all his flying gear under a pile of leaves in a wood, he too set out walking to get away from the crash area. The first village he reached was possibly Heiltz-le-Hunter, which he passed through rather quickly and lay up in some woods for the day of March 12th.

In the evening he began walking, but was soon caught by an armed German soldier and taken to a house where he was locked up in an outside lean-to building. At the house there were two other armed German soldiers, but not one of them attempted to get any personal details from Mackie or interrogate him. They did, however, take away his flying boots before locking him up. Just as it was getting dark Flight Lieutenant Mackie managed to force the lock of the door with the aid of a bar which he found inside the shed. Once out, he made off as fast as he could, in spite of being without footwear.

After walking about about 10 kms, he came to a large bridge and, as he could see some people on the opposite side, he got down to the river bank. He was seen and a French civilian carrying a rifle came across the bridge and asked whether or not he was English. After admitting to the fact, the Frenchman and another civilian took him across to a house on the opposite side of the bridge where they gave Mackie shoes and a haversack full of food and coffee. They told him that the Germans were out looking for an aircraft which had crashed nearby. They did not explain who they were or why they were armed, but Mackie presumed they were supposed to guard the bridge. They were unable to help Mackie any further, but pointed out directions to St Dizier and Vitry-le-Francois. Mackie unfortunately couldn't understand the directions given in French so he decided to set course south along a railway cutting until it started to get light.

Mackie then approached a house on the outskirts of a village, which as he recalls did not appear to have a name. The owner of the house, who looked to be a gardener, supplied some food and a map of the whole of France which was too small a scale to be of any help, but he also gave Mackie a cap to make him look less conspicious. He was directed to a wood, which he couldn't find, so Mackie opted to walk south to south west by means of his escape compass.

On March 14th Mackie managed to beg some food from an isolated farmhouse and as he was leaving the farm he was overtaken by a man on a motor cycle who warned him against going on to the next village, where some German soldiers were billetted and French collaborators lived. On instructions from the motor cyclist he waited in a nearby wood until another elderly man came along bringing some food and a set of overalls, but no other help was forthcoming. Continuing walking the Flight Lieutenant went through about four villages until he reached Bertignolle on whose outskirts he called at a farmhouse for food. Not only did the farmer oblige, but also supplied an axe to carry over his shoulders so as to divert any suspicion from him as he walked along.

Nine days after he had baled out Mackie reached Laignes where his luck was in. While at a small café he was approached by a French gendarme and a civilian. Thinking he was going to be arrested Mackie decided to act dumb. When asked for papers he pretended not to hear or understand. He was then asked if he was English or French and when Mackie shook his head the civilian asked if he was German, this time he nodded. The civilian then spoke fluent German, but Mackie had no idea what he meant. He was then taken into the back room of the café and searched. Very quickly they came upon his wings and to Mackie's amazement both men grinned, shook his hand and congratulated him. The men quickly put Mackie in touch with an escape organisation which arranged for his journey to Switzerland and freedom.

Although 405 Squadron lost four aircraft on the Stuttgart raid, a quarter of the squadron's bombers which took off, they were more fortunate in the number of aircrew who managed to evade capture after baling out as seven returned to the UK.

Only one man evades

906012 Sergeant Kenneth Elt, the flight engineer aboard Halifax BB250 V for Victor of 405 (RCAF) Squadron, piloted by J/16582 Pilot Officer H. D. Rea, was one of three airmen who evaded capture when the aircraft was shot down. The rest of the crew, including a second pilot on his first trip, were captured and made prisoners of war. The bomber had already reached and bombed the target at Stuttgart and was on its return flight when it was attacked just west of Chalons-sur-Marne, a notorious black spot for fighter interceptions. The aircraft was set on fire and in the course of the attack the Canadian bomb aimer, R/76136 Flight Sergeant W. A. McDonald, was wounded. Efforts to extinguish the fire were in vain and at about midnight the captain reluctantly had to give the bale out order. The aircraft was flying at an altitude of 12,000 feet at the time. Sergeant Elt landed in a grass field about 3 miles west of Chalons-sur-Marne and during his descent he could clearly see the flaming aircraft coming down. It hit the ground and exploded.

On landing Elt first buried his 'chute, harness and Mae West. Then to get away as quickly as possible from the area of the crash, he set out walking west for about three hours before he came to a farm and crawled into a barn nearby and slept. He was awoken at about 06.00 hours by the sound of traffic and saw a German lorry loaded with troops apparently travelling in the direction of his crashed aircraft. A few hours later he crept out of his hiding place unobserved and walked away from the farm buildings. Opening his escape box he took out the silk map to get an idea of his bearings. While doing so, he was quietly approached by a man and, as Sergeant Elt could speak a little French, he was told his approximate postion. Deciding that his best course of action would be to try and make for Switzerland, he removed his badges of rank and flying brevet and put them loose in his pocket. Then he pulled his trousers over to hide his flying boots. He started to walk in a south-westerly direction, walking by day and keeping off all roads, obtaining bread and wine from any farm workers who he passed.

On the evening of March 13th, he arrived tired out at the village of St Quentin-sur Coole, about 10 miles south Chalons-sur-Marne. He called at a lonely farm worker's house, where luckily he was given food and a bed. The farmworker also gave him a pair of old overalls to cover his RAF uniform. Early on March 15th, shaved and refreshed after his short stay, the farmworker took him by bicycle to another farm nearby. The farmer here was very frightened and immediately took him to a neighbour's house. This neighbour gave him some more food and an address in Chamonix. He told him to walk to St Dizier and then catch a train to Chalons-sur-Soane.

Carrying his food in a sack, Sergeant Elt looked just right as a French peasant land worker. He went along the road to St Dizier, where he bought a razor in a shop and slept that night in a shed. Next morning, March 16th, he walked to the railway station. From a notice displayed there he discovered that a train left for Dijon at about 15.00 hours, this meant that he had to wander about the town to avoid being particularly conspicious. When it was nearly time for the train's departure he returned to the station and approached a Frenchman in the ticket queue. He asked if he would purchase a ticket to Dijon for him, offering the money that was in his escape box. Without any qualms the Frenchman obliged after Sergeant Elt declared that he was an escaping airman. On boarding the train Sergeant Elt judged from the conversation of his compartment companions that he could also safely divulge to them who he was, this he did with out any difficulties. One of the Frenchmen said that he was trying to get to Lyons and when they arrived at Dijon, at about 20.00 hours, this Frenchman took him to buy a ticket for Chalons-sur-Soane.

At 06.00 hours on March 17th they both caught a train and arrived at Chalons-sur-Soane about two hours later. The Frenchman had ascertained that there was some sort of control check point between Chalons-sur-Soane and Macon. He therefore advised Sergeant Elt to get off the train and walk to Macon, where he would meet him again the following morning. Setting off on his walk, he reached Macon at 03.00 hours on 18th March and sheltered in the railway station lavatory until 07.00 hours. He waited around the vicinity of the station until that afternoon, but the French acquaintance did not turn up as arranged. By now extremely hungry, Sergeant Elt decided to go into the town in search of some food. Along the way he passed a small garage and, as he was a garage proprietor before joining the RAF, decided to try his luck there for help. He told a workman who was repairing a car who he was and asked whether he could give any help. As he had no identity discs on him, he showed the owner his badges of rank and flying badge which he had in his pocket. The garage owner seemed satisfied with this and provided a meal. That evening he brought two other men in to see Sergeant Elt. They gave him more food and took him to an hotel, where he remained the whole of the next day, 19th March. That evening another man came along and took him to a town nearby and from that point the subsequent journey to freedom was arranged for him by the underground. On his return to England Sergeant Elt was awarded the Distinguished Flying Medal.

Five more 405 Squadron aircrew evade

Halifax DT745 was another of the missing planes from 405 Squadron on the Stuttgart raid. It was piloted by J/16008 Pilot Officer B. C. Dennison. On this particular operation there was an eight man crew, for they were carrying a second pilot who went on the sortie for operational experience. Two of the crew were killed and a third was made a prisoner of war, but the remaining five all evaded capture.

The plane was on its return flight when it was attacked by a night fighter and set on fire. The blaze was so severe that the captain had no alternative but to give the bale out order over Hirson (Aisne) at about 01.00 hours. Two of the crew, wireless operator R/85952 Flight Sergeant Jennings, and the second pilot, C/1359 Squadron Leader S. E. Logan, landed about 100 yards apart in wooded country north-east of Hesdin. They saw and heard their burning aircraft crash about two miles away. Unaware of what had happened to the rest of the crew, the two gathered their 'chutes and carried them away from the immediate vicinty of the crash site, walking for about half an hour. They were hampered from going any further, for Squadron Leader Logan had lost his boots on the bale out. Believing that they were a sufficent distance away from the crash, the two men crawled into some dense undergrowth in a wood and rolled themselves up in their parachutes to rest a while and gather their thoughts about a future plan of action. They both awoke from a fitful sleep at about 05.00 hours and immediately set about burying their Mae Wests, harness and 'chutes. They also riped off their badges of rank and flying brevets from their battle dress. Although not really equipped for a long walk, they set out again and at daylight came near to the village of Hirson.

Unsure of what to do, they both hid in some bushes until 17.30 hours, when a passing woodcutter spotted them. Neither of the men could speak French, but they called out to him and by his gestures they guessed that he wanted them to stay hidden and that he would be back later.

At 19.00 hours the woodcutter did return along with another man with some welcome food in a basket. They also brought both men a civilan suit and a beret. Logan was supplied with a pair of old army boots and both were taken to a barn about half a mile away. They stayed there until March 18th. At 05.00 hours one of the helpers took them to the railway station at Hirson, gave them third class rail tickets and put them on a train. The helper also travelled on the train, but not in the same compartment. At 21.00 hours they had to change trains and on the platform saw the guide they had met at the barn talking to their helper. They were given further rail tickets which were marked Paris and went on another train, their helpers still with them. They all arrived at the Gare du Nord at about 12.00 hours on March 19th.

One of the helpers who had recently joined them and who could speak a little English explained that they were planning to send the two evaders by train on to Toulouse on their own, but that they could not provide any identity cards. Both Logan and Jennings said that they didn't think that they could make such a long journey successfully on their own. One of the helpers went to telephone someone and on returning said that they had changed their plans and were now going to send the two airmen via Bordeaux to Dax. Later at the café another Frenchman arrived with a girl who could speak fairly good English. Logan and Jennings were then given a considerable sum of money, a suitcase full of food and a razor. They had to sit in the café until 17.30 hours when they were taken by underground to Versailles Park. In the evening they were taken back to the Gare D'Austerlitz and boarded a train at 21.30 hours for Bordeaux. They arrived at Dax (Landes) at 08.30 hours on the 19th, and were told by the helper to walk about the station while he went to telephone a friend for further help. As the station environs were actively patrolled by German troops, the two airmen thought it would be prudent to get a little further away along a side street. After half an hour they returned to find their helper waiting for them with the bad news that he was unable to get any further assistance at Dax. He had been advised to go back to Bayonne and told that the two airmen should walk there alone along the main road. The two evaders thought that this was exceedingly risky and decided between them that they should try and walk south independently of any helpers. The helper gave them a map of the immediate area around Dax and also an English/French dictionary. With their suitcase full of food they took leave of the helper and walked south out of Dax, finally hiding in some bushes when Logan's feet became badly blistered in the ill fitting army boots. After a brief rest they continued through Mees and Tercis, where they saw some German guards near the road so they hid in a swamp for most of the night.

At 06.30 hours on March 20th they continued walking and skirted the village of St Lon Lesmines, stopping in a wood to have food and a quick shave. They arrived at Port-de-Lanne around midday and saw some people fishing from boats in the River Adour. They persuaded one of the fishermen to take them across the river in his boat. Once across they found some straw in a field, burrowed into it and fell asleep. About 17.00 hours they continued their journey and crossed the River La Bidouse north of Guiche by means of a small wooden bridge which was not guarded. At 20.00 hours they hid behind a church in Guiche and ate some more food, then continued to the little village of Bardos. They stopped at a farm here to fill up their water bottles and an old woman told them that two Englishmen had recently passed through the area. The police were looking around and she advised them to hide in the nearby woods. They immediately took her advice and shortly after they entered the wood they saw two figures wearing steel helmets walking along the road from which they had just come, it was a little too dark to see whether or not they were in uniform, but taking no chances the two evaders abandoned their heavy suitcase of food and escaped southwards as quickly as they could.

On the morning of the 21st they had arrived somewhere between Ayherre and Hasparren, where they hid up all day, now without any food. At 04.00 hours on the 22nd of March they approached the village of Greciettes and slept until daybreak.

With the help of their dictionary they prepared a note in French, asking for some food. This they showed to a nearby farmer, who shrugged his shoulders and pointed to the village saying, "Monsieur la Mairie". They then both went in search of the mayor's house in the village and finally saw him. The mayor gave them some bread and eggs, but refused to help them any further. Duly refreshed with the food they kept on walking, skirting the villages of Menionde, Macaye and Louhossa before finally spending the night in open country near Bidarray. They asked many times at farms for food, but the people either could not understand, were indifferent or maybe too scared, for they received no help at all. Eventually they found a lone fisherman who told them that there were some Germans in Bidarray, he also gave them three small fish. That night they followed the River Bohumba upstream, east of Montarsmendi. By now they were quite famished and early next morning, the 24th, they lit a fire and cooked the fish. On consulting their maps they reckoned that they were about half a mile away from the Spanish frontier. At 08.30 hours they saw ahead of them what they felt surely looked like Spanish Frontier guards. Making every effort to avoid them, they made a dash forwards and carried on until they felt sure that they were well into Spanish territory. By 14.00 hours they arrived at an isolated farm where they asked for food. The occupants said that they were Spanish and a young girl in the farm house gave them all the food that they could eat. They then left and slept in a field until 16.00 hours. That evening they continued up the main stream of the river and, as it was getting very cold, they moved to the outskirts of Errazu, where they went to sleep outside a house. At 07.00 hours on the 25th they woke up to find that the house was the station of the Spanish Civil Guard, who quickly took them to an hotel where they were allowed to spend some of their French francs on food.

The next morning, March 26th, the Civil Guard took them by bus to Pamplon where they were interrogated at the police station, by a Frenchman who could speak a little English and who acted as an interpreter. The airmen refused to answer any service questions except to say that they were Canadian aircrew. At first Jennings said he was a sergeant, but when he discovered that the other ranks would be housed in gaol and the officers in an hotel he quickly changed his mind and said that he was a pilot officer. Jennings need not have put on an act that he was an officer, for ironically his commission had come through during his evasion. Both men asked to see the British Consul, but the Frenchman who took them to the hotel told them that a representative from the British Consulate would visit them shortly.

The next day, March 27th, both men met Mr Michael Cresswell, who had the code name of Monday and was one of the attaches who had come from the Madrid consulate. (Cresswell did a great deal to assist the movements of many British escapers and evaders when they reached Spain, in spite of much opposition at that time from the Franco regime.) After staying in the hotel until April 7th both airmen left by train to Madrid in the company of another group of Frenchmen. On April 16th they arrived at Gibraltar and were back in the UK on April 20th, 1943.

On their return both men were awarded the Distinguished Flying Cross and were posted to Canada for a well deserved leave. Squadron Leader Logan DFC was shortly back with 405 Squadron on operations, a highly unusual posting after an evasion. His luck did not last for he and his crew were reported missing after an operation to Brunswick on September 27th, 1943. Logan, as a prisoner No. 1758 at Stalag 1 Barth Vogelsang, and the rest of the crew survived.

A Persistant Train Escaper

The only 408 Squadron aircraft lost on the Stuttgart raid of March 11th/12th was Halifax HR656, piloted by New Zealander Flying Officer Andrew Stewart. All the crew were on the sixth operation of their tour. The aircraft developed engine trouble before reaching the target and the pilot was forced to turn back for base. On the return flight the bomber was attacked by a night fighter and damaged to such an extent that the captain had no option but to give the bale out order. All the crew landed safely at Vassy, France.

The navigator was 921693 Flight Sergeant David Duncan Leitch, and from the time that he landed he became the enemy's biggest nuisance ever. After his bale out he rid himself of his 'chute and harness and from a nearby field stole a scarecrow's clothes to make himself look less conspicuous, From the start he was intent on getting away. He obtained some food and other clothing from the residents when he reached the village of Ville-en-Blaisois. With further help he reached Ambonville on 14th March, but here he was captured by some German troops. He was taken to a military prison in Paris before being transferred to Dulag Luft Oberusel, then on to Stalag Luft 3. He found little chance of escape during this period of imprisonment. Leitch, however, made his first attempt to escape on June 20th, 1943, when he was being taken by train from Stalag Luft 3 at Sagan to Stalag Luft 6 at Heydekrug. He left the train through a lavatory window, but was recaptured after travelling 100 miles in another train towards the Baltic coast.

His next escape attempt was made in February, 1944, again from a train in which he was being transferred from one camp to another. After two hours of liberty he was recaptured and taken back to the PoW train.

On March 22nd, 1944, Leitch yet again gave his guards the slip whilst travelling on a train. This time he was more fortunate in that he got in touch with some French forced labour workers who took him to their unguarded camp. They helped him take on the identity of a French worker, supplying him with a forged identity card and a written authority pass to travel to Danzig, where he planned to board a ship. With great coolness and resourcefulness he managed to reach Danzig, but his luck ran out for he was recaptured while getting on to a Swedish boat.

Not withstanding his previous failures, which would have daunted the average escaper, he made preparations for yet another escape early in April 1944, this time with the aid of Army and Navy personnel at Stalag XXB. Before the plan could be put into effect the Germans reorganised the defences to the camp. On discovering that the barrack windows were going to be wired up by the Germans, Leitch wasted no time and decided to make still another attempt. He managed to break out of camp wearing civilian clothes and remained at large until June 8th, 1944, when yet again he was recaptured. This time the Germans put him under close guard. He was eventually liberated by the Allied Forces at Velson on 16th April, 1945. For his unfailing determination to escape his captors and for setting such a fine example to his fellow prisoners Flight Sergeant Leitch was awarded the MBE after he returned to England and also found that he had been promoted to Warrant Officer rank during his period of captivity.

Four other members of Leitch's crew, Flying Officer Lamus the bomb aimer and Sergeant Hammond the flight engineer, along with Sergeants Hamilton and Sergeant Davidson the air gunners, were all fortunate to evade capture. Quite independently, but with the help of various escape organisations, they made it to Switzerland where they were all interned.

Casualties March 11th/12th, 1943. Target Stuttgart

83 Squadron 8 Group Lancaster ED313 OL/B
Crashed near St.Dizier, France after fighter attack.
Pilot. 88410 F/Lt N.A.Mackie DFC Evaded capture.
Nav. 1181464 W/O L.E.J.Humber PoW. Stalag 357, Kopernikus. 1006
B/A. 120865 F/Lt A.M.Ogilvie DFC* Evaded capture
W/OP. 1001787 F/Sgt L.A.Lynch Killed Sogny-en-L'Angle, France. 2
F/E. 1291378 Sgt R.Henderson Evaded capture.
A/G. 751810 W/O W.E.Barrett PoW. Stalag 357, Kopernikus. 886
A/G. 1105193 Sgt K.W.Chipchase Killed Sogny-en-L'Angle, France. 1
2nd pilot acted as flight engineer on this sortie.

7 Squadron 8 Group Stirling W7617 MG/K
Aircraft crashed at Minacourt, France.
Pilot. 79550 S/Ldr M.E.Thwaites DFC Killed Minacourt, France. 1
Nav. 120392 F/Lt F.D.J.Thompson DFC Killed Minacourt, France. CG 4/6
B/A. 132180 P/O L.R.S.Luton DFC Killed Minacourt, France. CG 4/6
W/OP. 49875 F/O A.H.Bywater DFC Killed Minacourt, France. CG 4/6
F/E. 517058 F/Sgt C.Stewart DFM Killed Minacourt, France. CG 4/6
A/G. 1014657 F/Sgt R.M.Urwin Killed Minacourt, France. 2
A/G. 1206512 F/Sgt A.Clift DFM Killed Minacourt, France 3

214 Squadron 3 Group Stirling BF469 BU/M
Aircraft crashed at Fagnieres, France after fighter attack.
Pilot. J/16064 P/O A.Carruthers Killed Chalons-sur-Marne, France. CG 1-1591
Nav. 655812 Sgt E.Parker Killed Chalons-sur-Marne, France. CG 1-1591
B/A. 1201575 Sgt P.P.Oakes Killed Chalons-sur-Marne.France. CG 1-1591
W/OP. 798585 F/Sgt B.Carnell Killed Chalons-sur-Marne, France. CG 1-1591
F/E. 629071 Sgt E.L.Eaglen Killed Chalons-sur-Marne, France. CG 1-1591
A/G. 1215579 Sgt B.R.Jennings Killed Chalons-sur-Marne, France. CG 1-1591
A/G. 1208901 F/Sgt A.J.Tyrrell PoW. Stalag 344, Lamsdorf. 27746

218 Squadron 3 Group Stirling BF343 HA/M
Aircraft crashed at Dieppe, France.
Pilot. NZ/41931 F/Sgt G.A.Parkinson Killed Dieppe (Canadian), France. H-40
Nav. 139491 P/O J.Millward Killed Dieppe (Canadian), France. H-41
B/A. 1379410 Sgt P.P.Jobling Killed Dieppe (Canadian), France. CG H-38/39
W/OP. 1376372 Sgt D.Collins Killed Dieppe (Canadian), France. CG H-38/39
F/E. 921793 Sgt R.B.P.H.Heath Killed Dieppe (Canadian), France. H-37
A/G. 1371363 Sgt J.H.Ross Killed Dieppe (Canadian), France. CG H-38/39
A/G. NZ/403757 F/Sgt C.J.Campbell Killed Dieppe (Canadian), France. H-42

158 Squadron 4 Group Halifax DT748 NP/J
Pilot. 1332048 Sgt H.E.Witham Killed Marson-sur-Barboure, France. CG 1-4
Nav. 1339498 Sgt J.Harris Killed Marson-sur-Barboure, France. CG 1-4
B/A. 655647 Sgt T.C.Laws Killed Marson-sur-Barboure, France. CG 1-4
W/OP. 143403 P/O P.G.Lyon Killed Marson-sur-Barboure, France. CG 1-4
F/E. 632681 Sgt E.F.Smith Killed Marson-sur-Barboure, France. CG 1-4
A/G. 657089 Sgt L.E.Ashdown Killed Marson-sur-Barboure, France. CG 1-4
A/G. A/406557 Sgt B.H.Bishop Killed Marson-sur-Barboure, France. CG 1-4

467 Squadron 5 Group Lancaster ED523 PO/
Pilot. A/405131 P/O G.S.Mant Killed Durnbach, Germany. 8-F-20
Nav. A/403058 F/Lt J.Leitke PoW. Stalag Luft 3, Sagan. 249
B/A. 104376 F/Lt V.G.T.Davis PoW. Stalag Luft 3, Sagan. 277
W/OP. A/404884 F/Sgt G.H.Millett Killed Durnbach, Germany. 8-F-21
F/E. 1157637 W/O J.J.Rider PoW. Stalag 344, Lamsdorf. 27738
A/G. A/420441 W/O G.R.Castle PoW. Stalag 344, Lamsdorf. 27700
A/G. 628624 W/O A.E.Spencer PoW. Stalag 344, Lamsdorf. 27741

405 Squadron 6 Group Halifax W7083 LQ/B
Pilot. J/7979 F/Lt H.G.Shockley Killed Septmonts, France. 6
2/Pilot. J/16635 P/O B.H.Labarge Killed Septmonts, France. CG 1-5
Nav. 132995 P/O W.W.Kirkpatrick Killed Septmonts, France. CG 1-5
B/A. 132994 P/O F.Holland Killed Septmonts, France. CG 1-5
W/OP. J/9256 F/O W.M.Palmer Killed Septmonts, France. CG 1-5
F/E. R/75353 Sgt C.O.Henderson Killed Septmonts, France. CG 1-5
A/G. 1355437 Sgt M.W.Mackenzie Killed Septmonts, France. CG 1-5
A/G. 133003 P/O J.Henderson Killed Septmonts, France. CG 1-5

405 Squadron 6 Group Halifax BB250 LQ/V
Crashed at Chalons-sur Marne, France after fighter attack.
Pilot. J/16582 F/O H.D.Rea PoW. Stalag Luft 3, Sagan. 934
2/Pilot. 1336541 W/O H.J.Mason PoW. Stalag 357, Kopernikus. 914
Nav. 138323 F/Lt K.P.C.Money PoW. Stalag Luft 3, Sagan. 932
B/A. R/76136 W/O W.A.MacDonald PoW. Stalag Luft 4, Sagan. 1014
W/OP. 1365330 W/O P.Johnston PoW. Stalag 344, Lamsdorf. 27718
F/E. 906012 Sgt K.W.Elt DFM Evaded capture
A/G. A/3358 F/O J.J.Maquire PoW. Stalag Luft 3, Sagan 1028
A/G. R/114740 Sgt P.Dmytruk Evaded capture, Killed fighting with the
Maquis 9 Dec 1943. Buried Les Martres-de-Veyre, Clermont Ferrand, France

405 Squadron 6 Group Halifax W7803 LQ/U
Pilot. J/16955 F/Lt G.T.Chretien DFM PoW. Stalag Luft 3, Sagan. 27706
Nav. J/16815 F/O T.E.Carlon DFM PoW. Stalag Luft 3, Sagan. 27701
B/A. J/16627 F/O J.S.Probert PoW. Stalag Luft 3, Sagan. 933
W/OP. R/82514 W/O H.G.Reynolds PoW. Stalag 344, Lamsdorf. 27737
F/E. R/60126 Sgt A.C.Collin PoW. Stalag 344, Lamsdorf. 27705
A/G. R/91221 W/O A.E.Danes PoW. Stalag 344, Lamsdorf. 27709
A/G. 1040804 Sgt R.Moore Killed Durnbach, Germany. 2-K-1

405 Squadron 6 Group Halifax DT745 LQ/E
Aircraft crashed at Hirson, France.
Pilot. J/16008 P/O B.C.Dennison Evaded capture
2/Pilot. C/1359 S/Ldr S.E.Logan Evaded capture
Nav. R/72937 F/Sgt E.L.Bulman Evaded capture
B/A. J/16834 P/O G.L.Spencer Evaded capture
W/OP. R/85952 F/Sgt H.J.Jennings Evaded capture
F/E. R/107026 Sgt E.G.Lacina Killed Longueval(London), France. 13-E-31
A/G. R/124691 Sgt R.G.Macdonald Killed Longueval(London), France. 13-E-30
A/G. R/102033 W/O R.F.Kennett PoW. Stalag 357, Kopernikus. 904

408 Squadron 6 Group Halifax HR656 EQ/
Aircraft crashed near Vassy, France.
Pilot. NZ/413502 F/Lt A.A.Stewart PoW. Stalag Luft 3, Sagan 260
Nav. 921693 W/O D.D.P.Leitch PoW. Stalag Luft 3, Sagan. 1024
B/A. 121779 F/Lt G.H.Lamus Evaded capture
W/OP. 1268458 F/Sgt L.S.Marsden PoW. Stalag 344, Lamsdorf. 27726
F/E. R/81832 Sgt J.A.Hammond Evaded capture
A/G. R/144478 Sgt R.D.Davidson Evaded capture
A/G. NZ/411240 Sgt C.T.Hamilton Evaded capture

76 Squadron 4 Group Halifax DT492 MP/
Crashed at Hand Cross, Sussex.
Pilot. 1074117 F/Sgt T.Gallantry Baled out.
Nav. Sgt L.Exton Baled out.
B/A. Sgt J.Higgins Baled out.
W/OP. J/9737 F/O A.McClure Baled out.
F/E. 1071462 Sgt W.Middleton Baled out.
A/G. Sgt S.Bayfield Baled out.
A/G. 1394402 Sgt K.Whitmore Baled out.

Gardening

March 11th/12th, 1943
One Stirling from 3 Group and three Lancasters from 5 Group went minelaying. One Lancaster was forced to return after failure of navigational equipment, but the remaining aircraft dropped 71 mines without loss.

Essen

March 12th/13th, 1943

The next big raid on the Ruhr was again on Essen. The 457 strong force consisted of 31 Pathfinders (10 Mosquitoes, 16 Lancasters, 3 Halifaxes and 2 Stirlings) and a main force of 426 bombers (140 Lancasters, 40 Stirlings, 88 Halifaxes and 158 Wellingtons.) 4 Group supplied the biggest contribution to the main force on this occasion. Early returners accounted for 46 of the main force and one PFF Mosquito which had technical problems with its *Oboe* set. Weather conditions were good for the German night fighters, there was no cloud and it was a bright moonlit night, but the moderate visibility did not make it ideal for them.

The *Oboe* equipped Mosquitoes again accurately marked the centre of the bombing area, which was the giant Krupps factory just west of the city centre. German post war records show that one third of the bombs dropped on this raid landed on the town of Bottrop, which is just north of Essen. As the towns in the Ruhr Valley had their built up areas overlapping each other very accurate bombing was extremely difficult, especially with creep back which occurred as the period of the raid went on. There were numerous searchlights which coned many bombers over the target and the *Flak* was very accurate. A total of 495.2 tons of high explosives were dropped and two very large explosions were observed at 21.29 and 21.36 hours. 231,584 incendiaries were also dropped (520.1 tons) and the Pathfinders dropped eighty-two 250lbs target indicators. Photographic reconnaissance after this raid assessed 30% more damage to the Krupps works than in the previous big raid. 500 German homes were destroyed and 198 people were killed in Essen. This total was divided with typical Teutonic detail as 64 men, 45 women, 19 children, 4 soldiers, 61 foreign workers and 5 prisoners of war. 39 people were killed in other areas around Essen, the town of Bottrop with the majority of these fatalities. The price paid by the RAF was high, twenty-three aircraft were lost, a loss rate from the attacking force of 5.9%. Fourteen aircraft were brought down by *Flak*, seven were claimed by night fighters and two were lost due to unknown causes. A further 69 aircraft were found to be damaged on return to their bases. 102 aircrew were killed, 26 were missing and 23 became prisoners of war.

425 Squadron Wellington Lost

One of the Wellingtons lost was BK340, KM/T of 425 (RCAF) Squadron based at Dishforth, Yorkshire. It was piloted by Canadian Sergeant J. Gilles Lamontagne. After succesfully bombing the target, the Wellington was on its homeward flight when it ran into trouble on the Dutch/German border after being attacked by a fighter. The pilot had no time to take any evasive action before the fighter's guns had caused a fire in the cockpit and in the bomb aimer's position. Sergeant Lamontagne remained at the controls while some of the crew members tackled the blaze with fire extinguishers. Again the fighter attacked, this time causing another fire in the main body of the fuselage. With all extinguishers used up the bomb aimer, Flight Sergeant J. A. V. Gauthier, managed to beat out the flames with his gloved hands. The crew's luck did not last, for the fighter was obviously intent on getting them down. A third attack was made, and this time the bomber became a blazing torch. The pilot knew there was no chance of saving his aircraft so he ordered the crew to bale out while he held the Wellington on an even keel as best he could.

Unfortunately, as so often happened in such an emergency, the forward escape hatch was jammed from the initial fire. The navigator, Flight Sergeant A. W. Brown, had to hack away with the fire axe before it finally opened and the crew all got clear. The now blazing bomber crashed 20 miles north east of Altmark, near Spaarbruck, Holland.

All the crew except the pilot were immediately arrested after their bale out. Two of them, Flight Sergeant M. J. A. Aumand, the rear gunner and Sergeant J. R. A. Goulet, the wireless operator, were badly wounded. Although made prisoners of war they were repatriated in a wounded prisoner of war exchange before the war was ended. The pilot, having been the last to bale out, was well separated from the rest of the crew and managed to hide up and avoid capture for two days. However, his luck ran out and he was captured, becoming an inmate of Stalag Luft III and VI with both the navigator and bomb aimer. The three remained as fellow prisoners until they were liberated by a British Armoured Division in May, 1945.

Three Wellingtons make Emergency Landings

Three other Wellingtons made it back to England for emergency landings at East Wretham and Stradishall. One was Wellington BK499, captained by Sergeant A. W. Jameson of 429 Squadron. This aircraft had collided with another bomber over the target. The rear gunner was jammed in his turret and the tail plane was badly damaged. Only the skill and courage of the pilot enabled this aircraft and its crew to make it back home.

Another Wellington, HE205 X-Xray of 431 Squadron, was captained by Flight Sergeant R. Hamby. This aircraft was badly shot up over the target by heavy anti-aircraft fire after being coned by a concentration of searchlights. The navigator, 126043 Pilot Officer J. T. Clarke, was killed instantly. All the hydraulics, radio and navigational aids were wrecked. Again it was only the exemplary airmanship of the pilot which enabled the bomber to make it back to Britain.

The third Wellington was badly hit by *Flak* at 21.10 hours, just before reaching the target. BK164 was captained by the Commanding Officer of 427 Squadron, Wing Commander Dudley H. Burnside DFC. The navigator, J 16756 Pilot Officer R. J. Heather, was killed instantly. The wireless operator, 923049 Flight Sergeant G. Frank Keen DFM, had half of his right foot blown off and also received several leg wounds. Keen had already completed one tour of operations with 51 Squadron and was on his 39th operation. The aircraft was very difficult to control due to severe aileron damage. The windscreen de-icing glycol tank burst drenching the bomb aimer, Pilot Officer R. J. Hayhurt, and filling the forward part of the Wellington with suffocating fumes. Despite this the bomb aimer directed the captain on his bombing run which was completed, the bombs being successfully dropped at 21.30 hours. During this time the badly wounded wireless operator, who had been standing in the astro dome, crawled back to his radio position. In spite of his terrible wounds, Keen laboured for two hours to repair the damaged radio. He also assisted in navigation by dragging himself to the chart table to get essential maps.

Shortly after leaving the target area the aircraft was again coned by searchlights for several minutes, but the pilot skilfully evaded the defences in his badly crippled bomber. However, the crew's ordeal was not yet over for they were attacked by enemy fighters on the return flight. Because of the alertness of the crew, the pilot's skill and the return fire from the rear turret manned by Pilot Officer D. B. Ross, they successfully evaded each attack. They eventually made it back for an emergency landing at Stradishall. For their outstanding actions the Wing Commander was awarded a Bar to his DFC and both the bomb aimer and wireless operator were given immediate awards of the DFC and CGM respectively.

Parachuting into the target

On the same raid flew Lancaster R5749, ZN-G 'George' from 106 Squadron, based at Syerston. This aircraft was captained by Australian Flight Sergeant A. L. McDonald who, with five other members of the crew, were not destined to return from this Essen raid. The only survivor was another Australian Flight Sergeant, Neil Lindsay, the bomb aimer. It was quite apparent that as his Lancaster was approaching the white TIs the searchlights and *Flak* were more active and intense than when they had been there on the 5th, a week previously. In fact the TIs had been dropped by the Pathfinders 15 miles short of the target as a datum point for the bomb run in. At this white marker, their aircraft was hit by *Flak*, but there was only superficial damage. As Neil lay in the nose of the Lancaster looking out through his perspex window he saw ahead two other bombers blow up directly over the target area at about 20,000 feet, the same altitude at which they were flying. After dropping the bomb load on to the glowing TIs below he glanced at his bomb panel to check that the bomb door closed indicator light was on. There was an almighty explosion and a white flash in front of his eyes. 'We've had it', he thought. On regaining conciousness he realised that he had been blown out through the nose of the Lancaster. Although dazed he quickly pulled the ripcord and a series of events in the next 10 to 12 minutes kept his adrenalin flowing. Firstly he felt as though he was sitting in an armchair in a darkened room. He felt no sensation of movement and was convinced that his parachute had not opened. As he glanced upwards he was relieved to see the reassuring white canopy overhead.

Then he became aware of the noise of passing aircraft and of the sharp blasts and staccato of the air battle. *Flak* and also searchlights were reaching up to the attacking bomber force whose falling bombs he could hear in erupting explosions. As the Lancasters were mainly in the rear of the bomber force, Neil realised that he was witnessing the closing stages of the attack. The defences were becoming less intense, but from his grandstand position he became aware that he was drifting rapidly towards the centre of the conflagration below. It really was a classic case of out of the frying pan and into the fire. Three searchlights suddenly coned him as he drifted down and as he was held in their beams some of the ground defence guns started to take pot shots at him. He was too weak to try and side slip his 'chute to get away and out of range, instead he just hung limply in his harness and feigned dead. Smoke drifting from the target obscured him at times from the sharpshooters below and his ruse of acting dead saved his life. He drifted past buildings to finally hit the ground between two rows of badly bombed and still burning buildings.

After releasing his parachute harness he lay on the ground wondering what to do when ghoulish figures appeared through the swirling smoke and flames. They turned out to be slave workers from the Krupps factory, into whose grounds he had landed. Only a short time before he had dropped his load of high explosive and incendiary bombs on this very factory. Using his schoolboy French he managed to communicate with the slave workers who indicated that they were prepared to try and help him to hide. When he made an effort to stand up he collapsed back to the ground. It was obvious to the slave workers that he required hospital treatment and they had no alternative but to go to the nearest *Flak* battery to inform of his presence.

The German officer who came to see him greeted him with the phrase which he and many more aircrew would hear as prisoners of war, "For you the war is over". After being carried away in a blanket, he was taken to an underground room which housed a telephone switchboard. Here his guards soon organised a slap and tickle schnapps party with the girls on the exchange, while he lay helpless on the floor in a corner of the room.

Next morning he was taken on the back of a lorry through the smoking devastation of the previous night's bombing to St Lambertus Krankhaus (Hospital), He was put into a ward with ten injured slave workers from the local armament factories and mines who were mainly Russian and French. Neil recalls that much to his surprise there was no discrimination in the very professional treatment of any of the patients. Later in hospital he was sad to learn that the rest of his crew had all perished in the mid-air explosion. He was the sole survivor. After his spell in hospital he was transferred to Stalag Luft 3 as prisoner of war No.1026. Neil Lindsay can certainly claim that he had a charmed life on the night of 12th/13th March, 1943.

Escape from a PoW camp

Piloting Halifax DT751 on the March 12th/13th Essen raid was 1231507 Pilot Officer Peter Nevines of 76 Squadron. They had bombed the target and were on the return flight when their Halifax was attacked by a fighter and set on fire. After he had checked that all his crew had baled out, Nevines jumped and landed in a marshy field near Venraij, a village 30 miles north-east of Eindhoven. As soon as he had landed and taken off his harness and Mae West he was approached by a Dutchman who quickly took him to two nearby houses, but the occupants would not help them. At about 04.00 hours a group of civilians, who obviously worked for the Germans, came along in a car and took him to the local Police Station. From there he was taken to a nearby aerodrome where he spent the night under guard. The next day all his crew were rounded up and after spending eight days in Holland they were transported to Dulag Luft to be interrogated. From there Nevines was sent in to Stalag 344 at Lamsdorf in April 1943. He stayed until October 1944, during which time he changed identity with a soldier to join an outside working party which would allow him to get into an outside camp. Although under guard this would give him a greater opportunity for making an escape. RAF aircrew were never allowed to go on these working parties because the Germans thought that the risk of them escaping was much too high. Nevines' first escape attempt was from a working party outside camp at E351, Hansdorf, in February 1944. In the company of another RAF airman, Flight Sergeant W. S. Wright who had also swopped identity, both airmen planned an escape with the assistance of the camp committee who supplied them with money, food, papers and clothing. This escape plan was frustrated by an English Army Sergeant in the camp. Nevines had reported this man some months previously for suspicious conduct.

Undeterred, a second escape attempt took place in April, 1944. A tunnel had been built with the help of over a dozen other prisoners and once again their escape had met with the full approval of the camp escape committee. This second attempt was made with Lance Corporal E. Egan of the Kings Royal Rifles and their plan was to reach Sweden. Supplied with 500 Marks and some food, they had both been advised by the committee to make for Stettin by train. On arrival there they had been told to go to a brothel in Oder Klein Strasse to seek help. Then they should go on to a café called the Golden Bullet.

After getting out through the tunnel, both escapers lay low for about six hours awaiting the time of the train departure. When they arrived at the local railway station Egan, who spoke good German, bought two tickets for Stettin. Just as the train was arriving they were both approached by a German Railway Guard and asked for their travel papers. Egan began to explain to the guard that they were both Dutch machinists travelling to Stettin, but as the papers were being examined Nevines realised that they would not get through the check. Realising that they would be recaptured he destroyed his papers and then created a diversion for Egan to get rid of his papers too. Both were quickly back in camp after only a brief taste of freedom.

Their third attempt was from Working Camp 283 at Ratibor in October 1944. This was to be Pilot Officer Nevines' lucky one when he at last got away. Again he had been considerably helped by the Camp's Escape Committee who had supplied the essential false papers, food and clothing. This time Nevines had changed identity with yet another soldier, Guardsman Grubb of the Coldstream Guards PoW No. 202. His escape partner was 633406 Keith Graley of the RAF. Some Polish workers had been contacted and they had given names of people in Blomberg who might be prepared to help.

The escape was made from the camp when the perimeter lights were fused, this having been arranged by the Camp Committee. Both escapers went by train to Chybie, near Bielitz, where they stayed a short while before making for the Carpathian foothills. According to the helpers in Blomberg another Polish contact would be waiting for them there. On arrival they were unable to find their contact, so they had to make their way back to Chybie and then to Blomberg. There they stayed in the house of a relative of an earlier helper and were fortunate to meet an English speaking Pole who was able to supply them with food ration cards. After a stay of a week, another Pole made arrangements for both escapers to reach a point between Gydnia and Danzig on the Baltic coast, where there was a possibility of making contact with Swedish smugglers who would take them across to Sweden. This plan was abandoned when news was received that the Germans had now mined the inshore areas around the coast near Danzig. After further delay the two airmen decided that it would be best to go by train to Kutno and meet the Russian Army advance, which according to reports was imminent in that area. They carried out their plan, but the Russian advance came sooner than expected and both men contacted the Russians on the west side of the River Vistula on January 24th, 1945. On contact both had great difficulty, apart from the language barrier, of convincing the Russian troops of their true identity. After two lengthy interrogations both men were put in gaol for several weeks. At the goal they met up with other British prisoners from Thorn Prisoner of War Camp. Later they were all marched to Wreschen where they met about 500 American officers. After spending a week there all the escaped prisoners were repatriated via Odessa, Port Said, Cairo and then to UK, which they reached on March 18th, 1945.

Casualties March 12th/13th, 1943. Target Essen

83 Squadron 8 Group Lancaster W4928 OL/S
Pilot. 41596 S/Ldr D.A.J.McClure DFC Killed Reichswald Forest. 10-B-17
Nav. 50667 P/O D.G.Lovell Killed Reichswald Forest, Germany. 10-C-3
B/A. J/7520 F/Lt O.R.Waterbury DFC Killed Reichswald Forest. 10-C-4
W/OP. 1254843 F/Sgt P.J.Musk DFM Killed Reichswald Forest. 10-C-5
F/E. 566978 Sgt J.Macfarlane Killed Reichswald Forest, Germany. 10-C-2
A/G. 111483 F/Lt A.F.Macqueen DFC Killed Reichswald Forest 10-C-1
A/G. 136720 P/O L.E.Warren Killed Reichswald Forest, Germany. 10-B-18

7 Squadron 8 Group Stirling BK592 MG/P
Pilot. 113682 F/Sgt D.E.Street Missing, Runnymede Memorial 139
Nav. 656188 Sgt D.C.Wilson Missing, Runnymede Memorial 170
B/A. 1102605 Sgt W.M.Meiklejohn Missing, Runnymede Memorial 159
W/OP. R/108329 F/Sgt R.A.W.Sharpe Missing, Runnymede Memorial 185
F/E. 1138074 Sgt T.E.Hastings Missing, Runnymede Memorial 152
A/G. R/115981 F/Sgt D.Neale Missing, Runnymede Memorial 185
A/G. 1068137 F/Sgt W.S.Berry Missing, Runnymede Memorial 135

101 Squadron 1 Group Lancaster W4862 SR/E
Pilot. J/15518 F/O J.R.Kee Killed Reichswald Forest, Germany. 10-B-5
Nav. 1316054 Sgt A.D.Slade Killed Reichswald Forest, Germany. 10-B-6
B/A. 1331034 Sgt S.G.Smith Killed Reichswald Forest, Germany. 10-B-7
W/OP. 1194273 Sgt W.E.Greasley Killed Reichswald Forest, Germany. 10-B-9
F/E. 969248 Sgt W.Hynd Killed Reichswald Forest, Germany. 10-B-8
A/G. 1074934 Sgt E.Shaw Killed Reichswald Forest, Germany. 10-B-10
A/G. 1322158 Sgt E.A.Steed Killed Reichswald Forest, Germany. 10-B-11

103 Squadron 1 Group Lancaster W4827 PM/
Pilot. 125680 F/O H.W.Dugard Killed Reichswald Forest, Germany. 21-F-3
Nav. 130388 P/O P.G.Harris Killed Reichswald Forest, Germany. 21-F-6
B/A. 1392628 Sgt R.A.Gerrard Killed Reichswald Forest, Germany. 21-F-8
W/OP. 1026151 Sgt W.R.Jones Killed Reichswald Forest, Germany. 21-F-7
F/E. 1222496 Sgt E.C.Fermanian Killed Reichswald Forest, Germany. 21-F-9
A/G. 651327 Sgt W.Andrews Killed Reichswald Forest, Germany. 21-F-4
A/G. 1394248 Sgt P.E.Trew Killed Reichswald Forest, Germany. 21-F-5

100 Squadron 1 Group Lancaster ED544 HW/Q
Pilot. A/408871 Sgt R.M.Peake Killed Reichswald Forest.. CG 3-C-11/12
Nav. A/414580 Sgt R.F.R.Sides Killed Reichswald Forest. CG 3-C-11/12
B/A. 1506082 Sgt E.Hodgson Killed Reichswald Forest. CG 3-C-11/12
W/OP. A/707909 Sgt A.R.Roberts Killed Reichswald Forest, Germany. 3-C-10
F/E. 945664 Sgt H.Jowitt Killed Reichswald Forest, Germany. 3-B-17
A/G. 50778 P/O D.I.Arthur Killed Reichswald Forest, Germany. 3-C-14
A/G. 1476619 Sgt W.E.Chamberlain Killed Reichswald Forest. 3-C-13

199 Squadron 1 Group Wellington HX263 EX/
Pilot. 41712 F/Lt W.J.King Missing, Runnymede Memorial 119
Nav. A/406964 Sgt C.R.Townsend Missing, Runnymede Memorial 197
B/A. 1160293 Sgt D.A.Nunn Missing, Runnymede Memorial 160
W/OP. 1312741 Sgt C.F.White Missing, Runnymede Memorial 169
A/G. R/153973 F/Sgt R.I.Edwards Killed Bergen, Holland. 2-C-10

199 Squadron 1 Group Wellington HE819 EX/
Pilot. 1332298 Sgt D.J.Clifford Missing, Runnymede Memorial 145
Nav. 119474 F/Lt C.M.Kitson PoW. Stalag Luft 3, Sagan. 925
B/A. 1337745 Sgt L.M.Jones Missing, Runnymede Memorial 155
W/OP. R/86416 W/O J.G.Richardson Missing, Runnymede Memorial 180
A/G. 1525044 Sgt R.Lambert Missing, Runnymede Memorial 156

149 Squadron 3 Group Stirling EF330 OJ/P
Crashed Beek, Holland at 22.03 hours, (13/3/43). Victim of Hptm.Dormann,
II/NJG1
Pilot. 1125798 F/Sgt F.A.Pearson Killed Bergh (Beek), Holland. CG 3/8
2/Pilot. 656429 Sgt V.Page Killed Bergh (Beek), Holland. CG 3/8
Nav. NZ/41498 Sgt P.H.Skinnel Killed Bergh (Beek), Holland. CG 3/8
B/A. J/13767 F/O G.W.Sellers Killed Bergh (Beek), Holland. CG 3/8
W/OP. 1377386 Sgt W.H.Clayton Killed Bergh (Beek), Holland. CG 3/8
F/E. 573564 Sgt J.Misseldine Killed Bergh (Beek), Holland. CG 3/8
A/G. 137664 P/O L.H.R.Binning Killed Bergh (Beek), Holland. 2
A/G. R/118377 W/O G.W.Miller Killed Bergh (Beek), Holland. 1

115 Squadron 3 Group Wellington BJ756 KO/
Pilot. 552269 Sgt L.P.Fallon Missing, Runnymede Memorial 149
Nav. 1436200 Sgt W.E.Akrill Missing, Runnymede Memorial 140
B/A. 655677 Sgt L.Collinge Missing, Runnymede Memorial 145
W/OP. 1295572 Sgt C.J.J.W.Lamb Missing, Runnymede Memorial 156
A/G. R/105883 Sgt C.M.Moffatt Killed Amersfoort, Holland. 13-7-137

10 Squadron 4 Group Halifax DT778 ZA/R
Pilot. 968735 F/Sgt L.Barker Killed Jonkerbos, Holland. 24-E-1
Nav. 125563 F/O R.J.Paul Killed Jonkerbos, Holland. 24-E-2
B/A. 1440297 Sgt K.A.Mills Killed Jonkerbos, Holland. 24-E-3
W/OP. 1291773 Sgt L.E.Thomas Killed Jonkerbos, Holland. 24-E-4
F/E. R/89257 Sgt W.L.G.Thompson Killed Jonkerbos, Holland. 24-E-7
A/G. 1318574 Sgt G.A.Hyatt Killed Jonkerbos, Holland. 24-E-6
A/G. 1126762 Sgt J.Freel Killed Jonkerbos, Holland. 24-E-5

10 Squadron 4 Group Halifax HR692 ZA/
Pilot. 142572 P/O J.Dickinson Killed Reichswald Forest, Germany. 2-B-9
Nav. 1035756 Sgt J.H.Harris Killed Reichswald Forest, Germany. CG 2-B-5/8
B/A. 1038690 Sgt F.W.Stanners Killed Reichswald Forest. CG 2-B-5/8
W/OP. 1263058 Sgt J.E.Smith Killed Reichswald Forest, Germany. 2-B-10
F/E. 634581 Sgt H.E.Henden Killed Reichswald Forest, Germany. CG 2-B-5/8
A/G. 1315144 Sgt L.J.Gait Killed Reichswald Forest, Germany. 2-B-11
A/G. 63115 Sgt F.P.Crawford Killed Reichswald Forest, Germany. CG 2-B-5/8

102 Squadron 4 Group Halifax DT739 DY/
Pilot. 1386718 Sgt E.W.L.Charlesbois Killed Reichswald Forest. 23-B-10
Nav. 1330509 W/O D.A.P.Horne PoW. Stalag 344, Lamsdorf. 27711
B/A. 1344406 F/Sgt A.D.Williams PoW. Stalag 344, Lamsdorf. 27748
W/OP. 1380186 W/O W.S.Hedges PoW. Stalag 344, Lamsdorf. 27713
F/E. 1104795 W/O H.R.Kemp PoW. Stalag 344, Lamsdorf. 27719
A/G. 547802 F/Sgt H.F.Powers PoW. Stalag 344, Lamsdorf. 27734
A/G. 1467789 Sgt E.A.Hughes Killed Reichswald Forest, Germany. 23-B-11

102 Squadron 4 Group Halifax DT799 DY/
Pilot. 1294257 Sgt H.C.A.Newland Killed Reichswald Forest. 16-G-15
Nav. 1338298 Sgt R.W.Floyd Killed Reichswald Forest, Germany. 16-G-16
B/A. 1295400 Sgt J.D.Haigh Killed Reichswald Forest, Germany. 10-C-12
W/OP. 1380230 Sgt D.J.Druett Killed Reichswald Forest, Germany. CG 12-A-4
F/E. 1207834 W/O C.S.Jones PoW, Stalg 344, Lamsdorf. 27716
A/G. 1555573 Sgt M.H.C.Crow Killed Reichswald Forest, Germany. CG 12-A-4
A/G. 1358410 Sgt A.E.Beaven Killed Reichswald Forest, Germany. CG 12-A-4

102 Squadron 4 Group Halifax JB836 DY/
Pilot. 109004 F/O A.D.A.Barnes Missing, Runnymede Memorial 123
Nav. 1286488 Sgt A.L.Thurlow Missing, Runnymede Memorial 167
B/A. 1396129 Sgt G.C.Felsentein Missing, Runnymede Memorial 149
W/OP. 126624 F/O E.H.Beeton Missing, Runnymede Memorial 123
F/E. 1290929 Sgt J.S.Lowdell Missing, Runnymede Memorial 147
A/G. 1330229 Sgt V.N.Elkins Missing, Runnymede Memorial 148
A/G. 1267977 Sgt W.P.Quinlivan Missing, Runnymede Memorial 162

76 Squadron 4 Group Halifax DT751 MP/C
Crashed 3 Kms SW of America, Holland
Pilot. 1231507 Sgt P.Nevines PoW. Escaped on 18-3-45
Nav. 126891 F/Lt J.B.Locke PoW. Stalag Luft 3, Sagan. 926
B/A. 658309 Sgt R.G.Poland PoW. Died 19/1/44.Cracow, Poland. 3-A-8
W/OP. 921130 W/O W.S.Wright PoW. Stalag 344, Lamsdorf. 27750
F/E. 9191130 Sgt A.C.Sharpe Killed Jonkerbos, Holland. 18-C-8
A/G. 1049713 F/Sgt P.C.Ratcliffe PoW. Stalag 344, Lamsdorf. 27736
A/G. 578097 F/Sgt F.G.Stapleton PoW. Stalag 344, Lamsdorf. 27740

78 Squadron 4 Group Halifax DT774 EY/
Pilot. R/107744 F/Sgt F.A.Marean Killed Uden, Holland. 4-C-2
Nav. 658077 Sgt H.Bentley Killed Uden, Holland. 4-C-5
B/A. 1586313 Sgt W.H.Gosnell Killed Uden, Holland. 4-C-6
W/OP. 644941 Sgt W.J.McLelland Killed Uden, Holland. 4-C-3
F/E. 533448 Sgt C.G.Dyer Killed Uden, Holland. 4-C-4
A/G. 1143366 Sgt G.E.Benson Killed Uden, Holland. 4-C-7
A/G. 975582 Sgt B.M.Singleton Killed Uden, Holland. 4-C-1

431 Squadron 4 Group Wellington HE205 SE/X
Pilot. F/Sgt R.Hamby
Nav. 126043 P/O J.T.Clarke Killed Edinburgh (Mount Vernon). G-421
Aircraft coned by searchlights and badly shot up by *Flak*. Navigator killed
instantly by shell splinter.

207 Squadron 5 Group Lancaster ED604 EM/
Pilot. 68816 F/O M.E.Noble DFC Killed Reichswald Forest, Germany. 30-A-4
Nav. 116125 F/O B.Clitheroe DFC Killed Reichswald Forest, Germany. 30-A-2
B/A. 979995 Sgt B.L.Litoloff Killed Reichswald Forest, Germany. JG 30-A-6/7
W/OP. 51295 P/O I.A.H.Linklater DFM Killed Reichswald Forest. JG 30-A-6/7
F/E. 527199 Sgt A.Garden Killed Reichswald Forest, Germany. 30-A-5
A/G. 969796 F/Sgt T.J.Walker Killed Reichswald Forest, Germany. 30-A-3
A/G. 1378749 F/Sgt R.S.Carr DFM Killed Reichswald Forest, Germany. 30-A-1

106 Squadron 5 Group Lancaster R5749 ZN/G
Pilot. A/403069 P/O A.L.McDonald Killed Reichswald Forest. 10-B-12
Nav. 1147352 Sgt H.S.F.Bishell Killed Reichswald Forest, Germany. 10-B-15
B/A. A/404815 F/O R.N.Lindsay PoW. Stalag Luft 3, Sagan. 1026
W/OP. 1376454 Sgt B.J.Eckett Killed Reichswald Forest, Germany. 10-B-13
F/E. 572584 Sgt K.R.Young Killed Reichswald Forest, Germany. 10-B-14
A/G. 1437145 Sgt R.C.C.Owen Killed Reichswald Forest, Germany. 10-B-13
A/G. R/114787 F/Sgt E.B.Clampitt Killed Reichswald Forest 10-B-16

50 Squadron 5 Group Lancaster ED449 VN/
Pilot. R/105321 F/Sgt F.Ward Killed Jonkerbos, Holland. 24-C-2
Nav. 1318904 Sgt F.Stephens Killed Jonkerbos, Holland. 24-C-1
B/A. 1501112 Sgt R.Heslop Killed Jonkerbos, Holland. 24-C-4
W/OP. 523635 F/Sgt A.Allan Killed Jonkerbos, Holland. 24-C-7
F/E. 1104498 Sgt R.Wilson Killed Jonkerbos, Holland. 24-C-6
A/G. 134184 Sgt R.J.Jenkins Killed Jonkerbos, Holland. 24-C-5
A/G. R/106357 Sgt V.R.D.Kissick Killed Jonkerbos, Holland. 24-C-3

97 Squadron 5 Group Lancaster R5607 OF/
Pilot. R/103187 W/O D.C.Plaunt Killed Reichswald Forest, Germany. 17-B-4
Nav. J/16380 P/O A.J.Smith Killed Reichswald Forest, Germany. 17-B-5
B/A. R/95518 F/Sgt J.A.J.L.Viau Killed Reichswald Forest, Germany. 17-B-3
W/OP. 637240 F/Sgt W.C.Burr Killed Reichswald Forest, Germany. 17-B-6
F/E. 965881 Sgt T.L.Williams Killed Reichswald Forest, Germany. 17-B-2
A/G. 1397293 Sgt G.W.Dillon Killed Reichswald Forest, Germany. 17-B-1
A/G. 1601091 Sgt A.W.Taylor Killed Reichswald Forest, Germany. 17-B-7

420 Squadron 6 Group Wellington HE690 PT/
Pilot. R/122227 W/O G.H.Cooke PoW. Stalag 344, Lamsdorf. 27707
Nav. 657790 F/Sgt J.Morris PoW. Stalag 344, Lamsdorf. 27729
B/A. 657972 W/O R.G.Mercer PoW. Stalag 344, Lamsdorf. 27728
W/OP. 1365781 Sgt A.R.Dawson Killed Rotterdam, Holland. LL-1-29
Killed by *Flak* in aircraft.
A/G. R/132284 W/O T.S.McKinnon PoW. Stalag 357, Kopernikus. 912

424 Squadron 6 Group Wellington BK348 GB/J
Pilot. J/16785 P/O R.G.Caldwell Killed Uden, Holland. CG 4-C-8/9
Nav. J/11240 F/O G.J.Cory Killed Uden, Holland. CG 4-C-8/9
B/A. R/103759 F/Sgt W.F.Topping Killed Uden, Holland. CG 4-C-8/9
W/OP. R/102165 Sgt A.P.Larson Killed Uden, Holland. CG 4-C-8/9
A/G. R/92418 Sgt L.A.Parker Killed Uden, Holland. CG 4-C-8/9

425 Squadron 6 Group Wellington BK340 KW/T
Aircraft crashed 20 mls.NE of Altmark nr.Spaarbruck, Holland.
Pilot. R/104784 W/O J.C.G.Lamontagne PoW. Stalag 357, Kopernikus. 905
Nav. R/104832 W/O A.W.Brown PoW. Stalag 357, Kopernikus. 888
B/A. R/72626 W/O J.V.Gauthier PoW. Stalag 357, Kopernikus. 899
W/OP. R/56139 Sgt J.R.A.Goulet PoW. Badly Wounded (Repatriated)
A/G. R/104875 F/Sgt M.J.A.J.Aumand PoW. Badly Wounded (Repatriated)

Minelaying

March 12th/13th, 1943
As Essen was being bombed, nine Stirlings from 3 Group were
out on their lonely, but important task of minelaying around the
Frisians. All aircraft were successful in finding their exact
locations and 50 mines were laid without an aircraft being lost.

No let up for the Gardeners

March 13th/14th, 1943
A much larger than usual force of bombers were allocated to
minelaying operations. Seventeen Lancasters from 5 Group and
51 Wellingtons from 1, 4 and 6 Groups were out in three areas.
The Lancasters laid 73 mines in the southern Baltic, while the
Wellingtons dropped 58 mines in the Bay of Biscay and along
the north German coast. 5 Group crews reported at debriefing
that light *Flak* was seen from many towns in southern Sweden
before and after the passage of the aircraft. One crew reported
fairly accurate *Flak* at Karlskrona. One aircraft was lost from
each of the minelaying areas with no aircrew survivors.

Casualties March 13th/14th, 1943. Minelaying

300 Squadron 1 Group Wellington BK516 BH/K
Pilot. P/783169 Sgt T.Kuzinski Missing, Northolt Memorial.
Nav. P/780226 F/Sgt K.Kramarczyk Missing, Northolt Memorial.
B/A. P/782742 Sgt N.Napora Missing, Northolt Memorial.
W/OP. P./703539 Sgt A.Papkow Missing, Northolt Nemorial.
A/G. P/794726 Sgt F.Polom Missing, Northolt Memorial.

9 Squadron 5 Group Lancaster ED494 WS/M
Pilot. R83454 W/O H.C.Lewis Missing, Runnymede Memorial 180
Nav. 1392825 Sgt R.L.Laycock Missing, Runnymede Memorial 146
B/A. 1801303 Sgt J.I.Mitchell Missing, Runnymede Memorial 159
W/OP. 1270145 Sgt R.C.Hitchcock Missing, Runnymede Memorial 153
F/E. 967384 Sgt D.Cowie Missing, Runnymede Memorial 146
A/G. 1494009 Sgt R.F.Cunningham Missing, Runnymede Memorial 146
A/G. 1575692 Sgt J.H.Howorth Missing, Runnymede Memorial 154

420 Squadron 6 Group Wellington BK296 PT/
Pilot. R/108882 F/Sgt C.H.Tidy Missing, Runnymede Memorial 186
Nav. J/13815 F/O J.D.Macfarlane Missing, Runnymede Memorial 174
B/A. R/108825 F/Sgt G.R.D.Hall Missing, Runnymede Memorial 182
W/OP. 1128944 Sgt H.Reddy Missing, Runnymede Memorial 162
A/G. R/88388 F/Sgt J.A.Corbett Missing, Runnymede Memorial 181

A Temporary Pause in Bombing

March 14th/15th, 1943
While the main bombing force was having a stand down period,
minor minelaying sorties were still being carried out. Thirteen
Wellingtons went once more to the well visited minelaying areas
around the Frisians. There were no early returners and 26 mines
were laid without any loss.

Explosion on an English airfield

During this stand down period Bomber Command suffered one
of its worst bombing up accidents to date as far as loss of
aircraft was concerned. This accident happened at Scampton
airfield in Lincolnshire, the home base at that time of 50 and 57
Squadrons who were equipped with Lancasters. The incident
occurred at 09.15 hours on March 15th, when the Lancasters
were being bombed up. One 4,000 lbs bomb dropped from an
aircraft's bomb bay and exploded, causing a chain reaction with
neighbouring bombs. Three Lancasters (W4196, W4823 and
W4112) of 50 Squadron and three Lancasters (ED306, ED594
and W4834) of 57 Squadron blew up and were complete write
offs. Another five aircraft were damaged. Fortunately no lives
were lost in this disaster. Why the order to bomb up these
aircraft had been given is still a mystery, for no operation had

been scheduled for that day or night. In fact the stand down from operations for the main force bombing squadrons lasted from 12th/13th to 22nd/23rd March, 1943.

Bombing Up

Bombing up was an important part of the ground crew operations before a raid. Depending on the target and the rôle the squadron was to play, the loads could vary from fourteen 250 lb or 500 lb bombs to a single bomb of 8,000 lbs. The smaller bombs were of varying types:- general purpose, armour piercing or semi-armour piercing. They could also be of low, medium or high capacity. Low capacity bombs had a small charge to weight ratio and therefore penetrated further before exploding, while the high capacity bombs would explode on impact. The type of bombs used depended on the target for the night and the type of aircraft being used. A typical Lancaster bomb load to the Ruhr would be one 4,000 lbs 'cookie', four 500 lbs GP bombs and small bomb containers which held either eight 30lbs or ninety 4lbs incendiary bombs. A Stirling load could be one 2,000 lbs bomb plus two 1000 lbs bombs. 1,740 four pound and thirty-two 30 pound incendiary bombs could also be carried. A Halifax typical load would be three 1,000 lbs bombs plus one 2,000 lbs bomb with 90 thirty lbs incendiaries.

For obvious reasons the bomb dumps on all airfields were situated in remote corners, well away from other installations. Bombs were brought out from the dumps on special bomb trolleys and pulled along by tractors to the well spread dispersal points or hard standings where the aircraft were parked. Feverish activity on airfields in the mornings would herald that operations were on that night and aircrew would always anxiously look at the bomb and fuel loads for an indication as to whether it was going to be a long haul that night or a short visit to Happy Valley. Bombs were winched up into the aircraft's bomb bay in a special sequence so that on their release the aircraft would still maintain its centre of gravity. Rigid checks were made to ensure that each bomb was held securely and locked. The jaws for the big bomb carriers were locked by a small lever near the bomb release handle. Sometimes errors were

made in the loading operation and bombs would drop accidentally. Electrical faults could also cause premature release.
Normally no great damage would result, except to the men of the
bomb crews who could have accidents involving crushed arms or
legs. Explosions did not normally occur for the drop was
insufficent for the fuse action to go off or the casing of the bomb
to crack. But there were always exceptions to the rule. Apart
from bombing up accidents, aircrew were not immune from
making a premature release of bombs while checking their
aircraft in the dispersal area. Many aircraft were burnt out in
this way, for any incendiaries which were dropped were sure to
ignite.

Minelaying goes on

March 16th/17th, 1943
During the lull in the main force bombing, minelaying was again
undertaken by 12 Wellingtons from 1 Group when they went to
the Frisians to lay 24 mines. No aircraft were lost from these
operations.

March 20th/21st, 1943
Minelaying operations were chalked up again on the target
boards for 1 Group Wellington squadrons and 3 Group Lancasters. Twelve of the Wellingtons had a recall signal when they
were half way to the Bay of Biscay to return to base due to a
sudden change in base weather conditions for landing. The four
Lancasters carried out their sortie, laying 16 mines without any
loss.

St Nazaire

March 22nd/23rd, 1943
The Atlantic coast port of St Nazaire was the target on the night
of March 22nd/23rd for the next heavy raid by the main force
bombers. This port was the key base for U boat operations in the
North Atlantic and for this attack 357 aircraft would take part.
46 of the force were Pathfinders consisting of 6 Mosquitoes, 25

Lancasters, 10 Halifaxes and 5 Stirlings. The main force of four engined bombers, 164 Lancasters, 89 Halifaxes and 58 Stirlings, left their bases for zero hour, 21.30 hours, over the target. Twenty-two aircraft returned early for various reasons. The remainder met fairly favourable weather en route with patches of odd cloud at 6,000 feet. The weather over the target was good with no cloud and moderate visibility. *Flak* defences were spasmodic with very few searchlights, but a heavy smoke screen was set off during the early part of the raid, which obscured the aiming point for many of the bombers. Only one Lancaster was lost on this raid. It was probably shot down over the target area for many crews brought back reports of seeing two parachutes going down in the target area. Some aircraft reported heavy *Flak* from Guernsey.

The U-Boat War

It was not until April 6th that Bomber Command was released from its obligation to bomb the Atlantic French ports, which were classed by the High Command as high priority targets because of the U-Boat menace. Sir Arthur Harris was not overly enthusiatic about mounting these sorties, but a letter from the Assistant Chief of Air Staff (Operations) had instructed him that an increase in enemy U-Boat operations demanded a policy of area bombing against their bases on the west coast of France. Even an order of priority was spelt out:- Lorient, St Nazaire, Brest and La Pallice in that order. This bombing was to take priority, but there was a let out for Harris in the letter. It continued to say that operations were not to prejudice any attacks that Harris might be planning on Berlin, or any concentrated attacks on important targets in Germany or Italy, when suitable weather allowed these to take place. Harris later said that this instructive letter was a misdirection of the bomber force, for he was convinced that no damage could be caused to the U-Boat pens. They had been constructed by the Todt organisation, which was the German para-military work force that designed and built defence structures along the entire French coast against possible Allied invasion. The U-Boat pens, when completely finished, were covered by many feet of reinforced concrete which was impenetrable to any bomb that the RAF possessed at that juncture of the war. An amendment to the Casablanca Directive (Pointblank) was made in June 1943 which made other targets, rather than the U boat shipyards and pens, a much higher priority in the Allied bombing. This was obviously a specific preparation for the invasion of Western Europe.

In spite of his strong views, Harris followed his orders and between January 14th and February 17th, 1943, he had despatched 1,960 sorties against Lorient and dropped just over 4,000 tons of high explosive on it. Between 18th February and the 29th March, 1943, he had again despatched 1,117 sorties against St Nazaire dropping another 2,600 tons of high explosive bombs. Harris, however, stated that he would have much preferred that those 6,600 tons of bombs been dropped on Germany, where he was confident that they would have done more to win the war. Harris's views on these pointless bombings of U-Boat pens were proved correct. After the war was over, when records attributed to Grand Admiral Doenitz were seen, it was found that he had written early in 1943 the following.

"The towns of St Nazaire and Lorient have been rubbed out as main submarine bases. No dog or cat is left .... nothing but the important submarine shelters remain."

Casualties March 22nd/23rd, 1943. Target St Nazaire

101 Squadron 1 Group Lancaster ED775 SR/V
Aircraft crashed at Moulins de Per, near St.Nazaire, France.
Pilot. 1230404 Sgt G.R.Lewis Killed Escoublac-la-Baule, France. CG 2-F-20/21
Nav. 1078040 Sgt J.Conroy Killed Escoublac-la-Baule, France. CG 2-F-20/21
B/A. 127290 F/O J.L.Metcalfe Killed Escoublac-la-Baule, France. CG 2-F-20/21
W/OP. 1383168 Sgt J.H.Sibley Killed Escoublac-la-Baule. CG 2-F-20/21
F/E. 1066150 Sgt W.Rishton Killed Escoublac-la-Baule, France. CG 2-F-20/21
A/G. 1490509 Sgt E.Davies Killed Escoublac-la-Baule, France. 2-F-18
A/G. 1314398 Sgt J.R.Jeffrey Killed Escoublac-la-Baule, France. 2-F-19

Minelaying

March 22nd/23rd, 1943
While the main force of bombers were at St Nazaire, six Wellingtons from 6 Group were laying 12 mines around Texel without suffering any loss.

Minelaying

March 23rd/24th, 1943
Before returning to the Ruhr there was one more night of minelaying operations for Bomber Command. A force of 45 aircraft, 33 Wellingtons, ten Stirlings and two Lancasters, were out over the north German coast. Three aircraft were unable to obtain an accurate fix for dropping their mines and aborted their mission, but the remainder dropped 120 mines in strategic shipping lanes. One Wellington was lost on this operation.

Casualties March 23rd/24th, 1943. Minelaying

196 Squadron 4 Group Wellington HE167 ZO/A
Pilot. NZ/414603 Sgt H.C.Duckmanton Killed Terschelling, Holland. 88
Nav. 1101027 Sgt D.R.Jeffrey Killed Terschelling, Holland. 90
B/A. 1331344 Sgt B.S.F.Crook Killed Terschelling, Holland. 87
W/OP. 1190213 Sgt S.R.O.Hermon Killed Terschelling, Holland. 86
A/G. 986071 F/Sgt E.W.Booth PoW. Stalag 357 Kopernikus. 980

Bomber Command very rarely operated at full strength on three succesive nights. Fatigue slowed a crew's reflexes and therefore decreased efficency. Sir Arthur Harris also believed that the odds against aircrew survival were already stacked high enough without loading the dice. However, he broke this unwritten rule and major bombing operations were scheduled the next four consecutive nights of March 26th to the 29th, 1943.

Duisburg

March 26th/27th, 1943

On the night of March 26th, 455 bombers took off from their bases in England. It was another big raid, to be mounted this time, on the town of Duisburg in the Ruhr. The force consisted of seventeen Pathfinders (9 Mosquitoes, 4 Lancasters, 2 Halifaxes and 2 Stirlings). The main force was 153 Lancasters from 1, 3 and 5 Groups, 112 Halifaxes from 4 and 6 Groups, and 173 Wellingtons from 1, 4 and 6 Groups. From the outset the raid was doomed to failure, for six of the important *Oboe* Mosquitos had to return to base with faulty sets. One back-up Lancaster which had engine trouble also aborted. As a consequence there was a lack of continuous marking in the 10/10ths cloud conditions over the target. The bombing became very scattered, especially in the early stages of the attack which started at 21.13 hours and lasted for 95 minutes.

There was moderate to heavy *Flak* in barrage form, especially in the north and north-east of the town. Searchlights were fairly ineffective as they were unable to penetrate the thick cloud. 64 aircraft did not arrive over the target, having to abort for a variety of reasons, an abortive loss rate of 14.1%. A total of 449.6 tons of high explosive bombs were dropped as well as 233.5 tons of incendiaries (14,128 thirty pounders and 165,836 four pounders). Three large explosions were reported at 21.56 hours. German post war records show that only minimal damage was caused by such a large force of bombers. 15 houses were reported destroyed with 70 damaged. Eleven people were killed and 36 injured. Four aircraft ditched in the North Sea on their return, one being a 109 Squadron Mosquito. This was the first *Oboe* casualty. One of the others was a Wellington from 426 Squadron, X3696 captained by 1216854 Sergeant E. Hall. No trace of aircraft or crew was ever found. Of the 32 aircrew who did not return from this raid, 7 were killed, 18 missing, 6 became prisoners and one evaded capture.

Casualties March 26th/27th, 1943. Target Duisburg

109 Squadron 8 Group Mosquito DK318 HS/
Ditched in Thames Estuary.
Pilot. 114192 F/Lt L.I.Ackland Missing, Runnymede Memorial 119
Nav. J/17228 P/O F.S.Strouts Missing, Runnymede Memorial 178

460 Squadron 1 Group Lancaster ED354 UV/O
Pilot. A/413468 F/Sgt R.E.Wilson Missing, Runnymede Memorial 194
Nav. 1384132 Sgt D.J.Cooper Missing, Runnymede Memorial 146
B/A. 1388573 Sgt P.J.Haseman Missing, Runnymede Memorial 152
W/OP. 130450 P/O C.O.Bramham Missing, Runnymede Memorial 130
F/E. 1158748 Sgt F.V.Harrison Missing, Runnymede Memorial 152
A/G. 1382768 Sgt H.D.Brown Missing, Runnymede Memorial 144
A/G. 1601778 Sgt N.A.Lever Missing, Runnymede Memorial 156

78 Squadron 4 Group Halifax W7931 EY/
Crashed 22.00 hours at Gaanderen, Holland.
Pilot. 1063628 F/Sgt J.M.Tait Killed Doetinchem (Loolan), Holland. 1-10
2/Pilot. NZ/413923 Sgt J.A.Wilson Killed Doetinchem (Loolan), Holland. 1-9
Nav. 51297 F/O S.Hauxwell PoW. Stalag Luft 3, Sagan. 1014
B/A. R/122377 W/O G.R.Johnstone PoW. Stalag 357, Kopernikus. 1020
W/OP. 48697 F/Lt R.W.Keen PoW. Stalag Luft 3, Sagan. 982
F/E. 520885 W/O F.E.Lemon PoW. Stalag 357, Kopernikus. 1025
A/G. 532057 Sgt A.Wilson Killed Doetinchem (Loolan), Holland. 1-11
A/G. 1059832 Sgt R.R.H.Huleatt PoW. Stalag 357, Kopernikus. 1018

429 Squadron 4 Group Wellington MS487 AL/
Pilot. 123109 F/O G.Fox Killed The Hague, Holland. AP-2-40
Nav. 1235043 Sgt A.A.Skelly Killed The Hague, Holland. AP-3-47
B/A. 1082668 Sgt G.H.Murray Evaded capture
W/OP. 126739 P/O P.S Bastian Killed The Hague, Holland. AP-3-53
A/G. 1108414 Sgt J.Mc.Murray PoW. Stalag 357, Kopernikus. 42730

431 Squadron 4 Group Wellington HE503 SE/S
Pilot. 62464 F/Lt G.H.T.Eades Missing, Runnymede Memorial 131
Nav. J/8621 F/Lt A.M.Hill Missing, Runnymede Memorial 172
B/A. 120704 F/Lt N.J.Gardner Missing, Runnymede Memorial 119
W/OP. R/75458 W/O B.V.L Ducker Killed Kviberg, Gothenburg, Sweden. 3-A-5
A/G. R/85301 W/O J.M.Rogal Missing, Runnymede Memorial 180

426 Squadron 6 Group Wellington X3696 KW/
Ditched 60 miles east of Withernsea, Yorkshire. Hull. Radio obtained fix on
aircraft at 02.05 hours - 5347N 0120E. Beaufighter was sent on sea search, but
nothing was found.
Pilot. 1216854 Sgt E.Hall Missing, Runnymede Memorial 152
Nav. 657755 Sgt J.J.Reade Missing, Runnymede Memorial 162
B/A. 1238939 Sgt F.Simpson Missing, Runnymede Memorial 164
W/OP. 1369435 Sgt W.Stevenson Missing, Runnymede Memorial 165
A/G. 710081 Sgt C.D.Reed Missing, Runnymede Memorial 162

Berlin

March 27th/28th, 1943

Three major raids followed, although not to the Ruhr. The first, on 27th/28th March, was on Germany's capital city Berlin. A completely four engined force made up of 23 Lancasters, 16 Halifaxes and 15 Stirlings in the Pathfinding section, with a main force consisting of 168 Lancasters, 108 Halifaxes and 66 Stirlings were despatched. The raid again was not a success. The important Pathfinding aircraft had eleven of their number return early, the six Stirlings from 7 Squadron being the most serious handicap in this group. The main force suffered 45 aborted sorties. The Pathfinder heavy bombers approached the city from the south-west and, although there was no moon, the weather conditions were fairly reasonable with 3/10ths layer cloud at 14,000 feet and only a slight haze over the target itself. The Pathfinders dropped their markers at two separate points 5 miles away from the planned aiming point and well away from the city, with the result that the raid became very scattered. This illustrates the navigation and target identification problems of Pathfinders relying purely on H^2S and dead reckoning. They were forced to operate without the help of *Oboe* equipped Mosquitos as the *Oboe* range could not be extended accurately to Berlin. 439.6 tons of high explosives and 394.7 tons of incendiaries, as well as 153 target indicators, were dropped during the raid which commenced at 23.00 hours and lasted half an hour.

In spite of the scattered nature of the raid, 102 people were killed and 260 injured, the casualties mainly being caused by two apparently fluke bombs falling on Berlin's Anhalter station. A military train had just arrived, bringing back forces on leave from the Russian front, when the bombs fell. According to German records there was also one other lucky strike in this raid, when a secret *Luftwaffe* radio equipment depot was completely destroyed. The Germans even believed that this depot must have been the aiming point and purpose of the raid, such was the importance of the depot. Two large explosions were reported by some crews at 23.10 hours and could well have been one of the depot hits. Nine aircraft failed to return from this raid and from the missing crews 45 were killed, 11 became prisoners with 7 being interned in Sweden.

Bale out over Sweden

One Halifax from 408 (RCAF) Squadron, captained by 1299738 Sergeant R. H. Batchelor, was hit by *Flak* over Hanover on their way to the target. The aircraft was badly hit, both port engines being damaged, and the petrol tanks holed. The captain decided that they had no hope of crossing heavily defended Denmark alone if they returned early, so he decided to set course for Sweden. The bombs were jettisoned allowing a reasonable altitude was to be maintained. At around 00.30 hours, running very low on fuel, they presumed that the coastline they were flying across was Sweden. The bale out order was given.

On landing in wooded countryside near Ulricehamm (Borg), the pilot and flight engineer, R/68020 Sergeant H. L. Grayson, landed in close proximity to each other. Uncertain of where exactly they had landed, either in Norway or in Sweden, they buried their 'chutes and then approached a group of people who were standing near the burning wreckage of their bomber. They found to their relief that they were in Sweden.

The bystanders took them to a farm, where they were given food and hot drinks. At about 02.00 hours, the local Chief of Police and an English speaking Swede arrived to interview them and gave the two airmen the glad news that the rest of the crew were safe and had landed in the vicinity of the farm.

Eventually all the crew were placed in a local hotel under military guard. They were interviewed by a Swedish Army Officer and a Captain from the Swedish Air Force, who spoke excellent English. This particular officer was keen to find out the aircraft's details and was disappointed to find that the crew were not co-operative in disclosing this information. The whole crew were transported to a military camp at Boras, before being taken under guard by train to Stockholm and then on to an internment camp at Falun, north of Stockholm.

Captain's self sacrifice

Another 6 Group Halifax which failed to return was from 419 Squadron. DT634 'E-Edward', was being captained by J/9668 Flying Officer C. E. Porter. At briefing the crew, most of whom were nearing the end of their tour of operations, were informed that their usual aircraft 'K for King' was not available. It was due for a major overhaul and they had to take a substitute aircraft 'E for Edward'. They were not, therefore, in the best of spirits. Each crew became attached to one aircraft, for every plane had a kind of personality of its own with its whims and oddities to which the regular crew grew accustomed and felt happy with. On checking out 'E - Edward', their aircraft for the Berlin raid, the flight engineer found that the emergency fire axe was missing from its normal mounting near the escape hatch. He asked the ground crew to supply a replacement, a wise order as circumstances turned out. Even the wireless operator complained of what he considered a temperamental radio.

On the outward flight the Halifax ran into a heavy barrage of anti-aircraft fire from the German coastal *Flak*. Shortly after, flying at twenty thousand feet in the area south of Bremen, further heavy *Flak* rocked the heavily laden bomber. Away to port the crew saw a sheet of flame burst from an exploding Lancaster which had received a direct hit. Their Halifax was hit by the *Flak* and suffered damage. The starboard outer engine began to seriously overheat until it finally had to be feathered. With still a long way to go before reaching their target of Berlin, the captain had a quick vote amongst the crew as to whether they should continue or abort because of this complete engine failure. The crew's reaction was mixed, some suggested that it would be prudent to bomb Bremen and then cut back to base, rather than risk continuing on to Berlin. The captain, however, was persuasive and told the crew that as they had already survived much *Flak* it would be a waste if they did not press on towards the target as they still had three good engines.

Still on course, but with a decreased airspeed, they flew on. By now they were well behind in the bomber stream and being a lone bomber over Berlin was not a healthy situation to be in. An attack on Magdeburg was decided on and successfully carried out. A new course was then set for home. Some forty minutes later the Halifax was attacked by a night fighter which raked the fuselage with cannon and machine gun fire. The port inner and outer engines both caught fire. Other fires broke out in the wireless operator's compartment and bomb bay. Although seriously wounded, the pilot managed to feather the port inner engine and tried to dive the aircraft in an attempt to blow out the fire in the outer engine, which surprisingly still appeared to be functioning. Almost immediately the situation looked hopeless because the fires in the fuselage were completely out of control. Reluctantly the captain had to give the bale out order to the crew.

To their horror, when they tried to open the escape hatches they were all jammed, due either to being frozen up or having been damaged in the fighter attack. The flight engineer, Sergeant M. W. Bishop, struggled along with the two gunners, Sergeant D. London and Flight Sergeant A. H. Taylor, to hack away with the fire axe which thankfully had been replaced. By now the altimeter was beginning to unwind at a startling speed. The pilot struggled to keep the bomber from plunging down and tried to turn back inland as he knew that they were somewhere near the coast. He wanted to avoid his crew having to bale out into the bitterly cold sea.

The bomb aimer, Flying Officer G. J. Sweanor, went forward to open the pilot's top escape hatch and clip the pilot's 'chute on to his harness, urging him to get out immediately as the rest of them had little chance of releasing their escape hatch in time. Porter, however, stayed at his controls, unwilling to leave either by choice or because of his extensive injuries. Still he wrestled with the controls to keep the plane from hurtling down out of control. Each crew member knew that they were racing to a certain death if the hatch would not open. Finally, because of the frenzied hacking by the fire axe, the door gave way. Falteringly, but with deliberate speed, each member of the crew slid or leapt out into the dark night. The first out was Sergeant London and the last was Flying Officer George Sweanor who hoped that his skipper had already jumped from the front hatch. Unknown to George, the pilot was still at the controls when the aircraft crashed.

As Sweanor jumped, the slipstream caught him just as a sheet of flame passed over. The drill called for a ten second delay before pulling the rip cord, but the bomb aimer knew that he did not have that luxury of time and pulled it immediately. Right after the parachute opened there was a muscle tearing jerk as the canopy caught the upper branches of a tree. 'E - Edward', the stricken Halifax, crashed and exploded in a nearby field. Sweanor could even feel the heat from the flames. Had he delayed the jump by another few seconds he knew that he would still have been aboard the aircraft when it crashed. A tall tree, the only one in the vicinity, had broken his fall and probably saved his life.

A gun emplacement nearby was still firing into the bomber which was burning furiously amid the explosions of machine gun ammunition. From his lofty perch George Sweanor could hear German voices and, realising that his position was a little too obvious, he released his harness. The tree was taller than he had imagined and he crashed to the ground. In a daze he dragged himself to his feet and found that his leg wound, which he had sustained in the aircraft, was very painful and was bleeding badly. Only minutes had passed since the aircraft was hit and the crew had baled out, but to George it seemed like an eternity. Realising that to stand any chance of getting away he must move quickly from the area of the crashed bomber,he bound his scarf tightly around his wound and moved into a nearby orchard. On his way he almost bumped into a group of Germans who were moving towards the site of the crashed aicraft. In the darkness George was not noticed and was able to limp away. Being unsure of the area where the plane had crashed, but knowing that were in Germany, the crew's chances of escape were practically nil. Soon George, along with the rest of his crew, were rounded up and made prisoners of war. Afterwards the deeply sad feeling among the six survivors was that their trusty skipper had skilfully managed to keep the aircraft under some sort of control, so giving them sufficent time to bale out safely. By doing so he sacrificed his own life.

Casualties March 27th/28th, 1943. Target Berlin

156 Squadron 8 Group Lancaster W4895 GT/
Pilot. 143228 P/O R.J.Wallis Killed Berlin, Germany. CG 1-B-5/9
Nav. 1071280 F/Sgt J.G.Shepherd Killed Berlin, Germany CG 1-B-5/9
B/A. 1386586 Sgt F.J.Walder Killed Berlin, Germany. CG 1-B-5/9
W/OP. 1286345 Sgt U.Thomas Killed Berlin, Germany. 1-B-11
F/E. 971820 Sgt A.Mackenzie Killed Berlin, Germany. CG 1-B-5/9
A/G. 1698523 Sgt S.Poole Killed Berlin, Germany. 1-B-10
A/G. R/88514 W/O G.T.Hillman Killed Berlin, Germany CG 1-B-5/9

35 Squadron 8 Group Halifax W7907 TL/M
Pilot. J/118575 F/O H.J.Espy Killed Grave not known.
Nav. 1501437 Sgt G.C.Dynes Killed Becklingen, Germany. 11-G-1/6
B/A. NZ/413111 F/O J.H.Naylor Killed Becklingen, Germany. 11-G-1/6
W/OP. 1377817 Sgt R.C.Smith Killed Becklingen, Germany. 11-G-1/6
F/E. 575820 Sgt R.A.Thomas Killed Becklingen, Germany. 11-G-1/6
A/G. 632331 Sgt C.Pattison Killed Becklingen, Germany. 11-G-1/6
A/G. 1390540 Sgt G.H.Yeates Killed Becklingen, Germany. 11-G-1/6

7 Squadron 8 Group Stirling BF317 MG/X
Aircraft crashed at Bremen, Germany.
Pilot. NZ/413096 P/O M.Lord Killed Sage, Germany. 14-B-6
Nav. NZ/405459 F/Sgt D.Wellington Killed Sage, Germany. 10-C-12
B/A. 131998 P/O T.H.Brown Killed Sage, Germany. 10-D-2
W/OP. 1265860 Sgt N.Young Killed Sage, Germany. CG 14-B-1/5
F/E. 979904 Sgt L.Nash Killed Sage, Germany. CG 14-B-1/5
A/G. 1303883 Sgt R.McKerrill Killed Sage, Germany. 10-C-11
A/G. 1312946 Sgt J.R.Oliver Killed Sage, Germany. 10-C-10

101 Squadron 1 Group Lancaster W4322 SR/0
Pilot. 1134764 Sgt W.Bell Killed Hanover, Germany. 11-F-18
Nav. J/16407 P/O F.Prosperine Killed Hanover, Germany. 12-F-4
B/A. 1349775 Sgt G.Wilson Killed Hanover, Germany. 12-F-19
W/OP. 929736 Sgt J.S.Priestley Killed Hanover, Germany. 12-F-7
F/E. 529282 Sgt G.E.Moore Killed Hanover, Germany. 12-F-18
A/G. 1289974 Sgt P.J.Edwards Killed Hanover, Germany. 12-F-1
A/G. R/79184 W/O R.W.G.Hogan Killed Hanover, Germany. 12-F-5

214 Squadron 3 Group Stirling BF453 BU/L
Aircraft crashed at Finkenwerder, Germany.
Pilot. 140914 P/O E.Challis Killed Hanover, Germany. CG 10-B-9/12
Nav. 942664 Sgt R.Anderson Killed Hanover, Germany. 10-B-8
B/A. 1349598 Sgt C.K.Phin Killed Hanover, Germany. 10-B-7
W/OP. 1379905 Sgt E.Greenhalgh Killed Hanover, Germany. CG 10-B-9/12
F/E. 1171555 Sgt R.G.Martin Killed Hanover, Germany. CG 10-B-9/12
A/G. 933968 Sgt S.A.Woodrow Killed Hanover, Germany. 10-B-6
A/G. A/406681 Sgt D.J.Rae Killed Hanover, Germany. CG 10-B-9/12

158 Squadron 4 Group Halifax HR753 NP/B
Pilot. 1199434 F/Sgt E.C.Hibburt Killed Sage, Germany. 1-B-1
Nav. 1039478 Sgt J.B.Kelly PoW. Stalag 357, Kopernikus. 903
B/A. 128623 F/Lt H.B.Pearson PoW. Stalag Luft 3, Sagan. 929
W/OP. 1268195 F/Sgt J.G.Hawkesworth PoW. Stalag 357, Kopernikus. 901
F/E. R/57798 Sgt W.H.Penrose Killed Sage, Germany. 1-B-7
Killed in aircraft by *Flak*.
A/G. 1245902 W/O R.D.Harding PoW. Stalag 357, Kopernikus. 900
A/G. 1378860 W/O M.B.Budd PoW. Stalag 357, Kopernikus. 890

44 Squadron 5 Group Lancaster W4839 KM/F
Pilot. 1289611 F/Sgt A.J.Horwood Killed Berlin, Germany. 1-D-2
Nav. 1126336 Sgt R.L.Cole Killed Berlin, Germany. CG 1-A-3/11
B/A. R/78908 W/O J.A.Newton Killed Berlin, Germany. 1-D-1
W/OP. R/79076 W/O F.W.Guild Killed Berlin, Germany. CG 1-A-3/11
F/E. 572620 Sgt L.W.J.Schultz Killed Berlin, Germany. 1-D-4
A/G. 1556644 Sgt G.M.Sheridan Killed Berlin, Germany. 1-D-5
A/G. R/104277 F/Sgt H.H.Clements Killed Berlin, Germany. 1-D-3

408 Squadron 6 Group Halifax BB332 EQ/
Aircaft crashed in Blindberg, Sweden. Crew baled out.
Pilot. 1299738 Sgt R.H.Batchelor Interned in Sweden.
Nav. 1391852 Sgt H.Wein Interned in Sweden.
B/A. 124316 P/O R.V.Fisher Interned in Sweden.
W/OP. R/79080 Sgt R.Hall Interned in Sweden.
F/E. R/68020 Sgt H.L.Grayson Interned in Sweden.
A/G. R/118088 Sgt F.W.Grant Interned in Sweden.
A/G. R/128359 Sgt A.Sieben Interned in Sweden.

419 Squadron 6 Group Halifax DT634 VR/
Pilot. J/9668 F/O C.E.Porter Killed Hamburg, Germany. 5A-D-8
Nav. 143991 P/O A.T.Budinger PoW. Stalag Luft 3, Sagan. 891
B/A. J/11114 F/Lt G.J.Sweanor PoW. Stalag Luft 3, Sagan. 936
W/OP. R/55933 W/O J.G.Lanteigne PoW. Stalag 357, Kopernikus. 906
F/E. R/65139 Sgt M.W.Bishop PoW. Stalag Luft 4, Sagan. 887
A/G. 1247844 F/Sgt D.London PoW. Stalag 357, Kopernikus. 910
A/G. R/97354 W/O A.H.Taylor PoW. Stalag 357, Kopernikus. 42783

Minelaying

March 27th/28th, 1943
A small force of 24 aircraft, 16 Stirlings and one Lancaster from
3 Group with seven Wellingtons from 1 Group, were out laying
81 mines. All aircraft dropped their mines and returned safely to
their bases.

St Nazaire

March 28th/29th, 1943.

The next major raid was to St Nazaire on the evening of March 28th/29th, when a force of 298 bombers was led into the attack by six Mosquitoes, backed up by 18 heavy Pathfinders. All had operated on the long flight to Berlin the previous night. There was a lower rate of early returners on this mission, 8% (26 aircraft) the majority of these being the two engined Wellingtons with fuel shortage problems. Only one Mosquito returned early, with faulty equipment. There were no heavy Pathfinder early returners. Weather conditions were reasonably good with 4/10 to 6/10 cloud at 18,000 feet over the target. Crews reported the *Flak* intensive, but mainly inaccurate, although it was responsible for the loss of the two bombers which did not return from this raid. One was Halifax BB283 from 419 RCAF Squadron, captained by R/120117 Flight Sergeant R. F. Beckett. The bomber was coned by searchlights for quite a long time over the target and in spite of its twisting and turning was firmly held before finally going down in flames due to anti-aircraft fire. The other lost bomber, a Lancaster from 97 Squadron, was also the victim of *Flak*. A total of 340.7 tons of high explosive bombs and 319.9 tons of incendiaries (142,601) were dropped on this raid.

Casualties March 28th/29th, 1943. Target St Nazaire

97 Squadron 5 Group Lancaster ED754 OF/A
Pilot. 119155 F/O R.E.Weight Killed Escoublac-la-Baule, France. 2-G-11
Nav. 1334656 Sgt E.F.Ball Killed Escoublac-la-Baule, France. 2-G-10
B/A. 623524 Sgt R.J.Whatley Missing, Runnymede Memorial 169
W/OP. 1123389 Sgt A.Kemp Missing, Runnymede Memorial 155
F/E. 574948 Sgt K.F.Green Missing, Runnymede Memorial 151
A/G. 137547 Sgt L.C.A.Fisk Killed Escoublac-la-Baule, France. 2-G-9
A/G. R/103890 F/Sgt J.Tongue Missing, Runnymede Memorial 186

419 Squadron 6 Group Halifax BB283 VR/
Pilot. R/120117 F/Sgt R.F.Beckett Killed Escoublac-la-Baule, France. 2-G-7
Nav. 1183277 Sgt D.Ainsley Killed Escoublac-la-Baule, France. 2-G-6
B/A. R/119623 F/Sgt R.M.McLeod Killed Escoublac-la-Baule, France. 2-G-8
W/OP. 1379357 Sgt W.J.S.Boyd Killed Escoublac-la-Baule, France. 2-G-5
F/E. R/70200 F/Sgt C.S.Foster Killed Escoublac-la-Baule, France. 2-G-2
A/G. R/148539 Sgt J.J.Goldspink Killed Escoublac-la-Baule, France. 2-G-3
A/G. R/99387 F/Sgt G.McGrath Killed Escoublac-la-Baule, France. 2-G-4

419 Squadron 6 Group Halifax DT669 VR/
Pilot. R/105312 Sgt G.K.Smallwood
B/A. R/106758 W/O R.G.Douglas PoW, Stalag Luft 4, Sagan. 897
Baled out over Enemy territory. W/O Douglas was killed along with 26 other prisoners, when 4 RAF Typhoon Fighter bombers strafed a PoW marching column near Grasse (19-04-45). He was buried at Grasse, but reinterred in Berlin Cemetery at the end of the War (Grave: 6-B-7)

Minelaying

March 28th/29th, 1943
On the same night seven Wellingtons from 1 Group were also minelaying around St Nazaire. One aircraft failed to get an accurate pin point and brought the mines back to base, while the remainder laid twelve mines without losses.

Berlin

March 29th/30th, 1943
Bomber Command mounted a major raid on Berlin. It was doubtful whether the operation would take place because of bad weather conditions en route, but at the last minute the go ahead was given. A total of 329 aircraft took off from their bases, but an exceptionally large number of aircraft, 95 (28.9%), returned after meeting very severe icing and electrical storm conditions over the North Sea. Many of the bombers were unable to climb with their heavy loads of bombs and fuel through 10/10 cloud which had layers up to 14,000 or 15,000 feet. Those bombers which did manage to struggle through found no cloud cover over the target itself. Searchlights were operating in groups of 30 to 40 with predicted moderate to heavy *Flak* over the capital city. Route markers had been dropped by the Pathfinders over Muggel See, so that the main force bombers could do a timed run to the target. The concentrated marked aiming point was, however, too far south of the planned aiming point. All this was compounded by the main force which had struggled through terrible weather conditions and arrived late. This was mainly due to the badly forecasted winds en route. Many crews were so

far off track they did not even bother to go to the datum point at Muggel See, so bombed well south of the markers instead.

Although 288.2 tons of high explosive bombs and 226.3 tons of incendiaries were dropped, not a great deal of damage was caused in relation to this tonnage. The Command suffered bad losses because of this ill advised operation. Twenty-one aircraft failed to return and from their crews 93 were killed, 35 were missing, 18 became prisoners and one successfully evaded capture.

Two Stirlings from 214 Squadron, EF362 and BK663, collided in mid air on return to their base at Chedburgh. The crews baled out safely, except for the pilot of EF362, 115186 Flying Officer W. G. Cooper, and the rear gunner of BK663, NZ411789 Sergeant H. L. Burt, who were killed.

A 97 Squadron Lancaster W4175, captained by 116782 Flying Officer P. H. Norton, crashed at Woodhall Spa on return and all the crew were killed. Halifax JB848 of 102 Squadron, piloted by R/95452 Warrant Officer W. P. Comrie, crashed at Pocklington on its outward flight, killing all the crew.

Of those bombers which actually landed back at their bases, 31 had returned with *Flak* or fighter attack damage. The Pathfinder force lost only one Lancaster, R5754 from 83 Squadron, but two other Halifaxes from 35 Squadron were extremely fortunate in getting back to base.

The Halifax captained by Flight Lieutenant B. McDonald was coned by 30 searchlights over the target and was held for so long that the only escape was to dive from 18,000 feet to 10,000 feet to elude the predicted *Flak* that poured into the apex of the cone. Fortunately the pilot managed to climb his bomber back to 15,000 feet to join the safety in numbers of the bomber stream on the homeward leg. Later, however, he flew too near the Bremen defences, which for some reason were particularly active and heavy on that night. The aircraft was caught again in a searchlight cone which blinded the pilot completely. Dropping his seat below the cockpit window eye level to get away from the glare, the pilot threw his bomber about like a fighter, twisting and weaving in the heavy *Flak*. His luck held out that night, for down at 1,000 feet he managed to clear the area relatively unscathed. Then he coaxed his bomber to gain more altitude, for a captain always considered that height was a good safety measure in any evasive action that he might have to make. It was just as well that he had that philosophy, for just off Terschelling he flew directly over a *Flak* ship, positioned to give any minelaying aircraft a very warm welcome. The German *Flak* gave the Halifax the full treatment. One shell burst under the aircraft, putting its nose up in a stalling position. The pilot quickly recovered, even at the low altitude. Now very low on petrol, it was touch and go as to whether the battered bomber would make it back to base. The English coast was a most welcome sight to the crew and the landing at the first available aerodrome, Coltishall, must have been a great relief.

Another 35 Squadron Halifax, piloted by Flight Lieutenant Rees, was also coned by searchlights over Berlin and badly damaged by *Flak*. Rees managed to struggle back to base, testimony to the well built and sturdy Halifax aircraft which appeared to take such heavy punishment.

An Evader is Betrayed

Flight Lieutenant A. T. L. Cullum from 49 Squadron was the navigator in Lancaster ED435, which was hit by *Flak* over Berlin and also attacked by a night fighter on its return flight over Holland. The bomber sustained severe damage which resulted in the crew having to bale out.

Cullum landed in the outskirts of Nijverdaal and for the rest of the night hid in some woods. The next morning he contacted a friendly farmer who took him to a doctor's house in Holten, where he became the doctor's guest for three weeks. Eventually the doctor was able to make contact with the underground movement and Cullum was then taken to the town of Meppel where he stayed in another house for two months until arrangements for his further travel could be completed.

On June 21st, he was taken by train to a small village near Tilburg and then into some woods nearby where he spent four days before crossing the border into Belgium. Then he was sent on by train to Brussels, where he stayed in the house of the wife of a former BBC announcer. He was then taken to a school house for two weeks during which time Cullum met a man who claimed to be an English Intellience Officer and who wished to be addressed as 'The Captain'. This man took Cullum to a chateau in the outskirts of the city where he spent five days before he was taken by train to Paris. In an hotel in Paris he met up with nine other Allied personnel. The next day the whole party was taken to the railway station to catch the train to Bordeaux, but while walking to the station they were surrounded by plain clothes Gestapo agents, arrested and taken to Fresnes Prison in Paris. Cullum remained there until August 21st, when he was transferred to Stalag Luft III at Sagan before being finally liberated by Allied troops at Lubeck on May 2nd, 1945.

Cullum bitterly remembers the Paris betrayal and realised that it was quite obviously a carefully planned job. Sadly many other aircrew were caught in a similar way.

Casualties March 29th/30th, 1943. Target Berlin

83 Squadron 8 Group Lancaster R5754 OL/X
Message to base at 23.33hours returning early bad weather. Position given as 5402N 0442E. Nothing further heard.
Pilot. 80238 F/O N.C.Johnson Missing, Runnymede Memorial 125
Nav. 1348644 Sgt G.B.MacFarlane Missing, Runnymede Memorial 157
B/A. 1016380 Sgt G.T.Still Missing, Runnymede Memorial 166
W/OP. 1196615 Sgt D.H.Harper Missing, Runnymede Memorial 152
F/E. R/110280 F/Sgt R.D.McCullagh Missing, Runnymede Memorial 183
A/G. 127276 F/O W.F.Coldwell Missing, Runnymede Memorial 123
A/G. R/87263 F/Sgt A.H.Penner Missing, Runnymede Memorial 185

12 Squadron 1 Group Lancaster W4858 PH/A
Aircraft crashed near Rotterdam, Holland on return flight, shortage of fuel.
Pilot. 1028921 Sgt F.W.Pinkerton Evaded capture
Nav. 1452049 F/Sgt I.C.Clunas PoW. Stalag 357, Kopernikus. 1005
B/A. 1341383 Sgt W.A.Lees PoW. Stalag 357, Kopernikus. 1023
W/OP. 1214528 Sgt F.Morton Killed Rotterdam, Holland LL-2-33
Killed in aircraft by *Flak*
F/E. 1257644 Sgt R.G.Irons PoW. Stalag 357, Kopernikus. 1019
A/G. 1580874 Sgt G.C.W.Warren Killed Rotterdam, Holland LL-1-31
Baled out parachute did not open.
A/G. 1320597 F/Sgt N.H.S William PoW. Stalag 357, Kopernikus. 1046

460 Squadron 1 Group Lancaster ED391 UV/E
Aircraft shot down over Holland.
Pilot. A/403735 F/Lt K.H.Grenfell Killed Hardenburg, Holland. A-6
Nav. A/403754 P/O S.F.S.McCullach Killed Hardenburg, Holland. A-8
B/A. 1008290 Sgt R.Cordingley Killed Hardenburg, Holland. A-7
W/OP. A/411010 F/Sgt P.W.Dunn Killed Hardenburg, Holland. A-4
F/E. 573570 Sgt G.E.Lewis Killed Hardenburg, Holland. A-9
A/G. A/406680 F/Sgt R.L.Potter Killed Hardenburg, Holland. A-10
A/G. 955673 Sgt S.G.Webb Killed Hardenburg, Holland A-5

460 Squadron 1 Group Lancaster W4327 UV/S
Aircraft shot down at Lievelde, Holland at 04.46 hours, (30/3/43). Victim of
Hptm.Geiger, II/NJG1
Pilot. A/416322 F/Sgt D.H.V.Charlick Killed Lichtenvoorde, Holland. 13
Nav. A/405381 F/O T.H.McNeil Killed Lichtenvoorde, Holland. 12
B/A. A/403502 F/Sgt E.N.Cooper Killed Lichtenvoorde, Holland. 15
W/OP. A/411445 F/Lt F.J.Falkenmire PoW, Stalag Luft 3, Sagan. 976
F/E. 980250 Sgt P.Perry Killed Lichtenvoorde, Holland. 14
A/G. 1316314 Sgt W.P.D.Chapman Killed Lichtenvoorde, Holland. 11
A/G. A/408578 F/Sgt G.V.Hampton Killed Lichtenvoorde, Holland. 10

149 Squadron 3 Group Stirling BK708 OJ/P
Aircraft crashed at Lindenburg, Germany.
Pilot. 138658 P/O J.T.S.Fulton Missing, Runnymede Memorial 131
Nav. 1386592 Sgt A.J.Crosson Missing, Runnymede Memorial 146
B/A. 1236492 Sgt E.D.Edwards Missing, Runnymede Memorial 148
W/OP. 1268390 Sgt E.G.Hunt Missing, Runnymede Memorial 154
F/E. 1037662 Sgt J.W.Houlgrave Missing, Runnymede Memorial 154
A/G. 1601119 Sgt R.P.T.Saunders Missing, Runnymede Memorial 164
A/G. 527344 W/O C.L.Blackford PoW. Stalag 357, Kopernikus 42723

218 Squadron 3 Group Stirling BK702 HA/O
Aircraft crashed at Bremen, Germany.
Pilot. J/17189 P/O W.G.Hoar Killed Sage, Germany. 10-D-4
Nav. 1383288 Sgt R.E.Jeffreys Killed Sage, Germany. CG 14-B-1/5
B/A. 659110 Sgt R.A.Mears Killed Sage, Germany. CG 14-B-1/5
W/OP. 1167366 Sgt E.T.Howard Killed Sage, Germany. CG 14-B-1/5
F/E. 1017385 Sgt J.E.Turnbull Killed Sage, Germany. CG 14-B-1/5
A/G. 530734 Sgt W.M.Robertson Killed Sage, Germany. CG 14-B-1/5
A/G. R/129563 Sgt J.H.M.Fraser Killed Sage, Germany. 10-D-3

218 Squadron 3 Group Stirling BK716 HA/J
Aircraft crashed into North Sea off Vlieland, Holland.
Pilot. 118128 F/O J.F.Harris Missing, Runnymede Memorial 124
Nav. J/11241 F/O H.G.Farrington Missing, Runnymede Memorial 149
B/A. 1027864 Sgt C.A.Bell Missing, Runnymede Memorial 142
W/OP. 122910 F/O J.M.Campbell Missing, Runnymede Memorial 123
F/E. 1487492 Sgt R.Kennedy Missing, Runnymede Memorial 155
A/G. 1251519 Sgt L.R.J.Shrubshall Missing, Runnymede Memorial 164
A/G. R/105188 F/Sgt J.F.McCaw Missing, Runnymede Memorial 183

115 Squadron 3 Group Lancaster DS625 KO/
Pilot. J/16873 P/O H.J.Ross Missing, Runnymede Memorial 177
Nav. 1331022 Sgt S.P.Shaw Missing, Runnymede Memorial 164
B/A. 1312186 F/Sgt D.Dray Missing, Runnymede Memorial 136
W/OP. NZ/413769 Sgt F.W.Marshall Missing, Runnymede Memorial 199
F/E. 1088307 Sgt F.L.Godden Missing, Runnymede Memorial 150
A/G. R/125961 W/O J.M.Bradford Missing, Runnymede Memorial 179
A/G. 1166981 Sgt J.McKenny Missing, Runnymede Memorial 158

51 Squadron 4 Group Halifax BB244 MH/
Shot down Vorden, Holland at 03.47 hours, (30/3/43). Victim of Hptm.Geiger II/NJG1
Pilot. 124802 F/O R.G.Harris Killed Vorden, Holland. 13
Nav. 1503619 F/Sgt E.Williams PoW. Stalag 357, Kopernikus 42731
B/A. 127304 F/O V.J.Dowling Killed Vorden, Holland. 15
W/OP. 1293332 Sgt D.M.Reed Killed Vorden, Holland. 11
F/E. 1374466 Sgt J.M.Taylor Killed Vorden, Holland. 12
A/G. 528021 F/Sgt A.Heponstall Killed Vorden, Holland. 14
A/G. R/74870 F/Sgt J.P.Young Killed Vorden, Holland. 10

76 Squadron 4 Group Halifax DT744 MP/K
Shot down at Welmbuttel, Germany.
Pilot. 82716 F/Lt J.H.Wetherly DFC Killed Kiel, Germany. 4-J-15
2/Pilot. 1315989 Sgt A.H.J.Whittle Killed Kiel, Germany. 4-J-14
Nav. 137522 P/O A.H.G.Paxton Killed Kiel, Germany. 4-J-10
B/A. 131167 F/lt H.J.Beck Killed Kiel, Germany. 4-J-11
W/OP. 991727 F/Sgt J.R.Orr Killed Kiel, Germany. 4-J-13
F/E. 549090 Sgt C.H.Mitton Killed Kiel, Germany. 4-J-12
A/G. 1459226 Sgt L.Havenhand Killed Kiel, Germany. 4-J-16
A/G. 900952 Sgt S.A.Bayfield Killed Kiel, Germany. 4-J-11

76 Squadron 4 Group Halifax DT563 MP/0
Crashed off Vlieland, Holland
Pilot. 51291 P/O L.J.Cursley Missing, Runnymede Memorial 131
Nav. 142008 P/O T.Edwards Missing, Runnymede Memorial 131
B/A. R/98145 W/O J.Taylor Missing, Runnymede Memorial 180
W/OP. 1376657 Sgt A.B.Boyd Missing, Runnymede Memorial 143
F/E. 969970 Sgt F.J.Platt Missing, Runnymede Memorial 161
A/G. 142491 P/O R.G.Wright Killed Westdongeradeel(Wierum), Holland 58
A/G. R/103992 F/Sgt R.W.MacNeill Missing, Runnymede Memorial 184

77 Squadron 4 Group Halifax JB/842 KN/E
Damaged by fighter at Berlin. Crashed in Fehmarn Belt, Denmark.
Pilot. 1201836 F/Sgt C.H.Newman Killed Berlin. Buried 8/4/43 CG 2-L-12/16
Nav. 996625 Sgt J.M.Donald Killed Svino, Denmark. 34
B/A. 74586 F/O J.R.Armstrong Killed Berlin, Germany. 8-D-7
W/OP. 125424 F/O A.Metcalf Killed Berlin, Germany.Buried 16/6/43 8-D-6
F/E. 982880 F/Sgt A.F.Smith Missing, Runnymede Memorial 139
A/G. 1336488 Sgt E.S.Bowen Missing, Runnymede Memorial 143
A/G. 1179979 F/Sgt R.Brough Killed Berlin, Germany. CG 2-L-12/16

158 Squadron 4 Group Halifax HR757 NP/M
Pilot. 926963 W/O H.Holcombe Killed Hamburg, Germany. 5A-D-7
Nav. 1380632 F/Sgt H.F.R.Stettiner Killed Hamburg, Germany. 5A-D-13
B/A. R/848004 F/Sgt H.V.Tracey Killed Hamburg, Germany. 5A-D-14
W/OP. R/82496 F/Sgt J.H.Dillon Killed Hamburg, Germany. 5A-D-9
F/E. 1006135 Sgt T.Dawson Killed Hamburg, Germany. 5A-D-10
A/G. 995124 Sgt E.Milne Killed Hamburg, Germany. 5A-D-11
A/G. 1070425 Sgt R.M.Wilson Killed Hamburg, Germany. 5A-D-12

44 Squadron 5 Group Lancaster W4199 KM/H
Pilot. NZ/414986 Sgt K.J.Johnson Killed Berlin, Germany. 7-E-18
Nav. 143988 P/O I.F.Leng Killed Berlin, Germany. 7-E-20
B/A. 656269 Sgt R.A.Edmonds Killed Berlin, Germany. 7-E-24
W/OP. 1376410 Sgt T.C.Somerville Killed Berlin, Germany. JG 7-E-22/23
F/E. 1197149 Sgt W.H.Shipp Killed Berlin, Germany. 7-E-19
A/G. 1395042 Sgt C.G.L.Marlin Killed Berlin, Germany. 7-E-21
A/G. 1333546 Sgt R.T.Widdy Killed Berlin, Germany. JG 7-E-22/23

49 Squadron 5 Group Lancaster ED435 EA/
According to post war interrogations, the parachutes of B/A, W/Op and rear gunner not seen to open.
Pilot. 1343309 F/Sgt D.W.Fyffe PoW. Stalag 357, Kopernikus 1012
Nav. J/22563 F/Lt A.T.L.Cullum PoW. Stalag Luft 3, Sagan. 2084
B/A. R/849998 W/O F.A.McNutt Killed Raalte, Holland. 8
W/OP. 614144 Sgt T.Fazackerley Killed Raalte, Holland. 6
F/E. 1016477 F/Sgt E.R.McCracken PoW. Stalag 357, Kopernikus 1030
A/G. 1199524 Sgt R.C.Link PoW. Stalag Luft 6, Heydekrug. 1027
A/G. 1374201 Sgt J.Robertson Killed Raalte, Holland. 7

49 Squadron 5 Group Lancaster ED469 EA/
Pilot. J/12562 F/O G.F.Mabee Killed Hanover, Germany. 12-F-13
Nav. 658715 Sgt W.Carr Killed Hanover, Germany. 12-F-9
B/A. 658431 Sgt R.W.Brown Killed Hanover, Germany. 12-D-19
W/OP. 970305 Sgt A.S.McLaren Killed Hanover, Germany. 12-F-14
F/E. 1092054 Sgt J.A.Cross Killed Hanover, Germany. 12-F-12
A/G. 1334688 Sgt J.G.Jewell Killed Hanover, Germany. 12-F-8
A/G. 1411530 Sgt G.A.Jones PoW. Camp not known

57 Squadron 5 Group Lancaster ED761 DX/
Crashed in Holland
Pilot. 143669 P/O A.E.Fisher Killed Bergen-op-Zoom, (Can). CG-8-H-10/12
Nav. 1147351 Sgt H.Richardson Killed Bergen-op-Zoom, (Can). CG-8-H-10/12
B/A. 1187123 Sgt R.H.G.Taylor Killed Bergen-op-Zoom, (Can). CG-8-H-10/12
W/OP. 1112260 Sgt J.Westerdale Killed Bergen-op-Zoom, (Can). CG-8-H-10/12
F/E. 1374522 Sgt F.A.Bandeen Killed Bergen-op-Zoom, (Can). CG-8-H-10/12
A/G. 1197803 Sgt A.G.Deane Killed Bergen-op-Zoom, (Can). CG-8-H-10/12
A/G. 1335631 Sgt D.J.Simmonds Killed Bergen-op-Zoom, (Can). CG-8-H-10/12

106 Squadron 5 Group Lancaster ED596 ZN/
Shot down Lievelde, Holland at 04.29hours, (30/3/43). Victim of
Hptm.Geiger II/NJG1.
Pilot. 86633 S/Ldr R.L.Hayward DFC Killed Lichtenvoorde, Holland. 28
Nav. 61960 F/Lt J.O.Young DFC Killed Lichtenvoorde, Holland. 26
B/A. 141415 P/O A.Urquhart Killed Lichtenvoorde, Holland. 23
W/OP. 141279 P/O E.H.Mantle DFM * Killed Lichtenvoorde, Holland. 29
F/E. 570635 Sgt G.W.F.Baker Killed Lichtenvoorde, Holland. 25
A/G. 1549636 Sgt D.Brown Killed Lichtenvoorde, Holland. 27
A/G. 142021 P/O G.V.Pryor DFM Killed Lichtenvoorde, Holland. 24

207 Squadron 5 Group Lancaster W4931 EM/
Pilot. 123026 F/O D.O.Street Killed Berlin, Germany 3-A-24
Nav. 985099 F/Sgt B.A.Rawlinson PoW. Stalag 357, Kopernikus 1034
B/A. 1270446 W/O G.V.Eld PoW. Stalag 357, Kopernikus 1011
W/OP. 1379814 F/Sgt W.L.Blake PoW. Stalag 357, Kopernikus 999
F/E. 988436 W/O P.Dudley PoW. Stalag Luft 6, Heydekrug. 1008
A/G. R105872 W/O J.E.Taylor PoW. Stalag Luft 4, Sagan. 1040
A/G. 1578131 F/Sgt B.H.Nutt PoW. Stalag 357, Kopernikus 1031

408 Squadron 6 Group Halifax HR654 EQ/
Pilot. 1148932 Sgt G.Jennings Killed Kiel, Germany. 4-B-1
Nav. J/13840 F/Lt J.S.Acheson PoW. Stalag Luft 3, Sagan. 965
B/A. 909501 Sgt R.S.V.Lewis Killed Kiel, Germany. 4-B-4
W/OP. 1332233 Sgt F.J.Cherry Killed Kiel, Germany. 4-A-19
Died shortly after bale out.
F/E. R/62274 Sgt H.Davenport Killed Kiel, Germany. 4-B-3
A/G. R/110955 F/Sgt N.W.Roberts Killed Kiel, Germany. 4-B-2
A/G. R/150671 F/Sgt J.F.Barnes Killed Kiel, Germany. 4-A-20

408 Squadron 6 Group Halifax DT679 EQ/
Pilot. J/13482 F/O F.N.S.Cavanaugh Killed Sage, Germany. JG-14-B-11
Nav. J/13421 F/O H.E.Tanner Killed Sage, Germany. 5-F-1
B/A. 1432430 Sgt T.W.Harris Killed Sage, Germany. 5-F-3
W/OP. 1210605 Sgt E.A.Biggs Killed Sage, Germany. 11-B-1
F/E. 578060 Sgt R.H.Holtham Killed Sage, Germany. 14-B-11
A/G. R/137373 F/Sgt G.W.Herrington Killed Sage, Germany. 5-F-4
A/G. R/137398 F/Sgt W.A.Kopacz Killed Sage, Germany. 5-F-2

214 Squadron 3 Group Stirling EF362 BU/
Collided in mid air 1,300 ft over Chedburgh with Stirling BK663 and crashed
at Oldham, near Hadleigh, 17 miles south east of Cambridge, after operations
to Berlin.
Pilot. 115186 F/O W.G.Cooper Killed Shirley (St James), Birmingham. 22/18D
Nav. NZ/415271 Sgt C.R.Logan Baled out.
B/A. 997120 Sgt F.E.Smith Baled out.
W/OP. 1331148 Sgt A.T.Boosma Baled out.
F/E. 1612432 Sgt R.D.T.Kearns Baled out.
A/G. 1433724 Sgt E.R.H.Dyde Baled out.
A/G. NZ/418229 Sgt F.T.Lovegrave Baled out.

214 Squadron 3 Group Stirling BK663 BU/
Collided with Stirling EF362 over Chedburgh and crashed on aerodrome after minelaying operations.
Pilot. 123105 F/O J.C.Dixon Safe
Nav. P/O W.Rowley Safe
B/A. Sgt T.H.McShane Safe
W/OP. Sgt H.W.Bennett Safe
F/E. Sgt R.F.Dewsbury Safe
A/G. Sgt T.E.Drew Safe
A/G. NZ/411789 Sgt H.L.Burt Killed Haverhill, Suffolk U/196

102 Squadron 4 Group Halifax JB848 DY/
Crashed out of control on take off at Pocklington after being caught in the slipstream of another aircraft on outward flight for operations Berlin.
Pilot. R/95452 W/O W.P.Comrie Killed Barmby Moor, Yorkshire. A-1
Nav. 127313 F/O D.W.F.Harper Killed Barmby Moor, Yorkshire. F-8
B/A. 129161 F/O W.H.Jenkins Killed Birmingham Crematorium.
W/OP. 1330802 Sgt F.W.Dorrington Killed Brighton & Preston, Surrey C-178
F/E. 1365664 Sgt W.J.McGrath Killed Glasgow (St Peter's R.C.) 16-1126
A/G. 1609738 Sgt J.King Killed East London (Plaistow). 17571
A/G. 1478651 Sgt M.C.C.Squires Killed Barmby Moor, Yorkshire. G-8

97 Squadron 5 Group Lancaster W4175 OF/U
Crashed in circuit at Woodhall Spa after ops Berlin.
Pilot. 116782 F/O P.H.Norton Killed Coningsby, Lincolnshire. 64-1250A
Nav. 126038 F/O G.C.Francis Killed Coningsby.Lincolnshire. 64-1251
B/A. 1035770 Sgt W.Standrigg Killed Sacriston, Durham. 16-4
W/OP. R/84415 Sgt R.Frank Killed Nottingham(Jewish). 38
F/E. 104220 Sgt J.A.Peel Killed Knockbreda, Co.Down, Ireland L-390
A/G. 751476 F/Sgt F.R.Birtwhistle Killed Gilroes, Leicester. 534
A/G. 1601035 Sgt W.H.Whiting Killed Branksome, Poole. C6/31

78 Squadron 4 Group Halifax W7939 EY/
Abandoned after engine lost power through icing, ex ops Berlin. and crashed at North Grimston near Malton, Yorkshire.
Pilot. NZ/415206 Sgt A.Toon Baled out.
Nav. 185837 Sgt R.Falcus Baled out.
B/A. 1379810 Sgt H.J.Burridge Baled out.
W/OP. A/403883 Sgt J.Whelan Baled out, injured.
F/E. 1280330 Sgt J.Donaldson Baled out.
A/G. 1577824 Sgt J.Sands Baled out, injured.
A/G. 1071995 Sgt G.Campbell Baled out.

Bochum

March 29th/30th, 1943

A Wellington force of 157 aircraft led by eight *Oboe* Mosquitos also left to attack Bochum on the same night. Again, because of weather conditions similar to those encountered by the four engined force to Berlin, 47 aircraft returned to their bases early. This left less than a hundred bombers to attack the target with 65.2 tons of high explosive and 74.9 tons of incendiaries.

Over the target it was a moonless and cloudy night, so the target was marked by the *Musical Wanganui* method, the code name for blind dropped sky markers. For some reason, perhaps because of wind conditions, the Mosquitos were unable to keep to their planned timetable and there were long gaps when the target was left completely unmarked. The Wellington bombers dropped their loads on estimated time of arrival, which resulted in very fragmented results. Little damage was caused at Bochum for the high price of thirteen aircraft lost. Of their crews 36 were killed, 24 missing and 5 became prisoners.

One of the lost Wellingtons was HE175 of 428 Squadron, captained by NZ/415001 Sergeant J. B. Martyn, which was forced to ditch in the North Sea. The last radio fix was obtained by Hull Radio when the aircraft was ditching at 01.55 hours at a position 5524N 0055E. A sea search was made, but nothing was found. A similar fate must also have met Wellington BK540 of 429 Squadron. This was piloted by 1334945 Sergeant H. D. G. Carty. Hull Radio received a distress call from this aircraft on its outward flight at 20.43 hours from a position of 5333N 0140E. The body of the navigator from this aircraft, R/106671 Warrant Officer D. L. Bain, was washed ashore at Esbjerg, Denmark. There was no trace of the other members of the crew.

Casualties March 29th/30th, 1943. Target Bochum

166 Squadron 1 Group Wellington X3965 AS/L
Pilot. NZ/414961 Sgt O.E.Collins Missing, Runnymede Memorial 199
Nav. 125603 F/O L.Young Missing, Runnymede Memorial 130
B/A. 1377312 Sgt J.G.Hubbard Missing, Runnymede Memorial 154
W/OP. A/412098 F/Sgt J.B.Bayliss Missing, Runnymede Memorial 192
A/G. A/401744 F/Sgt S.N.Curtis Missing, Runnymede Memorial 192

166 Squadron 1 Group Wellington HE545 AS/H
Pilot. 142863 P/O J.R.A.Hodgson Killed Arnhem, Holland. 9
Nav. 143877 P/O S.R.Farley Killed Arnhem, Holland. 6
B/A. J/16408 P/O F.L.E.Dupre Killed Groesbeek, (Can), Holland. XV-C-5
W/OP. 1376154 Sgt D.Keenan Killed Arnhem, Holland. 8
A/G. J/17467 P/O R.A.Weese Killed Groesbeek, (Can), Holland. XV-C-6

196 Squadron 4 Group Wellington HE548 ZO/
Pilot. 1135766 Sgt A.Lucas Missing, Runnymede Memorial 157
Nav. 112534 F/O K.F.Smart Missing, Runnymede Memorial 129
B/A. 1196327 Sgt A.W.E.Wilson Missing, Runnymede Memorial 170
W/OP. R/78939 W/O H.G.Allen Missing, Runnymede Memorial 179
A/G. 645577 Sgt D.Andrew Missing, Runnymede Memorial 140

196 Squadron 4 Group Wellington HE385 ZO/
Crashed at Lochem/Laren, Holland at 23.10 hours, (30/3/43).
Pilot. 125676 F/O E.R.Culff Killed Laren (Barchem), Holland. CG 2-A-7/11
Nav. 658578 Sgt T.A.Dew Killed Laren (Barchem), Holland. CG 2-A-7/11
B/A. J/11183 F/O L.D.McAllister Killed Laren (Barchem). CG 2-A-7-11
W/OP. 1378911 Sgt A.C.A.Veeck Killed Laren (Barchem). CG 2-A-7/11
A/G. 1231055 Sgt H.R.Wilmore Killed Laren (Barchem), Holland. CG 2-A-7/11

429 Squadron 4 Group Wellington HE635 AL/
Pilot. 1379057 Sgt K.A.Burini Killed Reichswald Forest, Germany. 10-E-9
Nav. 1314645 Sgt W.G.J.Aplin Killed Reichswald Forest, Germany. 10-E-6
B/A. 1378669 Sgt J.W.Kerr Killed Reichswald Forest, Germany. 10-E-10
W/OP. 1192438 Sgt W.E.Jones Killed Reichswald Forest, Germany. 10-D-5
A/G. 638615 Sgt R.Dolbear Killed Reichswald Forest, Germany. 10-D-4

429 Squadron 4 Group Wellington BK540 AL/
Hull Radio gave a fix to this aircraft at 20.43 hours, (29/3/43). Position 5333N
0140E. Nothing further heard.
Pilot. 1334945 Sgt H.D.G.Carty Missing, Runnymede Memorial 144
Nav. R/106671 W/O D.L.Bain Killed Esbjerg (Fourfelt), Denmark. A111-7-22
B/A. 1115190 F/Sgt E.K.Hart Missing, Runnymede Memorial 137
W/OP. 1126204 Sgt R.E.Scott Missing, Runnymede Memorial 164
A/G. 1336444 Sgt W.F.Whitelands Missing, Runnymede Memorial 169

431 Squadron 4 Group Wellington HE182 SE/A
Pilot. 1236891 Sgt E.J.Aspden Killed Reichswald Forest, Germany. 33-C-8
Nav. 1315711 W/O D.T.Dudley-Jones PoW. Stalag Luft 6, Heydekrug. 1009
B/A. 1319181 Sgt J.H.Kimber Killed Reichswald Forest, Germany. 23-C-11
W/OP. R/77427 W/O P.F.Yellin Killed Reichswald Forest, Germany. 23-C-9
A/G. 1338839 Sgt R.Davies Killed Reichswald Forest, Germany. 23-C-10

420 Squadron 6 Group Wellington MS484 PT/
Pilot. J/21941 F/O B.A.Grant Killed Groesbeek, (Canadian), Holland. XV1-D-7
Nav. R/107770 F/Sgt P.E.Barron Killed Groesbeek, (Canadian). XV1-D-9
B/A. 1384027 W/O A.G.Skiggs PoW. Stalag 357, Kopernikus 1037
W/OP. 1218403 Sgt R.Dyson Killed Eindhoven (Woensel), Holland. JJB-36
A/G. R/128173 F/Sgt S.V.Bradshaw Killed Groesbeek, (Can), Holland. XVI-D-6

420 Squadron 6 Group Wellington X3814 PT/
Pilot. R/134525 Sgt R.L.Brandow Killed Reichswald Forest, Germany. 10-C-15
Nav. R/99552 Sgt C.W.Cockaday Killed Reichswald Forest, Germany. 10-C-16
B/A. R/129209 F/Sgt H.C.Sleep Killed Reichswald Forest, Germany. 10-C-14
W/OP. 1206582 Sgt L.G.Jones Killed Reichswald Forest, Germany. 10-C-18
A/G. R/125227 F/Sgt J.M.Greer Killed Reichswald Forest, Germany. 10-C-17

426 Squadron 6 Group Wellington BJ762 KW/
Pilot. R/126792 F/Sgt R.E.Todd Killed Gassterland, 2-A-3 Holland.
Nav. R/136325 W/O H.Martin PoW. Stalag 357, Kopernikus 1029
B/A. R/145232 Sgt J.F.Gubb Killed Gassterland, 2-A-2 Holland.
Baled out, parachute not seen to open.
W/OP. 1128679 F/Sgt J.Taylor PoW. Stalag 357, Kopernikus 1039
A/G. R/141776 Sgt J.A.Bailey Killed Gassterland, 2-A-1 Holland.

427 Squadron 6 Group Wellington HE744 ZL/
Pilot. R/99534 F/Sgt D.F.McFadden Missing, Runnymede Memorial 184
Nav. R/136065 F/Sgt W.M.Bissett Missing, Runnymede Memorial 181
B/A. 1270967 Sgt A.R.Dove Missing, Runnymede Memorial 148
W/OP. R/126478 Sgt C.A.Boyd Missing, Runnymede Memorial 186
A/G. J/14813 F/O L.T.E.Sweet Missing, Runnymede Memorial 175

428 Squadron 6 Group Wellington BK564 NA/L
Pilot. J/17165 P/O J.L.R.F.Cartier Killed Reichswald Forest. 19-A-18
Nav. R/113728 F/Sgt P.B.Gustavsen Killed Reichswald Forest. 18-A-18
B/A. 124650 F/O J.F.Spencer Killed Reichswald Forest, Germany. 18-A-17
W/OP. 1380860 Sgt H.F.Rhodes Killed Reichswald Forest, Germany. 18-D-17
Died shortly after bale out.
A/G. 1343110 Sgt D.J.King PoW, Stalag Luft 6, Heydekrug. 331

428 Squadron 6 Group Wellington HE175 AL/U
Ditched 25 miles off Acklington. Last fix given by Hull Radio at 01.55 hours.
Position given as 5524N 0055E.
Pilot. NZ/415001 Sgt J.B.Martyn Missing, Runnymede Memorial 199
Nav. 1237623 Sgt N.S.Farr Missing, Runnymede Memorial 149
B/A. 1331554 Sgt K.Benjamin Missing, Runnymede Memorial 142
W/OP. 1270441 F/Sgt L.Hayward Missing, Runnymede Memorial 137
A/G. NZ/411746 Sgt J.C.Donaldson Missing, Runnymede Memorial 199

Minor Operations

29th/30th March, 1943

To finish operations for the month of March, a force of seven
Stirlings laid 30 mines in the Frisians. They suffered no losses,
no doubt because the night fighters and *Flak* defences had been
deployed elsewhere. A single Mosquito also dropped three 500 lb
bombs on Dortmund.

April 1943

Lone Attack

April 1st, 1943
On Thursday, April 1st, at 04.29 hours a Lancaster of 103 Squadron piloted by Squadron Leader C. O'Donoghue took off for a lone daylight raid to Emmerich. This was second time that O'Donoghue had attempted such a mission. It was planned that this single aircraft would bomb at dawn and use cloud cover for protection on the return flight. This type of operation was called *'Moling'*. The plane was last heard at 07.35 hours attempting to get an M/F fix. Later that day the German radio stated that a Lancaster had been shot down after it had dropped its bombs. This type of raid was against the policy of Bomber Command at that time and it is difficult to find out how the flight was authorised. The aircraft did not return on this April Fool's raid and the entire crew were killed and are buried in Holland.

Casualties April 1st, 1943. Target Emmerich

103 Squadron 1 Group Lancaster ED626 PM/
Took off alone at 04.29 hours to bomb target at dawn. Crashed at Hulhurst, Holland.
Pilot. 39828 S/Ldr C.O'Donaghe Killed Harderwijk, Holland. 2-19
Nav. 658467 Sgt A.H.Fry Killed Harderwijk, Holland. 2-25
B/A. 126517 F/O E.R.V.Ashcroft Killed Harderwijk, Holland. 2-27
W/OP. 1212281 Sgt J.E.Winn Killed Harderwijk, Holland. 2-23
F/E. 1459176 Sgt J.E.Callaghan Killed Harderwijk, Holland. 2-29
A/G. 1033931 Sgt S.Stafford Killed Amersfoort, Holland. 13-5-97
A/G. 115731 F/O I.C.Burns Killed Harderwijk, Holland. 2-21

St Nazaire / Lorient

April 2nd/3rd, 1943
St Nazaire and Lorient were the two targets for the night of April 2nd/3rd. Fifty-five bombers were despatched to St Nazaire, 20 Pathfinders and 35 main force bombers. The target conditions were excellent with only slight cloud and fair visibility. Smoke screen defences were quickly in operation after the attack commenced, but not before the eighteen Pathfinders accurately

dropped forty-two 250 lbs target indicators. The thirty main force bombers which attacked dropped 161.8 tons of high explosive bombs, but no incendiaries were carried on this raid. Major explosions were seen about a quarter of a mile from the town centre. One Lancaster from 5 Group failed to return to base after this attack. All the crew were killed and are buried at Nantes, France.

It was a different story when 47 bombers, thirteen Pathfinders and 34 main force bombers, were despatched to the nearby town of Lorient. The ten Pathfinders which attacked, dropped their twelve target indicators into the sea instead of the dock area. When the subsequent 36 bombers arrived at the target the error was seen and their 117.1 tons of bombs were dropped visually. There were no losses from this operation.

Casualties April 2nd/3rd, 1943. St Nazaire

57 Squadron 5 Group Lancaster W4257 DX/
Pilot. 144185 P/O R.L.Pickup Killed Pont-du-Cens, Nantes. CG L-B-16/18
Nav. 1236213 Sgt A.E.Bagley Killed Pont-du-Cens, Nantes. CG L-B-16/18
B/A. 1332920 Sgt H.P.Hunter Killed Pont-du-Cens, Nantes. CG L-B-16/18
W/OP. 1379802 Sgt W.G.Barnes Killed Pont-du-Cens, Nantes, France. L-B-15
F/E. 577749 Sgt R.W.Lea Killed Pont-du-Cens, Nantes, France. CG L-B-16/18
A/G. 1397311 Sgt K.A.Tester Killed Pont-du-Cens, Nantes. CG L-B-16/18
A/G. R/102105 F/Sgt C.W.Dahl Killed Pont-du-Cens, Nantes. CG L-B-16/18

Minelaying continues

April 2nd/3rd, 1943
Minelaying operations took place when a mixed force of 33 aircraft from 1, 3 and 5 Groups laid 136 mines. Three Lancasters from 5 Group were unable to get an accurate fix for mining and brought their loads back to base. One Lancaster from 50 Squadron, captained by Flight Lieutenant A. H. Nichols, failed to return from this operation. The crew's bodies were never found.

Casualties April 2nd/3rd, 1943. Minelaying

50 Squadron 5 Group Lancaster ED482 VN/
Pilot. 101051 F/Lt A.H.Nichols Missing, Runnymede Memorial 120
Nav. 124756 F/O J.Parsons Missing, Runnymede Memorial 128
B/A. 126678 F/O J.C.Davies Missing, Runnymede Memorial 124
W/OP. 1330745 Sgt A.E.Roberts Missing, Runnymede Memorial 163
F/E. 951417 Sgt J.W.Moon Missing, Runnymede Memorial 159
A/G. 1503503 Sgt C.M.Skelton Missing, Runnymede Memorial 164
A/G. 614099 F/Sgt A.G.Maguire Missing, Runnymede Memorial 138

Essen

April 3rd/4th, 1943
Essen was the Ruhr target on the night of 3rd/4th April. A large
force of 348 aircraft, 225 Lancasters and 113 Halifaxes, led by
ten *Oboe* Mosquitoes went to Happy Valley again. As the
weather forecast was unreliable, with two layers of cloud, the
Pathfinders had two plans prepared. *Musical Paramatta*, (the
code name for target marking by blind dropped *Oboe* ground
markers) would be used if the ground was visible, or *Musical
Wanganui* (sky markers) if there was cloud or thick haze over
the target area.

The original idea for target marking was to first let off white
flares and then the target would be initially bombed with
incendiaries. After this the first bombers would visually identify
the target aiming point in the flares' light and the following
bombers would then aim their bombs on to the burning
incendiaries. Early armament experts thought that an effective
coloured marker system was an impossible problem to solve.
Fortunately, however, a Dr. Coxen of the Ministry of Aircraft
Production came up with a perfect target marking device. This
which was to put 60 large 'candles' made of Verey Light
cartridge-like material into a canister. This was fitted with a
barometric fuse which would explode the canister and ignite the
candles at a predetermined height. Initially this was 3,000 feet,
but later on this height was reduced. When exploded, the target
indicator bloomed out into a magnificent splurge of colour - red,
green or yellow, which slowly drifted to the ground and stayed
burning for about three minutes. If there were sky markers, the
main problem was to allow sufficent margin for wind drift over

the target area. The colours of these markers were predetermined before each raid so it became very difficult for the German defenders to drop decoy flares. They tried many times in later Ruhr raids to emulate the RAF markers, but without much success.

On the night of April 3rd/4th, there was no cloud over the Essen target and conditions were reasonably clear so ground markers were dropped. Unfortunately some Pathfinder Mosquito crews also dropped sky markers over the target area and according to debriefing reports many crews from the main force were quite confused by this double marking. Intense night fighter activity was reported even in the areas of heavy *Flak*. There were no Stirlings or Wellingtons flying that night. They normally flew at lower altitudes and took some of the *Flak* and fighter attention. There was an enormous number of active searchlights and the *Flak* was the hottest, and to date the most intense, experienced over this target. Nevertheless the raid was successful and bombing was quite concentrated, 465.9 tons of high explosive and 210.7 tons of incendiaries being dropped. Reconnaissance later showed widespread damage in the centre and in the western half of the city. After this particular raid Goebbels visited the stricken city and afterwards wrote in his diary.

"We arrived in Essen before 7 a.m. Deputy Gauleiter Schlossman and a large staff called for us at the railway station. We went to the hotel on foot because driving was impossible in many parts of Essen. This walk enabled us to make a first hand estimate of the damage inflicted in the last three raids. It is colossal and indeed ghastly. The city, must for the most part be written off completely. The city's building experts estimate that it will take twelve years to repair the damage .... Nobody can tell how Krupps can go on. Everybody wants to avoid transplanting Krupps from Essen. There would be no purpose in doing so, for the moment Essen is no longer an industrial centre, the English will pounce upon the next city, Bochum, Dortmund or Düsseldorf."

After the raid the Essen military authorities asked their counterparts at Düsseldorf how many homeless families from Essen they could accommodate temporarily. The answer they received was "Impossible to help, we have already 18,000 uninhabitable apartments."

This was the first raid in which more than 200 Lancasters had taken part and augured well for the future growth of squadrons to be equipped with this famous bomber. There was a high rate of aborted flights, 36 bombers turned back to their bases for a variety of reasons. 21 aircraft were lost on this raid with 104 aircrew killed, 21 missing and 24 made prisoners of war. A further two 4 Group Halifaxes were lost returning from this raid. One from 51 Squadron crashed at Selby, Yorkshire, and three of the crew were killed. The other aircraft was from 158 Squadron based at Lissett, Yorkshire. This crashed into Hornsea Mere, killing four of the crew.

Flying Officer Johnstone's Dicey Do

One aircraft which was extremely fortunate to return from this Essen raid was Halifax DT686 of 51 Squadron. It was captained by Flying Officer Johnstone. At 21.40 hours, when flying about 20 miles from the target, the Halifax was suddenly attacked by a Ju88. The rear gunner, Sergeant H. R. Kennedy, was unable to give his skipper any warning before the enemy fighter raked the bomber from nose to tail. In this initial attack, five of the crew were injured by the cannon and machine gun fire. Fearing another attack, the pilot immediately went into violent evasive action, but much damage had already been done to the bomber. The IFF and *Gee* navigation sets had blown up and the radio set was also out of action. The navigator, Flying Officer R. A. Short, gave his pilot a new course for the target and then had to go back to the plane's rest position to seek treatment for the shrapnel splinters in his legs. On his new course, the pilot opened the bomb doors and the bomb aimer, Flight Sergeant L. G. Patterson, dropped the load of bombs. It was found later that some of them remained hung up in the bomb bay. During this time the wireless operator, who was uninjured, assisted the seriously injured flight engineer, Sergeant S. Scott, back to the rest position to give him a morphine jab. The pilot's evasive action had thrown off a second attack from the fighter and after dropping the bombs the bomb aimer used his own compass on the bomb sight to help the pilot steer a course back to England. The DR compass had been put of action when the fighter attacked. When the French coast had been safely crossed the bomb aimer assisted the wireless operator in caring for the other wounded crew members. He had not disclosed that he too had been injured in the fighter attack. When the English coast had been reached, under the pilot's instructions, the wireless operator acted as flight engineer and fired off the colours of the day by Verey pistol. Ahead the pilot saw the welcoming sight of a searchlight cone, which was a sign that an airfield was nearby and was prepared to accept any bomber in trouble. He called up the emergency *Darkie* on his TR9 radio set. Circling the airfield he called for medical and ambulance assistance and then made a safe flapless landing without any further damage to the plane. The whole crew had shown an excellent spirit in the most difficult situations and the pilot, by his exemplary courage and leadership, had brought the Halifax safely back. Even more importantly, he had saved the lives of his crew. For his action he was awarded an immediate Distinguished Flying Cross.

A Halifax Limps Home

Another Halifax which managed to return to base from Essen was from 419 Squadron. It was captained by Sergeant P. S. Johnson. The plane was pounced upon by an Me110, and in the ensuing attack the two gunners, Sergeants L. A. Wallis and J. H. Thompson, with the bomb aimer, Sergeant R. E. Ross, were seriously wounded. Extensive damage was done to the rear turret, rudders and flaps. Nevertheless the pilot, without the aid of his gunners' all important commentaries, and with a very badly damaged plane managed to shake off the fighter's second attack. Johnson struggled back to the UK to make a landing at Coltishall, where his injured crew members received emergency hospital treatment.

Pyrenees guide loses his way and an evader is caught

405 Squadron lost two of its Halifaxes on the Essen raid. From DT723, LQ/V, captained by Canadian Warrant Officer McAlpine only the two gunners survived. The rear gunner was the

Squadron's Gunnery Leader, Flight Lieutenant Wilfred Murphy, and he relates his story of how he nearly made it into Spain.

"On the way into the target we were hit by *Flak* and the aircraft was severely damaged. We were given the bale out order. I don't know where I landed, but on hitting the deck and getting rid of my 'chute and Mae West, I started walking. I kept on going for over a week, hiding by night and walking in a south-westerly direction by day. At last, through lack of food, I was forced to make contact with a farmer I met in some fields. Fortunately he was quite friendly and he took me along to the local priest who sheltered me before arranging for me to be sent to an address in Hasselt, Holland. Here I stayed for four days before being taken along to Brussels by train to spend two weeks there. From Belgium's capital I was moved on to Paris where I was accommodated in a doctor's house. Two weeks went by before arrangements were finalised and I was taken on to Lyons to the Headquarters of the organisation which had been responsible for my evasion. They finally got me to Perpignan, where I met up with four other RAF evaders and seven French civilians. With a guide this party set out towards the mountains to cross over into Spain. Unfortunately, during the night, the guide lost his way and we were forced to wait until first light. Unsure of his position the guide went away and returned a few hours later driving a truck. We all clambered aboard and after about half an hours drive we were stopped by a German patrol. We were all arrested. The guide decide to make a run for it, but was shot by the soldiers. The whole party was taken back to Perpignan and from there to Fresnes Prison, Paris, where I was kept for three months and interrogated by the *Gestapo*. They would not accept my identity as an RCAF officer and threatened to shoot me as a saboteur. They finally relented and believed my story. Then I was taken on to Dulag Luft on 15th September, before finally being sent to Stalag Luft III at Sagan. On January 27th, 1945, the camp at Sagan was evacuated and we were all marched for ten days to Nestertim, where we remained until April 10th. From here we were again marched to Lübeck where we arrived on 24th April. A few days later we were liberated by the Allied Forces."

Casualties April 3rd/4th, 1943. Target Essen

83 Squadron 8 Group Lancaster ED334 OL/R
Shot down at Winterswijk, Holland at 23.54 hours (3/4/43).Victim of Hptm. Lütje 8/NJG1
Pilot. 79541 S/Ldr F.T.Flower Killed Winterswijk, Holland. 16
Nav. 67049 F/O F.A.Southon Killed Winterswijk, Holland. 15
B/A. 655814 Sgt D.McEwan Killed Winterswijk, Holland. CG 10/14
W/OP. 1111801 F/Sgt L.Fieldhouse Killed Winterswijk, Holland. CG 10/14
F/E. 964395 F/Sgt F.W.T.Routledge DFM Killed Winterswijk. CG 10/14
A/G. 1380892 F/Sgt E.L.Shandley Killed Winterswijk, Holland. CG 10/14
A/G. R/142054 W/O C.M.McCoghill Killed Winterswijk, Holland. CG 10/14

83 Squadron 8 Group Lancaster R5626 OL/M
Pilot. 122129 F/Lt R.B.Hope DFC Killed Reichswald Forest, Germany. 10-E-12
Nav. R/104008 W/O L.N.McArthur Killed Reichswald Forest. 10-E-13
B/A. 1502415 Sgt C.L.Billington Killed Reichswald Forest, Germany. 10-E-15
W/OP. 623478 W/O J.S.Keay Killed Reichswald Forest, Germany. 10-F-2
F/E. 1238512 Sgt R.G.Pegg Killed Reichswald Forest, Germany. 10-E-16
A/G. 1600210 Sgt D.Brennen Killed Reichswald Forest, Germany. 10-E-14
A/G. 1080356 Sgt W.Billington Killed Reichswald Forest, Germany. 10-E-11

83 Squadron 8 Group Lancaster LM302 OL/H
Pilot. 137298 P/O C.D.Calvert DFM Killed Rheinberg, Germany. 2-D-13
Nav. 126037 P/O G.Mackay Killed Rheinberg, Germany. 2-D-17
B/A. 1209308 Sgt J.C.Aston Missing, Runnymede Memorial 141
W/OP. 137523 P/O J.H.Ridd Killed Rheinberg, Germany. 2-D-15
F/E. 1059604 Sgt R.Bee Killed Rheinberg, Germany. 2-D-14
A/G. 1065692 Sgt R.O'Brien Killed Rheinberg, Germany. 2-D-18
A/G. 591747 Sgt L.R.Tomlinson Killed Rheinberg, Germany. 2-D-16

156 Squadron 8 Group Lancaster W4894 GT/
Pilot. A/416410 F/Sgt R.H.Byass Missing, Runnymede Memorial 187
Nav. A/409519 F/O G.J.Black Missing, Runnymede Memorial 187
B/A. A/41500 Sgt R.S.Trigwell Missing, Runnymede Memorial 197
W/OP. 1391936 Sgt G.R.Mains Missing, Runnymede Memorial 159
F/E. A/414102 Sgt N.R.Thurecht Missing, Runnymede Memorial 197
A/G. R/102097 Sgt D.L.Robertson Missing, Runnymede Memorial 185
A/G. 1321533 Sgt S.R.Crooks Killed Peronnes-lez-Binche, Belgium. 30-A-11

101 Squadron 1 Group Lancaster ED736 SR/W
Pilot. 124414 F/O R.N.Johnson Killed Reichswald Forest, Germany. 21-E-18
Nav. 1125794 Sgt G.W.Jones Killed Reichswald Forest. CG 21-E-13/14
B/A. 1338144 Sgt I.W.L.Llewellyn Killed Reichswald Forest. CG 21-E-13/14
W/OP. 1294067 Sgt R.C.Horton Killed Reichswald Forest. CG 21-E-16/17
F/E. 1132947 Sgt F.J.Hackett Killed Reichswald Forest. 21-E-15
A/G. 656856 Sgt R.L.Hodgson Killed Reichswald Forest. CG 21-E-16/17
A/G. 1456815 Sgt H.A.Ramsey Killed Reichswald Forest. CG 21-E-16/17

51 Squadron 4 Group Halifax DT738 MH/D
Pilot. 1238965 Sgt J.Rawcliffe Killed Reichswald Forest, Germany. 10-D-9
Nav. 996588 F/Sgt J.Richards Killed Reichswald Forest, Germany. 10-D-7
B/A. 1365885 Sgt R.K.Guy Killed Reichswald Forest, Germany. 10-D-11
W/OP. 1188860 Sgt W.G.Richardson Killed Reichswald Forest. 10-D-8
F/E. 574488 Sgt J.V.Branscombe Killed Reichswald Forest, Germany. 10-D-6
A/G. 652711 Sgt A.Howarth Killed Reichswald Forest, Germany. 10-D-12
A/G. 1346417 Sgt D.B.Ralston Killed Reichswald Forest, Germany. 10-D-10

76 Squadron 4 Group Halifax W7805 MP/M
Crashed east of Dorsten, Germany.
Pilot. 655475 Sgt J.K.Howarth Killed Reichswald Forest, Germany. 17-C-5
Nav. 1210640 W/O G.A.Egan PoW. Stalag Luft 6, Heydekrug. 1010
B/A. 1000093 F/Sgt J.W.S.Blakey PoW. Stalag 357, Kopernikus. 1000

W/OP. 49686 F/O P.W.Digby Killed Reichswald Forest, Germany. 17-C-4
F/E. 1192387 Sgt W.C.Pitt Killed Reichswald Forest, Germany. 17-C-6
A/G. 1304115 Sgt F.G.Williams Killed Reichswald Forest, Germany. 17-C-7
A/G. R/115122 Sgt H.N.Richards PoW. Stalag 357, Kopernikus. 1035

78 Squadron 4 Group Halifax W7937 EY/
Pilot. 125685 F/O T.N.Forster Missing, Runnymede Memorial 124
Nav. R/128566 W/O G.Sendall PoW. Stalag 357, Kopernikus. 1036
B/A. J/22559 F/Lt H.Jamieson PoW. Stalag Luft 3, Sagan. 980
W/OP. 1292222 F/Sgt E.A.Drury PoW. Stalag Luft 6, Heydekrug. 1007
F/E. 612461 Sgt W.F.Hodgson PoW. Stalag 357, Kopernikus. 1016
A/G. 1213920 F/Sgt C.Wayte PoW. Stalag 357, Kopernikus. 10431
A/G. 1545156 F/Sgt N.V.Thornton PoW. Stalag Luft 6, Heydekrug. 1041

78 Squadron 4 Group Halifax DT780 EY/
Pilot. 141465 P/O G.Riach Killed Rheinberg, Germany. 2-D-11
2/Pilot. C/245 S/Ldr B.J.Bourchier PoW, Stalag Luft 3, Sagan. 42722
Nav. 1385128 F/Sgt E.C.Lacey PoW, Stalag 357, Kopernikus. 1022
B/A. 1365115 W/O W.Ingles PoW, Stalag Luft 7, Bankau. 362
W/OP. 1258426 W/O D.H.Howard PoW. Stalag 357, Kopernikus. 1017
F/E. 1259549 Sgt A.M.Parker Killed Rheinberg, Germany. 2-D-12
A/G. 987834 Sgt A.Wright PoW, Camp not known.
A/G. 1238453 Sgt L.L.Stas PoW. Stalag 357, Kopernikus. 1038

78 Squadron 4 Group Halifax JB845 EY/
Pilot. 88657 F/Lt T.H.O.Richardson Killed Woensel, Eindhoven. JJB-50
Nav. 127293 F/O C.R.C.A.Allberry Killed Woensel, Eindhoven. JJB-51
B/A. 1338395 Sgt R.J.Kernick Killed Woensel, Eindhoven, Holland. JJB-57
W/OP. 49298 F/O L.R.C.Shadwell Killed Woensel, Eindhoven, Holland. JJB-49
F/E. R/70006 Sgt R.O.M.Dunlop Killed Groesbeek (Can), Holland. XVI-F-6
A/G. 1382258 Sgt T.H.Webb Killed Woensel, Eindhoven, Holland. JJB-52
A/G. 639959 Sgt J.McCormick Killed Woensel, Eindhoven, Holland. JJB-54

102 Squadron 4 Group Halifax JB867 DY/K
Pilot. S/Ldr J.D.H.Matthews DFC
A/G. 131658 F/O T.McCoughlin Killed Darlington (West). W-7G-357
Air gunner killed by *Flak* over the target.

158 Squadron 4 Group Halifax DT635 NP/F
Pilot. 118067 F/Lt J.D.Cole Killed Rheinberg, Germany. 9-B-8
Nav. 141802 P/O R.C.Stamp Killed Rheinberg, Germany. CG 2-D-20/24
B/A. 1391138 Sgt B.J.Warr Killed Rheinberg, Germany. CG 2-D-20/24
W/OP. 1074938 Sgt A.Ward Killed Rheinberg, Germany. CG 2-D-20/24
F/E. 941531 Sgt R.Gowing Killed Rheinberg, Germany, CG 2-D-20/24
A/G. 141810 P/O C.G.Dawson Killed Rheinberg, Germany. 2-D-19
A/G. 142019 P/O W.A.Robinson Killed Rheinberg, Germany. CG 2-D-20/24

158 Squadron 4 Group Halifax DT795 NP/N
Aircraft crashed after fighter attack near Apeldoorn Canal, Amersfoort, Holland.
Pilot. R/78495 W/O F.H.Blake Killed Amersfoort, Holland. 13-5-95
Nav. 1316309 Sgt W.D.Hawkins Missing, Runnymede Memorial 152
B/A. 1386043 Sgt J.C.Jones Missing, Runnymede Memorial 155
W/OP. 1293257 Sgt P.H.Eldridge Missing, Runnymede Memorial 148
F/E. 1271369 Sgt G.S.Walters Missing, Runnymede Memorial 168
A/G. 1352234 Sgt T.V.Trollope Killed Amersfoort, Holland. 13-5-94
A/G. R/106709 Sgt R.Webber Killed Amersfoort, Holland. 13-5-96

9 Squadron 5 Group Lancaster ED694 WS/G
Crashed near Stevensbeek, Holland.
Pilot. 144641 P/O W.H.Swire Killed Woensel, Eindhoven, Holland. JJB-46
Nav. 906747 Sgt E.W.Cook Killed Woensel, Eindhoven, Holland. JJB-48
B/A. 1317037 Sgt G.H.Evans Killed Woensel, Eindhoven, Holland. JJB-45
W/OP. 1269942 Sgt R.D.Francis Killed Woensel, Eindhoven, Holland. JJB-56
F/E. 1047153 Sgt G.R.Gilbert Killed Woensel, Eindhoven, Holland. JJB-47
A/G. 1011474 Sgt W.Watt Killed Woensel, Eindhoven, Holland. JJB-44
A/G. 1162929 F/Sgt R.R.Feeley Killed Woensel, Eindhoven, Holland. JJB-55

9 Squadron 5 Group Lancaster ED479 WS/Z
Pilot. 27088 S/Ldr G.W.J.Jarrett Killed Reichswald Forest, Germany. 9-D-1
Nav. 142872 P/O G.Smith Killed Reichswald Forest, Germany. 10-D-14
B/A. 124711 F/O A.G.Seymour Killed Reichswald Forest, Germany. 10-D-17
W/OP. 1025976 Sgt I.Francis Killed Reichswald Forest, Germany. 10-D-13
F/E. 531170 Sgt H.Precious Killed Reichswald Forest, Germany. 10-D-15
A/G. 777922 Sgt J.Miles Killed Reichswald Forest, Germany. 10-D-16
A/G. 128962 F/O G.R.Dale Killed Reichswald Forest, Germany. 10-D-18

106 Squadron 5 Group Lancaster ED542 ZN/
Pilot. 1314248 Sgt T.J.Ridd Killed Reichswald Forest, Germany. 2-A-13
Nav. 127980 F/O J.W.Simpson Killed Reichswald Forest, Germany. 2-A-11
B/A. 128509 F/O A.C.Palmer Killed Reichswald Forest, Germany. 2-A-10
W/OP. 1271016 Sgt A.C.Burson Missing, Runnymede Memorial 144
F/E. 932584 Sgt R.C.H.Webb Killed Reichswald Forest, Germany. 2-A-14
A/G. 646001 Sgt R.S.Sabell Killed Reichswald Forest, Germany. 2-A-12
A/G. 1337304 Sgt E.Williams Killed Reichswald Forest, Germany. 2-A-9

467 Squadron 5 Group Lancaster ED524 PO/
Pilot. 36192 S/Ldr A.M.Paape DFC * Killed Reichswald Forest. 10-E-1
Nav. 116791 F/O H.North Killed Reichswald Forest, Germany. 10-E-4
B/A. 778674 Sgt D.J.Robinson Killed Reichswald Forest, Germany. 10-E-5
W/OP. 129462 F/O T.Dring DFC Killed Reichswald Forest, Germany. 10-E-8
F/E. R/61529 Sgt L.T.Fulcher Killed Reichswald Forest, Germany. 10-E-2
A/G. 131808 F/O J.M.Stewart AFM Killed Reichswald Forest. 10-E-3
A/G. 1220311 Sgt W.Johnson Killed Reichswald Forest, Germany. 10-E-7

405 Squadron 6 Group Halifax DT723 LQ/V
Pilot. R/93277 W/O W.J.McAlpine Killed Groesbeek (Can). JG XVI-F-9/10
Nav. R/91819 W/O J.D.White Killed Groesbeek (Can), Holland. JG-XVI-F-9/10
B/A. J/15434 F/Lt F.E.Luxford Killed Groesbeek (Can), Holland. XVI-F-13
W/OP. R/95419 W/O J.W.Halikowski Killed Groesbeek (Can), Holland. XVI-F-8
F/E. R/10748 Sgt H.McQueen Killed Groesbeek (Can), Holland. XVI-F-7
A/G. J/90044 P/O E.Bradley PoW. Stalag 357, Kopernikus. 1001
A/G. J/15166 F/Lt W.L.Murphy PoW. Stalag Luft 3, Sagan. 2480

405 Squadron 6 Group Halifax DT808 LQ/F
Pilot. J/16960 F/Lt J.Lago PoW. Stalag Luft 3, Sagan. 983
2/Pilot. R/87712 W/O K.O.Perry PoW. Stalag Luft 1, Bankau. 1032
Nav. J/10418 F/Lt J.H.Colwell PoW. Stalag Luft 3, Sagan. 973
B/A. R/119427 W/O W.S.Beatty Missing, Runnymede Memorial 179
W/OP. J/9848 F/O W.H.Hoddinott PoW. Stalag Luft 3, Sagan. 979
F/E. R/54222 W/O W.W.Phipps PoW. Stalag Luft 4, Sagan. 1033
A/G. R/58818 W/O H.C.Waugh PoW. Stalag 357, Kopernikus. 1042
A/G. R/102442 W/O A.B.Granbois PoW. Stalag 357, Kopernikus. 1013

408 Squadron 6 Group Halifax HR713 EQ/F
Pilot. J/9337 F/Lt R.H.P.Gamble Missing, Runnymede Memorial. 172
Nav. R/90781 W/O D.L.Jarrett Missing, Runnymede Memorial 180
B/A. 919537 Sgt A.J.Hawkins Missing, Runnymede Memorial 152
W/OP. A/405437 P/O C.N.Black Missing, Runnymede Memorial 190
F/E. 989712 Sgt R.W.Barker Missing, Runnymede Memorial 141
A/G. A/401712 P/O K.S.McColl Missing, Runnymede Memorial 191
A/G. J/11851 F/O E.R.Ray Missing, Runnymede Memorial 174

408 Squadron 6 Group Halifax JB866 EQ/T
Pilot. J/16946 P/O E.A.Sirett Killed Uden, Holland. 4-F-8
Nav. R/114615 W/O M.G.Church Killed Uden, Holland. 4-G-13
B/A. J/17222 P/O G.A.Fletcher Killed Uden, Holland. 4-F-5
W/OP. J/9850 F/O J.D.McBride Killed Uden, Holland. 4-F-10
F/E. 922835 Sgt K.O.Brice Killed Uden, Holland. 4-F-6
A/G. R/90535 Sgt G.D.Boyer Killed Uden, Holland. 4-F-7
A/G. R/104185 F/Sgt F.R.Burke Killed Uden, Holland. 4-F-9

419 Squadron 6 Group Halifax DT617 VR/
Pilot. 125482 F/O P.D.Boyd Killed Olst (Duur), Holland. 7
Nav. J/12970 F/O G.W.Lawry Killed Olst (Duur), Holland. 8
B/A. 1511061 Sgt J.B.Langley Killed Olst (Duur), Holland. 9
W/OP. 1079156 Sgt L.H.Ransome Killed Olst (Duur), Holland 10
F/E. R/65638 Sgt S.N.Hall Killed Olst (Duur), Holland. 6
A/G. 132735 P/O H.T.Macdonald Killed Olst (Duur), Holland. 12
A/G. R/105759 F/Sgt B.W.Agar Killed Olst (Duur), Holland. 11

51 Squadron 4 Group Halifax DT666 MH/
Aircraft crashed at Shortlands Farm, Carlton, Selby, Yorkshire. after
operation to Essen
Pilot. NZ/415200 Sgt C.E.Pheloung Killed Selby 5348
Nav. NZ/412794 Sgt W.R.McKenzie Injured
B/A. 1390577 Sgt D.G.Fakley Injured
W/OP. 1380457 Sgt F.H.Knight Killed Horsham Hills U-314
F/E. 1162793 Sgt B.W.Kemp Injured
A/G. 1252255 Sgt J.J.Merritt Killed Beaufort, Ebbw Vale. 1A-3A
A/G. NZ/412776 Sgt B.Williams Injured

158 Squadron 4 Group Halifax HR754 NP/K
Crashed west end of Hornsea Mere, 8 miles from Lissett, Yorkshire after
operation to Essen
Pilot. 925015 Sgt J.Keedwell Killed Slimbridge (St Johns).
Nav. 130239 P/O W.R.Simpson Injured
B/A. 128714 F/O J.Burgess Killed Carmoney, Antrim. ZZ-16
W/OP. 1496525 Sgt R.S.Nurse Injured
F/E. 998499 Sgt J.R.Franks Killed Lawnswood, Leeds. Y-969
A/G. 1395954 Sgt R.V.Loose Killed Staines.(London Rd). F-444
A/G. 1379219 Sgt L.P.Froud Injured

Mines Dropped Again

April 3rd/4th, 1943
On the same night 20 Wellingtons from 1 and 4 Groups went to
Lorient and St Nazaire, an area code named *Artichokes* and
Beeches, to lay mines. Although 32 mines were laid, three
aircraft returned with their mines still on board and one
Wellington from 1 Group failed to return.

Casualties April 3rd/4th, 1943. Minelaying

166 Squadron 1 Group Wellington HE631 AS/V
Pilot. 1385948 Sgt A.H.Radbourne Killed Moelan-sur-Mer, France. 1
Nav. 1202459 Sgt E.W.Aldridge Missing, Runnymede Memorial 140
B/A. 1071349 Sgt W.Carter Missing, Runnymede Memorial 144
W/OP. 1021498 Sgt J.Stock Missing, Runnymede Memorial 166
A/G. 1170005 Sgt T.H.Luscombe Missing, Runnymede Memorial 157

Kiel

April 4th/5th, 1943

The next big raid, the largest non 1,000 bomber force so far in the war, was on the 4th/5th April, to the German port of Kiel when 577 aircraft went on the attack, 203 Lancasters, 168 Wellingtons, 116 Halifaxes and 90 Stirlings. The Pathfinders encountered thick cloud and very strong winds over the target, the latter making the *Wanganui* markers drift considerably away from the aiming point. 108 target indicators and 24 flares were dropped, but the only indication that some crews knew that they were over the target was the amount of *Flak* being thrown up and the reflected fire glow on the low cloud. According to debriefing reports the main force bombers were also distracted by decoy fire sites. Twelve aircraft were lost on this raid, a 2.1% loss rate. From the crews, 51 were killed, 34 missing and one became a prisoner.

426 Squadron Wellington Ditches

Five minutes before reaching the Kiel target Wellington X3699 from 426 (RCAF) Squadron, captained by Flying Officer D. L. Kennedy, was damaged in the main fuselage and rear turret by *Flak*. The damage was such that the captain decided to jettison his bomb load and return to base. After releasing the bombs at 8,000 feet he set course for Dishforth. Some time later it was noticed that there was a light on under the fuselage and despite all efforts it could not be switched off so it shone out like a beacon. It was not long before the aircraft was attacked by a Ju88 fighter. In the attack the hydraulics were badly damaged causing the wheels to drop and the bomb doors fall open. In spite of many attempts to rectify this dangerous situation they refused to close. The navigator found that his Gee set was u/s, so the wireless operator endeavoured to obtain an M/F fix, but was unsuccessful. The captain decided against sending out an SOS as the fighter had broken off his attack, but the IFF button was put on the automatic emergency stud 3 for some considerable time.

As none of the crew had been injured in the fighter attack and the pilot had calculated that there was sufficent petrol in the tanks, he decided it would be possible to make it back to England and attempt a crash landing. Fatefully, five minutes flying time away from the English coast, both engines cut out and the pilot was forced to make a gliding approach to ditch the aircraft. The stricken plane hit the sea with force and immediately went under and broke up. The bomb aimer Pilot Officer D. Laskey and the wireless operator Sergeant L. L. Anderson were fortunate in being able to get clear and swim to the overturned dinghy, helping each other to scramble on top of it. They could hear the rear gunner, Sergeant C. N. Beaton and the navigator, Pilot Officer K. M. Walley calling out in the darkness, but both were finding it dificult to right the dinghy and paddle towards the other crew members to give assistance. It was four and half hours later that the two survivors, still sitting on top of the overturned dinghy, were picked up by a British naval destroyer and put ashore at Grimsby. The pilot, Flying Officer D. L. Kennedy was killed instantly in the ditching and his body was washed ashore the next day, but the bodies of the other two crew members were never found. Both Pilot Officer Laskey and Sergeant Anderson were respectively awarded the Distinguished Flying Cross and Medal. Pilot Officer Laskey returned to the squadron and crewed up with another pilot, Sergeant I. R. A. Runciman and resumed operational duties. He was later shot down on the Duisburg raid of May 12th/13th, 1943 and became a prisoner of war.

Casualties April 4th/5th, 1943. Target Kiel

156 Squadron 8 Group Lancaster W4850 GT/
Pilot. 142446 P/O C.H.Davies Killed Kiel, Germany. 1-E-4
Nav. 1250340 F/Sgt J.A.Holderness Killed Kiel, Germany. 1-E-11
B/A. 1105617 F/Sgt E.T.McHugh Killed Kiel, Germany. CG 5-E-9/12
W/OP. 630984 F/Sgt R.Rixon Killed Kiel, Germany. CG 5-E-9/12
F/E. 647282 Sgt K.W.Taylor Killed Kiel, Germany. CG 5-E-9/12
A/G. 1585825 Sgt A.R.Baker Killed Kiel, Germany. 1-H-10
A/G. 1159783 Sgt P.J.W.Grimwood Killed Kiel, Germany. 1-E-5

156 Squadron 8 Group Lancaster ED615 GT/
Pilot. 84667 S/Ldr B.Grimston DFC Missing, Runnymede Memorial. 118
2/Pilot. A/407712 F/O K.Girrbach Killed Kiel, Germany. 5-D-14
Nav. 107993 F/O A.B.Marsh Killed Kiel, Germany. 1-J-16
B/A. 143771 P/O S.J.Volante DFM Killed Kiel, Germany. 1-H-13
W/OP. 51888 P/O A.L.S.Portch Killed Kiel, Germany. 1-E-16
F/E. 1218440 Sgt T.J.Woodward Missing, Runnymede Memorial 170
A/G. 937603 F/Sgt K.R.Hazelwood Killed Kiel, Germany. 1-E-9
A/G. 1128910 W/O G.C.Stafford DFM Missing, Runnymede Memorial 134

460 Squadron 1 Group Lancaster W4310 UV/
Pilot. A/400595 F/O K.Moore DFC Killed Kiel, Germany. 1-H-16
Nav. A/411192 F/O B.K.Rust Killed Kiel, Germany. 1-H-17
B/A. A/403363 P/O J.G.Lee Killed Kiel, Germany. 1-E-13
W/OP. A/401209 W/O R.Gooding Killed Kiel, Germany. 1-E-7
F/E. 1058003 F/Sgt H.Lloyd Killed Kiel, Germany. 1-J-15
A/G. A/405502 W/O W.B.Ranclaud Killed Kiel, Germany. 1-E-14
A/G. 1335476 F/Sgt R.F.Cooksey Killed Kiel, Germany. 1-E-12

149 Squadron 3 Group Stirling R9327 OJ/M
Aircraft shot down at Obbekaer/Ribe, Denmark at 22.57 hours (4/4/43)
Pilot. 1389078 Sgt K.A.Way Killed Esbjerg, Denmark. AIII-7-8
Nav. 1040061 Sgt J.Palmer Killed Esbjerg, Denmark. AIII-7-14
B/A. 1439456 Sgt R.G.Woodfield Killed Esbjerg, Denmark. AIII-7-12
W/OP. 1293131 Sgt R.P.Bilham Killed Esbjerg, Denmark. AIII-7-13
F/E. 541514 Sgt N.Macleod Killed Esbjerg, Denmark. AIII-7-11
A/G. 634371 Sgt E.G.King Killed Esbjerg, Denmark. AIII-7-9
A/G. 1214816 Sgt W.E.Norman Killed Esbjerg, Denmark. AIII-7-10

214 Squadron 3 Group Stirling W7621 BU/G
Aircraft crashed in North Sea.
Pilot. 1385331 Sgt K.R.Burton DFM Missing, Runnymede Memorial 14
Nav. 1334740 Sgt G.H.J.Cash Missing, Runnymede Memorial 144
B/A. 1332551 Sgt H.M.Parsons Missing, Runnymede Memorial 161
W/OP. 1376471 Sgt A.J.Gordon Missing, Runnymede Memorial 151
F/E. 996460 Sgt J.H.Starthern Missing, Runnymede Memorial 166
A/G. 1560563 Sgt E.McGloin Missing, Runnymede Memorial 157
A/G. 1254086 Sgt J.Broderick Killed Kiel, Germany. 5-B-13

10 Squadron 4 Group Halifax HR699 ZA/J
Pilot. J/9543 F/O J.A.Wann Missing, Runnymede Memorial 175
Nav. 144198 P/O N.Bertram Missing, Runnymede Memorial 130
B/A. 1089365 Sgt W.E.Scanlon Missing, Runnymede Memorial 164
W/OP. 144260 P/O H.Wheen Missing, Runnymede Memorial 134
F/E. R/137144 F/Sgt W.M.Maisenbacher Missing, Runnymede Memorial 185
A/G. 51701 P/O D.C.T.Jagger Missing, Runnymede Memorial 132
A/G. 144261 P/O E.V.Frankland Missing, Runnymede Memorial 131

51 Squadron 4 Group Halifax DT686 MH/
Pilot. 45801 F/Lt A.A.Emery DFM Killed Kiel, Germany. CG 5-A-9/12
Nav. 1348043 Sgt J.B.Veal Killed Kiel, Germany. CG 5-A-9/12
B/A. 1343175 Sgt W.Fleming Killed Kiel, Germany. 5-A-8
W/OP. 1203965 Sgt W.Woosnam Killed Kiel, Germany. 5-A-14
F/E. R/73542 Sgt G.E.McDonald Killed Kiel, Germany. 5-A-13
A/G. 1332933 F/Sgt S.G.Adams Killed Kiel, Germany. CG 5-A-9/12
A/G. 710101 Sgt F.W.Austin Killed Kiel, Germany. CG 5-A-9/12

9 Squadron 5 Group Lancaster ED696 WS/T
Pilot. 778564 F/Sgt J.H.C.Walsh Killed Hamburg, Germany. 4A-A-8
Nav. 144762 P/O R.E.Raven Killed Hamburg, Germany. 4A-A-14
B/A. 126958 F/O K.E.Fraser Killed Hamburg, Germany. 4A-A-9
W/OP. R/106683 W/O T.W.Telfer Killed Hamburg, Germany. JG 4A-A-10/11
F/E. 570542 Sgt H.L.Jones Killed Hamburg, Germany. 4A-A-12
A/G. 953122 Sgt E.S.Wood Killed Hamburg, Germany. JG 4A-A-10/11
A/G. 49285 F/O S.M.Hobson Killed Hamburg, Germany. 4A-A-13

57 Squadron 5 Group Lancaster W4252 DX/
Aircraft ditched, last position on W/T fix at 0148 hours (5/4/43), 5420N 0425E.
Pilot. 33350 S/Ldr S.N.T.Wallace Missing, Runnymede Memorial 119
Nav. 130519 P/O F.E.F.Weldon Missing, Runnymede Memorial 134
B/A. 1393578 Sgt B.E.Spicer Missing, Runnymede Memorial 165
W/OP. 1365803 Sgt A.Haddow Missing, Runnymede Memorial 151
F/E. 538409 Sgt G.R.Harbottle Missing, Runnymede Memorial 152
A/G. 1492250 Sgt A.R.Evans Missing, Runnymede Memorial 148
A/G. 1230388 Sgt A.R.Wood Missing, Runnymede Memorial 170

405 Squadron 6 Group Halifax DT704 LQ/M
Pilot. R/90930 F/Sgt W.J.Foley Killed Kiel, Germany. 1-J-13
Nav. J/22531 F/O R.J.Wright Killed Kiel, Germany. CG 5-E-9/12
B/A. R/109394 Sgt H.B.J.Sargent Killed Kiel, Germany. 1-J-14
W/OP. R/69379 W/O W.F.Jordan Killed Kiel, Germany. 1-H-12
F/E. 942345 Sgt R.A.Damas Killed Kiel, Germany. 1-H-14
A/G. R/118056 F/Sgt R.E.Goldney Killed Kiel, Germany. 1-E-3
A/G. R/130695 F/Sgt J.A.C.Taylor Killed Kiel, Germany. 1-E-8

408 Squadron 6 Group Halifax BB336 EQ/
Pilot. C/1036 S/Ldr E.G.Gilmore DFC Missing, Runnymede Memorial 172
Nav. 121551 F/Lt J.B.Darroch Missing, Runnymede Memorial 119
B/A. 1475434 F/Sgt J.W.T.Smith DFM Missing, Runnymede Memorial 139
W/OP. 1254722 F/Sgt P.G.Oyler Missing, Runnymede Memorial 138
F/E. 1087533 Sgt K.W.Haynes Missing, Runnymede Memorial 152
A/G. J/16063 P/O M.P.Hall Missing, Runnymede Memorial 175
A/G. J/90359 P/O R.T.Wiggett PoW. Stalag 357, Kopernikus. 1045

428 Squadron 6 Group Wellington HE432 NA/C
Pilot. J/9416 F/Lt R.G.Tighe Killed Westdongeradeel(Wierum), 2-6 Holland.
Nav. J/11956 F/O H.C.Irwin Missing, Runnymede Memorial 174
B/A. R/103151 F/Sgt K.W.Rosevear Missing, Runnymede Memorial 185
W/OP. J/17171 P/O W.D.Heslip Missing, Runnymede Memorial 175
A/G. R/98510 F/Sgt L.D.Ryan Killed Sage, Germany. 7-E-2

426 Squadron 6 Group Wellington X3699 KW/
Aircraft ditched 10 miles off Cromer, Norfolk
Pilot. J/20024 F/O D.L.Kennedy Killed Scotton, Norfolk. 296
Nav. J/13830 P/O K.M.Walley Missing, Runnymede Memorial 175
B/A. J/22525 P/O D.Laskey Rescued
W/OP. R/101990 Sgt L.L.Anderson Rescued
A/G. R/67642 Sgt C.N.Beaton Missing, Runnymede Memorial 175

Minelaying

April 6th/7th, 1943
A mixed force of 14 Stirlings, 5 Lancasters, 10 Halifaxes and 18
Wellingtons went minelaying in the Lorient and St Nazaire
areas on the night of April 6th/7th laying 123 mines. Six of the
bombers failed to drop their mines, some had technical problems
and others were unable to get a satisfactory pinpoint for their
run in. Two aircraft were lost on this operation. From their
crews five were killed and the bodies of the other seven were
never found.

Casualties April 6th/7th, 1943. Minelaying

166 Squadron 1 Group Wellington BK299 AS/Q
Pilot. 72105 F/Lt N.S.H.Brown Missing, Runnymede Memorial 119
Nav. 1239621 Sgt R.Lankester Missing, Runnymede Memorial 156
B/A. A/413617 F/Sgt E.E.Lankester Missing, Runnymede Memorial 193
W/OP. 1315566 Sgt M.H.V.Lewis Missing, Runnymede Memorial 156
A/G. 1454107 Sgt I.Caulton Missing, Runnymede Memorial 144

405 Squadron 6 Group Halifax DT699 LQ/G
Pilot. J/21216 F/O J.H.Edwards Killed St.Martin-de-Re, France. 3-1
Nav. R/133386 F/Sgt R.V.Stuart Killed St.Martin-de-Re, France. 1-1
B/A. R/106431 F/Sgt R.J.Jones Killed St.Martin-de-Re, France. 1-2
W/OP. 1333384 Sgt L.R.Wallace Missing, Runnymede Memorial 168
F/E. R/61133 Sgt A.D.Gordon Killed Pornic, France. 1-AB-5
A/G. R/98929 F/Sgt F.R.W.Anderson Missing, Runnymede Memorial 181
A/G. R/119606 F/Sgt F.D.Roberts Killed St.Martin-de-Re, France. 2-2

Duisburg

April 8th/9th, 1943

It was back again to the Ruhr on the night of the 8th/9th April, when Duisburg was the target for the night. 392 aircraft - 156 Lancasters, 97 Wellingtons, 73 Halifaxes, 56 Stirlings and 10 Mosquitoes left their English bases, but only 289 actually bombed, a high percentage (21.5%) returning early because of extremely bad weather conditions encountered en route. Bombing was only a moderate success, for thick cloud covered the target area and the resultant bombing was scattered. Most bombers dropped the 406.3 tons of high explosive and 392.3 tons of incendiaries on their estimated time of arrival, the 18 target indicators and 21 flares not being visible. This type of raid attempted in unsuitable bad weather conditions was to be repeated too often in the coming months. On this Duisburg raid, 19 aircraft were lost, a loss rate of 4.8% and from the crews 79 were killed, 32 were missing, 15 being made prisoners and one managed to evade capture. One of the Pathfinding Mosquitoes crashed at Wyton after take off and Stirling BK770 from 75 Squadron, captained by New Zealand Warrant Officer J. A. E. Walsh, crashed on return at Bressingham, Norfolk, killing all the crew.

Only Four Crew Return in Bomber

A Halifax from 405 Squadron, 6 Group captained by Pilot Officer C. C. Stovell had an especially shaky trip on this Duisburg raid. The aircraft was caught in a heavy box of *Flak* and the pilot attempted to try and escape by climbing. Heavy icing was encountered at the higher altitude and control of the aircraft was lost causing the Halifax to go into a vicious spin in which three of the engines cut out so the captain warned the crew to stand by for a bale out order. Unfortunately four of the crew, the second pilot Pilot Officer G. E. Bisson, the flight engineer Sergeant A. Whitterton and the two gunners Flight Sergeants W. A. Wagner and A. Cox DFM, apparently misunderstood this preparatory order and left the aircraft prematurely. Their actions were completely understandable for in that situation there was no time to question an order, the intercom would have been indistinct and the plane's circumstances would not have inspired any other command but a bale out order. Miraculously at only 1, 000 feet the captain regained control of the aircraft and made his way back to England, struggling again when the engines temporarily cut out a second time on the return flight. Pilot Officer Stovell and the remaining three crew members finally made it safely back to base. Of the four who baled out, three became prisoners of war, but Flight Sergeant Cox was killed in the bale out.

Rear Turret Blown Off

Sergeant Leonard Franklin Williamson was the captain of Wellington HE239 NA/Y from 428 'Ghost' Squadron (RCAF) which was severely damaged when it encountered accurate and intense *Flak* four miles north of Duisburg at 23.15 hours. A shell blew off the rear turret and half the rudder and all the fuselage fabric was stripped off the rear of the aircraft. Seconds later the bomber began to vibrate badly and the rudder bar beneath the pilot's feet swung uselessly to and fro. Struggling to keep the bomber on a straight and level course for the bomb run the pilot succeeded in enabling the bomb aimer to drop the bombs dead on target at 23.20 hours. Then the bomber became exceedingly difficult to handle so the pilot decided that a bale out order was necessary, but before giving the command he checked on his crew. He received no reply from his rear gunner, Sergeant. Lorenzo Bertrand, so the navigator was asked to go back and check to if he was OK. The navigator reported that the turret had sheared off and there was no trace of the gunner.

With bomb doors still open and both wheels hanging down because of hydraulic failure the Wellington was in a very poor state to attempt the homeward flight. But in spite of this the pilot found that although the airspeed was much reduced the bomber was still able to maintain height, so he decided to make to get back to England. With great skill he nursed his crippled bomber slowly along and finally made landfall at West Malling, the nearest airfield to the coast.

For his exemplary airmanship and tenacity Sergeant William-son was awarded an immediate CGM on this his 7th operation. The body of the unfortunate gunner, 10500195 Sergeant Bertrand, was found and buried by the Germans, but was later reinterred at the Reichswald Forest War Cemetry. Germany (Grave 12-G-1).

166 Squadron Navigator Evades Capture

Pilot Officer B. H. Marion J/22552, a Canadian navigator on Wellington BK361 'F for Freddie' from 166 Squadron, was the lucky member of the crew who baled out over France, for he within a short time managed to have the help of the underground to evade capture.

On the return flight from Duisburg when conditions were very misty the engines started to give serious trouble and as they were nearing the Channel, an SOS was sent out by the wireless operator Sergeant Conrad, who was unsuccessful in asking for a fix on their position. Aware of the danger of having to ditch in the sea, the pilot, Sergeant Barclay, decided that it would be better to turn inland and chance their luck with a bale out over France. So the order was given and Pilot Officer Marion landed in a ploughed field, the aircraft crashing and bursting into flames about 300 yards away. His first reaction was to get away from the crash site as soon as possible so he ran into a nearby wood, where he hid his parachute and Mae West, then continued walking across open country for about three miles. Before resting, he consulted his maps and guessed that he was somewhere near Mezerolles about 10 kilometres north west of Doullens.

Pilot Officer Marion was fortunate in that he was able to speak French, so when he saw a French boy he approached him and asked for help. The boy confirmed that he was near Mezerolles and advised him to hide in a bush while he went for his father. When the boy's father arrived he told Marion to remain where he was and that some help would be sent to him. Later the young boy's older brother accompanied by another man brought food and civilian clothes and took away Pilot Officer Marion's uniform and identity disc. These men were connected with the underground movement, who arranged his passage back to England through Spain. On returning to England he heard that his crew were safe but prisoners. Whilst Pilot Officer Marion was evading capture another of his crew, the rear gunner Warrant Officer Ronald Limage was also on the run in France and he too was helped by a resistance group but he was not so lucky in making a home run, for he was one of the party which included Flight Lieutenant Murphy (who baled out on the Essen raid of April 3rd/4th). They were captured in the foothills of the Pyrenees when their guide lost his way and the party were taken on by a truck which was intercepted by a German patrol.

Warrant Officer Limage spent three months in Fresnes prison, Paris before being transferred to a PoW camp where he was kept for the rest of the war.

419 Squadron's 1,000th Sortie

419 Canadian Bomber Squadron made their 1,000th sortie of the war on the Duisburg raid. Unfortunately the celebrations in the mess that night were marred by the fact that they had lost one crew, that of Halifax BB327 captained by R/125703 Sergeant John H. Morris, who were on their 4th operation. Later it was reported that there was only one survivor, the flight engineer Sergeant L. E. Turner, who became a prisoner of war. In his post war interrogation, Sergeant Turner could not recall what had happened to his aircraft, he stated that nothing extraordinary had happened until the target was reached. The only thing he remembers was becoming conscious for a short time as he floated down in his parachute and hitting the ground. Then his next recollection was waking up in a bed in what appeared to be a Police Station and being told that the rest of his crew were dead and for him the war was over.

April 8th/9th, 1943 Target Duisburg

156 Squadron 8 Group Lancaster ED622 GT/
Pilot. A/401344 F/Sgt R.G.Younger Killed Rheinberg, Germany. 4-E-5
Nav. 656400 Sgt N.Stopford Killed Rheinberg, Germany. 4-E-9
B/A. A/404716 P/O N.Ferguson Killed Rheinberg, Germany. 4-E-6
W/OP. A/15319 Sgt S.M.White Killed Rheinberg, Germany. 4-E-8
F/E. A/403691 F/Sgt R.H.Flett Killed Rheinberg, Germany. 4-E-7
A/G. 1322187 Sgt A.J.Jackson Killed Rheinberg, Germany. 4-E-11
A/G. A/404582 F/Sgt J.P.M.Grace Killed Rheinberg, Germany. 4-E-10

7 Squadron 8 Group Stirling R9199 MG/T
Pilot. J/9196 F/O L.J.Stewart Missing, Runnymede Memorial 175 2/
Pilot. 139579 P/O G.M.DeMeillac Missing, Runnymede Memorial 131
Nav. J/11217 F/O A.Jackson Missing, Runnymede Memorial 174
B/A. 1270391 Sgt R.S.Hamilton-Fox Missing, Runnymede Memorial 152
W/OP. 1377506 Sgt V.Walters Missing, Runnymede Memorial 168
F/E. 1495951 Sgt G.M.Boardman Missing, Runnymede Memorial 143
A/G. 1302847 Sgt R.Wilson Missing, Runnymede Memorial 170
A/G. R/107927 Sgt G.C.Gale Missing, Runnymede Memorial 181

100 Squadron 1 Group Lancaster ED568 HW/T
Pilot. J/4965 S/Ldr J.A.McKinnon Killed Rheinberg, Germany. CG 2-E-9/19
Nav. 1331520 Sgt R.J.B.Montigue Killed Rheinberg, Germany. 2-E-6
B/A. 1029829 Sgt R.S.Sweetlove Killed Rheinberg, Germany. CG 2-E-9/19
W/OP. 1025847 Sgt H.Jenkinson Killed Rheinberg, Germany. CG 2-E-9/19
F/E. 625153 Sgt S.F.Chappell Killed Rheinberg, Germany. 2-E-7
A/G. 649407 Sgt C.J.Grimshaw Killed Rheinberg, Germany. CG 2-E-9/19
A/G. 1575223 Sgt M.H.Knowles Killed Rheinberg, Germany. 2-E-8

460 Squadron 1 Group Lancaster W4785 UV/
Pilot. A/408949 Sgt J.H.Ball Killed Reichswald Forest, Germany. 9-C-18
Nav. 658374 Sgt C.E.Frampton Killed Reichswald Forest. CG 9-C-7/8
B/A. 1330750 Sgt D.M.Gray Killed Reichswald Forest, Germany. CG 9-C-7/8
W/OP. 1025415 Sgt D.G.Mordecai Killed Reichswald Forest. CG 9-C-7/8
F/E. 1251372 Sgt W.C.Langley Killed Reichswald Forest. CG 9-C-7/8
A/G. 1090929 Sgt G.G.Dobson Killed Reichswald Forest, Germany. CG 9-C-7/8
A/G. A/403806 F/Sgt A.A.Garven Killed Reichswald Forest. CG 9-C-7/8

166 Squadron 1 Group Wellington HE658 AS/S
Aircraft crashed due to heavy icing.
Pilot. 124467 F/O D.W.H.Morgan Killed Reichswald Forest. CG 4-G-2/3
Nav. J/22551 F/O J.E.Hardy Killed Reichswald Forest, Germany. CG 4-G-2/3
B/A. 1148269 Sgt W.Myerscough Killed Reichswald Forest. CG 4-C-2/3
W/OP. 130155 F/Lt P.P.Stevens PoW. Stalag Luft 3, Sagan. 1090
A/G. 129041 F/O C.C.Lee PoW. Stalag Luft 3, Sagan. 1082

166 Squadron 1 Group Wellington BK/361 AS/F
Pilot. NZ/413369 W/O G.S.Barclay PoW. Stalag 357, Kopernikus. 977
Nav. J/22552 P/O B.H.Marion Evaded capture
B/A. 1391223 W/O R.W.Hart PoW. Stalag Luft 6, Heydekrug. 1001
W/OP. 1263438 F/Sgt A.H.Conrad PoW. Stalag 357, Kopernikus. 986
A/G. 1391336 W/O R.F.Limage PoW. Stalag 4B, Muhleberg(Elbe). 222830

300 Squadron 1 Group Wellington HE148 BH/T
Pilot. P/1916 P/O S.Tomicki Missing, Northolt Memorial.
2/Pilot. P/792051 Sgt S.Slusarski Missing, Northolt Memorial.
Nav. P/2021 F/O J.Rudek Killed Bergen-am-Zee, Holland.
B/A. P/780782 Sgt T.Kniazycki Missing, Northolt Memorial.
W/OP. P/794308 Sgt W.Marczuk Missing, Northolt Memorial.
A/G. P/792832 Sgt S.Stepien Killed Bergen-am-Zee, Holland.

15 Squadron 3 Group Stirling EF359 LS/B
Aircraft crashed at Woltershoff, Germany.
Pilot. 143231 P/O A.J.Gurr Killed Rheinberg, Germany. 2-E-3
Nav. 1235760 Sgt P.Lutwyche Killed Rheinberg, Germany. 14-D-22
B/A. 1339473 Sgt F.G.Lambert Killed Rheinberg, Germany. 2-D-25
W/OP. 1290705 Sgt J.E.Kimber Killed Rheinberg, Germany. JG 2-E-1/2
F/E. 621785 Sgt W.S.Bragg Killed Rheinberg, Germany. JG 2-E-1/2
A/G. 1527292 Sgt J.Hall Killed Reichswald Forest, Germany. 26-G-16
A/G. 1504193 Sgt I.W.Williams Killed Reichswald Forest, Germany. 9-C-15

218 Squadron 3 Group Stirling BF502 HA/
Pilot. 143676 P/O D.A.S.Tomkins Missing, Runnymede Memorial 133
Nav. 1151777 Sgt J.R.Tait Missing, Runnymede Memorial 166
B/A. 1056063 Sgt A.Ridge Missing, Runnymede Memorial 163
W/OP. 1122799 Sgt D.C.L.Guest Missing, Runnymede Memorial 151
F/E. 576406 Sgt D.L.N.Eggleton Missing, Runnymede Memorial 148
A/G. 1385043 Sgt T.R.Davidson Missing, Runnymede Memorial 147
A/G. 656323 Sgt J.Forrest Missing, Runnymede Memorial 149

76 Squadron 4 Group Halifax W1236 MP/G
Pilot. 117489 F/O M.A.S.Elliott Missing, Runnymede Memorial 124
2/Pilot. 1014935 Sgt J.D.Armstrong Missing, Runnymede Memorial 140
Nav. 141803 P/O R.R.Johnston Missing, Runnymede Memorial 132
B/A. 113484 F/O H.H.Rogers DFM Missing, Runnymede Memorial 129
W/OP. 121569 F/O A.M.Houston Missing, Runnymede Memorial 125
F/E. 1187176 Sgt R.J.Matthews Missing, Runnymede Memorial 158
A/G. 1101248 F/Sgt J.Appleton Missing, Runnymede Memorial 134
A/G. 655937 F/Sgt T.K.Wagstaff Missing, Runnymede Memorial 139

77 Squadron 4 Group Halifax JB/847 KN/
Pilot. 122321 F/Lt J.W.N.Balley Killed Creil, France. 2-351
Nav. 1375108 Sgt T.S.McStay Killed Creil, France. 2-348
B/A. A/415186 Sgt L.F.Samson Killed Creil, France. 2-350
W/OP. 1109116 F/Sgt P.A.Greene Killed Creil, France. 2-349
F/E. 1211129 Sgt J.W.R.H.Woodley Killed Creil, France. 2-352
A/G. 1580165 Sgt T.Crossland Killed Creil, France. 2-347
A/G. 1318167 Sgt R.W.Hedicker Killed Creil, France. 2-353

466 Squadron 4 Group Wellington HE155 HD/
Pilot. 143087 P/O S.M.Wood Missing, Runnymede Memorial 134
Nav. 142881 P/O A.C.Kneeshaw Missing, Runnymede Memorial 132
B/A. 1321621 Sgt J.G.Chalmers Missing, Runnymede Memorial 145
W/OP. 1187020 Sgt A.D.Pennycord Missing, Runnymede Memorial 161
A/G. R/107739 W/O L.R.Crowe Missing, Runnymede Memorial 179

44 Squadron 5 Group Lancaster ED/351 KM/Y
Pilot. 1257965 F/Sgt I.C.Haines Killed Rheinberg, Germany. CG 2-E-9/19
Nav. 1241805 Sgt R.A.Asbury Killed Rheinberg, Germany. CG 2-E-9/19
B/A. 1218594 Sgt R.G.Prince Killed Rheinberg, Germany. CG 2-E-9/19
W/OP. 1020872 Sgt F.G.Ward Killed Rheinberg, Germany. CG 2-E-9/19
F/E. 949104 Sgt S.Richardson Killed Rheinberg, Germany. CG 2-E-9/19
A/G. 1314128 Sgt L.J.Yeo Killed Rheinberg, Germany. CG 2-E-9/19
A/G. R/134019 W/O E.Strandberg Killed Rheinberg, Germany. 2-E-4

49 Squadron 5 Group Lancaster ED590 EA/
Pilot. 107910 F/O D.J.N.Southern Killed Reichswald Forest. 10-F-12
Nav. 47652 F/O J.B.Lapping Killed Reichswald Forest, Germany. 10-F-13
B/A. 656957 Sgt G.S.Pring Killed Reichswald Forest, Germany. 10-F-5
W/OP. 125353 F/O A.L.Munro Killed Reichswald Forest, Germany. 10-F-1
F/E. 578008 Sgt C.J.Tiley Killed Reichswald Forest, Germany. 10-F-3
A/G. 1576209 Sgt H.Chatterton Killed Reichswald Forest, Germany. 10-F-6
A/G. A/407030 P/O J.L.Rollins Killed Reichswald Forest, Germany. 10-F-4

106 Squadron 5 Group Lancaster W4156 ZN/
Pilot. 144005 P/O J.L.Irvine Killed Reichswald Forest. CG 27-B-11/17
Nav. 1380953 Sgt F.A.Smith Killed Reichswald Forest. CG 27-B-11/17
B/A. 1575776 Sgt L.J.Tate Killed Reichswald Forest, Germany. CG 27-B-11/17
W/OP. A/408725 F/Sgt F.W.G.Limbrick Killed Reichswald Forest.CG27B11/17
F/E. 570212 Sgt S.Cordery Killed Reichswald Forest, Germany. CG 27-B-11/17
A/G. 1314276 Sgt W.G.Harvey Killed Reichswald Forest. CG 27-B-11/17
A/G. 1232887 Sgt L.J.Hemus Killed Reichswald Forest. GC 27-B-11/17

405 Squadron 6 Group Halifax HR809 LQ/X
Pilot. J/16835 P/O C.C.Stovell
2/Pilot. J/16354 F/Lt G.E.Bisson PoW. Stalag Luft 3, Sagan. 1075
F/E. R/66720 Sgt A.Whitterton PoW. Stalag 357, Kopernikus. 1052
A/G. R/126995 W/O W.A.Wagner PoW. Stalag 4B, Muhlberg(Elbe). 1046
A/G. 952028 F/Sgt A.Cox DFM Killed Rheinberg, Germany. 2-E-20
Four crew members baled out over the target misunderstanding pilot's orders
after the aircraft went into a spin and three engines cut out during violent
evasive action. Remainder of the crew brought the bomber safely back to base.

419 Squadron 6 Group Halifax BB327 VR/
Pilot. R/125703 Sgt J.H.Morris Killed Reichswald Forest, Germany. 2-G-17
Nav. 655464 Sgt K.H.Godbold Killed Reichswald Forest, Germany. 2-G-18
B/A. J/22556 F/O A.R.Hickey Killed Reichswald Forest, Germany. CG 2-F-2/4
W/OP. 1330644 Sgt R.J.Amos Killed Reichswald Forest, Germany. CG 2-F-2/4
F/E. R/85055 Sgt L.E.Turner PoW. Stalag Luft 1, Barth Vogelsang.1105
A/G. R/107044 Sgt P.J.Ireland Killed Reichswald Forest, Germany. CG 2-F-2/4
A/G. R/92992 F/Sgt D.C.Way Killed Reichswald Forest, Germany. 2-F-5

420 Squadron 6 Group Wellington MS479 PT/
Pilot. J/16151 P/O W.A.Walkinshaw Killed Reichswald Forest. 10-E-18
Nav. J/16935 P/O K.W.McDonald Killed Reichswald Forest, Germany. 10-F-11
B/A. R/95730 W/O D.F.Evans Killed Reichswald Forest, Germany. 10-E-17
W/OP. R/74917 W/O F.Bemi Killed Reichswald Forest, Germany. 10-F-8
A/G. R/86912 W/O R.G.Rispin Killed Reichswald Forest, Germany. 10-F-7

425 Squadron 6 Group Wellington HE592 KW/Q
Pilot. R/94963 W/O J.F.Smith Killed Jonkerbos, Holland. 24-D-2
Nav. 1219354 Sgt P.A.Smith Killed Jonkerbos, Holland. JG 24-A-9
B/A. R/95765 W/O C.W.G.Burke Killed Jonkerbos, Holland. 24-D-1 W/OP.
J/10020 F/O R.G.Cook Killed Jonkerbos, Holland. JG 24-A-9
A/G. J/19312 P/O O.E.E.Schulz Killed Jonkerbos, Holland. 24-D-3

428 Squadron 6 Group Wellington DF635 NA/I
Pilot. J/16784 F/Lt R.M.Buckham PoW. Stalag Luft 3, Sagan. 1076
Nav. J/10716 F/Lt N.W.Rodin PoW. Stalag Luft 3, Sagan. 1087
B/A. 124755 F/Lt G.C.Fletcher PoW. Stalag Luft 3, Sagan. 1079
W/OP. R/107078 W/O J.D.Fraser PoW. Stalag 357, Kopernikus. 995
A/G. 1502391 Sgt T.Whitehead PoW. Stalag 357, Kopernikus. 1051

428 Squadron 6 Group Wellington HE239 NA/Y
Pilot. R/107665 Sgt L.F.Williamson
R/G. 1050195 Sgt L.Bertrand Killed Reichswald Forest, Germany. 12-G-1
Rear turret blown off aircraft by anti aircraft fire.

109 Squadron 8 Group Mosquito DZ430 HS/
Crashed on take off for Duisburg.
Pilot. 117425 F/O J.Walker Killed Hull (Northern) 264-50
Nav. J/6665 F/O C.D.McKenna Killed Altrincham, Cheshire. X-429-B

75 Squadron 3 Group Stirling BK770 AA/L
Crashed at Valley Farm, Bressingham, Norfolk after operation to Duisburg.
Pilot. NZ/401294 W/O J.A.E.Walsh Killed Newmarket. O-378
Nav. R/80237 W/O B.A.Moffatt Killed Newmarket. P-431
B/A. 1030797 Sgt F.H.Reddicliffe Killed Newmarket. P-415
W/OP. 1211835 Sgt J.W.Scudder Killed Mitcham (Streatham Pk). 24-31609
F/E. 574819 Sgt J.Worthington Killed Worthing(Durrington), Sussex. 9-8-42
A/G. 1386838 Sgt S.A.Curtis Killed Newmarket. O-397
A/G. R/93568 Sgt P.G.Stuart Killed Newmarket. P-446

Minelaying

April 8th/9th, 1943

A mixed force of 27 aircraft from 1, 3 and 5 Groups did some
minelaying in the Biscay area. Five aircraft did not drop their
mines, as they had engine or technical troubles. A total of 64
mines were laid. One aircraft was lost from this sortie, only the

rear gunner's body was found and he is buried at Guidel, France.

Casualties April 8th/9th, 1943. Minelaying

199 Squadron 1 Group Wellington HE495 EX/
Pilot. 1313873 Sgt K.A.Pinchin Missing, Runnymede Memorial 161
Nav. 120231 F/O L.C.Wheeler Missing, Runnymede Memorial 130
B/A. J/16397 P/O L.R.Townsend Missing, Runnymede Memorial 178
W/OP. R/90548 W/O J.H.Paquin Missing, Runnymede Memorial 180
A/G. 1310815 Sgt J.W.Green Killed Guidel, France. 5-30

Frankfurt

April 10th/11th, 1943

Complete cloud cover again thwarted the next raid which was on Frankfurt on the night of April 10th/11th, when 144 Wellingtons, 16 Lancasters, 124 Halifaxes and 98 Stirlings, a total of 502 aircraft went on the attack. More aircraft could have become available, but 6 Group records show that there was a serious shortage of overload tanks for their Wellingtons, which had to undertake long flights. Many of the squadrons in the 6 Group had aircraft standing by on call, but only a limited number were ordered on to this Frankfurt operation, because suffcient tanks were not available. More disturbing for some Station and Squadron Commanders was that there was a forecast of a further three months delay in the supply of these overload tanks. It was obvious that Bomber Command was gearing its bomber committment to four engined aircraft for long range targets and was not prepared to divert valuable production time and materials to these tanks for two engined aircraft.

Route markers were clearly seen but target markers were not as clear, although 91 target indicators were dropped. 479.9 tons of high explosive and 532. 2 tons of incendiaries were dropped but there was little success from this high bomb tonnage. Frankfurt records noted only slight damage and little loss of life. Nineteen aircraft did not return from this raid, a loss rate of 3.8%. From the aircrew manning these bombers, 102 lost their lives (84 killed and 18 missing), 12 were made prisoners and 7 were fortunate in making a successful evasion.

Spitfire Escort After Ditching

One of the aircraft on the raid, a Stirling of 75 Squadron piloted by Flight Sergeant Rothschild, ditched in the English Channel off Shoreham. The bomber floated for 25 minutes giving the crew plenty of time to board their dinghy. Before ditching Sergeant E. R. Todd, the wireless operator, had radioed a *Mayday* message and the crew sitting in their dinghy soon saw an escort of Spitfires circle overhead in response to this distress call. Later an Air Sea Rescue Walrus aircraft flew over and landed, but unfortunately it taxied into the dinghy, capsizing it and throwing all the crew into the sea. Fortunately they were all recovered safely and became members of the Goldfish Club, the exclusive club for those who have survived after ditching their aircraft.

Lost on Return from Frankfurt

After this raid on Frankfurt a Wellington, HE422 from 420 Squadron captained by Pilot Officer C. W. Jackson, must have strayed off course on its way back to its home base at Middleton St George in County Durham, for the crew were ordered to bale out over Tenby in South Wales. Unfortunately the pilot landed in the sea and was drowned, but the remaining four crew members were unhurt after baling out over land. The plane crashed into the sea at Monkstone Point, Wales.

Second Jump for Lucky Rear Gunner

Another Wellington, HE159 from 424 Squadron based at Topcliffe, Yorkshire, captained by Canadian Sergeant R. M. Buie was carrying a load of incendiaries. It crashed and burnt out near Hastings, Sussex at 00.58 hours on the outward flight. All the crew were killed except for the rear gunner, Canadian Sergeant A. G. Lees who baled out and only suffered minor abrasions and shock. According to his report the aircraft had developed engine trouble and had been losing height steadily all the way from its base. The captain had ordered the crew to bale out, but by the time the order was given the plane was down to about 600 feet. The rear gunner saw the aircraft crash before he landed by parachute so the remainder of the crew obviously had insufficent time to bale out. When the gunner managed to approach the crash site, the aircraft was already a mass of flames and unhappily he could do nothing to save the rest of his crew. As this was the second occasion that the rear gunner had baled out since his recent arrival on the squadron, he must have considered himself to have a charmed life.

Group Captain's Evasion

A Halifax, JB871 'V for Victor' of 76 Squadron, piloted by Flight Lieutenant A. H. Hull was another victim of night fighters on the Frankfurt raid. Aboard and acting as a second pilot was the Station Commander of Linton upon Ouse, Group Captain J. R. Whitley AFC who went along on this operation to gain first hand experience. But he got more than he bargained for on that night, for not only did he bale out, he evaded capture along with three other members of the crew and made it back to England.

The Halifax was en route to Frankfurt when after a sudden attack by an Me110 at 02.00 hours, the aircraft caught fire and the bale out order was given. The Group Captain baled out after the navigator, Sergeant W. J. Painter and the bomb aimer, Sergeant M. A. J. Davies, and floated down landing uninjured in a street between two rows of houses. The aircraft crashed in flames, in open country on the outskirts of a village. Although unsure of his exact location, the Group Captain realised that he was in France when he heard a Frenchwoman's voice and then later when two Frenchmen emerged from a house protesting loudly about the parachute which was festooned around the house roof. Fortunately the Group Captain could speak French and immediately attracted their attention. After dropping his Mae West near to the parachute one of the men took him into the house, where he explained who he was and showed his RAF badge. The Group Captain was told that he had landed in the village of Hirson. A number of neighbours then visited the house to see the stranger who had dropped in from the sky. By this time the two Frenchmen had ably disposed of the parachute and Mae West.

Group Captain Whitley was more prepared and equipped for evasion than most aircrew, because before leaving England he had put on a pair of grey civilian trousers and a civilian shirt under his uniform and he also carried a haversack, which contained a 'pepper and salt' jacket and a striped tie. What the rest of the crew must have thought when they saw the 'Groupie' getting aboard their aircraft with this 'kit' is not difficult to imagine, but one thing for sure, it can't have given them a boost of confidence.

When the Group Captain had peeled off his service tunic, trousers and shirt to emerge in his 'civilian rig out', the Frenchman roared with laughter and gave him a soft black hat to complete his disguise. They also provided him with food. He was told that there were twelve German soldiers billeted in the village who were guarding the local railway line. As curfew ended at 05.30 hours, his helpers took him to an unoccupied house nearby and told him to stay there for the rest of the night and that he would be helped in the morning. When alone in the empty house one of the first things he did was to shave off his rather large distinctive RAF type moustache, which would have been a dead give away. He was able to use his own Rolls Razor and soap from his escape haversack. At this house the Group Captain had second thoughts about remaining in the area as it was so near the crashed aircraft site. After hiding his service tunic and trousers in an empty stove in the house, he decided to move away from the village. He planned to walk in a south westerly direction and on his way he filled up his water bottle and wisely removed all the wrappers bearing English words from the contents of his RAF escape kit, and stowed the various items about his person.

At 07.00 hours he hid in a hedgerow near a wood and while lying there he saw a German light aircraft circling the wood flying at about 50 feet apparently looking for escapees. Finally it flew directly over him then disappeared from view. After eating the Horlicks tablets and some of the biscuits that the helpers had given him he studied his maps and set off and walked most of the day.

At 17.30 hours he saw an old woman working in a field and approached her and explained to her who he was. She replied that the Germans were looking for the airmen from the crashed bomber. She then disappeared but soon brought a man back with her, who began singing the Marseillaise. After he had talked to the man and explained that he needed help, the man left promising to come back. He did return later bringing some bread, eggs and coffee and reported that there were so few Germans in the neighbourhood that it would be quite safe to walk across country. Later that evening the Frenchman led the Group Captain towards the village of Bucilly and pointed the direction in which he should continue to walk. Further on near Martigny, the Group Captain found a lonely farmhouse, and chancing his luck, he knocked up the occupants. A woman who came to the door seemed rather scared when she learnt his true identity, but took him in and gave him a pair of civilian shoes as well as food and allowed him to stay the night in the outside hayloft. The next morning he persuaded the woman to try to get him a French identity card, she didn't think this possible but cycled to the neighbouring village to fetch her father. He arrived with a friend and after listening to the Group Captain's story allowed him to stay in the hayloft until the evening of the 13th April, when he was visited by another man and taken by truck to a house in a nearby village. From there he was taken to yet another house where he was told that an RCAF officer named Dennison, who had broken three ribs, had been sheltered there three days before. In fact the Canadian officer was Pilot Officer B. C. Dennison from 405 Squadron who had baled out on March 12th. It was from this house that the Group Captain's journey back to England, was arranged for him by the underground movement.

"For You the War is Over"

Sergeant Stan Reed was the rear gunner of Halifax DT 775 from 78 Squadron, which was captained by 1330122 Sergeant Jack Adams. All the crew except for the mid upper gunner, 988200 Sergeant J. E. Enright who was killed, baled out safely. The pilot and navigator, Warrant Officer Philip Hyden, landed quite near to each other and in view of advantage that Hyden was able to speak French they decided to keep together in their attempt to evade capture. But luck was not on their side, for although they were able to catch a train to Paris, when crossing the city by Metro to catch another train for Montauben, a town 80 miles from the Spanish border, their luck ran out at Vierzon when the train was stopped for a travel document check and they were arrested by two German soldiers. They had been on the run for eight days. Warrant Officer Hyden's commission came through during his period of captivity and he returned to the UK at the end of the war with the rank of Flight Lieutenant.

Stan and his crew had left their Yorkshire base of Linton on Ouse, a 4 Group Station, at 23.55 hours on Saturday April 10th. Bound for Frankfurt their aircraft joined the rest of the bombing armada at the assembly point at Start Point on the Devonshire coast. The Halifax they were flying was a brand new kite, a Mark B2 Series 1 Special, which had the nose and mid upper turrets removed in an attempt to improve the rather poor peformance of the aircraft, leaving only the rear turret with its four Brownings for defence. The mid upper gunner, now without a gun, had to man a small perspex blister which had been fitted in the floor of the fuselage, just aft of the entrance hatch. Not the most popular innovation or modification, as it entailed the mid upper gunner laying flat on the very cold and draughty metal floor for hours on end with his head stuck into the perspex blister. This so called ventral position, with its intercom, oxygen points and signal light switches, was an attempt to give the crew more warning of the ever increasing and deadly below and astern fighter attacks, which the enemy were beginning to favour, because there was an increasing bomber toll.

On this Frankfurt raid, Stan had flown down to the English coast, sitting in the second dickie's seat up front with his skipper whilst Joe Enright, the mid upper gunner, had manned the rear turret until it was time for Stan to take over. After leaving the English coast on this very dark moonless night, they had no sighting of another aircraft but on several occasions were aware of their presence as they flew through the slip stream of other unseen bombers. Stan made his way aft to take up his normal rear turret position but he found that the microphone on his face mask was not working and no one could hear what he was saying. No amount of banging, the usual remedy employed, would clear the fault, although he could hear perfectly well through his headphones in his flying helmet what the rest of the crew were saying. As there was no spare face mask aboard, the skipper decided that the gunner who was already in the rear turret should remain there and Stan would have to take up the dreaded blister position. He was to use the signal light to flash the letter F in Morse code if any fighters were about, so that the pilot could start to weave and corkscrew, until hopefully they were out of danger. Settling down in his blister position, Stan lay on some canvas covers which were kept inside the aircraft and peered down into the inky darkness below. He could hear in his headphones the sounds of the crew proceeding with their work. Jack the skipper, quietly in charge, saying very little. Phil Hyden, the navigator, trying his best with his Gee set, which was being jammed. Stan Hurrel, the bomb aimer, was up front looking out for the PFF flares and turning point markers. Cliff Price, the wireless operator, was searching his given wave bands, hoping to pick up German night fighter controllers giving instructions to their fighters, so that he could give them a shot from the microphone situated alongside one of the Merlin engines and interrupt their broadcasts with engine noises. Nobby Clarke, the flight engineer, was engaged in checking his petrol tanks and effecting change over from various tanks to preserve the balance of the aircraft in its flight. Joe in the rear turret was asking his skipper's permission to test fire his four 303 Browning guns from the rear turret.

On crossing the French coast just north of Dieppe, always a gut tightening occasion, the pilot commenced his gentle weaving across the general flight path. There was no *Flak* near them, at least as far as Stan could see from his blister and no member of the crew up front had made any comment of *Flak* ahead. All was well on board F for Freddie. The engines were roaring on as they were approaching Metz in eastern France, where there was to be a change of course on PFF markers. The skipper had warned all the crew that they were approaching the well known German night fighter belt and to keep their eyes peeled. Nothing kept a crew more on its toes than the prospect of being caught by a German night fighter, it demanded 100% concentration. All was completely black until the markers went down and the pilot turned on to his new heading at Metz, but they saw nothing of the town below because of the 10/10ths cloud. Everyone on board was now extremely alert not only searching for German fighters but on the look out for any other bombers which would be all around in the stream, in case one might get too close for comfort. Still head down in the blister Stan probed into the pitch black darkness when suddenly came several blinding lines of very bright lights. Tracer and lots of it! The enemy had caught them from astern and below. This tracer from a night fighter had torn into the bomber, raking it from nose to tail with one savage burst of 20mm cannon and machine gun fire, which lasted for not more than two or three seconds. Stan recalls that the noise was terrific, just like a giant tearing up sheets of corrugated iron, and he was lucky to escape being hit. He never caught sight of the fighter which attacked them, but the enemy pilot must have known his trade well, for he had crept up unseen, no doubt using his radar and had hit the Halifax plumb amidships where most damage could be done. The *Monica* set fitted in the tail of the bomber, a rear warning radar, which should have given an audible warning to the pilot that an aircraft was approaching from the rear must have been on the blink that night, for it failed to give a single beep during the encounter. Immediately fire broke out amidships, where the petrol tanks and load of incendaries were sited. The wireless operator had been hit and was uttering choice words into the intercom and there was lots of shouting going up forward of the plane, but certainly no panic. Stan had heard nothing from Joe back in the tail turret, nor had he heard the guns firing, so the rear gunner couldn't have seen the fighter either. From up forward it seemed that the plane was well alight and it was impossible to control the fire let alone put it out. All this happened with such speed although at the time to Stan it seemed to last for an age, in fact from the moment of the attack to all the crew hearing the bale out order less than 30 seconds had elapsed. Stan still couldn't believe it was happening, it all appeared so unreal. This he thought was what happened to other crews, not to his. But reality soon took over, he heard the flight engineer hollering that he had been burnt and the skipper's calm voice ordering, "Better get out chaps, this is it". When he heard this Stan pulled out his intercom plug and made his way quickly to the rear door, having grabbed his 'chute which lay on the floor beside him.

He remembers opening the entrance hatch inwards and seeing the flames tearing by underneath the fuselage and hearing the ear splitting noise and soon realised that he had to get out fast. Pausing momentarily at the open door and looking down into the pitch black darkness below, he saw two bodies flash by with their parachutes streaming out behind them. Sitting with his legs out of the door, he made no conscious effort to jump, he must have been sucked out, for the next thing he remembers was that he was out and the tail of the Halifax was shooting by overhead. To his amazement he experienced no sensation of falling, rather he got the impression that he was just sitting in the sky, suspended. Stan had seen two parachutes opening and he thought of Jack, the skipper who would be the last one out and of his slender chance of escaping from the diving burning aircraft. All this flashed through his mind as he hung there in the cold night air.

Realising it was time that he pulled the ripcord of his 'chute, he felt he could have counted up to a hundred, whilst he sat there in the sky. He reached across his chest for the parachute pack in order to grasp the metal D ring which one had to pull to open the 'chute and found to his horror that there was no pack there, his chest was bare. He died several deaths realising that he must have left the damn thing on the floor of the plane, as he opened the hatch door. This he thought was his lot. Well at least it didn't hurt and wouldn't take long and there was nothing at all that he could do about it, but what a way to go and all his own stupid fault for leaving the 'chute on the floor.

Then Stan became aware of two straps dangling from his parachute harness hanging up above, he grabbed them and pulled them and there was his parachute pack firmly clipped at the end of the straps. It was as if the good Lord had taken pity on him and had issued him with a new 'chute, but he soon realised what must have happened. Because of his unexpectedly quick exit from the Halifax, he must have broken the stitching on the straps, which are about five feet in length and are normally folded neatly on to the parachute harness and stitched to keep them in position. Large clips are attached to the straps to which the parachute pack is connected. Normally when a parachute is opened by using the D ring, the stitching breaks and the straps unfold leaving the parachute pack above one's head.

Clutching the parachute pack firmly as if it was a pot of gold, he pulled the rip cord, thinking as he did, of a sardonic corporal back in his squadron parachute section, who delighted in saying when handing out the 'chutes, "If it doesn't work bring it back to me and I will give you another one". With a bang, Stan's 'chute opened with a full smack into his face, which caused an aerial nose bleed, the only war injury that he sustained. Then he felt the excruciating jerk cutting hard into his crotch. Continuing slowly to descend Stan began to feel very cold, mainly the result of the shock of the last few minutes. In spite of wearing his flying helmet, he could still hear the roar of the bomber stream overhead, the bomber force which his Halifax had been a part of only a few minutes ago.

At last he thought he could see the ground coming up to meet him. So relaxing himself, with his knees slightly bent in the approved manner, he was at the ready, but the ground looked a bit light in colour and to his amazement his feet went right through the ground, the terra firma turned out to be a large cloud. Then Stan found himself in a kind of light clammy darkness, but not for long for within a few seconds he hit the ground like a sack of wet potatoes. His knees came up and struck him sharply under the chin with almost a knock out blow. Rolling over he was relieved to find himself on the ground at last, even if it was somewhere in darkest France.

Quickly he managed to free himself from his harness, his precious 'chute was streaming out and showing very white in the darkness and it appeared to Stan that it would be seen for miles around. On the ground all was deathly quiet, only overhead was the noisy bomber stream on its way to Frankfurt. At that point Stan had a feeling of intense loneliness for his thoughts were with the boys up there and he envied them their impending return to their bases and their bacon and egg breakfast, before they turned into their billets for welcome sleep. What would he have given to be back up there instead of being in this wretched ploughed field somewhere in France?

He remembered a lecture that he had once attended during training, given by an airman who baled out over France and who managed to get back to England, a lecture in which he now ruefully recalled that he had slept more than half way through. This airmen had hidden his 'chute in a furrow of a ploughed field and concealed it by kicking earth all over it. Stan decided to try the same proceedure but found that he must have been issued with the longest and whitest parachute in the RAF for there certainly seemed to be more parachute than furrows and loose earth. Scratching around in the dark he could still see too much white so he abandoned the 'chute in a nearby ditch and stuffed his Mae West and flying helmet up a convenient land drain pipe.

As he left the field he saw in the distance what appeared to be red railway warning lights, and walking towards them, Stan's thoughts were of a passing goods train which he could board and that would take him straight through to Switzerland, or perhaps with his present bad luck straight into Germany! He quickly put this idea out of his head until he found out more information. By now he was beginning to suffer from what many baled out airmen had gone through, the feeling that there might be a German behind every tree or bush and that he was very much on his own. Unfortunately it was not long before he was captured. This was at Briey, a coal mining district, which abounded in slag heaps, Russian prisoner of war cages and a good supply of Germans. The three other surviving members of the crew, Stan Hurrel, Cliff Price, Nobby Clark were flushed out of their hiding places by Russian PoW's, who under orders of their German guards were being used as beaters, as in a grouse shoot. Joe Enright, who took Stan Reed's place as the tail gunner was killed in the fighter action, his body being recovered from the wreckage of the Halifax the next day.

A Pathfinder Pilot Evades Capture

Altogether seven aircrew managed to evade capture after being brought down on the Frankfurt raid, this higher than usual number was due to the fact that the bombers' route was on that night mainly through France, where the chances of a successful evasion were greater with the help and the courage of many French people who often whisked away baled out aircrew from under the Germans' noses. One pilot who managed to get through to Switzerland was 63419 Flight Lieutenant G. F. Lambert, the captain of a Pathfinding Halifax DT 806 from 35 Squadron which was shot down by a fighter in the neighbourhood of Luxembourg.

The bomber caught fire and Lambert had to give the bale out order. At about 01.30 hours he parachuted down into the middle of a wood, having no idea of his exact whereabouts. After burying his flying gear, he started to walk westwards as he thought that he might have landed in Germany and that his best chance of escape would be in France. For the same reason he decided to avoid making contact with people.

For the next few days and nights he walked by night and lay low during the day, during which time he saw no sign posts, so he still had no idea of his exact position. He cut off his badges of rank and flying brevet and put his blue pullover over his battle dress top and tied his white scarf around his neck, his only disguise until the day before he reached the Swiss frontier. He was fortunate that he had worn his ordinary shoes, for he had been in the habit of not wearing his flying boots on operations. Many aircrew, except for the gunners who needed the warmth of fur lined flying boots, later found that their chance of a successful evasion was greatly improved if they wore ordinary boots or shoes. Apart from the ease of walking in normal footwear, many flying boots of those who baled out came off in the bale out. At a later period the RAF did issue flying boots whose tops could easily be cut off leaving a laced up walking black shoe.

On about April 15th, Lambert was seen by a man who turned out to be a Russian tending some cows in a field. The man approached and after Lambert had identified himself the Russian brought him some bread, meat and a bottle of milk. This was the first real food that Lambert had eaten since baling out. He had sustained himself until then on the contents of his escape kit. From the Russian he found that the town which lay ahead was Sedan. Now with a better picture of his position, Lambert hid for the rest of the day before walking that evening south-eastwards towards Switzerland.

Crossing the River Meuse by a bridge, which fortunately was not guarded, he headed towards Stenay. On the way he tried to make contact with single people he met in open fields, but on each occasion he found no one prepared to help. At Stenay on about 17th April, Lambert turned off just before crossing a railway at Laneuville and approached a farmhouse. The farmer was friendly and gave him food and shelter for the night. After telling the farmer of his intentions of getting to Switzerland,

Lambert was advised not to travel through Verdun, but to take the train at Montmedy. Following this advice, the next morning he walked to Montmedy and caught a train to Nancy, using the money from his escape kit, to purchase the ticket. On arrival at Nancy he discovered that there was no train to Belfort, a town nearer to Switzerland, until the next morning, so he had no option but to walk out of Nancy to spend the night in some woods on the outskirts. The following morning, 18th April, he caught a train from Nancy to Belfort, his luck was in, for although Lambert had no identity card, there were no control checks on the train that morning.

At Belfort he walked out from the town to wait on a hillside until late afternoon, before again starting to walk south east to the Swiss frontier in the direction of Delle. Just before Froidefontaine it was necessary to cross a bridge which was guarded by two French civilians who were armed wth rifles. Lambert tried to avoid them, but was seen and he tried to bluff his way out by pretending that he was a Polish worker, his ruse failed and he had to finally admit his identity. The older man wanted to let Lambert go and have nothing to do with him, but the younger one wanted to help and took him to a nearby field, returning later to take Lambert to his home on the outskirts of the town, where he spent the night and the next day. He was given food and more important by very detailed instructions about the remainder of the journey and how to cross the Swiss frontier.

Wearing an old coat and beret that he had also been given, Lambert set out on April 20th after being finally warned that the frontier was well guarded. Proceeding very cautiously after going through Delle, he crossed the frontier with no problems, the only indication that he had done so, were the milestones in the woods on the Swiss side, with what appeared in the moonlight, to have blue crosses on the them. When he was certain that he was well inside the frontier, Lambert let himself be arrested by a Swiss frontier guard on the Delle - Porrentruy road. He was then taken by guard to the police station at Boncourt before being escorted the next morning to Porrentruy. Here he asked to see the British Consul, telling the Swiss the false story that he had been captured by the Germans and escaped in transit in the hope that this would improve his chances for an early return to England. He was told that it would take about a week to make contact with the British, especially as it was the Easter holidays. On April 27th he was taken along with several Russians to Berne, where he was handed over to the Assistant Military Attache. From that time Lambert was free and he returned to the UK on January 8th, 1944, in company of another evader a Canadian J/15177 Squadron Leader F. V. Taylor, a Wellington pilot from 420 Squadron who was shot down on the Stuttgart raid of April 14th, 1943. From Lambert's crew, only two others survived, the bomb aimer 1334366 Sergeant J. R. Jones and wireless operator 1377258 Sergeant R. A. Kempsell, both of whom were made prisoners.

Casualties April 10th/11th, 1943. Target Frankfurt

35 Squadron 8 Group Halifax DT806 TL/Z
Pilot. 63419 F/Lt G.F.Lambert Evaded capture
Nav. 122220 F/O V.R.Mathews Killed Fleigneux, France. CG
B/A. 1334366 W/O J.R.Jones PoW. Stalag Luft 6, Heydekrug. 1012
W/OP. 1377258 F/Sgt R.A.Kempsell PoW. Stalag Luft 6, Heydekrug. 1013
F/E. 904734 Sgt A.Beddoe Killed Fleigneux, France. CG
A/G. 1397903 Sgt R.A.Nason Killed Fleigneux, France. CG
A/G. 1311941 Sgt S.J.Knight Killed Fleigneux, France. CG

7 Squadron 8 Group Stirling R9275 MG/Y
Shot down at Koerich, Grand Duchy of Luxembourg
Pilot. 139509 P/O F.A.Terry Killed Hollerton, Luxembourg. CG 12/17
Nav. J/6659 F/O P.G.Freburg DFC Killed Hollerton, Luxembourg. CG 12/17
B/A. R/90501 W/O H.E.Nesbitt Killed Hollerton, Luxembourg. CG 12/17
W/OP. 143402 P/O T.J.Ryder Killed Hollerton, Luxembourg. CG 12/17
F/E. 51687 P/O R.H.Genesis DFM Killed Hollerton, Luxembourg. CG 12/17
A/G. J/92604 P/O E.A.Allen Killed Hollerton, Luxembourg. CG 12/17
A/G. 1389145 F/Sgt F.N.Barley Killed Hollerton, Luxembourg. CG 12/17

7 Squadron 8 Group Stirling BK760 MG/X
Crashed south of Tongerloo, Belgium at 03.45 hours (11/4/43). Victim of Major Walter Ehle, II/NJG1.
Pilot. 26198 S/Ldr H.W.A.Chesterman AFC Killed Heverlee, Belgium. 8-G-4
Nav. 1387099 Sgt S.J.Moore Evaded capture
B/A. 1378392 Sgt E.Tolson Killed Heverlee, Belgium. 8-G-1
W/OP. 1313959 Sgt L.Ellis Killed Heverlee, Belgium. 8-G-5
F/E. 1021760 Sgt D.Ferguson Evaded capture
A/G. 1396272 Sgt B.S.G.Bugg Killed Heverlee, Belgium. 8-G-3
A/G. 1235122 Sgt W.Moore Killed Heverlee, Belgium. 8-G-2

100 Squadron 1 Group Lancaster ED760 HW/L
Aircraft crashed near Kleve, Germany.
Pilot. NZ/416151 Sgt F.A.Partridge Killed Rheinberg, Germany. 8-H-24
Nav. 1410281 Sgt N.F.Hallett Killed Rheinberg, Germany. JG 8-H-22/23
B/A. 1504180 Sgt J.D.Law Killed Rheinberg, Germany. JG 8-H-22/23
W/OP. 1124468 Sgt W.H.Hargreaves Killed Rheinberg, Germany. 8-H-17
F/E. 1101161 Sgt P.Plowright Killed Rheinberg, Germany. 8-H-18
A/G. R/92475 F/Sgt W.Bodley Killed Rheinberg, Germany. 8-H-19
A/G. R/60321 F/Sgt C.F.Rimmer Killed Rheinberg, Germany. 8-H-20

166 Squadron 1 Group Wellington BK749 AS/F
Aircraft crashed 7 miles NW of Laon, France.
Pilot. 119783 F/O J.M.Everill Killed Couvron-et-Aumencourt. CG A-9/11
Nav. 129352 F/O F.D.Clarke Killed Couvron-et-Aumencourt. CG A-9/11
B/A. 131965 P/O R.Brown. Killed Couvron-et-Aumencourt, France., CG A-9/11
W/OP. 919478 Sgt J.R.Gordon Killed Couvron-et-Aumencourt, France. A-8
A/G. R/122409 F/Sgt T.E.Richardson Killed Couvron-et-Aumencourt. A-7

166 Squadron 1 Group Wellington BK464 AS/N
Pilot. 1312003 Sgt P.R.Hall Missing, Runnymede Memorial 152
Nav. 966317 Sgt T.L.Edwards Missing, Runnymede Memorial 148
B/A. 1435429 Sgt H.Elliott Missing, Runnymede Memorial 148
W/OP. 631242 F/Sgt R.L.Castellari Missing, Runnymede Memorial 135
A/G. 1295569 Sgt E.J.Peacock Killed St.Marie, Le Havre, France. 67-F-6

166 Squadron 1 Group Wellington X3334 AS/W
Pilot. 142864 P/O A.Urquhart Killed Durnbach, Germany. 7-H-1
Nav. 656290 Sgt W.Kinniburgh Killed Durnbach, Germany. 7-H-2
B/A. 1237135 Sgt H.E.Williams Killed Durnbach, Germany. JG 7-H-4/5
W/OP. 1379731 Sgt R.G.Edwards Killed Durnbach, Germany. JG 7-H-4/5
A/G. R/99543 Sgt M.R.Dixon Killed Durnbach, Germany. 7-H-3

15 Squadron 3 Group Stirling BF475 LS/T
Crashed at Montcornet, France
Pilot. 1316038 Sgt E.J.Trezise Killed Mountcornet, France. GG-11
Nav. 1389462 Sgt T.J.Letbe Killed Mountcornet, France. GG-9
B/A. 126826 F/O P.S.McCaughey Killed Mountcornet, France. GG-8
W/OP. 1271406 Sgt J.Harrison Killed Mountcornet, France. GG-6
F/E. 1004605 Sgt A.Loudon Killed Mountcornet, France. GG-10
A/G. 1389244 Sgt F.R.Burton Killed Mountcornet, France. GG-12
A/G. 1411732 Sgt H.Wakefield Killed Mountcornet, France. GG-7

75 Squadron 3 Group Stirling BF456 AA/J
Crashed near Kleve, Germany.
Pilot. 657412 Sgt J.Webb Killed Rheinberg, Germany. CG 18-E-3/7
Nav. 1337506 Sgt D.V.Jones Killed Rheinberg, Germany. CG 18-E-3/7
B/A. 1315996 Sgt D.T.Anthony Killed Rheinberg, Germany. CG 18-E-3/7
W/OP. 1380534 Sgt R.W.Lowther Killed Rheinberg, Germany. 18-E-1
F/E. 979322 Sgt J.R.Inglis Killed Rheinberg, Germany. 18-E-2
A/G. 643601 Sgt L.R.Cunningham Killed Rheinberg, Germany. CG 18-E-3/7
A/G. 1315524 Sgt E.J.Letherbarrow Killed Rheinberg, Germany. CG 18-E-3/7

75 Squadron 3 Group Stirling BF455 AA/Y
Ditched 3 miles off Shoreham, Sussex. Hit by *Flak* over target and running out of petrol.
Pilot. F/Sgt C.Rothschild Rescued
Nav. Sgt G.Samson Rescued
B/A. Sgt J.Richards Rescued
W/OP. R/91742 Sgt R.E.Tod Rescued
F/E. 625045 Sgt E.Grainger Rescued
A/G. NZ/413274 Sgt H.E.Moss Rescued
A/G. Sgt W.A.Hardy Rescued
A/G. R/91741 Sgt E.R.Todd Rescued

115 Squadron 3 Group Lancaster DS604 KO/B
Crashed near Rheims, France
Pilot. 1312656 Sgt A.B.Thomas Killed Le Thour, Rethel, France. 8
Nav. 1389001 Sgt V.R.Wilson Killed Le Thour, Rethel, France. JG 4/5
B/A. 1335131 Sgt D.S.Andrew Killed Le Thour, Rethel, France. JG 4/5
W/OP. R/84121 W/O C.M.Smith Killed Le Thour, Rethel, France. 2
F/E. R/70699 Sgt M.A.Lambert Killed Le Thour, Rethel, France. 1
A/G. 1332433 Sgt L.C.Fitt Killed Le Thour, Rethel, France. 3
A/G. 1393093 Sgt E.V.Hudson Killed Le Thour, Rethel, France. 6

76 Squadron 4 Group Halifax JB871 MP/V
Crashed at Hirson, France
Pilot. 83244 F/Lt A.H.Hull Killed Bergen, Holland. 4
2/Pilot. 24002 G/Cpt J.R.Whitley DSO Evaded capture
Nav. 143985 Sgt W.J.Painter Killed Bergen, Holland. 2
B/A. 1072959 Sgt M.A.J.Davies Evaded capture
W/OP. 144715 Sgt G.A.Bozier Killed Bergen, Holland. 1
F/E. 1071615 Sgt M.B.Strange DFM Evaded capture
A/G. 1322010 Sgt P.E.Matthews Killed Bergen, Holland. 3
A/G. 125991 P/O J.A.A.M.David Evaded capture

78 Squadron 4 Group Halifax DT775 EY/
Pilot. 1330122 W/O H.J.Adams PoW. Stalag 357, Kopernikus. 1229
Nav. 127316 F/Lt P.Hyden PoW. Stalag Luft 3, Sagan. 1346
B/A. 924025 W/O S.V.F.Hurrell PoW. Stalag 357, Kopernikus. 1007
W/OP. 1330737 F/Sgt C.J.Price PoW. Stalag 357, Kopernikus. 1028
F/E. 615894 F/Sgt M.Clarke PoW. Stalag 357, Kopernikus. 985
A/G. 1336707 F/Sgt S.G.Reed PoW. Stalag 357, Kopernikus. 1030
A/G. 988200 Sgt J.N.Enright Killed Briey, France. 1

431 Squadron 4 Group Wellington HE213 SE/F
Crashed off Guernsey. Last fix given from Southampton, Position 4956N 0159W
Pilot. 657234 W/O W.E.Bidmead PoW. Stalag Luft 6, Heydekrug. 978
Nav. 591390 Sgt A.Holden Killed St Helier, Jersey, Channel Is. 2
B/A. 657064 W/O E.A.Odling PoW. Stalag 357, Kopernikus. 1024
W/OP. 1380047 F/Sgt L.C.Bolke PoW. Stalag 357, Kopernikus. 42727
A/G. R/135580 F/Sgt G.A.Booth Missing, Runnymede Memorial 181

466 Squadron 4 Group Wellington HE506 HD/
Pilot. 141711 P/O F.E.Booy Missing, Runnymede Memorial 130
Nav. 1385897 Sgt D.F.Gage Missing, Runnymede Memorial 150
B/A. 1023525 Sgt G.Myers Missing, Runnymede Memorial 160
W/OP. 553822 Sgt D.W.Williams Missing, Runnymede Memorial 170
A/G. NZ/41993 Sgt J.G.Morgan Missing, Runnymede Memorial 199

9 Squadron 5 Group Lancaster ED501 WS/
Crashed near Rhein, Germany
Pilot. 36042 W/Cdr K.B.Smith DSO Killed Rheinberg, Germany. 8-A-6
2/Pilot. 1387857 Sgt A.G.Stone Killed Rheinberg, Germany. 8-A-9
Nav. 125631 F/O A.J.Turner Killed Rheinberg, Germany. 8-A-11
B/A. NZ/413997 F/O D.J.Smith PoW. Stalag Luft 3, Sagan. 1629
W/OP. NZ/413283 Sgt G.A.Taylor Missing, Runnymede Memorial 200
F/E. 1111480 Sgt W.Thompson Killed Rheinberg, Germany. 8-A-7
A/G. 51285 P/O R.V.C.Pleasance Killed Rheinberg, Germany. 8-A-12
A/G. 122746 F/O B.Smith Killed Rheinberg, Germany. 8-A-10

50 Squadron 5 Group Lancaster ED478 VN/
Crossed English coast at 03.10 hours, asked permission to land after jettisoning bomb load. Nothing further heard.
Pilot. R/108260 W/O F.G.McGrath Missing, Runnymede Memorial 180
Nav. 620764 Sgt R.F.Wilson Missing, Runnymede Memorial 170
B/A. 1212998 Sgt R.Coulson Missing, Runnymede Memorial 146
W/OP. 134030 F/O A.Cheetham Missing, Runnymede Memorial 123
F/E. 925934 F/Sgt P.L.Mansfield Missing, Runnymede Memorial 138
A/G. 1338726 Sgt A.H.Jeffery Missing, Runnymede Memorial 155
A/G. 955619 Sgt C.Birtles Missing, Runnymede Memorial 142

57 Squadron 5 Group Lancaster ED766 DX/
Pilot. R/85651 W/O J.H.Lemon Killed Durnbach, Germany. 9-J-5
Nav. R/82280 W/O L.J.Lalonde Killed Durnbach, Germany. 9-J-3
B/A. R/86847 W/O G.R.Holm Killed Durnbach, Germany. 9-J-4
W/OP. R/80654 W/O R.G.Griffin Killed Durnbach, Germany. 9-J-2
F/E. 911475 Sgt H.J.Coombes Killed Durnbach, Germany. 9-J-1
A/G. 1124720 Sgt R.H.Roberts Killed Durnbach, Germany. 9-J-6
A/G. J/17314 P/O D.O.McMahon Killed Durnbach, Germany. 9-J-7

426 Squadron 6 Group Wellington HE652 KW/
Shot down at Virelles, Belgium at 03.30 hours. Victim of GruppenKommandeur Wilhelm Herget, I/NJG4.
Pilot. J/16941 P/O J.H.Sammett Killed Florennes, Belgium. 2-16
Nav. J/19730 P/O J.Hehir Killed Florennes, Belgium. CG 2-17/20
B/A. 1487005 Sgt D.A.W.Weller Killed Florennes, Belgium. CG 2-17/20
W/OP. 1077553 Sgt G.Leving Killed Florennes, Belgium. CG 2-17/20
A/G. J/17497 P/O J.G.Budreau Killed Florennes, Belgium. CG 2-17/20

429 Squadron 6 Group Wellington HE636 AL/
Pilot. 908611 W/O D.W.Jeffries Killed Rheinberg, Germany. 8-K-11
Nav. 127847 F/O L.S.Knott Killed Rheinberg, Germany. CG 8-K-12/17
B/A. 970018 W/O S.N.Beckett Killed Rheinberg, Germany. CG 8-K-12/17
W/OP. 946288 F/Sgt A.G.Lewis Killed Rheinberg, Germany. CG 8-K-12/17
A/G. 1377502 F/Sgt K.D.Franklin Killed Rheinberg, Germany. 8-G-18

420 Squadron 6 Group Wellington HE422 PT/
Aircraft crashed into sea at Monkstone Point, S.Wales on return flight from operations to Frankfurt due to fuel shortage. Crew baled out near Tenby, South Wales.(5140N 0440W)
Pilot. J/20125 F/O C.W.Jackson Killed St Mary's, Carew, S.Wales B-6
Nav. R/130655 Sgt H.B.Elhorn Baled out.
B/A. R/124964 Sgt A.M.Macdonald Baled out.
W/OP. 1342646 Sgt J.T.Kydd Baled out.
A/G. R/73769 Sgt K.T.P.Allan Baled out.

424 Squadron 6 Group Wellington HE159 QB/P
Crashed at Hastings at 00.58 hours (11/4/43) on outward flight from operation to Frankfurt
Pilot. R/103915 W/O R.M.Buie Killed Maidstone. CC1-84
Nav. 130160 P/O R.W.Thompson Killed Castle Bromwich. No Grave No.
B/A. J/19427 P/O L.K.Taylor Killed Maidstone. CC1-106
W/OP. R/82402 F/Sgt A.W.Kimmerley Killed Maidstone. CC1-61
A/G. R/103647 Sgt A.G.Lees Baled out.

Minelaying

April 10th/11th, 1943
Seven Stirlings from 3 Group also went minelaying to the Frisians on the same night, laying 42 mines without suffering any loss.

Minelaying

April 11th/12th, 1943
Three areas, Brittany, Biscay and Texel were visited by a mixed force of 46 aircraft on minelaying missions on the night of April 11th/12th, a total of 130 mines being laid. Three aircraft returned early without dropping any mines and two aircraft a Stirling and Wellington were lost on these operations. From their aircrew, two are buried in France and one in Denmark, while the remaining nine men were never found.

Casualties April 11th/12th, 1943. Minelaying

214 Squadron 3 Group Stirling BK612 BU/Z
Pilot. 1005717 W/O G.A.Davie Missing, Runnymede Memorial 134
Nav. 1330321 Sgt J.B.Woods Killed Royan, France. K-3-1
B/A. 975343 Sgt D.O.Dawson Missing, Runnymede Memorial 148
W/OP. 638850 F/Sgt L.Copley Killed Royan, France. K-3-2
F/E. 943745 Sgt A.C.Wade Missing, Runnymede Memorial 168
A/G. 951197 Sgt T.F.Richardson Missing, Runnymede Memorial 163
A/G. 1452264 F/Sgt A.Bowers Missing, Runnymede Memorial 35

425 Squadron 6 Group Wellington HE491 KW/U
Pilot. R/124106 F/Sgt E.R.Carvajal Missing, Runnymede Memorial 181
Nav. J/13369 F/O G.W.Elliott Missing, Runnymede Memorial 173
B/A. 1313763 Sgt B.W.A.Perry Missing, Runnymede Memorial 161
W/OP. J/22496 F/O R.J.Howard Missing, Runnymede Memorial 173
A/G. J/13838 F/O E.Kitt Killed Esbjerg (Fourfelt), Denmark. AIII-7-17

La Spezia

April 13th/14th, 1943

La Spezia in Italy was the next target for a force of 208
Lancasters and 3 Halifaxes on the night of April 13th/14th. The
weather was good over the target area and the visibility such
that the bomb aimers were able to visually identify the dock
area, which was the aiming point. 369.2 tons of high explosive
and 92.1 tons of incendiary bombs were dropped and they
caused heavy damage in the dock area of the city. Four aircraft
were lost and others which were damaged made the crossing of
the Mediterranean to the recently captured airstrips in North
Africa rather than risk, in their damaged state, the dangerous
return crossing over the Alps. One Lancaster of 61 Squadron
which made the return flight did not make it safely back to base,
for the pilot, Flying Officer Chivers, and his crew had to ditch in
the Atlantic south west of the Scillies, spending 63 hours in
their dinghy before being found and rescued by an RAF High
Speed Rescue Launch. Another Lancaster also made a ditching
on its return from La Spezia. It was from 103 Squadron and
came down 20 miles south of Plymouth. Fortunately all the crew
were rescued by the ever vigilant Air Sea Rescue services who
were always on alert when Bomber Command aircraft were
returning from their operations.

Casualties April 13th/14th, 1943. Target La Spezia

12 Squadron 1 Group Lancaster ED714 PH/
Pilot. 1385841 Sgt W.E.F.Clark Killed Le Mans (West), France. CG 21-B-12
Nav. J/21817 F/O E.F.Dynarski Killed Le Mans (West), France. 21-B-15
B/A. 1455851 Sgt J.L.A.Mulligan Killed Le Mans (West), France. 21-B-11
W/OP. 1379629 Sgt C.N.Clay Killed Le Mans (West), France. CG 21-B-12
F/E. 814160 Sgt F.G.Sayers Killed Le Mans (West), France. 21-B-7
A/G. R/103626 F/Sgt E.A.Applegate Killed Le Mans (West), France. 21-B-8
A/G. R/141597 F/Sgt E.H.Bakeman Killed Le Mans (West), France. 21-B-10

103 Squadron 1 Group Lancaster W4318 PM/
Aircraft hit by *Flak* and lost fuel.Ditched 50 miles off Falmouth. Crew in
dinghy for 4 hours. Aircraft floated for 30 hours. Attempts were made to tow it
to port, but aircraft broke up and sank.
Pilot. 1336851 Sgt J.S.Stoneman Rescued.
Nav. 129359 F/O D.C.Elder Rescued.
B/A. 131166 P/O C.E.T.Bryan Rescued.
W/OP. 970979 F/Sgt J.Flynn Rescued.
F/E. 1095183 Sgt T.Stanley Rescued.
A/G. Sgt S.Dixon Rescued.
A/G. F/Sgt J.H.McMahon Rescued.

103 Squadron 1 Group Lancaster W4828 PM/
Pilot. 125695 F/Lt E.C.Lee-Brown Killed Le Mans (West), France. CG 21-B-12
Nav. 144753 P/O J.Smart Killed Le Mans (West), France. 21-B-13
B/A. R/74721 W/O J.W.Toon Killed Le Mans (West), France. 21-B-16
W/OP. 551549 F/Sgt J.J.O'Brien DFM Killed Le Mans (West). CG 21-B-12
F/E. 974219 Sgt G.W.Houliston Killed Le Mans (West), France. 21-B-9
A/G. 1351789 Sgt S.Moseley Killed Le Mans (West), France. CG 21-B-12
A/G. 657170 Sgt A.M.Munn Killed Le Mans (West), France. 21-B-143

61 Squadron 5 Group Lancaster ED717 QR/
Aircraft ditched at 07.45 hours SW of Bishop's Rock. Sighted by crew of
Whitley bomber 63 hours after ditching. Picked by Air Sea Rescue boat.
Pilot. 124436 F/O M.E.Chivers Rescued.
Nav. 1434394 Sgt V.A.Rimmer Rescued.
B/A. 1339048 Sgt M.James Rescued.
W/OP. 1293499 Sgt D.C.Shea Rescued.
F/E. 571568 Sgt E.A.Vale Rescued.
A/G. 618899 Sgt S.A.White Rescued.
A/G. 1316567 Sgt E.G.Smith Rescued.

Mosquito Nuisance Raids

April 13th/14th, 1943

Also on this same night six Mosquito aircraft of 105 Squadron in 2 Group, which to date was still attached to Bomber Command, started the series of their nuisance raids to many German cities and towns. This was the forerunner of the Light Night Striking Force of Mosquito aircraft which caused such harassment to the German defences for the remaining period of the war. Three towns were bombed, Bremen, Hamburg and Wilhelmshaven, 1.8 tons of bombs being dropped on each place. Not a heavy tonnage, but enough to keep the Germans guessing if it was the beginning of a major raid.

Minelaying

Ten Lancasters also went to the Frisians, two returned early but the remainder laid 32 mines, without suffering any loss.

Stuttgart

April 14th/15th, 1943

Stuttgart was again on the target sheet for 462 aircraft - 146 Wellingtons, 135 Halifaxes, 98 Lancasters and 83 Stirlings. 74 of the despatched aircraft aborted and returned early, a very high rate of 16% of early returners. Although many of the crews had returned with good reasons such as engine failure or trouble with essential equipment, Bomber Command headquarters had a growing concern for some of the reasons given by captains for their early return and inability to complete their mission. Listed were such reasons as crew member sick, navigation error made it so that aircraft would be too late to arrive over the target, petrol flap on wing left unlocked and wireless operator forgot his helmet. Weather conditions for the raid were very good, there being no cloud, bright moonlight and excellent visibility for the Pathfinders to mark their aiming point. Stuttgart's Bad Cansatt, the main industrial area, was reputed to be a difficult target to mark accurately and again this proved to be the case. The

Pathfinder heavies although claiming to have dropped their 126 target indicators and 316 flares marking the centre accurately, in fact did not do so. The main area where the 328.6 tons of high explosive and 416.2 tons of incendiary bombs were dropped by the main force was on the bomber's approach run, which was from the north-east. It could be argued that this might have been caused by the creep back which sometimes occurred as a raid progressed. In this case the creepback fell in an industrial suburb, where some considerable damage was caused. German records show that only a few bombs fell in the centre of the city, but one which did, made a direct hit on an air raid shelter packed with French and Russian prisoners of war, 400 of whom were killed as a result. Bomber Command's loss on this raid was 23 aircraft, a 5% loss rate. Many crews who returned had great difficulty in landing at their bases, because the fog although forecast had thickened considerably and was earlier than expected. From the missing aircraft 96 aircrew were killed, 41 were made prisoners and the high number of 12 managed to evade capture.

The Naval Bomb Aimer

On Lancaster ED752 ZN/H from 106 Squadron, captained by Flight Lieutenant L. C. J. Brodrick which was lost on this raid, was an unusual bomb aimer, a Royal Naval Lieutenant. He was one of three naval officers who had been temporarily attached to 106 Squadron in mid December, 1942. Their attachment had caused much speculation amongst the aircrew on the station as to the likelihood of the squadron being used on a mission to attack capital German warships. The three Lieutenants were G. Muttrie, P. M. McGrath and D. Lee DSO (an award he was given for his rôle in a torpedo bombing attack by 825 Fleet Air Arm Squadron on the German warship *Gneisenau*, from which there were only five survivors). During the earlier part of their stay, the three Naval officers joined in squadron life except for taking part in operations. After the flap of December 1942, when there was a stand to for bombing the German Fleet, there were no further developments about any impending operations and the naval officers eventually obtained permission from the

Admiralty to fly as bomb aimers on air operations. Two of them, McGrath and Muttrie, lost their lives, McGrath on the Nuremburg raid of 25th/26th February, 1943 and Muttrie on this Stuttgart raid.

It was on the return flight from the Stuttgart raid that Flight Lieutenant Les Brodrick's Lancaster got into trouble. The aircraft had been hit over the target which resulted in it losing considerable altitude. Flying at about 100 feet over Amiens the bomber was raked with ground machine gun fire and was set on fire. With no height for a bale out, Brodrick crash landed near Amiens at 03.30 hours. In the crash, five of the crew, including the Royal Naval Officer Muttrie and second pilot Squadron Leader Latimer DFC were killed. The navigator, Flying Officer Burns, was very badly injured and one gunner Sergeant H. Jones and the pilot were slightly injured.

After scrambling from the wreckage the pilot and gunner realised that any chance of evasion was very slim as urgent medical help was required for their navigator. Both airmen went to a nearby farmhouse to ask for help. A message was sent from the farm and soon a party of German soldiers arrived on the scene and arrested both airmen. Sergeant Jones was asked to indentify the bodies of his comrades before the three survivors were taken by ambulance to the nearby aerodrome, from where Flying Officer Burns was taken to hospital. Jones and Brodrick were taken to Dulag Luft and then on to prisoner of war camps, Jones to Stalag Luft I at Barth Vogelsang and Brodrick to Stalag Luft III at Sagan.

During his stay at Sagan, Brodrick escaped through the tunnel known as Harry in the north compound of the camp on March 24th, 1944. He was the 52nd of the escapers to leave the tunnel, dressed in his own battle dress over which he wore an airman's greatcoat, the buttons of which had been covered with dark cloth. With false indentity papers and some survival rations he joined up with a party of ten other airmen led by a Canadian Flight Lieutenant Birkland in a nearby wood as soon as he had scrambled out of the tunnel. The party walked together for about 2 kilometres before splitting up into smaller groups. Flight Lieutenants Birkland and Brodrick staying together.

They continued walking this time in a southerly direction resting up in the woods the next day. Before dark they set off once more but by now they were very wet from the heavy rain which been falling steadily all the time. Just before dawn on the 27th, the three were soaking wet and suffering terribly from the bitter cold. They realised that their chances of getting any further away were now practically nil and decided to give themselves up. They approached a small cottage, probably near Kalkbrugh and discovered that it was occupied by four German soldiers who were out on a search party looking for the many escaped prisoners. They were quickly arrested and taken to the local police station before being transferred to the Civil Prison at Gorlitz for interrogation. They all managed to get rid of their false papers by burning them in a fire at the police station on the pretence of getting warm.

From Gorlitz it was back to Sagan to serve 21 days of solitary confinement for their brief taste of freedom, which they considered well worth the effort because of the disruption and chaos that the escapes had caused the Germans. Brodrick was finally liberated at Lubeck on May 2nd 1945.

420 Squadron Wellington Lost

A Wellington, HE683 from 420 Squadron captained by Squadron Leader F. V. Taylor, was one of the aircraft which failed to return to its base. It was attacked on its return flight by an enemy night fighter near St Quentin and it quickly caught fire. One of the first who baled out was Flying Officer G. C. Crowther who was extremely lucky to be helped by the underground in evading capture. On landing he broke his ankle, but managed to crawl away from the aircraft crash site, and hide his 'chute and Mae West. After a brief rest, in spite of his injury, he carried on hobbling for another three quarters of an hour, until he came to a dense wood where he hid and slept. Awakened by the sound of someone else moving about in the wood, he found that it was Sergeant H. N. McKinnon, the wireless operator on his plane. After spending the rest of the day in hiding and sharing McKinnon's escape pack, for he had lost his own on the bale out, it was decided that McKinnon should carry on alone, because by now Crowther's ankle had swollen quite badly. Left on his own, later that day at about 22.00 hours, McKinnon managed to hobble along for another two hours, by which time he guessed that he was somewhere south of St Quentin. After unsuccessfully trying to get any help from several people in a nearby village and as he could walk no further he hid up in a barn, where some gypsies, who were passing, gave him some food. Later some French people came along and took him to a house in Mezieres where they tried to treat his ankle, they also supplied him with food and gave him a complete outfit of civilian clothes and 500 francs. He stayed there until the 19th April, when another man came along and took him to yet another house at Urvillers, from where the rest of his journey was taken care of by the underground and he finally arrived in Gibraltar on 1st June, 1943. Without the help of the underground he would have never made it on his own. Sergeant McKinnon was not so lucky for he was captured and made a prisoner of war. The pilot, J/15177 Squadron Leader F. V. Taylor made it to freedom through Switzerland.

Casualties April 14th/15th, 1943. Target Stuttgart

35 Squadron 8 Group Halifax HR678 TL/N
Pilot , W/OP and R/G killed in fighter attack.
Pilot. 141103 P/O R.E.Wilkes DFM Killed Rheinberg, Germany. CG 8-C-12/15
Nav. 1262920 W/O T.G.O'Shaughnessy PoW. Stalag 357, Kopernikus. 115
B/A. A/412053 F/O R.Wheatley Killed Rheinberg, Germany. CG 8-C-12/15
W/OP. 1174030 W/O F.W.Vincent PoW. Stalag 357, Kopernikus. 1045
F/E. 570690 W/O T.L.Brown PoW. Stalag 357, Kopernikus. 983
A/G. 1002505 F/Sgt F.Hay Killed Rheinberg, Germany. CG 8-C-12/15
A/G. A/411478 F/Sgt M.A.E.Bradford Killed Rheinberg, Germany. CG 8-C-12/15

7 Squadron 8 Group Stirling R9278 MG/E
Aircraft crashed at Reims, France after night fighter attack.
Pilot. 143232 F/O J.T.R.Taylor DFC PoW. Stalag Luft 3, Sagan. 2543
Nav. 109920 F/Lt R.H.Lunney PoW. Stalag Luft 3, Sagan. 1449
B/A. 1348526 W/O D.Ness PoW. Stalag 357, Kopernikus. 1156
W/OP. 940254 W/O T.Morley PoW. Stalag 4B, Muhlberg(Elbe). 226448
F/E. 1150890 F/Sgt A.H.Smith PoW. Stalag 4B, Muhlberg(Elbe). 83695
A/G. 914890 Sgt F.G.A.Weight Evaded capture.
A/G. R/82650 F/Sgt D.K.Nolan Evaded capture.

7 Squadron 8 Group Stirling BK709 MG/P
Aircraft crashed at Biblis, Germany.
Pilot. J/16626 P/O M.Mank Killed Durnbach, Germany. 1-C-23
Nav. R/85483 W/O H.E.Budd Killed Durnbach, Germany. 1-C-22
B/A. R/56194 W/O J.R.Roy Killed Durnbach, Germany. 1-C-24
W/OP. R/66305 Sgt H.D.Oke Killed Durnbach, Germany. 1-C-27
F/E. 1112914 Sgt A.Walker Killed Durnbach, Germany. 1-C-25
A/G. 1230170 Sgt R.R.Fox Killed Durnbach, Germany. 1-C-26
A/G. 1393810 Sgt P.Wadding Killed Durnbach, Germany. 1-C-28

7 Squadron 8 Group Stirling BK769 MG/G
Aircraft crashed at Lembach, Germany.
Pilot. 40239 S/Ldr R.W.McCarthy Killed Durnbach, Germany. 5-E-9
Nav. J/17453 P/O A.L.Foster Killed Durnbach, Germany. 9-D-21
B/A. 1337496 Sgt R.V.Jennings Killed Durnbach, Germany. 9-D-20
W/OP. R/92543 W/O L.Bartman Killed Durnbach, Germany. 9-D-22
F/E. 568514 Sgt G.Wade Killed Durnbach, Germany. CG 9-D-23/24
A/G. 1377951 Sgt L.F.Harris Killed Durnbach, Germany. CG 9-D-23/24
A/G. 1336022 F/Sgt F.J.Britton Killed Durnbach, Germany. CG 9-D-23/24

100 Squadron 1 Group Lancaster ED653 HW/E
Pilot. 66495 F/Lt R.J.Shufflebotham Killed Bohain, France. Coll Grave
Nav. 130237 F/O A.F.Towers Killed Bohain, France. Coll Grave
B/A. 129921 F/O S.H.West Killed Bohain, France. Coll Grave
W/OP. 1202182 Sgt J.H.Nunn Killed Bohain, France. Coll Grave
F/E. 546505 Sgt G.P.Tyrer Killed Bohain, France. Coll Grave
A/G. 913763 Sgt P.H.R.Hunt Killed Bohain, France. Coll Grave
A/G. 1585869 Sgt G.E.Pascoe Killed Bohain, France. Coll Grave

101 Squadron 1 Group Lancaster W4951 SR/O
Pilot. 1043580 Sgt R.G.Hamilton Killed Maubeuge (Centre), France. A-16
Nav. 127970 F/O H.E.Clements Killed Maubeuge (Centre), France. A-20
B/A. 1391065 Sgt A.Ottolangui Killed Mausbeuge (Centre), France. JG A-17
W/OP. 1129644 Sgt J.L.Cartmell Killed Maubeuge (Centre), France. A-19
F/E. 1149392 Sgt F.Wood Killed Maubeuge (Centre), France. JG A-17
A/G. 1601428 Sgt G.W.H.Northover Killed Maubeuge (Centre), France. A-18
A/G. 1307587 Sgt P.D.Steed Killed Maubeuge (Centre), France. A-21

75 Squadron 3 Group Stirling BF513 AA/E
Shot down at Regniessart near Couvin, Belgium and exploded in mid air.
Pilot. NZ/13573 P/O D.G.McCaskill Killed Florennes, Belgium. 2-27
Nav. NZ/42295 P/O J.K.Grainger Killed Florennes, Belgium. CG 2-22/26
B/A. 519416 Sgt B.Elwell Killed Florennes, Belgium. CG 2-22/26
W/OP. 1211032 Sgt T.C.Green Killed Florennes, Belgium. CG 2-22/26
F/E. 1371651 Sgt A.McVicar Killed Florennes, Belgium. CG 2-22/26
A/G. 1609864 Sgt E.D.Cook Killed Florennes, Belgium. CG 2-22/26
A/G. NZ/415378 Sgt R.A.Smith Killed Florennes, Belgium. CG 2-22/26

90 Squadron 3 Group Stirling BF462 WP/P
Aircraft crashed at Soude-Notre Dame, France.
Pilot. 139276 F/Lt R.J.Beldin PoW. Stalag Luft 3, Sagan. 1095
Nav. 1232268 Sgt E.A.Shaw Killed Soude-Notre Dame-ou-le-Petit, France. 6
B/A. 1230761 Sgt R.J.Palmer Killed Soude-Notre Dame-ou-le-Petit, France. 1
W/OP. R/9529 W/O R.B.Blake Killed Soude-Notre Dame-ou-le-Petit, France. 2
F/E. 977618 Sgt H.Noar Killed Soude-Notre Dame-ou-le-Petit, France. 4
A/G. 1384731 Sgt S.F.Gould Killed Soude-Notre Dame-ou-le-Petit, France. 5
A/G. 1031693 Sgt S.Hammond Killed Soude-Notre Dame-ou-le-Petit, France. 3

149 Squadron 3 Group Stirling BF500 OJ/M
Aircraft crashed at Tounes, France.
Pilot. J/16896 P/O D.B.White Killed Belval, Mezieres, France. CG 1
Nav. J/10684 F/O L.G.Vallance Killed Belval, Mezieres, France. CG 1
B/A. R/121566 F/Sgt T.W.Foran Killed Belval, Mezieres, France. CG 1
W/OP. R/91336 W/O R.R.Stover Killed Belval, Mezieres, France. CG 1
F/E. 1445443 Sgt A.J.White Killed Belval, Mezieres, France. CG 1
A/G. 985405 Sgt E.Farnen Killed Belval, Mezieres, France. CG 1
A/G. 1339292 Sgt K.S.A.Payne Killed Belval, Mezieres, France. CG 1

149 Squadron 3 Group Stirling BK759 OJ/X
Aircraft crashed at Studernheim, Germany.
Pilot. 139614 P/O T.G.Ogle Killed Rheinberg, Germany. CG 19-1-1/5
Nav. J/16487 P/O E.M.Merritt Killed Rheinberg, Germany. CG 19-1-1/5
B/A. 1312026 Sgt D.Lenahan Killed Rheinberg, Germany. CG 19-1-1/5
W/OP. 1113094 Sgt L.Jones Killed Rheinberg, Germany. CG 19-1-1/5
F/E. 1258142 Sgt V.J.Upson Killed Rheinberg, Germany. CG 19-1-1/5
A/G. 1059267 F/Sgt W.Stephen Killed Rheinberg, Germany. CG 19-1-1/5
A/G. 1313880 Sgt H.Walters Killed Rheinberg, Germany. CG 19-1-1/5

214 Squadron 3 Group Stirling EF331 BU/H
Aircraft crashed at Sept-Saulx, France after fighter attack.
Pilot. 144037 P/O L.Powell Killed Sept-Saulx, France. 1
Nav. 127266 F/O E.H.Scott Killed Sept-Saulx, France. 4
B/A. 1338700 Sgt R.E.Dutton Killed Sept-Saulx, France. 2
W/OP. 1384029 Sgt H.C.Dent Killed Sept-Saulx, France. 3
F/E. 573650 Sgt T.Shepherd Killed Sept-Saulx, France. 5
A/G. 1094029 Sgt J.W.Williams Killed Sept-Saulx, France. 6
A/G. R/119142 F/Sgt E.H.Ingram Killed Sept-Saulx, France. 7

10 Squadron 4 Group Halifax DT746 ZA/
Pilot. 1375756 F/Sgt J.E.G.Hancock Killed St.Hilaire-le-Petit, France. 5
Nav. 1387138 Sgt H.G.Owen Killed St.Hilaire-le-Petit, France. 4
B/A. 963888 Sgt D.B.Everitt Killed St.Hilaire-le-Petit, France. 3
W/OP. 1292366 Sgt D.E.Funnell Killed St.Hilaire-le-Petit, France. 6
F/E. 1219685 Sgt J.L.Lee PoW. Stalag Luft 6, Heydekrug. 1076
A/G. 1375614 Sgt F.W.Griggs Killed St.Hilaire-le-Petit, France. 2
A/G. 798691 Sgt J.D.Culleton Killed St.Hilaire-le-Petit, France. 1

431 Squadron 4 Group Wellington HE357 SE/S
Pilot. 1438344 Sgt L.Denby Killed Rheinberg, Germany. CG 18-E-15/18
Nav. NZ/415335 F/Lt A.J.McDonald PoW. Stalag Luft 3, Sagan. 1101
B/A. 1396315 Sgt W.A.W.Hunter Killed Rheinberg Germany. CG 18-E-15/18
W/OP. 1029111 Sgt J.G.Adam Killed Rheinberg, Germany. CG 18-E-15/18
A/G. 1305606 Sgt J.J.O'Hagan Killed Rheinberg, Germany. CG 18-E-15/18

431 Squadron 4 Group Wellington HE374 SE/U
Pilot. 1041098 Sgt J.V.Avery Evaded capture.
Nav. 1334523 Sgt W.M.Shields Evaded capture.
B/A. 1577663 F/Sgt W.Boddy Evaded capture.
W/OP. 1078263 F/Sgt J.C.Cash Evaded capture.
A/G. R/6190A Sgt R.A.McEwan Evaded capture.

431 Squadron 4 Group Wellington HZ256 HD/
Pilot. Sgt E.F.Hicks C.G.M
A/G. 628161 Sgt F.J.Field Killed Littlehampton. D-4274
Air Gunner fatally wounded in fighter attack.

106 Squadron 5 Group Lancaster ED752 ZN/H
Pilot. 122363 F/Lt L.C.J.Brodrick PoW. Stalag Luft 3, Sagan. 1219
2/Pilot. 39286 S/Ldr J.Latimer DFC Killed Sauvillers Mongival, France. 3
Nav. J/14197 F/Lt J.A.Burns PoW. Stalag Luft 3, Sagan. 1342
B/A. R.N.V.R Lt G.Muttrie Killed Sauvillers Mongival, France. 5
W/OP. 1177603 Sgt H.Buxton Killed Sauvillers Mongival, France. 1
F/E. 576889 Sgt G.W.Hancock Killed Sauvillers Mongival, France. 4
A/G. 1551176 Sgt W.T.McLean Killed Sauvillers Mongival, France. 2
A/G. 1320799 F/Sgt H.Jones PoW. Stalag luft 1, Barth Vogelsang. 1011

408 Squadron 6 Group Halifax JB909 EQ/G
Aircraft attacked by fighter and caught fire over Reims, France at 03.30 hours, (15/4/43)
Pilot. A/405005 P/O I.C.Mackenzie Killed Clichy, Paris, France. 16-3-2
2/Pilot. R/127907 Sgt W.L.Canter Evaded capture.
Nav. 118652 F/Lt A.Playfair PoW. Stalag Luft 3, Sagan. 1103
B/A. 1343940 F/Sgt T.J.Coupland PoW. Stalag Luft 3, Sagan. 987
W/OP. A/403033 F/Lt C.O.O'Connell PoW. Stalag Luft 3, Sagan. 1451
F/E. C/92946 P/O L.W.McKenzie PoW. Stalag 357, Kopernikus. 1017
A/G. 50572 F/Lt W.A.McIlroy PoW. Stalag Luft 3, Sagan. 3267
A/G. R/62945 F/Sgt J.S.Murray PoW. Camp not known.

408 Squadron 6 Group Halifax BB311 EQ/L
Pilot. J/14135 F/Lt L.E.Usher PoW. Stalag Luft 3, Sagan. 1352
Nav. J/13820 F/Lt G.M.Parkinson PoW. Stalag Luft 3, Sagan. 2280
B/A. R/137824 W/O I.R.Macdonald PoW. Stalag 357, Kopernikus. 3038
W/OP. 1086282 Sgt J.J.Courtney Killed Montescourt Lizerolles, France. 1
F/E. R/59857 Sgt R.E.Dressler PoW. Stalag 4B, Muhlberg(Elbe). 222686
A/G. R/105201 F/Sgt W.E.Reed PoW. Stalag 357, Kopernikus. 2879
A/G. J/16465 F/Lt R.H.Jay PoW. Stalag Luft 3, Sagan. 1347

420 Squadron 6 Group Wellington HE863 PT/
Pilot. R/105169 W/O P.J.Cozens Killed Rocquiny, France.
Nav. R/115483 W/O W.G.Blight Killed Rocquiny, France.
B/A. R/134457 F/Sgt S.G.Giffin Killed Rocquiny, France.
W/OP. R/105866 W/O J.Paplowski Killed Rocquiny, France.
A/G. R/136360 F/Sgt L.Dutton Killed Rocquiny, France.

420 Squadron 6 Group Wellington HE550 PT/
Pilot. J/15177 S/Ldr F.V.Taylor Evaded capture.
Nav. J/12975 P/O G.C.Crowther Evaded capture.
B/A. J/15744 F/O S.Brown Evaded capture.
W/OP. 623970 W/O H.N.McKinnon PoW. Stalag 4B, Muhlberg(Elbe). 222620
A/G. J/17113 P/O J.Simpson Evaded capture.

424 Squadron 6 Group Wellington HZ273 QB/G
Pilot. R/105255 W/O A.R.Harrison PoW. Stalag 357, Kopernikus. 1000
Nav. J/17379 F/O F.Rath PoW. Stalag Luft 3, Sagan. 1158
B/A. 657735 F/Sgt J.E.Malkin PoW. Stalag 357, Kopernikus. 42761
W/OP. R/102405 W/O E.A.McQuarrie PoW. Stalag 357, Kopernikus. 1018
A/G. R/90414 Sgt A.J.Cockaday PoW. Repatriated Oct 1944

425 Squadron 6 Group Wellington X3763 KW/L
Aircraft shot down at Mussey sur Marne, France, by enemy fighter.
Pilot. J/15960 F/O A.T.Doucette DFC Killed Mussey-sur-Marne. CG 151/154
2/Pilot. 1234135 Sgt A.Jones Killed Mussey-sur-Marne, France. CG 151/154
Nav. J/15820 F/O J.O.Desrouches Killed Mussey-sur-Marne. CG 151/154
B/A. 656175 Sgt D.Vollans Killed Mussey-sur-Marne, France CG 151/154
W/OP. J16270 F/O G.P.H.Ledoux Killed Mussey-sur-Marne, France. 149
A/G. R/79441 W/O P.P.Trudeau Killed Mussey-sur-Marne, France. 150

425 Squadron 6 Group Wellington HE753 KW/S
Pilot. R/131679 W/O R.B.Dingman PoW. Stalag 4B, Muhlberg(Elbe). 889
Nav. J/13412 F/Lt H.E.Garland PoW. Stalag Luft 3, Sagan. 1081
B/A. 1295535 F/Sgt C.A.F.Griffin PoW. Stalag Luft 6, Heydekrug. 998
W/OP. J/22523 F/Lt T.R.C.Irwin PoW. Stalag Luft 3, Sagan. 1408
A/G. 1337613 F/Sgt E.C.M.Guyatt PoW. Stalag Luft 6, Heydekrug. 999

428 Squadron 6 Group Wellington HE176 NA/F
Pilot. R/114556 W/O W.S.Harris Killed Durnbach, Germany. 8-G-25
Nav. R/102739 W/O R.T.Sutton PoW. Stalag Luft 4, Sagan. 1042
B/A. J/16838 F/Lt D.H.Ferry PoW. Stalag Luft 3, Sagan. 1098
W/OP. R/107238 W/O J.L.Warren PoW. Stalag 357, Kopernikus. 1049
A/G. R/100561 W/O T.H.White PoW. Stalag Luft 4, Sagan. 1050

196 Squadron 4 Group Wellington HE166 ZO/
Crashed at Tangmere on take off after landing on diversion after operation to Stuttgart.
Pilot. 1313694 Sgt R.V.Rosser Killed Llangendeirne, S.Wales. 4-3
Nav. 1235964 Sgt P.G.Conwell Killed Manchester.(Moston). 208
B/A. 1393627 Sgt J.R.G.Calvert Killed St Andrews, Tangmere. 3-505
W/OP. 1283142 Sgt D.C.Grocock Killed St Andrews, Tangmere. 3-504
A/G. 1007194 Sgt H.Wilcock Killed Lancaster. D-386

Pilsen

April 16th/17th, 1943

A raid to distant Pilsen in Czechoslovakia took place on the 16th/17th April, where the Skoda armament factory was to be the main target in a complicated battle plan. Main force bombers had on this occasion been instructed to use only the Pathfinder markers as a guide and that they should confirm the target visually before bombing. Why this plan was made is not clear. The main force of 327 aircraft, 197 Lancasters and 130 Halifaxes despatched, were soon depleted by 48 early returners (14.7%). Weather conditions en route were good, there was bright moonlight over the target with a thin layer of strato cumulus cloud at 2,000 to 3,000 feet. The Pathfinders dropped 32 target indicators and a larger than usual number of flares (368), but the factory was not touched at all by the 395.2 tons of high explosive and 129.4 tons of incendiary bombs which were dropped and damaged instead a large mental hospital at Dobrany and a German barracks nearby in which 200 German soldiers were killed. Weather conditions were ideal for a great number of fighter interceptions. 37 aircraft went missing, 11. 3% of the force despatched and 15. 3% of the attacking aircraft.

Ditched

Through shortage of fuel some of the missing planes ditched in the North Sea, after their long flight but fortunately some of their crews were rescued. One of these was the crew of Lancaster ED437 from 50 Squadron, 5 Group which was luckily spotted by a patrolling Spitfire from 41 Squadron. The fighter pilot saw the dinghy about 6 miles off Le Touquet, France and although two Motor Gun Boats from Dover rushed there, they only managed to rescue four of the crew. Two of the remainder, the bomb aimer 1147367 Sergeant H. Hinchcliffe and the second pilot, 130513 Pilot Officer P. C. Cotter, were missing and the captain 125506 Flying Officer H. Elderfield was believed to have tried to swim ashore in an attempt to get help, but was never seen again.

Four Crew Members Evade Capture

Halifax HF663 of 102 Squadron, 4 Group, captained by Squadron Leader W. I. Lashbrook DFM was one of the aircraft shot down by night fighters, which obviously had a field day in the nigh perfect weather conditions, when bombers could be spotted so easily. Fortunately for this bomber crew the underground movement played their important role in helping shot down aircrew evade capture. It was on their return flight at about 04.00 hours, six hours after they had left their base at Pocklington, that the Halifax was attacked by a fighter over Belgium. The bomber immediately caught fire and the order to bale out was passed along, as the intercomm had failed. Sergeant W. R. Laws the wireless operator was the third out after the navigator, Flying Officer K. J. Bolton and the bomb aimer, Pilot Officer Martin with Flight Sergeant Knight, the flight engineer and the pilot immediately behind. Sergeant Laws in his report did not think that the gunners had a chance to get the bale out message. On his parachute descent he saw his aircraft break in two and fall in flames. He landed uninjured in a wood, and like all airmen buried his 'chute and Mae West straight away and walked quickly south to get away from the crash site.

He rolled down his trousers to cover his conspicuous flying boots, then using his escape compass, he walked through a village. He saw a signpost indentifying it as Montbliart. Here he left the road and walked across country, through some woods for about two hours, before stopping in a field to eat some chocolate and Horlicks tablets from his kit. After it became light he studied his map but he was unable to make out his position at Montbliart and did not know whether he was in France or Belgium. At nightfall on the 17th, he continued walking south and used his water bottle to acquire some water from a brook, making sure to put in the purifying tablets before drinking and taking a benzadrine tablet to stay awake. Walking on he passed through the villages of Seloignes and Villers La Tour before he decided to lay up and rest.

On the morning of the 18th he removed his badges from his uniform before continuing on. Eventually he came to an isolated chateau, where a man who looked as if he might be the game keeper, came up to him and spoke in French. Luckily Sergeant Laws could speak French fairly fluently and explained to the man that he was an English airman and wanted to know where he was. The man stated that he was a Pole and was the caretaker of the chateau which was unoccupied. He also said the chateau was in Belgium, near Les Taillettes, about 7 kilometres from the French frontier. The man took him into the chateau and allowed him to shave with his razor and later gave him some food. He was also given an old blue mackintosh. In return Sergeant Laws gave him 500 Francs from his escape pack. The caretaker, however, was quite scared to have the airmen about the place and advised him to carry on and keep to the woods and walk south into France.

About midnight on the 18th/19th, he again set out and at daybreak crossed the French frontier north of Watigny. He then sheltered in a bombed out house where he ate some of the bread and cheese he had been given by the Pole and went to sleep. When he awoke he set off once again walking along the road to Fligny, which he reached at 14.00 hours and continued on to Auge. It was here that a bad storm broke, with exceptionally heavy rain, so soaking wet he approached an isolated farmhouse and sheltered under its front door porch. A girl of about 24 opened the door and spoke to him then invited him into the house to shelter from the storm. As Sergeant Laws replied in French, the girl did not know who he was, but when inside he had explained that he was an RAF airman. She and her family became very frightened when they found he had no indentity discs to show and his ability to speak French so fluently made them even more suspicious of him, but they did give him some food and allowed him to sleep in the barn for the night.

Meanwhile one of the family told a friend about Sergeant Laws, who sent a message asking that he should write down on a piece of paper the names of the rest of his crew and approximately where he had landed. This paper was taken back by the girl that night. Next day he was told that someone would come for him, this in fact did not happen and he stayed in the barn. On April 21st, the man who had asked for the paper arrived and told Laws to stay where he was and that help would be forthcoming. He stayed in and around the barn until May 4th, when at last the man returned with a car and took Sergeant Laws to another village. There he met up with Group Captain Whitley, who had baled out on the Frankfurt raid on April 11th. From here the necessary arrangements were made by the underground movement and finally Laws returned safely to England.

Two Years as a Prisoner

A survivor from Halifax HR758 of 158 Squadron which did not return from the Pilsen raid was air gunner Sergeant Reg Newdick. The plane was attacked by an Me109F, near Bormstadt, Frankfurt. Both the bomber's gunners and the fighter pilot opened fire simultaneously at each other, but the Halifax was hit in the port wing and the incendiaries caught fire. The captain, Australian Flying Officer B. P. Jay, gave the order to bale out, but not before the bomber crew saw the fighter being hit by the return fire from the bomber's gunners and go down with smoke trailing from its engine. Five of the crew managed to escape the fire which engulfed the bomber. The bomb aimer, Flying Officer K. A. Barratt, held open the forward escape hatch, as it could not be jettisoned, so that the crew in the forward section of the fuselage could escape. Flying Officer Barratt and Flying Officer Jay lost their lives in the bomber. Sergeant Newdick remembers little of the bale out, except that he received a blow on the head as he tumbled out and has a small scar still showing to this day. He felt the 'chute harness quite loose on his descent and when he released the main toggle after landing, it fell away having broken off the main strap.

The bomber's survivors were soon rounded up by the inhabitants of Bormstadt. They were lucky to avoid being mal treated by the civilians, as many aircrew felt that it was safer to be captured by the military or police rather than the irate people of a town that had been subjected to bombing. Sergeant Newdick met up with his crew the next day, but they found that their rear gunner Sergeant, C. D. Fawcett, had been badly burned about the hands and face as he escaped from the blazing turret. The five were taken to Dulag Luft and then on to various Luft camps before finally ending up in Stalag 357 having survived the transfer by sea in the hold of the infamous *SS Instaburg* and the well known prisoner of war episode of the 'Run up the road'. All were liberated on April 16th 1945, two years to the day on which they had baled out.

Bomber Returns, But Three Crew Bale Out

Lancaster W4366 PH/R from 12 Squadron based at Wickenby, Lincolnshire, was captained on the Pilsen operation by Sergeant W. F. Mizon. Their flight plan on this raid was to fly through the German fighter belt at low level and then to quickly climb when they were near the target to bomb from 4,000 feet.

As the aircraft approached the target the wireless operator, Sergeant T. H. Hutton was standing in the main body of the fuselage near the flare chute in readiness to check that the photo flash was safely dropped when he saw a huge flash below the aircraft and felt the fuselage shudder. He made a quick check around but found no apparent damage and reported this to his skipper. The bomb run was continued and the bombs released from 5,000 feet The captain then quickly climbed to 10,000 feet and set course for home base.

At 02.30 hours the Flight Engineer, Sergeant H. E. Peckham, noticed that the oil pressure in the starboard outer engine was beginning to fall rapidly. Shortly afterwards the engine failed and every effort to feather it was to no avail. The drag caused by the windmilling propeller made the aircraft extremely difficult to handle. It was not long before the defective engine caught fire, but fortunately this was extinguished by using the engine Graviner system. At 03.40 hours the flight engineer noticed that the oil pressure in the faulty and windmilling engine was starting to build up again. He knew that restarting a defective engine after using the fire extinguisher was not a recommended procedure, but the captain was having such difficulty in handling the plane that a decision was made to try and restart the faulty engine. This caused more flames to issue from the cowling, but luckily these died down. Fearing a more serious fire problem with the engine, at 03.41 hours the captain ordered as a precautionary measure that his crew should stand by in case it would be necessary to give a bale out order.

There must have been some confusion over the intercom concerning this order because the wireless operator, Sergeant Tom Hutton and the two gunners, Sergeant J. A. McKay and Sergeant L. Rudkin, heard what they they believed to be an abandon aircraft order which naturally they did not question and obeyed immediately.

At 03.50 hours the pilot, on checking his crew positions, found that the three crew members in the rear of the aircraft were missing, having presumably baled out. The rest of the crew were in luck for the three engined Lancaster eventually struggled back to England calling up the *Darkie* emergency procedure after crossing the English coast at Beachy Head. The answering searchlights pointed the aircraft in the direction of Ford airfield where it landed at 06.30 hours. After his bale out Sergeant McKay was quickly captured, due to his fracturing a hip on landing, but Sergeants Rudkin and Hutton landed uninjured and quickly met up with each other on the ground. Unsure of their exact position and whether they were in Germany or France they very wisely left their landing site as quickly as possible, before considering their plan of action. After wading into a nearby stream they trudged along before they decided, after becoming very cold, to leave the stream and find a hiding place before daybreak.

After they came to a main road they hid behind some hedges, having first agreed not to go to an isolated house, which they came to immediately after leaving the stream, in case they were still in Germany. From their spot behind the hedge they saw and heard some passing cyclists talking to each other in French and with relief realised that at least they were either in Belgium or France, where the prospect of help was very much more favourable.

Their first encounter was with another cyclist, who realised that they were RAF aircrew and he advised them to get away from the main road and to keep to the fields. Their luck was in for they met up with a farmer, who spoke excellent English, having lived in Canada for many years, but it took some time to convince him that they were actually evading RAF aircrew and not Germans masquerading as aircrew to break into the Resistance escape line. After considerable questioning he was finally convinced, but was unable to harbour them in his own home, because of many Germans in the area. He took them instead to a nearby wood, where he advised them to lay low until he returned later. That night, April 17th, he returned with some food and ersatz coffee and told the two fliers that he had arranged for them to be picked up by a Resistance worker. Later the worker arrived and took them to the village of Musson, where they were sheltered by a very patriotic and courageous village priest, Father Goffinet, who had a passionate hatred of the Germans. He was responsible for helping many Allied airman to safety, Hutton and Rudkin being the first, but eventually he was suspected by the Germans and to avoid being taken by them he decided to go to England with his next group of evaders. He was however betrayed by a fellow priest, in fact a German, who claimed he was anti-Nazi and wished to join Father Goffinet in his escape bid. Father Goffinet was arrested on his escape journey and after being tortured in an effort to obtain secrets of the escape line, he was eventually imprisoned at the infamous Buchenwald Concentration Camp. Sadly he did not survive. He was shot by the German guards only 24 hours before the camp was liberated by the American Forces.

Sergeants Hutton and Rudkin were duly passed down through the homes of many brave French helpers, until finally they crossed the Pyrennes on a 12 hour walk, which considerably taxed their stamina and strength. They eventually reached the British Embassy in Madrid before proceeding to Gibraltar and arrived home on July 24th, 1943.

Casualties April 16/17th, 1943. Target Pilsen

83 Squadron 8 Group Lancaster R5484 OL/V
Message returning on 2 engines. Last fix given north east of Paris at 04.11 hours (17/4/43). Nothing further heard.
Pilot. J/17109 F/O G.A.McNichol Killed Pontavert, Laon, France. 1
Nav. J/16378 F/Lt H.H.P.Beaupre PoW. Stalag Luft 3, Sagan. 1253
B/A. 622657 W/O G.C.Mott PoW. Stalag 357, Kopernikus. 1152
W/OP. 1359980 W/O G.S.MacFarlane PoW. Stalag 357, Kopernikus. 1079
F/E. R/85583 W/O C.E.Hobbs PoW. Stalag Luft 6, Heydekrug. 1071
A/G. J/16111 F/Lt T.W.Lewis PoW. Stalag 357, Kopernikus. 1270
A/G. 1314029 F/Sgt H.R.Willis PoW. Stalag 357, Kopernikus. 1113

83 Squadron 8 Group Lancaster R5622 OL/
Pilot. 65667 P/O F.C.Milt Killed Prague, Czechoslavkia. 11-D-7
Nav. 123044 F/Lt W.B.Wells Killed Prague, Czechoslavkia. 11-D-1
B/A. J/8807 F/O N.M.McLellan Killed Prague, Czechoslavkia. 11-D-4
W/OP. 1381145 F/Sgt J.Rodgers Killed Prague, Czechoslavkia. 11-D-2
F/E. 626944 F/Sgt R.Beaven DFM Killed Prague, Czechoslavkia. 11-D-3
A/G. R/86547 Sgt A.Podolsky Killed Prague, Czechoslavkia. 11-D-5
A/G. 965184 Sgt M.Kleinhorn Killed Prague, Czechoslavkia. 11-D-6

156 Squadron 8 Group Lancaster W4854 GT/
Pilot. 146157 P/O H.B.Gonce Killed Chalons-sur-Marne, France. 1-1630
Nav. 1452042 Sgt J.G.K.Dean Killed Conde-sur-Marne, France. 17
B/A. 129920 P/O M.C.Anastassiades Killed Chalons-sur-Marne. 1-1631
W/OP. 1078082 Sgt H.D.Rowe Killed Chalons-sur-Marne. CG 1-1632/35
F/E. 979328 Sgt M.M.Muirhead Killed Chalons-sur-Marne. CG 1-1632/35
A/G. 577658 Sgt J.Boyd Killed Chalons-sur-Marne, France. CG 1-1632/35
A/G. R/126738 F/Sgt L.E.Corley Killed Chalons-sur-Marne. CG 1-1632/35

156 Squadron 8 Group Lancaster W4930 GT/
Pilot. 143758 P/O H.R.Anderson DFC Killed Brimont, Rheims, France. 4
Nav. 139927 P/O K.Bordycott DFC DFM Killed Brimont, Rheims, France. 5
B/A. 1331855 Sgt B.H.Godding Killed Brimont, Rheims, France. 2
W/OP. 138424 P/O F.Smith DFM Killed Brimont, Rheims, France. 3
F/E. 577758 Sgt P.L.Brougham-Faddy Killed Brimont, Rheims, France. 1
A/G. 1585561 Sgt J.T.Stephens Killed Brimont, Rheims, France. 6
A/G. 519840 F/Sgt W.O.Woolnough Killed Brimont, Rheims, France. 7

35 Squadron 8 Group Halifax W7873 TL/
Pilot. 115429 F/Lt W.R.Owen PoW. Stalag Luft 3, Sagan. 1272
Nav. R/13280 Sgt J.R.Martyn Killed Liesse, Laon, France. CG A-3/6
B/A. 136732 P/O G.Cruickshank Killed Liesse, Laon, France. CG A-3/6
W/OP. 1377851 F/Sgt D.R.Bradley DFM Evaded capture
F/E. 903697 F/Sgt W.G.Allen DFM Evaded capture
A/G. 933423 F/Sgt J.F.Bourne Killed Liesse, Laon, France. CG A-3/6
A/G. 1216336 Sgt J.Young Killed Liesse, Laon, France. CG A-3/6

12 Squadron 1 Group Lancaster W4366 PH/R
Pilot. Sgt W.F Mizon
Nav. Sgt H.O.Spenbourge
B/A. Sgt P.J.Smale
W/OP. 1108958 Sgt T.H.Hutton Evaded capture
F/E. Sgt H.E.Peckham
A/G. Sgt J.A.McKay PoW. Camp not known.
A/G. 950233 Sgt L.Rudkin Evaded capture
Three crew members baled out over Belgium. Confusion in bale out order due to intercom failure. Remaining crew brought aircraft back to base. One gunner broke hip in bale out.

100 Squadron 1 Group Lancaster ED564 HW/H
Pilot. NZ/413451 F/Lt R.E.Milliken Killed Rheinberg, Germany. CG 8-K-1/5
Nav. R/95479 F/Sgt W.H.George Killed Rheinberg, Germany. CG 8-K-1/5
B/A. 144757 P/O W.H.Walton Killed Rheinberg, Germany. CG 8-K-1/5
W/OP. 1271097 Sgt R.E.J.Hunt Killed Rheinberg, Germany. CG 8-K-1/5
F/E. 610787 Sgt T.E.Jones Killed Rheinberg, Germany. CG 8-K-1/5
A/G. 900793 Sgt G.J.Good Killed Rheinberg, Germany. CG 8-K-1/5
A/G. 143395 Sgt M.Whitby Killed Rheinberg, Germany. CG 8-K-1/5

100 Squadron 1 Group Lancaster ED563 HW/G
Pilot. NZ/416075 Sgt D.K.Atkinson Killed Rheinberg, Germany. 8-J-19
Nav. R/124176 F/Sgt I.S.Brown Killed Rheinberg, Germany. 8-J-21
B/A. 1535677 Sgt J.Rutter Killed Rheinberg, Germany. 8-J-22
W/OP. 1292995 Sgt R.F.Clutterbuck Killed Rheinberg, Germany. 8-J-24
F/E. 1128891 Sgt N.Vanston Killed Rheinberg, Germany. 8-J-20
A/G. R/140995 F/Sgt P.Rudick Killed Rheinberg, Germany. 8-J-25
A/G. A/416383 P/O P.V.Monk Killed Rheinberg, Germany. 8-J-23

101 Squadron 1 Group Lancaster ED379 SR/F
Pilot. A/416594 F/Sgt C.K.Menzies Killed Durnbach, Germany. 5-F-2
Nav. 1387863 Sgt H.Evans Killed Durnbach, Germany. 5-F-1
B/A. A/408888 F/O T.M.Taylor Killed Durnbach, Germany. 5-F-5
W/OP. 1384192 Sgt L.Green PoW. Stalag 357, Kopernikus. 996
F/E. 651156 Sgt H.A.Upton Killed Durnbach, Germany. 5-F-3
A/G. 1451283 Sgt J.Monks Killed Durnbach, Germany. 5-F-4
A/G. R/157039 F/Sgt J.H.Fitch Killed Durnbach, Germany. 5-F-6

103 Squadron 1 Group Lancaster W4848 PM/
Pilot. NZ/416141 P/O J.O.B.Mooney Killed Durnbach, Germany. 7-C-2
Nav. J/13143 F/O A.H.Gipson Killed Durnbach, Germany. CG 7-C-9/11
B/A. 144768 F/O H.J.D.Rowse PoW. Stalag 357, Kopernikus. 1033
W/OP. 129518 F/O F.J.Hudson Killed Durnbach, Germany. 7-C-7
F/E. 810100 Sgt S.Biggs PoW. Stalag 357, Kopernikus. 979
A/G. 1587160 Sgt V.J.Merefield Killed Durnbach, Germany. CG 7-C-9/11
A/G. 1578786 Sgt R.W.Harley Killed Durnbach, Germany. 7-C-5

460 Squadron 1 Group Lancaster W4331 UV/
Pilot. A/411165 F/Sgt I.G.Miller Killed Durnbach, Germany. 7-C-6
Nav. 1391946 Sgt N.P.Richmond Killed Durnbach, Germany. 7-C-4
B/A. 1333550 Sgt M.G.W.Capon Killed Durnbach, Germany. 7-C-8
W/OP. 1383005 Sgt G.J.Wilson Killed Durnbach, Germany. 7-C-3
F/E. 814139 Sgt D.Curtis Killed Durnbach, Germany. CG 7-C-9/11
A/G. 1810453 Sgt R.A.Hall Killed Durnbach, Germany. 7-C-1
A/G. 1601542 Sgt R.F.Beaumont Killed Durnbach, Germany. CG 7-C-9/11

460 Squadron 1 Group Lancaster W4942 UV/
Pilot. A/416135 F/Sgt J.N.Williams Killed Durnbach, Germany. 9-F-27
Nav. A/411355 F/Sgt E.R.King Killed Durnbach, Germany. 9-F-26
B/A. A/409034 F/Sgt E.C.Ebbott Killed Durnbach, Germany. 9-F-28
W/OP. 1271734 Sgt L.C.Smith Killed Durnbach, Germany. 9-F-22

F/E. A/205848 Sgt J.C.Bell Killed Durnbach, Germany. 9-F-23
A/G. 1387144 Sgt A.W.Clark Killed Durnbach, Germany. 9-F-25
A/G. 1433368 Sgt E.J.Ablewhite Killed Durnbach, Germany. 9-F-24

460 Squadron 1 Group Lancaster ED711 UV/
Pilot. A/408896 P/O D.E.White Killed Durnbach, Germany. 8-A-8
2/Pilot. A/409331 F/Sgt J.S.Stewart Killed Durnbach, Germany. CG 8-A-13/15
Nav. A/411121 P/O W.R.K.Charlton Killed Durnbach, Germany. 8-A-9
B/A. A/411207 F/Sgt F.H.Ward DFM Killed Durnbach, Germany. CG 8-A-13/15
W/OP. A/412265 P/O A.K.Parker Killed Durnbach, Germany. 8-A-12
F/E. A/9431 Sgt B.Knilands Killed Durnbach, Germany. 8-A-11
A/G. 1378794 F/Sgt A.K.Smith Killed Durnbach, Germany. CG 8-A-13/15
A/G. A/401730 F/Sgt R.H.Baker Killed Durnbach, Germany. 8-A-10

51 Squadron 4 Group Halifax DT690 MH/
Pilot. 1385745 Sgt J.E.McCrea Evaded capture.
Nav. 121737 F/O D.G.Spencer PoW. Stalag Luft 6, Heydekrug. 2195
B/A. 143654 F/O C.B.Ings PoW. Stalag 4B, Muhleberg(Elbe). 222519
W/OP. 1076981 W/O J.E.C.Simpson PoW. Stalag 4B, Muhleberg(Elbe). 222554
F/E. 1095982 Sgt J.Alderdice DFM Evaded capture.
A/G. 1440300 Sgt D.L.Jones DFM Evaded capture.
A/G. 1231259 F/Sgt A.W.Davis PoW. Stalag Luft 6, Heydekrug. 1147

51 Squadron 4 Group Halifax DT561 MH/
Pilot. 1334812 Sgt E.W.Cox Killed Durnbach, Germany. 6-H-26
Nav. 1336282 Sgt R.C.Burt Killed Durnbach, Germany. 6-H-24
B/A. R/115429 W/O F.G.McCardle Killed Durnbach, Germany. 6-H-28
W/OP. 1377421 Sgt W.A.Rogers Killed Durnbach, Germany. 6-H-25
F/E. 1402515 Sgt S.J.Briffett Killed Durnbach, Germany. 6-H-23
A/G. 1159492 Sgt L.R.Bray Killed Durnbach, Germany. 6-H-22
A/G. 1343837 Sgt R.A.McLaren Killed Durnbach, Germany. 6-H-27

51 Squadron 4 Group Halifax DT578 MH/
Pilot. 1271750 Sgt D.F.Inch Killed Chalons-sur-Marne, France. 1-1627
Nav. 1079476 Sgt H.Riley Evaded capture.
B/A. 124706 F/O R.F.Clements Killed Chalons-sur-Marne, France. 1-1628
W/OP. A/408770 F/Sgt E.L.Lancaster Killed Choloy, Nancy, France. 1-B-1
F/E. 1244010 Sgt T.F.Hayden Killed Chalons-sur-Marne, France. 1-1626
A/G. 1691788 Sgt F.P.Dards PoW. Stalag Luft 6, Heydekrug. 1146
A/G. 700735 Sgt R.M.Mumms Killed Chalons-sur-Marne, France. 1-1629

51 Squadron 4 Group Halifax HR729 MH/
Pilot. 1167329 W/O J.G.Edwards Killed Reichswald Forest, Germany. 22-C-11
Nav. 125668 F/O W.C.Brisbane Killed Reichswald Forest, Germany. 22-C-8
B/A. 1387933 Sgt A.O.Lewis Killed Reichswald Forest, Germany. 22-C-7
W/OP. 111788 F/Lt J.W.Marriott PoW. Stalag Luft 3, Sagan. 42734
F/E. 651771 Sgt G.E.Roberts Killed Reichswald Forest, Germany. 22-C-6
A/G. 145786 P/O A.D.Kitchen Killed Reichswald Forest, Germany. 22-C-9
A/G. 49233 F/O L.Walters Killed Reichswald Forest, Germany. 22-C-10

51 Squadron 4 Group Halifax HR784 MH/
Pilot. J/17100 P/O R.H.Stewart Killed Maucourt, Amiens, France 3
Nav. 519422 W/O W.R.Kiernan DFM PoW. Stalag 357, Kopernikus. 14
B/A. 120669 F/O T.C.Robinson Killed Maucourt, Amiens, France 4
W/OP. 62674 F/Sgt D.Axtell DFM Killed Maucourt, Amiens, France 1
F/E. 51909 P/O W.R.McBriar Killed Maucourt, Amiens, France 5
A/G. 1316069 Sgt D.H.Reid Killed Maucourt, Amiens, France 2
A/G. 144266 P/O F.M.Thompson Killed Maucourt, Amiens, France 6

76 Squadron 4 Group Halifax DT575 MP/Y
Crashed near Liesse, France.
Pilot. 1335713 Sgt B.W.E.Wedderburn Killed Liesse, Laon, France. CG - 6/11
Nav. 1384438 Sgt B.J.Clinging Killed Liesse, Laon, France. CG - 6/11
B/A. R/99150 F/Sgt F.O.Ross Killed Liesse, Laon, France. CG - 6/11
W/OP. 1196513 Sgt F.C.Fidgeon Killed Liesse, Laon, France. CG - 6/11
F/E. 1013892 Sgt J.Strachan Killed Liesse, Laon, France. CG - 6/11
A/G. R/180403 Sgt L.N.Jonasson Killed Liesse, Laon, France. B - 12
A/G. 1336567 Sgt S.H.C.Brown Killed Liesse, Laon, France. CG - 6/11

76 Squadron 4 Group Halifax JB800 MP/U
Aircraft cashed at Mundelsheim, Germany.
Pilot. 1213927 Sgt G.C.Wright Killed Durnbach, Germany CG 4-J-18/21
Nav. 126887 F/O H.E.Smith Killed Durnbach, Germany. CG 4-J-18/21
B/A. 49280 F/O A.N.Cooper Killed Durnbach, Germany. CG 4-J-18/21
W/OP. 49997 F/O J.F.Webb Killed Durnbach, Germany. 4-J-17
F/E. 1186489 W/O A.G.C.Read PoW. Stalag 357, Kopernikus. 1029 Killed In
RAF air attack (19-4-45) Buried in Berlin, Germany. 11-D-10
A/G. 1413863 F/Sgt D.B.Wombwell PoW. Stalag 357, Kopernikus. 1054
A/G. R/122884 Sgt F.A.Robb Killed Durnbach, Germany. CG 4-J-18/19

76 Squadron 4 Group Halifax DK165 MP/E
Aircraft crashed between Lachen and Speyerdorf, Germany.
Pilot. 1315766 Sgt K.E.Webb Killed Rheinberg, Germany. 18-H-1
Nav. 1315633 Sgt K.R.G.Williams Killed Rheinberg, Germany. 18-H-6
B/A. 10794-7 Sgt J.Kay Killed Rheinberg, Germany. 18-H-5
W/OP. R/115601 F/Sgt A.R.Ross Killed Rheinberg, Germany. 18-H-4
F/E. 653562 Sgt S.Braybrook Killed Rheinberg, Germany. 18-H-2
A/G. 553053 Sgt L.B.Mitchell Killed Stalag Luft 4, Sagan. 42735
A/G. 751279 F/Sgt G.Brown Killed Rheinberg, Germany. 18-H-3

77 Squadron 4 Group Halifax JB908 KN/
Aircraft attacked by enemy fighter. Post war interrogations state that Nav,
W/Op and F/E.'s parachutes not seen to open.
Pilot. 1334628 W/O F.S.Wall PoW. Stalag 357, Kopernikus. 1163
Nav. 1383533 Sgt G.R.Fernee Killed Durnbach, Germany. 8-F-22
B/A. 1394664 Sgt R.M.Tullett PoW. Stalag 357, Kopernikus. 1044
W/OP. 1380422 Sgt A.K.Edgar Killed Durnbach, Germany. 8-F-24
F/E. 646201 Sgt D.I.Pullen Killed Durnbach, Germany. 8-F-23
A/G. 1332631 Sgt R.W.Robinson Killed Durnbach, Germany. 8-F-25
A/G. 1332764 F/Sgt L.Johnson PoW. Stalag 357, Kopernikus. 1010

78 Squadron 4 Group Halifax HR659 EY/
Aircraft attacked by Me 109 and then shot down by Me110 at Trier, France
Pilot. 117484 F/Lt E.G.Mortenson Killed Rheinberg, Germany. 8-E-23
Nav. 141800 P/O R.C.W.Dennis PoW. Stalag Luft 3, Sagan. 1096
B/A. 122486 F/Lt W.G.F.Fisher PoW. Stalag Luft 3, Sagan. 1099
W/OP. 1375494 Sgt A.Steven PoW. Camp not known
F/E. 1010574 Sgt J.A.Bell PoW. Stalag 357, Kopernikus. 1144
A/G. 1578344 Sgt D.A.Pitman Killed Rheinberg, Germany. 8-E-24
A/G. 1391083 Sgt L.C.Minshaw PoW. Stalag 357, Kopernikus. 1155

78 Squadron 4 Group Halifax DT773 EY/
Aircraft crashed near River Neckar, Stuttgart, after two fighter attacks.
Pilot. 88035 F/Lt A.P.Dowse DFC Killed Durnbach, Germany. 11-D-28
Nav. R/79743 W/O R.Des-Jardins PoW. Stalag 357, Kopernikus. 1148
B/A. 655036 Sgt H.E.Thompson PoW. Repatriated.
W/OP. NZ/412343 F/O P.Langsford PoW. Stalag Luft 3, Sagan. 1154
F/E. 1042698 F/Sgt T.T.Slater PoW. Stalag 357, Kopernikus. 1038
A/G. 121341 F/Lt A.N.Orr PoW. Stalag Luft 3, Sagan. 1102
A/G. 1421354 W/O A.Hoare PoW. Stalag 357, Kopernikus. 1002

102 Squadron 4 Group Halifax HR663 DY/
Pilot. 45895 S/Ldr W.I.Lashbrook DFC DFM Evaded capture.
Nav. 45525 F/O J.K.Bolton Evaded capture.
B/A. 120240 F/O A.Martin DFC Evaded capture.
W/OP. 745880 Sgt W.R.Laws Evaded capture.
F/E. 51677 F/Sgt D.C.Knight PoW. Stalag 4B Muhleberg(Elbe). 250739
A/G. 1055567 W/O L.Neill PoW. Stalag Luft 4, Sagan. 1192
A/G. 136044 F/O G.M.Williams Killed Maubeuge, France. A-15

158 Squadron 4 Group Halifax HR758 NP/Y
Pilot. A/403745 F/O B.P.Jay Killed Rheinberg, Germany. 9-E-3
Nav. 1234186 F/Sgt G.D.W.Scholes PoW. Stalag 357, Kopernikus. 1162
B/A. 123848 F/O K.A.Barratt Killed Rheinberg, Germany. 9-E-4 Believed
parachute failure.
W/OP. 1379992 F/Sgt A.Ford PoW. Stalag 357, Kopernikus. 993
F/E. 1262524 F/Sgt F.E.Holmes PoW. Stalag 357, Kopernikus. 1004
A/G. 1382016 Sgt R.Newdick PoW. Stalag Luft 4, Sagan. 1020
A/G. R/115932 Sgt C.D.Fawcett PoW. Stalag 357, Kopernikus. 991

49 Squadron 5 Group Lancaster ED441 EA/
Pilot. 1385187 Sgt D.T.Penry Killed Camon, Amiens, France. 2-2
Nav. 1254892 F/Sgt A.N.Dixon Killed Camon, Amiens, France. 2-3
B/A. 1452712 Sgt C.L.James Killed Camon, Amiens, France. 2-1
W/OP. 1379852 Sgt T.C.Robertson Killed Camon, Amiens, France. 2-5
F/E. 575897 Sgt C.G.Bamford Killed Camon, Amiens, France. 2-4
A/G. 1579349 Sgt J.F.Fletcher Killed Camon, Amiens, France. 2-6
A/G. 1348823 Sgt H.W.G.Kerr PoW. Camp not known.

49 Squadron 5 Group Lancaster ED427 EA/
Pilot. 48898 F/O A.V.Bone Missing, Runnymede Memorial 123
Nav. 1578189 Sgt C.W.Yelland Missing, Runnymede Memorial 170
B/A. 1238955 Sgt R.J.Rooney Missing, Runnymede Memorial 163
W/OP. 1314359 Sgt R.C.White Missing, Runnymede Memorial 169
F/E. 575719 Sgt R.N.P.Foster Missing, Runnymede Memorial 149
A/G. 1086776 Sgt R.Cope Missing, Runnymede Memorial 146
A/G. J/90946 P/O B.E.Watt Missing, Runnymede Memorial 178

50 Squadron 5 Group Lancaster ED800 VN/
Shot down at Yves-Gomezee, Belgium at 04.00 hours (17/4/43).Victim of
GruppenKommandeur Wilhelm Herget, I/NJG4.
Pilot. 1346423 Sgt J.G.Duncan Missing, Runnymede Memorial 148
Nav. 947859 Sgt J.Spiers Missing, Runnymede Memorial 165
B/A. 1345207 Sgt D.M.Smellie Missing, Runnymede Memorial 165
W/OP. 1078000 Sgt J.A.Bates Missing, Runnymede Memorial 142
F/E. 1475694 Sgt C.Payne Missing, Runnymede Memorial 161
A/G. 1162200 Sgt A.W.Berry Missing, Runnymede Memorial 142
A/G. 1412081 Sgt H.R.Barnes Missing, Runnymede Memorial 141

50 Squadron 5 Group Lancaster ED691 VN/
Pilot. 124456 P/O H.H.Day Killed Epense, France. 1
2/Pilot. 124438 F/Lt D.A.Trotman Evaded capture
Nav. A/411090 F/O H.E.Holland PoW. Stalag Luft 3, Sagan. 1072
B/A. 1243280 W/O G.A.E.Hodgkinson PoW. Stalag 357, Kopernikus. 1151
W/OP. 1199030 W/O J.A.Rossbotham PoW. Stalag Luft1, Barth Vogelsang.
F/E. 578213 F/Sgt R.C.Salmon PoW. Stalag 357, Kopernikus. 1161
A/G. 1334839 F/Sgt N.I.Evans PoW. Stalag 357, Kopernikus. 1241
A/G. R/188012 Sgt S.R.Syms PoW. Repatriated May 1944

50 Squadron 5 Group Lancaster ED784 VN/
Ditched 6 mls off French coast.Rescued by Motor Torpedo Boat at 02.00 hours.
Pilot. 125506 F/O H.Elderfield Missing, Runnymede Memorial 124
2/Pilot. 130513 P/O P.C.Cotter Missing, Runnymede Memorial 131
Nav. 155280 Sgt J.M.Laing Rescued.
B/A. 1147367 Sgt H.Hinchcliffe Missing, Runnymede Memorial 153
W/OP. 129221 Sgt R.S.Harman Rescued.
F/E. 942459 Sgt R.Chambers Rescued.
A/G. 1575365 Sgt H.Webster Rescued.
A/G. 999074 Sgt J.Hammond Rescued

61 Squadron 5 Group Lancaster W4317 QR/
Shot down at Givry, Belgium at 04.30 hours (17/4/43). Victim of Staffel
Kapitan R.Altendorf I/NJG4
Pilot. 142540 P/O W.Macfarlane Killed Chievres, Belgium. CG 10-A
Nav. 123048 F/O C.F.Williams Killed Chievres, Belgium. JG 9/10 2/
Nav. 1338539 Sgt E.R.Davidson Killed Chievres, Belgium. JG 9/10
B/A. 1123166 F/Sgt W.W.Dawson Killed Chievres, Belgium. 12
W/OP. 143652 P/O J.F.Edwards DFM Killed Chievres, Belgium. 13
F/E. A/15302 Sgt P.J.Keay Killed Chievres, Belgium. 11
A/G. 1321234 Sgt J.V.Rees Killed Chievres, Belgium. CG 10-A
A/G. 144654 P/O D.A.Holdsworth Killed Chievres, Belgium. CG 10-A

467 Squadron 5 Group Lancaster ED651 PO/
Pilot. A/408545 W/O B.C.Wilson PoW. Stalag 357, Kopernikus. 10623
Nav. 127982 F/Lt R.Stitt PoW. Stalag 6G, Bonn-Duisdorf. 10621
B/A. 127118 P/O F.G.Boswell PoW. Camp not known
W/OP. 1382764 Sgt H.F.Goode Killed Rheinberg, Germany. 1-H-25
Died in hospital (23/4/43)
F/E. 640100 Sgt R.H.Pallender Killed Rheinberg, Germany. JG 1-H-23/24
A/G. 944720 Sgt R.Dunn Killed Rheinberg, Germany. 1-H-22
A/G. 1564310 Sgt W.W.Bannatyne Killed Rheinberg, Germany. JG 1-H-23/24

467 Squadron 5 Group Lancaster ED780 PO/
Pilot. A/406702 F/Sgt R.C.Stuart Killed Poix-de-la-Somme, France. E-15
Nav. 80418 F/O B.R.McNair DFC Killed Poix-de-la-Somme, France. E-14
B/A. 1338233 Sgt A.F.McDonald Killed Poix-de-la-Somme, France. JG E-18/19
W/OP. NZ/415980 Sgt R.C.Anderson Killed Poix-de-la-Somme, France. E-17
F/E. 636646 Sgt T.Martin Killed Poix-de-la-Somme, France. E-16
A/G. A/405819 F/Sgt P.L.Boase Killed Poix-de-la-Somme, France. E-13
A/G. 1453416 Sgt R.J.Johnson Killed Poix-de-la-Somme, France. JG E-18/19

408 Squadron 6 Group Halifax BB343 EQ/X
Pilot. R/55551 W/O J.J.A.Guay Killed Liesse, Laon, France. B-5
Nav. R/90867 F/Sgt F.R.Pilon Killed Liesse, Laon, France. CG B-1/4
B/A. R/117684 F/Sgt L.G.Haines Killed Liesse, Laon, France. CG B-1/4
W/OP. 1314142 Sgt R.H.Winter Killed Liesse, Laon, France. CG B-1/4
F/E. R/81030 Sgt H.W.Fill Killed Liesse, Laon, France. CG B-1/4
A/G. R/88100 F/Sgt I.Macdonald Killed Liesse, Laon, France. CG B-1/4
A/G. 996048 Sgt A.P.Gielty Killed Liesse, Laon, France. CG B-1/4

408 Squadron 6 Group Halifax JB854 EQ/D
Aircraft crashed at Louppy-le-Chateau, 10 miles west of Verdun, France.
Pilot. R/120606 F/Sgt G.C.Heming Killed Louppy-le-Chateau, France. CG 3/5
Nav. R/90351 W/O R.Birchall Killed Louppy-le-Chateau, France. CG 3/5
B/A. R/115908 F/Sgt D.Zaleschuk Killed Louppy-le-Chateau, France. CG 3/5
W/OP. 1333188 Sgt R.W.Mason Killed Louppy-le-Chateau, France. CG 3/5
F/E. R/73825 Sgt A.C.Cantley Killed Louppy-le-Chateau, France. 2
A/G. R/149986 Sgt S.J.Jorgensen Killed Louppy-le-Chateau, France. 1
A/G. R/139949 Sgt S.Archie Killed Louppy-le-Chateau, France. CG 3/5

408 Squadron 6 Group Halifax DT752 EQ/W
Shot down near Nassogne, Belgium. Victim of Adjutant Ludwig Meister
I/NJG4
Pilot. J/20028 F/O J.R.L.Sergent Killed Heverlee, Belgium. 4-F-1
Nav. 1435573 Sgt G.M.Hill Killed Heverlee, Belgium. CG 4-F-4
B/A. 1216483 Sgt F.R.Cocks Killed Heverlee, Belgium. 4-F-3
W/OP. 1272498 Sgt D.F.Gargrave Killed Heverlee, Belgium. CG 4-F-4
F/E. R/81119 Sgt H.G.Machell Killed Heverlee, Belgium. CG 4-F-4
A/G. R/134910 F/Sgt W.Kwasney Killed Florennes, Belgium. B-24
A/G. R/70986 F/Sgt C.D.Heming Killed Heverlee, Belgium. 4-F-2

408 Squadron 6 Group Halifax JB925 EQ/R
Pilot. J/9407 F/Lt C.O.Hatle Killed Rheinberg, Germany. CG 8-L-6/11
2/Pilot. C/20765 F/O T.H.O'Connell Killed Rheinberg, Germany. CG 8-L-6/11
Nav. 135023 F/O L.H.Holmes Killed Rheinberg, Germany. CG 8-L-6/11
B/A. 1391764 Sgt S.F.Osmond Killed Rheinberg, Germany. CG 8-L-6/11
W/OP. R/97633 W/O H.Richmond Killed Rheinberg, Germany. CG 8-L-6/11
F/E. R/80897 Sgt W.G.Kapuscinski Killed Rheinberg, Germany. CG 8-L-6/11
A/G. R/75614 W/O J.W.Gibson Killed Rheinberg, Germany. CG 8-L-6/11
A/G. R/144193 F/Sgt A.A.Tschantre Killed Rheinberg, Germany. CG 8-L-6/11

10 Squadron 4 Group Halifax DT791 ZA/
Crash landed at Lewes, Sussex after operation to Pilsen.
Pilot. F/Lt J.A.Wood Slightly Injured.
2/Pilot. Sgt R. Rooney Slightly Injured.
Nav. P/O K.F.Whynes Slightly Injured.
B/A. P/O G.C.Stepney Slightly Injured.
W/OP. Sgt G.Walshaw Slightly Injured.
F/E. Sgt F.Beare Slightly Injured.
A/G. Sgt P.G.O'Kill Slightly Injured.
A/G. Sgt S.Prebble Slightly Injured.

Mannheim

April 16th/17th, 1943

Mannheim was the other major target on the same night as the Pilsen raid. It was successfully marked by the heavy Pathfinders and effectively bombed, by a force of 271 aircraft, 159 Wellingtons, 95 Stirlings and 17 Halifaxes. Again on this raid there was a high percentage of early returners (19.6%), but of the 53 aircraft which turned back, 34 of them were the two engined Wellingtons, many of which had various engine problems and flying on to a distant target with a doubtful engine was not to be recommended. There were good weather conditions for the raid, bright moonlight with no cloud over the target area. The 71 target indicators were well concentrated and the 233 flares which were also dropped by the Pathfinders helped the main bomber stream to visually indentify the Rivers Rhine and Neckar. A large amount of damage was caused especially in the industrial areas where production was stopped or temporarily reduced. The 220 tons of high explosive and 78.7 tons of incendiary bombs mainly fell south of the I. G. Farbenindustrie Works. The price paid was high for 18 aircraft failed to return, 9% of the attacking force of bombers. From the aircrew manning these bombers 69 were killed, three were missing, 20 were made prisoners of war and the high number of 19 made successful evasions.

Five Days in a Dinghy

One aircraft which did not return was Wellington HE862 of 166 Squadron, 1 Group and based in Kirmington, Lincolnshire. Its crew captained by Flying Officer Lupton took off for Mannheim at 21.19 hours and by 22.50 hours had ditched in the North Sea after engine trouble. First the port engine cut out after crossing the English coast at a height of 13,000 feet, but picked up revs again. Soon after the starboard engine began to act erratically and the aircraft lost height rapidly. The ditching order was given by the captain at 200 feet after he had jettisoned the bombs. The aircraft struck the sea nose first at an angle of about ten degrees and sank in four or five seconds. The captain was dead when two of the survivors, navigator Flying Officer R. A. Lord and rear gunner, Flying Officer E. G. Hadingham tried in vain to pull him into the dinghy a few minutes after ditching. The wireless operator, Sergeant J. P. Merton, who was badly injured, was also pulled into the dinghy, but died three hours later at about 02.00 hours. Nothing was seen or heard of the bomb aimer, Sergeant W. F. Whitfield, either immediately before or after the ditching. It was five days later that the dinghy which the survivors had launched was found drifting in the sea. The remaining two crew members had kept themselves alive on the meagre rations in their emergency flying packs. It must have been a terrible ordeal and later they admitted they had almost given up hope of being rescued after such a long time adrift. They received hospital treatment and eventually both survivors returned to their squadron.

Another Wellington from 196 Squadron, captained by Wing Commander A. G. Duguid, bombed the target and then when they had almost completed the return flight ran out of fuel. The crew were forced to bale out over Croydon, fortunately all without any injury.

Counting the Cost

From these two operations, a total of 54 aircraft were missing, the worst casualties that Bomber Command had suffered to date. In some Halifax squadrons, there had been very severe losses. 51 Squadron in 4 Group flying Halifaxes was especially hard hit losing five of its 17 strong force, although there were a number of aircrew from these missing planes who managed to evade capture, finally making it back to England. From the Halifaxes from 158 Squadron based at Lissett, Yorkshire one of the missing planes was HR779 NP/R captained by Flying Officer D. Bertera.

The whole crew of this bomber was so new to the squadron that they had only arrived at RAF Lissett, on the Friday morning of the Mannheim raid from training at 1658 Heavy Conversion Unit based at Riccall, Yorkshire. Normally crews were given some settling in period and often a second pilot trip for the captain. But there was a crew shortage on the squadron and within a few hours they went straight into their first raid briefing and were fated not to sleep in the billets they had been allocated.

Their aircraft was en route to the target when it was attacked by two Ju88 fighters near to Saarbrucken. Three engines of the Halifax bomber were badly damaged, one of which caught fire and the plane went into a dive before eventually coming into contact with a hill. With the greatest amount of luck possible, the angle of the bomber's dive coincided with the slope of the hill and the aircraft skidded down the hillside, coming to a standstill at the bottom. All the crew escaped uninjured from this miraculous landing. The only major injury was to the flight engineer, Flight Sergeant Berkeley, who sustained some broken ribs. After scrambling from the wreckage, the plane was set on fire and all the secret code papers were destroyed and the whole crew started walking in a westerly direction, hoping to get into France.

That evening the crew split up into smaller parties as they realised that a group of seven young men was too conspicious, Flight Sergeant Berkeley joined up with the bomb aimer Warrant Officer Jenkins. After the pair had walked for about two hours they came to a fairly wide river which they knew they had to cross. Both hunted around for a boat, which they eventually found but which was padlocked by a chain to its moorings. With the aid of the flexible wire saw from his escape kit Berkeley began to saw through one of the links and as he was completing the job his pilot and navigator turned up so they together all safely crossed the river in the boat. After hiding up in a wood on the 17th they set out at dusk and carried on walking for the next three days. On the evening of the 21st they saw an old woman working in a field and went across to ask for help. She told them that they were near the village of Bar-le-Duc whose villagers were quite friendly and it would be safe for them to go into the village to ask for assistance, but only after dusk. All decided that it would be best if only two went into the village to investigate so the pilot and navigator went in and met a young girl, who obviously was waiting for them. The pilot soon returned for the other two crew members and all went to the young girl's home for a meal. After two to three hours they left, but not until the flight engineer had been given some help to strap up his damaged ribs.

That Thursday evening, 22nd April, they walked until daybreak when they came to the area of Neufchateau where they decided to split up again, Berkeley going along with Fuge, the navigator. Their plan was to skirt the town and go through an area between the town and a new aerodrome which was being built on the outskirts. It had been raining heavily and both found the going very tough. While they were cautiously making their way through a wood they heard the command 'Halt' and were quickly arrested by a German patrol. Both were taken to Nancy and then on to the Gestapo headquarters at the Avenue Marechal Foch in Paris. There they were interrogated by the assistant Gestapo Chief Schneiders. Refusing to divulge any further information than their name rank and number they were transferred to Fresnes Prison.

During the seven weeks there Fuge and Berkeley occupied neighbouring cells and by chipping away a piece out of a window were able to talk to each other. They decided to cook up a story between them, as they had agreed it might be better than refusing to talk. A few days later they were again taken for interrogation and hoped that they would remember their new stories and more important that they would tally. Fuge was taken out first and Berkeley immediately afterwards and it seems that because to the Germans their stories tallied both were transferred to Dulag Luft where again they were further interrogated and subjected to the hot and cold treatment in the cells. Finally they were transferred to PoW Camp 357 at Kopernikus, Germany, where they spent the rest of the war in captivity. The other four members of the crew managed to evade capture, eventually getting back to the UK, two through Spain and two of them via Switzerland.

No. 51 Squadron Evaders

From the five Halifaxes from 51 Squadron lost on the Pilsen raid, the navigator, 1079476 Sergeant H. Riley, from Halifax DT578 managed to evade capture. From Halifax DT690 captained by 1385745 Sergeant J. McCrea, two of the crew, 1095982

Sergeant James Alderdice and 1440300 Sergeant David Jones, the flight engineer and air gunner respectively also evaded capture.

Halifax DT690 was on its way to the target over north-eastern France when it was attacked by a night fighter and although slightly damaged in the attack, continued towards the target. Another attack was made shortly afterwards by a Ju88 and according to the crew, this night fighter was destroyed by the gunner's return fire. Passing six miles south of Mannheim, the engineer reported that the aircraft was losing petrol, it was obvious that the tanks had been holed in the first attack and after a quick calculation, the captain decided that there would be insufficent fuel to fly to the target and back to base at their present rate of fuel consumption, so he decided to abort the mission and dropped the bombs on a railway line before turning back towards France. After flying for some time the petrol loss was such that the captain ordered a controlled bale out at 03.25 hours, about 7 miles east of Laon.

Sergeant Jones landed in the most inappropriate place, on a German aerodrome, just north of Glisy and in the process broke his two front teeth. After burying his 'chute outside the aerodrome perimeter, he began to walk south to the village of Glisy. Here, while cautiously making his way along the street, he met up with Sergeant Alderdice, who had also landed on the outskirts of the aerodrome. On landing Alderdice must have hit his head rather badly, for he states that he was quite silly, remembering clearly spending a lot of time around his landing site, looking for some locker keys and the exact sum of 3s 4d which had fallen out of his trouser pocket. He witnessed his own aircraft burning on the ground to the north and heard Germans on the aerodrome shouting and firing light *Flak* at another aircraft, a Stirling which was passing overhead at about 500 feet.

Both airmen, glad of each other's company, decided to hide in an old hay shed, where they cut off their badges of rank and flying badges and also the tops of Jones' flying boots to make them look like shoes. After eating some Horlicks tablets and also two raw eggs which they found in the hay, they decided to remain there for the rest of the day. At 21.30 hours they spotted a farmer walking past and as Alderdice could speak a little French decided to approach him for help. After showing him their maps, the farmer tried to indicate to them where exactly they had landed. He also gave them some food, but on a request for civilian clothes, he said that he would have to go back into the house for them. Both airmen watched the house and saw the farmer jump on his bike and pedal away quickly in the direction of the German aerodrome. It was obvious he intended to report their presence to the Germans. Wasting no more time the two airmen walked away eastwards until they came to the village of Liesse. Here they visited the railway station and tried to find out the time of the first train south. The porter to whom they spoke was very scared and would not help them at all. They then walked along the Laon - Charleville railway line, hoping that they might be able to jump on a passing train.

By now they were becoming very tired and hungry and when they came upon an old wood shed they went in and spent the night of April 17th/18th there. At 10.00 hours they saw and approached an old man who gave them some food and he later brought back to the wood shed his friend who had an English/French dictionary. They explained to the men what they needed, some civilian clothes and one or two other items. Jones gave the old man his chevrons as a souvenir and again the old man disappeared, but in a short while returned with yet another helper who could speak English. This helper brought them civilian clothes, a little food, razors and soap and a pair of shoes for Jones to replace the cut down flying boots, Alderdice was wearing his own shoes. The new helper advised them to make for Switzerland via Dijon, but both men did not think this a good plan and produced money from their escape kits, and asked the helper to buy them tickets to Bordeaux . The helper was happy to do this and took not only the French francs, but also changed the airmen's Dutch and Belgian money. The train tickets cost 400 Francs apiece.

Leaving the wood shed at 08.30 hours on April 19th, the helper accompanied them to a village called St Erme, on the main Laon/Reims railway line and after giving them their railway tickets and also some Paris Metro tickets for Gare d'Austerlitz he left the airmen on the platform. About mid day they caught a train for Reims, arriving there about 13.00 hours, but found that they had a five hour wait for the Paris train. They arrived in Paris around 20.30 hours and after noticing some discarded Metro tickets on the railway station floor which appeared quite different from those given to them by their helper, Alderdice decided to buy two new tickets to the Gare d'Austerlitz. At 22.30 hours they boarded the Bordeaux express and it was fortunate there was no control at the station barrier or on the train. As the train was crowded and both airmen were now confidently wearing civilan clothes they brazenly stood next to two German soldiers who were standing in the corridor and who travelled as far as Toulouse. The train arrived at Bordeaux at 07.30 hours on April 20th and after having some coffee in a café, both men decided to walk southwards out of the town, their intention being to cross the Line of Demarcation near Langon. Jones' new shoes were far too big for him and caused painful blisters, so they stopped to rest at the small village of Begles, three miles south of Bordeaux, where they tried several times to get food, but were only successful when they showed they had money. After spending another night in a shed they decided to return to Bordeaux.

They knew that the bridge across the River Garonne was heavily guarded, so they looked for a boat which would take them to Toulouse via the river. At 14.30 hours, they found a man in charge of a boat and revealed to him who they were and showed him their RAF uniforms which they still wore under their civilian clothes. After introducing them to yet another person, both airmen were fortunate that the man, Monsieur Larrose Desire, the captain of the barge, was prepared to take them on board but they were to hide in the hold of the barge. On Thursday April 22nd they started their journey up river and by 23rd April they had crossed the Line of Demarcation at Langon, where German officers boarded the barge to inspect the ship's papers but fortunately it was around lunch time and they did not bother to search the hold where the two airmen were hidden. Maybe the officers were anxious and ready for their mid day meal. They remained on the barge until May 4th when they left the river by the Canal Lateral de la Garonne and travelled via Agen, Castelsarrasin and on to Toulouse. During the journey on the barge Alderdice was advised to have his distinctive and conspicious red hair dyed. In Toulouse, the barge captain contacted an Escape organisation and the subsquent part of their bid for freedom was organised. On their arrival in Spain, the diary that Sergeant Jones kept illustrates that it was not easy for them even when they crossed the French - Spanish border on July 2nd, for both men were arrested by the Spanish authorities on the charge that they were trying to smuggle French currency into the country. They were detained for more than a month in Huesca Prison, which was situated about 60 miles north of Sargagossa, in what Jones describes as a hell of a place. It housed many nationalities, some even under sentence of death. Conditions were atrocious and the food was mostly watered down bean soup. It was seemingly interminable waiting and the monotony of prison life wore down the two airmen. But at last release came and at 11.00 hours on Friday August 6th 1943, Sergeant Jim Alderdice and Sergeant David Jones left in the company of a British Air Attache after spending 32 days in prison since crossing the frontier. Soon it was to Gibraltar and home to UK on August 15th, 1943.

On their return both airmen were awarded the Distinguished Flying Medal for their outstanding efforts in evading. The five remaining crew members became prisoners of war.

Casualties April 16th/17th, 1943. Target Mannheim

166 Squadron 1 Group Wellington HE862 AS/L
Ditched in North Sea
Pilot. 125539 F/O S.J.Lupton Missing, Runnymede Memorial 125
Nav. 121315 F/O R.A.Lord Rescued.
B/A. R/129438 Sgt J.P.Merton Missing, Runnymede Memorial 186
W/OP. 1063748 Sgt W.F.Whitfield Missing, Runnymede Memorial 169
A/G. 80370 F/O E.G.Hadingham Rescued.

15 Squadron 3 Group Stirling BF474 LS/H
Aircraft crashed at St.Erme, France.
Pilot. 143451 P/O J.L.Shiells DFM Killed St.Erme, Laon, France CG D-13/20
2/Pilot. J/17357 P/O K.M.Piche Killed St.Erme, Laon, France CG D-13/20
Nav. 143422 P/O C.B.Perring Killed St.Erme, Laon, France CG D-13/20
B/A. R/94993 F/Sgt B.J.A.Bessette Killed St.Erme, Laon, France CG D-13/20
W/OP. 1182265 Sgt J.Gould Killed St.Erme, Laon, France CG D-13/20
F/E. 547135 Sgt J.P.Lacy Killed St.Erme, Laon, France CG D-13/20
A/G. 1249758 Sgt D.J.A.Hyde Killed St.Erme, Laon, France CG D-13/20
A/G. 1332170 Sgt L.A.James Killed St.Erme, Laon, France CG D-13/20

15 Squadron 3 Group Stirling BK691 LS/F
Aircraft crashed at Hetzerath, Germany.
Pilot. 117422 F/Lt D.H.Haycock DFC Killed Rheinberg, Germany. CG 8-H-1/4
Nav. 1357462 Sgt J.S.Blackburn Killed Rheinberg, Germany. CG 8-H-1/4
B/A. 143396 P/O H.C.Fiddes Killed Rheinberg, Germany. CG 8-H-1/4
W/OP. 1179661 Sgt H.Fortune Killed Rheinberg, Germany. CG 8-H-1/4
F/E. 171703 F/O C.W.Hobgen PoW. Stalag Luft 3, Sagan. 410
A/G. 625668 Sgt T.L.Bromley Killed Rheinberg, Germany. CG 8-H-1/4
A/G. 1360248 Sgt J.W.Greenwood Killed Rheinberg, Germany. CG 8-H-1/4

75 Squadron 3 Group Stirling BF451 AA/Z
Aircraft crashed at Chigny les Roses, France.
Pilot. NZ/415819 P/O K.H.Groves Killed Choloy, Nancy, France. 2-A-6
2/Pilot. R/102353 W/O J.O Way Killed Choloy, Nancy, France. 2-A-7
Nav. 1149715 Sgt T.G.Shergold Killed Choloy, Nancy, France. 2-A-6
B/A. 656462 Sgt R.F.Wanstall Killed Choloy, Nancy, France. 2-A-1
W/OP. 1376120 Sgt R.L.Pierson Killed Choloy, Nancy, France. 2-A-2
F/E. 971743 Sgt L.C.Cameron Killed Choloy, Nancy, France. 2-A-8
A/G. 1187983 Sgt L.L.Everden Killed Choloy, Nancy, France. 2-A-4
A/G. NZ/413281 Sgt R.C.Stone Killed Choloy, Nancy, France. 2-A-3

75 Squadron 3 Group Stirling W7469 AA/O
Aircraft crashed at Katzenbach, Germany.
Pilot. NZ/412211 P/O K.F.Debenham Killed Rheinberg, Germany. 20-A-10
Nav. R/87330 W/O R.J.Barnes Killed Rheinberg, Germany. CG 20-A-13/14
B/A. 1312572 Sgt D.M.T.Watts Killed Rheinberg, Germany. CG 20-A-13/14
W/OP. 1377412 Sgt P.B.Pearson Killed Rheinberg, Germany. 20-A-12
F/E. 1193816 F/Sgt D.Wainwright PoW. Stalag Luft 6, Heydekrug. 1108
A/G. 629241 Sgt J.J.Davis Killed Rheinberg, Germany. 20-A-11
A/G. 1353768 Sgt J.L.Marlow Killed Rheinberg, Germany. CG 20-A-13/14

90 Squadron 3 Group Stirling BK725 WP/M
Aircraft crashed at Commenchou, north-west of Chauny, France.
Pilot. 117423 F/Lt P.D.White PoW. Stalag Luft 3, Sagan. 1104
2/Pilot. R/125293 Sgt W.E.Phillips Evaded capture.
Nav. 126042 F/O S.F.Everiss Evaded capture.
B/A. 120911 F/O G.D.Ross Evaded capture.
W/OP. 1376850 Sgt R.G.Gaisford Evaded capture.
F/E. 1102463 Sgt A.Smith Evaded capture.
A/G. 1217375 Sgt J.B.Ford Evaded capture.
A/G. NZ/413875 Sgt W.J.Fitzgerald Evaded capture.

214 Squadron 3 Group Stirling BK653 BU/A
Attacked by 3 Me 109s on way to target. Crew baled out at 00.15 hours (17/4/43)
20 miles north of Beauvais, France. Aircraft crashed at Bonneuil, France.
Pilot. R/92762 F/Sgt D.E.James Evaded capture.
2/Pilot. 921996 Sgt W.G.Grove Evaded capture. Returned to ops with 15 Sqd.
(146424 F/Lt) Killed Rheinberg, Germany. (24/3/44) 11-E-16
Nav. 123112 Sgt J.A.Smith Evaded capture.
B/A. 911341 Sgt J.Hall Evaded capture.

W/OP. 130224 Sgt R.W.Adams Evaded capture.
F/E. 1322140 F/Sgt C.G.Walton PoW. Stalag 357, Kopernikus. 1165
A/G. 1334827 F/Sgt G.B Gallagher PoW. Stalag 357, Kopernikus. 1067
A/G. 1132944 Sgt E.M.Lee Killed Poix-de-la-Somme, France. E-12

218 Squadron 3 Group Stirling BF514 HA/X
Aircraft crashed at Raucourt, 10 miles east of Sedan, France.
Pilot. 125987 F/O K.S.Bird Killed Choloy, Nancy, France. CG 1A-A-18/20
Nav. 138684 P/O D.F.Howlett Killed Choloy, Nancy, France. 1A-A-17
B/A. R/125806 F/Sgt D.E.Roberts Killed Choloy, Nancy, France. 1A-A-16
W/OP. 1126345 Sgt H.N.Hamilton Evaded capture.
F/E. 1160100 Sgt L.W.Canning Evaded capture
A/G. 1236043 Sgt F.J.Knight Killed Choloy, Nancy, France. CG 1A-A-18/20
A/G. R/135092 F/Sgt E.J.Longstaff Killed Choloy, Nancy. CG 1A-A-18/20

78 Squadron 4 Group Halifax JB870 EY/
Pilot. 1387760 Sgt W.Illingworth Killed Roye, Amiens, France 1-AA-13
Nav. 1316504 Sgt C.G.West Killed Roye, Amiens, France 1-AA-15
B/A. 125643 F/O H.D.Dixon Killed Roye, Amiens, France 1-AA-16
W/OP. 1270671 Sgt E.G.Thomas Killed Roye, Amiens, France 1-AA-14
F/E. 995589 Sgt R.Woodall Killed Roye, Amiens, France 1-AA-11
A/G. 1384483 Sgt S.W.Patton Killed Roye, Amiens, France 1-AA-12
A/G. 1652776 Sgt D.A.Watkins Killed Roye, Amiens, France 1-AA-17

51 Squadron 4 Group Halifax HR779 NP/R
Aircraft belly landed at Saarbrucken.
Pilot. 118605 F/O D.Bertera Evaded capture.
Nav. 1388991 W/O A.J.Fuge PoW. Stalag 357, Kopernikus. 8
B/A. 1316316 Sgt W.J.Jenkins Evaded capture.
W/OP. 1987496 Sgt J.W.E.Lawrence DFM Evaded capture.
F/E. 1436315 W/O F.R.Berkeley PoW. Stalag 357, Kopernikus. 3
A/G. 1539234 F/Sgt E.Durant PoW. Stalag Luft 6, Heydekrug. 386
A/G. 1319207 Sgt W.J.Barber DFM Evaded capture.

196 Squadron 4 Group Wellington HE397 ZO/
Aircraft crashed near Couvron-et-Aumencourt, France.
Pilot. 143666 P/O I.M.Morgan Killed Couvron-et-Aumencourt. CG A-12/13
Nav. 959541 F/Sgt R.Hill Killed Couvron-et-Aumencourt, France. CG A-12/13
B/A. 127120 F/O A.W.A.Trevarthen Killed Couvron-et-Aumencourt CGA12/13
W/OP. 1068572 Sgt N.Bruce Killed Couvron-et-Aumencourt. CG A-12/13
A/G. 998431 Sgt L.Pickford Killed Couvron-et-Aumencourt. CG A-12/13

431 Squadron 4 Group Wellington HE379 SE/H
Pilot. 655895 W/O H.Sutterby PoW. Stalag Luft 6, Heydekrug. 1041
Nav. J/22562 F/Lt W.E.Paton PoW. Stalag Luft 3, Sagan. 1085
B/A. R/130665 W/O R.G.Rudd PoW. Stalag Luft 4, Sagan. 1034
W/OP. 1271192 F/Sgt P.F.Cartwright PoW. Stalag Luft 6, Heydekrug. 984
A/G. 572631 Sgt M.R.Hadland Killed Rheinberg, Germany. 18-C-15

466 Squadron 4 Group Wellington HE501 HD/
Pilot. A/406585 P/O C.F.Tozer Killed Seraincourt, Mezieres, France. CG 4/6
Nav. R/90189 W/O G.K.Young Killed Seraincourt, Mezieres, France. CG 4/6
B/A. 137584 Sgt H.E.Jones Killed Seraincourt, Mezieres, France. CG 4/6
W/OP. 1193463 Sgt R.K.White Killed Seraincourt, Mezieres, France. CG 4/6
A/G. 1531620 Sgt G.Errington Killed Seraincourt, Mezieres, France. CG 4/6

420 Squadron 6 Group Wellington HE682 PT/
Shot down at Froidlier, Belgium at 01.30 hours (17/4/43)
Pilot. R/127884 F/Sgt L.M.Horahan Killed Heverlee, Belgium. JG 4-F-6/7 *
Nav. R/124524 F/Sgt J.E.Isaacs Killed Heverlee, Belgium. JG 4-F-6/7 *
B/A. R/113191 F/Sgt L.K.Plank Killed Sohier, Dinant, Belgium. 1
W/OP. 1206738 Sgt H.S.P.Radford Killed Heverlee, Belgium. 4-F-5 *
A/G. R/73769 F/Sgt K.T.P.Allan PoW. Stalag 357, Kopernikus. 54 *
*Originally buried by *Luftwaffe* at St Trond, Belgium.

425 Squadron 6 Group Wellington HE475 KW/E
Pilot. R/107207 W/O P.L.Bujold PoW. Stalag 357, Kopernikus. 1057
Nav. 1231462 F/Sgt W.Harris PoW. Stalag 357, Kopernikus. 1150
B/A. 124318 P/O H.Gray Killed Cologne, Germany. 4-AA-19
W/OP. A/412184 W/O W.F.Redding PoW. Stalag 357, Kopernikus. 1159
A/G. R/95511 F/Sgt J.M.Leblanc Killed Cologne, Germany. 3-AA-1

426 Squadron 6 Group Wellington HE591 OW/
Pilot. 1004634 Sgt L.Thompson Killed Rheinberg, Germany. JG 8-F-19/20
Nav. R/109126 W/O J.C.Kennedy Killed Rheinberg, Germany. 8-F-16
B/A. 130506 F/O R.G.Wood Killed Rheinberg, Germany. 8-F-17
W/OP. 1078306 Sgt J.Parkinson Killed Rheinberg, Germany. JG 8-F-19/20
A/G. R/53979 W/O E.A.Whalen Killed Rheinberg, Germany. 8-F-18

427 Squadron 6 Group Wellington HE547 ZL/
Pilot. R/130533 F/Sgt S.Tomyn Killed Rheinberg, Germany. 8-D-25
Nav. 1578210 F/Sgt G.W.Hall PoW. Stalag 357, Kopernikus. 1149
B/A. 1332016 Sgt A.F.Johnson PoW. Stalag Luft 6, Heydekrug. 1009
W/OP. 657419 W/O A.T.Symons PoW. Stalag 357, Kopernikus. 1043
A/G. R/140353 Sgt W.Ostaficuik PoW. Stalag 357, Kopernikus. 1025

429 Squadron 6 Group Wellington BK162 AL/
Aircraft attacked by fighter at 02.15 hours over Septmonts, south of Soissons,
France and caught fire.
Pilot. 37015 S/Ldr F.A.Holmes DFC Killed Septmonts, Soissons, France. 2
2/Pilot. 658498 Sgt J.Milne Evaded capture.
Nav. 50436 P/O J.McMaster Killed Septmonts, Soissons, France. 3
B/A. R/104442 Sgt D.S.Ritchie Killed Septmonts, Soissons, France. 4
W/OP. 940017 F/Sgt G.Gill Killed Septmonts, Soissons, France. 1
A/G. J/10875 F/Lt G.A.Lunn Killed Septmonts, Soissons, France. 5

196 Squadron 4 Group Wellington HE469 ZO/
Aircraft ran out of petrol over the Croydon area after operation to Mannheim.
Pilot. 37468 W/Cdr A.G.Duguid Baled out.
Nav. 119477 P/O E.H.Swain Baled out.
B/A. 126819 P/O F.Darbyshire Baled out.
W/OP. R/87333 Sgt A.M.Long Baled out.
A/G. 911418 Sgt J.F.Ray Baled out.

Minelaying

April 17th/18th, 1943

On the night of 17th/18th April, a mixed force of 20 aircraft continued minelaying around the Bay of Biscay ports, again without any loss, after laying 42 mines. Two returned early from the general mining area as they were unable to get an accurate pinpoint to drop their mines.

A Minelaying op

A Wellington captain, Warrant Officer Peter Stead, who was fortunate to finish his tour of operations, describes in his wartime diary, his experiences on a particular minelaying operation and illustrates the dangers and difficulties encountered on such an operation.

"We were detailed to lay mines in the bay off Brest, and pretty close in shore. The run down England was quiet and mostly in daylight, so we were able to map read most of the way. On leaving the English coast I came down to 700 feet above the sea and stayed there until we were due west of Brest. Then turning towards the coast, I came down to 500 feet and opened up full throttle. We saw some islands ahead of us which showed us that we were about eight miles too far north, so I came down to 200 feet and turned over them, doing about 210 mph. We flew south for two minutes out to sea, then back towards the coast. This time we were on track and got a pin point in the right position and turned towards our dropping area. I climbed back to 500 feet, our dropping height and dropped the mines in the exact spot we had been briefed, before turning back seawards.

"Just then a *Flak* ship opened upon us. We must have been a lovely target, so low and silhouetted against the moon. The first burst of fire went underneath and anticipating the second, I dived towards the sea to about 200 feet. The second burst of *Flak* was even longer and luckily passed above and to starboard. Lovely shooting and very close. We were properly caught in it, but nothing actually hit us, although there were bursts all around the aircraft. The rear gunner gave a very long burst from his guns at the point from where the tracer was coming and this made them stop firing, but there was no means of telling if our return fire did any damage. It was most exciting and we ran well out to sea before turning for home, having a quiet run to base."

La Spezia

April 18th/19th, 1943

The Ruhr continued to have some respite, for on the 18th/19th April, La Spezia again was the target when it was visited by 158 Lancasters and 5 Halifaxes. 15 Lancasters had to abort their mission early. This time the city centre appeared to have borne the brunt of the attack with a more concentrated attack than the previous raid. Crews reported a large orange explosion between 02.02 and 02.04 hours, which appeared to be an ammunition dump. The harbour was mined with 28 mines by eight Lancaster aircraft at the same time as the city raid. One PFF Lancaster was lost on this La Spezia bombing raid, a 0.6% loss rate. The Lancaster minelayers came back to their bases unscathed. On the same night ten Stirling minelayers were also out in the Bay of Biscay, laying 30 mines, without suffering any loss.

Casualties April 18th/19th, 1943. Target La Spezia

156 Squadron 8 Group Lancaster W4849 GT/
Pilot. 1313990 Sgt G.S.Cooper Missing, Runnymede Memorial 146
Nav. 1496446 Sgt K.Coulson Missing, Runnymede Memorial 146
B/A. 1198784 Sgt D.R.Edwards Missing, Runnymede Memorial 148
W/OP. 1210696 Sgt R.Harrison Missing, Runnymede Memorial 152
F/E. 1485877 Sgt J.J.Vaulkhard Missing, Runnymede Memorial 168
A/G. R/50471 Sgt N.O.Robinson Missing, Runnymede Memorial 185
A/G. 1579640 Sgt A.K.Eley Killed Merville-Franceville-Plage, France. 1

Stettin

April 20th/21st, 1943

A target more than 600 miles away, well beyond *Oboe* range was the next to be attacked. It was the city of Stettin on the night of 20th/21st April. A force of 339 aircraft, 194 Lancasters, 134 Halifaxes and 11 Stirlings left their English bases but were soon depleted by 13 early returners (3.8%). The city was illuminated by 46 Pathfinders who dropped their 95 target indicators and 248 flares. Their marking, commencing at 01.02 hours, was well nigh perfect in the clear visibility and cloudless skies over the target area which enabled the main force bombers to identify the ground features of the River Oder and dock area, and drop their 387.5 tons of high explosive and 383.3 tons of incendiaries accurately. So many fierce fires were caused that they were still burning when the photographic reconnaisance plane saw them clearly 36 hours after the attack. German records show that approximately 100 acres of the city was devastated, with severe damage to a chemical factory, where production was completely stopped. 586 people were killed. Twenty one aircraft were lost, a 7.2% loss rate, and from their crews 83 were killed, 48 were never found, 21 became prisoners of war, 7 were interned in Sweden and one lucky airman evaded capture in Denmark and eventually escaped to Sweden.

Aircraft Struck by Incendiaries

At 01.08 hours over the Stettin target Halifax JB785 from 35 Squadron, captained by Pilot Officer W. S. Sherk DFC, was struck by incendiary bombs which had been dropped from above by another attacking bomber. The Halifax temporarily went out of control when the pilot's seat caught fire and other incendiaries exploded in the flight engineer's position. Two members of the crew, 151973 Flying Officer R. G. Morrison, the bomb aimer and rear gunner, R/60901 Flight Sergeant H. T. Woonton, baled out on the captain's orders, before he rescinded the order when he managed to regain control. When a bale out order is given there is no time to question the command and the two crew who baled out acted correctly. They were prisoners of war until hostilities ceased. The pilot and the rest of the crew brought the bomber safely back to base.

Rear Gunner Killed by Gunfire

After a running battle with a night fighter, Stirling BK720 from 214 Squadron and captained by Flight Lieutenant A. F. Wallace managed to limp back to base, but sadly the rear gunner, Sergeant R. E. Thompson, was killed in the air fight.

First Allied Airman to Escape from Denmark to Sweden

One of the aircraft lost on the Stettin raid was a Pathfinder Stirling, R9261 from 7 Squadron captained by Flight Lieutenant C. W. Parish. On arriving over the target the port inner engine began to give trouble and the bomb sight was out of order. As they were Pathfinders, the pilot decided that he was unable to drop any of his target indicators with sufficent accuracy so he turned the aircraft away from the target and flew in a NNW direction. At about 02.00 hours the Stirling was attacked by an enemy fighter while flying over Korsor on the west of Zealand, Denmark. Such was the ferocity of the attack that the bomber was a mass of flames by the time the crew heard the bale out order. The first and only member of the crew to get out was the Canadian flight engineer, Sergeant D. V. Smith, who managed to bale out at about 800 feet before the bomber blew up. The remainder of the crew, including a Squadron Leader W. A. Blake, who was acting as a second pilot, were all killed.

Sergeant Smith landed north-east of Korsor and quite near the sea in a field which had recently been sown with grain. Like all aircrew who had landed in occupied territory, his first job was to dispose of his 'chute and Mae West which he hid in a mud hole and covered them with some branches from a nearby bush. He found that he was on the north bank of a river which ran south west into Musholm Bay. He walked north-east along the banks of the river and crossed a railway line and road before he left the river bank around dawn and he hid in a clump of trees. From his hiding place he could see a farmer working in a feld about 20 to 30 feet away, but he was unsure of what to do so he did not approach him. About midday, when the farmer had gone and the field was empty, Sergeant Smith walked to an empty house about 400 yards away, where he went to sleep in the attic until 17.30 hours. Still dressed in his battle dress but minus the blouse badges which he had cut off, he went to a nearby farm to ask the way to Copenhagen. A woman at the farm pointed out the town of Slagelse about two and half miles away, but didn't offer any further help, maybe she did not understand he was an evader or was too frightened to offer any assistance. Making use of any cover he could Sergeant Smith kept on walking across country, crossing two main roads as he went. At 21.00 hours when he was very tired he came upon another farmer working in a field near a farm house, so he decided to approach him and ask again the way to Copenhagen. The farmer certainly could not understand him, but his wife came out of the house and Sergeant Smith explained by signs that he was a British airman. He was taken into the farmhouse and given bread, eggs, coffee and milk. While the young son kept a look out for any Germans, he ate the most welcome meal. He was then shown the way to Soro. On leaving the farm he walked on until he reached a large wood beside a railway line, where he hid until dawn of the next day, the 22nd of April.

Leaving the wood he kept to the railway track and skirted Soro on the south to avoid some marshes and small lakes. Seeing a small isolated farmhouse he stopped to ask for water, but instead was given breakfast and shown the position of the next town of Ringsted. Continuing to walk, he reached another farm south of Ringsted, where the farmer gave him a small bottle of beer to quench his thirst. Again skirting the town he walked through a very heavily wooded area before coming to a main road which appeared to run from Ringsted to Koge where he was forced to rest at an empty stable on the outskirts of a hamlet. By this time Sergeant Smith's feet were very badly blistered and as he was sitting outside the stable trying to cut off the tops of his flying boots, he was noticed by a Dane who was out walking with his wife and children. Sergeant Smith asked him the way to Copenhagen and explained that he was an English flier. Although he was unable to speak English, the Dane understood the general gist of what was said and by signs told Smith to stay where he was and that he would be back at 21.00 hours. When, as promised, he did return he brought with him a jacket, a pair of old plus four trousers, a sweater, a pair of rubber boots and a trilby hat. Again by signs he told Sergeant Smith to spend the night in the stable and that he would come again early next day.

At 05.30 hours on 23rd April the Dane returned and took Sergeant Smith to his home at Dalby for breakfast, where he was supplied with a Shell motor map on which a route had been marked for Copenhagen with Swastika signs drawn in to show areas which were heavily guarded by Germans. Smith was also given 20 Krone in money, a clasp knife and a shaving mirror. In return for all this generous help, Sergeant Smith gave the Dane, who was obviously not well off 1500 francs from his escape kit. The Dane, George Rasmussen, then took the Sergeant to the main Ringsted to Koge road and left him. After walking along this road, shortly before Koge, he took a by-pass road which led north east to the coast road. On this by-pass Sergeant Smith called at yet another farmhouse where he was given bread, cheese and milk by the friendly Danes. Fearing that the Germans might be more active on the coast, he took a branch road inland to Taastrup. It was here that he found a farm where the people spoke a little English, the Sorenson family. They provided him with supper and marked his road map with yet another route to avoid the police. They also suggested that it would be of little use going on to Copenhagen and that he should aim for the town of Elsinore. From the farm he continued through Taastrup, but as there were many German soldiers about, he left the roads and cut across country. At about 20.30 hours he came to a farm on the outskirts to Glostrup and here with the aid of an English/Danish dictionary, which he had been given by the last farmer, he was able to explain his identity more easily. The people at the farm telephoned a friend, the local school head teacher, Mr E. Marbrog who spoke English fluently. It was then arranged that Sergeant Smith should meet Mr Marborg in the main street of Glostrup at 07.00 hours the next morning. As there were six young children in the farmhouse from whom he had to be concealed, in case they talked about him, Smith spent the night outside in the barn.

The next morning, 24th April, the people at the farm gave him a supply of sandwiches and 5 Kroner and bade him farewell, before the children awoke. After walking to Glostrup, about 6 Kilometres away, he met the schoolteacher who bought some rail tickets and accompanied him to Elsinore, going via Copenhagen where they had to wait for about an hour to change trains. The station was full of Germans and Smith and his helper had an anxious time waiting for their connecting train. They reached Elsinore at 10.30 hours and looked around in vain for a boat which would safely take Sergeant Smith the short distance across to Sweden.

Ships left Elsinore every half hour for Sweden, but it was hopeless to try to board such a ferry as they were heavily guarded by German soldiers. Unfortunately the school master, who had no links with any underground movement, had to leave, bitterly disappointed that he had been unable to get in touch with anyone who could continue to help, but he suggested that Smith should contact the local fishermen. Alone once again the Sergeant continued to walk northwards along the shore from Elsinore still trying to locate local boats but with no success. By nightfall he came upon an unlocked, empty, beach summer house which had a table, chair and some blankets. He took possession of the summer house and during the night a patrolling Danish policeman looked in, but luckily uttered no word as either he didn't see Smith curled up in the blankets or he knew all about him and was prepared to look the other way. The next day, Sunday, April 25th, was wet and miserable and Smith walked disconsolately up and down the coast between Elsinore and Aalasgaarde. Finally he went to a house at Hellebaek, where a Danish flag was flying, a good sign that at least the occupants were proud Danes living under the German occupation. In answer to his knock, a young lady opened the door and Smith was lucky for she spoke very good English, but she was unable to help him with information about a boat. As Smith was leaving he was called back by a young man from the house, who gave him his first real meal for three days. The house belonged to a Mr and Mrs Folmer who also allowed him to listen to the BBC news, before he returned to the beach hut for the night.

The next day Smith approached an old fisherman, who although unable to speak English, realised what he wanted and by gestures showed that the Germans had confiscated his boat. By now Smith thought that his chances of getting away were hopeless and he was beginning to feel the strain of the last few days. But his luck had not run out, for across the road he spotted a man reading a newspaper in the sun lounge of a house. Thinking he had now nothing to lose, he knocked at the door. A woman answered and to Smith's surprise she too spoke fluent English. After he had explained his plight, she called her husband and he quickly took Smith in, locking the door after him. After a typical English meal of roast meat and potatoes, Smith was shown to the bathroom to take a welcome hot bath and then to a bedroom to rest. Unable to sleep, because of all the tension, he heard the bedroom door suddenly open and a short portly stranger shouting, "We will get you to Sweden". Apparently this newcomer had spent some time in America and had an English wife. He checked Smith's identity and left the airman with soaring hopes of an early getaway.

At 18.00 hours on April 25th, he left his newly found host Mr & Mrs Knudsen and was taken to the portly man's house, where he was interrogated about his bale out and Smith was told that this story would need to be checked with London and by being pointedly shown a small revolver he realised what would happen if his story could not be verified. After dinner on the evening of 26th April, a distinguished gentleman, Mr. Tjoern, called and took Smith by taxi to the nearest town, then on by train and taxi once more to Hellerup, where after many diversions to make sure they were not being followed they arrived at Mr. Tjoern's home. Smith stayed there until the following evening when Mr. Tjoren returned from work and announced that Smith would immediately be going to Sweden. They took a taxi to Skodsberg, where they hoped to get a boat but unfortunately there was a further delay and Lars Tjoern and Smith had to spend the night there. But the next day they met Chris Hanson, a Danish Resistance worker, who had made the final arrangements for the escape.

Under cover of darkness, Danish Resistance workers had assembled their collapsible canoe and a warming measure of

Schnapps. They were off on their paddle to Sweden and freedom. They had been given the correct colours of the day to switch on their torch should a patrol boat spot them. The sea was quite rough and after a short time their canoe was picked up by a patrol boat's swinging searchlight beam, but by keeping their heads down low, the patrol boat passed by with out sighting them again. Early on the morning of May 1st, Smith's worries were over when they landed on a stretch of beach near Helsinborg, Sweden and after making sure they were well inland they surrendered to the Swedish police, who treated Smith with great kindness. After an interview with the Consul, he was quickly taken to Stockholm before being flown back to Leuchars, Scotland on May 13th. Later Smith was repatriated to his home town of Toronto, Canada.

Casualties April 20th/21st, 1943. Target Stettin

83 Squadron 8 Group Lancaster ED312 OL/
Message received at base at 01.14 hours (21/4/43) that crew were baling out.
Aircraft crashed at Klagshamm, Sweden.
Pilot. J/16989 P/O C.P.McDonald Interned in Sweden.
Nav. 141403 P/O V.W.J.Nunn Interned in Sweden.
B/A. 1076453 Sgt C.M.Paley Interned in Sweden.
W/OP. 798663 Sgt M.A.Coles Interned in Sweden.
F/E. 941046 Sgt T.J.Parrington Interned in Sweden.
A/G. 1311907 F/Sgt C.J.Ford Interned in Sweden.
A/G. 48603 F/O J.P.Crebbin DFC Interned in Sweden.

7 Squadron 8 Group Stirling R9261 MG/M
Shot down Konigsmark/Slagelse, Denmark.Victim of Uffz Berg 7/NJG3
Pilot. 81927 F/Lt C.W.Parish Killed Svino, Denmark. CG 9
2/Pilot. 40202 S/Ldr W.A.Blake Killed Svino, Denmark. 7
Nav. J/16604 P/O E.R.Vance Killed Svino, Denmark. CG 9
B/A. R/86762 W/O J.R.Marshall Killed Svino, Denmark. JG 6
W/OP. R/89611 W/O L.J.Krulicki Killed Svino, Denmark. 10
F/E. R/70152 Sgt D.V.Smith Evaded capture *
A/G. 1575746 Sgt D.C.Farley Killed Svino, Denmark. JG 6
A/G. 1004486 Sgt J.Lees Killed Svino, Denmark. 8
* First Allied airmen to escape from Denmark to Sweden in World War II.

35 Squadron 8 Group Halifax JB785 TL/F
Pilot. J/16137 P/O W.S.Sherk DFC
B/A. 151973 F/O R.G.Morrison PoW. Stalag Luft 1, Barth Vogelsang 5180
A/G. R/60901 F/Sgt H.Woonton PoW. Stalag 357, Kopernikus. 1114
Both baled out on orders over target. Order countermanded and aircraft flown back to base.

12 Squadron 1 Group Lancaster ED326 PH/
Pilot. A/413208 F/Sgt N.C.Keeffe Missing, Runnymede Memorial 193
Nav. 658400 Sgt J.Goulding Missing, Runnymede Memorial 151
B/A. 1531353 Sgt K.C.Eagland Missing, Runnymede Memorial 148
W/OP. 1029629 Sgt A.Bone Missing, Runnymede Memorial 143
F/E. 569552 Sgt R.E.Dadd Missing, Runnymede Memorial 146
A/G. 657501 Sgt G.Brady Missing, Runnymede Memorial 153
A/G. 1574058 Sgt F.McPhillips Missing, Runnymede Memorial 158

12 Squadron 1 Group Lancaster ED326 PH/
Shot down Vregeno, Denmark at 02.20 hours (21/4/43) by *Flak II/Zug 1/Lei.*
Pilot. 37480 S/Ldr J.C.Richards Missing, Runnymede Memorial 119
Nav. 128518 F/O G.F.Jones Killed Nyborg, Denmark G-7
B/A. 1321620 Sgt L.A.Rummery Killed Odense, Denmark. BD-347
W/OP. 1029848 Sgt F.T.Peake Killed Copenhagen, Denmark. X-1-127
F/E. 577654 Sgt H.V.Durrant Missing, Runnymede Memorial 148
A/G. 143859 P/O R.P.Cryer Killed Nyborg, Denmark G-5
A/G. 1600059 Sgt W.J.Colwill Missing, Runnymede Memorial 145

100 Squadron 1 Group Lancaster ED709 HW/S
Shot down Ringkobing Fiord, Denmark at 03.25 hours (21/4/43) by *Flak II/Zug 3/742.*
Pilot. 39136 W/Cdr J.G.W.Swain Killed Esbjerg, (Fourfelt), Denmark. A-9-19
Nav. A/411043 F/Lt B.F.Myers Killed Lemvig, Denmark. 734
B/A. 131125 P/O C.E.Wellard Killed Lemvig, Denmark. 706
W/OP. 1197663 Sgt R.S.Sidwell Missing, Runnymede Memorial 164
F/E. 652617 Sgt T.Carter Missing, Runnymede Memorial 144
A/G. A/420327 F/Sgt M.A.B.Watkins Missing, Runnymede Memorial 194
A/G. 1333520 Sgt R.A.Whelans Missing, Runnymede Memorial 169

100 Squadron 1 Group Lancaster ED557 HW/Y
Shot down Sprogo, Denmark at 01.31 hours (21/4/43) by *Flak II/zug 1/Lei.*
Pilot. 124510 F/Lt W.A.Jones Missing, Runnymede Memorial 119
Nav. A/411783 F/O G.B.Herring Missing, Runnymede Memorial 188
B/A. 1320280 Sgt C.Walker Killed Copenhagen, Denmark. X-7-131
W/OP. 1377124 Sgt B.W.D.Cooper Missing, Runnymede Memorial 146
F/E. 1171532 Sgt D.R.Ling Missing, Runnymede Memorial 157
A/G. 1339519 Sgt A.M.Hodges Missing, Runnymede Memorial 153
A/G. 1531156 Sgt S.J.Houston Missing, Runnymede Memorial 154

103 Squadron 1 Group Lancaster ED614 PM/
Shot down V.Vedsted/Ribe, Denmark by fighter at 00.45 hours (21/4/43).
Pilot. 145158 P/O G.M.Pettigrew Killed Esbjerg, (Fourfelt), Denmark. A-10-24
Nav. 1238287 Sgt W.D.Ramsay Killed Esbjerg, (Fourfelt), Denmark. A-10-20
B/A. 1559316 Sgt A.I.Mackay Killed Esbjerg, (Fourfelt), Denmark. A-10-22
W/OP. A/405676 F/Sgt P.J.Cramer Killed Esbjerg, (Fourfelt). A-10-26
F/E. 542661 Sgt J.Cooper Killed Esbjerg, (Fourfelt), Denmark. A-10-19
A/G. 976368 Sgt R.G.Elkins Killed Esbjerg, (Fourfelt), Denmark. A-10-21
A/G. 47871 F/O A.Daley DFM Killed Esbjerg, (Fourfelt), Denmark. A-10-23

460 Squadron 1 Group Lancaster W4330 UV/H
Shot down by fighter Vestbrick, Denmark at 03.12 hours (21/4/43).
Pilot. A/408656 F/Sgt K.James Killed Esbjerg, (Fourfelt), Denmark. A-11-17
Nav. A/409175 F/Sgt B.M.Muir Killed Esbjerg, (Fourfelt), Denmark. A-11-18
B/A. A/413482 F/Sgt B.Finnane Killed Esbjerg, (Fourfelt), Denmark. A-11-19
W/OP. 1128672 Sgt W.D.Mayoh Killed Esbjerg, (Fourfelt), Denmark. A-11-20
F/E. 1475502 Sgt B.Smith Killed Esbjerg, (Fourfelt), Denmark. A-11-16
A/G. A/405921 P/O E.A.Mahoney Killed Esbjerg, (Fourfelt), Denmark. A-11-21
A/G. A/412957 F/Sgt B.H.Harvey Killed Esbjerg, (Fourfelt), Denmark. A-11-22

460 Squadron 1 Group Lancaster W4956 UV/J
Pilot. A/409221 F/Sgt W.F.Pridgeon Missing, Runnymede Memorial 193
Nav. A/416552 F/O R.E.Dollar Missing, Runnymede Memorial 187
B/A. A/411469 F/Sgt P.M.Mackenzie Killed Kiel, Germany. 4-H-8
W/OP. 1384232 Sgt F.A.Solly Missing, Runnymede Memorial 165
F/E. 1394694 Sgt C.A.Wills Missing, Runnymede Memorial 170
A/G. 1522573 Sgt R.J.Chapman Missing, Runnymede Memorial 145
A/G. A/409146 F/Sgt R.S.King Missing, Runnymede Memorial 193

460 Squadron 1 Group Lancaster W4325 UV/O
Pilot. A/416574 F/Sgt R.S.Hogben Missing, Runnymede Memorial 193
Nav. 966164 Sgt J.Pomfret Missing, Runnymede Memorial 162
B/A. 1558122 Sgt T.Boland Missing, Runnymede Memorial 143
W/OP. 1293036 Sgt R.E.Smith Missing, Runnymede Memorial 165
F/E. 1430231 Sgt A.J.Cousins Missing, Runnymede Memorial 146
A/G. 1810602 Sgt H.E.Dixon Missing, Runnymede Memorial 147
A/G. A/412633 F/Sgt F.McGlinchy Missing, Runnymede Memorial 193

10 Squadron 4 Group Halifax JB930 ZA/H
Crashed Tjaereborg (Esbjerg), Denmark at 23.20 hours (21/4/43).
Pilot. 1098307 W/O F.Glover PoW. Stalag 357, Kopernikus. 146
Nav. 1388419 W/O D.E.Taylor PoW. Stalag 357, Kopernikus. 1103
B/A. 1148678 Sgt R.Bell PoW. Stalag Luft 6, Heydekrug. 42773
W/OP. 1379856 F/Sgt E.J.Phillips PoW. Stalag 357, Kopernikus. 42688
F/E. 1486008 Sgt R.S.Burr PoW. Stalag 357, Kopernikus. No Number
A/G. 45552 F/Lt T.B.Baker PoW. Stalag 9C, Mulhausen. 39677
A/G. 920750 W/O R.E.Everett PoW. Stalag Luft 6, Heydekrug. 130

51 Squadron 4 Group Halifax DT628 MH/
Pilot. 1312833 Sgt B.T.Brett Missing, Runnymede Memorial 143
2/Pilot. 1393417 Sgt D.B.Martin Missing, Runnymede Memorial 158
Nav. 1090703 Sgt R.F.Lyster Missing, Runnymede Memorial 157
B/A. 49935 P/O R.H.Glover Missing, Runnymede Memorial 131
W/OP. 1123560 Sgt P.Shortland Missing, Runnymede Memorial 164
F/E. 635944 Sgt J.C.Waring Missing, Runnymede Memorial 168
A/G. 1316342 Sgt C.Vandy Missing, Runnymede Memorial 168
A/G. 1313503 Sgt A.Barrie BEM Missing, Runnymede Memorial 141

77 Squadron 4 Group Halifax HR714 KN/
Aircraft crashed at Mando, Denmark.
Pilot. 1561631 Sgt R.Watson Killed Esbjerg, (Fourfelt), Denmark. A-11-23
Nav. 611793 Sgt R.C.M.Douglas Killed Esbjerg, (Fourfelt), Denmark. A-10-18
B/A. 1383346 Sgt A.P.Deighton Killed Esbjerg, (Fourfelt), Denmark. A-11-24
W/OP. 1349949 Sgt J.B.Watt Killed Esbjeeg, (Fourfelt), Denmark. A-11-8
F/E. 1123153 Sgt T.Pearson Killed Esbjerg, (Fourfelt), Denmark. A-11-25
A/G. 1339381 Sgt A.Luke Killed Esbjerg, (Fourfelt), Denmark A-11-26
A/G. R/116029 F/Sgt R.G.Hume Killed Esbjerg, (Fourfelt), Denmark. A-10-25

77 Squadron 4 Group Halifax JB804 KN/
Pilot. 109093 F/Lt T.S.Lea DFC Killed Berlin, Germany. CG 14-G-1/6
Nav. 1181067 F/Sgt R.J.White Killed Berlin, Germany. CG 14-G-1/6
B/A. 128516 F/O D.J.D.Chitty Killed Berlin, Germany. CG 14-G-1/6
W/OP. 84885 F/Lt J.R.Harries Killed Berlin, Germany. CG 14-G-1/6
F/E. 1547554 Sgt G.H.Cruxton Killed Berlin, Germany. 14-H-12
A/G. 1515873 Sgt E.Carter Killed Berlin, Germany. 14-H-11
A/G. 1323203 Sgt R.W.Lambert Killed Berlin, Germany. 14-H-10

102 Squadron 4 Group Halifax HR712 DY/
Shot down Slipshavn, Denmark at 02.26 hours (21/4/43) by *Flak II/zug/I/lei*
and 8 MAA
Pilot. 1294744 W/O P.R.Oliver PoW. Stalag 357, Kopernikus. 1086
Nav. 1336841 Sgt G.L.Doidge Killed Nyborg, Denmark. G-8
B/A. 1316841 Sgt A.F.Warner Killed Nyborg, Denmark. G-4
W/OP. R/103506 W/O G.H.Bartman Killed Nyborg, Denmark. G-2
F/E. 547356 Sgt G.S.Meldrum PoW. Stalag 357, Kopernikus. 1084
A/G. 1447790 Sgt F.W.Day Killed Nyborg, Denmark. G-1
A/G. 1342405 Sgt J.B.M.Irving Killed Nyborg, Denmark. G-3

102 Squadron 4 Group Halifax DT747 DY/
Crashed Saedden (Esbjerg), Denmark at 01.40 hours (21/4/43).
Pilot. 1316333 Sgt W.A.Griffiths Killed Esbjerg (Fourfelt). CG A-10-10/15
2/Pilot. NZ/415055 F/Sgt T.S.Dennett Killed Esbjerg (Fourfelt). CG A-10-10/15
Nav. 1312151 Sgt W.C.Marsh Killed Esbjerg (Fourfelt), Denmark. A-10-17
B/A. 1065510 Sgt J.K.Campbell Killed Esbjerg (Fourfelt). CG A-10-10/15
W/OP. 1380237 Sgt A.Jenkinson Killed Esbjerg (Fourfelt). CG A-10-10/15
F/E. 1053959 Sgt J.T.Smith Killed Esbjerg (Fourfelt), Denmark. A-10-9
A/G. R/123705 F/Sgt A.C.Weir Killed Esbjerg (Fourfelt). CG A-10-10/15
A/G. 1339032 Sgt B.C.J.White Killed Esbjerg (Fourfelt), Denmark. CG
A-10-10/15

158 Squadron 4 Group Halifax HR722 NP/C
Shot down Drosselbjerg/Slagelse, Denmark at 02.01 hours (21/4/43).
Pilot. 43924 F/Lt D.J.Donaldson Killed Svino, Denmark. 17
2/Pilot. 1338445 Sgt D.F.R.Banks Killed Svino, Denmark. CG-9
Nav. 120073 F/Lt W.J.Parsons Killed Svino, Denmark. 23
B/A. 987264 Sgt H.F.D.Lay Killed Svino, Denmark. 12
W/OP. 1382074 Sgt G.W.Cole Killed Svino, Denmark. 13
F/E. 541136 Sgt L.Whyatt Killed Svino, Denmark. 19
A/G. 922593 Sgt M.J.Fitzgerald Killed Svino, Denmark. 11
A/G. 124109 P/O G.H.Willis Killed Svino, Denmark. 24

49 Squadron 5 Group Lancaster ED620 EA/K
Shot down Stadil near Ringkobing, Denmark at 23.35 hours (21/4/43) by *Flak*
5/HKB/180.
Pilot. 1347713 Sgt A.Anderson Killed Lemvig, Denmark. 737
Nav. 658832 Sgt G.Boulton PoW. Repatriated (May 1944)
B/A. 1005936 Sgt W.A.Cook Killed Lemvig, Denmark. 735
W/OP. 1218571 Sgt G.J.Evans Killed Lemvig, Denmark. 702
F/E. 1371009 Sgt A.Telfer Killed Lemvig, Denmark. 736
A/G. 1236949 W/O W.P.Heyworth PoW. Stalag Luft 6, Heydekrug. 1134
A/G. 995998 F/Sgt G.Barclay PoW. Stalag 357, Kopernikus. 42754

57 Squadron 5 Group Lancaster W4254 DX/
Pilot. J/21614 F/O R.F.Collins Missing, Runnymede Memorial 172
Nav. 130434 F/O F.R.H.Tate Missing, Runnymede Memorial 129
B/A. 574341 Sgt R.V.Emerson Missing, Runnymede Memorial 148
W/OP. 1083876 Sgt H.C.Fazakerly Missing, Runnymede Memorial 149
F/E. 1352700 Sgt D.O'Loughlin Missing, Runnymede Memorial 160
A/G. 1149026 Sgt K.Morris Missing, Runnymede Memorial 160
A/G. 1601565 Sgt K.R.A.Whitcombe Missing, Runnymede Memorial 169

57 Squadron 5 Group Lancaster ED770 DX/
Pilot. 88871 F/Lt I.S.Jenks Killed Poznan, Poland 6-A-1
Nav. R/116194 F/Sgt T.A.McDowell Killed Poznan, Poland CG 6-A-3/5
B/A. 1333706 Sgt A.J.Britton Killed Poznan, Poland 6-A-2
W/OP. 1293011 Sgt A.Smithdale Killed Poznan, Poland CG 6-A-3/5
F/E. 530868 Sgt J.Bryant Killed Poznan, Poland CG 6-A-3/5
A/G. 1492388 Sgt G.Cooper Killed Poznan, Poland CG 6-A-3/5
A/G. 656192 Sgt L.Turvey Killed Poznan, Poland CG 6-A-3/5

61 Squadron 5 Group Lancaster W4795 QR/
Pilot. J/16747 P/O J.L.Rossignol Killed Berlin, Germany. 2-L-18
Nav. 1290933 Sgt P.T.Smith Killed Berlin, Germany. 2-L-19
B/A. 1193202 Sgt G.Fellows Killed Berlin, Germany. CG 2-L-12/16
W/OP. 1375739 F/Sgt T.C.J.Grist Killed Berlin, Germany. CG 2-L-12/16
F/E. 651866 Sgt W.J.Jackson Missing, Runnymede Memorial 154
A/G. 1613718 Sgt M.C.Burgoine Killed Berlin, Germany. 2-L-17
A/G. 1550627 Sgt J.F.McNeill Killed Berlin, Germany. CG 2-L-12/16

419 Squadron 6 Group Halifax JB912 VR/
Pilot. J/16939 F/Lt T.E.Jackson PoW. Stalag Luft 3, Sagan. 1267
2/Pilot. R/66448 W/O J.F.Westerman PoW. Stalag 357, Kopernikus. 1111
Nav. R/103168 F/Sgt J.M.Carlton PoW. Stalag Luft 4, Sagan. 1058
B/A. J/16934 F/Lt J.R.Fry PoW. Stalag 357, Kopernikus. 1220
W/OP. R/85964 Sgt T.M.Crandell PoW. Stalag 357, Kopernikus. 1061
F/E. R/64004 Sgt C.J.Sebastien PoW. Stalag Luft 4, Sagan. 1094
A/G. 653173 F/Sgt E.Jury PoW. Stalag Luft 1, Barth Vogelsang. 1074
A/G. 938881 F/Sgt D.A.Watkins DFM Killed Berlin, Germany. 13-H-7 *
* 2nd tour of operations. Killed in aircraft by *Flak.*

Rostock

April 20th/21st, 1943

While Stettin was being attacked by a main force of Lancasters and Halifaxes. 86 Stirlings from 3 Group were winging their way to nearby Rostock. 67 of them reached the target, the Heinkel works, which was illuminated by flares from two 7 Squadron Pathfinder Stirlings. Although visiblity was excellent and there was no cloud, the works were obscured by smoke and twenty-four of the bombers had to bomb the secondary target in the town itself. A total of 43 tons of high explosive bombs were dropped, there being no incendiaries in the bomb loads. Eight Stirlings were missing as a result of this raid, a high loss rate of 11.6% of the attacking force. From the aircrew aboard these aircraft 21 were killed, 21 were never found and 16 were captured by the Germans and made prisoners for the rest of the war.

Casualties April 20th/21st, 1943. Target Rostock

15 Squadron 3 Group Stirling BF476 LS/P
Shot down Kragelund, Denmark by fighter at 04.45 hours, (21/4/43).
Pilot. NZ/415334 F/Lt C.S.Lyons PoW. Stalag Luft 3, Sagan. 1225
Nav. NZ/413315 F/Sgt J.R.Marshall PoW. Repatriated (6/2/45)
B/A. 124928 F/Lt R.Lockwood PoW. Stalag Luft 3, Sagan. 1224
W/OP. 1380104 F/Sgt R.P.Howland PoW. Stalag 357, Kopernikus. 1139
F/E. 746197 Sgt M.Hipwell PoW. Stalag 357, Kopernikus. 1070
A/G. 997727 Sgt J.Shaw PoW. Stalag 357, Kopernikus. 1097
A/G. 1394941 F/Sgt M.C.Huggett PoW. Stalag Luft 6, Heydekrug. 1250

75 Squadron 3 Group Stirling BF506 AA/P
Shot down Bogeballe, Denmark by fighter at 03.26 hours, (21/4/43)
Pilot. NZ/411954 P/O A.G.Tolley Killed Esbjerg, (Fourfelt). CG A-11-11/14
Nav. 1021328 F/Sgt W.H.Ellis Killed Esbjerg, (Fourfelt). CG A-11-11/14
B/A. NZ/404430 F/Sgt F.W.Upton Killed Esbjerg, (Fourfelt). CG A-11-11/14
W/OP. NZ/412315 F/Sgt C.T.Cobb Killed Esbjerg, (Fourfelt). A-9-6 Buried 12/5/43
F/E. 1217965 Sgt G.A.R.Town Killed Esbjerg, (Fourfelt), Denmark. A-11-15
A/G. 1332585 Sgt F.J.Earle Killed Esbjerg, (Fourfelt). CG A-11-11/14
A/G. NZ/404046 F/Sgt I.C.Salt Killed Esbjerg, (Fourfelt). CG A-11-11/14

90 Squadron 3 Group Stirling BF442 WP/K
Aircraft crashed into Baltic Sea.
Pilot. NZ/416196 P/O R.F.Elliott Missing, Runnymede Memorial 198
Nav. 1027587 Sgt C.B.Barrott Missing, Runnymede Memorial 141
B/A. R/111483 F/Sgt C.McKerns Missing, Runnymede Memorial 184
W/OP. 1214519 Sgt A.Chadwick Missing, Runnymede Memorial 145
F/E. 1539922 Sgt B.L.Neal Missing, Runnymede Memorial 160
A/G. 931566 Sgt N.L.Fauvel Missing, Runnymede Memorial 149
A/G. J/18269 P/O C.L.Maunder Killed Berlin, Germany. 8-2-19

90 Squadron 3 Group Stirling BF508 WP/S
Crashed at Faenosund, Denmark at 00.48 hours, (21/4/43).
Pilot. 41061 F/Lt A.S.W.Prioleau Killed Odense, Denmark. BD-348
Nav. 1312210 Sgt D.Stowe Killed Esbjerg, (Fourfelt), Denmark. A111-7-16
B/A. 1034351 Sgt W.T.Leahtly Missing, Runnymede Memorial 156
W/OP. 1075572 Sgt C.D.Mackelvie Killed Esbjerg, (Fourfelt). A111-723
F/E. 1217276 Sgt H.Munnery Missing, Runnymede Memorial 160
A/G. 1602348 Sgt R.H.Dunstan Missing, Runnymede Memorial 148
A/G. 1314807 Sgt M.Leoaward Missing, Runnymede Memorial 156

90 Squadron 3 Group Stirling BF463 WP/Q
Shot down Halsskov/Korsar, Denmark by *Flak* 1/Lei/985 at 00.19 hours.
Pilot. NZ/414258 P/O S.N.Cross Killed Svino, Denmark 31
Nav. 1148284 Sgt N.Shield Killed Svino, Denmark 25
B/A. 1425260 Sgt L.Tagg Killed Copenhagen, Denmark. X-7-45
W/OP. 1359883 Sgt T.E.Hall Killed Copenhagen, Denmark. X-7-130
F/E. 977000 Sgt C.L.Cruttenden Killed Svino, Denmark 30
A/G. 1252002 Sgt E.M.Offen Killed Svino, Denmark 33
A/G. 1585760 Sgt J.D.Lindrea Killed Svino, Denmark 28

149 Squadron 3 Group Stirling BK714 OJ/L
Flown into ground at Broendum (Esbjerg), Denmark. Pilot low flying to avoid
Flak. Front turret broke off when aircraft hit the ground.
Pilot. 39418 S/Ldr T.L.Howell PoW. Stalag Luft 3, Sagan. 1222
Nav. 1332425 Sgt F.L.Parker PoW. Stalag 357, Kopernikus. 1088
B/A. 1097776 Sgt E.Lewis Killed Esbjerg (Fourfelt), Denmark. CG A-10-10/15
W/OP. 1295004 F/Sgt A.W.Dowie PoW. Stalag Luft 1, Barth Vogelsang. 1064
F/E. 570229 W/O G.W.Herring PoW. Stalag 357, Kopernikus. 1069
A/G. 132384 F/Lt M.S.Winston PoW. Stalag Luft 3, Sagan. 1230
A/G. 1388704 F/Sgt G.C.Carter PoW. Stalag 357, Kopernikus. 1059

149 Squadron 3 Group Stirling BF507 OJ/S
Aircraft attacked by fighter and crashed at Dormagen, Germany.
Pilot. NZ/414269 F/Lt G.I.Ellis Missing, Runnymede Memorial 197
2/Pilot. 147192 P/O I.A.M.Holloway Missing, Runnymede Memorial 132
Nav. 139949 F/O E.Booth Missing, Runnymede Memorial 130
B/A. NZ/405299 F/O D.McNarey Killed Lemvig, Denmark. 703
W/OP. 1291765 Sgt E.R.Ginn Missing, Runnymede Memorial 150
F/E. 573042 Sgt F.L.Kelly Missing, Runnymede Memorial 155
A/G. 1322316 Sgt F.Sheppard Missing, Runnymede Memorial 164
A/G. 1385980 Sgt P.B.Mills Missing, Runnymede Memorial 159

214 Squadron 3 Group Stirling BK720 BU/Y
Pilot F/Lt A.F.Wallace
A/G. Sgt R.E.Thompson Killed.
Rear gunner killed in fighter attack.

218 Squadron 3 Group Stirling BK596 HA/B
Aircraft crashed at Stralsund, Germany.
Pilot. 657303 Sgt T.Jopling Missing, Runnymede Memorial 155
Nav. 1498587 Sgt N.L.Fairhurst Missing, Runnymede Memorial 149
B/A. 1391293 Sgt K.R.Faulconbridge Missing, Runnymede Memorial 149
W/OP. 1288529 F/Sgt J.Warnes Missing, Runnymede Memorial 139
F/E. 1064857 F/Sgt L.H.Shackleton PoW. Stalag 357, Kopernikus. 1095
A/G. 1324887 F/Sgt D.W.Lewin PoW. Stalag 357, Kopernikus. 42760
A/G. 631248 Sgt C.Robinson PoW. Stalag 357, Kopernikus. 3595

Diversion to Berlin

Losses for the two raids at Stettin and Rostock were heavy, a total of 30 aircraft in spite of a diversionary raid by 11 Mosquitoes dropping 8 tons of bombs on a clear moonlit night over Berlin. From this raid one Mosquito of 139 Squadron was lost and the body of the pilot, Wing Commander Shand DFC, was never found. His navigator, Pilot Officer C. D. Handley DFM, is buried in Holland.

Additionally a small force of 18 Wellingtons from 1 and 6 Groups were out laying 29 mines around the coast of Brittany. All returned safely.

Casualties April 20th/21st, 1943. Target Berlin

139 Squadron 8 Group Mosquito DZ386 XD/
Pilot. 33285 W/Cdr W.P.Shand DFC Missing, Runnymede Memorial 118
Nav. 144203 P/O C.D.Handley DFM Killed Bergh (Beek), Holland. N-103

Minelaying

April 22nd/23rd, 1943
A mixed force of 32 aircraft laid 80 mines, but this force was depleted by three who could not get accurate fix positions, despite reaching the general mining area. Two aircraft failed to return, there were no survivors from the crews

300 Squadron 1 Group Wellington HE291 BH/V
Pilot. P/76635 F/Lt E.Przysiecki Killed Escoublac-la-Baule, France. 11-H-2
Nav. P/784001 Sgt B.Prozmowski Killed Escoublac-la-Baule, France.
B/A. P/794182 Sgt C.Krelowski Killed Escoublac-la-Baule, France.
W/OP. P/781264 Sgt P.Debowski Killed Escoublac-la-Baule, France.
A/G. P/703599 Sgt T.Szeremeta Killed Escoublac-la-Baule, France.

9 Squadron 5 Group Lancaster ED799 WS/G
Pilot. 144183 P/O R.Brown Missing, Runnymede Memorial 131
Nav. 125672 F/O B.Carey Missing, Runnymede Memorial 123
B/A. 47665 F/Lt R.Y.Higginson DFM Missing, Runnymede Memorial 119
W/OP. 1379148 Sgt H.Jenkins Missing, Runnymede Memorial 155
F/E. 650050 Sgt R.A.Storey Missing, Runnymede Memorial 166
A/G. 1384385 Sgt R.J.M.Cox Missing, Runnymede Memorial 146
A/G. 778988 Sgt J.A.Bland Missing, Runnymede Memorial 142

Duisburg

April 26th/27th, 1943

The night of 26th/27th April saw a large force of 557 bombers leave their English bases, - 215 Lancasters, 135 Wellingtons, 119 Halifaxes, 78 Stirlings and 14 Mosquitoes, from which 496 made another attack on the Ruhr where Duisburg was the target. Nos. 97 and 405 Squadrons who had joined the Pathfinder Force earlier in the month were operating for the first time as Pathfinder squadrons. The PFF laid foundations for what should have been a successful raid, with their 151 target indicators. There had been full cloud cover over most of the route, but the target was cloudless. A high tonnage of bombs was dropped 781.2 tons of high explosive and 647 tons of incendiaries. Crews on debriefing reported to have seen the target fires 100 miles away. But daylight reconnaissance afterwards told a different story, for most of the bombs had been dropped north-east of the aiming point so the raid was a partial failure.

Although Duisburg was the largest inland port in Europe with its heavy industries and high priority targets, the fact that more sorties were flown to it than any other target during the Battle of the Ruhr, over-emphasised its importance. The plain truth was that in four raids little lasting damage had been done. 17 aircraft were lost on this raid, a 3.0% loss rate, many from the very intense *Flak* and active searchlight defences on that night. Aircrew losses in these planes were 89 killed, 9 missing, 14 made prisoners of war and there was one solitary evader.

A New Zealand Wireless Operator Gets Help

One of the lost Stirlings, BK657, was from 15 Squadron based at Mildenhall and captained by Pilot Officer Watson. At approximately 01.30 hours the bomber was attacked by a fighter about 30 miles inland from the Dutch coast between The Hague and Haarlem. The cannon fire from the enemy fighter hit the load of incendiaries, which erupted into a mass of flames. Immediately the main fuselage was well alight and the bomber was doomed. The bale out was given. The wireless operator, New Zealand Sergeant C. M. Mora, takes up the story.

"I was the first out of the plane, having crawled along the floor to reach the escape hatch. I parachuted down at Breukelen, north-west of Utrecht and landed in a market garden greenhouse, going right through the glass roof. I released my 'chute and left the tangled 'chute in the broken glass of the greenhouse roof and got away immediately. I went through the gardens, skirted a very large house, remembering the advice I had received in escape lectures about avoiding large houses. I hid in the garden for about an hour, but as no one came near me I walked about 300 yards along the side of a road, leading from the garden, until I reached a small house. I knocked at the door and explained that I was a member of the RAF. Luckily I was taken in immediately and given some coffee. Later that night before I went to bed, I returned to the greenhouse with a young Dutchman to retrieve my 'chute, which would have been a dead giveaway to any Germans in daylight.

"The next day I discarded my uniform for civilian clothes, which were provided for me by my kind helpers and later that afternoon I was taken by bicycle by the young Dutchman to his father's house in Utrecht. Here I was given another change of clothes and stayed the night. On April 28th I was handed over to an escape organisation, which arranged the rest of my journey back to UK."

Three hours after the air raid sirens had sounded the all clear at Duisburg, there was another warning when three nuisance Mosquitoes flew over and dropped their bomb loads.

Lucky Escape After a Fighter Attack

One aircraft which was lucky to return from the main raid was Wellington HE867 of 426 Squadron, captained by Wing Commander Crooks DFC. The bomber was attacked by a night fighter at Wesel at 02.26 hours when flying at 14,000 feet towards the target. The attack came from port astern and caused considerable damage. The rear turret was put out of action, all the fabric was ripped from the port tail plane and the trailing edge of the port mainplane was shot away three feet from the fuselage. All the hydraulics went out of action and to make matters worse the port engine began to overheat badly. In view of the aircraft's condition the captain wisely decided to abandon the attack and return to base. On the return flight efforts were made to jettison the bombs, but this was found to be impossible due to an electrical failure. On reaching home base at Dishforth, Yorkshire, the landing wheels would not go down, so rather than risk a belly landing with a full load of bombs, the captain instructed all the crew to bale out. The bomber crashed at Stonegrave, Yorkshire, but without damaging any civilian property or causing any casualties. The captain sprained his back on landing from his parachute descent, while the navigator Pilot Officer Power fractured his ankle, but the remaining crew members were uninjured. The fact that this Wellington ever returned to England was due to the very commendable work of the whole crew and leadership of the pilot. For his action the Wing Commander was awarded the Distinguished Service Order.

420 Squadron's Last Operation

It was a sad ending for 420 Squadron's association with Bomber Command, for the Duisburg raid of April24th/25th 1943, was their last operation before going to the Middle East. Although normally based at Middleton St George, for this operation they flew from nearby Croft airfield, as all the squadron's belongings had been packed into crates ready for their impending move. One of their aircraft did not return from the Duisburg raid and three others had to land in airfields in southern England because of bad *Flak* damage. Another of their Wellingtons, HE771 piloted by Sergeant G. Hall, got into difficulties on the final approach for landing after the operation and crashed near to the base. The second pilot, Canadian Sergeant P. C. Alder on his first operation, was killed and the rest of the crew received severe injuries. Sergeant Alder was buried at Darlington on April 30th. His own crew, who had not flown on operations with their skipper, acted as pall bearers before they set off for North Africa to be crewed up with a new pilot.

Casualties April 26th/27th, 1943. Target Duisburg

156 Squadron 8 Group Lancaster W4140 GT/
Pilot. R/108809 F/Sgt D.H.Waugh Killed Reichswald Forest. CG 9-C-9/12
Nav. 1392125 Sgt C.N.Bonar Killed Reichswald Forest, Germany. 10-F-15
B/A. 131905 F/O L.E.Lindsey Killed Reichswald Forest, Germany. CG 9-C-9/12
W/OP. 1330590 Sgt R.E.Funnell Killed Reichswald Forest. CG 9-C-9/12
F/E. 1034865 Sgt S.C.Brown Killed Reichswald Forest, Germany. CG 9-C-9/12
A/G. 1699995 Sgt B.P.Ashcroft Killed Reichswald Forest, Germany. 10-F-14
A/G. A/413495 F/Sgt L.H.Watters Killed Reichswald Forest, Germany. 9-D-2

405 Squadron 8 Group Halifax JB920 LQ/F
Pilot. J/17418 P/O D.E.Crockatt Killed Reichswald Forest, Germany. 9-D-6
2/Pilot. J/17446 P/O C.B.Dixon Killed Reichswald Forest, Germany. 9-D-7
Nav. J/17600 P/O J.R.Marriott Killed Reichswald Forest, Germany. 9-D-4
B/A. R/84338 W/O S.Sleeth Killed Reichswald Forest, Germany. 9-D-5
W/OP. 51838 P/O F.E.O'Hare Killed Reichswald Forest, Germany. 9-D-3
F/E. R/61926 Sgt I.A.Penner Killed Reichswald Forest, Germany. 9-D-9
A/G. R/104320 F/Sgt J.L.Stordy Killed Reichswald Forest, Germany. 9-D-8
A/G. R/70608 W/O T.L.Bentley Killed Reichswald Forest, Germany. 9-D-10

15 Squadron 3 Group Stirling BK657 LS/C
Shot down by enemy fighter at Portengen, Holland.
Pilot. 138654 P/O R.Watson PoW. Repatriated (2/2/45)
Nav. 1387489 W/O W.A.Dyson PoW. Stalag Luft 1, Barth Vogelsang. 1065
B/A. 1382532 Sgt H.L.Phillips PoW. Stalag Luft 4, Sagan. 1089
W/OP. NZ/404652 Sgt C.M.W.Mora Evaded capture.
F/E. 913540 Sgt W.A.Spencer PoW. Stalag Luft 6, Heydekrug. 1100
A/G. 1315940 Sgt G.C.Whittaker Killed Amersfoort, Holland. 13-5-98
A/G. R/83259 F/Sgt K.L.Bearnes PoW. Stalag Luft 3, Sagan. 259848

90 Squadron 3 Group Stirling BF383 WP/T
Aircraft crashed into Zuider Zee, Holland.
Pilot. 123952 F/O I.F.McKenzie Missing, Runnymede Memorial 126
Nav. 127545 F/O P.A.Walker Killed Amsterdam, Holland. CG 69-C-6
B/A. 1312110 Sgt R.F.Cocking Killed Amsterdam, Holland. CG 69-C-7
W/OP. 1194348 Sgt V.G.Leak Missing, Runnymede Memorial 156

F/E. 1372169 Sgt J.Wilson Killed Amsterdam, Holland. CG 69-C-6
A/G. 1101061 Sgt J.R.Boyes Missing, Runnymede Memorial 143
A/G. 927795 Sgt R.E.Hardingham Killed Amersfoort, Holland. 13-6-106

115 Squadron 3 Group Lancaster DS609 KO/
Pilot. J/16658 P/O H.Minnis DFC Killed Reichswald Forest, Germany. 9-D-12
Nav. 655955 Sgt W.C.Snook Killed Reichswald Forest, Germany. 9-D-18
B/A. 1220111 Sgt W.A.Timms DFM Killed Reichswald Forest. 9-D-15
W/OP. 1077194 Sgt N.Law DFM Killed Reichswald Forest, Germany. 9-B-15
F/E. 523101 Sgt L.G.Webster Killed Reichswald Forest, Germany. 9-D-14
A/G. J/17091 P/O E.A.Foster Killed Reichswald Forest, Germany. 9-D-11
A/G. 1800350 Sgt C.E.Thorpe Killed Reichswald Forest, Germany. 9-D-13

51 Squadron 4 Group Halifax HR778 MH/
Pilot. 1238789 Sgt G.Fisher Killed Rheinberg, Germany. CG 11-B-13/19
Nav. 1335785 Sgt B.H.James Killed Rheinberg, Germany. CG 11-B-13/19
B/A. 1387514 Sgt J.S.Boyce Killed Rheinberg, Germany. CG 11-B-13/19
W/OP. 1269939 Sgt W.H.Stacey Killed Rheinberg, Germany. CG 11-B-13/19
F/E. 633506 Sgt S.Hawkins Killed Rheinberg, Germany. CG 11-B-13/19
A/G. 1127540 Sgt J.L.Readman Killed Rheinberg, Germany. CG 11-B-13/19
A/G. 1600465 Sgt A.L.W.Pond Killed Rheinberg, Germany. CG 11-B-13/19

51 Squadron 4 Group Halifax HR787 MH/
Pilot. A/411439 F/Sgt C.M.Brigden Killed Rheinberg, Germany. 2-F-2
2/Pilot. 1334603 Sgt N.Thompson Killed Rheinberg, Germany. 2-F-3
Nav. 1237253 Sgt W.D.Griffith Killed Rheinberg, Germany. 2-F-4
B/A. 657052 Sgt G.C.Peters Killed Rheinberg, Germany. 2-F-5
W/OP. 1078836 Sgt W.Holding Missing, Runnymede Memorial 153
F/E. 577651 Sgt R.G.H.Sees Missing, Runnymede Memorial 164
A/G. A/406804 F/Sgt B.F.K.Green Killed Rheinberg, Germany. 2-F-6
A/G. A/408564 F/Sgt W.V.Chittock Missing, Runnymede Memorial 192

76 Squadron 4 Group Halifax DG423 MP/H
Crashed at Amsterdam, Holland.
Pilot. NZ/415416 Sgt D.G.McNab Killed Amsterdam, Holland. CG 69-C-4
Nav. 658262 Sgt F.N.Slingsby Killed Amsterdam, Holland. CG 69-C-4
B/A. 129158 F/O N.D.Fleming Killed Amsterdam, Holland. 69-C-3
W/OP. 1295228 Sgt B.F.Keable Killed Amsterdam, Holland. 69-C-2
F/E. 1047244 Sgt J.Wood Killed Amsterdam, Holland. CG 69-C-4
A/G. R/127567 Sgt C.C.Strain Killed Amsterdam, Holland. CG 69-C-4
A/G. 656810 Sgt J.Clegg Killed Amsterdam, Holland. CG 69-C-19

77 Squadron 4 Group Halifax DT796 KN/D
Pilot. A/404262 P/O J.D.Pye Killed Reichswald Forest, Germany. 9-C-14
Nav. 176728 F/O R.C.Stewart PoW. Stalag Luft 3, Sagan. 6633
B/A. 129046 F/Lt D.W.Atter PoW. Stalag Luft 3, Sagan. 1251
W/OP. 934366 W/O G.E.Barfoot PoW. Stalag 357, Kopernikus. 1056
F/E. 1430017 F/Sgt E.J.Tassell PoW. Stalag 357, Kopernikus. 1102
A/G. 1389097 F/Sgt P.D.Gibbs PoW. Stalag 357, Kopernikus. 1068
A/G. 1600931 Sgt J.R.Wells Killed Reichswald Forest, Germany. 9-C-13

102 Squadron 4 Group Halifax JB918 DY/
Pilot. R/78456 W/O J.G.Grainger Killed Vlieland, Holland. 60
Nav. 1410437 Sgt K.Oatridge Killed Texel, Holland. K-2-38
B/A. 1348996 Sgt W.Foley Killed Texel, Holland. K-2-34
W/OP. 1331200 Sgt W.A.Willis Missing, Runnymede Memorial 170
F/E. 1291074 Sgt F.G.Harris Missing, Runnymede Memorial 152
A/G. 1237059 Sgt H.Beck Killed Texel, Holland. K-2-32
A/G. 1448179 Sgt T.A.Wells Killed Esbjerg (Fourfelt), Denmark. A111-7-18
Buried (26/6/43)

158 Squadron 4 Group Halifax HR737 NP/U
Pilot. J/16487 F/O C.W.Gebhard Killed Rheinberg, Germany. 2-E-21
Nav. 1384833 Sgt E.W.J.Bennett Killed Rheinberg, Germany. 2-F-1
B/A. 1313128 F/Sgt R.H.Barnes Missing, Runnymede Memorial 135
W/OP. J/16978 P/O A.E.Taylor Killed Rheinberg, Germany. 2-E-25
F/E. 649870 Sgt E.G.Goodfellow Killed Rheinberg, Germany. 2-E-22
A/G. 1611324 Sgt F.C.Brownlow Killed Rheinberg, Germany. 2-E-24
A/G. 1382125 Sgt H.L.Barnes Killed Rheinberg, Germany. 2-E-23

196 Squadron 4 Group Wellington HE168 ZO/
Pilot. 1383620 Sgt G.F.Fletcher Killed Poederoijen, Holland. CG 1-2/5
Nav. 143571 P/O E.G.Francis Killed Poederoijen, Holland. CG 1-2/5
B/A. 1382065 Sgt E.T.D.Hardee Killed Poederoijen, Holland. CG 1-2/5
W/OP. 1189940 Sgt F.T.Pratt Killed Poederoijen, Holland. CG 1-2/5
A/G. 976658 Sgt J.A.Hawkins Killed Poederoijen, Holland. 1-1

207 Squadron 5 Group Lancaster W4171 EM/J
Shot down at Mol, Belgium.
Pilot. 1337890 Sgt I.B.Jones Killed Schoonselhoof, Belgium. II-G-31
Nav. 657118 Sgt G.J.Glare Killed Schoonselhoof, Belgium. II-G-28
B/A. 124201 F/O B.P.M.Hyland Killed Schoonselhoof, Belgium. II-G-30
W/OP. 1382650 Sgt W.A.Hollett Killed Schoonselhoof, Belgium. CG II-G-12/14
F/E. R/56637 Sgt J.Gillespie Killed Schoonselhoof, Belgium. CG II-G-12/14
A/G. 815114 Sgt F.W.Davies Killed Schoonselhoof, Belgium. CG II-G-12/14
A/G. 1183725 Sgt B.B.Jones Killed Schoonselhoof, Belgium. II-G-29

420 Squadron 6 Group Wellington HE693 PT/
Pilot. R/120905 F/Sgt E.L.Newburg Killed Bergen-op-Zoom (Can). 11-F-5
Nav. R/115915 F/Sgt F.J.Duffy Killed Bergen-op-Zoom (Can), Holland. 11-F-6
B/A. R/150882 Sgt R.Mucklow Killed Bergen-op-Zoom (Can), Holland. 11-F-3
W/OP. R/120563 Sgt O.K.Glascock Killed Bergen-op-Zoom (Can). 11-F-11
A/G. 914766 Sgt K.B.Cooke Killed Bergen-op-Zoom (Can), Holland. 23-C-4

428 Squadron 6 Group Wellington HZ365 NA/U
Pilot. R/123973 F/Sgt L.R.Coutts Killed Reichswald Forest, Germany. 2-B-2
Nav. R/123492 F/Sgt J.A.Smith Killed Reichswald Forest, Germany. 2-B-3
B/A. 1388118 Sgt P.H.Snow PoW. Stalag 357, Kopernikus. 1099
W/OP. 1150881 Sgt R.W.Stockton Killed Reichswald Forest, Germany. 2-B-4
A/G. R/98354 W/O W.C.Hencke Killed Reichswald Forest, Germany. 2-B-1

429 Squadron 6 Group Wellington HE737 AL/
Pilot. 42692 S/Ldr J.C.Cairns DFC PoW. Stalag Luft 3, Sagan. 1321
2/Pilot. 1333360 Sgt K.E.Rabbitt Killed Bergen, Holland. 2-E-10
Nav. 117853 F/O R.H.Larkins Killed Bergen, Holland. 2-E-12
B/A. J/15639 F/Lt C.M.S.Awad Killed Bergen, Holland. 2-E-9
W/OP. 544898 W/O R.T.Lang PoW. Stalag Luft 6, Heydekrug. 1187
A/G. J/15702 F/O S.M.N.Pozer PoW. Stalag Luft 3, Sagan. 1334

429 Squadron 6 Group Wellington HE382 AL/
Pilot. R/101482 W/O S.Hanan Killed Borne (Bornerbroek), Holland. CG 4/6
2/Pilot. 1038224 Sgt G.K.Thompson Killed Borne (Bornerbroek), Holland. 2
Nav. 778810 Sgt M.P.Brown Killed Borne (Bornerbroek), Holland. CG 4/6
B/A. R/105100 W/O F.H.Purchase Killed Borne (Bornerbroek), Holland. 3
W/OP. 776126 Sgt E.G.Litchfield Killed Borne (Bornerbroek), Holland. CG 4/6
A/G. R/81411 F/Sgt F.S.Lane Killed Borne (Bornerbroek), Holland. 1

420 Squadron 6 Group Wellington HE771 PT/
Aircraft crashed at base coming in to land after operation to Duisburg.
Pilot. 1319273 Sgt G.Hall Injured.
2/Pilot. R/4607 Sgt C.D.Alder Killed Darlington W-7K-359
Nav. R/133344 Sgt J.P.Bishop Injured.
B/A. R/124453 Sgt G.W.Bedford Injured.
W/OP. 1333553 Sgt E.A.Shaul Injured.
A/G R/100619 Sgt L.D.Annis Injured.

Minelaying

April 27th/28th, 1943
The night of 27th/28th April saw a sizable force of Lancasters, 58 Halifaxes, 25 Stirlings and 31 Wellingtons despatched to three minelaying areas, Biscay, Brittany and the Frisians. There was the large number of 37 early returners, the majority of those being unable to get an accurate fix on their position. One aircraft was lost from which there were no survivors.

Casualties April 27th/28th, 1943. Minelaying

101 Squadron 1 Group Lancaster ED728 SR/Y
Pilot. 1335003 Sgt C.A.Margerum Killed Biarritz (Du-Sabrou). CG 9-6730
Nav. 1046330 Sgt R.N.Dixon Killed Biarritz (Du-Sabrou), France. CG 9-6730
B/A. 1396828 Sgt R.D.Balfour Killed Biarritz (Du-Sabrou), France. CG 9-6730
W/OP. 1294117 Sgt D.J.Park Killed Biarritz (Du-Sabrou), France. CG 9-6730
F/E. 947632 Sgt H.Clegg Killed Biarritz (Du-Sabrou), France. CG 9-6730
A/G. 1302662 Sgt J.W.Stotter Killed Biarritz (Du-Sabrou), France. CG 9-6730
A/G. 710084 Sgt J.J.Veldsman Killed Biarritz (Du-Sabrou), France. CG 9-6730

Minelaying

April 28th/29th, 1943

On the night of 28th/29th of April an even larger force was scheduled for mining in the dangerous Heligoland and River Elbe areas, which were always heavily defended by *Flak* and night fighters. 207 aircraft - 68 Lancasters, 60 Halifaxes, 32 Stirlings and 47 Wellingtons reduced to 189 by early returners met very heavy opposition and 23 bombers failed to return. A heavy loss rate for a minelaying operation of 14.1%. Fighter and *Flak* over Denmark accounted for the majority of these lost aircraft. There were only four aircrew survivors from this operation and they became prisoners. Of the other lost aircrew 84 were killed and unhappily the bodies of the remaining 61 airmen were never found. On the same night six Mosquitoes made a diversionary attack on Wilhelmshaven, three aircraft dropped flares to simulate the beginning of a big raid and three dropped bombs. They suffered no loss.

Casualties April 28th/29th, 1943. Minelaying

12 Squadron 1 Group Lancaster LM313 PH/D
Aircraft crashed at Kritzmov, 5 kilometres SW of Rostock.
Pilot. 70691 S/Ldr E.F.Tyler Killed Berlin, Germany. 8-B-37
Nav. 1474209 Sgt F.Grant Killed Berlin, Germany. 8-D-1
B/A. 132025 F/O W.J.Dowdell Killed Berlin, Germany. 8-B-36
W/OP. 1386011 Sgt N.E.Lind Killed Berlin, Germany. JG 8-D-3/4
F/E. 1260533 Sgt K.W.Jury Killed Berlin, Germany. 8-D-2
A/G. 905022 Sgt R.E.Haywood Killed Berlin, Germany. 8-D-5
A/G. 935454 Sgt H.Wilford Killed Berlin, Germany. JG 8-D-3/4

12 Squadron 1 Group Lancaster ED408 PH/A
Aircraft crashed in Baltic Sea near Leba, Poland.
Pilot. 1315743 Sgt G.Elsworthy Killed Malbrook, Danzig, Poland. CG 3-A-1/3
Nav. J/10677 F/O B.V.L.Veira DFC Killed Malbrook, Danzig. CG 3-A-1/3
B/A. 143857 P/O J.L.Haddow Killed Malbrook, Danzig, Poland. CG 3-A-1/3
W/OP. 1311073 F/Sgt W.E.Freeman Missing, Runnymede Memorial 181
F/E. 621910 Sgt E.A.Pye Missing, Runnymede Memorial 167
A/G. 989136 Sgt C.W.S.Downes Missing, Runnymede Memorial 148
A/G. 930059 Sgt R.C.Grant Missing, Runnymede Memorial 151

12 Squadron 1 Group Lancaster ED325 PH/J
Aircraft crashed in Baltic Sea.
Pilot. 143900 P/O L.W.G.Head DFM Killed Malbrook, Danzig, Poland. 3-B-9
Nav. 1043825 Sgt J.Short Killed Malbrook, Danzig, Poland. 3-B-8
B/A. 1236693 Sgt J.Willatt Missing, Runnymede Memorial 289
W/OP. 1268389 Sgt F.G.R.Gibbs Killed Malbrook, Danzig, Poland. 3-B-11
F/E. 548014 Sgt H.H.Wensley Killed Malbrook, Danzig, Poland. 3-B-7
A/G. 976496 Sgt P.Y.Murphy Killed Malbrook, Danzig, Poland. 3-B-10
A/G. 1317460 Sgt D.W.Payne Missing, Runnymede Memorial 289

12 Squadron 1 Group Lancaster W4954 PH/V
Aircraft crashed in Eastern Baltic Sea.
Pilot. 41814 F/Lt R.H.Ashton Killed Poznan, Poland. CG 5-B-6
Nav. 1317349 Sgt E.G.Buscombe Killed Poznan, Poland. CG 5-B-6
B/A. 1430161 Sgt J.Mackintosh Killed Poznan, Poland. CG 5-B-6
W/OP. 1080386 Sgt M.Savage Killed Poznan, Poland. CG 5-B-6
F/E. 1101483 Sgt A.Goodhand Killed Poznan, Poland. CG 5-B-6
A/G. 1578183 Sgt P.Lees Killed Poznan, Poland. CG 5-B-6
A/G. A/35488 F/Sgt J.S.Huggard Killed Poznan, Poland. CG 5-B-6

103 Squadron 1 Group Lancaster ED733 PM/
Shot down by fighter at Jordrup, Denmark at 02.20 hours (29/4/43).
Pilot. 1098136 Sgt A.D.Nicholson Killed Esbjerg (Fourfelt), Denmark. A-10-4
Nav. 128666 F/O L.Meakin Killed Esbjerg (Fourfelt), Denmark. A-10-6
B/A. 1391041 Sgt J.C.Lilley Killed Esbjerg (Fourfelt), Denmark. A-10-8
W/OP. 1129286 Sgt T.J.Daley Killed Esbjerg (Fourfelt), Denmark. A-10-7
F/E. 574552 Sgt G.L.K.McCallum Killed Esbjerg (Fourfelt), Denmark. A-10-5
A/G. 1323630 Sgt M.D.Peters Killed Esbjerg (Fourfelt), Denmark. A-9-1
A/G. 1810747 Sgt A.Segal Killed Esbjerg (Fourfelt), Denmark. A-11-2

166 Squadron 1 Group Wellington HZ278 AS/N
Shot down by *Flak* at Esbjerg ved Saedding, Denmark at 01.04 hours (29/4/43).
Pilot. J/20082 F/O L.M.Clark Killed Esbjerg (Fourfelt), Denmark. A-10-2
Nav. R/123266 F/Sgt D.E.Giles Killed Esbjerg (Fourfelt), Denmark. A-11-1
B/A. J/20887 P/O J.A.Dalton Killed Esbjerg (Fourfelt), Denmark. A-10-3
W/OP. R/104348 F/Sgt H.A.MacEachen Killed Esbjerg (Fourfelt). A-10-1
A/G. R/95749 W/O H.R.Fisher PoW. Stalag 4B, Muhlberg(Elbe). 1066

75 Squadron 3 Group Stirling BK807 AA/M
Shot down in Langelandsbaelt, Denmark at 00.23 hrs by *MAA 508* (Naval *Flak*).
Pilot. 141713 P/O D.V.Hamer Missing, Runnymede Memorial 131
Nav. NZ/411451 Sgt D.R.Ross Missing, Runnymede Memorial 199
B/A. NZ/411206 F/Sgt R.C.Buckley Missing, Runnymede Memorial 198
W/OP. NZ/411737 F/Sgt W.L.F.Brian Missing, Runnymede Memorial 198
F/E. 950013 Sgt G.L.Lennox Missing, Runnymede Memorial 156
A/G. 1301281 Sgt H.P.Holme Killed Svino, Denmark. 37
A/G. NZ/415375 Sgt M.E.J.Shogreen Killed Svino, Denmark. 27

75 Squadron 3 Group Stirling W7513 AA/G

Shot down in Fehmarn Belt area, Denmark at 00.18 hours by Naval *Flak*.
Pilot. NZ/415411 Sgt K.Halliburton Missing, Runnymede Memorial 199
Nav. NZ/42297 Sgt P.T.Hunter Missing, Runnymede Memorial 199
B/A. 1261331 Sgt L.T.Scarfe Missing, Runnymede Memorial 164
W/OP. 1196564 Sgt D.Church Missing, Runnymede Memorial 145
F/E. 946455 Sgt D.S.Sidhu Missing, Runnymede Memorial 147
A/G. 1393248 Sgt C.H.G.Boxall Missing, Runnymede Memorial 143
A/G. NZ/392104 Sgt A.C.Howell Missing, Runnymede Memorial

75 Squadron 3 Group Stirling R9290 AA/X

Aircraft crashed at Ostero Veaternas, Laaland, Denmark.
Pilot. A/412458 F/Sgt A.E.Lewis Missing, Runnymede Memorial 193
Nav. NZ/417269 Sgt H.G.Corrin Missing, Runnymede Memorial 199
B/A. 49977 F/O C.J.Bickham Missing, Runnymede Memorial 123
W/OP. 1292879 Sgt F.A.Moulton Missing, Runnymede Memorial 160
F/E. 1369996 Sgt A.Graham Missing, Runnymede Memorial 151
A/G. 964185 Sgt J.H.Whitehart Missing, Runnymede Memorial 169
A/G. NZ/413418 Sgt V.C.Howes Missing, Runnymede Memorial 199

75 Squadron 3 Group Stirling BF467 AA/W

Aircraft shot down Baltic/Nakskov, Denmark at 00.08 hours by Naval *Flak*.
Pilot. NZ/413152 P/O D.L.Thompson Killed Svino, Denmark. 15
Nav. R/93418 W/O J.A.Ramsay Killed Svino, Denmark. 18
B/A. A/401341 F/Sgt J.M.Williams Killed Svino, Denmark. 14
W/OP. NZ/405780 W/O E.R.Jenkins Killed Svino, Denmark. 21
F/E. 1098896 Sgt C.Abbott Killed Svino, Denmark. 16
A/G. 1070166 Sgt J.T.Glendinning Killed Svino, Denmark. 20
A/G. 930235 Sgt G.Phillips Killed Svino, Denmark. 26

218 Squadron 3 Group Stirling BF447 HA/F

Shot down by fighter at Vroending, Denmark at 00.35 hours (29/4/43).
Pilot. 51130 P/O D.J.Brown Killed Esbjerg (Fourfelt), Denmark. A-11-7
Nav. 1316509 Sgt W.T.Jones Killed Esbjerg (Fourfelt), Denmark. A-11-4
B/A. 118600 F/O J.W.Scott Killed Esbjerg (Fourfelt), Denmark. A-11-6
W/OP. 658035 Sgt T.Rich Killed Esbjerg (Fourfelt), Denmark. A-11-5
F/E. 541024 F/Sgt W.Lowery PoW. Stalag Luft 6, Heydekrug. 1189
A/G. 1016960 W/O L.Turner PoW. Stalag 357, Kopernikus. 1106
A/G. 1209339 Sgt G.Sutton Killed Esbjerg (Fourfelt), Denmark. A-11-3

218 Squadron 3 Group Stirling EF356 HA/O

Shot down by fighter Aanum/Tarn, Denmark at 03.52 hours (29/4/4/3).
Pilot. 143386 P/O K.S.Hailey Killed Oddum, Denmark. CG B-68
Nav. 1315664 Sgt A.G.P.Sindrey Killed Oddum, Denmark. CG B-68
B/A. 128621 F/O S.M.Holliman Killed Esbjerg (Fourfelt), Denmark. A-9-2
W/OP. 1271695 Sgt R.J.Barton Killed Oddum, Denmark. CG B-68
F/E. 944647 Sgt A.G.Surtees Killed Oddum, Denmark. CG B-68
A/G. 650927 W/O H.Bliss PoW. Stalag 357, Kopernikus. 1119*
A/G. 1302953 Sgt J.A.Head Killed Esbjerg (Fourfelt), Denmark. AIII-7-15
*Died in PoW camp. Buried Becklingen, Germany. 16-D-11

218 Squadron 3 Group Stirling BF515 HA/N
Shot down by fighter Taagerup/Slagelse, Denmark at 00.56 hours (29/4/43).
Pilot. 47736 F/Lt G.F.Berridge Killed Reerslev, Denmark. CG 248
Nav. 139400 F/O J.M.Traynor Killed Reerslev, Denmark. CG 248
B/A. 119901 F/O T.C.Wheelhouse Killed Copenhagen, Denmark. X-7-128
W/OP. 120735 F/O C.V.Parsloe Killed Reerslev, Denmark. CG 248
F/E. 574108 Sgt K.F.Erne Killed Reerslev, Denmark. CG 248
A/G. 1333378 Sgt J.A.Bolton Killed Copenhagen, Denmark. X-7-129
A/G. 1499616 Sgt A.A.Fitzpatrick Killed Reerslev, Denmark. CG 248

90 Squadron 3 Group Stirling BF346 WP/G
Probably shot down by fighter west of Blaavandshuk/Esbjerg, Denmark.
Pilot. 40409 S/Ldr R.S.May Missing, Runnymede Memorial 118
Nav. J/17258 P/O W.G.Monk Killed Kiel, Germany. 1-J-17
B/A. 1320949 Sgt K.G.Horne Missing, Runnymede Memorial 154
W/OP. 1267828 Sgt L.Hainin Missing, Runnymede Memorial 151
F/E. 817293 Sgt N.Marshall Missing, Runnymede Memorial 158
A/G. 134917 P/O G.Heathcote-Pierson Missing, Runnymede Memorial 132
A/G. 1388458 Sgt B.H.Reeve Missing, Runnymede Memorial 162

158 Squadron 4 Group Halifax HR773 NP/A
Shot down by fighter in the Kattegat, Denmark.
Pilot. 143094 P/O R.D.Roberts DFM Missing, Runnymede Memorial 133
Nav. 141827 P/O A.R.Schofield Missing, Runnymede Memorial 133
B/A. R/74320 W/O W.E.E.B.Pridden Missing, Runnymede Memorial 180
W/OP. NZ/402557 F/Sgt J.D.D.Mackie Missing, Runnymede Memorial 199
F/E. R/89376 Sgt W.G.Dent Missing, Runnymede Memorial 146
A/G. 1031824 Sgt E.J.Culley Missing, Runnymede Memorial 186
A/G. 1585098 Sgt M.A.Gibson Missing, Runnymede Memorial 150

196 Squadron 4 Group Wellington HE220 ZO/
Pilot. 749747 Sgt J.F.Atkins Missing, Runnymede Memorial 141
Nav. 1335916 Sgt F.Guy Missing, Runnymede Memorial 151
B/A. 1318170 Sgt R.H.Tayler Missing, Runnymede Memorial 166
W/OP. 1083266 Sgt W.McDonough Missing, Runnymede Memorial 157
A/G. 521097 Sgt P.W.J.Morrow Missing, Runnymede Memorial 159

196 Squadron 4 Group Wellington HE170 ZO/
Shot down by fighter, Bjerndrup/Logum Kloster, Denmark at 00.57 hours.
Pilot. 1336737 Sgt F.C.Swain Killed Aabenraa, Denmark. AMP-3-17
Nav. 1254714 Sgt A.Wheatley Killed Aabenraa, Denmark. AMP-3-19
B/A. 1317194 Sgt E.G.Quick Killed Aabenraa, Denmark. JG AMP-3-18
W/OP. 1311769 Sgt G.R.Burgess Killed Aabenraa, Denmark. JG AMP-3-18
A/G. 1610909 Sgt E.D.Curling Killed Aabenraa, Denmark. AMP-3-20

196 Squadron 4 Group Wellington HE395 ZO/
Shot down Jerstal, Denmark by fighter at 00.58 hours (29/4/43).
Pilot. 39487 F/Lt I.N.Bonard Killed Aabenraa, Denmark. CG AMP-6-7
Nav. 119906 F/O J.J.Burns Killed Aabenraa, Denmark. CG AMP-6-7
B/A. 143772 P/O A.R.Potter Killed Aabenraa, Denmark. CG AMP-6-7
W/OP. 51673 P/O B.A.Curtis DFM Killed Aabenraa, Denmark. CG AMP-6-7
A/G. 51286 P/O J.I.P.Ford Killed Aabenraa, Denmark. CG AMP-6-7

61 Squadron 5 Group Lancaster W4898 QR/

Crashed Kattegat/Hesselo, Denmark.
Pilot. 742200 W/O M.B.Collenette DFM Killed Frederikshavn. AP-38
Nav. A/404657 P/O I.D.Robertson Killed Copenhagen, Denmark. X-6-46
B/A. J/17075 P/O R.D.Mix Missing, Runnymede Memorial 176
W/OP. A/401236 P/O N.R.Gyles Missing, Runnymede Memorial 191
F/E. 541519 Sgt J.Norman Killed Halsingborg, Sweden. XV-7
A/G. R/119531 Sgt F.G.Moore Missing, Runnymede Memorial 180
A/G. 1301892 Sgt A.W.Bond Missing, Runnymede Memorial 143

207 Squadron 5 Group Lancaster W4945 EM/Z

Shot down at Oddesunbroen, Denmark at 01.30 hours (29/4/43) by *Flak* from
Oddesund Bridge
Pilot. 930246 W/O K.R.Rees Killed Lemvig, Denmark. 700
Nav. 145353 P/O P.A.K.Mockford Killed Lemvig,704 Denmark.Buried 16/5/43
B/A. 1383884 Sgt T.E.Ellingham Killed Lemvig, Denmark. 696
W/OP. 136345 F/O L.Foulds Killed Lemvig, Denmark. 698
F/E. C/14063/A Sgt G.Tyler Killed Lemvig, Denmark. 699
A/G. 1578147 Sgt S.W.Cowham Missing, Runnymede Memorial 146
A/G. 1370576 Sgt A.W.Cochrane Missing, Runnymede Memorial 145

428 Squadron 6 Group Wellington HE728 NA/B

Pilot. R/118160 W/O K.E.Radcliff Missing, Runnymede Memorial 180
Nav. R/112619 F/Sgt W.M.Manson Killed Sage, Germany. 11-A-8 Buried 4/5/43
B/A. R/121039 F/Sgt J.V.Agate Missing, Runnymede Memorial 181
W/OP. 1250272 Sgt I.P.D.Rushton Missing, Runnymede Memorial 163
A/G. R/107964 F/Sgt H.V.Smith-Jones Missing, Runnymede Memorial 185

428 Squadron 6 Group Wellington HE543 NA/D

Pilot. 144180 P/O R.A.Parkinson Killed Sage, Germany. 11-D-5
Nav. 1500013 Sgt W.Collier Missing, Runnymede Memorial 145
B/A. 126748 F/O G.Meakins Killed Sage, Germany. 11-C-7
W/OP. 1382466 Sgt K.P.Garnett Killed Sage, Germany. 4-D-2
A/G. J/17747 P/O C.R.Balcer Killed Sage, Germany. 11-C-4

419 Squadron 6 Group Halifax JB923 VR/

Shot down in the sea north of Hjorring, Denmark by fighter at 01.29 hours
(29/4/43).
Pilot. R/105312 W/O G.K.Smallwood Missing, Runnymede Memorial 180
Nav. R/98829 F/Sgt J.W.Carley Missing, Runnymede Memorial 181
B/A. R/68264 W/O J.M.B.O'Connor Missing, Runnymede Memorial 180
W/OP. R/91189 W/O J.G.Acker Missing, Runnymede Memorial 179
F/E. R/80235 Sgt J.A.L.Allan Missing, Runnymede Memorial 186
A/G. R/146613 F/Sgt L.J.C.Murphy Missing, Runnymede Memorial 185
A/G. R/134921 F/Sgt R.R.Gourde Missing, Runnymede Memorial 181

Essen

April 30th/May 1st, 1943

On the last night of April, Essen was to be the focal point of Bomber Command's attack when 305 aircraft consisting of 190 Lancasters, 105 Halifaxes and 10 *Oboe* equipped Mosquitoes took off. Again there was a high number of aborted flights, 53, which made only 252 bombers available for the attack. At Zero hour (02.30 hours) and regularly at five minute intervals throughout the raid , the Pathfinders dropped their 36 flares. Cloudy weather conditions had been forecast and the *Musical Wanganui* (air marking plan) was used, which did not always give such good results as *Parmatta* markers. A few minutes after the attack opened, a glow from many fires was reflected on the cloud base and a flash from a very large explosion which lasted for several seconds was seen by crews 20 minutes flying time away from the target. Damage was widespread, but in spite of 401.6 tons of high explosive and 391 tons of incendiaries being dropped there were no areas of high bombing concentration. Many other Ruhr towns bordering Essen reported some bombing on this night. German records show that the Krupps factory was again hit and that 53 people were killed and 218 injured. The losses for the night were relatively light, 12 aircraft being lost. Aircrew losses were 54 killed, 15 missing and 16 became prisoners. In the last four raids on the town of Essen, 5th/6th, 12th/13th March, 3rd/4th April and 30th/1st May, 1,552 aircraft had dropped 3,967 tons of bombs, for the loss of 70 aircraft and a human loss of 298 killed, 99 missing, 80 prisoners of war and one succesful evader.

Bomb Aimer's Evasion Ends in Betrayal

Flying as a bomb aimer in Halifax JB783, KN/N from 77 Squadron, was 1010089 Sergeant N. Aubrey Fearneyhough. He was one of two from the crew who survived, the other being the wireless operator Flight Sergeant Butlin. Their aircraft was attacked over Holland on the way to the target and the bale out order was given. Fearneyhough landed in a tree in a forest and although he made every effort to hide his 'chute, it was so entangled in the branches that he had to abandon it. After walking most of the night, by dawn he came to a group of people working in a field and unsure of his exact location decided to hide up in a nearby wood for the rest of the day. Whilst dozing under some branches he heard someone approach and decided to speak to the person in broken German. Fortunately the man was Dutch and promised to help, but warned Fearneyhough to remain in his hiding spot for the rest of the day. After dark the Dutchman returned and took him to his home which was about 10 minutes walk away and near the village of Hoenderloo. The Sergeant was kept hidden there for two nights before he was moved by bicycle to another house belonging to the Dutchman's married sister, which was situated about 10 Kilometres away. He remained there for another two days and during his stay he was examined by a Dutch doctor and given civilian clothes, then moved again by bicycle to Roeekamperweg (Garderen), where he remained in a country bungalow for four weeks, sleeping in the loft. Also in the bungalow, the brave Dutch owner was sheltering a number of Dutch Jews.

At the end of the four weeks the bungalow was raided by the Germans, but Fearneyhough managed to remain hidden in the loft during the eight hour search. A Dutch Jewish doctor in the loft also managed to avoid being caught in the loft and both the Sergeant and the doctor made their way to a new address they had been given in Roeekamperweg, but the owner there had also made a hurried exit. Both men wandered about the countryside for two days until they finally made it back to Hoenderloo and to the people who had originally helped Fearneyhough. After about four hours both were taken by car to a farm approximately 25 kilometres away at Staverden and from there the Sergeant was taken by bicycle to a shipping magnate's estate about 15 kms away at Ermelo, where he remained hidden for two weeks sleeping outside in the woods but being fed in the house.

It was here that Sergeant Fearneyhough was put into contact with the underground movement when one of its members came to visit him to take a photograph for his false identity card. Then he was taken by tandem to Amersfoort where he remained for one night before moving on for another two night's stay at yet another Dutchman's home.

The next day he was instructed to follow a guide to the railway station, where he boarded a train for a small village near Eindhoven. He stayed with the guide for two days and then by bicycle and by foot they crossed the frontier into Belgium. Here another guide took over and in the company of another RAF evader, Sergeant F. Sanders, both were taken to Bray, Belgium where they stayed the night in a large bakery, a refuge which became well known to many other RAF evaders. The next morning with yet another guide they set off for Brussels, where they were met by two elderly ladies and escorted to a large office block for the night. The next day they were both taken to a block of luxury flats where to their great surprise they met up with about 30 Allied personnel all dressed in civilian clothing and awaiting instructions on how to proceed on the next stage of their attempted evasions. Fearneyhough was taken to the large store *Bon Marche* in Brussels where he was able to have a photograph taken and in the next few days was supplied with permits for travelling in Belgium and France. After three days the Sergeant, in company of 12 other personnel, was taken from Brussels to Paris by a main line train. In Paris they changed over to a suburban train which transported them to Place D'Italie where they were taken to a third class hotel and given a room. Then as a large party of 12 they were taken out to dinner at a local restaurant, which made Fearneyhough uneasy as he was greatly concerned about their security. On their return they were given instructions that the next morning, July 25th, they were to make their way to the hotel lounge and then quietly leave and follow the two guides who had brought them from Brussels. The party of evaders had been told that when they reached a large square the guides would be changed and they should then follow the new guides.

As the guides changed, Fearneyhough noticed that the new guides acted quite suspiciously in that they kept slowing down the pace in such a way that the original rather scattered party became a compact group. After crossing a main thoroughfare the party was led up a side street where they were quickly surrounded by waiting plain clothes Gestapo, who bustled them into a waiting bus nearby and they were taken to the Gestapo HQ in Paris. All the evaders blamed their betrayal on the Head of the Organisation in Brussels, the man known as 'The Captain' whose facade of great desire to plan and initate escape routes aroused the suspicion in many airmen. This man later betrayed or was instrumental in many RAF evaders being captured either in Paris or Bordeaux.

After being interrogated at Gestapo HQ Fearneyhough was taken to Fresnes Prison, Paris where he was kept in solitary confinement with practically no food for three and half weeks and was regularly interrogated in an effort to extract information about those who had initially helped him. Having no success the Germans moved him to Dulag Luft before transferring him in November 1943 to Stalag Luft 6, Heydekrug. He was liberated at Neubradenburg about 50 Kilometres north of Berlin by the Russians on 28th April 1945.

Casualties April 30th/May 1st, 1943. Target Essen

405 Squadron 8 Group Halifax DT741 LQ/P
Pilot. 47360 F/Lt H.P.Atkinson Killed Uden, Holland. 4-E-12
2/Pilot. C/11767 F/Lt E.P.Nurse PoW. Stalag Luft 3, Sagan. 1271
Nav. J/10054 F/O W.A.G.Hardy Killed Uden, Holland. 4-E-13
B/A. J/16628 F/O R.M.Reilly PoW. Stalag Luft 3, Sagan. 1277
W/OP. R/76187 W/O G.L.MacCullum PoW. Stalag 357, Kopernikus. 1078
F/E. R/102333 W/O G.K.Collopy PoW. Stalag 357, Kopernikus. 1060
A/G. J/18604 F/O N.H.Weiler PoW. Stalag 7A, Moosburg(Isar). 1110
A/G. R/7808 W/O F.R.O'Neill PoW. Stalag Luft 4, Sagan. 1087

12 Squadron 1 Group Lancaster W4925 PH/
Shot down Winterswijk, Holland at 02.40 hours (1/5/43). Victim of Hptm Dormann III/NJG1.
Pilot. 123653 F/Lt J.Potts Killed Winterswijk, Holland. 17
Nav. 1318406 Sgt W.Woodland Killed Winterswijk, Holland. 22
B/A. A/409042 F/Sgt F.B.Gillan Killed Winterswijk, Holland. 20
W/OP. 635059 F/Sgt K.Hall DFM Killed Winterswijk, Holland. 18
F/E. 1010657 Sgt R.Martin Killed Winterswijk, Holland. 21
A/G. 1312247 Sgt J.S.Harris Killed Winterswijk, Holland. 19
A/G. 1351297 Sgt L.Gill Killed Winterswijk, Holland. 23

51 Squadron 4 Group Halifax HR733 MH/
Pilot. 1316141 F/Sgt D.R.Wilson Killed Reichswald Forest, Germany. 21-F-16
Nav. 1338893 F/Sgt L.Allen PoW. Stalag Luft 3, Sagan. 43255
B/A. 1577617 Sgt H.A.Briggs Killed Reichswald Forest, Germany. 21-F-12
W/OP. 1283056 Sgt C.H.Longley Killed Reichswald Forest, Germany. 21-F-17
F/E. 1216634 F/Sgt J.W.Peacock PoW. Stalag 357, Kopernikus. 42787
A/G. R/100196 F/Sgt H.P.Spencer Killed Reichswald Forest, Germany. 21-F-14
A/G. R/78896 W/O W.R.Hewitt Killed Reichswald Forest, Germany. 21-F-13

76 Squadron 4 Group Halifax DK171 MP/J
Crashed at Estern, Germany.
Pilot. A/416466 F/Sgt B.W.Thomas Killed Reichswald Forest. 12-C-11
Nav. 1311885 Sgt E.H.Wood Killed Reichswald Forest, Germany. 12-C-13
B/A. 646266 F/Sgt F.Norris PoW. Stalag 357, Kopernikus. 1153
W/OP. 1032376 Sgt F.J.Chandler Killed Reichswald Forest, Germany. 12-C-12
F/E. 814218 Sgt A.Hanley Killed Reichswald Forest, Germany. 12-C-10
A/G. 1515941 F/Sgt G.E.Testal PoW. Stalag 357, Kopernikus. 1104
A/G. 1472158 F/Sgt R.E.Hemsworth PoW. Stalag 357, Kopernikus. 164

77 Squadron 4 Group Halifax JB803 KN/G
Pilot. 1383608 Sgt G.Watson Killed Muiden, Holland. E-84
Nav. J/11636 F/O A.E.Parsons Killed Muiden, Holland. E-85
B/A. 1383305 Sgt L.Hannam Killed Muiden, Holland. E-82
W/OP. 1198324 Sgt W.R.Lough Missing, Runnymede Memorial 157
F/E. 634710 Sgt I.D.Crawford Killed Muiden, Holland. E-80
A/G. 929961 Sgt R.Shepherd Killed Muiden, Holland. E-81
A/G. R/95040 F/Sgt T.D.Scarff Killed Muiden, Holland. E-83

77 Squadron 4 Group Halifax JB846 KN/L
Pilot. 43195 S/Ldr F.C.Bertram Killed Reichswald Forest, Germany. 17-E-5
Nav. 1090550 Sgt C.W.Warne Killed Reichswald Forest, Germany. 17-E-6
B/A. 1220683 Sgt C.H.Herbert Killed Reichswald Forest, Germany. 17-E-2
W/OP. 1289968 Sgt J.P.H.Brownlee Killed Reichswald Forest. 17-E-1
F/E. 1104327 Sgt K.Ambler Killed Reichswald Forest, Germany. 17-E-3
A/G. 1376911 Sgt W.C.Bostock Killed Reichswald Forest, Germany. 17-E-4
A/G. 913181 Sgt J.D.Olding Killed Reichswald Forest, Germany. 17-E-7

77 Squadron 4 Group Halifax JB783 KN/N
Pilot. 1092905 Sgt A.R.Camburn Killed Apeldoorn, Holland. 4-287
Nav. 1314531 Sgt R.E.Hawkins Killed Apeldoorn, Holland. 4-289
B/A. 1010089 Sgt N.A.Fearneyhough PoW. Stalag Luft 6, Heydekrug. 1304
W/OP. 1383141 F/Sgt A.J.Butlin PoW. Stalag Luft 6, Heydekrug. 1122
F/E. R/76935 Sgt L.Dubetz Killed Groesbeek (Can), Holland. XV-A-8
A/G. 1691928 Sgt T.T.Jardine Killed Apeldoorn, Holland. 4-290
A/G. 1478299 Sgt J.K.Hendry Killed Apeldoorn, Holland. 4-291

9 Squadron 5 Group Lancaster ED838 WS/R
Pilot. 146436 P/O G.A.Nunez Missing, Runnymede Memorial 132
Nav. 1535181 Sgt A.Beard Missing, Runnymede Memorial 142
B/A. 1505512 Sgt E.F.Doolittle Missing, Runnymede Memorial 147
W/OP. 1312487 Sgt R.A.Knapman Missing, Runnymede Memorial 156
F/E. 1200432 Sgt C.H.Collins Missing, Runnymede Memorial 145
A/G. 1300620 Sgt J.Baylis Missing, Runnymede Memorial 142
A/G. 1354869 Sgt D.R.Barber Missing, Runnymede Memorial 141

44 Squadron 5 Group Lancaster ED783 KM/F
Pilot. 145792 P/O L.J.Ellis Killed Dalfsen, Zwolle, Holland. 6-1-9
Nav. J/21818 F/O W.A.Rollings Killed Dalfsen, Zwolle, Holland. 6-1-12
B/A. 1336517 Sgt J.B.Browne Killed Dalfsen, Zwolle, Holland. 6-1-8
W/OP. 1270431 Sgt H.C.Ellis Killed Dalfsen, Zwolle, Holland. 6-1-10
F/E. 577884 Sgt R.L.Le Page Killed Dalfsen, Zwolle, Holland. 6-1-11
A/G. 1384317 Sgt S.S.McCellan Killed Dalfsen, Zwolle, Holland. 6-1-6
A/G. 974495 Sgt R.Williams Killed Dalfsen, Zwolle, Holland. 6-1-7

57 Squadron 5 Group Lancaster ED706 DX/
Pilot. 957981 Sgt W.J.Glotham Missing, Runnymede Memorial 150
Nav. 1390280 Sgt A.V.Ansell Missing, Runnymede Memorial 140
B/A. 1335182 Sgt M.J.Grace Missing, Runnymede Memorial 151
W/OP. 1130071 Sgt J.Hodgson Missing, Runnymede Memorial 153
F/E. 1068163 Sgt J.K.Mansley Missing, Runnymede Memorial 158
A/G. 613267 Sgt W.C.Nugent Missing, Runnymede Memorial 160
A/G. 1579155 Sgt C.D.Todd Missing, Runnymede Memorial 167

106 Squadron 5 Group Lancaster ED451 ZN/
Pilot. 1335643 Sgt S.Abel Killed Reichswald Forest, Germany. 17-B-12
Nav. 127018 P/O V.A.Nono Killed Reichswald Forest, Germany. 17-B-10
B/A. 145328 P/O S.Plaskett Killed Reichswald Forest, Germany. 17-B-11
W/OP. 1377395 Sgt C.M.Harrower Killed Reichswald Forest. 17-B-14
F/E. R/89283 Sgt J.G.Alderson Killed Reichswald Forest, Germany. 17-B-13
A/G. 1200694 Sgt A.L.Barber Killed Reichswald Forest, Germany. JG 17-B-8/9
A/G. 1004817 Sgt D.Brown Killed Reichswald Forest, Germany. JG 17-B-8/9

467 Squadron 5 Group Lancaster ED771 PO/
Pilot. 40210 F/Lt R.A.Craigie PoW. Stalag Luft 3, Sagan. 1261
Nav. 127066 F/O R.H.Capron Killed Harderwijk, Holland. JG 2-31
B/A. 130512 F/O G.J.Phillips PoW. Stalag Luft 3, Sagan. 1276
W/OP. 1078045 Sgt G.H.Edwards Killed Harderwijk, Holland. JG 2-31
F/E. 929876 F/Sgt W.T.Fair PoW. Stalag Luft 6, Heydekrug. 1128
A/G. 1520433 Sgt J.A.Proctor Killed Harderwijk, Holland. JG 2-31
A/G. 1559144 Sgt T.D.Peat Killed Harderwijk, Holland. JG 2-33

78 Squadron 4 Group Halifax W7929 EY/
Aircraft crashed at Docking at 04.47 hours (1/5/43) after operation to Essen.
Pilot. A/416288 F/Sgt J.C.Rudd DFM Killed Great Bircham 1-3-3
Nav. 546 293 Sgt E.J.Wilson Killed Hammersmith,(Kensal Green). E-856
B/A. 657492 Sgt R.J.Pike Killed St Johns,Skewen,S.Wales.
W/OP. 1380052 Sgt H.Mason Killed St Chad, Prees, Shropshire.
F/E. 645244 Sgt R.Davies Injured.
A/G. 1124471 Sgt W.Oldroyd Killed Hanging Heaton,Batley 420
A/G. 2206682 Sgt J.Rashbrook Injured.

Bocholt Training Raid

April 30th/May 1st, 1943

12 aircraft, 4 Halifaxes and 8 Stirlings from Pathfinder force were on an H^2S (airborne radar) target identifying training raid to Bocholt, but although training they carried a total bomb load of 16 tons. Five aircraft had to abort with faulty H^2S sets. The remaining seven dropped bombs by their navigational aids. One aircraft, Stirling R9263 MG/D from 7 Squadron captained by Canadian Pilot Officer E. C. Hallding, failed to return. It crashed at Akkerwoude, Holland after a fighter attack. The flight engineer, Sergeant F. Painter was the only survivor and he became a prisoner of war.

Casualties April 30th/May 1st, 1943. Target Bocholt

7 Squadron 8 Group Stirling R9263 MG/D
After fighter attack aircraft crashed at Akkerwoude, Holland.
Pilot. J/17288 P/O E.C.Hallding Killed Dantumadeel(Akkermoude). 16-17
Nav. 139947 P/O G.Wragge Killed Dantumadeel(Akkermoude), Holland. 16-19
B/A. 1221520 Sgt N.A.Peachey Killed Dantumadeel(Akkermoude). 16-18
W/OP. R/94118 W/O L.Nutik Killed Dantumadeel(Akkermoude). 16-15
F/E. 572221 Sgt F.Painter PoW. Stalag Luft 4, Sagan. 42763
A/G. 1576201 Sgt A.E.Emms Killed Dantumadeel(Akkermoude). 16-16
A/G. R/133756 F/Sgt H.Sobel Killed Dantumadeel(Akkermoude). 16-14

May 1943

A Three Day Respite

May 1st/2nd, 1943
A respite of three days was given to the Ruhr until the night of 4th/5th May, but in the interim period Bomber Command kept up its work. It was minelaying on the target boards for 30 crews on the night of May 1st/2nd, when 12 Stirlings from 3 Group and 18 Wellingtons from 1 and 4 Groups mined areas as far apart as Brittany , Biscay and the Frisians, laying altogether 66 mines. One Stirling, from 149 Squadron was lost on these sorties, crashing near Havant, Hampshire on its return. Fortunately the crew baled out safely.

Casualties May 1st/2nd, 1943. Minelaying

149 Squadron 3 Group Stirling BK696 OJ/L
Crashed near Windmill Hill, Havant, after running out of fuel returning from minelaying.
Pilot. NZ/41865 P/O J.L.Blair Baled out.
Nav. R/89695 F/Sgt J.Giacomelli Baled out.
B/A. 1346491 Sgt A.G.Davidson Baled out.
W/OP. R/7038 Sgt N.K.Sutherland Baled out.
F/E. 633304 Sgt W.F.Johnston Baled out.
A/G. 1322578 Sgt R.Zambra Baled out.
A/G. 1442933 Sgt J.G.Barker Baled out.

Dortmund

May 4th/5th, 1943
The Ruhr once again was the focus of attention for the heavy bombers on the night of 4th/5th of May, when a large force of 596 aircraft - 255 Lancasters, 141 Halifaxes, 110 Wellingtons, 80 Stirlings and 10 Mosquitoes made a major attack, dropping 844.1 tons of high explosive bombs and 269, 343 incendiaries on Dortmund. Weather conditions over the target were not the most favourable for a large bomber force. There was no protective cloud cover but there was excellent visibility, although this changed when heavy smoke caused by the fires during the course of the attack began to rise. The initial Pathfinder

marking was extremely accurate, as most crews reported seeing the PFF coloured markers clearly on their run up to the target. During the course of the raid the backers up had great difficulty in maintaining the main aiming point but over the full period of the raid, 137 target indicators were dropped. Many bombers of the main force were distracted by the decoy fires, a ploy that the Germans were beginning to use more frequently in an effort to hamper the bombers finding the correct aiming point. Nevertheless the central and northern areas of the city had very serious damage. A number of explosions were observed, and many returning crews reported an exceptionally large explosion in the northern area of the city. The glow from the fires could be seen by crews 150 miles after leaving the target area. The city records state that 1218 buildings were destroyed and 2,141 damaged. 693 people were killed (which included 200 prisoners of war) and 1075 people were injured. The cost in bombers for this raid was 31 aircraft, 5.2% of the force. From the 204 aircrew manning these bombers. 104 were killed, 38 were missing and 62 were made prisoners of war. A further seven aircraft crashed on return to their various bases, killing 20 and seriously injuring 15 aircrew.

No Chance of Escape in Stockinged Feet

408 Squadron (RCAF) lost two aircraft on this raid. One of those Halifaxes was JB898 EQ/Q piloted by J17313 Pilot Officer R. O. Blackhall which was attacked by a German night fighter at 23.00 hours on the way to the target over Akkrum, Holland and quickly caught fire. Five of the crew, including a second pilot managed to bale out in spite of the lack of intercom in the plane. The remaining crew were killed when the aircraft crashed. One of the lucky crew was bomb aimer 146147 Flight Lieutenant George Semper. He landed uninjured in a field about two miles outside the town. Unfortunately he lost both flying boots on the parachute descent and this handicap was no doubt the cause of his quick capture. As soon as it became dawn Semper buried his equipment and approached a number of farmhouses for assistance, but the people he met were extremely frightened and he had to begin walking away from the crash site in his stockinged

feet. After about six miles, his socks were in tatters and he had no choice but to ask for help at the next farmhouse. He was given some food but almost immediately the Dutch police arrived and arrested him. Obviously the farmer had informed the police of Semper's presence. The other four crew members were also captured on the same day.

After being in two prisoner of war camps Flight Lieutenant Semper finally ended up at Stalag Luft 3 at Sagan in November 1943. In April 1945, the prisoners of war were moved to a temporary camp at the Artillery Barracks, in Lübeck. At this time the advancing British forces were only 25 miles away and in the general confusion Semper, along with Flight Lieutenant L. Kenyon and a French PoW officer, managed to sneak aboard a Red Cross lorry ready to leave the camp. The lorry was only superficially searched at the prison gates, as by this time the German guards had lost interest. The vehicle was bound for the docks where there were anchored some Swedish mercy ships taking aboard refugees from Belsen. Mingling with these refugees the three escapers succeeded in boarding the ship the 'Lily Mathieson' and eventually reached Trelleborg, in Sweden. All the passengers on board were put into 14 days quarantine by the Swedish authorities to prevent the spread of any diseases. Semper declared that he was an escaping RAF officer and he avoided quarantine and was sent on to Stockholm before being flown back to the UK on Whit Monday, 1945.

Pathfinder's Training Raid

May 4th/5th, 1943
Pathfinders continued with their H^2S training when they sent two Halifaxes and six Stirlings to bomb Rheine. All eight aircraft returned safely.

Casualties May 4th/5th, 1943. Target Dortmund

83 Squadron 8 Group Lancaster R5629 OL/J
Pilot. 1077886 Sgt J.R.Leigh Killed Reichswald Forest. CG 3-A-14/17
2/Pilot. 34042 W/Cdr J.R.Gillman Killed Reichswald Forest. CG 3-A-14/17
Nav. 1023959 Sgt T.Griffith Killed Reichswald Forest, Germany. 3-A-12
B/A. J/10884 F/O O.M.Cornish Killed Reichswald Forest. CG 3-A-14/17
W/OP. 1066778 Sgt F.Johnson Killed Reichswald Forest. CG 3-A-14/17

F/E. 126613 Sgt P.R.Smith Killed Reichswald Forest, Germany. 3-A-11
A/G. 1236544 Sgt D.H.Rock Killed Reichswald Forest, Germany. CG 3-A-14/17
A/G. 516664 Sgt F.J.Cleasby Killed Reichswald Forest. CG 3-A-14/17

156 Squadron 8 Group Lancaster ED877 GT/
Pilot. 114170 F/Lt A.G.Lang DFC PoW. Stalag Luft 3, Sagan. 1409
Nav. NZ/404998 F/Lt E.N.Gray Killed Reichswald Forest, Germany. 3-A-10
B/A. J/17759 P/O R.J.Lee Killed Reichswald Forest, Germany. 3-A-9
W/OP. NZ/412354 F/Sgt D.G.Ridings Killed Reichswald Forest. 3-A-8
F/E. 1247451 Sgt J.L.Clark DFM PoW. Camp not known.
A/G. 1314161 F/Sgt F.M.Venn Killed Reichswald Forest, Germany. 3-B-2
A/G. 1435587 Sgt N.H.Wood Killed Reichswald Forest, Germany. 3-B-1

405 Squadron 8 Group Halifax JB904 LQ/E
Aircraft crashed after fighter attack.
Pilot. J/16481 P/O J.W.Lennox Killed Reichswald Forest, Germany. 15-F-14
Nav. 1384356 F/Sgt A.T.Knight PoW. Stalag Luft 1, Barth Vogelsang. 1143
B/A. 124317 F/Lt J.B.Graham PoW. Stalag Luft 3, Sagan. 1266
W/OP. 1288940 F/Sgt F.V.Roberts PoW. Stalag Luft 4, Sagan. 1156
F/E. 6266241 F/Sgt A.A.A.Adlam PoW. Stalag 357, Kopernikus. 42753
A/G. R/108161 Sgt J.L.Prieur PoW. Stalag 357, Kopernikus. 1265
A/G. 1987282 Sgt B.Moody Killed Reichswald Forest, Germany. 15-F-16
Killed in aircraft.

7 Squadron 8 Group Stirling BK773 MG/T
Crashed in Zuider Zee, south of Einkhuisen, Holland.
Pilot. J/17213 P/O W.Holden Killed Bergen, Holland. 2-E-27
Nav. 1313665 Sgt A.J.Phillips Missing, Runnymede Memorial 161
B/A. 1585820 Sgt T.W.Hunt Killed Bergen, Holland. 2-E-18
W/OP. 1063033 Sgt J.Avery Missing, Runnymede Memorial 141
F/E. 571115 Sgt R.W.Conuel Killed Amsterdam, Holland. CG 69-C-7
A/G. 1602507 Sgt J.B.J.Hook Killed Amsterdam, Holland. 69-B-12
A/G. 1321784 Sgt P.E.C.Flood Missing, Runnymede Memorial 149

101 Squadron 1 Group Lancaster W4784 SR/E
Pilot. 919205 Sgt W.Nicholson Missing, Runnymede Memorial 160
Nav. 49737 F/O N.Ainsworth Missing, Runnymede Memorial 122
B/A. 126745 F/O H.K.Wainer Missing, Runnymede Memorial 130
W/OP. 1078947 Sgt G.Eastwood Missing, Runnymede Memorial 148
F/E. 654516 Sgt B.W.Squires Missing, Runnymede Memorial 165
A/G. 1580102 Sgt G.Brick Missing, Runnymede Memorial 143
A/G. 1434822 Sgt D.W.Rowley Missing, Runnymede Memorial 163
First operation for crew.

101 Squadron 1 Group Lancaster W4888 SR/P
Pilot. 80378 F/O N.J.Stanford Killed Workum (Spoordyk), Holland. D-1-4
Nav. 128664 F/Lt R.D.Patterson PoW. Stalag Luft 3, Sagan. 42744
B/A. 1336486 Sgt A.J.L.Lyon Killed Workum (Spoordyk), Holland. D-1-3
W/OP. J/16982 F/O W.Lewis DFM Killed Workum (Spoordyk), Holland. D-1-2
F/E. 1203348 Sgt A.H.Clark Killed Workum (Spoordyk), Holland. D-1-5
A/G. R/131490 F/Sgt G.W.F.Reynolds Killed Workum (Spoordyk). D-1-6
A/G. 1132867 Sgt J.M.Hadfield Killed Workum (Spoordyk), Holland. D-1-7

460 Squadron 1 Group Lancaster W4818 UV/
Pilot. A/416680 F/Sgt D.N.Jaekel Killed Reichswald Forest, Germany. 3-A-1
Nav. A/414506 P/O S.M.Russ Killed Reichswald Forest, Germany. 3-A-6
B/A. A/412479 F/Sgt E.J.Candish Killed Reichswald Forest, Germany. 3-A-4
W/OP. A/412139 F/Sgt A.Hilton Killed Reichswald Forest, Germany. 3-A-5
F/E. 1476394 Sgt W.J.Turpin Killed Reichswald Forest, Germany. 3-A-8
A/G. A/20047 F/Sgt J.L.Barry Killed Reichswald Forest, Germany. 3-A-2
A/G. A/405597 F/Sgt W.Williams Killed Reichswald Forest, Germany. 3-A-3

166 Squadron 1 Group Wellington HE923 AS/R
Pilot. R/135043 F/Sgt A.P.Uditsky Killed Vlagtwedde, Holland. CG A-6-1
Nav. R/110747 F/Sgt J.T.Macksimchuk Killed Vlagtwedde, Holland. CG A-6-1
B/A. R/138918 F/Sgt E.N.Moore Killed Vlagtwedde, Holland. CG A-6-1
W/OP. 1123751 Sgt T.A.S.Buchanan Killed Vlagtwedde, Holland. CG A-6-1
A/G. R/125223 F/Sgt G.E.Armstrong Killed Vlagtwedde, Holland. CG A-6-1

166 Squadron 1 Group Wellington HE244 AS/D
Pilot. 1030871 Sgt A.I.Stark Killed Werkendam, Holland. 8-10
Nav. 744714 Sgt D.High Killed Werkendam, Holland. 8-8
B/A. R/97340 F/Sgt H.J.Salisbury Killed Werkendam, Holland. 8-9
W/OP. 1133751 Sgt J.A.Beedim Killed Werkendam, Holland. 8-12
A/G. R/10542 F/Sgt T.Lafontaine Killed Werkendam, Holland. 8-11

15 Squadron 3 Group Stirling BK782 LS/X
Shot down by night fighter at Houten/Schalkwijk, Holland.
Pilot. 143225 P/O T.E.Emberson Killed Amersfoort, Holland. 13-6-104
Nav. 127063 F/O W.C.Lambie Killed Amersfoort, Holland. 13-6-105
B/A. 1585062 Sgt G.Rutherford Killed Amersfoort, Holland. 13-6-101
W/OP. 1292168 Sgt G.A.Rodway Killed Amersfoort, Holland. 13-6-99
F/E. 545569 Sgt H.G.Brown Killed Amersfoort, Holland. 13-6-103
A/G. 1585534 Sgt P.F.Hanberger Killed Amersfoort, Holland. 13-6-102
A/G. 1600330 Sgt H.G.Mugridge Killed Amersfoort, Holland. 13-6-100

15 Squadron 3 Group Stirling BK658 LS/K
Aircraft crashed at Midwolda, Holland after fighter attack.
Pilot. NZ/414655 W/O W.M.McLeod PoW. Stalag Luft 4, Sagan. 1149
Nav. 1335153 W/O A.H.Law PoW. Stalag Luft 6, Heydekrug. 1144
B/A. 1392698 F/Sgt A.E.J.Eaton PoW. Stalag Luft 1, Barth Vogelsang. 1127
W/OP. 1189201 F/Sgt E.Willis PoW. Stalag Luft 6, Heydekrug. 1275
F/E. 576667 F/Sgt E.Routh PoW. Stalag Luft 4, Sagan. 1157
A/G. 1269263 Sgt H.S.Flowerday PoW. Stalag Luft 6, Heydekrug. 1130
A/G. 1452090 Sgt P.McNulty Killed Midwolda, Holland. E-1 Killed in fighter attack

15 Squadron 3 Group Stirling EF345 LS/M
Aircraft crashed at Anholt, Germany.
Pilot. NZ/415384 P/O J.H.Stowell Killed Reichswald Forest, Germany. 21-A-2
2/Pilot. 1123558 W/O T.Malcolm PoW. Stalag Luft 4, Sagan. 1081
Nav. 137217 P/O D.Spooner Killed Reichswald Forest, Germany. 21-A-3
B/A. 1039745 F/Sgt J.Banyer Killed Reichswald Forest, Germany. JG 21-A-4

W/OP. 146098 P/O L.H.Pattison Killed Reichswald Forest, Germany. 21-A-5
F/E. 577192 Sgt P.R.Sharman Killed Reichswald Forest, Germany. 10-D-17
A/G. 1322986 Sgt W.Jennings Killed Reichswald Forest, Germany. JG 21-A-4
A/G. 951369 F/Sgt F.Stevens PoW. Stalag Luft 6, Heydekrug. 1101

90 Squadron 3 Group Stirling BK814 WP/T
Aircraft crashed at Derne, Germany.
Pilot. 1344526 Sgt F.C.Maxwell Missing, Runnymede Memorial 158
Nav. 1451293 Sgt J.Kay Killed Reichswald Forest, Germany. 3-A-7
B/A. 1331271 Sgt J.T.Pooley Missing, Runnymede Memorial 162
W/OP. 1186818 Sgt H.W.Burton Missing, Runnymede Memorial 144
F/E. 574880 Sgt L.S.Bromfield Missing, Runnymede Memorial 143
A/G. 1587150 Sgt S.Sweet Missing, Runnymede Memorial 166
A/G. 132626 F/O R.J.Davis Missing, Runnymede Memorial 124

149 Squadron 3 Group Stirling EF343 OJ/B
Shot down by night fighter at Ijpecolsga, Holland.
Pilot. 120435 F/O W.E.Davey Killed Wymbritseradeel(Ijpecolsga). E-12
Nav. 1384532 F/Sgt R.F.Whitaker Killed Wymbritseradeel(Ijpecolsga). E-15
B/A. 125606 F/O T.C.Timney Killed Wymbritseradeel(Ijpecolsga). E-13
W/OP. 1291126 Sgt D.R.Higgs Killed Wymbritseradeel(Ijpecolsga). E-17
2/W/OP 1033308 Sgt J.J.O'Neill Killed Wymbritseradeel(Ijpecolsga). E-14
F/E. 345474 Sgt C.W.E.Leach Killed Wymbritseradeel(Ijpecolsga). E-18
A/G. 1396863 Sgt G.J.C.Hall Killed Wymbritseradeel(Ijpecolsga). E-19
A/G. A/406674 F/Sgt E.H.Finch Killed Wymbritseradeel(Ijpecolsga). E-16

218 Squadron 3 Group Stirling BF505 HA/Z
Aircraft exploded in mid air near Murmerwoude and crashed at Dokkum, Holland.
Pilot. J/8378 F/Lt W.L.Turner Killed Dantumadeel (Murmurwoude). E-7-4
2/Pilot. 1094894 Sgt F.N.Robinson Killed Dantumadeel (Murmurwoude). E-7-8
Nav. 926552 W/O J.L.White PoW. Stalag Luft 6, Heydekrug. 1165
B/A. 116535 F/Lt P.S.Beck PoW. Stalag Luft 3, Sagan. 1254
W/OP. 636817 W/O J.M.T.Smith PoW. Stalag 4B, Muhleberg(Elbe). 222555
F/E. 1329885 Sgt W.N.Forth Killed Dantumadeel (Murmurwoude). E-7-6
A/G. 1322090 Sgt H.W.Sawkings Killed Dantumadeel (Murmurwoude). E-7-7
A/G. 550977 F/Sgt G.A.Hinshelwood Killed Dantumadeel. E-7-5

76 Squadron 4 Group Halifax DK134 MP/Y
Shot down Kilder, Holland at 01.55hours (5/5/43). Victim of Hptm Dormann II/NJG1.
Pilot. 124841 F/Lt J.I.M.Bell PoW. Stalag Luft 3, Sagan. 1255
2/Pilot 1384825 W/O A.E.Bumstead PoW. Stalag Luft 1, Barth Vogelsang. 1121
Nav. 1236937 W/O H.M.Farrington PoW. Stalag Luft 6, Heydekrug. 1129
B/A. 1337099 F/Sgt H.J.Hamlyn PoW. Stalag Luft 1, Barth Vogelsang 1133
W/OP. 1186999 F/Sgt D.J.Marshall PoW. Stalag Luft 4, Sagan. 1148
F/E. 1247777 W/O A.Forster PoW. Stalag Luft 6, Heydekrug. 1242
A/G. R/98439 F/Sgt D.B.Brown PoW. Stalag 7A, Moosburg (Isar). 1120
A/G. 1332033 Sgt B.Thompson PoW. Stalag Luft 6, Heydekrug. 1202

78 Squadron 4 Group Halifax JB973 EY/
Pilot. 655643 F/Sgt A.Burns Missing, Runnymede Memorial 135
Nav. 1218379 W/O H.Gamble PoW. Stalag Luft 6, Heydekrug. 1131
B/A. 127508 F/Lt J.B.Thompson PoW. Stalag Luft 3, Sagan. 1282
W/OP. 1201189 Sgt J.R.Heslop PoW. Repatriated in May 1944
F/E. 1507185 F/Sgt F.G.Hockin PoW. Stalag Luft 3, Sagan. 1136
A/G. 1802400 F/Sgt W.Ashley PoW. Stalag Luft 6, Heydekrug. 1116
A/G. 1387976 F/Sgt H.Tyler PoW. Stalag Luft 6, Heydekrug. 1161

78 Squadron 4 Group Halifax JB903 EY/
Pilot. 657098 Sgt A.C.Leppard Missing, Runnymede Memorial 156
Nav. 1321404 Sgt V.C.G.Moody Missing, Runnymede Memorial 159
B/A. 989148 Sgt R.Boydell Missing, Runnymede Memorial 143
W/OP. 1382734 Sgt P.E.Mellish Missing, Runnymede Memorial 159
F/E. 1337080 Sgt D.N.Brown Missing, Runnymede Memorial 143
A/G. 1485071 Sgt C.Lowis Missing, Runnymede Memorial 157
A/G. 1510059 Sgt F.Moore Missing, Runnymede Memorial 159

78 Squadron 4 Group Halifax JB915 EY/
Aircraft crashed after fighter attack.
Pilot. 37650 S/Ldr J.H.B.Chapple PoW. Stalag Luft 3, Sagan. 1260
Nav. J/13808 F/Lt B.A.G.Campbell PoW. Stalag Luft 3, Sagan. 1259
B/A. 109939 F/Lt H.J.King PoW. Stalag Luft 3, Sagan. 1269
W/OP. 1027348 F/Sgt E.K.Blackweall PoW. Stalag 357, Kopernikus. 1118
F/E. 1289735 Sgt B.Legg Killed Reichswald Forest, Germany. 23-F-9
Killed in fighter attack
A/G. 1272409 F/Sgt R.Hillary PoW. Stalag 357, Kopernikus. 1135
A/G. 122904 F/Lt E.W.Barnes PoW. Stalag Luft 3, Sagan. 1252

102 Squadron 4 Group Halifax W7820 DY/V
Ditched 75 miles off Flamborough Head at 03.14 hours (5/4/43).
Pilot. 11804 F/Sgt J.Bowman Rescued.
Nav. 1344926 Sgt D.Galbraith Rescued.
B/A. 1388188 Sgt J.H.Loveless Rescued.
W/OP. 1265766 Sgt G.C.Parry Rescued.
F/E. 1402631 Sgt H.R.H.Mock Rescued.
A/G. 778947 Sgt J.J.Prinsloo Rescued.
A/G. 1031723 Sgt S.J.Treguno Rescued.

102 Squadron 4 Group Halifax JB869 DY/H
Pilot. 1092623 Sgt W.B.J.Happold Killed Rheinberg, Germany. 2-F-8
Nav. 657168 W/O H.Barratt PoW. Stalag Luft 6, Heydekrug. 1168
B/A. 127296 F/O J.Baxter Killed Rheinberg, Germany. 2-F-9
W/OP. 1070175 F/Sgt J.Brownlie PoW. Stalag Luft 6, Heydekrug. 1234
F/E. 1219595 Sgt G.S.Bowles Killed Rheinberg, Germany. 2-F-10
A/G. 1338943 W/O T.H.Jones PoW. Stalag 357, Kopernikus. 1142
A/G. 1602585 Sgt D.R.McGregor Killed Rheinberg, Germany. 2-F-11

102 Squadron 4 Group Halifax HR667 DY/U
Pilot. 37542 S/Ldr J.B.Flowerdew Missing, Runnymede Memorial 118
Nav. 133564 P/O D.E.Grant Missing, Runnymede Memorial 131
B/A. 134570 P/O H.G.R.Chiverton Missing, Runnymede Memorial 131
W/OP. 1209360 Sgt J.G.S.Dutton Missing, Runnymede Memorial 148
F/E. 576698 F/Sgt P.E.Tiller Missing, Runnymede Memorial 139
A/G. R/83572 F/Sgt K.H.Buck Killed Kollumerland (Westergeest). SE-2-2
A/G. 1356376 Sgt G.Rose Killed Kollumerland (Westergeest), Holland. SE-2-1

196 Squadron 4 Group Wellington HE162 ZO/
Pilot. 1525019 Sgt J.Staniforth Killed Reichswald Forest, Germany. 19-F-9
Nav. 1344743 Sgt H.G.Graham Killed Reichswald Forest, Germany. 19-F-11
B/A. 1336379 Sgt R.W.Lynn Killed Reichswald Forest, Germany. 19-F-8
W/OP. 1174187 Sgt G.W.C.James Killed Reichswald Forest, Germany. 19-F-10
A/G. 710151 Sgt B.E.Taylor Killed Reichswald Forest, Germany. 19-F-7

466 Squadron 4 Group Wellington HE530 HD/
Pilot. A/414299 W/O L.F.James PoW. Stalag Luft 4, Sagan. 1140
Nav. A/414212 W/O R.E.Dolby PoW. Stalag Luft 4, Sagan. 1125
B/A. A/413214 Sgt R.L.Lutton PoW. Stalag Luft 4, Sagan. 1146
W/OP. 1148282 Sgt J.R.Baxter PoW. Stalag Luft 1, Barth Vogelsang. 1146
A/G. A/412543 Sgt F.G.Latham Killed De Wijk, Meppel, Holland. 141

57 Squadron 5 Group Lancaster ED390 DX/
Pilot. 158305 P/O V.D.Farmer Killed Reichswald Forest, Germany. 15-F-13
Nav. 134072 P/O T.Armstrong Killed Reichswald Forest, Germany. 13-F-15
B/A. 1319816 Sgt L.A.W.Sanders Killed Reichswald Forest. CG 15-F-9/10
W/OP. 751507 F/Sgt J.T.Taylor Killed Reichswald Forest. CG 15-F-9/10
F/E. 1178891 Sgt A.M.James Killed Reichswald Forest, Germany. 15-F-17
A/G. 1600961 Sgt L.H.Leaney Killed Reichswald Forest. CG 15-F-9/10
A/G. 988528 Sgt N.Long Killed Reichswald Forest, Germany. CG 15-F-9/10

408 Squadron 6 Group Halifax HR658 EQ/V
Pilot. R/123858 F/Sgt G.A.Johannesson Missing, Runnymede Memorial 182
Nav. J/22204 F/O W.A.Grant Missing, Runnymede Memorial 173
B/A. R/104383 F/Sgt M.R.E.Metcalfe Missing, Runnymede Memorial 185
W/OP. R/106380 W/O D.C.R.Nault Missing, Runnymede Memorial 180
F/E. R/51529 Sgt C.W.Ellard Missing, Runnymede Memorial 186
A/G. R/108256 F/Sgt R.V.Clithoroe Missing, Runnymede Memorial 181
A/G. R/141130 F/Sgt J.C.Archer Missing, Runnymede Memorial 181

408 Squadron 6 Group Halifax JB898 EQ/Q
Pilot. J/17313 P/O R.O.Blackhall Killed Utingeradel(Akkrum), Holland. K-110
2/Pilot. 129339 F/Lt F.H.Scythes PoW. Stalag Luft 3, Sagan. 1278
Nav. R/95595 F/Sgt C.B.Norton PoW. Stalag Luft 4, Sagan. 1154
B/A. 146147 F/O G.I.Semper PoW. Stalag Luft 6, Heydekrug. 1158
Escaped April 1945
W/OP. 1187129 F/Sgt K.E.Godfrey PoW. Stalag 357, Kopernikus. 42756
F/E. R/52795 Sgt K.E.Emmons Killed Utingeradel(Akkrum), Holland. K-112
A/G. J/17692 P/O A.J.Sutton Killed Utingeradel(Akkrum), Holland. K-111
A/G. R/119868 W/O C.L.Horn PoW. Stalag 357, Kopernikus. 1138

419 Squadron 6 Group Halifax DT794 VR/
Pilot. J/14866 F/O W.G.Elliott Killed Reichswald Forest, Germany. 20-E-17
Nav. J/14521 F/O E.E.Kennedy Killed Reichswald Forest. JG 20-E-14/15
B/A. J/21737 F/O H.M.Metcalfe Killed Reichswald Forest. JG 20-E-14/15
W/OP. 1062023 Sgt G.Sandfield Killed Reichswald Forest, Germany. 20-E-11
F/E. R/89099 Sgt G.D.Menzies Killed Reichswald Forest, Germany. 20-E-16
A/G. R/127620 F/Sgt J.W.McIntosh Killed Reichswald Forest. 20-E-12
A/G. R/152210 F/Sgt J.A.Farrel Killed Reichswald Forest, Germany. 20-E-13

419 Squadron 6 Group Halifax W7817 VR/
Aircraft shot down by night fighter.
Pilot. J/12563 F/Lt C.J.L.Vaillancourt PoW. Stalag Luft 3, Sagan. 1284
Nav. 131904 F/Lt D.Grimshaw PoW. Stalag Luft 3, Sagan. 1265
B/A. 1501737 W/O N.M.Douglas PoW. Stalag Luft1, Barth Vogelsang. 1126
W/OP. R/91314 W/O A.S.Morrison PoW. Stalag Luft 4, Sagan. 1151
F/E. R/18054A Sgt A.Jaynes PoW. Stalag Luft 4, Sagan. 1141
A/G. R/120248 W/O J.L.Peck PoW. Stalag 4B, Muhlberg(Elbe). 1155
A/G. R/134212 Sgt F.T.Stanley Killed Zwollerkerspel(Voorst), Holland. 3

428 Squadron 6 Group Wellington HE727 NA/K
Pilot. R/74234 W/O R.B.Moulton Killed Wilnis, Holland. 4
Nav. R/119839 Sgt G.C.Carter PoW. Stalag 357, Kopernikus. 1123
B/A. R/114141 F/Sgt J.White Missing, Runnymede Memorial 186
W/OP. 1344173 F/Sgt H.H.Hoddinott PoW. Stalag Luft 6, Heydekrug. 1137
A/G. R/94389 Sgt J.E.A.Thibaudeau Missing, Runnymede Memorial 186

428 Squadron 6 Group Wellington HE864 NA/D
Pilot. R/120884 F/Sgt D.W.Johnson Killed Zwollerkerspel(Voorst), Holland. 2
Nav. R/61778 Sgt J.L.Boyd PoW. Camp not known
B/A. R/110932 Sgt J.Prosnyck Killed Zwollerkerspel(Voorst), Holland. 1
W/OP. R/79019 Sgt D.E.Thompson PoW. Stalag Luft 4, Sagan. 1273
A/G. R/113949 W/O J.J.Levasseur PoW. Stalag 357, Kopernikus. 1145

97 Squadron 8 Group Lancaster ED880 OF/N
Crashed on overshoot, landing at Waterbeach, on diversion after operations.
Pilot. 1005145 Sgt A.Reilly Killed Cambridge 14533
Nav. 1063026 Sgt M.McFarlane Injured.
B/A. 120544 F/O R.J.Hopps Injured.
W/OP. 1323807 Sgt L.A.Horne Safe.
F/E. 988693 Sgt R.Gibbon Injured.
A/G. 639470 Sgt R.L.Griffiths Safe.
A/G. 868664 Sgt F.Fisher Safe.

156 Squadron 8 Group Lancaster ED715 GT/
Crashed near Chatteris, ran out of fuel in fog after operations.
Pilot. 43377 S/Ldr B.L.Duigan DFC Baled out.
Nav. 127482 F/O J.C.Eade Baled out.
B/A. 1301464 Sgt R.Drysdale Baled out.
W/OP. 47872 F/O D.J.Drake Baled out.
F/E. 655809 F/Sgt J.R.Hood Baled out.
A/G. 1356283 Sgt K.Richards Baled out.
A/G. 24029 F/Lt J.A.Rogers Baled out.

35 Squadron 8 Group Halifax DT489 TL/Y
Aircraft crashed west of Portland/Gelling crossroads, Graveley after operations.
Pilot. 145671 P/O J.A.Cobb Killed Ringwood. 2-284
Nav. 124952 F/O S.A.Coles Killed Talbot, Bournemouth. 988
B/A. 1183357 Sgt S.E.A.Russell Killed Dorking. 1-5277
W/OP. 1026403 Sgt J.D.Collinge Killed Castleton, Rochdale. 150
F/E. 1144928 Sgt F.R.Beech Killed Wrexham. D-8653
A/G. 1055777 Sgt C.H.Fisher Killed Houghton, Wyton. 352
A/G. Sgt J.H.Robertson Injured,

35 Squadron 8 Group Halifax W7887 TL/E
Aircraft crashed near Grafton Underwood after operations to Dortmund.
Pilot. 1332303 Sgt J.J.Williams Baled out.
Nav. 1319061 Sgt B.C.Tucker Baled out.
B/A. 657145 Sgt J.Casey Baled out.
W/OP. 61485 F/Sgt E.G.Brown Baled out.
F/E. 999563F Sgt G.J.Hurley Baled out.
A/G. 1252904 Sgt T.D.Bishop Baled out.
A/G. 1010564 Sgt J.I.Barrie Baled out.

101 Squadron 1 Group Lancaster W4863 SR/G
Crashed near Scorton, Catterick, Yorkshire after take off for operations.
Pilot. NZ/413376 Sgt J.R.Browning Killed Catterick. O-14
Nav. 953183 Sgt R.Allison Killed West Hartlepool. 10-B-979
B/A. Sgt Hogben Injured.
W/OP. Sgt Granville Injured.
F/E. 949546 Sgt J.H.Stretton Killed Dalbeattie, Scotland. 883
A/G. R/140082 Sgt M.D.Davis Killed Catterick. N-G-1
A/G. F/Sgt Rays Injured.

101 Squadron 1 Group Lancaster ED608 SR/T
Crashed at 03.42 hrs near Hotham, East Yorkshire after hitting trees returning from Dortmund. Aircraft badly damaged by *Flak*.
Pilot. 1058798 F/Sgt G.Hough Killed Holme on Spalding, Yorkshire. A-36
Nav. F/O S.H.Beason Injured
B/A. Sgt P.W.Ratcliffe Injured.
W/OP. 126623 F/O F.W.Gates DSO Killed Sutton and Cheam. F-209
F/E. 574248 Sgt H.C.Hooper Killed Plymouth (Old). T-I-49
A/G. Sgt W.D.G.Merlin Injured.
A/G. F/Sgt C.L.Outhouse Injured.

101 Squadron 1 Group Lancaster ED776 SR/U
Overshot on landing at base 03.20 hrs after operations.Struck DF Hut mistook approach lights for flare path in poor visibility.
Pilot. A/412023 F/Sgt F.J.Kelly Safe.
Nav. Sgt E.Wheelwright Safe.
B/A. Sgt R.R.Sparkes Safe.
W/OP. Sgt D.T.Hone Safe.
F/E. Sgt L.Mooney Safe.
A/G. Sgt C.J.Wearmouth Safe.
A/G. Sgt D.H.Flack Safe.

10 Squadron 4 Group Halifax JD105 ZA/
Crashed at Hood Range Farm, Sutton Bank, Yorkshire, returning from operations.
Pilot. A/401939 F/Sgt R.H.Geddes Injured.
2/Pilot. 1334006 Sgt E.B.Hill Killed Southall, Middlesex. 56-26
Nav. 1575418 Sgt T.Cox Killed Elmdon, Solihull
B/A. 1334645 Sgt H.S.Taylor Killed Talbot, Bournemouth 939
W/OP. 1295368 Sgt H.H.Way Killed Brantham, Suffolk
F/E. 614225 Sgt W.A.Dunbar Injured.
A/G. 1641825 Sgt G.F.Ward Killed Onehouse, Suffolk
A/G. Sgt K.Hart Injured.

Frisians Mined Again

May 5th/6th, 1943.
21 Stirlings, from 3 Group laid 101 mines around the Frisians.
One aircraft failed to return, no trace of the crew was found.

Casualties May 5th/6th, 1943. Minelaying (Frisians)

75 Squadron 3 Group Stirling EF340 AA/Q
Aircraft crashed into North Sea.
Pilot. A/416471 P/O R.F.Westwood Missing, Runnymede Memorial 191
Nav. NZ/414580 P/O R.H.W.Bentley Missing, Runnymede Memorial 142
B/A. NZ/413709 Sgt E.H.R.Lamb Missing, Runnymede Memorial 163
W/OP. 1127681 Sgt W.Harkness Missing, Runnymede Memorial 152
F/E. 1281626 Sgt F.H.Bennetton Missing, Runnymede Memorial 142
A/G. 1382746 Sgt G.H.Rogers Missing, Runnymede Memorial 163
A/G. NZ/414491 Sgt J.M.Boswell Missing, Runnymede Memorial 199

Minelaying Switches to the French West Coast

May 9th/10th, 1943.
21 Stirlings made a minelaying operation to the La Pallice area of the western coast of France. They laid 62 mines and all the aircraft returned safely.

Fourth Heavy Attack on Duisburg

May 12th/13th, 1943
A week elapsed before Duisburg had its fourth and final attack in this period. This occurred on the night of 12th/13th May, at

the end of which the people of Duisburg knew from experience what cities like Essen had suffered. 238 Lancasters, 142 Halifaxes, 112 Wellingtons, 70 Stirlings and 10 Mosquitoes, a total of 572 aircraft, left their English bases for the attack with the city centre and the port area just off the River Rhine, as the main aiming points in Germany's largest inland port. Fifty of the bombers failed to reach the target and returned early to their bases. Very good weather conditions prevailed all along the route and over the target area. Visibility was good except for a slight ground haze. The perfect marking and timing of the Pathfinders on this raid contributed a great deal to the well concentrated bombing by the main force. Early arrivals were able to clearly see the built up areas and the River Rhine. 80% of the 174 target indicators dropped were plotted within 2 miles of the aiming point. 864.6 tons of high explosives and 248,074 incendiaries were dropped during the course of the raid. A spectacular explosion at 02.17 hours was plainly seen by aircraft 40 miles away. Such widespread damage was caused that 2,000 prisoners of war were drafted into Duisburg to temporarily repair the damage. The old town was gutted and four of Thyssen's steel plants were among the targets showing new damage. The port area suffered a great deal and records show that 21 barges and 13 ships, totalling 18,921 tons, were sunk and 60 other ships damaged. The price paid by the bomber force for this attack was the loss of 34 aircraft, 5.9 % of the total force. Aircrew losses were 149 killed, 44 missing, 27 prisoners and two were succesful in evading.

Back to Base Without a Gunner

Halifax DT777, EY/T from 78 Squadron captained by 1086886 Sergeant G. E. Clay, returned to base minus the mid-upper gunner 1559133 Sergeant A. Scott. After bombing the target, the bomber was caught in a group of searchlights and the pilot during his evasive action stated to his crew over his intercom "We will have to get out of this lot quick." The aircraft was put into a steep starboard diving turn and as it dived it shuddered excessively. When eventually clear of the searchlights and supporting *Flak* the pilot called up each member of his crew to check their safety after such a violent manoeuvre. When he received no reply from the mid-upper gunner, the flight engineer was sent back to check personally. He reported that the back escape hatch was open and that the gunner was missing. On landing back at base the bomber was found to have a deep score mark under its port main wing, probably caused by an anti aircraft shell which had scored a hit but had not exploded. No doubt this was the reason for the aircraft's shudder during the dive.

The following night on a raid on Bochum, Sergeant Clay and his crew were shot down by anti-aircraft fire over Bochum and some days later unexpectedly met up with Sergeant Scott in a prisoner of war camp. He explained why he had baled out. Apparently the last thing that Scott heard was the pilot saying "We had better get out of this quick," and the intercom had then gone dead. Scott presumed that a bale out order had been given, especially as the aircraft was already in a very steep dive, so he wasted no time in making a quick exit from the Halifax and so became a prisoner for the rest of the war.

Post War Interrogations

From post war PoW questionnaires, the reasons for some losses were revealed. A typical answer is found in the reports of five survivors from Halifax JB791 of 419 Squadron, lost on this Duisburg raid. Apparently the bomber had reached the target without any difficulty, but being five minutes early, the captain, R/79669 Warrant Officer McMillan began orbiting north of Duisburg, as instructed at briefing. On the bombing run, the Halifax was coned by a group of searchlights and in the violent evasive action taken by the pilot, the bomber was placed too far east of the target, so the bombing run was made west to east instead of the briefed north to south. To complicate matters, just after the bomb doors were closed, it was found that some incendiaries were still hung up in the bomb bay. So the pilot went through the bombing procedure again, holding the aircraft straight and level, "Bomb doors open, bombs gone, bomb doors closed," in an effort to get rid of the incendiaries. Shortly after this second run, the predicted heavy *Flak* hit the Halifax so it was obvious that the anti aircraft gunners had been patiently tracking the bomber on its straight and level flight. The starboard wing and forward part of the fuselage were badly damaged and the cockpit perspex smashed open, leaving the pilot facing an airstream of over 200 mph. Fortunately no member of the crew had been injured, but the danger was such that the pilot had to immediately protect his eyes with goggles.

Shortly afterwards tongues of flame began to leap from the starboard engine and quickly enveloped the whole wing. As the flames spread, it became evident that the pilot's plan of making every effort to get to the Zuider Zee and ditch was out of the question so he had no alternative but to order an immediate bale out. According to J/14982 Pilot Officer Wallace, in the air gunner's report, the bale out was made at 12,000 feet about 50 miles west of Duisburg, which should have given ample height for all the crew to bale out safely. But a remark in the report of navigator R114160 Sergeant Klein gave an explanation as to why the pilot failed to make it out. He states that shortly after leaving the plane he heard an explosion from inside the aircraft and as so often happened in an emergency bale out the captain must have remained at the controls to make sure that all the crew were safely out a little too long. The loss of the wireless operator, 1377990 Sergeant W. H. D. Alison, will forever remain a mystery. Sergeant Klein reports that when he jumped the wireless operator was standing at the hatch with his parachute pack on and ready to immediately follow him out of the bomber.

Two Aircrew Evade Capture

There were two evaders from aircraft shot down on this Duisburg raid, one being J/9929 Flight Lieutenant Julian Sale, a Canadian who came from Toronto, the pilot of Halifax DT801, A for Apple from 35 Pathfinder Squadron. Sale was awarded the Distinguished Service Order for his very commendable efforts in evading capture and returning to the UK.

Halifax DT801 was crossing the Zuider Zee on its outward flight and had almost reached the turning point before going south to the target, when it was attacked by a night fighter, as a result of which the bomber was very severely damaged and the order to prepare for bale out was given. The pilot removed the escape hatch cover above his head and then gave the bale out order to his crew. No sooner had he relayed this message than a large explosion occured inside the plane and the pilot can only recall being thrown out through the open hatch, cracking his head as he went through. As he parachuted down he saw only one other 'chute opening. Just before landing he saw his aircraft hit the ground in a ball of fire. Happily four other members of the crew did bale out successfully and were made prisoners, but the bomb aimer and mid-upper gunner were killed. Flight Lieutenant Sale's account of his evasion shows not only his grit and tenacity but it also illustrates the unstinting aid given to evaders by Dutch, Belgian and French patriots, who by their help, generosity and their brave actions, were willing to risk their lives. Flight Lieutenant Sale reports :-

"I landed on top of a pine tree in the vicinity of what I found later to be Oldenzaal at about 00.30 hours on May 13th. Leaving my 'chute at the top of the tree, I climbed down. One of my legs was bruised and I had also lost one of my flying boots in the descent. I did not bother about hiding my Mae West and left it at the bottom of the tree, as I knew the 'chute would be visible in the tree top. Next I put both of my socks on the foot which was minus a boot. I looked around and gave a few calls for the gunner, who I thought I saw parachuting down, but got no reply. At the time I thought I was in Germany, so I started walking across some very sandy fields in a north-westerly direction, guided by the stars. It was lucky that I was wearing a ski jacket which had no outward distinguishing marks because my battle dress top was at the cleaners. My RAF blue trousers had been badly torn when I landed in the branches of the tree and I tried my best to patch the rents with tape which I found in my escape kit. By now it was near dawn, so I filled my water bottle from a nearby stream and hid in a thicket between two farms, so that I could try to find out whether the people were German or Dutch. I lay hidden all day, eating one of my chocolate bars I had in my pocket, but saw no one about.

"At 23.00 hours I set out, planning to do another night's march westward. At dawn on 14th May, after walking about 20 miles along sandy secondary roads, keeping my general direction by the North Star, I came to a piece of very thick undergrowth, which seemed an ideal place to hide up for the day. I had already taken the precaution of filling up my water bottle with milk which I found in a can outside a farm gate. During the day I ate a Horlicks tablet and drank my milk. At dusk, on coming out of my hiding place, I thought that I must be well into Holland by now and felt that I could not go very much further without footwear and more substantial food, so I decided to call at the first farmhouse, where I used sign language to the farmer, who I approached. He seemed to understand who I was , but although friendly was very nervous. On calling his wife, she was at first unwilling to help at all, but when I showed the farmer my identity discs, as he wanted to see proof of who I was, the couple seemed more relaxed and gave me hot milk, bread and butter and more important a pair of wooden shoes. The farmer then gave me directions for the road to Arnhem. After leaving this farm, I tried another farm, where in spite of the black out, there were lights burning, but my call was useless. I carried on walking all through the night on secondary roads, but I could see that I was going too much in a southerly direction to hit Arnhem, so at dawn on May 15th, I decided to lie up for another day, the wooden shoes had badly blistered my feet and by now my trousers were practically falling to pieces. I had to take off my shoes when passing through the villages, owing to the noise they made on the cobble stones. By now I was feeling very hungry and on the evening of May 15th, I approached two or three farmers, but beyond establishing that I was on the outskirts of Eibergen, I got no friendly response.

"That night I started again for Arnhem, wearing only socks on my feet and towards dawn on the 16th I reconnoitred a house on the outskirts of the village of Linde, which is about six miles west of Ruurlo. I was now pretty desperate and felt that I must get some shoes at all costs, having walked about 30/40 miles. I knocked at the back door of the first house and declared myself by signs, to the man who opened it. My luck was in, I was well received and found myself in the middle of a most helpful, but extremely frightened Dutch family. They gave me a complete set of clothes, shoes, socks, sweater, shirt, overcoat and the important pair of trousers. The son of the family brought in a friend, a former Dutch officer, who could speak English, who strongly advised me to give myself up, on the grounds that I was needlessly endangering Dutch lives and that I would be unable to cross the frontier into Belgium. I maintained that it was my duty to continue to try and escape. He then offered me Dutch money, which I declined, as I found that the neighbourhood had already been heavily penalised for assisting RAF aircrew. On the first two nights of my evasion, I had seen 12 British planes shot down in the neighbourhood. The owner of the house told me that his tools and working plant had even been very recently burnt out by a British incendiary bomb. I was put to bed in the attic and the family brought food up to me during the day. It was Sunday and there were visitors to the house all day, to see the damage recently done by the fire bomb. That night the family, who were intensely patriotic Dutch Royalists and very pro British, gave me a large scale road map and set me on my way.

"I walked all the next night to Brummen which I reached about 04.30 hours on the 17th. It was more or less a straight main road and I ducked down by the side if I saw any approaching traffic. As I now was wearing civilian clothes, I decided that I could get further if I walked by day as well. I crossed the River Ijssel by a duck punt, which I found on the bank side and entered a large reafforestation area north east of Arnhem. Unfortunately I found myself inside an artillery range, when I saw some danger warning signs, so I had to make a long detour back to the Ijssel. I reached Dieren and walked south-west along the Arnhem road. There was much military traffic and on one occasion I helped a German officer push his broken down car. I passed Arnhem to the north and came round via Oosterbeek to reconnoitre a crossing of the lower Rhine. By nightfall on the 17th I had reached the Nijmegen / Arnhem railway bridge, which at first I thought was not guarded. When I had got on to the bridge, however, I was hailed and saw a man coming towards me. Fortunately a train came between us and I had time to notice, looking under the train, that the man was in German uniform and armed. I at once ran off the bridge. As soon as the train had passed, he shouted again and fired at me as I ran down westward along the river bank. I could not find any unchained boat, so stripped off my clothes and bundled them in my overcoat, placed them on a plank of wood I had found and swam naked, propelling the plank ahead of me across the river. The river looked to be about 100 yards wide and although I am a good swimmer, I let the strong current carry me along and I landed about a quarter of a mile down stream. It was brilliant moonlight and the water was not too cold.

"By the morning of the 18th I had walked to Druten on the River Waal, where I found there was a ferry crossing. I was also told by a friendly Dutch boy, who spoke a little English, that there would be no German control on the ferry, but there was a charge. I exchanged a half crown piece I had on me, with the boy, for a few cents, sufficient to get me across. The fare was collected by a Dutchman, who asked no questions. After crossing I walked to Maasbommel on the River Meuse. I crossed this river by a private rail ferry which was used for carrying gravel from a pit to a plant. I managed this by hailing and using deaf and dumb language to some workers who put no difficulty in my way.

"On the outskirts of Maasbommel I called at a house, which to my good fortune was occupied by a school teacher, who could speak some English. He kept me on his back porch and was not anxious for me to go inside. Instead he brought me some food, a tweed sports coat and some socks. That night, 18th/19th, I slept outside near Maasbommel. The next day, the 19th, I passed through Oss, Heeswijt, Schijndel and on to St Oedenrode which I reached in the evening. On the way I was stopped and asked for my papers by a Dutch policeman, who wore a black uniform. He made things easy for me, by suggesting to me in broken French, that I was a Frenchman going home from Germany. I readily agreed with him and he shook hands and wished me good luck. In St Oedenrode I knocked at the door of a house, which I thought might be the priest's house, as it was next door to the church, but instead I found it was the home of three elderly Dutch ladies. They gave me food and introduced me to a friend, who spoke English and appeared friendly, but I had difficulty in convincing him that I had no other forms of identity, other than my discs. He introduced me to three other residents of the town and I stayed two nights and the intervening day, the 20th, in the home of one of these people. My new friends supplied me with a new road map, food for three days and a pair of boots, as my shoes were pinching badly, and most important of all, a bicycle.

"I decided to go westwards to Roosendaal, 15 miles west of Breda, from which place I could cross the border to Nispen, where my friends knew there was a good spot to cross, this was a hole in the barbed wire barricade on the outskirts of Nispen. At the Belgian frontier town of Esschen, having memorised the Dutch words I required and which had been given to me by my helpers at St Oedenrode, I asked in Dutch the occupants of the house near the border whether there were any German soldiers on guard at the frontier. I was quite relieved to be told that there were no such guards.

"I crossed the frontier at Esschen at 15.00 hours on 22nd May and turned on to the main road heading south in the direction of Antwerp. After going about a kilometre, I was signalled to stop by two Belgian customs officers, who must have changed their minds as they waved me on again. A little later I was stopped by two Belgian policemen, who asked for my papers. I declared myself to them. They were very friendly, but advised against keeping the bicycle, as it had no Belgian licence plates on it. My Dutch bicycle had a blue plate on the front fork. I decided to keep the bicycle as I could travel much quicker with it, but improvised from a cigarette carton, something similar to the appropriate Belgian licence plate and kept it in position on the handlebars with my hand, discarding the Dutch plate.

"That day I went through Brasschlet, which was full of German soldiers, also Louvain and Charleroi, where trying to avoid the numerous gendarmes who were about, I got lost. I had to use my escape compass to find a road which went south out of the town, Finally I went westwards and I spent the night of May 22nd at Haulchin, just north of the French border and south east of Mons, where a farmer gave me a bed for the night.

"The next day a lad took me to a farm house on the border, where the owner after hearing who I was, took me personally through the town of Grandreng, thus avoiding the Customs Post. I could have crossed unaided on foot, but I did not want to lose the use of my cycle. After crossing the frontier on the night of the 23rd I nearly ran into a crossing point outside the town. As I know a little French, my general idea now that I was able to cycle, was to get south to Spain going east of Paris. Having made useful contacts at Fismes I had high hopes of being able to get some organised help, but nothing materialised, except that one of my helpers at Fismes gave me food coupons sufficient to get a large loaf of bread. With this exception, I held on to my main idea to get south on my own. Throughout I contacted people only in the evening and confined myself to farmers. In nearly every case I was given permission to sleep in the barns, but on many occasions, with the stipulation that I did not smoke in the barns. As I am a non smoker this was an easy request which I could comply with. I was hardly ever allowed to pay for meals, which were generous, and as a rule I was given something to help me through the following day. I supplemented this ration with raw potatoes and cherries, the latter especially as I made my way south. In Holland I got a small glass screw topped bottle, which was useful to carry water and which I carried in my cycle bag. Once I had to cycle with one pedal, but otherwise apart from innumerable punctures towards the end, my bicycle never really broke down. As I had no repair kit, if I was unlucky to get a puncture, I used to push the bike until I could get to a town or village, where I got it repaired. By the end of my journey, the tyres were practically worn out with no tread. Throughout the journey my device of imitating the local licence plate by shaping a piece of coloured paper and holding it on the handlebars with my hand proved to work quite well. I always maintained a close look out for police patrols on the outskirts of towns, as I thought my distinctive Dutch cycle which was much higher off the ground than the low French ones would involve me in some questioning.

°As I am fairly fair of colour, I found it served me well to declare myself as Polish to any daytime casual enquiry in shops. My route as I cycled was from Grandreng - Guise - Laon - Fismes - Chateau-Thierry - Montmirail - Provins - Sens - Montargis - Gien - Bourges. In the Marne/Paris area I noticed that yellow plates were carried on the back of bicycles and at Laon I had to cycle over part of a German aerodrome, which had a lot of ground staff moving about. I crossed the Line of Demarcation between St Just and Levet, ten miles south of Bourges. There I had dinner with a land owner who told me that in the past he had helped refugees across the line. In my case I had no difficulty and there were no road controls. My route took me through Le Chatre - Gueret - Eymoutiers - Tulle - Figeac - Albi and Castres. Just north of Albi at Condez I was stopped by French police, who let me go after some discussion. I reached Revel about 15 miles SW of Castres on 1st June, having come from the Belgian border in eight days. My target, sometimes exceeded and sometimes not achieved, was 125 kilometres per day. Near Figeac I went fishing and using grub bait, I caught several small trout in a stream, with the fish hook and linen thread I had with me.

°The bread coupons which I had been given at Fismes were available for other food items on the two or three occasions when I had to eat in a restaurant. In the south the farmers seemed less well off and I often had to pay for my meals. I stayed two nights in Revel, where I met a young Frenchman, who was bound for Switzerland. I spent 10 days in a farm outside Revel and then returned to Revel for a further 8 days. During this time plans were considered for me to go to Toulouse. The young Frenchman returned from Grenoble as he was unable to get into Switzerland so we both then decided to join forces to get to England. I left my well used and faithful bike at Revel and we both went by train to

Toulouse, where we stayed the night, before going on by train to Carcassone. We changed trains for Quillan about 25 miles south of Carcassone and from Quillan we took a bus to Belcaire, where we spent the night in a hotel. As we had no papers for the Zone Interdite Sud, we walked to Le Castelet and had to stay another night in an hotel. There we contacted a guide who was prepared to guide us across the Andorran frontier for 3,000 francs.

*We were in a party of eight and started out on June 24th. Soon two of the party had to return because they could not keep up with the heavy luggage that they insisted on carrying. The remaining six of us got lost on the way up the hill from Le Castelet and had to spend the first night half way up. In the morning, a shepherd told us that there were no German sentries near the border, so we continued climbing all day. About 05.00 hours on 25th June, we arrived about 4 to 5 kilometres from the Andorran border. The guide would not continue any further, so my French friend and I decided to go on ourselves by daylight and we left the others. We crossed the high peak, passing through some snow drifts during the day. We were not particularly bothered about German guards, as we had opted for the stiffest route for climbing. I was fortunate that I had a pocket spy glass, which I had with me in my aircraft and which I found very useful for observing the slopes for any sign of other people and I also had a very stout walking stick, which helped a great deal on the stiffer slopes.

*We slept inside a shepherd's hut just inside the Andorran border and walked into Canillo on the morning of 26th June. The shepherd had told us that German soldiers had sometimes chased fugitives well inside the Andorran border and taken them back into France. In Canillo we stopped at an hotel. A man we casually met there put us in touch with a Spanish refugee, who was a tobacco smuggler, he agreed to guide us to Barcelona. We went to St Julia by car and that night crossed the mountains on foot with the Spaniard. The Andorran and Spanish frontier was very closely guarded. Our descent route through the mountains skirted Solsona and Cardona and we arrived at Manressa ten days after leaving Andorra, a journey of about 80 to 90 miles, which tested our endurance much more than the earlier part of the crossing. The tobacco smuggler went into Barcelona on his own to alert the Consul, who came out to collect us the next day, July 7th. I arrived in Gibraltar on August 5th and returned to the UK on August 11th, 1943.

Flight Sergeant O. W. Forland, Air Gunner 426 Squadron

At 03.40 hours on 13th May, Manston Radio Station received a message from Wellington HE905 of 426 Squadron, which was captained by Sergeant I. R. Runciman. "Rudderless SOS. 2nd pilot k. . . " then the message signal faded out. The QDM (Course to steer) was 280 degrees from Manston, Kent and at the same time the Radio Direction Finding Station also plotted a hostile aircraft in S/2473 (Fighter Grid Map) which corresponded to the above QDM. Twelve fighter aircraft were sent to search the relevant area, but nothing was found. The Wellington had been been hit by *Flak* over the target and the second pilot, J/8216 Flying Officer D. G. Fraser had been killed. The captain found his plane so badly damaged and losing petrol so seriously that he decided to head for the Belgian coast. Then the aircraft lost height so rapidly that the bale out order was given at 03.45 hours at 5,000 feet north-east of Spa, Belgium. The remaining five crew baled out safely, the pilot, navigator Flying Officer G. Miller, bomb aimer Flying Officer D. Laskey DFC and wireless operator Sergeant D. H. Pennock were made prisoners of war. The rear gunner, Canadian Flight Sergeant O. W. Forland, successfully evaded capture and with the help of the undergound movement finally reached Gibraltar in June, the first aircrew member from the squadron to evade capture.

Crashes in Bad Weather on Return to Bases

From the Duisburg raid another two bombers crashed on return to their bases, both from 4 Group. One was a 466 Squadron Wellington, HZ530, captained by Australian Flight Sergeant C. W. Trinder who lost contact with his base airfield Leconfield, Yorkshire in deteriorating weather conditions and crashed into high ground on the Yorkshire Wolds at Towthorpe Farm, Sledmere killing all the five man crew. The other aircraft was a Halifax from 77 Squadron, JB865, which was also captained by an Australian, Flying Officer T. Archibald diverted from its home base at Elvington, Yorkshire to Pocklington airfield. Because of bad weather conditions it too crashed on the slopes of the Yorkshire Wolds at Bishop Wilton, killing the pilot and bomb aimer, the rest of the crew being seriously injured. Many aircrew returning to or going on operations from the many wartime airfields in the Vale of York met untimely deaths on the Yorkshire Wolds.

Take off Crash with a Full Bomb Load

One Stirling, BK721, captained by New Zealander Sergeant R. F. Harvey of 75 Squadron crashed on take off from its base at

Chedburgh with a full bomb load. The wireless operator, Flight Sergeant S. G. Cocks, although badly injured was the only survivor.

Casualties May 12th/13th, 1943. Target Duisburg

156 Squadron 8 Group Lancaster ED857 GT/
Pilot. 119179 S/Ldr L.Verdon-Roe DFC Killed Reichswald Forest. 5-B-11
Nav. 144766 P/O F.Giles DFM Killed Hotton, Belgium. VIII-C-9
B/A. 777836 F/Sgt E.W.Banks DFM Killed Reichswald Forest, Germany. 5-B-7
W/OP. 1205018 F/Sgt T.J.Pritchard DFM Killed Reichswald Forest. 5-B-8
F/E. 1346451 Sgt J.C.Stewart Killed Reichswald Forest, Germany. 5-B-10
A/G. 50612 P/O H.F.Jolley Killed Reichswald Forest, Germany. 5-B-9
A/G. 1439229 Sgt K.C.Harrison Killed Reichswald Forest, Germany. 5-B-6

156 Squadron 8 Group Lancaster ED837 GT/
Pilot. A/403389 P/O W.M.Wendon Killed Reichswald Forest, Germany. 5-A-13
Nav. A/403146 P/O E.S.Mackenzie Killed Reichswald Forest, Germany. 5-A-9
B/A. A/404987 F/Sgt N.R.Mason Killed Reichswald Forest, Germany. 5-A-11
W/OP. A/411082 Sgt G.A.Williams PoW. Stalag Luft 4, Sagan. 1206
F/E. 936478 Sgt C.Askham Killed Reichswald Forest, Germany. 5-A-12
A/G. A/408605 F/Sgt R.G.Wynn Killed Reichswald Forest, Germany. 5-A-8
A/G. A/404684 F/Sgt A.C.Johnston Killed Reichswald Forest, Germany. 5-A-14

83 Squadron 8 Group Lancaster W4955 OL/
Aircraft crashed at Eemnes, Holland.
Pilot. 45901 F/Lt L.A.Rickenson DFC Killed Amersfoort, Holland. 13-7-127
Nav. A/404486 F/Lt H.D.M.Ransome DFC PoW. Stalag Luft 3, Sagan. 1726
B/A. 967727 F/Sgt D.B.Bourne Killed Amersfoort, Holland. 13-6-125
W/OP. A/404922 P/O W.L.Gibbs Killed Amersfoort, Holland. 13-7-126
F/E. 1209375 F/Sgt H.Plant Killed Amersfoort, Holland. 13-6-118
A/G. 1051616 F/Sgt T.R.Cairns Killed Amersfoort, Holland. 13-7-129
A/G. 1330482 F/Sgt S.A.Hathaway Killed Amersfoort, Holland. 13-7-128

35 Squadron 8 Group Halifax DT801 TL/A
Pilot. J/9929 F/Lt J.Sale DSO Evaded capture.
Nav. 126034 F/O G.E.Heard PoW. Stalag Luft 3, Sagan. 1407
B/A. 125574 F/Lt R.C.Sawyer Killed Haaksbergen, Holland. 4-2-8
W/OP. 798716 Sgt S.A.Moores PoW. Stalag Luft 4, Sagan. 1261
F/E. 1160639 Sgt C.W.Rowley PoW. Stalag Luft 4, Sagan. 42788
A/G. 1418379 Sgt D.J.Richards Killed Haaksbergen, Holland. 4-2-9
A/G. R/103805 W/O R.O.Elford PoW. Stalag Luft 4, Sagan. 1239

12 Squadron 1 Group Lancaster ED476 PH/
Pilot. NZ/39668 P/O I.H.Alexander Missing, Runnymede Memorial 198
Nav. R/119693 F/Sgt R.D.Fraser Missing, Runnymede Memorial 181
B/A. 1455360 Sgt E.D.Harrison Killed Reichswald Forest, Germany. 5-8-15
W/OP. 1179576 Sgt J.A.Stephens Missing, Runnymede Memorial 165
F/E. 1377787 Sgt E.Rome Missing, Runnymede Memorial 163
A/G. 1021071 Sgt R.Bell Killed Reichswald Forest, Germany. 5-8-14
A/G. 618117 F/Sgt D.H.Williams Killed Reichswald Forest, Germany. 5-8-13

199 Squadron 1 Group Wellington HE702 EX/Y
Pilot. 1383863 Sgt L.Waldorf Killed Harderwijk, Holland. CG 2-26/30
Nav. 1450605 Sgt R.Hughes Killed Harderwijk, Holland. CG 2-26/30
B/A. 1386132 Sgt J.G.Wilson Killed Harderwijk, Holland. CG 2-26/30
W/OP. 127864 F/O R.H.D.Cook Killed Harderwijk, Holland. CG 2-26/30
A/G. 1236751 Sgt T.Wharmby Killed Harderwijk, Holland. CG 2-26/30

300 Squadron 1 Group Wellington HE295 BH/D
Pilot. P./782668 Sgt S.Werner Missing, Northolt Memorial.
Nav. P/0368 F/O R.Tabaczynski Missing, Northolt Memorial.
B/A. P/794517 Sgt H.Szymanowicz Missing, Northolt Memorial.
W/OP. P/794322 Sgt H.Lercel Missing, Northolt Memorial.
A/G. P/784413 F/Sgt M.Galas Missing Northolt Memorial.

90 Squadron 3 Group Stirling BF523 WP/G
Shot down Harderwijk, Holland by a fighter from II/NJG/1.
Pilot. R/120226 F/Sgt W.Morey Missing, Runnymede Memorial 185
Nav. 1320220 Sgt B.A.Bacon Missing, Runnymede Memorial 141
B/A. 658018 Sgt W.Murray Killed Harderwijk, Holland. 1-24
W/OP. 1332191 Sgt E.W.Eke Killed Amersfoort, Holland. 13-7-131
F/E. 575244 Sgt R.S.Shaw Missing, Runnymede Memorial 164
A/G. 785082 Sgt A.J.Buxton Killed Amersfoort, Holland. 13-7-132
A/G. 614909 Sgt C.Green Missing, Runnymede Memorial 151

90 Squadron 3 Group Stirling BK661 WP/O
Pilot. J/17721 P/O J.I.Gedak Missing, Runnymede Memorial 175
Nav. 1239026 Sgt D.H.Robinson Missing, Runnymede Memorial 163
B/A. 1432354 Sgt A.V.Edwards Missing, Runnymede Memorial 148
W/OP. 1380640 Sgt L.Urry Missing, Runnymede Memorial 168
F/E. 992896 Sgt S.James Missing, Runnymede Memorial 154
A/G. 1194377 Sgt S.Owen Missing, Runnymede Memorial 160
A/G. 1419572 Sgt T.G.Matthews Missing, Runnymede Memorial 158

149 Squadron 3 Group Stirling EF357 OJ/V
Aircraft shot down near Rotterdam, Holland.
Pilot. 1388099 Sgt E.G.Bass Killed Rotterdam, Holland. LL-1-32
Nav. 127104 F/O R.F.Kingham Killed Rotterdam, Holland. LL-2-40
B/A. 1322042 Sgt K.G.Roots Killed Rotterdam, Holland. LL-234
W/OP. 1083960 Sgt J.G.Newall Killed Rotterdam, Holland. JG LL-2-35/36
F/E. 1263273 Sgt F.G.Salter Killed Rotterdam, Holland. JG LL-2-35/36
A/G. 530757 Sgt R.D.Evans Killed Rotterdam, Holland. LL-1-33
A/G. 133827 Sgt D.B.Sach Killed Rotterdam, Holland. LL-2-37

214 Squadron 3 Group Stirling BF381 BU/
Aircraft crashed at Duisburg/Ruhrort, Germany.
Pilot. 143698 P/O H.Broadbent Killed Reichswald Forest, Germany. 5-B-2
Nav. 142892 P/O H.Catch Killed Reichswald Forest, Germany. 5-A-18
B/A. 1411154 Sgt N.Douglas Killed Reichswald Forest, Germany. 5-B-4
W/OP. 1332273 Sgt W.F.Hards Killed Reichswald Forest, Germany. 5-B-1
F/E. 1445870 Sgt S.F.Dean Killed Reichswald Forest, Germany. 5-B-5
A/G. 1303478 Sgt J.A.Brown Killed Reichswald Forest, Germany. 5-B-3
A/G. 1349970 Sgt W.Duthie Killed Reichswald Forest, Germany. 5-A-17

218 Squadron 3 Group Stirling BK705 HA/K
Aircraft crashed into North Sea.
Pilot. J/17097 P/O R.J.Bryans Missing, Runnymede Memorial. 175
Nav. 657132 Sgt J.R.Thompson Missing, Runnymede Memorial 167
B/A. 1318543 Sgt J.Davies Missing, Runnymede Memorial 147
W/OP. 1017549 Sgt S.Fitton PoW. Stalag Luft 3, Sagan. 260473
F/E. 1029217 Sgt F.B.Holmes Missing, Runnymede Memorial 153
A/G. R/134226 F/Sgt K.L.Garman Missing, Runnymede Memorial 181
A/G. 656686 Sgt K.G.Money Missing, Runnymede Memorial 132

51 Squadron 4 Group Halifax DT645 MH/
Pilot. 1239555 F/Sgt D.C.Smith Killed Harlingen, Holland. E-3-11
Nav. 1313414 Sgt E.W.Thomson Killed Harlingen, Holland. JG E-4-9/11
B/A. 1384948 Sgt B.A.Bunting Killed Harlingen, Holland. JG E-4-9/11
W/OP. 1382661 Sgt C.L.King Killed Harlingen, Holland. E-3-12
F/E. 1213091 Sgt E.F.Kinerman Killed Harlingen, Holland. E-3-13
A/G. R/70337 Sgt M.H.Nesbitt Killed Harlingen, Holland. E-3-14
A/G. 1398030 Sgt W.J.Merrigan Killed Harlingen, Holland. E-3-15

51 Squadron 4 Group Halifax DT685 MH/
Pilot. 656955 F/Sgt N.E.Jones Killed Reichswald Forest, Germany. 5-A-2
Nav. 1091719 Sgt K.S.Hobkirk Killed Reichswald Forest, Germany. 5-A-4
B/A. 1148650 Sgt E.G.Brown Killed Reichswald Forest, Germany. 5-A-5
W/OP. 1084046 Sgt L.Wakenshaw PoW. Stalag 357, Kopernikus. 1203
F/E. 1283558 Sgt P.C.W.Rich Killed Reichswald Forest, Germany. 5-A-3
A/G. 1622398 Sgt H.Goddard Killed Reichswald Forest, Germany. 5-A-6
A/G. 1338590 Sgt P.R.J.Blake Killed Reichswald Forest, Germany. 5-A-1

51 Squadron 4 Group Halifax JB806 MH/
Pilot. A/413162 W/O B.Brown PoW. Stalag Luft 4, Sagan. 1170
Nav. 657014 Sgt W.Henderson PoW. Stalag Luft 6, Heydekrug. 11
B/A. 658424 Sgt H.Ray Killed Reichswald Forest, Germany. 22-C-17
W/OP. 1330530 F/Sgt K.A.Goodchild PoW. Stalag Luft 6, Heydekrug. 319
F/E. 1454177 Sgt A.L.G.Knight PoW. Stalag Luft 6, Heydekrug. 327
A/G. 929468 W/O W.North-Lewis PoW. Stalag Luft 1, Barth Vogelsang. 1193
A/G. R/144970 Sgt P.L.M.D.De-Bourbon PoW. Stalag 4B, Muhlberg. 1277

51 Squadron 4 Group Halifax HR786 MH/
Pilot. 143389 P/O G.W.Locksmith Missing, Runnymede Memorial 132
Nav. 146287 P/O R.Tunstall Missing, Runnymede Memorial 133
B/A. 146447 P/O A.J.Hendry Missing, Runnymede Memorial 132
W/OP. 1056193 F/Lt H.A.Roberts Missing, Runnymede Memorial 132
F/E. 146104 P/O J.I.Noble Missing, Runnymede Memorial 132
A/G. 1352803 Sgt C.N.V.Cogdell Killed Amsterdam, Holland. CG 69-C-5
A/G. 121055 F/O G.Massip-de-Turville Killed Amsterdam, Holland. CG 69-C-5

77 Squadron 4 Group Halifax DT632 KN/
Pilot. R/105579 W/O T.M.Moran Killed Reichswald Forest, Germany. 23-C-4
Nav. 1312924 Sgt L.A.Stimpson Killed Reichswald Forest. CG 23-C-5/7
B/A. 128520 F/O F.A.Clark Killed Reichswald Forest, Germany. 23-C-1

W/OP. 1377449 Sgt R.G.Miles Killed Reichswald Forest. CG 23-C-5/7
F/E. 577547 Sgt J.D.Mahony Killed Reichswald Forest, Germany. CG 23-C-5/7
A/G. 1467008 Sgt J.T.Murray Killed Reichswald Forest, Germany. 23-C-2
A/G. 1547158 Sgt W.A.Pasqual Killed Reichswald Forest, Germany. 23-C-3

78 Squadron 4 Group Halifax DT777 EY/T
Pilot. 1086886 Sgt G.E.Clay
A/G. 1559133 Sgt A.Scott PoW. Stalag 357, Kopernikus. 1199
Air gunner baled out, misunderstood captain's intercom remark.

102 Squadron 4 Group Halifax JB799 SR/E
Pilot. J/17464 P/O M.Q.Moffatt Killed Sage, Germany. 11-A-9
Nav. J/7023 F/O J.D.Erzinger Missing, Runnymede Memorial 173
B/A. 658627 Sgt D.F.Moon Missing, Runnymede Memorial 159
W/OP. 1193559 Sgt C.H.Hurle Killed Bevermijk, Holland. CG J-7
F/E. R/71815 Sgt C.G.Gowen Killed Kiel, Germany. 3-G-19
A/G. 137587 P/O G.Davies Killed Bergen-op-Zoom, Holland. 33-A-6
A/G. 1190817 Sgt W.J.Holman Missing, Runnymede Memorial 153

196 Squadron 4 Group Wellington HE398 ZO/
Pilot. 1315254 F/Sgt J.Greenfield Missing, Runnymede Memorial 136
Nav. 1385003 F/Sgt R.Burridge Missing, Runnymede Memorial 135
B/A. 1367121 Sgt W.O'Neill Missing, Runnymede Memorial 160
W/OP. 1165211 Sgt K.F.Bell Missing, Runnymede Memorial 142
A/G. 553011 Sgt W.Eddington Missing, Runnymede Memorial 148

431 Squadron 4 Group Wellington HE440 SE/Y
Aircraft crashed at Winterswijk, Holland at 02.25 hours (13/5/43)
Pilot. 658403 Sgt G.R.Y.Wood Killed Winterswijk, Holland. 27
Nav. 1379214 Sgt E.Gummer Killed Winterswijk, Holland. 26
B/A. 1575533 Sgt I.Mobley Killed Winterswijk, Holland. 28
W/OP. 1210978 Sgt A.Cresswell Killed Winterswijk, Holland. 24
A/G. 993817 Sgt T.H.Smith Killed Winterswijk, Holland. 25

50 Squadron 5 Group Lancaster W4762 VN/
Pilot. 143453 P/O F.H.Huntley DFM Killed Amsterdam, Holland. 69-C-7
2/Pilot. 111118 F/O G.D.Priestley Killed Amersfoort, Holland. 13-7-135
Nav. 144446 P/O C.W.Clarke Killed Amersfoort, Holland. 13-7-134
B/A. 145180 P/O E.Hough Killed Amsterdam, Holland. 69-C-12
W/OP. J/17654 P/O H.M.Ivatt Missing, Runnymede Memorial 176
F/E. 570468 Sgt M.Bates Killed Amersfoort, Holland. 13-7-136
A/G. 985652 Sgt A.Stott DFM Killed Amersfoort, Holland. 13-7-133
A/G. 1317229 Sgt F.C.Greening Killed Amersfoort, Holland. 13-7-135

57 Squadron 5 Group Lancaster ED329 DX/
Pilot. 126985 F/O V.A.Wilson Killed Jonkerbos, Holland. 24-D-6
Nav. 130163 F/O J.D.Wallace Killed Jonkerbos, Holland. 24-D-4
B/A. 1335521 F/Sgt P.G.Kehl PoW. Stalag 6G, Bonn-Duisdorf. 11026
W/OP. 1198322 Sgt R.B.Loverseed Killed Jonkerbos, Holland. 24-D-8
F/E. 980462 Sgt S.Laughlin Killed Jonkerbos, Holland. 24-D-7
A/G. 1409336 Sgt A.Steel Killed Jonkerbos, Holland. 24-D-9
A/G. R/115979 F/Sgt C.L.Gerding Killed Jonkerbos, Holland. 24-D-5

57 Squadron 5 Group Lancaster ED778 DX/
Aircraft crashed at Netterden, Holland at 02.13 hours (13/5/43).
Pilot. R/93921 F/Sgt G.B.Leach PoW. Stalag 357, Kopernikus. 197
Nav. J/17016 F/O H.C.McNeil Killed Gendringen, Holland. B-25
B/A. 996725 Sgt T.J.Gregory Killed Gendringen, Holland. B-24
W/OP. R/81445 W/O H.A.Sheeham Killed Gendringen, Holland. B-26
F/E. 1204743 F/Sgt N.Rees PoW. Stalag 357, Kopernikus. 1197
A/G. R/116417 F/Sgt M.G.T.Levins Killed Gendringen, Holland. B-23
A/G. R/90950 W/O A.L.Home Killed Gendringen, Holland. B-27

61 Squadron 5 Group Lancaster W4269 QR/
Pilot. 1331632 F/Sgt P.H.Alderton Killed Amsterdam, Holland. CG 69-C-10
Nav. 1089371 Sgt R.E.Sloan Killed Amsterdam, Holland. CG 69-C-10
B/A. J/22547 F/O J.V.O.Wood Killed Amsterdam, Holland. CG 69-C-10
W/OP. R/93374 W/O W.J.Reid Killed Amsterdam, Holland. CG 69-C-11
F/E. 633604 Sgt S.Lupton Killed Amsterdam, Holland. CG 69-C-11
A/G. 1386883 Sgt J.Thomas Killed Amsterdam, Holland. CG 69-C-11
A/G. 1415511 Sgt C.D.Whiteall Killed Amsterdam, Holland. CG 69-C-10

207 Squadron 5 Group Lancaster ED418 EM/
Pilot. 145836 P/O W.D.Hawkes Killed Amersfoort, Holland. 13-6-109
Nav. 1383312 Sgt H.R.Dick Killed Amersfoort, Holland. CG 13-6-110/113
2/Nav. 1149749 Sgt A.W.Whiteoak Killed Amersfoort. CG 13-6-110/113
B/A. 1376119 Sgt G.R.Nipper Killed Amersfoort, Holland. CG 13-6-110/113
W/OP. R/84846 W/O W.A.McNair Killed Amersfoort, Holland. CG 13-6-110/113
F/E. 1232284 Sgt E.S.Tomkins Killed Amersfoort, Holland. 13-6-108
A/G. 45813 F/Lt A.D.Coldicott DFM Killed Amersfoort. CG 13-6-110/113
A/G. 1313558 Sgt J.Smith Killed Amersfoort, Holland. 13-6-107

207 Squadron 5 Group Lancaster W4938 EM/A
Pilot. 128897 F/O D.W.H.Evans Missing, Runnymede Memorial 124
Nav. 1473356 Sgt S.Ogden Missing, Runnymede Memorial 160
B/A. 1331635 Sgt T.H.Skelton Killed Reichswald Forest, Germany. 5-A-15
W/OP. 1330620 Sgt R.C.Meyer Missing, Runnymede Memorial. 159
F/E. 628839 Sgt S.L.Goodwin Missing, Runnymede Memorial. 151
A/G. 132389 F/O F.A.Alp Killed Reichswald Forest, Germany. 5-A-16
A/G. R/109372 F/Sgt S.L.Whitehead Killed Reichswald Forest. 5-A-10

419 Squadron 6 Group Halifax JB791 VR/
Pilot. R/79669 W/O G.A.McMillan Killed Rheinberg, Germany. 2-F-12
Nav. R/114160 F/Sgt W.J.Klein PoW. Stalag 357, Kopernikus. 1186
B/A. 126872 F/Lt H.Enever PoW. Stalag Luft 3, Sagan. 1323
W/OP. 1377990 Sgt W.H.D.Alison Killed Hotton, Belgium. XI-C-6
F/E. R/112596 W/O W.J.Howell PoW. Stalag 357, Kopernikus. 1183
A/G. J/14982 F/Lt A.R.Wallace PoW. Stalag Luft 3, Sagan. 1338
A/G. R/124488 W/O H.G.Bees PoW. Stalag 357, Kopernikus. 1169

419 Squadron 6 Group Halifax JB861 VR/

Pilot. R/98515 W/O J.Palmer Killed Rotterdam, Holland. LL-1-38
Nav. 1084155 Sgt H.Walsh Killed Rotterdam, Holland. LL-1-36
B/A. 127127 F/O T.Brown Killed Rotterdam, Holland. LL-1-37
W/OP. R/87956 W/O R.C.Weedy Killed Rotterdam, Holland. LL-2-38
F/E. R/70265 Sgt W.A.Simonett Killed Rotterdam, Holland. LL-2-39
A/G. R/120191 F/Sgt R.E.L.Ratelle Killed Rotterdam, Holland. LL-1-34
A/G. 1384115 Sgt A.J.Gearing Killed Rotterdam, Holland. LL-1-35

426 Squadron 6 Group Wellington HE157 OW/

Pilot. R/106603 W/O K.F.Fighter Killed Bergen-op-Zoom (Can). JG 6-F-4/5
Nav. J/14772 F/O G.McMillan Killed Bergen-op-Zoom (Can). JG 6-F-4/5
B/A. R/123618 F/Sgt D.C.Maxwell Killed Bergen-op-Zoom (Can). 7-E-7
W/OP. 1219830 Sgt E.W.Betts Killed Bergen-op-Zoom (Can), Holland. 7-E-8
A/G. J/14815 F/O H.R.Drake Killed Bergen-op-Zoom (Can), Holland. 12-F-6

426 Squadron 6 Group Wellington HE905 OW/

Pilot. J/17588 F/O I.R.A.Runciman PoW. Stalag Luft 3, Sagan. 1269
2/Pilot. J/8216 F/O D.G.Fraser Killed Hotton, Belgium. II-C-12
Nav. J/11239 F/O G.Miller PoW. Stalag Luft 3, Sagan. 1411
B/A. J/22525 F/Lt D.Laskey DFC PoW. Stalag Luft 3, Sagan. 1410
W/OP. 145721 F/O D.H.Pennock PoW. Stalag Luft 6, Heydekrug 1194
A/G. R/84207 F/Sgt O.W.Forland Evaded capture.

428 Squadron 6 Group Wellington HE656 NA/A

Pilot. R/107981 F/Sgt W.E.Mann Killed Dieppe (Can), France. H-23
Nav. J/14520 F/O W.W.O'Brien Killed Dieppe (Can), France. JG H-22
B/A. J/20822 F/O L.A.Dingley Killed Dieppe (Can), France. H-19
W/OP. J/19451 P/O P.G.Kelly Killed Dieppe (Can), France. JG H-22
A/G. R/91200 Sgt E.E.Lundy Killed Dieppe (Can), France. H-21

428 Squadron 6 Group Wellington HE321 NA/Z

Pilot. R/120614 F/Sgt A.E.Hatch Killed Weerselo(Deuringen). CG 1-1/5
Nav. J/14523 F/O R.L.Baumgarter Killed Weerselo(Deuringen). CG 1-1/5
B/A. R/127814 F/Sgt D.R.Horwood Killed Weerselo(Deuringen). CG 1-1/5
W/OP. 1077731 Sgt W.Leven Killed Weerselo(Deuringen), Holland. CG 1-1/5
A/G. R/145781 F/Sgt C.C.Hildreth Killed Weerselo(Deuringen). CG 1-1/5

429 Squadron 6 Group Wellington HE423 AL/

Pilot. 131641 F/O B.A.A.Geale Killed Amersfoort, Holland. 13-6-117
Nav. J/16322 P/O H.A.Tennis Killed Amersfoort, Holland. 13-6-114
B/A. R/93441 F/Sgt J.S.Vose Killed Amersfoort, Holland. 13-6-116
W/OP. 1232904 Sgt J.Piggott Killed Amersfoort, Holland. 13-6-119
A/G. R/131089 W/O R.T.Crimmins Killed Amersfoort, Holland. 13-6-115

429 Squadron 6 Group Wellington HE913 AL/

Pilot. 1313054 F/Sgt A.F.Halstead Killed Jonkerbos, Holland. 16-D-5
Nav. 130271 P/O P.J.Dunger Killed Jonkerbos, Holland. 15-D-6
B/A. 49765 F/O S.A.Willoughby Killed Jonkerbos, Holland. 16-D-8
W/OP. 1219035 Sgt C.Taylor Killed Jonkerbos, Holland. 16-D-7
A/G. R/110293 F/Sgt D.O.Broughton Killed Jonkerbos, Holland. 16-D-9

75 Squadron 3 Group Stirling BK721 AA/
Aircraft crashed NW of Newmarket on take off for operations to Duisburg.
Pilot. 42473 F/Lt E.R.M.Appleton Seriously Injured.
2/Pilot. NZ/416483 Sgt R.F.Harvey Killed Newmarket. P-414
Nav. NZ/416198 F/O J.Johnston Killed Newmarket. P-445
B/A. NZ/414593 F/O S.J.Clubb Killed Newmarket. P-430
W/OP. NZ/404623 F/Sgt S.G.Cocks Injured
F/E. 634968 Sgt J.S.Andrews Killed Guildford. 985
A/G. 1106308 Sgt B.A.Moore Killed Cheltenham. D1-1425
A/G. 1127228 Sgt J.Wykes Killed Dalbeattie. 879-880

77 Squadron 4 Group Halifax JB865 KN/J
Crashed in bad weather conditions at Bishop Wilton, East Yorks. returning
from operations to Duisburg.
Pilot. A/412606 F/O T.Archibald Killed Barmby Moor, Yorkshire. C-8
Nav. Sgt J.Gerry Injured.
B/A. 1219445 Sgt G.Scully Killed Olton, Solihull. G - 475
W/OP. Sgt G.Marlow Injured.
F/E. Sgt C.Hewitson Injured.
A/G. Sgt F.K.Smith Injured.
A/G. Sgt J.Currie Injured.

466 Squadron 4 Group Wellington HZ530 HD/
Crashed at Towthorpe Farm, Sledmere, E.Yorkshire returning from ope-
rations to Duisburg.
Pilot. A/411970 F/Sgt C.W.Trinder Killed Driffield, Yorkshire. 6209
Nav. NZ/411865 Sgt D.Davidson Killed Driffield, Yorkshire. 6224
B/A. 1320125 Sgt H.Russell Killed Cheshunt, Hertfordshire. I-V-27
W/OP. 657397 Sgt D.Trail Killed Driffield, Yorkshire. 6218
A/G. 1323461 Sgt E.G.L.Giggs Killed Hammersmith (New). 9-A-12

Bochum

May 13th/14th, 1943

The Bochum attack force consisted of 442 aircraft made up of 135 Halifaxes, 104 Wellingtons, 98 Lancasters, 95 Stirlings and 10 Mosquitoes. The start of the raid went well in good weather conditions with no moonlight. The Pathfinders were accurate and well timed with the 74 markers which they dropped during the course of the attack, but the German decoys again drew many of the bombs away from the aiming point. The Germans fired their decoy TIs from the ground and although they burst and cascaded at a lower height the simulation was good. Burning time on the ground varied from 30 seconds to 2.5 minutes. They also cunningly varied the method they used in employing decoy TIs, on occasions using them on their own and at other times in conjunction with decoy fires or smoke screens. It was later in August 1943, that Bomber Command developed the use of a Red Spot Fire Target Indicator. This was a 250 lbs casing, filled with cotton wool soaked in a solution of metallic perchlorate dissolved in alcohol. It burnt on the ground as a single deep red spot for 15 to 20 minutes, and its light was so intense, bomber crews had little difficulty in differentiating it from the German decoys. 529.6 tons of high explosive and 164,962 incendiaries were dropped from the attacking force on Bochum. Some 394 buildings were reported damaged with 302 people killed. 24 aircraft were missing and from their crews 82 were killed, 16 were missing, 56 became prisoners and one navigator, 1333556 Sergeant R. G. Goddard from Halifax JB873 of 78 Squadron, managed to evade capture. His plane was shot down by a German fighter piloted by Lt. Schnaufer (II/NJG1).

One Stirling, EF367 from 218 Squadron 3 Group, crashed on its return to base. Five of the crew were killed and the pilot, Sergeant. T. J. Nicholls, and navigator, Pilot Officer E. G. Pierce, were seriously injured.

Mid Upper Gunner is Missing

Flying Officer C. W. Smith, the captain of Halifax JB968 from 408 Squadron, had an unusual happening to report on his de-briefing. After they had bombed the target at 02.40 hours, the bomber was coned by searchlights, but after some evasive action managed to get away. Shortly afterwards they were again caught in a cone so this time the pilot put the aircraft into a more violent corkscrew to shake off the glaring lights. During these manoeuvres the flight engineer, Sergeant A. E. Dutton, noticed that the mid upper gunner, Sergeant R. Elmes who was on his eighth operation was trying to open the back fuselage escape hatch. At 02.55 hours, after the pilot had lost considerable altitude and was down to about 200 feet, he successfully evaded the probing beams of light. It was then observed by the wireless operator, Pilot Officer G. Klein, that the mid upper gunner was not in his proper position. The captain was informed and he instructed the flight engineer to make a thorough search in the back of the darkened fuselage. On proceeding there he found the escape hatch wide open and an oxygen tube hanging out of the opening, but no trace of the gunner or his parachute. Records show that Sergeant Elmes was captured after his untimely bale out and made a prisoner of war.

Crew Bale Out But the Pilot Crash Lands

The crew of another Wellington, HZ271 of 466 Squadron captained by Sergeant E. F. Hicks CGM, also had a lucky escape after the Bochum raid. The bomber developed port engine trouble after leaving the target and while limping back across the North Sea, the starboard engine also gave trouble. The pilot, however, coaxed his plane back over the English coast, where he ordered the crew members to bale out. The bomb aimer, Flight Sergeant Fyffe, and wireless operator, Sergeant F. C. Blair DFM, made a succesful landing. The navigator, 6ft 4ins tall, Flying Officer R. Clayton DFC was injured on landing. The pilot found that after these three had baled out one engine seemed to pick up and he decided to opt for a forced landing, which he successfully made one mile west of Winterton, Norfolk. The rear gunner, Pilot Officer Bluey Cairns, elected to remain with his skipper rather than hit the silk.

A Bad Omen

When the crew of Halifax JB873 of 78 Squadron, 4 Group, went to their aircraft at the dispersal bay at their Linton on Ouse airfield, they found that the 'Saint' motif painted on the side of their aircraft's fuselage had for some reason been painted out overnight. The mid upper gunner, Flight Sergeant A. Beatson, in keeping with many aircrew, was superstitious and as he was the first to notice that their good luck motif was missing, he forecast trouble on the forthcoming trip. On this occasion, he was right, for the bomber lost the use of its starboard engine with mechanical trouble on the outward flight and it had to be feathered. The pilot, Pilot Officer G. Dale, found that the heavily laden bomber had great difficulty in maintaining height and slowly the Halifax fell behind and below the main stream, a sitting target for any fighter attack. The pilot realised that it was wiser to abort his mission and after jettisoning the bombs, turned for home still gradually losing height.

A short time later there was a brief burst of exploding cannon shells in the aircraft. Prior to this there had been no *Flak* or searchlight activity and the gunners had given no warning of any fighters around. It was obvious that the bomber had been followed by radar and a fighter had made its attack from underneath, the blind spot in a bomber. The shells set fire to both inner engines and made a large hole in the starboard wing, from which spewed flames, reaching well past the tail. The aircraft suddenly went into a diving starboard turn, whilst the pilot struggled to hold the control column back firmly into his chest and over to full port. In spite of his efforts, the dive steepened and the centrifugal force was such that the flight engineer, Sergeant Arthur Minnitt, was unable to reach and press the fire extinguisher buttons in an attempt to control the flames.

Deciding that conditions were hopeless, the captain gave the order to abandon the aircraft. As there was a second pilot on board that night, the flight engineer realised that there were too many crew members to go out of the front hatch, so he handed his captain a parachute pack and informed him that he was going aft to the rear escape hatch. Struggling from the front to the back of a Halifax was always a difficult task as airmen had to climb over the main spar in the rest position of the fuselage and negotiate the many metal projections and the mid upper turret. On this occasion in spite of the angle of the diving bomber, the engineer made extra bulky with a parachute firmly clipped on to his chest, made the distance back to the rear hatch in double quick time. He found the mid upper gunner sitting on the edge of the already open hatch, ready to bale out. Sergeant Minnitt needed no help to quickly follow suit. As he pulled his ripcord, he saw small pieces of the burning Halifax falling away and a few seconds later the bomber exploded in mid air. The rest of the crew's successful exit was entirely due to the efforts of the two pilots who continued to struggle with the controls to enable their crew members to get out safely before they both lost their own lives in the following explosion. This was an exceedingly brave and selfless act, an act so often repeated by Bomber Command's aircrew.

Losing his left flying boot in the bale out, Sergeant Minnitt was handicapped at the start. Unsure of whether he was in Germany or Belgium, it was his intention to lay doggo for a few days and then to try to get to Switzerland. Initially he made his way to a small thicket and hid himself deep in the undergrowth. But he was quickly combed out and captured by a German army squad later in the same day and for him the war was over. The navigator, Sergeant R. G. Goddard, was luckier for when he landed, he was fortunate to call at the house of a Resistance worker and with the help of the underground movement was soon back in the UK.

12 Squadron Lancaster Ditches

Lancaster R5688 G for George from 12 Squadron based at Wickenby, Lincolnshire was being captained by Sergeant G. V. Scott. It was hit by *Flak* over the target area and suffered severe damage to the port mainplane as well as to the port engines which had to be feathered. Flying on only two starboard engines the aircraft gradually lost height until the skipper decided that he had little option but to attempt to ditch in the North Sea. Jettisoning fuel to lighten the Lancaster and so aid flotation, the aircraft was eventually ditched at a position 5125N 0255E at 02.10 hours on May 14th. Sea conditions were good for ditching with waves two to three feet high and a wind speed of 10 to 15 mph.

The bomber remained in one piece after the ditching, but the water rapidly came in and was up to the pilot's waist before he managed to extricate himself from the cockpit. In the meantime bringing into action the practised dinghy drill, the bomb aimer, Sergeant A. F. Rees, released the dinghy successfully but it drifted away from the plane and was only retrieved by the valiant efforts of the bomb aimer who dived into the sea and towed it back. Soon all the crew managed to heave themselves on board but to their chagrin they discovered that the emergency food, the Verey pistol, paddles and half the aerial mast had been lost. The crew were left with only 24 tins of water and their own escape kits. The two carrier pigeons carried in some bombers were rescued from the now sinking Lancaster, but one of them was found already drowned. The other one had its feathers dried by the pilot, but when it was released it circled the dinghy and quickly landed back aboard. On its second attempt it flew off, but to the crew's dismay not in the direction in which they believed the United Kingdom should be.

On their first day the crew set up a make shift sail by using a canvas cover with half the radio aerial as a mast but they made little headway. Also on this day an aircraft swooped low overhead and all the crew waved back madly to attract its attention until they recognised that it was a German Ju88. They decided not to drink any water on this their first day as a conservation measure and they tried to fill their time by singing songs and having debates, one of the crew even made a rough deck of cards and they all played Nap in the bouncing dinghy in the middle of the sea. The second and third day passed without any sign of any help coming, but their spirits were still high and they kept to rigid rations of their water and meagre food supply. On the fourth day their spirits soared as their dinghy drifted so close to a town, which they thought to be Dover, that the crew could even see the cars in the streets. But in spite of their yells, whistles and flashes from a mirror no one managed to notice them. On the sixth day they sighted three Royal Navy minesweepers steaming close by, the crew thought they had not been spotted but fortunately one of the vessels, that captained by Lt. Harry Collier, had developed engine trouble and drifted closer to the dinghy. At last they were seen by a sailor on lookout duty and the ship approached them with its deck machine guns trained on the solitary dinghy. On being asked if they were RAF and giving a typical unprintable response the crew were thankfully hauled aboard. On eyeing the machine guns at close quarters they dreaded to think what might have happened had they been an enemy crew. Their ordeal had lasted 129 hours and their rescue ship with engines now repaired, took them the seven miles to Dover. In spite of their exposure to the elements, for which they received medical treatment they were soon back at their base.

Casualties May 13th/14th, 1943. Target Bochum

405 Squadron 8 Group Halifax JB966 LQ/D
Pilot. J/10119 F/O H.D.Beattie Killed Avereest, Meppel, Holland. 1
Nav. J/11941 F/O J.S.Hawtin PoW. Stalag Luft 3, Sagan. 1329
B/A. 1376493 W/O K.W.Clarke PoW. Stalag Luft 1, Barth Vogelsang. 1172
W/OP. 1269142 Sgt S.B.Hawley Killed Avereest, Meppel, Holland. 3
F/E. R/75127 W/O J.D.Gibson PoW. Stalag Luft 4, Sagan. 1180
A/G. R/141618 Sgt R.Ferguson PoW. Stalag Luft 4, Sagan. 1177
A/G. R/95244 F/Sgt R.Hart Killed Avereest, Meppel, Holland. 2

12 Squadron 1 Group Lancaster W4366 PH/R
Pilot. A/412618 F/Sgt F.W.Morgan Killed Reichswald Forest, Germany. 17-G-2
Nav. 1600221 F/Sgt G.L.Fountain PoW. Stalag Luft 6, Heydekrug. 1178
B/A. 657569 Sgt K.J.G.Walker PoW. Stalag Luft 6, Heydekrug. 1204
W/OP. 1218718 Sgt R.Maginnis PoW. Stalag Luft 6, Heydekrug. 1190
F/E. 1061305 Sgt K.Foster Killed Reichswald Forest, Germany. 17-G-3
A/G. R/114345 F/Sgt J.R.Richmond Killed Reichswald Forest. 17-G-4
A/G. R/141385 W/O G.T.Spiece PoW. Stalag Luft 4, Sagan. 1200

12 Squadron 1 Group Lancaster R5688 PH/G
Aircraft ditched in North Sea (5125N 0255E) at 02.10 hours, >May 14th.
Pilot. Sgt G.V.Scott Rescued
Nav. Sgt G.H.Russell Rescued
B/A. Sgt A.F.Rees Rescued
W/OP. Sgt G.D.Mitchell Rescued
F/E. Sgt H.T.Redford Rescued
A/G. P/O P.H.Phillips Rescued
A/G. Sgt L.F.Range Rescued

166 Squadron 1 Group Wellington HZ280 AS/Q
Pilot. J/20354 F/O W.Wahl Killed Amsterdam, Holland. 69-C-14
Nav. 751409 Sgt S.A.T.Davies PoW. Stalag Luft 3, Sagan. 593
B/A. J/20835 F/O H.W.Newby PoW. Stalag Luft 3, Sagan. 1349
W/OP. R/114771 F/Sgt W.N.Partridge Killed Bergen-op-Zoom (Can). 8-I-30
A/G. R/87125 Sgt J.A.Wright PoW. Repatriated.

15 Squadron 3 Group Stirling BK704 LS/Z
Aircraft crashed at 01.30 hours at Barlo, Germany. Shot down by *Flak*.
Pilot. 118812 S/Ldr C.C.Bowyer Killed Reichswald Forest, Germany. 21-B-15
2/Pilot. 142039 P/O D.C.Smith PoW. Stalag Luft 3, Sagan. 1335
Nav. J/11115 F/Lt W.G.M.Olivier PoW. Stalag Luft 3, Sagan. 1333
B/A. 146452 F/O J.B.Craggs PoW. Stalag Luft 6, Heydekrug. 1175
W/OP. 970685 W/O T.P.Hanarahan PoW. Stalag 357, Kopernikus. 1182
F/E. 942498 Sgt H.C.Cooper PoW. Stalag Luft 6, Heydekrug. 1174
A/G. R/133151 Sgt E.E.Warner PoW. Stalag 4B, Muhlberg(Elbe). 1205
A/G. 655574 W/O C.E.Keik PoW. Stalag 357, Kopernikus. 1185

149 Squadron 3 Group Stirling BF479 OJ/E
Aircraft crashed at Kasterlee, Belgium at 03.15 hours (14/5/43).
Pilot. 124513 F/O L.C.Martin Killed Schoonselhoof, Belgium. CG II-G-6/9
2/Pilot. R/115045 F/Sgt R.C.Ferguson Killed Schoonselhoof, Belgium. II-G-11
Nav. 1387239 Sgt N.H.Frank Killed Schoonselhoof, Belgium. CG II-G-6/9
B/A. 118604 F/O G.R.Royde Killed Schoonselhoof, Belgium. CG II-G-6/9
W/OP. 1268287 Sgt E.Hazlden-French Killed Schoonselhoof. CG II-G-6/9
F/E. 961492 Sgt J.E.Butt Killed Schoonselhoof, Belgium. II-G-10
A/G. 1578408 Sgt H.A.J.Berry Killed Schoonselhoof, Belgium. IV-B-43
A/G. R/76310 F/Sgt H.P.Fudge Killed Schoonselhoof, Belgium. CG II-G-6/9

149 Squadron 3 Group Stirling BK726 OJ/Z
Aircraft crashed at Immerath, (Erkelenz), Germany after fighter attack.
Pilot. J/17672 P/O H.E.Forsyth Killed Rheinberg, Germany. 2-F-20
Nav. R/93881 F/Sgt D.F.McDonald Killed Rheinberg, Germany. CG 2-G-1/12
B/A. R/108356 W/O Y.J.B.Guepin Killed Rheinberg, Germany. 2-F-21
W/OP. 144690 P/O D.E.Sharpe Killed Rheinberg, Germany. 2-F-22
F/E. 614624 Sgt J.J.Ryan Killed Rheinberg, Germany. CG 2-G-1/12
A/G. 1319840 Sgt L.P.Barnett Killed Rheinberg, Germany. 2-F-23
A/G. 651839 Sgt W.McCall Killed Rheinberg, Germany. CG 2-G-1/12

214 Squadron 3 Group Stirling R9242 BU/O
Aircraft attacked by night fighter and crashed atHeerlerheide, Holland.
Pilot. 1527965 Sgt R.M.Gibbney Missing, Runnymede Memorial 150
Nav. 128458 F/Lt A.R.Minton PoW. Stalag Luft 3, Sagan. 1412
B/A. 1319706 F/Sgt R.F.Gullick PoW. Stalag 357, Kopernikus. 155
W/OP. 1025590 F/Sgt L.Sutcliffe PoW. Stalag Luft 3, Sagan. 10582
F/E. 996460 Sgt F.D.Stannard Missing, Runnymede Memorial 166
A/G. 1699563 Sgt L.Leake Missing, Runnymede Memorial 156
A/G. 1320307 Sgt S.R.Tinkler Missing, Runnymede memorial. 167

10 Squadron 4 Group Halifax DT732 ZA/X
Aircraft crashed in Zuider Zee, Holland. Wreckage recovered after the war.
Pilot. 415040 F/Sgt J.F.Mills Missing, Runnymede Memorial 193
Nav. 1347046 Sgt J.S.Macadam Killed Bergen-op-Zoom (Can). C-8-236
B/A. 1336690 Sgt J.W.Avent Killed Amsterdam, Holland. CG 69-C-12
W/OP. 1211847 Sgt A.Jones Killed Amsterdam, Holland. CG 69-C-12
F/E. 1284957 Sgt J.C.Howie Killed Amsterdam, Holland. CG 69-C-12
A/G. 1260589 Sgt E.J.C.Howard Killed Amsterdam, Holland. CG 69-C-12
A/G. 1055780 Sgt C.Maltby Killed Amsterdam, Holland. CG 69-C-12

10 Squadron 4 Group Halifax HR695 ZA/D
Captain :- Sgt C.Beveridge
A/G. R/123498 W/O A.F.McCoy Missing, Runnymede Memorial 181
Air gunner baled out.

51 Squadron 4 Group Halifax HR790 MH/
Pilot. 128065 F/O G.W.H.Byres PoW. Stalag Luft 3, Sagan. 1343
Nav. 120338 F/Lt R.H.Stark PoW. Stalag Luft 3, Sagan. 1351
B/A. 1294118 W/O D.J.Emes PoW. Stalag Luft 1, Barth Vogelsang. 1240
W/OP. 1290307 F/Sgt R.T.Howell PoW. Stalag Luft 6, Heydekrug. 1248
F/E. 922222 Sgt G.Steer Killed Weerselo (Rossum), Holland, A-9
A/G. 1581536 Sgt C.Stringer Killed Weerselo (Rossum), Holland, A-11
A/G. 649808 F/Sgt J.A.C.Jacobs Killed Weerselo (Rossum), Holland, A-10

51 Squadron 4 Group Halifax DT526 MH/
Aircraft shot down over Bochum, Germany by FW 190 after being hit by *Flak.*
Pilot. 123522 F/Lt R.D.Johnstone PoW. Stalag Luft 3, Sagan. 1330
Nav. 120628 F/Lt A.G.Wingrave PoW. Stalag Luft 3, Sagan. 1339
B/A. 131773 F/Lt M.Gibb PoW. Stalag Luft 3, Sagan. 1324
W/OP. 107458 F/Lt G.I.Donkersley PoW. Stalag Luft 3, Sagan. 1322
F/E. 975105 Sgt F.Tipton PoW. Camp not known.
A/G. 1322336 Sgt B.R.Byfield Killed Reichswald Forest, Germany. 3-B-3
A/G. 121057 F/Lt P.Parnham DFC Killed Reichswald Forest, Germany. 3-B-4

77 Squadron 4 Group Halifax JB892 KN/
Pilot. 136541 F/O D.P.Uddephatt Killed Sleen, Holland CG 12-289/293
Nav. 1391746 Sgt L.W.Bolton Killed Sleen, Holland. CG 12-289/293
B/A. 1338378 Sgt J.I.P.Morgan Killed Sleen, Holland. CG 12-289/293
W/OP. 1380500 Sgt G.S.Walton Killed Sleen, Holland. 12-288
F/E. 574090 Sgt M.J.H.Brookes Killed Sleen, Holland. CG 12-289/293
A/G. 1464887 Sgt R.A.Halestrap Killed Sleen, Holland. 12-294
A/G. 1007370 Sgt A.W.McKillop Killed Sleen, Holland. CG 12-289/293

78 Squadron 4 Group Halifax JB924 EY/
Pilot. 145473 P/O R.E.Bragg Killed Barrandeel(Wijnaldum), Holland. 6-A-2
2/Pilot. 1431810 Sgt E.Pritchard Killed Barrandeel(Wijnaldum). 6-A-5
Nav. R/103820 W/O J.M.Farrell Killed Bergen-op-Zoom (Can). 1-A-13
B/A. 1147374 W/O H.E.Gell PoW. Stalag 357, Kopernikus. 1244
W/OP. 1266729 Sgt R.D.Matchjes Killed Barrandeel(Wijnaldum). 6-A-4
F/E. 50952 F/Lt R.Grey Killed Barrandeel(Wijnaldum), Holland. 6-A-5A
A/G. 1011881 Sgt D.Baxter Killed Barrandeel(Wijnaldum), Holland. 6-A-1
A/G. R/135246 F/Sgt A.A.Kew Killed Barrandeel(Wijnaldum), Holland. 6-A-3

78 Squadron 4 Group Halifax JB873 EY/
Shot down at Haasrode, near Leuven, Belgium at 03.10 hours (14/5/43).Victim of Lt.Schnaufer and Lt.Baro of II/NJG1.
Pilot. 146425 P/O G.H.Dane Killed Haasrode, Leuven, Belgium. 1
2/Pilot. 658465 Sgt J.H.Body Killed Haasrode, Leuven, Belgium. 2
Nav. 1333556 Sgt R.G.Goddard Evaded capture,
B/A. 1390851 W/O L.Adams PoW. Stalag 357, Kopernikus. 42750
W/OP. 1380502 F/Sgt J.W.Pople PoW. Stalag Luft 4, Sagan. 1264
F/E. 1166617 F/Sgt A.C.P.Minnitt PoW. Stalag Luft 4, Sagan. 1260
A/G. 1698487 F/Sgt A.Beatson PoW. Stalag Luft 1, Barth Vogelsang 1231
A/G. 1388371 F/Sgt F.W.Webb PoW. Stalag Luft 6, Heydekrug. 42765

78 Squadron 4 Group Halifax DT777 EY/T
Pilot. 1086886 W/O G.E.Clay PoW. Stalag Luft 1, Barth Vogelsang. 1173
Nav. 1269442 F/Sgt J.O'Reilly PoW. Stalag Luft 4, Sagan. 1263
B/A. 658181 F/Sgt L.D.E.Marriott PoW. Stalag 357, Kopernikus. 1256
W/OP. 650905 F/Sgt E.A.Coates PoW. Stalag Luft 6, Heydekrug. 1237
F/E. 930627 Sgt L.Jakes Killed Rheinberg, Germany. 1-D-25
A/G. 146624 F/O C.F.Leverett PoW. Stalag Luft 3, Sagan. 201
A/G. R/110347 W/O W.J.H.Perry PoW. Stalag Luft 4, Sagan. 1195

102 Squadron 4 Group Halifax JB964 DY/G
Pilot. 1392608 Sgt V.H.Hatchard Killed Rheinberg, Germany. CG 2-G-1/12
Nav. 127975 F/Lt F.A.James PoW. Stalag Luft 3, Sagan. 1446
B/A. 1322948 Sgt S.Brown Killed Rheinberg, Germany. CG 2-G-1/12
W/OP. 1291992 Sgt J.Leedham Killed Rheinberg, Germany. CG 2-G-1/12
F/E. 577037 Sgt W.T.Lee Killed Rheinberg, Germany. CG 2-G-1/12
A/G. R/155989 Sgt J.A.Coughlin PoW. Stalag 357, Kopernikus. 7
A/G. 1576327 Sgt J.S.W.Fowles Killed Rheinberg, Germany. 2-F-24

102 Squadron 4 Group Halifax W7935 DY/Y
Aircraft ditched 21 miles East of Great Yarmouth.
Pilot. 937481 F/Sgt A.M.Sargent Rescued.
Nav. 1239952 Sgt A.Campbell Rescued.
B/A. 129475 F/O J.R.Bullock Rescued.
W/OP. 1137146 Sgt M.Galloway Rescued.
F/E. 1211978 Sgt C.R.Webb Rescued.
A/G. 1312030 Sgt A.G.Newberry Rescued.
A/G. 1094915 Sgt J.C.Smith Rescued.

431 Squadron 4 Group Wellington HE183 SE/J
Pilot. 39618 S/Ldr T.B.Marshall Missing, Runnymede Memorial. 118
Nav. 125513 F/O D.S.Gooderham Missing, Runnymede Memorial 124
B/A. 127277 P/O D.Coales Missing, Runnymede Memorial 121
W/OP. 910228 Sgt A.E.Quaife Missing, Runnymede Memorial 162
A/G. J/12160 F/O D.J.Macmillan Missing, Runnymede Memorial 174

466 Squadron 4 Group Wellington MS473 HD/
Pilot. NZ/411032 P/O T.Sampson Killed The Hague, Holland. AP-4-72
Nav. 1382389 Sgt C.W.Jones PoW. Stalag Luft 6, Heydekrug. 1184
B/A. A/403633 F/O J.F.Cahill PoW. Stalag Luft 3, Sagan. 1171
W/OP. A/403621 F/Sgt K.S.Murphy PoW. Stalag Luft 4, Sagan. 1191
A/G. 1282544 W/O R.J.T.Lester PoW. Stalag Luft 1, Barth Vogelsang. 1188

408 Squadron 6 Group Halifax JB931 EQ/C
Pilot. 87059 S/Ldr H.D.Campbell DFC Killed Flushing, Holland. D-31
Nav. J/12987 F/Lt A.W.Thompson PoW. Stalag Luft 3, Sagan. 1336
B/A. 130409 F/Lt M.H.J.Hammill PoW. Stalag Luft 3, Sagan. 1328
W/OP. 938849 F/Sgt A.C.Ross PoW. Stalag 357, Kopernikus. 240
F/E. R/70275 Sgt J.M.Harrison Killed Flushing, Holland. E-2
A/G. A/402461 P/O A.E.Horne DFM Killed Flushing, Holland. D-32
A/G. R/116452 Sgt L.A.Stinson Killed Flushing, Holland. E-1

408 Squadron 6 Group Halifax JB968 EQ/R
Pilot. J/8371 F/O C.W.Smith
A/G. 1295474 W/O R.Elmes PoW. Stalag Luft 1, Barth Vogelsang. 1176
Air gunner baled out over target.

419 Squadron 6 Group Halifax DT672 VR/
Pilot. 1078804 Sgt G.Adams Killed Rheinberg, Germany. 2-F-13
Nav. J/14738 F/O E.B.Ruto Killed Rheinberg, Germany. 2-F-14
B/A. R/135010 F/Sgt W.H.Bowden Killed Rheinberg, Germany. 2-F-15
W/OP. 1128371 Sgt E.Kurring Killed Rheinberg, Germany. 2-F-17
F/E. 985412 Sgt F.S.Neal Killed Rheinberg, Germany. 2-F-16
A/G. R/131571 Sgt O.J.Haralson Killed Rheinberg, Germany. 2-F-19
A/G. R/120920 F/Sgt L.D.McEwen Killed Rheinberg, Germany. 2-F-18

419 Squadron 6 Group Halifax JD113 VR/
Pilot. R/120100 F/Sgt W.H.S.Buckwell Killed Dalen, Holland. 1N-7-167
Nav. J/13812 F/Lt R.H.Lowry PoW. Stalag Luft 3, Sagan. 1332
B/A. R/105405 Sgt W.M.Reid PoW. Stalag 357, Kopernikus. 1268
W/OP. R/88090 Sgt W.J.N.Duggen PoW. Stalag 4B, Muhlberg, Elbe. 259865
F/E. R/63806 Sgt F.W.Walkerdine Killed Dalen, Holland. 1N-7-166
A/G. R/149121 F/Sgt A.E.Hurteau Killed Dalen, Holland. 1N-7-168
A/G. R/113737 F/Sgt W.L.Bovaird Killed Dalen, Holland. 1N-7-165

426 Squadron 6 Group Wellington HE243 OW/
Pilot. J/17383 P/O J.B.Pettigrew Missing, Runnymede Memorial 177
Nav. J/16323 P/O R.E.Wagner Missing, Runnymede Memorial 178
B/A. 1397003 Sgt W.E.Delaney Missing, Runnymede Memorial 147
W/OP. 1380131 Sgt S.E.Herbert Missing, Runnymede Memorial 153
A/G. 1383116 Sgt E.D.Dwelly Missing, Runnymede Memorial 148

426 Squadron 6 Group Wellington HE691 OW/
Pilot. R/121044 F/Sgt J.A.Thomson Killed Amersfoort, Holland. 13-6-121
Nav. R/136282 F/Sgt A.F.Hopley Killed Amersfoort, Holland. 13-6-122
B/A. R/55816 Sgt J.P.O.Ethier Killed Amersfoort, Holland. 13-6-123
W/OP. 1126718 Sgt N.Hudspith Killed Amersfoort, Holland. 13-6-120
A/G. R/132630 F/Sgt T.F.How Killed Amersfoort, Holland. 13-6-124

429 Squadron 6 Group Wellington LN439 AL/
Pilot. R/103246 F/Sgt F.R.Windibank Killed Rheinberg. CG 2-G-1/12
Nav. R/142433 F/Sgt W.J.Reid Killed Rheinberg, Germany. CG 2-G-1/12
B/A. R/134035 Sgt A.E.Atkinson Killed Rheinberg, Germany. CG 2-G-1/12
W/OP. R/126252 Sgt N.R.McKinley PoW. Stalag 357, Kopernikus. 1259
A/G. R/139686 Sgt D.I.Havard Killed Rheinberg, Germany. CG 2-G-1/12

218 Squadron 3 Group Stirling EF367 HA/
Aircraft crashed at Chedburgh returning from operations.
Pilot. Sgt T.J.Nicholls Injured
Nav. P/O E.G.Pierce Injured
B/A. 1441087 Sgt J.P.V.Hargest Killed St David's, Brecon, S.Wales. A-B-11
W/OP. 1333534 Sgt T.A.Jamieson Killed Wandsworth (Streatham) 17-27
F/E. 547504 Sgt D.Wurr Killed Hull (Northern), Yorkshire. 265-76
A/G. R/17445 Sgt S.G.Cleveland Killed Haverhill, Suffolk. U-248
A/G. 1132050 Sgt J.S.Howard Killed Greenacres, Oldham. B-16-213

218 Squadron 3 Group Stirling BF480 HA/
Swung on landing and crashed into Control Tower on return from operations to Bochum.
Pilot. Sgt W.C.Carney Safe.
Nav. Sgt I.A.Jordan Safe.
B/A. Sgt A.R.Taylor Safe.
W/OP. Sgt A.G.Ives Safe.
F/E. Sgt B.Garland Safe.
A/G. Sgt L.W.J.Durrant Safe.
A/G. Sgt W.Stewart Safe.

Pilsen

May 13th/14th, 1943

The long flight to Pilsen which was made by 124 Lancasters of 5 Group and 24 Lancasters and 12 Halifaxes from 8 Group, proved to be a fruitless operation. The Pathfinders dropped 61 target indicators and 272 flares. The aiming point was the Skoda works on the edge of the town, and although all the 486 tons of bombs fell within three miles of this aiming point, the majority of them fell in open countryside well north of the Skoda armament works. If the aiming point had been in the centre of the town, the raid would have been classed as excellent. Air Marshal Harris had repeatedly pointed out the risk of failure if a target was at the edge of a town, as there was always a tendency for the bombers to undershoot as a raid progressed, this raid proved that his theory was correct. It can only be assumed that the planners of this particular raid from 5 Group had on this occasion disregarded his words of advice. Nine aircraft were lost in this raid, with 38 aircrew killed, 12 missing, 12 becoming prisoners and one pilot evading to make a 'home run'.

The airman who managed to evade capture was 142599 Pilot Officer J. B. M. Haye, who was originally in the Dutch Air Force and with his background the odds were very much in his favour to make a successful escape. He was the pilot of Lancaster ED667 from 57 Squadron, 5 Group which left its home base of Scampton, Lincolnshire at 22.00 hours for the long flight to Pilsen. After only an hour's flying time, whilst still over the German/Dutch border the aircraft was attacked by a night fighter and as a result the bomber was quickly set on fire and the flying controls were badly damaged. The pilot, however, managed to make a 180 degree turn and headed back for Holland. A bale out order was given and he ensured that the crew in the forward part of the plane had successfully baled out. He was unable to check whether the gunners had baled out because there was an intercom failure so the pilot left the plane and parachuted down, landing in a cornfield, which he later found to be near Tubbergen, 15 miles east of Enschede. With no sign of any German patrols and having the ability to speak fluent Dutch, Pilot Officer Haye was in an admirable position if he could avoid capture within the first few hours. He immediately hid his Mae West, chute and harness among the corn and as he was wearing a civilian shirt, he took off his battle dress top and hid that too. To prevent his flying boots being too conspicuous he rolled his trousers over the tops, he then emptied his escape box and purse and put the contents in his trouser pockets. There was a farm about 20 yards away from his landing spot, from which he heard voices but was unable to ascertain what language they were using. Pilot Officer Haye then started to walk westwards, as he was unsure at that time of exactly where he had landed. After a while he decided to try his luck at a lonely farm. Although he knocked at the door, the occupants would not open it, but from behind the locked door, the language sounded like some form of Dutch dialect. The pilot had declared who he was, but the man behind the door seemed very scared and told him to go away. A little time afterwards Haye saw a notice board with the words No Entry on it in Dutch, and was relieved to find he was in Holland. He continued walking along sand tracks and through fields and at about 01.00 hours on May 14th called at another farm, but again the occupants would not come out. Later he found the reason for this was because there was a very strict curfew in Holland from 20.00 hrs to 04.00 hours.

He walked on for about five miles and then as he was very tired he found and slept in a barn. In the morning he saw some farmworkers about, but waited until they had gone away, before he approached a woman at the farmhouse. Speaking to her in Dutch, Haye told her that he was a Dutchman serving in the RAF. The woman was very scared and called her husband, who suggested that Haye should carry on walking westwards. With the aid of his escape compass he continued, crossing a small canal by means of a plank bridge. Skirting the village of Almelo, Haye approached a farm on the outskirts, where he asked the farmer if he could let him have a spare pair of trousers. The farmer wanted to know if Haye was a student, but when told he was an RAF pilot he was taken into a barn where he was given bread and milk, but no trousers. Haye then continued walking south and noticed a number of civilians riding bicycles and from his recollection of living in Holland, he noticed that they were riding the distinctive tall bicycle, with a saddle bag at the back, which was normally used by Dutch police. When they came nearer Haye pretended to squat down and eat some bread that he had been given, in an effort to hide his conspicious blue trousers.

When he felt it was safe he continued walking through the village of Bornerbroen until he came to a canal called the Twikkelsche Vaart, and to a ferry where a number of people were awaiting a boat to be taken across. At about 11.00 hours, when there was no one else about, Haye approached the ferryman and asked him in Dutch, "Do you know who I am?". Without hesitation the ferryman replied that he did and after Haye had explained that he really was a Dutchman in the RAF and that he had only 20 Dutch guilders in notes, the ferryman helpfully took him across without payment.

On the other side there was a man with a farm cart, who was known to the ferryman and who gave Haye a ride on his cart to a farm where he was given some milk. The farmer also cut the tops off some old wellington boots and gave Haye the bottom halves. As with so many of the Dutch, the man appeared frightened, but it was here that Haye had a real stroke of luck, for near the farm he saw a boy on a bicycle. As he was walking away Haye was followed by the boy and although he did not ask to see Hayes identity discs he asked a number of questions about the aircraft and where it had crashed. The boy seemed satisfied with the reply and he escorted Haye to a farm near Enter, a hamlet, south west of Almelo. The occupants of this farm welcomed Haye very warmly and gave him a meal. They also changed his Dutch guilder notes into small coinage and gave him a complete civilian outfit and most importantly a bicycle which was an asset many evaders found invaluable. The occupants also gave Haye advice on how to reach Amsterdam and refused any payment for the many things they had supplied.

After leaving his helpers, Haye made a serious mistake, but luckily he managed to get away with it. In the village of Enter he asked a man for guidance and unwittingly spoke to him in English. Haye tried to make amends by speaking to him in German and finally in Dutch, giving the excuse that he was a German visitor to Holland, who wanted to know the way. He then cycled through Goor, Borculo, Barchem, Lochem, Almen and he reached Eefde at 16.00 hours. He still had some time before curfew and continued on through Zutphen, where he saw many German soldiers and then took the main road through Apeldoorn.

Just before curfew time, Haye stopped near Klarenbeek and went to a farm where, after declaring his identity, he was given some food and taken to a barn to sleep. The farmer told him that the back of his bike should be painted white to comply with the regulations and while Haye slept, the farmer kindly painted the bike. Next morning, May 15th, at 06.00 hours he filled his water bottle, hung it across the handlebars of the bike and set off for Amersfoort. He stopped on the way to have a drink and was shocked to notice that embossed on the rubber bottle the words MADE IN ENGLAND a dead give away to any sharp eyed enemy soldier. Haye quickly disposed of the bottle.

He had once lived in Hilversum, and thought it would be wiser to avoid that town in case he was recognised by someone. Instead he cycled through Baarn and Laren, where he met another lad who told Haye that he knew an English family in nearby Naarden, who might help. Haye visited this couple. The man was English and had lived in Holland for many years and on one occasion had been held by the Germans, although his wife was Dutch. He spent a few hours chatting with them and could see that they were not in a position to offer much help, but the man advised him that he should try to reach Warmoestraat an area in Amsterdam and a notorious resort for prostitutes, where one of the ladies might be willing to hide him.

After continuing his journey from Naarden, Haye stopped at Muiden, where he went into a cafe just before curfew time. He made a cautious approach and declared himself to a man he met there. He was taken out to a barn where he sheltered for the night. His new found hosts had only been released from a concentration camp a month previously. They were naturally very apprehensive and were taking an enormous risk, but they gave Haye food and also some bread coupons which would last for two weeks. Next morning, May 16th, Haye decided to venture into Amsterdam, but as his bicycle was conspicious with its rubber tyres, which was unusual in Holland at that time, he decided to throw it away and continue his journey on foot. Once in the city he saw a number of Jews walking about all wearing the yellow star on their clothing. Haye stopped one of them and asked directions to the Warmoestraat. On entering a bar in this street, Haye struck up a conversation with the barmaid and eventually told her that he was in the RAF. The barmaid replied speaking in a very low voice said that she did not care who he was but informed him that her father and sister who were sitting nearby were very pro-German and that it would be safer if he left. Haye departed and made his way into another bar where he saw a number of unpleasant looking prostitutes, so again he left. As he stepped outside he saw a police car stop outside the first bar at which he had called, no doubt in answer to a phone call reporting his presence. So he made himself scarce and went into the darkness of a cinema and safer surroundings.

When he left the cinema, Haye tried to buy a meal at a cafeteria, but found that practically all the food obtainable required coupons, which he did not possess. He then went to the railway station and with the money from his escape purse, bought a ticket for The Hague. This ticket cost 6 guilders and 75 cents and turned out to be a worker's season ticket valid for one week, a fact that Haye did not notice at the time. The train only went as far as Zandvoort. Here one of the railway officials explained that Haye was carrying the wrong type of ticket and that he had also boarded the wrong train and that if he wanted a correct ticket or a refund of the money, that he should see the station master at Haarlem. Haye thought that this could be rather a risky procedure, but decided that it would arouse more suspicion if he didn't take the advice. After a lengthy explanation the station master issued the correct ticket and refunded several guilders, but asked Haye to sign a receipt for the money, stating his name and address. Haye was alert and signed his correct name, but gave a fictitious address.

He then caught a train to the Hague and arrived there about 17.00 hours. His final stroke of luck came at The Hague railway station, where he saw a woman, whom he had known before the war. The woman was accompanied by her husband who was also known to Haye, so he decided to approach them. They were extremely surprised to meet him again and after he had explained to them that he was serving as a pilot in the RAF and of his bale out, the couple took him to their home. From that point Haye's subsequent journey back to the UK was arranged for him and he arrived safely back to the UK on Friday, July 30th, 1943.

An Evasion That Failed

1383521 Warrant Officer Charles Saville was the bomb aimer in Pilot Officer Haye's crew. He parachuted down in a field just north of Nordhorn, but he was not so fortunate in his evasion as his skipper. He relates.

"I ran to a small pond when I landed, where I sank my harness which I tied to a log. Then tore off my badges and pocket tops in an attempt to make my uniform less conspicuous and started to walk westwards by the stars until I saw a farm, which I watched from a hayrick until midday. I spoke to a man from whom I gathered I was still in Germany, so I made a quick exit across open country walking until 22.00 hours that night when I was stopped by two dogs. The dog owners told me that they were Dutch, but could not help me as the Gestapo were about. So I started walking again, this time in a south westerly direction, following the roads when it got dark.

"I continued like this for four days, sleeping up at night, during which time I got a meal at a farm, which I left quickly owing to the suspicious behaviour of the farmer. I also received some sandwiches and a pair of clogs from a worker I came across in a field on my second day. I had passed through Almelo, crossed the railway and canal at Lochem, reaching the river about 5 miles south-east of Arnhem on the fourth day. I walked along the river towards Arnhem trying to find a crossing, when at the junction of the two rivers Rhine and Ijssel, a man who was going by in a small boat came alongside to the bank. He asked me for my identity papers, but I was unable to produce them. He asked me in English who I was and then he took me across the river and left me in some bushes. After returning to the other bank to fetch food, he took off his own clothes, consisting of a blouse and light trousers, but leaving himself in only a pair of swimming shorts. He then rowed me down the river to a boathouse at Arnhem. We put the boat away and walked out to the river bank nearby. He gave me the boathouse key and told me to return there only at dusk.

"I stayed there until the next morning, 19th May, when the man returned bringing me some other civilian clothes, shoes and also a railway ticket for Breda. He took me along to the railway station and I followed him on to the train, which we both thought was going through to Breda, but it stopped at Nijmegen, where everyone had to get off and change trains. I lost him in the milling crowd changing platforms, but fortunately we were quickly reunited. This time he put me into the correct train and left me after telling me to contact a man who would be waiting for me outside the station at Breda.

*The train journey was uneventful and on arrival at Breda I followed the instructions I had been given but I failed to contact the man who was supposed to meet me there. After waiting for about 20 minutes I thought I was too conspicuous so I walked through the town into open countryside, where I stopped to take a compass bearing and headed for Belgium. I kept to the main roads and crossed over the frontier the same night. I approached a farmhouse, but the occupants would not help me so I slept in a hayrick. Next day I continued walking through Turnhout on to Gheel, where I slept in an outbuilding and then continued to Diest the next day. I had been watching the tram service on the way and seeing a similar service from Diest, I took a tram to Louvain, which I reached on the evening of May 21st. At Louvain I bought some food and slept in some outbuildings again. The next day I hitched a ride in a civilian lorry to Brussels, where I had another meal before taking a tram to Halle, which according to my map I knew to be in the right direction. I was hoping all the time to make some contact to obtain help, but whenever I declared myself none was forthcoming. I felt that either the people were afraid or disinterested, but on occasions they behaved quite suspiciously. Therefore my objective was France, where I understood I could more easily contact some underground organisation. I slept at Halle, then hitched a lift by lorry to Mons, where I went into several shops for food. It was difficult with coupon restrictions, but I managed to buy some soup and carrots. I declared myself at a farmhouse on the outskirts of Mons, but the farmer asked for my papers and started telephoning so I moved quickly on across country. That night I went into a barn, where a man followed almost at once, but although he appeared to be looking around for someone he did not find me and after a while he went out and locked the door. Nothing happened after however and I remained there until the next morning when some children came along and opened the door. I quickly slipped out after they had gone and continued walking across country, crossing the French/Belgian frontier that day at Villers sur Nicole, 8 miles north-east of Maubeuge.

*Next morning, May 26th, I started off again and reached Beughes at midday, where I knocked at the door of an old restaurant. A woman answered my knock but I had great difficulty in satisfying her that I was an evader. I eventually succeeded by showing her various flying charms that I was carrying and also my feet, which by now were in a pretty bad state. When her husband arrived and had satisfied himself as to my true identity, he brought along an English speaking Doctor, who attended to my feet and told me to remain where I was for a time to rest up and get my feet better. He also said that he would bring me some identity papers to help me move along later on. I stayed here for eight days, until the doctor brought along a man and woman who took me by bus to Avesnes and from there by train to Arras. Another woman met us there and took me to a house where I remained for a further three days, only going out once to have my hair cut by a Resistance barber. The man and woman then took me by train to Paris without incident, where they handed me over to yet another man who met us at the station. He took me along to a café and then on to a house where I stayed for 21 days. I was to have been moved on after a few days, but a section of the organisation had been arrested which made the plans more difficult. My expected papers did not materialise and I was moved yet again to a flat where I lived by myself for a week, two men bringing in food for me every evening. A week later I was taken in turn to yet two other houses where I stayed about a week and ten days respectively. In the last house I was looked after by a man and his sister, he was engaged in various subversive activities and used to take photographs of military defences etc. He always carried arms and I declined his offer to arm me with a gun.

"On July 21st he had been out all the morning when a number of Gestapo men suddenly arrived breaking down the front door. Apparently when they came in they had seen my silhouette through a glass partition in the hall behind which I was hiding. They opened fire, but luckily only one bullet grazed the flesh of my back and I was quickly captured. They put me in handcuffs and then waited some time for the man's sister to return, whereupon they arrested her as well and took us both back to the Gestapo HQ. Here I met the brother who was lying on a stretcher with three bullets in him. He was conscious but in a bad way. We both deliberately avoided recognition of each other. We both were taken to a hospital where I maintained the pretence that I was deaf and dumb as stated on my identity card, but in the end I was obliged to tell them who I was. I later heard that the brother had been cornered by the Gestapo and had tried to shoot his way out of the ambush. Later that day the nurses told me that he had died. I was taken from the hospital back to the Gestapo HQ later in the same day where I again met up with the man's sister and I was interrogated in her presence. I told them in English, a language which I knew she could speak and would understand, that she had never spoken to me as she could not speak English, also that she had nothing to do with me. Nevertheless we were both taken to Fresnes Prison in Paris on the same day. That was the last time I saw or heard of her.

"I was kept in Fresnes for four months and for two months I shared a cell with an English captain, Henry Newton (also called Henri Normand). I believe he was connected with British Military Intelligence and he also had a brother, Alfred Newton, who was also a prisoner in another part of the gaol. I now believe they are both back in the UK. I was interrogated twice during that time about my helpers during my evasion period, but I can't have given them any satisfaction for I was moved to Dulag Luft on November 11th, 1943, before going on to Stalag IVB at Muhlberg on 17th November, where I remained a prisoner until being liberated by Russian troops on April 23rd, 1945."

Casualties May 13th/14th, 1943. Target Pilsen

83 Squadron 8 Group Lancaster W4981 OL/
Pilot. 535117 Sgt A.S.Renshaw Killed Lemsterland (Lemmer). C-9-240
Nav. 1393387 Sgt J.E.Lecomber Killed Bergen-op-Zoom, Holland. C-8-238
B/A. 1365974 Sgt H.R.Williamson Killed Lemsterland (Lemmer). C-9-241
W/OP. 47704 F/O S.W.Gould PoW. Stalag Luft 3, Sagan. 1325
F/E. 1083323 Sgt F.A.Worsnop Killed Lemsterland (Lemmer). C-9-239
A/G. 1333951 Sgt J.R.Stone Killed Lemsterland (Lemmer), Holland. C-8-237
A/G. 1310051 Sgt J.M.Hargreaves Killed Lemsterland (Lemmer). C-8-220

9 Squadron 5 Group Lancaster ED589 WS/O
Pilot. 1499180 Sgt G.H.Saxton Missing, Runnymede Memorial. 164
Nav. 149558 Sgt D.C.Ferris Missing, Runnymede Memorial 149
B/A. R/124685 Sgt W.R.McDonald Missing, Runnymede Memorial 184
W/OP. 571812 Sgt R.M.Morris Missing, Runnymede Memorial 159
F/E. 1211258 Sgt J.Reddish Missing, Runnymede Memorial 162
A/G. 954224 Sgt J.C.Owen Killed Flushing, Holland. 2
A/G. 1550979 Sgt J.Buntin Killed Flushing, Holland. 1

44 Squadron 5 Group Lancaster W4305 KM/G
Pilot. J/17622 F/O J.G.Olding PoW. Stalag Luft 3, Sagan. 220
Nav. 1391877 Sgt E.L.Orchard Killed Reichswald Forest. CG 24-H-3/6
B/A. 1391811 Sgt R.Dewey Killed Reichswald Forest, Germany. CG 24-H-3/6
W/OP. 1330788 Sgt N.E.Taylor Killed Reichswald Forest. CG 24-H-3/6
F/E. 1316715 Sgt P.Stephens Killed Reichswald Forest, Germany. 24-H-1
A/G. 1354608 Sgt D.Cram Killed Reichswald Forest, Germany. CG 24-H-3/6
A/G. R/124579 F/Sgt W.E.O'Halleron Killed Reichswald Forest. 24-H-2

44 Squadron 5 Group Lancaster W4110 KM/K
Pilot. 80131 F/O W.D.Rail Missing, Runnymede Memorial 129
Nav. 1392030 Sgt A.T.C.Bromwich Missing, Runnymede Memorial 143
B/A. 1315999 Sgt W.C.Digby Missing, Runnymede Memorial 147
W/OP. 1028039 Sgt R.C.Boardman Missing, Runnymede Memorial 143
F/E. 1000940 Sgt N.K.Underwood Missing, Runnymede Memorial 167
A/G. 1085432 Sgt R.S.A.Walker Missing, Runnymede Memorial 168
A/G. 1415510 Sgt G.Batty Missing, Runnymede Memorial 142

50 Squadron 5 Group Lancaster ED693 VN/
Pilot. J/17387 F/O W.G.Pickens PoW. Stalag 4B, Muhlberg(Elbe). 1196
Nav. 124701 F/Lt M.Hall PoW. Stalag Luft 3, Sagan. 1326
B/A. 127861 F/Lt T.Royds PoW. Stalag Luft 3, Sagan. 1413
W/OP. 1315443 W/O J.G.Hanby PoW. Stalag 357, Kopernikis. 1181
F/E. 923009 F/Sgt C.Taylor PoW. Stalag Luft 6, Heydekrug. 1201
A/G. 1323253 Sgt W.A.Roberts Killed Reichswald Forest, Germany. 15-F-11
A/G. R/114904 W/O W.B.Nicol Killed Reichswald Forest, Germany. 15-F-12

57 Squadron 5 Group Lancaster ED667 DX/
Aircraft shot down by enemy fighter at Tubbergen, 15 miles NW of Enschede, Holland.
Pilot. 142599 P/O J.B.M.Haye Evaded capture.
Nav. 755972 W/O J.A.Redgrave PoW. Stalag 357, Kopernikus. 231
B/A. 1383521 W/O C.F.Saville PoW. Stalag 4B, Muhleberg(Elbe).
W/OP. R/91346 W/O S.H.Allison PoW. Stalag 357, Kopernikus. 1230
F/E. 575598 F/Sgt R.S.J.Betteridge PoW. Stalag 357, Kopernikus. 1232
A/G. 1601131 Sgt R.F.R.Gulliver Killed Tubbergen (Albergen), Holland. JG 1/2
A/G. 1350714 Sgt R.F.Williams Killed Tubbergen (Albergen), Holland. JG 1/2

57 Squadron 5 Group Lancaster W4944 DX/
Pilot. J/17650 P/O M.E.Barker Killed Reichswald Forest, Germany. 15-E-16
Nav. 1239661 W/O J.D.Robertson PoW. Stalag 357, Kopernikus. 42745
B/A. 574356 Sgt W.M.Ewing Killed Rheinberg, Germany. CG 17-C-11/13
W/OP. 1330837 Sgt L.J.Beech Killed Reichswald Forest, Germany. 15-E-14
F/E. 578282 Sgt F.E.Lee Killed Reichswald Forest, Germany. 15-E-18
A/G. 2206621 Sgt F.Butterfield Killed Reichswald Forest, Germany. 15-E-17
A/G. R/133810 F/Sgt A.D.Monaghan Killed Reichswald Forest. 15-E-15

106 Squadron 5 Group Lancaster R5611 ZN/
Pilot. 1384397 Sgt F.J.Howell Killed Weerselo (Rossum), Holland. 3
Nav. R/115769 F/Sgt W.H.Hill Killed Weerselo (Rossum), Holland. 1
B/A. 1338277 Sgt E.G.R.Beacham Killed Weerselo (Rossum), Holland. 5
W/OP. 1294785 Sgt R.W.Littlefair Killed Weerselo (Rossum), Holland. 2
F/E. 1244614 Sgt D.Grey Killed Weerselo (Rossum), Holland. 7
A/G. 1320264 Sgt L.A.Dunmore Killed Weerselo (Rossum), Holland. 4

Mosquitoes Keep Berlin's Sirens Wailing

May 13th/14th, 1943.
On the same night as the Pilsen raid 8 aircraft, (7 Stirlings and 1 Lancaster) from 3 Group dropped 43 mines around the Frisians, without suffering any loss. 12 Mosquitoes also visited Berlin again, but this time lost one aircraft. The bodies of the crew were never found.

Casualties May 13th/14th, 1943. Target Berlin
139 Squadron 3 Group Mosquito DK302 XD/
Pilot. 109372 F/O S.Wilkinson Missing, Runnymede Memorial 130
Nav. 136523 P/O A.H.Eades Missing, Runnymede Memorial 131

May 15th/16th, 1943
Three Mosquitoes continued with their nuisance raids on Berlin. No aircraft was lost.

The Famous Dams Raid

May 16th/17th, 1943

In the Ruhr Battle by the heavy bomber squadrons of Bomber Command there was a nine day break, but one other major attack on the Ruhr was undertaken which was one of the most memorable missions of the war because of its exceptional technical and tactical qualities. Although far more detailed accounts of this raid have been written in the past, it is important to mention it briefly in the sequence of operations. It introduced the beginning of 5 Group's break away from the Pathfinder Force of 8 Group for target marking and its development as an independent group with its own target finding crews and techniques. Air Marshal Sir Arthur Harris had still clung on to his original idea of each Group being able to operate against targets with their own target finding and marking force so that major operations against German cities could take place simultaneously. In August 1942 he had been overruled, but now with a very much increased bomber strength he felt the time was opportune for the best brains and pilot skills in each of the Groups to work out their solutions to the problems confronting the bomber force and by so doing give each Group a pride of achievement which could produce greater co-operation and develop specialist tactics. However he was not in favour of the Dams operation, and in fact he strongly opposed it, as he was more intent on area bombing and he resented going back to pinpointing specific small objectives. The operation was allowed to go on after he had been overruled by his superiors on the Air Staff who decided that a raid on the Ruhr dams that supplied the Ruhr Valley with water and hydro electric power was well merited. They argued that by knocking out the Dams, the RAF bombers could not only flood the valley but also paralyse Germany's entire armaments industry. This assessment was later to be confirmed by Albert Speer, the Reich Minister of production. He wrote that had the mission entirely succeeded, or even been followed up, Speer said that it would have had a devastating effect on production in the German war industries.

The daring Dams Raid took place on 16th/17th May when 19 Lancasters from 617 Squadron in 5 Group took off led by Wing Commander Guy Gibson in an attack on the important Möhne, Eder, Sorpe and Schwelme Dams. This squadron with selected crews had trained in secret for six weeks in their Lancasters on low level bombing, which neccesitated flying at between 60 and 100 feet at exactly 240 mph and dropping bombs to within an accuracy of 40 yards from a precise point of release. Each was to be armed for the raid with the specially designed bouncing bomb developed by Barnes Wallis, (later knighted) the designer of the Wellington bomber.

It was twenty years after the war that the secret of the bouncing bomb was revealed, the bomb was not a sphere as had been suggested shortly after the raid. It was a cylinder, like an oil drum, five foot long and almost that in diameter, hung crossways in the partially open bomb bay of the Lancaster bomber and given a back spin of about 500 revs per minute by an auxiliary motor inside the modified bomb bay. This motor was started up ten minutes before the bomb was dropped. When the bomb hit the water, it skimmed like a stone, bouncing in shorter and shorter jumps until it hit the dam itself. Then, instead of rebounding away, the back spin forced it against the wall and made it crawl downwards until it exploded, on a hydrostatic fuse set for 30 feet below the surface, still clinging to the dam. The explosion, magnified by water pressure, would function like a small man made earthquake and breach the dam. It was a beautifully simple idea for positioning a bomb weighing almost 10,000 lbs to within a few feet. For some reason this type of bomb was not used by the RAF again, although there were many opportunities for its use.

The entire Dams operation, code named *Upkeep* was carried out at low level from start to finish to evade the fighters and also to maximise the effects in the bombing of the dams, which were all positioned in deep valleys among wooded hills which reached 1,000 .feet. All the dams were enormous piles of concrete, masonry and earth, 180 feet high and nearly as thick at the base. They were virtually impervious to conventional bombs. They were defended by anti aircraft guns postioned on the two towers on each side of the dam as well as along the dam shore line and in the water anti-torpedo nets were placed a short distance from the dam walls. It took four bombs before the first and most important Möhne dam broke, at 00.56 hours when Gibson in his Lancaster ED932 G for George signalled his Group Headquarters the pre arranged code-word *Nigger.* Two more bombs were needed to destroy the Eder dam, but the Sorpe and Schwelme survived the bombs that hit them. The Möhne reservoir alone contained nearly 140 million tons of water and the water released caused widespread flooding and disruption of rail and road communication as well as chaos to the vital Ruhr canal system. The headlines in the following day's newspapers told the story to the British people:- 'Growing devastation in the Ruhr,' 'Flood waters sweep into Kassel,' 'Damage to German War Industry,' 'Dam floods stretch for sixty miles'. The number of people estimated to have been drowned near the Möhne Dam alone was 1,294 and the town of Neheim-Husten, five miles downstream of the Mohne Dam, took the full impact. 859 people were killed in this community and by a quirk of fate 493 Ukranian forced labour workers died in their prison camp near the town. Post war research shows that if all the dams had been destroyed the raid would have had a major impact on the German war industry in the Ruhr valley. The squadron lost eight aircraft from the 17 which attacked, two of which had to return early, one because of being damaged by *Flak* and the other after the aircraft struck the sea a glancing blow and the bomb which projected from under the fuselage was torn off. From the aircrew in these lost planes, 47 were killed, 6 were missing and three became prisoners.

For his leadership in this unique operation and for his courage in attacking *Flak* positions at the Möhne Dam after having carried out his own unsuccessful bombing run, Wing Commander Gibson was awarded the Victoria Cross. Thirty-four other airmen who took part in this raid received decorations of various kinds.

In this raid *Flak* and accidents had cost Bomber Command fifty-six of its most highly trained aircrew, but the effect on the German war machine was not as great as the strategists in London had envisaged. Though both the Möhne and Eder reservoirs had virtually been emptied and flooding was extensive, the damage was repaired in three months. Experts summoned by Speer from all parts of Germany dried out the soaked electrical installations at the Möhne Dam's pumping station and where necessary replaced useless motors with others pre-emptorily removed from factories outside the Ruhr. The mission's most important advantage for the Allied cause, apart from the morale booster to the British people, was one that the planners had not forseen. Some 7,000 workers, German as well as foreign conscripts, had to be temporarily pulled back to the Ruhr from the Atlantic Wall, the fortifications that were still being built along the French coast in anticipation of an Allied invasion.

Wing Commander Gibson was to do only one more operation after the famous Dams raid, as a Master Bomber in a Mosquito aircraft in a raid on the 19th/20th September, 1944 on München-Gladbach from which he did not return. His aircraft crashed before crossing the Dutch coast. Reasons for its crash are unknown, it is more than likely the plane could have been damaged by *Flak* over the target area or developed engine trouble and was too low for a bale out. It certainly was not the result of a fighter attack for there were no German fighter claims against a twin engined plane that night. Wing Commander Guy Gibson, VC. DSO. DFC and Bar, 26 years of age, and his navigator Squadron Leader Warwick DFC were both killed and they are buried in a small cemetery at Steenbergen-en-Kruisland, north of Bergen-op-Zoom on the East Scheldt Estuary.

Casualties May 16th/17th, 1943. Target Ruhr Dams

617 Squadron 5 Group Lancaster ED937 AJ/Z
Hit by *Flak* at Emmerich, Germany, crashed at 02.35 hours at Klein Netterden, Germany.
Pilot. 62275 S/Ldr H.E.Maudsley DFC Killed Reichswald Forest. 5-C-3
Nav. J/9763 F/O R.A.Urquhart DFC Killed Reichswald Forest. CG 5-B-16/18
B/A. 143760 P/O M.J.D.Fuller Killed Reichswald Forest. CG 5-B-16/18
W/OP. R/93558 Sgt A.P.Cottam Killed Reichswald Forest, Germany. 5-C-1
F/E. 1003474 Sgt J.Marriott DFM Killed Reichswald Forest, Germany. 5-C-4
A/G. 120851 F/O W.J.Tytherleigh DFC Killed Reichswald. CG 5-B-16/18
A/G. 1503094 Sgt N.R.Burrows Killed Reichswald Forest, Germany. 5-C-2

617 Squadron 5 Group Lancaster ED910 AJ/C
Hit by *Flak* north of Hamm, Germany, crashed at 02.35 hours at Basellagerschen Wald, Germany.
Pilot. 141460 P/O W.Ottley DFC Killed Reichswald Forest, Germany. 31-F-11
Nav. 115775 F/O J.K.Barrett DFC Killed Reichswald Forest. 31-F-14

B/A. 1060657 F/Sgt T.B.Johnston Killed Reichswald Forest, Germany. 31-F-15
W/OP. 1172550 Sgt J.Guterman DFM Killed Reichswald Forest. 31-F-12
F/E. 568415 Sgt R.Marsden Killed Reichswald Forest, Germany. 31-F-10
A/G. 1332270 F/Sgt F.Tees PoW. Stalag Luft 6, Heydekrug. 42790
A/G. 1395453 Sgt H.J.Strange Killed Reichswald Forest, Germany. 31-F-13

617 Squadron 5 Group Lancaster ED927 AJ/E
Hit electricity cable S.E. of Emmerich, Germany, crashed at Heeren-
Herkern-Halden, Germany.
Pilot. A/401899 F/Lt R.N.G.Barlow DFC Killed Reichswald Forest. 5-C-9
Nav. 124881 F/O P.S.Burgess Killed Reichswald Forest, Germany. 5-C-7
B/A. 144205 P/O A.Gillespie DFM Killed Reichswald Forest, Germany. 5-C-10
W/OP. A/405224 F/O C.R.Williams DFC Killed Reichswald Forest. 5-C-11
F/E. 144618 Sgt S.L.Whillis Killed Reichswald Forest, Germany. 5-C-6
A/G. J/10212 F/O H.S.Glinz Killed Reichswald Forest, Germany. 5-C-8
A/G. 1338282 Sgt J.R.G.Liddell Killed Reichswald Forest, Germany. 5-C-5

617 Squadron 5 Group Lancaster ED934 AJ/K
Hit by *Flak* at Texel, Holland, crashed into the sea near Vlieland, Holland at
22.57 hours.
Pilot. J/17474 P/O V.W.Byers Missing, Runnymede Memorial 175
Nav. 128619 F/O J.H.Warner Missing, Runnymede Memorial 130
B/A. 144777 P/O A.N.Whitaker Missing, Runnymede Memorial 134
W/OP. 1025280 Sgt J.Wilkinson Missing, Runnymede Memorial 169
F/E. 575430 Sgt A.J.Taylor Missing, Runnymede Memorial 166
A/G. 1058757 Sgt C.M.Jarvie Missing, Runnymede Memorial 154
A/G. R/101749 Sgt J.McDowell Killed Bergen-op-Zoom, Holland. E-4-11

617 Squadron 5 Group Lancaster ED887 AJ/A
Hit by *Flak* on return flight, west of Amsterdam, Holland, crashed into N.Sea
off Holland.
Pilot. 72478 S/Ldr H.M.Young DFC Killed Flushing, Holland. 2-D-4
Nav. 1269445 Sgt C.W.Roberts Killed Flushing, Holland. 2-E-17
B/A. J/15309 F/O V.S.MacCausland Killed Flushing, Holland. 2-D-28
W/OP. 1377941 Sgt L.W.Nichols Killed Flushing, Holland. 2-E-28
F/E. 568924 Sgt D.T.Horsfall Killed Flushing, Holland. 2-D-5
A/G. 1317656 Sgt G.A.Yeo Killed Flushing, Holland. 2-D-2
A/G. 655431 Sgt W.Ibbotsen Killed Flushing, Holland. 2-D-6

617 Squadron 5 Group Lancaster ED865 AJ/S
Hit trees and crashed Gilze Rijen airfield at 01.53 hours.
Pilot. J/17115 P/O L.J.Burpee DFM Killed Bergen-op-Zoom, Holland. 23-B-3
Nav. 1299446 Sgt T.Jaye Killed Bergen-op-Zoom, Holland. CG 24-B-4/7
B/A. R/119416 Sgt J.L.Arthur Killed Bergen-op-Zoom, Holland. CG 24-B-4/7
W/OP. 142507 P/O L.G.Weller Killed Bergen-op-Zoom, Holland. 27-A-6
F/E. 573474 Sgt G.Pegler Killed Bergen-op-Zoom, Holland. CG 24-B-4/7
A/G. 1500540 Sgt C.A.Long Killed Bergen-op-Zoom, Holland. CG 24-B-4/7
A/G. R/93554 F/Sgt J.G.Brady Killed Bergen-op-Zoom, Holland. 23-A-1

617 Squadron 5 Group Lancaster ED864 AJ/B
Hit electricity cables near Dorsten airfield, on the outskirts of Borkem, Holland.
Pilot. 60283 F/Lt W.Astell DFC Killed Reichswald Forest, Germany. 21-D-13
Nav. J/18872 P/O F.A.Wile Killed Reichswald Forest, Germany. 21-D-15
B/A. 127817 F/O D.Hopkinson Killed Reichswald Forest. CG 21-D-16/18
W/OP. R/84377 Sgt A.Garshowitz Killed Reichswald Forest. CG 21-D-16/18
F/E. 635123 Sgt J.Kinnear Killed Reichswald Forest, Germany. 21-D-14
A/G. R/84377 Sgt F.A.Garbas Killed Reichswald Forest. CG 21-D-16/18
A/G. 1211045 Sgt R.Bolitho Killed Reichswald Forest, Germany. 21-E-1

617 Squadron 5 Group Lancaster ED925 AJ/M
Hit by *Flak* over coast, 3 crew injured and 1 killed. Crashed after dropping bomb on dam.
Pilot. 61281 F/Lt J.V.Hopgood DFC Killed Rheinberg, Germany. CG 17-E-2/6
Nav. J/10891 F/O K.Earnshaw Killed Rheinberg, Germany. CG 17-E-2/6
B/A. J/17696 P/O J.W.Fraser PoW. Stalag Luft 3, Sagan. 136
W/OP. 1181097 Sgt J.W.Minchin Killed Rheinberg, Germany. CG 17-E-2/6
F/E. 942037 Sgt C.Brennan Killed Rheinberg, Germany. CG 17-E-2/6
A/G. 141285 P/O G.H.F.Gregory DFM Killed Rheinberg. CG 17-E-2/6
A/G. A/403182 F/O A.F.Burcher DFM PoW. Stalag Luft 3, Sagan. 134

Minor operations

May 16th/17th, 1943

On the same night as the Dams raid, 54 aircraft from 3, 4 and 6 Groups were minelaying off the Frisians and around the Biscay ports laying 156 mines in various areas, while nuisance raids on Cologne, Düsseldorf, Münster and Berlin were made by 9 Mosquitoes. One minelaying aircraft was lost, no trace of the crew was found.

Casualties May 16th/17th, 1943. Minelaying (La Rochelle)

466 Squadron 4 Group Wellington HE386 HD/
Pilot. A/8686 F/Sgt J.W.Lawson Missing, Runnymede Memorial 193
Nav. A/414642 Sgt R.D.Carne Missing, Runnymede Memorial 192
B/A. A/413256 F/Sgt R.L.Robertson Missing, Runnymede Memorial 193
W/OP. 1270871 Sgt D.C.Robertson Missing, Runnymede Memorial 163
A/G. 1547702 Sgt G.E.Harmes Missing, Runnymede Memorial 152

May 17th/18th, 1943

Minor operations were continued when 6 aircraft from 3 Group went minelaying off La Pallice, one of which failed to return.

Three of the crew became prisoners while the remainder were killed when the aircraft ditched in the Loire Estuary. Three Mosquitoes were also despatched to Munich without any loss.

Casualties May 17th/18th, 1943. Minelaying

149 Squadron 3 Group Stirling BK701 OJ/G
Aircraft ditched in the Loire Estuary, France after being hit by *Flak* and sank immediately. Nav, B/A., F/E. and R/G failed to get out after hatch jammed.
Pilot. 144186 P/O J.E.Hill PoW. Stalag Luft 3, Sagan. 1345
Nav. 1482431 Sgt S.Biddulph Missing, Runnymede Memorial 142
B/A. 1482187 Sgt J.E.Boyes Killed St Hilaire-de-Riez, France, 1
W/OP. 1330592 F/Sgt J.A.Boland PoW. Stalag 357, Kopernikus. 1233
F/E. 1021395 Sgt T.Smith Killed St Gilles-sur-Vie, France. JG 1
A/G. 1430291 F/Sgt S.R.Shankster PoW. Stalag Luft 6, Heydekrug. 1270
A/G. 531018 Sgt C.C.D.Scotney Missing, Runnymede Memorial 164

May 18th/19th, 1943

Minelaying was the main operation when thirteen Lancasters from 1 Group and four Wellingtons from 6 Group were in the Brest and Biscay areas, where 67 mines were laid. No aircraft was lost.

May 19th/20th, 1943

Six Mosquitoes flew to Berlin, but only two of them managed to drop their bomb loads.

May 20th/21st, 1943

Eighty mines were dropped in the southern area of the Bay of Biscay by 23 Lancasters and Stirlings from 1 and 3 Groups. No aircraft was lost. On the same night three Mosquitoes continued to keep the air raid sirens sounding in Berlin. All aircraft returned safely.

Minelaying

21st/22nd May, 1943

99 aircraft consisting of 64 Wellingtons, 31 Stirlings and 4 Lancasters from 1, 3 and 6 Groups carried out extensive minelaying in three areas, the Frisians, La Pallice and the River Gironde, where 263 mines were dropped. Four aircraft failed to return from these operations, no trace of the 22 aircrew was found.

One Wellington, HE177, captained by Flight Sergeant A. J. Simpson from 428 Squadron, 6 Group, crashed while attempting to land on return to its home base, killing four Canadians of the crew and seriously injuring the remaining crew member, rear gunner Sergeant A. J. Howes.

The crew of another Wellington, HE917 piloted by Warrant Officer A. Harrison, returning from this minelaying raid were instrumental in saving some other aircrew. After they had planted their mines, the pilot spotted an SOS being flashed by a red Aldis lamp and later by a white light. He circled the position and saw in the darkness a round object with a dark centre from which a red star Verey Light was fired. He instructed his wireless operator to report the position to base by radio. On landing back at base the crew were told that the reported object had been a dinghy from which a crew was rescued by the Air Sea Rescue Services. No Bomber Command aircraft had been reported ditching that night, so the rescued crew could have come from either Coastal, Training Commands or were on Special Operations.

Casualties May 21st/22nd, 1943. Minelaying

149 Squadron 3 Group Stirling BF510 OJ/P
Pilot. 1435137 Sgt C.E.Tomlin Missing, Runnymede Memorial. 167
Nav. 1577790 Sgt A.James Missing, Runnymede Memorial 154
B/A. 1575168 Sgt W.H.A.Shelvington Missing, Runnymede Memorial 164
W/OP. 1215546 Sgt E.W.Hall Missing, Runnymede Memorial 152
F/E. 1133327 Sgt A.Camps Missing, Runnymede Memorial 144
A/G. 1094187 Sgt G.T.Cook Missing, Runnymede Memorial 146
A/G. 1565412 Sgt J.S.Warburton Missing, Runnymede Memorial 168

431 Squadron 4 Group Wellington HE200 HD/P
Pilot. 1385277 Sgt R.A.Buck Missing, Runnymede Memorial 144
Nav. 1239188 Sgt R.A.Williams Missing, Runnymede Memorial 170
B/A. 1389188 Sgt H.C.Williams Missing, Runnymede Memorial 170
W/OP. 1334932 Sgt A.G.McManus Missing, Runnymede Memorial 158
A/G. 1339496 Sgt A.J.Marshall Missing, Runnymede Memorial 158

466 Squadron 4 Group Wellington HZ257 SE/
Pilot. A/409306 F/Sgt E.T.Horner Missing, Runnymede Memorial 193
Nav. A/24818 F/Sgt A.D.M.Ross Missing, Runnymede Memorial 193
B/A. 1386890 Sgt A.F.Lane Missing, Runnymede Memorial 156
W/OP. A/409727 F/Sgt O.P.Morton Missing, Runnymede Memorial 193
A/G. A/412892 F/Sgt T.J.Brassel Missing, Runnymede Memorial. 192

428 Squadron 4 Group Wellington HE899 NA/B
Pilot. R/124246 F/Sgt C.N.Magnusson Missing, Runnymede Memorial 185
Nav. R/144189 F/Sgt W.C.Sutton Missing, Runnymede Memorial 185
B/A. R/135031 F/Sgt P.H.Brand Missing, Runnymede Memorial 181
W/OP. R/120914 F/Sgt R.Hagan Missing, Runnymede Memorial 182
A/G. R/105371 F/Sgt E.K.Edwards Missing, Runnymede Memorial 181

428 Squadron 6 Group Wellington HE177 NA/G
Aircraft crashed at Eastmoor after returning from operations.
Pilot. R/114570 F/Sgt A.J.Simpson Killed Dishforth, Yorkshire. 74
Nav. R/120897 F/Sgt S.D.Frewen Killed Dishforth, Yorkshire. 72
B/A. J/20854 F/O A.B.Douglas Killed Dishforth. Yorkshire. 71
W/OP. R/119705 F/Sgt A.J.Grenon Killed Dishforth. Yorkshire. 73
A/G. R/75311 Sgt A.J.Howes Seriously Injured.

Sirens Wail Again In Berlin

May 21st/22nd, 1943
Four Mosquitoes kept up with their niggling attacks on
Germany's capital city on the same night, without suffering any
loss.

Back to the Ruhr

It was back again with a vengenace to Happy Valley, the place that aircrew came to hate and fear because of the ferocity of the anti aircraft fire and night fighter defences, especially in those Ruhr towns, which appeared to be ringed by a wall of *Flak* and illuminated by thousands of searchlights. To operate there trip after trip, bomb run after bomb run, struggling to avoid the urge to veer away from such fierce ground opposition and being pounced upon from the air above by enemy night fighters required nerves of steel. No flier looking back on those dreadful times can truthfully say that he was not frightened rigid on scores of occasions when operating in this area of Germany.

Compounding these problems was also the fear of mid-air collisions because of the now concentrated large stream of bombers over the target area in such a realtively short period of time and the sheer terror of seeing another bomber overhead with its bomb doors open ready to shed its load. The poor weather conditions back at the home stations, which were often covered with a low cloud base or with the early morning fog so prevalent in bases in East Anglia and the Vale of York also made landing hazardous for the battle weary crews on their return. To bomber crews at this period of the war the thoughts uppermost in their mind was the intensity of the Battle of the Ruhr and the toll it was taking on crews.

Dortmund

May 23rd/24th, 1943

Dortmund was detailed for a major force of 826 aircraft when 343 Lancasters, 199 Halifaxes, 151 Wellingtons, 120 Stirlings and 13 Mosquitoes went in on the attack. 119 of these aircraft were from 8 Group Pathfinders.

The order for the battle was that the best 250 crews from all Groups should be in the first wave after the target was marked.

They were instructed to bomb the TIs and if there were none visible, they were to orbit the target and come in again on another bomb run when another salvo of TIs had been dropped. It was to be Dortmund's last raid for a year, but one that it would not forget. 1,100.3 tons of high explosive and 86,500 incendiaries rained down on the city. The clear weather conditions were perfect for the Pathfinders and they marked the target very accurately according to plan with 159 two hundred and fifty pound target indicators. Large areas of the city were devastated, nearly 2,000 buildings were destroyed and Hoesch, the biggest steel works in Germany was put out of action. 595 people were killed and 1,275 injured. The loss to the force was 38 aircraft, a 4.6% loss rate and from the 257 aircrew manning these bombers, 144 were killed, 44 were missing and 69 became prisoners.

Crashed On Return

51 Squadron, flying Halifaxes and based at Snaith, Yorkshire had very heavy losses on this particular night, for as well as the four planes missing a further two crashed in the UK. Halifax JB792 crashed at Woolfox Lodge with hydraulics failure and Halifax HR853 made a forced landing with starboard outer engine failure, at Highfield Farm on the Doncaster to Selby road.

Bomb Aimer Flies Back

Wellington, HE198 of 431 Squadron captained by Flight Lieutenant C. H. Hall, bombed the target from a height of 17,000 feet, but shortly afterwards was coned by searchlights over the target area and repeatedly hit by *Flak*. The rear gunner reported to the pilot that he believed the fuselage was on fire near his turret. By steep dives the pilot tried his best to evade the searchlight beams but was unsuccessful for the searchlights held grimly on, illuminating the bomber as a sitting target for any lurking fighters. There must have been some confusion on board for the pilot baled out, as did the rear gunner but whether the pilot gave the bale out order is not clear, but as the rear gunner had baled out as well, it appears that some sort of order must have been given. The pilot, however, should have been the last to leave the aircraft, when all the crew had got safely away. The bomb aimer, an English Sergeant S. N Sloan, managed to ease himself into the pilot's, seat took control and was able to shake off the searchlights. Now with only two other members of the crew left on board, Flying Officer J. B. G. Bailey, the wireless operator, and the navigator, (Sergeant G. C. W. Parslow), Sergeant Sloan miraculously flew the plane back to England, although not to his own home base. When crossing the English coast he was unable to get contact with the ground control so he fired a red Verey cartridge and was given a green Aldis lamp permission to land. He made a good and safe landing at Cranwell. For his outstanding airmanship he was given an immediate award of the Conspicuous Gallantry Medal, commissioned and sent on a pilot's course. The other two crew members received the DFC and DFM, but unfortunately they, did not survive the war for they were lost on the Krefeld raid on the night of 21st/22nd June, 1943.

Wellington HE995 of 426 Squadron, captained by Sergeant S. Gaunt, had bombed the target at 01.30 hours from a height of 16,000 feet, but was coned by searchlights west of the Dortmund target area. The predicted *Flak* which followed practically shot away the undercarriage and the front turret caught fire. The pilot ordered the crew to bale out and needing no second invitation the rear gunner, Canadian Sergeant L. C McCracken, turned his turret to the beam and was out, while the other Canadian, bomb aimer Sergeant L. R. Fadden, had lifted the front floor escape hatch and had also baled out. The action of opening the front hatch and the resultant draught of air extinguished the fire so the captain quickly countermanded the bale out order and the remaining crew stayed on board. They were not yet out of danger, for by now the bomber was being shadowed by an Me 110 night fighter, but the corkscrewing manoeuvres of the pilot and the aid of the navigator, Sergeant A. T. McCormick, who stood in the astro dome to help and direct his pilot, they eluded the intending attacker, east of Rotterdam. Finally the bomber with its three man crew managed to make it back to England and crash landed at Martlesham Heath. The two crew who correctly baled out, spent the next two years as prisoners of war.

Lancaster S for Sugar of 44 (Rhodesia) Squadron.

x BI LQ-R of 405 (RCAF) Squadron.

The ungainly looking Stirling ready to be bombed up.

Although dated, Wellingtons were still operational with Bomber Command in 1

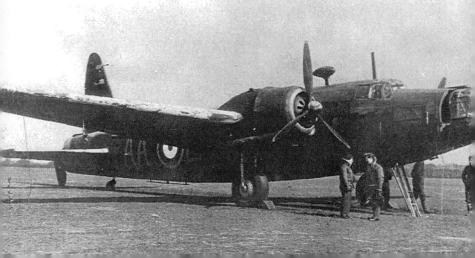

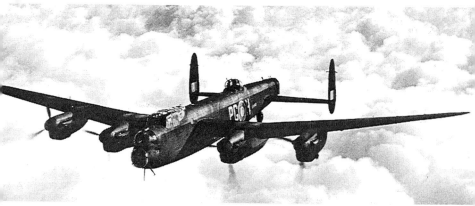

Lancaster PG-H of 619 Squadron based at Woodhall Spa in April 1943.

Lancasters of 207 Squadron, 5 Group.

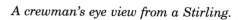

A crewman's eye view from a Stirling.

The cockpit of a Stirling.

A bomber pilot, as viewed from the tunnel leading to the nose of the aircraft.

The instruments and controls of a Halifax.

...lifax is waved off on its way to the Schneider works at Le Creusot on June 19th.

...uthor and his crew in front of JB797 of 405
...ron. L-R. Sgt J A Phillips, Sgt W King, Sgt V
...t, Sgt R A Andrews, Sgt H McLean, Sgt L Kohnke,
...t G Mainprie (kneeling).

The author

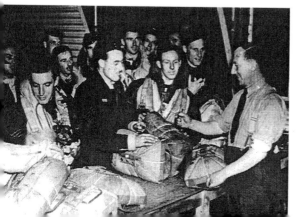

Issuing parachutes, 78
Squadron Linton on Ouse.

A Bf110G4b/R3 with Lichtenstein C1 and SN2 radar aerials.

The tail of Oblt Wilhelm Johnen's Bf110 showing tally of seventeen victories.

A Bf110G4a/R1 of IV/NJG3 with Lichtenstein BC radar aerials.

Ju88R1 of
NJG3 was
ed by its crew
yce in
land allowing
RAF to learn
secrets of the
tenstein BC
r.

he Schräge Musik
pward firing
rrangement of cannons
tted to a Ju88 of
JG102.

W190 day fighter modified to the night fighter rôle with I/NJGr10.

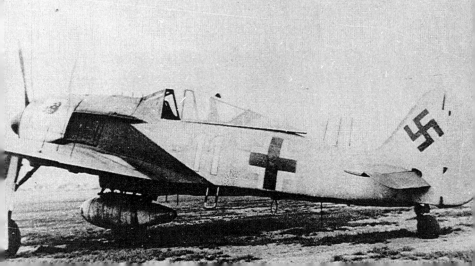

Major Martin Drews was beginning his career in 1943 , but went on to destroy 49 bombers.

Hauptman August Geiger s down 54 bombers before he killed in September 1943.

Below left. Herman Goerin; congratulates some of his p

Below. Major Heinrich Pri. Sayn-Wittgenstein shot dou bombers before he was kille January 1944.

George Barclay was the rear gunner in Lancaster ED620 of 49 Squadron which was shot down at Stadil in Denmark on April 21st, 1943.

45 years later he returned to the same spot to find it little changed.

The rear turret of Halifax JB873 from 78 Squadron after being shot down by Leutnant Schnaufer on May 13th/14th, 1943. The gunner baled out safely.

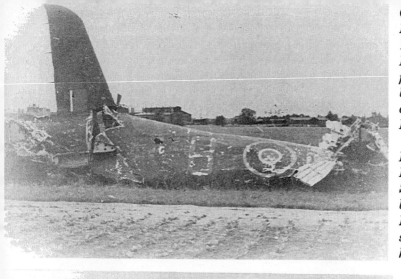

On the night
May 25th/26
1943, Major
Ehle shot do
four of the
bombers
attacking
Dusseldorf.

Left. Stirling
EF361 of 7
Squadron,
brought down
Major Ehle.
seven crew w
killed.

Left. Stirling
EH887 of 218
Squadron,
another of M
Ehle's victim.
Again all sev
crew were kil

Wellington
HE590 of 42
Squadron a
fell on May
25th/26th,
time to the
guns of Obl
Telge. All se
crew were
killed.

...x HR839 of 51 Squadron was shot down on the night of June 28th/29th, 1943 ...tnant Franz when attacking Cologne. Six were killed, one was captured and the ...pilot evaded successfully.

...ster ED781 of 57 Squadron was shot down on the night of June 24th/25th, 1943 ...rleutnant Telge when attacking Wuppertal. Six crew were killed and one ...ed.

Halifax JB793 of 419 Squadron, lost on the night of May 29th/30th, was anot
Oberleutnant Telge's victims. Three of the seven crew escaped with their lives.

Glad to be back. During the period covered by this book 22,893 sorties were flou
47,657 tons of bombs dropped. 1,048 aircraft were lost, a loss rate of 4.6%

Sergeant Lancaster's Lucky Escape

One of the Stirling crews from 214 Squadron based at Chedburgh was captained by Flight Lieutenant E. V. Miller DFC. The wireless operator on the crew was Sergeant Bert Lancashire and he vividly recalls an incident on this Dortmund operation.

It was his duty as a wireless operator to go down to the tail of the aircraft as the bombing run was made, to make sure that the photoflash was properly and safely released at a given time after the bomb load had been released, so that an accurate camera picture could be taken to plot the bomb hits. This meant a kind of obstacle race in the dark, in a pitching and bucking aircraft and without oxygen, until a connection for oxygen could be made at the point near the flare 'chute position, where there was a similar point for the intercom. The journey not only meant squeezing through or past all kinds of metal projections but also in Bert's aircraft, invariably a pile of frozen vomit which lay below the mid upper gunner's turret, because their gunner, poor chap, was always ill during a flight. The other obstacle, also unpleasant, especially if the pilot threw the bomber around in a corkscrew evasion, was the free rolling Elsan chemical toilet, which more often than not came adrift from its moorings and showered its contents on any unsuspecting crew member who happened to be around the main fuselage at the time. Such were some of the unseen hazards and rarely mentioned non lethal hazards with which aircrew had to cope whilst beneath and all around them all hell was unleashed.

On this particular Dortmund trip, Bert was just connecting his oxygen tube after checking the flash was in position and that it was attached to its static line, when suddenly the aircraft floor fell from below his feet, leaving him floating in the air, like some modern astronaut in training. However his flotation was brief, for he hit the floor of the bomb bay steps with some force. He doesn't remember much immediately after that bang, but he slowly recovered consciousness and saw the million candle power photo flash rolling against him on the floor. This horrific sight quickly brought Bert back to normality. He grabbed the photoflash with both hands and rammed it safely down the 'chute and out into the night. A flash of such intensity going off in the plane would have been a disaster. This photoflash had broken free of the static line releasing the striker, but luckily this must have been after it hit the floor and bent the aladdin type fuse, where it joined the main casing, thus stopping the fuse from functioning. At that time Bert's only thought was to get the flash out of the aircraft and because of the embarassment and ragging he had taken from the crew on an earlier trip when he raised a false alarm about an attacking fighter, he decided to keep the matter of the rolling photoflash on the Dortmund trip to himself. To this day, the rest of his crew are completely ignorant of what a lucky escape they had on that operation, which certainly would have been their last, had the flash gone off.

Sole Survivor

Flight engineer R/76929 Sergeant F. A. Dunn was aboard Halifax JB862 from 419 Squadron, which was captained by R/107004 Warrant Officer A. S. Green. He was extremely fortunate to be the only survivor from the crew after the aircraft crashed. He became a prisoner of war and in his post war interrogation, he describes the events of that fateful night and his miraculous escape.

"Forty minutes before we reached the target, the starboard outer engine emitted a long blue flame and minutes later the same engine's cylinder head and oil temperature soared off the scale and the engine had to be feathered. We continued towards the target and bombed on time at 01.10 hours, but the photoflash failed to release and in spite of the wireless operator, Sergeant M. A. Harrison's, efforts it could not be shaken free. A moment or two later the aircraft was coned at 18,000 feet by a large group of searchlights and subjected to very heavy *Flak*. In his efforts to escape the lights, the skipper took the plane down to 5,000 feet before finally clearing the glare from the lights and *Flak* barrage. It was only a temporary respite, for a single light picked the bomber up once more and a stream of tracer from a night fighter hit the bomber's port inner engine, which burst into flames. By now the bomber was down to 2,000 feet and was obviously severely damaged. The captain ordered through the intercom an immediate bale out, but by this time only three members of the crew were on intercom, the pilot, the mid upper gunner, Sergeant Prieur, who was standing by the pilot holding the pilot's chest parachute, and myself. I made an effort to get back down the fuselage with a fire extinguisher, intending to throw out the lethal photoflash and attempt to put out the fire. I have blurred recollection of the next chain of events, but do remember trying to get up after an explosion occured inside the plane and which must have knocked me out, then regaining consciousness amid the aircraft wreckage on the ground and crawling out of a hole in the fuselage, which was red hot and in flames, with ammunition popping about all over the place. The Germans picked me up later and told me that my six crew members' bodies had been recovered fom the wreckage. I had a miraculous escape and suffered no damage except for slight injuries and my broken watch which had stopped at 01.40 hours."

The Dortmund operation was the most successful attack in the heavy bombing campaign to date and after the raid Air Chief Marshal Sir Arthur Harris sent the following signal out to all his operational squadrons.

"In 1939 Goering promised that not a single enemy bomb would reach the Ruhr. Congratulations on having delivered the first 100,000 tons of bombs on Germany to refute him."

Casualties May 23rd/24th, 1943. Target Dortmund

35 Squadron 8 Group Halifax DT488 TL/Q
Pilot. A/416571 F/O A.H.Harvey Killed Reichswald Forest, Germany. 25-D-9
Nav. 130699 F/O D.A.Evans Killed Reichswald Forest, Germany. 25-C-17
B/A. 568210 Sgt S.Groom Killed Reichswald Forest, Germany. 25-D-6
W/OP. 1087702 Sgt J.R.Johnson Killed Reichswald Forest, Germany. 25-D-7
F/E. 570643 Sgt C.R.Shields Killed Reichswald Forest, Germany. 25-D-8
A/G. 1511162 Sgt R.G.Pritchard Killed Reichswald Forest, Germany. 25-D-10
A/G. 526109 F/Sgt W.R.Fairey PoW. Stalag 357, Kopernikus. 132

405 Squadron 8 Group Halifax JB896 LQ/C
Pilot. R/122787 W/O J.Martin Missing, Runnymede Memorial 179
Nav. J/13416 F/O F.P.Harrison Missing, Runnymede Memorial 173
B/A. 129643 F/O M.Gluck Missing, Runnymede Memorial 124
W/OP. R/107703 W/O G.Bancescu Missing, Runnymede Memorial 179
F/E. 574982 Sgt S.McGlory Missing, Runnymede Memorial 157
A/G. R/112668 F/Sgt R.McRae Missing, Runnymede Memorial 185
A/G. R/124657 F/Sgt R.W.Jennings Missing, Runnymede Memorial 182

12 Squadron 1 Group Lancaster W4861 PH/M
Pilot. 124550 F/O W.N.Mounsey Killed Markelo, Holland. 4-B-7
Nav. 130596 F/O W.R.Whitaker Killed Markelo, Holland. 4-B-10
B/A. 1000033 F/Sgt A.Dews PoW. Stalag Luft 6, Heydekrug. 117
W/OP. 1313750 Sgt R.S.G.Miller Killed Markelo, Holland. 4-B-9

F/E. 1004252 F/Sgt W.B.Jowett PoW. Stalag 357, Kopernikus. 183
A/G. 539691 Sgt K.G.Legg Killed Markelo, Holland. 4-B-8
A/G. 1181213 Sgt H.Pierpoint Killed Markelo, Holland. 4-B-6

101 Squadron 1 Group Lancaster W4919 SR/A
Pilot. A/411906 F/Sgt J.H.T.Hayes Killed Jonkerbos, Nolland. 16-C-1
Nav. 1361100 Sgt J.Park Killed Jonkerbos, Holland. CG 16-C-4/7
B/A. 1319738 Sgt P.G.Eames Killed Jonkerbos, Holland. CG 16-C-4/7
W/OP. 1334798 Sgt J.W.C.Evans Killed Jonkerbos, Holland. CG 16-C-4/7
F/E. 1116625 Sgt W.R.Cook Killed Jonkerbos, Holland. CG 16-C-4/7
A/G. R/175992 Sgt O.H.Sibson Killed Jonkerbos, Holland. 16-C-2
A/G. R/155648 F/Sgt L.G.Smith Killed Jonkerbos, Holland. 16-C-3

460 Squadron 1 Group Lancaster W4986 UV/E
Pilot. A/408533 W/O G.L.Stevens PoW. Stalag 357, Kopernikus. 238
Nav. A/411546 W/O D.L.Stubbs PoW. Stalag 357, Kopernikus. 259
B/A. A/405680 F/Sgt A.J.Harris PoW. Stalag 4B, Muhlberg(Elbe). 222477
W/OP. 1200597 F/Sgt E.L.Jones PoW. Stalag 357, Kopernikus. 13
F/E. 1039089 F/Sgt J.C.Waldron PoW. Stalag 357, Kopernikus. 274
A/G. A/409135 W/O T.S.Easton PoW. Stalag 357, Kopernikus. 128
A/G. A/403880 W/O P.H.Sara PoW. Stalag 357, Kopernikus. 242

460 Squadron 1 Group Lancaster W4984 UV/J
Aircraft shot down by fighter over Holland.
Pilot. A/405966 F/Sgt B.M.T.Davis Killed Schoonebeek, Holland. 3-1-752
Nav. A/412411 F/Sgt K.D.Dyce Killed Schoonebeek, Holland. 3-1-753
B/A. A/405849 F/Sgt C.Goldthorpe PoW. Stalag 357, Kopernikus. 1479
W/OP. A/411839 F/Sgt J.S.Biffen Killed Schoonebeek, Holland. 3-1-748
F/E. 1040539 Sgt E.Rowlands Killed Schoonebeek, Holland. 3-1-751
A/G. A/421066 F/Sgt C.S.Wright Killed Schoonebeek, Holland. 3-1-749
A/G. R/152317 F/Sgt F.W.Ralph Killed Schoonebeek, Holland. 3-1-750

166 Squadron 1 Group Wellington HE486 AS/L
Pilot. 116785 F/O A.E.Steward Killed Amsterdam, Holland. CG 69-C-15
Nav. 67652 F/Lt J.G.Eldridge DFC* Killed Amsterdam, Holland. CG 69-C-15
B/A. 1337841 Sgt J.H.Griffiths Killed Amsterdam, Holland. CG 69-C-15
W/OP. 146941 P/O S.B.Jobes Killed Amsterdam, Holland. CG 69-C-15
A/G. 146937 Sgt J.F.Saunders Killed Amsterdam, Holland. CG 69-C-15

166 Squadron 1 Group Wellington HE290 AS/J
Pilot. 656599 Sgt E.S.Morris Killed Haaksbergen, Holland. 4-3-17
Nav. 1483381 Sgt H.B.Thompson Killed Haaksbergen, Holland. 4-3-19
B/A. 1238809 Sgt F.V.G.Alloway Killed Haaksbergen, Holland. 4-3-15
W/OP. 1074636 Sgt R.F.Williamson Killed Haaksbergen, Holland. 4-3-18
A/G. R/138281 Sgt J.R.Stewart Killed Haaksbergen, Holland. 4-3-16

166 Squadron 1 Group Wellington HE655 AS/D
Pilot. 1333598 Sgt C.W.H.Westwood Killed Eindhoven(Woensel). JJB-60
Nav. 1450256 Sgt A.Benson Killed Eindhoven(Woensel), Holland. JJB-58
B/A. 574056 Sgt H.W.Fields Killed Eindhoven(Woensel), Holland. JJB-62
W/OP. 1381903 Sgt W.P.Baxter Killed Eindhoven(Woensel), Holland. JJB-59
A/G. 1375964 Sgt T.W.Shadgett Killed Eindhoven(Woensel), Holland. JJB-61

199 Squadron 1 Group Wellington HZ582 EX/
Pilot. 1331903 Sgt H.W.Austin Killed Flushing, Holland. 4-F-13
(Still trying to evade up to 19/6/43.)
Nav. A/420959 Sgt D.R.Keevers PoW. Stalag 357 Kopernikus, Germany 185
B/A. 958746 F/Sgt J.P.E.Last PoW. Stalag 9B Wegschelde, Germany. 42779
W/OP. 1212641 Sgt A.Herbert Killed Flushing, Holland. 4-F-11
A/G. R/99818 W/O R.M.Costello Killed Flushing, Holland. 4-F-12

300 Squadron 1 Group Wellington HZ374 BH/K
Pilot. P/1233 F/O H.Piatkowski Killed Reichswald Forest. CG 5-C-12/15
Nav. P/2017 F/O W.Jankowski Killed Reichswald Forest. CG 5-C-12/15
B/A. P/0967 F/O H.Lewicki Killed Reichswald Forest, Germany. CG 5-C-12/15
W/OP. P/783028 Sgt C.Ratajczyk Killed Reichswald Forest. CG 5-C-12/15
A/G. P/703387 Sgt E.Kulikowski Killed Reichswald Forest. CG 5-C-12/15

15 Squadron 3 Group Stirling BF482 LS/R
Aircraft crashed at Dortmund, Germany.
Pilot. J/17660 P/O W.Q.Johnson Killed Reichswald Forest, Germany. 3-D-5
2/Pilot. 658288 F/Sgt C.F.Ryall PoW. Stalag 357, Kopernikus. 241
Nav. J/13423 F/O H.N.Lyons Missing, Runnymede Memorial 174
B/A. 1318786 Sgt M.J.Flaherty Missing, Runnymede Memorial 149
W/OP. 656048 F/Sgt S.D.Hirst PoW. Stalag 357, Kopernikus. 169
F/E. 577724 Sgt H.C.C.Waite Missing, Runnymede Memorial 168
A/G. R/130123 Sgt T.Leonard PoW. Stalag Luft 6, Heydekrug.
A/G. 1336568 W/O N.R.Elford PoW. Stalag Luft 6, Heydekrug. 453

75 Squadron 3 Group Stirling BK783 AA/Q
Aircraft crashed at Beesd, Holland.
Pilot. NZ/415640 Sgt S.M.Tietjens Killed Beesd, Holland. CG 1/2
Nav. NZ/421342 Sgt G.W.Turnbull Killed Beesd, Holland. CG 1/2
B/A. NZ/417603 Sgt F.L.J.Joblin Killed Beesd, Holland. CG 1/2
W/OP. 1077692 Sgt R.Bell Killed Beesd, Holland. CG 1/2
F/E. 1391814 Sgt S.J.Wayman Killed Beesd, Holland. CG 1/2
A/G. 1809725 Sgt D.G.A.Storey Killed Beesd, Holland. CG 1/2
A/G. 1235008 Sgt L.R.Vale PoW. Stalag 357, Kopernikus. 272

214 Squadron 3 Group Stirling BF528 BU/L
Aircraft crashed at München-Gladbach, Germany.
Pilot. NZ/416581 Sgt J.K.Wilkins Killed Rheinberg, Germany. 2-G-20
Nav. NZ/417267 W/O W.S.Clifton-Mogg PoW. Stalag 357, Kopernikus. 1236
B/A. 1699808 F/Sgt W.A.Leslie PoW. Stalag 357, Kopernikus. 1253
W/OP. 1322558 Sgt L.G.Freeman Killed Rheinberg, Germany. 2-G-19
F/E. NZ/403765 W/O A.Mason PoW. Stalag 357, Kopernikus. 1258
A/G. 1353578 F/Sgt E.T.Hutchinson PoW. Stalag Luft 1, Barth Vogelsang.
A/G. 1064528 F/Sgt B.A.Kennedy PoW. Stalag 357, Kopernikus. 1252

214 Squadron 3 Group Stirling BF478 BU/G
Aircraft crashed in the North Sea near Waddenzee, Holland.
Pilot. J/18037 P/O J.W.Evans Missing, Runnymede Memorial 175
Nav. 1330847 Sgt Z.Goldfinger Missing, Runnymede Memorial 150
B/A. 968999 F/Sgt R.Child Missing, Runnymede Memorial 145
W/OP. 1060035 F/Sgt H.Ward Missing, Runnymede Memorial 139

F/E. 1380192 Sgt V.N.Walker Missing, Runnymede Memorial 168
A/G. 1575811 Sgt R.V.Street Killed Schiermonnikoog, Holland. 101
A/G. 646478 Sgt E.D.Ager Missing, Runnymede Memorial 140

214 Squadron 3 Group Stirling MZ/261 BU/T
Aircraft crashed at Unna, Germany.
Pilot. A/415126 F/Sgt J.J.Egan Killed Reichswald Forest, Germany. 3-C-15
Nav. 129581 F/O P.H.Liddle Killed Reichswald Forest, Germany. 3-D-17
B/A. 1393222 Sgt D.E.Dealford Killed Reichswald Forest, Germany. 3-C-18
W/OP. 1294190 Sgt L.Martin Killed Reichswald Forest, Germany. 3-C-16
F/E. 1231672 Sgt F.J.North Killed Reichswald Forest, Germany. 3-D-1
A/G. 641651 Sgt V.H.Archer Killed Reichswald Forest, Germany. 3-D-2
A/G. 1107057 Sgt J.Dodd Killed Reichswald Forest, Germany. 3-D-18

218 Squadron 3 Group Stirling BK706 HA/Y
Aircraft crashed at Dortmund, Germany.
Pilot. 124870 F/O J.Phillips Missing, Runnymede Memorial 128
Nav. 1551786 Sgt G.S.Wishart Killed Reichswald Forest, Germany. 3-D-4
B/A. 1320174 Sgt D.A.F.Paveley Missing, Runnymede Memorial 161
W/OP. 1385246 Sgt W.G.Kirby Missing, Runnymede Memorial 156
F/E. 975397 Sgt M.L.S.Drabble Missing, Runnymede Memorial 148
A/G. R/155623 Sgt G.B.Leadbeater Missing, Runnymede Memorial 186
A/G. 1451681 Sgt C.E.Bryant Killed Reichswald Forest, Germany. 3-D-7

10 Squadron 4 Group Halifax DT789 ZA/B
Pilot. 1317618 Sgt J.Rees Killed Kiel, Germany.Buried 8/7/43. 1-H-18
Nav. 1336707 F/Sgt S.G.Reed PoW. Stalag 357, Kopernikus. 1030
B/A. 1393160 Sgt S.J.Gaywood Missing, Runnymede Memorial 150
W/OP. 1218839 Sgt D.Birkhead Missing, Runnymede Memorial 142
F/E. 1238185 Sgt W.E.Oliver Missing, Runnymede Memorial 160
A/G. 1296897 Sgt E.G.David Missing, Runnymede Memorial 147
A/G. 1038623 Sgt F.W.Farnell Missing, Runnymede Memorial 149

10 Squadron 4 Group Halifax HR696 ZA/G
Pilot. 146336 P/O J.B.Denton Killed Reichswald Forest, Germany. 5-D-7
2/Pilot. 1343173 Sgt I.B.Inglis Killed Reichswald Forest, Germany. 5-D-2
Nav. 1504640 Sgt N.P.Plenderleith Killed Reichswald Forest, Germany. 5-D-5
B/A. 146446 P/O D.H.G.Adams Killed Reichswald Forest, Germany. 5-D-4
W/OP. 1331835 Sgt P.Grimwood Killed Reichswald Forest, Germany. 5-D-3
F/E. 643364 F/Sgt M.Harrison Killed Reichswald Forest, Germany. 5-D-1
A/G. 1578208 Sgt A.E.Wallis Killed Reichswald Forest, Germany. 5-D-6
A/G. 658406 Sgt G.H.Lawson Killed Reichswald Forest, Germany. 5-C-18

10 Squadron 4 Group Halifax W1217 ZA/Z
Pilot. 1335229 Sgt C.J.J.Hine Killed Wonseradeel(Makkum), Holland. M-36
Nav. 121250 F/O J.W.T.King Killed Wonseradeel(Makkum), Holland. M-32
B/A. 1394127 Sgt H.G.Ashton Killed Wonseradeel(Makkum), Holland. M-27
W/OP. 1270457 Sgt E.C.Church Killed Bergen-op-zoom, Holland. 32-A-9
F/E. 577780 Sgt A.Hall Killed Wonseradeel(Makkum), Holland. M-33
A/G. R/155845 Sgt G.D.Nisbet Killed Wonseradeel(Makkum), Holland. M-35
A/G. 1436522 Sgt R.F.F.Baggaley Killed Bergen-op-zoom, Holland. 30-A-9

51 Squadron 4 Group Halifax HR844 MH/
Pilot. 1043276 W/O R.R.Mascall PoW. Stalag Luft 6, Heydekrug. 43232
Nav. 1525009 W/O D.Shepherd PoW. Stalag Luft 1, Barth Vogelsang. 1271
B/A. 657372 Sgt F.J.Clancy PoW. Repatriated.
W/OP. 1264911 F/Sgt C.D.Wilcox-Jones PoW. Stalag Luft 6, Heydekrug. 83709
F/E. 950902 F/Sgt C.Rands PoW. Stalag Luft 4, Sagan. 1267
A/G. 1311944 F/Sgt W.Fry PoW. Stalag Luft 6, Heydekrug 1243
A/G. R/125203 W/O G.F.D.Heumann PoW. Stalag Luft 4, Sagan. 1262

51 Squadron 4 Group Halifax HR842 MH/
Pilot. 1386266 Sgt J.W.G.Parker Killed Reichswald Forest, Germany. 21-B-16
Nav. 1434090 W/O M.J.J.Maher PoW. Stalag 357, Kopernikus. 206
B/A. 1248848 F/Sgt W.J.Osborn PoW. Stalag 357, Kopernikus. 221
W/OP. 918809 F/Sgt L.H.Burnet PoW. Stalag Luft 6, Heydekrug. 86
F/E. 1554113 F/Sgt D.A.Kirk PoW. Stalag 357, Kopernikus. 191
A/G. 1300790 F/Sgt A.Simpson PoW. Stalag 357, Kopernikus. 248
A/G. 1231000 W/O L.Willoughby PoW. Stalag 357, Kopernikus. 288

51 Squadron 4 Group Halifax HR836 MH/
Pilot. 127881 F/O J.E.Rigby Killed Oegstgeest, Holland. CG 11/12
Nav. R/133119 F/Sgt H.G.Freeman Killed Oegstgeest, Holland. CG 11/12
B/A. 112481 F/O T.H.Green Killed Oegstgeest, Holland. 7
W/OP. 1206439 Sgt A.E.P.Rochester Killed Oegstgeest, Holland. 9
F/E. 526799 Sgt A.M.H.Black Killed Oegstgeest, Holland. 8
A/G. 1290012 Sgt H.J.Gibbs Killed Oegstgeest, Holland. CG 11/12
A/G. R/139842 F/Sgt M.E.Zapfe Killed Oegstgeest, Holland. 10

51 Squadron 4 Group Halifax HR835 MH/
Pilot. 1319421 F/Sgt L.A.Wright Killed Reichswald Forest. CG 5-C-13/17
Nav. 658922 Sgt J.D.Minton Killed Reichswald Forest. CG 5-C-13/17
B/A. 129479 F/O J.Cookson Killed Reichswald Forest, Germany. CG 5-C-13/17
W/OP. 1256599 Sgt J.L.Edwards Killed Reichswald Forest. CG 5-C-13/17
F/E. 1530092 Sgt C.Newman Killed Reichswald Forest. CG 5-C-13/17
A/G. 1451275 Sgt J.Jones Killed Reichswald Forest, Germany. 5-C-12
A/G. R/111993 F/Sgt W.Brown Killed Reichswald Forest. CG 5-C-13/17

76 Squadron 4 Group Halifax DK169 MP/M
Shot down by fighter near Zwolle, Holland. Victim of Lt.Augenstein, 7/NJG1.
Pilot. 1320792 W/O C.H.Cousins PoW. Stalag 357, Kopernikus. 103
Nav. 130592 P/O A.W.L.Pruce PoW. Stalag Luft 3, Sagan. 1452
B/A. 1147600 F/Sgt J.F.Hughes PoW. Stalag 357, Kopernikus. 173
W/OP. 1333001 Sgt A.G.Dale PoW. Stalag Luft 6, Heydekrug. 107
F/E. 1021354 Sgt J.Parr PoW. Stalag 357, Kopernikus. 222
A/G. 137555 F/O J.W.Coleman Killed Raalte, Zwolle, Holland. 10
A/G. R/97071 F/Sgt H.A.Crouse Killed Raalte, Zwolle, Holland. 9

76 Squadron 4 Group Halifax DK172 MP/L
Crashed 3 kilometres NW of Greven, Germnay.
Pilot. 146417 P/O E.S.Bawden Killed Reichswald Forest, Germany. 18-B-15
2/Pilot. Nor/1059 Lt P.E.R.Waaler PoW. Stalag Luft 3, Sagan. 1416
Nav. 145712 F/O L.W.S.Thick PoW. Stalag Luft 6, Heydekrug. 265
B/A. 1381332 F/Sgt T.Musgrove Killed Reichswald Forest. JG B-17/18
W/OP. 1176613 W/O J.W.Smith PoW. Stalag 344, Lamsdorf. 20
F/E. 988221 F/Sgt T.Knowles PoW. Stalag Luft 6, Heydekrug. 1482
A/G. 1001217 Sgt C.Greenhalgh Killed Reichswald Forest, Germany. 18-B-16
A/G. 1335371 Sgt T.L.V.Hitchcock Killed Reichswald Forest. JG B-17/18

78 Squadron 4 Group Halifax JD122 EY/
Pilot. 1334705 Sgt G.E.Schubert Killed Wierden, Almelo, Holland. CG B-3/7
Nav. 658522 Sgt D.C.Oliver Killed Wierden, Almelo, Holland. B-1
B/A. 129182 F/O A.B.Orme Killed Wierden, Almelo, Holland. CG B-3/7
W/OP. 553971 Sgt P.J.Wood Killed Wierden, Almelo, Holland. B-2
F/E. 929591 Sgt R.E.Goodyear Killed Wierden, Almelo, Holland. CG B-3/7
A/G. 1251710 Sgt J.Redman Killed Wierden, Almelo, Holland. CG B-3/7
A/G. 1272586 Sgt J.Goldflust Killed Wierden, Almelo, Holland. CG B-3/7

78 Squadron 4 Group Halifax JD160 EY/
Pilot. 1294565 W/O G.H.Tinniswood PoW. Stalag 357, Kopernikus. 1274
Nav. 133339 F/Lt H.Bear PoW. Stalag Luft 3, Sagan. 1399
B/A. 129477 F/O R.Donovan PoW. Stalag Luft 3, Sagan. 1403
W/OP. 1311949 F/Sgt G.J.Wallace PoW. Stalag 357, Kopernikus. 276
F/E. 1237680 Sgt F.M.Chaffey Killed Rheinberg, Germany. 2-F-25
Killed by *Flak* during parachute descent.
A/G. 1316888 W/O E.F.Harries PoW. Stalag 357, Kopernikus. 1245
A/G. R/134856 Sgt J.O.Mander PoW. Stalag 357, Kopernikus. 1255

78 Squadron 4 Group Halifax W7926 EY/
Aircraft shot down by fighter over Dutch coast. S.O.S sent at 01.56 hrs.
Position 5220N 0401E.Ditched and crew picked up from dinghy by German
convoy after 10 hours afloat. Two gunners baled out over target.
Pilot. 1314632 W/O B.W.T.Horn PoW. Stalag 357, Kopernikus. 172
Nav. 1478748 W/O G.Irving PoW. Stalag Luft 6, Heydekrug. 176
B/A. 1339764 F/Sgt W.H.Allely PoW. Stalag 357, Kopernikus. 56
W/OP. 1029741 Sgt D.R.Wilcox PoW. Stalag 357, Kopernikus. 286
F/E. 949595 F/Sgt R.F.Cumming PoW. Stalag 357, Kopernikus. 106
A/G. R/108763 F/Sgt F.Churchard PoW. Stalag 357, Kopernikus. 1235
A/G. 905183 W/O G.J.U.Stevens PoW. Stalag 357, Kopernikus. 257

102 Squadron 4 Group Halifax JD112 DY/H
Aircraft ditched in North Sea.
Pilot. 937481 F/Sgt A.M.Sargent PoW. Stalag 357, Kopernikus. 243
Nav. 1239952 Sgt A.Campbell Killed Flushing, Holland. 2-E-22
B/A. 129475 F/O J.R.Bullock Killed Flushing, Holland. 2-E-21
W/OP. 1137146 F/Sgt M.Galloway PoW. Stalag 357, Kopernikus. 141
F/E. 1211978 Sgt C.R.Webb PoW. Stalag 357, Kopernikus. 282
A/G. 1312030 Sgt H.D.Newberry Killed Flushing, Holland. 2-E-24
A/G. 1094915 Sgt J.C.Smith Killed Flushing, Holland. 2-E-23

158 Squadron 4 Group Halifax HR781 NP/F
Pilot. 1387485 F/Sgt N.Gillies Killed Reichswald Forest, Germany. 23-B-1
Nav. 1049999 Sgt R.C.Hall Killed Reichswald Forest, Germany. 23-A-18
B/A. 1318343 W/O T.S.J.Crawley PoW. Stalag 357, Kopernikus. 105
W/OP. 1078095 F/Sgt J.Roberts PoW. Stalag 357, Kopernikus. 235
F/E. 1029913 Sgt J.F.Hinds Killed Reichswald Forest, Germany. 23-A-17
A/G. 1493593 Sgt F.Warburton Killed Reichswald Forest, Germany. 23-A-16
A/G. 634191 F/Sgt R.M.E.Harrison PoW. Stalag Luft 6, Heydekrug. 42777

44 Squadron 5 Group Lancaster ED723 KM/U
Pilot. J/17333 P/O J.L.Drysdale Missing, Runnymede Memorial 175
Nav. 127010 F/O W.A.Marsden Missing, Runnymede Memorial 126
B/A. 655968 F/Sgt H.W.E.Hyett Missing, Runnymede Memorial 137
W/OP. 1057537 Sgt S.Jones Missing, Runnymede Memorial 155
F/E. 338714 Sgt J.F.Lester Missing, Runnymede Memorial 156
A/G. 1393670 Sgt A.S.Bushill Missing, Runnymede Memorial 144
A/G. J/17239 P/O F.A.Doherty Missing, Runnymede Memorial 175

49 Squadron 5 Group Lancaster ED813 EA/W
Pilot. 122751 F/Lt I.W.Thomas PoW. Stalag Luft 3, Sagan. 1414
Nav. 81674 F/Lt I.C.Duthie PoW. Stalag Luft 3, Sagan. 1405
B/A. 131994 P/O T.G.H.Lewis Killed Reichswald Forest, Germany. 5-E-4
W/OP. 143398 P/O R.Christy Killed Reichswald Forest, Germany. 5-E-3
F/E. 1561394 F/Sgt J.Grant PoW. Stalag 357, Kopernikus. 149
A/G. 1399793 Sgt R.H.Ancell Killed Reichswald Forest, Germany. 5-E-2
A/G. 1196508 Sgt G.R.Evans Killed Reichswald Forest, Germany. 5-E-5

57 Squadron 5 Group Lancaster ED970 DX/
Pilot. 1551139 Sgt A.R.Leslie Missing, Runnymede Memorial 156
Nav. 129500 P/O J.R.Morton Missing, Runnymede Memorial 132
B/A. 1392967 Sgt P.Hemingway Missing, Runnymede Memorial 153
W/OP. 1125769 Sgt A.K.Henderson Missing, Runnymede Memorial 153
F/E. 1455874 Sgt H.Kleiner Killed Leeuwarden, Holland. 24-32
A/G. 927900 Sgt W.J.Bennett Killed Bergen-op-Zoom, Holland. 96
A/G. 551847 Sgt P.Daly Killed Bergen-op-Zoom, Holland. D-13-8

57 Squadron 5 Group Lancaster ED707 DX/
Pilot. A/275238 F/O E.K.Chivers Killed Texel, Holland. K-4-92
Nav. 1434589 Sgt P.Parkin Killed Texel, Holland. K-3-64
B/A. 1237319 Sgt I.A.Jervis Killed Bergen-op-Zoom, Holland. 29-B-4
W/OP. 656009 Sgt D.A.Robb Killed Texel, Holland. K-3-62
F/E. 1002401 Sgt T.R.Bayles Killed Bergen-op-Zoom, Holland. 31-C-3
A/G. 1601751 Sgt W.B.Rawnsley Missing, Runnymede Memorial 162
A/G. 1473247 Sgt W.H.Bestwick Missing, Runnymede Memorial 142

408 Squadron 6 Group Halifax JB841 EQ/K
Pilot. J/7430 F/O J.M.Colvin Killed Reichswald Forest, Germany. 3-C-17
Nav. J/17974 P/O T.R.Livermore Missing, Runnymede Memorial 176
B/A. J/14818 F/O H.Uretzky Missing, Runnymede Memorial 175
W/OP. 1242384 Sgt F.Thompson Missing, Runnymede Memorial 167

F/E. R/70806 Sgt J.Hooper Missing, Runnymede Memorial 186
A/G. R/94489 F/Sgt D.Slabotsky Missing, Runnymede Memorial 185
A/G. R/123174 F/Sgt E.H.Alderson Killed Reichswald Forest, Germany. 3-D-6

419 Squadron 6 Group Halifax JB862 VR/
Pilot. R/107004 W/O A.S.Green Killed Rheinberg, Germany. 2-G-13
Nav. 128972 F/O D.Gartrey Killed Rheinberg, Germany. 2-G-14
B/A. 1310694 Sgt A.J.Brockway Killed Rheinberg, Germany. 2-G-15
W/OP. 1194276 Sgt M.A.Harrison Killed Rheinberg, Germany. 2-G-16
F/E. R/76929 W/O F.A.Dunn PoW. Stalag 357, Kopernikus. 124
A/G. R/132590 F/Sgt J.F.J.P.Prieur Killed Rheinberg, Germany. 2-G-17
A/G. R/139047 F/Sgt G.R.Gowling Killed Rheinberg, Germany. 2-G-18

426 Squadron 6 Group Wellington HE281 OW/
Pilot. R/99732 Sgt L.G.Sutherland Killed Haaksbergen, Holland. 4-2-11
Nav. 1450680 Sgt W.Dunkerley Killed Haaksbergen, Holland. 4-2-10
B/A. 1211239 Sgt S.Jepson Killed Haaksbergen, Holland. 4-2-13
W/OP. R/90238 W/O K.H.Masterton Killed Haaksbergen, Holland. 4-2-12
A/G. R/108468 W/O L.A.Rivet Killed Haaksbergen, Holland. 4-2-14

419 Squadron 6 Group Halifax BB384 VR/
Crashed through lack of fuel at Dinsdale, 2 mls from Middleton St George after
operations to Dortmund.
Pilot. J/10519 F/O P.G.Weedon Safe.
Nav. J/10420 F/O P.Campbell Safe.
B/A. F/O R.K.Shields Safe.
W/OP. Sgt M.Wigelsworth Safe.
F/E. Sgt C.W.Nevins Safe.
A/G. Sgt S.Poole Safe.
A/G. Sgt D.G.Plyley Safe.

431 Squadron 6 Group Wellington HE198 SE/
Pilot and rear gunner baled out after bombing target. Bomb aimer flew plane
back to UK and landed at Cranwell after operations to Dortmund. Three
remaining crew decorated for their action.
Pilot. 80550 F/Lt C.H.Hall PoW. Stalag Luft 3, Sagan. 1444
Nav. 1332251 Sgt G.C.W.Parslow DFM Safe
B/A. 1550960 Sgt S.N.Sloan CGM Safe
W/OP. 48551 F/O J.B.G.Bailey DFC Safe
A/G. NZ/412291 Sgt C.A.Warne PoW. Stalag 357, Kopernikus. 279

426 Squadron 6 Group Wellington HE995 OW/
Two of crew baled out on pilot's instructions after fire which was later
extinguished. Remaining crew flew aircraft back to UK after operations to
Dortmund and crash landed at Martlesham Heath. Pilot awarded immediate
DFM.
Pilot. R/120080 Sgt S.Gaunt Safe.
Nav. Sgt A.T.McCormick Safe.
B/A. R/97650 W/O L.R.Fadden PoW. Stalag 357, Kopernikus. 131
W/OP. Sgt J.H.Jones Safe.
A/G. R/64681 W/O L.C.McCracken PoW. Stalag 357, Kopernikus.

Düsseldorf

May 25th/26th, 1943

Another large force of 759 aircraft consisting of 323 Lancasters, 169 Halifaxes, 142 Wellingtons, 113 Stirlings and 12 Mosquitoes flew to attack Düsseldorf, but this raid was a failure. This was mainly due to the difficult weather conditions over the target area, which was covered by two distinct layers of cloud, 9/10ths at 18,000 to 21,000 feet and another lower layer at 8,000 feet, which made the Pathfinder markers almost impossible to see clearly. Again the main force was distracted by false ground fire sites laid out by the Germans and the decoy markers dropped by German planes. Conditions were ideal for this kind of deception plan with a result that the raid had very wide and scattered bombing from the 1,043.3 tons of high explosive and 336,845 incendiaries, although many explosions were observed and one particularly heavy one at 01.10 hours. *Flak* was moderate at first, but weakened as the attack developed, searchlights being ineffective because of cloud conditions, but these helped the very active night fighter defence which shot down most of the 27 aircraft which failed to return to their bases. There was a 3.6% loss rate, with 134 aircrew killed, 27 missing and 21 made prisoners.

One of those bombers intercepted and shot down by a night fighter was Lancaster ED768 from the Australian 467 Squadron and captained by Australian Flight Sergeant J. M. Parsons. The Lancaster was in sight of the target when attacked, but the engines were so badly damaged that there was no alternative but to turn back on a course for home. The limping bomber did not make it for it crashed at Gravenweel, Belgium shortly after a bale out order had been given. The pilot and rear gunner were unfortunately killed when the aircraft crashed. Of the five who baled out successfully the flight engineer was killed on the ground, the circumstances of which are not known. The other four were made prisoners but not before one of them, 1380187 Warrant Officer J. P. Egan, the navigator had evaded for quite a long period.

Egan had landed in a field north west of Antwerp and like all airmen his first act was to get rid of his flying equipment. Then he started walking and kept going until the next morning when he was stopped by a man on the road. Egan told him that he was RAF and the man said he was Belgian and told Egan, in French, to hide in a ditch until he returned. The man duly returned bringing with him a civilian jacket and 250 Belgian Francs and also advised Egan to get to the city of Antwerp where the chances were better for receiving more help.

Warrant Officer Egan took a bus to Antwerp and wandered around the city all day without making any contact until eventually he met a priest who advised him that his best chances of underground help would be in the capital city of Brussels and that he should travel there by train. On arriving in Brussels Egan found that it was nearly curfew time so he found an allotment near the city boundary and slept there for the night. The curfew expired at 5am. so at dawn Egan made his way to the city centre and entered a café. His luck was in, for after declaring himself to the woman owner, she gave him an enormous meal and then took him to a room over the café, telling him to wait until she made contact with an organisation. Later that day Egan was given a complete outfit of civilian clothes and met up with a girl called Ghilliane. This young girl took Egan to the home of a member of the organisation where he stayed for nine days during which time he was photographed and issued with an indentity card. Ghilliane was later captured and sent to a concentration camp for helping evaders. Sadly she died there.

Three days after his arrival at the house another RAF Sergeant, J. S. Wilkins, was brought there. On June 7th, along with three other airmen they picked up at the railway station by a guide who took the party to Menin where they crossed the border on foot. From there the party was taken by tram to Lille and from Lille by train to Paris, where Wilkins and one other airman got lost when the group became separated. At the Paris railway station the party was met by a Frenchman and his wife and while they were talking seven Germans suddenly appeared and arrested the French couple. Egan got away unnoticed by jumping on to a train which just happened to be leaving from the platform. He travelled as far as Place Sebastapool where he alighted and spent the night on a barge on the River Seine. He then decided that perhaps it would be better if he could make his own way to the Spanish border. The owner of the barge fed and sheltered him for a week while he obtained an address in Calais for Egan to have further shelter. However after Egan had travelled to Calais he was unable to locate the address he had been given so he decided to travel back to Brussels to make contact with his original helpers. He received further assistance from a Frenchman in Lille and he eventually arrived at the house in Brussels where he had obtained his identity card. Here he met two other airmen, Flight Sergeant E. Roede and Flying Officer B. Cooper.After staying in Brussels for three weeks at two different addresses, the house was raided by the Germans at 04.30 hours on Wednesday morning, June 30th, 1943. A gun fight broke out between the occupants and the Germans and eventually the Germans, who had automatic weapons, forced their way in and arrested everyone there. All were taken to St. Gilles Prison, Brussels, where Egan was kept for 15 days being regularly interrogated with some degree of violence. He was finally taken to Dulag Luft and then on to Stalag Luft 6 at Heydekrug on 31st July, 1943.

Whilst at the camp he made an escape attempt in the company of a Canadian, Warrant Officer Chisholm. In preparation they saved food from their Red Cross parcels and obtained maps and a compass from the Camp Escape Committee. They made wire cutters and under cover of darkness cut an opening through the fence of a new camp into which Egan and Chisholm had recently been moved. Sadly their freedom was short lived, for as soon as they were through the wire, the dogs began to bark which attracted the attention of the patrolling guard. The pair were quickly arrested and as a punishment spent 14 days in the 'Cooler'.

Undeterred by their failure and arrest, as soon as they were released from the Cooler, both Chisholm and Egan attempted to dig a tunnel from the latrines out of their new camp, but again they were caught in the act of digging and spent another 14 days in the Cooler. Warrant Officer Egan was finally liberated by the British Forces at Soltau on Monday, April 16th, 1945 and was flown back to the UK via Brussels on May 5th, 1945.

Casualties May 25th/26th, 1943. Target Düsseldorf

35 Squadron 8 Group Halifax W7825 TL/
Pilot. 1272433 W/O R.T.Hall PoW. Stalag 357, Kopernikus. 157
Nav. 937568 Sgt E.Garner Killed Reichswald Forest, Germany. 5-D-14
B/A. 1430645 Sgt R.H.Oats Killed Reichswald Forest, Germany. 5-D-16
W/OP. 745940 F/Sgt M.D.Fuller Killed Reichswald Forest, Germany. 5-D-17
F/E. 980521 Sgt T.C.E.Simmons Killed Reichswald Forest, Germany. 5-E-1
A/G. 1390159 Sgt J.Hogg Killed Reichswald Forest, Germany. 5-D-18
A/G. 1312458 Sgt L.D.Bryant Killed Reichswald Forest, Germany. 5-F-14

7 Squadron 8 Group Stirling EF361 MG/B
Aircraft crashed at Julich, Germany.
Pilot. J/17079 P/O J.F.E.G.Berthiaume Killed Rheinberg, Germany. 4-D-21
Nav. 1528408 Sgt A.Brotherton Killed Rheinberg, Germany. 4-D-24
B/A. 1129595 Sgt W.Denham Killed Rheinberg, Germany. CG 4-D-5/20
W/OP. R/107211 W/O W.J.Hills Killed Rheinberg, Germany. 4-D-22
F/E. 1137645 Sgt E.Broadhead Killed Rheinberg, Germany. CG 4-D-5/20
A/G. 925124 Sgt A.L.Fisher Killed Rheinberg, Germany. 4-D-25
A/G. 910591 Sgt N.Lagna Killed Rheinberg, Germany. 4-D-23

12 Squadron 1 Group Lancaster ED967 PH/F
Pilot. 655242 F/Sgt R.J.Steele Killed Reichswald Forest, Germany. 5-D-12
Nav. 129598 F/O C.B.Hooper Killed Reichswald Forest, Germany. 5-D-10
B/A. 1330741 Sgt D.W.Creevy Killed Reichswald Forest, Germany. 5-D-13
W/OP. 1082026 Sgt E.T.Powell Killed Reichswald Forest, Germany. 5-D-8
F/E. A/21144 Sgt A.A.Prouse Killed Reichswald Forest, Germany. 5-D-15
A/G. 1332267 Sgt S.A.J.Bailey Killed Reichswald Forest, Germany. 5-D-11
A/G. 1339266 F/Sgt L.C.Schroeder Killed Reichswald Forest, Germany. 5-D-9

12 Squadron 1 Group Lancaster ED995 PH/X
Pilot. F/O F.J.Wright
W/OP. 1178835 F/Sgt T.A.Routledge Killed Pershore, Worcs. S-29
Wireless Operator found dead in aircraft.Possible cause, lack of oxygen by
failure to plug into system, reason not known.

100 Squadron 1 Group Lancaster W4998 HW/J
Pilot. NZ/413106 F/Sgt A.T.W.Moore Killed Jonkerbos, Holland. 24-A-8
Nav. 1451978 Sgt D.C.Stone Killed Jonkerbos, Holland. 24-A-6
B/A. 130536 F/Lt S.W.J.Coventry PoW. Stalag Luft 3, Sagan. 2188
W/OP. 755138 F/Sgt J.C.Wood Killed Jonkerbos, Holland. 24-A-7
F/E. 940090 W/O J.S.Wilkins PoW. Stalag 4B, Muhlberg(Elbe). 222563
A/G. 1586059 Sgt M.Keogh Killed Jonkerbos, Holland. 24-A-5
A/G. NZ/414318 F/Sgt L.C.Maunsell Killed Jonkerbos, Holland. 24-A-4

100 Squadron 1 Group Lancaster LM320 HW/C
Pilot. 42542 S/Ldr P.R.Turgel DFC Killed Jonkerbos, Holland. CG 24-C-8/9
Nav. J/22555 F/O H.N.Petts Killed Jonkerbos, Holland. 18-E-6
B/A. 131938 F/O G.Russell Killed Jonkerbos, Holland. 18-E-5
W/OP. 129523 F/O J.M.Marnoch Killed Jonkerbos, Holland. CG 24-C-8/9
F/E. 146838 P/O I.A.Wynn Killed Jonkerbos, Holland. CG 24-C-8/9
A/G. 33456 F/O D.Harvey Killed Jonkerbos, Holland. CG 24-C-8/9
A/G. 1457263 Sgt J.Hudson Killed Jonkerbos, Holland. CG 24-C-8/9

101 Squadron 1 Group Lancaster ED660 SR/U
Pilot. 1480799 Sgt V.J.S.Tindale Killed Flushing, Holland. 5-C-2
Nav. 655863 Sgt A.T.M.Wright Killed Flushing, Holland. 5-D-13
B/A. 1211846 Sgt D.L.Berresford Killed Flushing, Holland. 5-C-1
W/OP. 1079641 Sgt B.C.Ainsworth Killed Flushing, Holland. 5-D-10
F/E. 1507344 Sgt E.Shackelton Killed Flushing, Holland. 5-D-9
A/G. 1586116 Sgt C.W.Bates Killed Flushing, Holland. 5-D-11
A/G. R/112455 Sgt A.S.Thomson Killed Flushing, Holland. 5-D-12

166 Squadron 1 Group Wellington HE699 AS/M
Pilot. 658480 Sgt R.Lowe Killed Eindhoven(Woensel), Holland. CG EE-34/35
Nav. 1389928 Sgt G.J.Mitchener Killed Eindhoven(Woensel). CG EE-34/35
B/A. 1390906 Sgt J.G.Watkins Killed Eindhoven(Woensel). CG EE-34/35
W/OP. 1386172 Sgt S.F.Barrow Killed Eindhoven(Woensel). CG EE-34/35
A/G. 1324736 Sgt L.M.Chisnall Killed Eindhoven(Woensel). CG EE-34/35

166 Squadron 1 Group Wellington HE535 AS/H
Pilot. 1432288 Sgt R.Batterbee Missing, Runnymede Memorial 142
Nav. R/92104 W/O E.A.Sproule Missing, Runnymede Memorial 180
B/A. 1476472 Sgt A.J.Railton Missing, Runnymede Memorial 162
W/OP. 1269078 Sgt J.T.Francis Missing, Runnymede Memorial 150
A/G. 1515864 Sgt K.McIntosh Missing, Runnymede Memorial 158

199 Squadron 1 Group Wellington HF488 EX/U
Attacked by fighter near target, exploded shortly after B/O order.Navigator
blown out of plane.
Pilot. 128577 F/O D.Makin Killed Jonkerbos, Holland. 20-A-4
Nav. 132494 F/Lt F.S.Reade PoW. Stalag Luft 3, Sagan. 1453
B/A. 134674 F/O R.T.Douglas Killed Jonkerbos, Holland. 20-A-3
W/OP. 1377796 Sgt W.H.Thompson Killed Jonkerbos, Holland. 20-A-1
A/G. 1785281 Sgt T.M.Scott Killed Jonkerbos, Holland. 20-A-2

15 Squadron 3 Group Stirling BF534 LS/L
Aircraft crashed at Julich, Germany.
Pilot. J/15487 F/O I.S.Thompson Killed Rheinberg, Germany. CG 4-D-5/20
Nav. R/84977 W/O C.T.Smith Killed Rheinberg, Germany. CG 4-D-5/20
B/A. 136531 P/O R.E.Newman Killed Rheinberg, Germany. CG 4-D-5/20
W/OP. 1370964 Sgt H.J.Morris Killed Rheinberg, Germany. 4-D-2
F/E. 549434 Sgt D.P.O'Riordan Killed Rheinberg, Germany. CG 4-D-5/20
A/G. 1609625 Sgt T.C.L.Orchard Killed Rheinberg, Germany. CG 4-D-5/20
A/G. 1446946 Sgt L.R.Smith Killed Rheinberg, Germany. 4-D-1

15 Squadron 3 Group Stirling BK611 LS/U
Aircraft crashed near Grubbenvorst, Holland after fighter attack.
Pilot. A/413329 Sgt J.Wilson Killed Jonkerbos, Holland. 24-A-2
Nav. 130589 F/Lt B.E.Cooper PoW. Stalag Luft 3, Sagan. 1770
B/A. 1333984 Sgt P.Arnott Killed Jonkerbos, Holland. 24-A-3
W/OP. 1333008 Sgt S.J.Maxted PoW. Stalag 4B, Muhlberg(Elbe). 222529
F/E. 1387554 Sgt R.W.Pittard Killed Jonkerbos, Holland. 24-A-1
A/G. Sgt B.Seabolt PoW. Camp not known
A/G. 1104451 W/O A.W.Edgeley PoW. Stalag 4B, Muhlberg(Elbe). 222506

75 Squadron 3 Group Stirling BK602 AA/R
Aircraft crashed in sea near Ijmuiden, Holland after fighter attack.
Pilot. NZ/414465 F/Sgt T.W.Darton Missing, Runnymede Memorial 148
Nav. NZ/421318 Sgt D.D.Coates Killed Ostend, Belgium. 9-5-17
B/A. NZ/422668 Sgt J.M.P.Riordan Missing, Runnymede Memorial 199
W/OP. 1234862 Sgt J.C.L.Whiteman Killed Ostend, Belgium. 9-5-18
F/E. 1369879 Sgt A.McQuater Missing, Runnymede Memorial 158
A/G. 1572718 Sgt S.Redpath Killed Dunkirk, France. 2-4-11
A/G. 1170594 Sgt F.P.Wilsher Killed Bergen-op-Zoom, Holland. 33-5-4

90 Squadron 3 Group Stirling EH876 WP/J
Aircraft crashed in North Sea near Texel, Holland.
Pilot. J/16906 P/O G.W.Young DFC Missing, Runnymede Memorial 179
2/Pilot. R/118286 W/O M.G.K.East Missing, Runnymede Memorial 180
Nav. NZ/404949 F/Sgt C.L.Saundercock Missing, Runnymede Memorial 199
B/A. 1534581 F/Sgt J.L.Poulter Missing, Runnymede Memorial 138
W/OP. 1376718 Sgt R.Wadsworth Missing, Runnymede Memorial 168
F/E. 1294010 Sgt W.H.Bryant Missing, Runnymede Memorial 144
A/G. R/124287 W/O E.S.Pollon Missing, Runnymede Memorial 180
A/G. 126607 F/O C.F.O'Connell Killed Texel, Holland. K-4-76

149 Squadron 3 Group Stirling BK710 OJ/A
Aircraft crashed in North Sea.
Pilot. 1334077 Sgt J.H.Uden Missing, Runnymede Memorial 167
Nav. 127978 F/O W.E.L.Morse Missing, Runnymede Memorial 127
B/A. 128514 F/O H.S.Winchester Missing, Runnymede Memorial 130
W/OP. 1295227 Sgt F.A.Williams Missing, Runnymede Memorial 170
F/E. 949263 Sgt L.G.Hadden Missing, Runnymede Memorial 151
A/G. 901570 Sgt H.S.Scott Missing, Runnymede Memorial 164
A/G. 1600739 Sgt C.J.Percival Killed Hamburg, Germany. 6A-E-7

214 Squadron 3 Group Stirling BK659 BU/N
Aircraft attacked by night fighter and crashed in North Sea.
Pilot. A/409144 F/Sgt R.A.Kerr Missing, Runnymede Memorial 193
Nav. 1315154 Sgt B.M.Jubb Missing, Runnymede Memorial 155
B/A. 127105 F/O R.Paisley Missing, Runnymede Memorial 127
W/OP. 1220818 Sgt R.S.Blake Missing, Runnymede Memorial 142
F/E. 1456715 Sgt F.H.E.Pooley Killed Sage, Germany. 11-D-7
A/G. 1670565 Sgt D.Littlewood Missing, Runnymede Memorial 157
A/G. 1314365 Sgt G.T.Davies Missing, Runnymede Memorial 147

218 Squadron 3 Group Stirling EH887 HA/Z
Aircraft crashed at Duren, Germany.
Pilot. 1316430 Sgt N.S.Collins Killed Rheinberg, Germany. CG 4-D-5/20
Nav. 1478810 Sgt W.J.Ledbury Killed Rheinberg, Germany. 4-E-3
B/A. NZ/416445 F/O C.F.Blanchard Killed Rheinberg, Germany. 4-E-4
W/OP. 1334592 Sgt J.P.Roughan Killed Rheinberg, Germany. 4-E-2
F/E. 577642 Sgt A.W.Fincham Killed Rheinberg, Germany. CG 4-D-5/20
A/G. R/142748 F/Sgt J.C.Lamond Killed Rheinberg, Germany. 4-E-1
A/G. 1383527 Sgt D.C.Maynard Killed Rheinberg, Germany. CG 4-D-5/20

51 Squadron 4 Group Halifax HR747 MH/
Pilot. 657964 Sgt W.Davies Killed Flushing, Holland. 5-I-4
Nav. 1585002 Sgt C.A.Richardson Killed Flushing, Holland. 5-I-6
B/A. 1116913 F/Sgt J.C.Macpherson Killed Flushing, Holland. 5-I-3
W/OP. 1138659 Sgt S.Busby Killed Flushing, Holland. 5-I-7
F/E. 1508677 Sgt W.J.Chambers Killed Flushing, Holland. 5-I-5
A/G. 1860203 Sgt A.Brown Killed Flushing, Holland. 5-I-2
A/G. R/113195 F/Sgt A.C.Worden Killed Flushing, Holland. 5-I-1

77 Squadron 4 Group Halifax JB837 KN/D
Pilot. 1425912 Sgt R.Lewis Killed Rheinberg, Germany. CG 4-D-5/20
Nav. 1334179 Sgt J.A.Waterston Killed Rheinberg, Germany. 4-D-4
B/A. 1062314 Sgt J.W.Richardson Killed Rheinberg, Germany. CG 4-D-5/20
W/OP. 1077003 Sgt J.Kershaw Killed Rheinberg, Germany. CG 4-D-5/20
F/E. 1316152 Sgt W.R.Codd Killed Rheinberg, Germany. 4-D-3
A/G. R/104713 F/Sgt J.P.Laurence Killed Rheinberg, Germany. CG 4-D-5/20
A/G. R/88370 F/Sgt D.W.Macfarlane Killed Rheinberg, Germany. CG 4-D-5/20

77 Squadron 4 Group Halifax W7813 KN//C
Pilot. 657547 Sgt L.W.Rees Killed Ostend, Belgium. CG 4-F-8/14
Nav. 1392398 Sgt H.Roots Killed Ostend, Belgium. CG 4-F-8/14
B/A. 1322934 Sgt H.W.Moore Killed Ostend, Belgium. 4-F-19
W/OP. 1382656 Sgt J.R.McLeod Killed Ostend, Belgium. CG 4-F-8/14
F/E. 103626 Sgt E.V.Pass Killed Ostend, Belgium. CG 4-F-8/14
A/G. R/152522 F/Sgt D.R.Gilchrist Killed Ostend, Belgium. 4-F-18
A/G. 1063769 Sgt C.H.Sherwood Killed Ostend, Belgium. CG 4-F-8/14

431 Squadron 4 Group Wellington HE990 SE/Z
Pilot. 1343921 W/O R.T.Barclay PoW. Stalag 357, Kopernikus. 60
Nav. 1237232 Sgt K.Dix PoW. Stalag Luft 6, Heydekrug. 118
B/A. 124717 F/O A.C.Bonner Killed Jonkerbos, Holland. 7-H-2
W/OP. 1280562 Sgt M.C.Jeffries Killed Jonkerbos, Holland. 11-H-2
A/G. 1230519 Sgt H.Sweet Killed Jonkerbos, Holland. 11-H-1

9 Squadron 5 Group Lancaster ED834 WS/Z
Pilot. 110587 F/O H.W.Woodhouse Killed Flushing, Holland. JG E-18/19
Nav. 1388638 Sgt H.J.Warren Killed Flushing, Holland. E-17
B/A. 1553400 Sgt J.B.Corbett Killed Flushing, Holland. E-13
W/OP. 1034418 Sgt W.Smith Killed Flushing, Holland. E-14
F/E. 1579189 Sgt L.J.Daker Killed Flushing, Holland. JG E-18/19
A/G. 1457373 Sgt E.L.Matthews Killed Flushing, Holland. E-15
A/G. 1578186 Sgt A.G.Coffin Killed Flushing, Holland. E-16

207 Squadron 5 Group Lancaster ED600 EM/F
Pilot. 105169 F/O P.C.B.Drayton Killed Flushing, Holland. CG JJB-64/66
Nav. 1437922 Sgt G.L.Bottomley Killed Flushing, Holland. JJB-63
B/A. 1320927 Sgt D.A.Genever Killed Flushing, Holland. CG JJB-64/66
W/OP. 1314646 Sgt I.E.G.Hall Killed Flushing, Holland. CG JJB-64/66
F/E. 651754 Sgt K.J.Frost Killed Flushing, Holland. CG JJB-64/66
A/G. 931976 Sgt E.H.F.Barker Killed Flushing, Holland. CG JJB-64/66
A/G. 936820 Sgt T.W.T.Stoddart Killed Flushing, Holland. CG JJB-64/66

207 Squadron 5 Group Lancaster W5001 EM/J
Pilot. 26242 W/Cdr T.A.B.Parselle Stalag Luft 3, Sagan. 2281
2/Pilot. J/20351 F/O W.C.Reynolds Killed Flushing, Holland. 5-I-9
Nav. 138816 P/O G.E.Hopson Killed Flushing, Holland. 5-I-10
B/A. 1337519 Sgt R.E.H Hood-Morris PoW. Stalag 357, Kopernikus. 171
W/OP. 1257739 Sgt S.A.J.Cook Killed Flushing, Holland. 5-I-12
F/E. 570198 Sgt P.Falkingham Killed Flushing, Holland. 5-I-11
A/G. 1332269 Sgt W.F.Hayllar Killed Flushing, Holland. 5-I-8
A/G. 1333972 Sgt A.W.White Killed Flushing, Holland. 5-I-13

467 Squadron 5 Group Lancaster ED695 PO/
Pilot. A/6157 F/O R.S.Giddey PoW. Stalag Luft3, Sagan. 2364
Nav. 133467 P/O P.R.Collins PoW. Stalag Luft3, Sagan. 1443
B/A. 1337961 F/Sgt W.V.Morris PoW. Stalag 357, Kopernikus. 215
W/OP. 1335033 F/Sgt R.J.Avann PoW. Stalag 357, Kopernikus. 58
F/E. A/9430 Sgt S.G.Kiers PoW. Stalag 357, Kopernikus. 186
A/G. R/102142 F/Sgt A.F.Birbeck Killed Flushing, Holland. 2-E-26
A/G. 134377 P/O K.R.Langthorne Killed Flushing, Holland. 2-E-25

467 Squadron 5 Group Lancaster ED768 PO/
Aircraft shot down by *Flak* and crashed at Gravenweel, Belgium.
Pilot. A/409274 F/Sgt J.M.Parsons Killed Schoonselhof, Belgium. II-G-4
Nav. 1380187 F/Sgt P.J..Egan PoW. Stalag Luft 6, Heydekrug. 387
B/A. 1099743 F/Sgt N.J.Vaulkhard PoW. Stalag 357, Kopernikus. 273
W/OP. R/92596 W/O J.F.Selman PoW. Stalag 357, Kopernikus. 1483
F/E. 574332 Sgt B.Spencer Killed Schoonselhoof, Belgium. IVA-C-42
A/G. 1699818 Sgt R.A.Hunt PoW. Stalag 357, Kopernikus. 175
A/G. 1401894 Sgt T.Chalmers Killed Schoonselhoof, Belgium. II-G-5

426 Squadron 6 Group Wellington HE590 OW/
Aircraft crashed at Bosch, near Brussels, Belgium.
Pilot. J/18125 P/O S.Pennington Killed Brussels, Belgium. X-16-17
2/Pilot. R/123539 Sgt R.E.Talman Killed Brussels, Belgium. X-16-16
Nav. J/22809 F/O J.K.Watson Killed Brussels, Belgium. X-16-18
B/A. J/18243 P/O N.C.Swan Killed Brussels, Belgium. X-16-19
W/OP. 1331633 Sgt E.Thomas Killed Brussels, Belgium. X-16-20
A/G. R/124012 W/O D.L.Beatty Killed Brussels, Belgium. X-16-15

428 Squadron 6 Group Wellington HZ.476 NA/A
Aircraft crashed near Breed, Belgium.
Pilot. R/105665 W/O W.G.Pepper Killed Heverlee, Belgium. 4-F-16
2/Pilot. J/13710 F/O R.G.Madge Killed Heverlee, Belgium. 4-F-15
Nav. J/17661 P/O F.G.Baker Killed Heverlee, Belgium. 4-F-17
B/A. R/107768 W/O N.J.Waters Killed Heverlee, Belgium. CG 4-F-8/14
W/OP. 1380092 Sgt K.G.Higgs Killed Heverlee, Belgium. CG 4-F-8/14
A/G. R/102484 W/O W.E.Douglas Killed Heverlee, Belgium. 4-F-20

51 Squadron 4 Group Halifax HR747 MH/
Aircraft force landed at Highfield Farm, Doncaster, Yorkshire returning from operations after failing first approach in poor visibility.
Pilot. 1314662 Sgt R.J.Cribb Safe.
Nav. 127315 F/O W.J.A.Nicholson Safe.
B/A. 1387111 Sgt G.M.Lloyd Safe.
W/OP. 1383042 Sgt D.Samuels Safe.
F/E. Sgt D.White Safe.
A/G. R/144839 Sgt M.L.Hutchings Safe.
A/G. 1300797 Sgt P.E.M.Gosling Safe.

Essen

May 27th/28th, 1943

The night of 27th/28th May saw Essen's fifth massive attack. At Zero hour 00.45 hours, 518 aircraft - 274 Lancasters, 151 Halifaxes, 81 Wellingtons and 12 *Oboe* Mosquitoes went in on the attack. 761.6 tons of high explosive bombs and 235,116 incendiaries rained down from the attacking bombers. Two large explosions were reported at 01.10 hours and in the clouds there were silver blue flashes followed by a red glow. Weather conditions were fairly good up to the Dutch coast, but there was 7/10ths to 10/10ths cloud over the target area with only occasional gaps. There was fairly good visibility above the cloud. It was necessary for the Mosquitoes to use their 60 *Wanganui* sky markers which were so prone to wind drift, especially if the target winds were not accurately forecast. Bombing photographs taken by the main force bombers showed much undershooting. This type of creep back was due to a number of factors. Wind change caused the markers to float from the main aiming point as did the ferocity of the German anti-aircraft barrage, especially around the release point flares. Many crews reported unnerving experiences when debriefed after the raid. One aircraft was hit by falling incendiaries, a bomber was accidentally fired upon by another bomber, and a Halifax and Lancaster momentarily collided with each other but fortunately both were able to limp back to their bases. 23 aircraft were lost on the raid, a loss rate of 4.4%. 89 of the aircrew were killed, 11 reported missing and 42 were made prisoners of war.

A Wellington Ditches in the North Sea

Wellington MS481 from 428 Squadron, which was piloted by Sergeant W. Lachman, bombed the target as planned at 01.39 hours from a height of 15,000 feet, but shortly afterwards the starboard engine completely packed up and it had to be feathered. On the return flight just off the Dutch coast near Terschelling at 02.30 hours the now crippled one engined bomber met very heavy and accurate *Flak* which severely damaged the ailerons and as the pilot was unable to take any evasive action the aircraft was forced down to 6,000 feet. Labouring at this altitude at 01.45 hours, the one remaining (port) engine began to develop trouble and the aircraft began to slowly descend until it was unable to maintain any height at all, so the pilot had to quickly make plans to ditch in the North Sea. The ditching was made at 04.30 hours and although it was a good sea landing, the aircraft sank in about two minutes. The crew in the front part of the plane comprising pilot, navigator Sergeant J. C. Jette, bomb aimer, Sergeant R. Askew and wireless operator Sergeant J.E.R. Marchand were able to launch the dinghy without too much trouble. They hastily paddled to the rear of the bomber hoping to pick up the rear gunner, as he was unaccounted for after the ditching, but they found that on impact with the sea the rear turret had completely broken off from the main fuselage and there was no trace of the gunner. An SOS was sent out on their dinghy radio transmitter which was cranked around by hand to give it power. Their position was sent out, and they believed it was not too far from the English coast. At around 05.00 hours in the early dawn light they thought they could see land and that they were drifting towards it, so they cancelled their SOS signal hoping that they could paddle towards the shore. They were, however, safely picked up by the Air Sea Rescue Service boat which had already been despatched on the first SOS signal. The body of rear gunner, Flight Sergeant A. F. O'Rourke, was never found.

Casualties May 27th/28th, 1943. Target Essen

109 Squadron 8 Group Mosquito DZ432 HS/
Pilot. R/98909 F/Sgt C.K.Chrysler PoW. Stalag 357, Kopernikus. 28
Nav. 127104 P/O R.F.Logan Killed Rotterdam, Holland. LL-1-40

156 Squadron 8 Group Lancaster W4943 GT/
Pilot. A/415060 F/Sgt D.L.Wallace Killed Ede, Holland. JG H-5
Nav. 1391148 F/Sgt T.H.Harvey PoW. Stalag 357, Kopernikus. 162
B/A. 1213493 F/Sgt W.H.Moore PoW. Stalag Luft 6, Heydekrug. 213
W/OP. 1172279 F/Sgt R.J.Jackson PoW. Stalag 357, Kopernikus. 178
F/E. 1386995 F/Sgt R.J.Twinn PoW. Stalag 357, Kopernikus. 50
A/G. A/412844 F/Sgt D.Ross Killed Ede, Holland. H-4
A/G. NZ/415538 F/Sgt H.A.Lister Killed Ede, Holland. JG H-5

35 Squadron 8 Group Halifax HR795 TL/
Pilot. 1333632 F/Sgt R.J.Ayres Killed Reichswald Forest, Germany. 23-D-4
Nav. 1318075 F/Sgt A.H.Porter PoW. Stalag 357, Kopernikus. 44
B/A. 1338423 Sgt F.C.Cleaver Killed Reichswald Forest, Germany. 23-D-5
W/OP. 1129300 Sgt L.J.Miles Killed Reichswald Forest, Germany. 23-D-6
F/E. 569504 F/Sgt R.Hageman Killed Reichswald Forest, Germany. 23-D-9
A/G. 654206 Sgt E.Cavill Killed Reichswald Forest, Germany. 23-D-8
A/G. 983679 Sgt L.Marshall Killed Reichswald Forest, Germany. 23-D-7

405 Squadron 8 Group Halifax HR807 LQ/E
Pilot. R/113437 F/Sgt G.E.J.Lebihan Killed Reichswald Forest. 5-F-13
Nav. J/14175 F/O G.S.Wilson Killed Reichswald Forest, Germany. 5-E-10
B/A. J/20264 F/O L.S.P.Dalton PoW. Stalag Luft 3, Sagan. 1402
W/OP. R/52211 F/Sgt C.F.Sovereign PoW. Stalag 357, Kopernikus. 253
F/E. 977737 Sgt J.Holmes Killed Reichswald Forest, Germany. 5-E-9
A/G. R/139351 F/Sgt C.Maracle PoW. Stalag 357, Kopernikus. 208
A/G. R/90327 F/Sgt J.Y.Houston Killed Reichswald Forest, Germany. 5-E-8

100 Squadron 1 Group Lancaster ED821 HW/A
Pilot. NZ/415041 F/Sgt L.A.Townrow PoW. Died 11 months after capture
.(24/4/44) Leeuwarden, Holland. 1-5
Nav. J/13118 F/O S.A.Bishop Killed Wonseradeel(Witmarsum), Holland.36-18
B/A. 1319336 Sgt E.Short Killed Wonseradeel(Witmarsum), Holland.36-19
W/OP. 129941 F/Lt J.Bolderson PoW. Stalag Luft 3, Sagan. 1442
F/E. 1150600 Sgt J.P.Fitchett Killed Wonseradeel(Witmarsum), Holland.36-16
A/G. 1585898 Sgt P.M.Cosgrove Killed Wonseradeel(Witmarsum).37-17
A/G. A/414764 F/Sgt A.E.Chapman Killed Wonseradeel(Witmarsum).36-17

460 Squadron 1 Group Lancaster ED804 UV/
Pilot. 131027 F/O C.Harrison Killed Uden, Holland. 5-H-1
Nav. A/413434 W/O W.G.Schrader PoW. Stalag 357, Kopernikus. 42
B/A. A/415391 F/Lt C.C.Bates PoW. Stalag Luft 3, Sagan. 1441
W/OP. 1272014 Sgt W.A.Blackwell Killed Uden, Holland. 5-H-4
F/E. A221985 F/Sgt C.R.S.Morris PoW. Stalag 357, Kopernikus. 214
A/G. A/414697 F/Sgt E.J.Kerr Killed Uden, Holland. 5-H-2
A/G. A/420661 F/Sgt J.A.Grant Killed Uden, Holland. 5-H-3

166 Squadron 1 Group Wellington HE752 AS/W
Pilot. 51064 F/Lt D.T.Tonkinson Killed Hengelo(Overijssel). JG D-1-65
Nav. 1167534 Sgt P.Guest Killed Hengelo(Overijssel), Holland. D-1-63
B/A. 124924 F/O T.D.Brown Killed Hengelo(Overijssel), Holland. D-1-64
W/OP. 138812 P/O A.D.Johnson Killed Hengelo(Overijssel). JG D-1-65
A/G. 1385954 Sgt N.P.Rayner Killed Hengelo(Overijssel), Holland. D-1-62

199 Squadron 1 Group Wellington HE634 EX/S
Pilot. 1333615 Sgt J.R.S.Waller Killed Reichswald Forest. CG 15-F-5/8
Nav. 657375 Sgt F.R.Pym Killed Reichswald Forest, Germany. CG 15-F-5/8
B/A. 1077010 F/Sgt H.Coupe Killed Reichswald Forest, Germany. CG 15-F-5/8
W/OP. 1061009 Sgt D.W.Glover Killed Reichswald Forest. CG 15-F-5/8
A/G. 1473515 Sgt R.T.A.Hudson Killed Reichswald Forest, Germany. 18-G-17

115 Squadron 1 Group Lancaster DS655 KO/M
Pilot. NZ/415290 F/Lt G.W.Cammell PoW. Stalag Luft 3, Sagan. 1401
Nav. 124578 F/O G.W.Cooper Killed Reichswald Forest, Germany. 18-D-18
B/A. NZ/412736 F/O H.D.Pye Killed Reichswald Forest, Germany. 19-F-13
W/OP. 1293717 Sgt G.A.Parker Killed Reichswald Forest. JG 19-F-15
F/E. 578114 Sgt E.G.F.B.Baker Killed Reichswald Forest, Germany. 19-F-14
A/G. 130931 F/O R.R.Reid Killed Reichswald Forest, Germany. 19-F-12
A/G. 130932 F/O D.S.Williams Killed Reichswald Forest, Germany. JG 19-F-15

10 Squadron 4 Group Halifax JB960 ZA/N
Pilot. 520838 W/O H.W.Price Killed Reichswald Forest, Germany. CG 23-B-6/8
Nav. 1435154 Sgt R.Leyland Killed Reichswald Forest, Germany. 23-B-9
B/A. 128012 F/O E.R.Curtis Killed Reichswald Forest, Germany. CG 23-B-6/8
W/OP. 137569 F/O E.Parry Killed Reichswald Forest, Germany. CG 23-B-6/8
F/E. 613496 Sgt F.G.Williams Killed Reichswald Forest, Germany 23-B-3
A/G. 1392507 Sgt E.G.Halston Killed Reichswald Forest, Germany. 23-B-5
A/G. 1581818 Sgt W.E.Waggett Killed Reichswald Forest, Germany. 23-B-4

10 Squadron 4 Group Halifax JB958 ZA/W
Pilot. 128872 F/O G.Rawlinson Killed Sleen, Holland. JG 12-298
Nav. 1433350 Sgt W.K.Warren PoW. Stalag Luft 6, Heydekrug. 280
B/A. 1347709 Sgt S.G.Beattie Killed Sleen, Holland. 12-297
W/OP. 1125812 F/Sgt E.Williams PoW. Stalag 357, Kopernikus. 287
F/E. 1479264 Sgt J.Howarth Killed Sleen, Holland. JG 12-298
A/G. 1313328 Sgt E.S.Buck Killed Sleen, Holland. 12-295
A/G. 1317476 Sgt E.B.Blackborrow Killed Sleen, Holland. 12-296

51 Squadron 4 Group Halifax HR789 MH/
Pilot. 1410376 F/Sgt F.J.Prothero PoW. Stalag 357, Kopernikus. 228
Nav. 129361 F/O A.B.Wilson Killed Reichswald Forest, Germany. 18-G-2
B/A. 1395905 Sgt J.H.Mastin Killed Reichswald Forest, Germany. 18-B-3
W/OP. 1211893 Sgt D.J.Smith Killed Reichswald Forest, Germany. 18-B-5
F/E. 1367354 Sgt A.Aitken Killed Reichswald Forest, Germany. 18-B-1
A/G. 1216686 F/Sgt W.F.Turner PoW. Stalag 357, Kopernikus. 271
A/G. R/88868 F/Sgt E.J.Cotton Killed Reichswald Forest, Germany. 18-B-4

51 Squadron 4 Group Halifax HR750 MH/
Pilot. 903396 W/O A.H.Beeston PoW. Stalag 357, Kopernikus. 65
Nav. 52179 F/O R.Waker PoW. Stalag Luft 6, Heydekrug. 275
B/A. 948124 F/Sgt H.West PoW. Stalag 357, Kopernikus. 284
W/OP. 1267019 F/Sgt H.F.Court PoW. Stalag 357, Kopernikus. 102
F/E. 960207 Sgt E.D.Mathews PoW. Stalag 357, Kopernikus. 16
A/G. 924414 F/Sgt A.G.East PoW. Stalag Luft 6, Heydekrug. 127
A/G. 1319196 F/Sgt E.H.Perlman PoW. Stalag 357, Kopernikus. 226

76 Squadron 4 Group Halifax DK147 MP/A
Aircraft crashed near Laer, NW of Munster, Germany.
Pilot. J/16483 F/Lt D.S.Ross PoW. Stalag Luft 4, Sagan. 1653
Nav. 1435918 Sgt H.Anderson Killed Reichswald Forest, Germany. 24-D-18
B/A. 1256730 W/O G.J.Beckford PoW. Stalag 357, Kopernikus. 2

W/OP. 1200546 Sgt W.G.Styles PoW. Repatriated.
F/E. 1537949 Sgt R.Jones PoW. Stalag 357, Kopernikus. 182
A/G. J/20105 F/Lt H.Langlois PoW. Stalag Luft 3, Sagan. 1447
A/G. 126966 F/O E.F.Campbell Killed Reichswald Forest, Germany. 24-D-17
Died in hospital from injuries.

77 Squadron 4 Group Halifax JD152 KN/

Pilot. A/411811 F/Sgt F.J.O'Grady Killed Reichswald Forest. 12-F-10
Nav. 120663 F/O B.C.McGrath Killed Reichswald Forest, Germany. 12-F-13
B/A. 1497822 F/Sgt C.Clarke Killed Reichswald Forest, Germany. 12-F-9
W/OP. 1380112 Sgt W.R.Beadsmore Killed Reichswald Forest. 12-F-11
F/E. 1330009 Sgt G.H.Garrard Killed Reichswald Forest, Germany. 12-F-12
A/G. 955870 Sgt C.B.Anderson Killed Reichswald Forest, Germany. 12-F-14
A/G. 1300611 Sgt W.A.Manning Killed Reichswald Forest, Germany. 12-F-8

102 Squadron 4 Group Halifax JD149 DY/

Crashed near Wieringen (Hippolytushoef), Holland
Pilot. 128889 F/O J.D.Jeffrey Killed Hippolytushoef.CG C-13-378/380
Nav. 130288 F/O R.D.Fewtrell Killed Hippolytushoef CG C-13-378/380
B/A. 129576 F/O H.Entwhistle Killed Hippolytushoef. CG C-13-378/380
W/OP. J/17716 P/O S.Zareikin Killed Hippolytushoef. CG C-13-378/380
F/E. 1509397 Sgt K.J.Smith Killed Hippolytushoef. CG C-13-378/380
A/G. 1143480 Sgt T.Heslop Killed Hippolytushoef. CG C-13-378/380
A/G. 1322699 Sgt J.L.S.Lowings Killed Hippolytushoef. CG C-13-378/380

158 Squadron 4 Group Halifax HR775 NP/V

Aircraft crashed N.E. of Deventer, Holland.
Pilot. R/99557 F/Sgt W.H.Wyatt Killed Raalte, Holland. JG 15/16
Nav. 1436421 Sgt J.L.Atha Killed Raalte, Holland. 14
B/A. 1337416 Sgt R.A.Tilbury Killed Raalte, Holland. 17
W/OP. 1294468 Sgt G.Henderson Killed Raalte, Holland. JG 15/16
F/E. 1037117 Sgt W.J.Erdbeer Killed Raalte, Holland. 12
A/G. 1334759 Sgt J.Simmons Killed Raalte, Holland. 11
A/G. R/151473 Sgt R.R.Mantha Killed Raalte, Holland. 13

106 Squadron 5 Group Lancaster W4842 ZN/

Pilot. 1336699 W/O E.A.Robbins PoW. Stalag 357, Kopernikus. 333
Nav. 1433571 W/O L.C.Carpenter PoW. Stalag Luft 6, Heydekrug. 92
B/A. 1113920 W/O L.Calvert PoW. Stalag 357, Kopernikus. 90
W/OP. 1125243 F/Sgt G.F.Calvert PoW. Stalag 357, Kopernikus. 89
F/E. 645605 F/Sgt J.Seedhouse PoW. Stalag 357, Kopernikus. 246
A/G. 1209307 F/Sgt A.Taylor PoW. Stalag 357, Kopernikus. 528
A/G. 1410554 F/Sgt J.N.Denton PoW. Stalag Luft 6, Heydekrug. 116

467 Squadron 5 Group Lancaster ED504 PO/

Pilot. A/406641 F/Lt J.M.Desmond Killed Reichswald Forest. CG 22-E-9/13
Nav. 143426 P/O G.Cribbin Killed Reichswald Forest, Germany. CG 22-E-9/13
B/A. 143430 P/O J.N.Lockwood Killed Reichswald Forest. CG 22-E-9/13
W/OP. 650462 W/O G.F.Paddon Killed Reichswald Forest. CG 22-E-9/13
F/E. 575812 Sgt E.S.Davis Killed Reichswald Forest. CG 22-E-9/13
A/G. 132388 F/O C.K.Cazaly Killed Reichswald Forest. CG 22-E-9/13
A/G. A/405217 P/O J.R.Ryalls Killed Reichswald Forest. CG 22-E-9/13

408 Squadron 6 Group Halifax DT674 EQ/A

Pilot. A/401309 F/Sgt K.O.Greig PoW. Stalag 357, Kopernikus 153
Nav. J/18152 F/O W.V.Neumann PoW. Stalag Luft 3, Sagan. 217
B/A. J/11862 F/Lt C.A.Vogel PoW. Stalag Luft 3, Sagan. 1415
W/OP. R/87336 W/O W.A.Ivor PoW. Stalag 357, Kopernikus. 177
F/E. R/91430 Sgt J.D.Blewett PoW. Stalag 357, Kopernikus. 73
A/G. R/104910 F/Sgt J.V.J.R.Veys Killed Reichswald Forest, Germany. 5-E-6
A/G. R/117670 W/O J.N.P.E.Comeau Killed Reichswald Forest. 5-E-7

428 Squadron 6 Group Wellington MS481 NA/Q

Aircraft ditched off Grimsby at 04.30 hours (28/5/43).
Pilot. R/121729 Sgt W.Lachman Rescued.
Nav. R/135170 Sgt J.C.E.Jette Rescued.
B/A. 1535621 Sgt R.Askew Rescued.
W/OP. R/96762 Sgt J.E.R.Marchand Rescued.
A/G. R/148749 F/Sgt A.F.O'Rourke Missing, Runnymede Memorial 185

428 Squadron 6 Group Wellington HZ485 HA/G

Pilot. R/72344 W/O D.H.Thompson Missing, Runnymede Memorial 179
Nav. J/13842 F/O A.F.Beaton Missing, Runnymede Memorial 172
B/A. R/111333 F/Sgt G.G.Hart Missing, Runnymede Memorial 182
W/OP. 1076367 Sgt K.G.Chilvers Missing, Runnymede Memorial 145
A/G. R/110283 F/Sgt G.C.P.O'Hara Missing, Runnymede Memorial 185

432 Squadron 6 Group Wellington HE294 QO/P

Pilot. J/18109 P/O R.E.Taylor DFM Missing, Runnymede Memorial 178
Nav. J/16754 P/O R.G.Allan Missing, Runnymede Memorial 175
B/A. J/12974 F/O J.A.Farnham Missing, Runnymede Memorial 173
W/OP. J/17209 P/O R.M.Murray Missing, Runnymede Memorial 176
A/G. R/101346 W/O A.G.Bailey Missing, Runnymede Memorial 179

Minelaying

27th/28th May, 1943

On the same night 23 Wellingtons and Stirlings from 1 and 3 Groups went to the Frisians where 89 mines were laid. One aircraft failed to return from this operation, no trace of the crew was found.

Casualties May 27th/28th, 1943. Minelaying (Frisians)

218 Squadron 3 Group Stirling BF405 HA/U

Aircraft ditched 45 miles N. of Leeuwarden, Holland after fighter attack.
Pilot. 655255 F/Sgt W.D.Mills Missing, Runnymede Memorial 138
Nav. NZ/414548 F/O W.V.Fitzgerald Missing, Runnymede Memorial 195
B/A. NZ/415073 F/Sgt G.A.Mathias Missing, Runnymede Memorial 199
W/OP. 1331086 Sgt H.T.G.Hubbard Missing, Runnymede Memorial 154

F/E. 1455802 Sgt S.Smith Missing, Runnymede Memorial 165
A/G. 1125511 Sgt S.Moore Missing, Runnymede Memorial 159
A/G. 50285 P/O J.True Missing, Runnymede Memorial 133

28th/29th May, 1943
Thirty-four Wellingtons and Stirlings from 3, 4 and 6 Groups
were sent to three areas, the Frisians, River Gironde and the
Brittany ports on minelaying sorties. 108 mines were dropped.
No aircraft were lost.

Wuppertal / Barmen

29th/30th, 1943
719 aircraft consisting of 292 Lancasters, 185 Halifaxes, 118
Stirlings, 113 Wellingtons and 11 Mosquitoes were briefed to
attack the Barmen half of Wuppertal. It was one of the most
successful attacks that took place in the whole Battle of the
Ruhr. Pathfinder marking was not, however, very accurate and
the *Oboe* Mosquitoes had serious timing problems throughout
the raid. If it had not been for the accurate marking of the first
Mosquito, at 00.46 hours - two minutes late, the attack would
have been a shambles. As it was the raid was a triumph for the
backers up from 83, 156 amd 405 Pathfinder Squadrons who
kept the 160 aiming point markers going down throughout the
long periods when there were gaps in the *Oboe* marking and so
achieved a concentration never before accomplished and rarely
afterwards surpassed. Credit must also be given to the early
wave of bombers' incendiaries which kept the target area well
illuminated. The 538 main force bombers which finally made it
to Barmen, 65 having returned early, were exceptionally
accurate with their 349,500 incendiaries causing a large
conflagration in the town centre, a type of firestorm which later
was to become associated with the Hamburg raids. 859.6 tons of
high explosive bombs were also dropped in this raid and there
was such a large explosion at 01.26 hours that the shock waves
were felt in some aircraft flying over the target. It was a
Saturday night raid and many of the city's chief officers were
spending the week end in the country so there was a shortage of
people with authority to give essential orders. This caused great

confusion amongst the rescue and fire services. Fires raged all through the night and all day Sunday. Fire services and appliances from neighbouring towns had to be drafted in to help, even though they were aware that they might be the recipients of the next air raid. Daylight reconnaissance photographs showed 1,000 acres of havoc, 34,000 houses were made uninhabitable, the main railway station was completely immobilised and the gas, water and electric services badly affected. Losses for this raid were 33 aircraft, a loss rate of 4.6%. Aircrew casualties being 138 killed, 27 missing and 53 being made prisoners of war. Two aircraft crashed on return to their bases, the first, a Stirling of 90 Squadron, crashed at Newmarket killing all the crew except the rear gunner. The second was a Wellington from 432 Squadron which crashed at Richmond, Yorkshire where the pilot and second pilot were killed and four others injured.

50 Squadron 'Haggis Bashers' Belly Lands

The crew of Lancaster W5004, affectionately known on 50 Squadron as the 'Haggis Bashers' because of the predominant number of Scotsmen in the crew, were fortunate to make it back to base on this their 10th operation.

Their Lanc was flying at 21,000 feet and had just entered the Ruhr area, when the crew saw dead ahead a distant row of searchlights directly on their course. The skipper, Sergeant J. M. McCrossan, was undecided whether he should turn port or starboard, as he thought that the row of searchlights were some form of trap working in conjunction with German night fighters. He chose the starboard option and as nothing happened for a while, the crew began to dismiss the theory that the lights were some form of trap, when suddenly they were bombarded with *Flak* and were hit continuously. It was obvious they had been carefully tracked by radar and were well within the *Flak* range. The starboard outer engine was hit and caught fire and within seconds the port outer engine was also hit and it too caught fire. Luckily the flight engineer, Sergeant J. Wilkinson, was quick with his reactions and pressed the fire extinguishers to douse the flames before they had a firm hold, but the two engines were left u/s and had to be feathered.

By this time the bomber had lost considerable altitude and was down to 12,000 feet. As they were so near the target, the pilot decided to press on with his bomb run and successfully dropped the load of bombs on the target indicators. As they turned for home, they found that the bomb doors would not close and the plane's wheels were hanging half down because the hydraulics were out of action. Now down to 1,500 feet and still losing height, the skipper gave the order to prepare to abandon, but asked the crew to first jettison everything that was possible to get out of the aircraft in a last effort to maintain height. All the crew lent a hand and with great gusto they set about getting rid of any moveable equipment. Eventually the pilot was able, with the two remaining Merlin engines going flat out, to maintain a height of 800 feet. Morale began to return among the crew and a few jokes were cracked as to who was going to pay for the heavy bulkhead doors that had been dumped from the aircraft. Meanwhile the navigator, Sergeant D. Buchan, was busy working out a new course home across Holland to avoid any high ground. As they were now well down below radar height their chances of a fighter interception was minimised, but the two gunners kept themselves busy shooting at any searchlights that were trying to pick them up. Eventually the Lancaster made it back to its base at Skellingthorpe, just one hour late and the pilot made an excellent job of getting the plane down safely in a superb belly landing. For their efforts on this particular trip the pilot and the flight engineer were awarded immediate Distinguished Flying Medals. The next day, when the crew saw their beloved Lanc lying on its fuselage at the end of the runway, they realised how extremely lucky they had been to have escaped injury, for the bomber was riddled with 47 holes, some in the floor and roof of the fuselage the size of a bucket. However their luck did not last much longer, for all except the bomb aimer were to perish in a different Lancaster on their 12th operation, to Bochum on June 12/13th.

Casualties May 29th/30th, 1943. Target Wuppertal

35 Squadron 8 Group Halifax W7876 TL/K
Pilot. 1332756 W/O A.R.Sargent PoW. Stalag 357, Kopernikus. 244
Nav. 1382953 F/Sgt R.G.Hands PoW. Stalag 357, Kopernikus. 160
B/A. 1098526 F/Sgt W.D.Gray Killed Rheinberg, Germany. 6-A-14
W/OP. 1079005 Sgt J.B.J.Knowles PoW. Stalag 357, Kopernikus. 103
F/E. 645001 Sgt G.H.Gardner PoW. Stalag 357, Kopernikus. 143
A/G. 530348 F/Sgt C.H.Garner Killed Rheinberg, Germany. 6-A-15
A/G. 1193315 Sgt D.R.Brown PoW. Camp not known.

35 Squadron 8 Group Halifax HR793 TL/J
Pilot. 68139 S/Ldr P.Johnston DFC Missing, Runnymede Memorial 118
2/Pilot. 1375983 W/O E.A.Roede PoW. Stalag 357, Kopernikus. 427
Nav. J/22541 F/Lt R.Wood PoW. Stalag Luft 3, Sagan. 1512
B/A. 121556 F/Lt R.G.Houston PoW. Stalag Luft 3, Sagan. 1445
W/OP. A/403819 F/Sgt B.T.Royall PoW. Stalag 4B, Muhlberg(Elbe). 83713
F/E. R/115366 W/O A.W.Gowan PoW. Stalag 357, Kopernikus. 104
A/G. 1394079 Sgt M.T.Byrne PoW. Stalag 357, Kopernikus. 88
A/G. 567590 Sgt F.J.Jarvis Missing, Runnymede Memorial 154

35 Squadron 8 Group Halifax HR833 TL/F
Aircraft crashed at Turnhout, Belgium.
Pilot. R/68499 W/O J.L.Lee Killed Schoonselhoof, Belgium. II-F-18
Nav. 81378 F/Lt W.A.Tetley DFC Killed Schoonselhoof, Belgium. II-G-3
B/A. 1334366 Sgt J.R.Jones PoW. Stalag Luft 6, Heydekrug. 1012
W/OP. A/405233 F/Sgt H.J.Ross Killed Schoonselhoof, Belgium. II-G-2
F/E. 51805 F/O J.C.Goodson DFM PoW. Stalag Luft 3, Sagan. 1497
A/G. 1384388 Sgt V.S.Platt Killed Schoonselhoof, Belgium. II-F-20
A/G. 1055872 Sgt F.M.Traynor Killed Schoonselhoof, Belgium. II-F-19

35 Squadron 8 Group Halifax DT804 TL/C
Aircraft crashed St Trond, Belgium at 01.43 hours (30/5/43).
Pilot. 49586 F/O R.Hoos Killed Heverlee, Belgium. 4-C-5
Nav. 1097285 Sgt R.W.Hodge Killed Heverlee, Belgium. CG 4-C-9/10
B/A. 1083975 Sgt J.G.Kennedy Killed Heverlee, Belgium. CG 4-C-9/10
W/OP. 1368705 F/Sgt J.Davidson PoW. Stalag Luft 6, Heydekrug. 112
F/E. 548837 Sgt E.Bell Killed Heverlee, Belgium. 4-C-6
A/G. 1561460 Sgt A.M.Taylor Killed Heverlee, Belgium. 4-C-7
A/G. 1361367 Sgt A.Tannock Killed Heverlee, Belgium. 4-C-8

12 Squadron 1 Group Lancaster ED996 PH/J
Pilot. 42562 F/Lt I.P.C.Goudge Killed Reichswald Forest, Germany. 5-E-14
Nav. 1501247 F/Sgt J.Gorton PoW. Stalag 357, Kopernikus. 148
B/A. 1348445 Sgt R.S.Richmond Killed Reichswald Forest, Germany. 5-E-12
W/OP. 1113723 Sgt V.Wells Killed Reichswald Forest, Germany. 5-E-16
F/E. 1444939 Sgt H.E.Graham Killed Reichswald Forest, Germany. 5-E-13
A/G. 1508882 Sgt J.Hardman Killed Reichswald Forest, Germany. 5-E-11
A/G. 1398671 Sgt N.M.Hatch Killed Reichswald Forest, Germany. 5-E-15

460 Squadron 1 Group Lancaster ED759 UV/
Pilot. A/413924 Sgt H.E.Bull Killed Reichswald Forest, Germany. 5-F-11
Nav. 1338999 Sgt F.C.Sherratt Killed Reichswald Forest. CG 5-F-6/9
B/A. 1321629 Sgt D.R.Munday Killed Reichswald Forest, Germany. 5-F-12
W/OP. 1333621 Sgt P.C.Willars Killed Reichswald Forest. CG 5-F-6/9
F/E. 650303 Sgt G.G.Powis Killed Reichswald Forest, Germany. CG 5-F-6/9
A/G. 1561599 Sgt R.M.Anderson Killed Reichswald Forest, Germany. 5-F-10
A/G. 1244865 Sgt A.W.G.Meech Killed Reichswald Forest. CG 5-F-6/9

460 Squadron 1 Group Lancaster W4985 UV/
Pilot. 1347861 Sgt T.P.Russell Killed Reichswald Forest. CG 9-C-19/21
Nav. A/414971 W/O R.W.Dunn PoW. Stalag 357, Kopernikus. 123
B/A. A/413917 F/Sgt T.Taylor Killed Reichswald Forest. CG 9-C-19/21
W/OP. 1342595 Sgt P.W.Findlay Killed Reichswald Forest, Germany. 9-C-17
F/E. 1070408 Sgt W.F.Clague Killed Reichswald Forest, Germany. 9-C-18
A/G. 1349618 Sgt D.B.Gordon Killed Reichswald Forest. CG 9-C-19/21
A/G. A/409057 W/O S.A.Kirk PoW. Stalag 357, Kopernikus. 190

460 Squadron 1 Group Lancaster ED664 UV/T
Pilot. A/412986 Sgt R.O.Vaughan
B/A. A/412448 W/O N.C.Hopwood PoW. Stalag Luft 6, Heydekrug. 34
Aircraft coned by searchlights over target and went into a spin. Pilot recovered
at 12,000 feet to find that bomb aimer had baled out.

75 Squadron 3 Group Stirling BF561 AA/O
Aircraft crashed at Gladbeck-Rentford, Germany.
Pilot. NZ/40109 F/Sgt S.R.Thornley Killed Reichswald Forest. CG 29-E-15/18
Nav. NZ/416586 Sgt A.McWilliam Killed Reichswald Forest. CG 29-E-15/18
B/A. NZ/41194 Sgt A.C.McPhail Killed Reichswald Forest. CG 29-E-15/18
W/OP. 1383593 Sgt D.Ruocco Killed Reichswald Forest. CG 29-E-15/18
F/E. 904570 Sgt C.W.Larkin Killed Reichswald Forest. CG 29-E-15/18
A/G. 1811761 Sgt J.V.Dartnall Killed Reichswald Forest. CG 29-E-15/18
A/G. 1234152 Sgt F.G.Hooper Killed Reichswald Forest. CG 29-E-15/18

75 Squadron 3 Group Stirling EH881 AA/Z
Aircraft crashed at Gut Deltourserb, Germany.
Pilot. NZ/414242 F/Sgt J.H.R.Carey Killed Rheinberg, Germany. 6-A-11
Nav. NZ/411593 W/O J.L.Roberts PoW. Stalag 357, Kopernikus. 236
B/A. NZ/417282 Sgt P.G.Knight PoW. Stalag 357, Kopernikus. 192
W/OP. NZ/39987 W/O M.Brady PoW. Stalag 357, Kopernikus. 79
F/E. 1276184 Sgt T.Beaver PoW. Repatriated.
A/G. 1250494 F/Sgt W.A.Owens Killed Rheinberg, Germany. 6-A-13
A/G. NZ/404079 F/Sgt N.A.McLeod Killed Rheinberg, Germany. 6-A-12

75 Squadron 3 Group Stirling EF398 AA/A
Aircraft crashed between Vlodorp and Roermond, Holland.
Pilot. NZ/416185 F/O R.B.Vernazoni Missing, Runnymede Memorial 198
Nav. NZ/421935 Sgt O.A.Innes Missing, Runnymede Memorial 199
B/A. NZ/416648 F/O H.Tong Missing, Runnymede Memorial 198

W/OP. NZ/41190 F/O C.H.Riddle Missing, Runnymede Memorial 198
F/E. 1051374 Sgt W.Bramwell Missing, Runnymede Memorial 143
A/G. 1522196 Sgt A.R.Cardoo Killed Jonkerbos, Holland. 24-B-1
A/G. 1699810 Sgt J.J.Chandler Killed Jonkerbos, Holland. 24-B-2

75 Squadron 3 Group Stirling BK776 AA/B
Aircraft shot down near Roermond, Holland.
Pilot. NZ/415282 P/O R.F.Bennett Killed Rheinberg, Germany. 4-G-11 2/
Pilot. NZ/416145 F/Sgt R.F.Norman Killed Reichswald Forest. CG 31-B-15/17
Nav. NZ/411864 W/O A.L.Davidson PoW. Stalag 357, Kopernikus. 111
B/A. 1318948 F/Sgt F.A.Bandy Killed Reichswald Forest. CG 31-B-15/17
W/OP. NZ/403579 W/O S.L.Kavanaugh Killed Reichswald. CG 31-B-15/17
F/E. 1052293 F/Sgt J.B.Harrison PoW. Stalag Luft 3, Sagan. 10646
A/G. R/108000 F/Sgt J.A.Pirie Killed Reichswald Forest. CG 31-B-15/17
A/G. NZ/413337 W/O C.P.Middleton PoW. Stalag 357, Kopernikus. 212

90 Squadron 3 Group Stirling EF349 WP/Y
Aircraft crashed at Cambrai, France.
Pilot. 128953 F/O R.W.J.Letters Killed Cambrai, France. 1-B-4
Nav. NZ/421328 W/O L.L.King PoW. Stalag 357, Kopernikus. 188
B/A. NZ/417042 F/O K.Estcourt Killed Cambrai, France. 1-B-5
W/OP. 1332103 Sgt F.A.Wells Killed Cambrai, France. 1-B-6
F/E. 1221156 Sgt C.W.Hughes Killed Cambrai, France. 1-B-7
A/G. 701032 Sgt R.Raven Killed Cambrai, France. 1-B-8
A/G. 1324260 F/Sgt H.Maskell PoW. Stalag Luft 6, Heydekrug. 210

149 Squadron 3 Group Stirling BF507 OJ/S
Attacked by fighter and crashed at Dormagen, Germany.
Pilot. NZ/413833 P/O A.W.Flack Killed Rheinberg, Germany. 4-G-12
Nav. 146166 P/O J.Shepherd Missing, Runnymede Memorial 133
B/A. 1085002 Sgt F.C.Detley Missing, Runnymede Memorial 147
W/OP. 1325871 Sgt T.B.Morris Missing, Runnymede Memorial 159
F/E. 621384 Sgt H.Lloyd Missing, Runnymede Memorial 157
A/G. R/95347 W/O R.W.Stanley Missing, Runnymede Memorial 180
A/G. R/122267 W/O H.Spoonsler Missing, Runnymede Memorial 180

218 Squadron 3 Group Stirling BK688 HA/A
Aircraft hit by *Flak* and crashed at Schaffen, Belgium at 02.00 hours (30/5/43).
Pilot. A/408278 F/Sgt W.A.M.Davis Killed Schaffen, Diest Belgium. CG 12/14
Nav. 1527169 Sgt T.W.Dixon Killed Schaffen, Diest, Belgium. CG 12/14
B/A. 1284892 Sgt W.R.Howes Killed Schaffen, Diest, Belgium. CG 12/14
W/OP. 1030622 Sgt T.L.Portrey Killed Schaffen, Diest, Belgium. CG 12/14
F/E. 572554 Sgt G.A.A.Grant Killed Schaffen, Diest, Belgium. CG 12/14
A/G. 653941 Sgt J.A.Bramble Killed Schaffen, Diest, Belgium. CG 12/14
A/G. 82184 F/Lt L.W.Abbiss Killed Schaffen, Diest, Belgium. CG 12/14

218 Squadron 3 Group Stirling BF565 HA/H
Aircraft crashed at Kathrinemplei near Kettenis, Belgium
Pilot. A/416404 P/O S.G.Allan Killed Hotton, Namur, Belgium. VII-C-11
Nav. NZ/42313 Sgt H.N.Wade Killed Hotton, Namur, Belgium. VII-C-12
B/A. 132096 F/O E.S.Garai Killed Hotton, Namur, Belgium. VII-C-10
W/OP. 1072483 Sgt W.F.Henderson Missing, Runnymede Memorial 153

F/E. 620927 Sgt J.C.Thomas Missing, Runnymede Memorial 167
A/G. 614965 Sgt K.M.Campbell Missing, Runnymede Memorial 144
A/G. NZ/411614 Sgt D.P.Strong Missing, Runnymede Memorial 200

115 Squadron 3 Group Lancaster DS627 KO/R
Pilot. 1349738 Sgt C.R.Fleming Killed Heverlee, Belgium. 10-B-1
Nav. 1483499 Sgt R.Adair Killed Heverlee, Belgium. 10-B-2
B/A. J/17259 P/O C.K.Coker Killed Heverlee, Belgium. 10-B-4
W/OP. 1367283 Sgt J.Currie Killed Heverlee, Belgium. 10-B-3
F/E. 612466 Sgt H.G.Thomas Killed Heverlee, Belgium. 10-B-7
A/G. 1601720 Sgt A.R.Tickner Killed Heverlee, Belgium. 10-B-6
A/G. 975799 Sgt K.G.Berry Killed Heverlee, Belgium. 10-B-5

10 Squadron 4 Group Halifax DT787 ZA/S
Pilot. NZ/402539 F/Sgt J.E.Clarke Killed Reichswald Forest. CG 3-D-10/13
Nav. 1385756 F/Sgt W.R.Scott Killed Reichswald Forest, Germany. 3-D-9
B/A. 1457107 Sgt J.H.Pickles Killed Reichswald Forest, Germany. 3-D-8
W/OP. 1270693 Sgt R.H.Harris Killed Reichswald Forest. CG 3-D-10/13
F/E. 537108 Sgt J.R.Cranham Killed Reichswald Forest. CG 3-D-10/13
A/G. 1550840 Sgt J.W.S.Birrell Killed Reichswald Forest. CG 3-D-10/13
A/G. 1293909 F/Sgt J.A.Saunders Killed Reichswald Forest. CG 3-D-10/13

102 Squadron 4 Group Halifax W7934 DY/
Pilot. 1388250 Sgt R.A.Ward Killed Rheinberg, Germany. 11-D-25
Nav. 1334923 Sgt P.H.Sheerman Killed Rheinberg, Germany. 2-G-22
B/A. 129579 F/O R.E.C.Allen Killed Rheinberg, Germany. 2-G-21
W/OP. 1028891 Sgt J.Martland Killed Rheinberg, Germany. 2-G-24
F/E. 1538261 Sgt R.L.Hoddle Killed Rheinberg, Germany. 2-G-23
A/G. 1460283 Sgt P.Smith Killed Rheinberg, Germany. 3-A-1
A/G. 1391507 Sgt J.A.Stewart Killed Rheinberg, Germany. 2-G-25

158 Squadron 4 Group Halifax HR717 NP/E
Aircraft crashed near Bourg-Leopold, Belgium.
Pilot. R/86182 W/O J.Cooper Killed Heverlee, Belgium. CG 4-C-12/17
Nav. 125696 F/O W.C.Luther B.D. Killed Heverlee, Belgium. 4-C-11
B/A. 127130 F/O D.R.Woodroffe Killed Heverlee, Belgium. CG 4-C-12/17
W/OP. 1376146 Sgt H.D.Young Killed Heverlee, Belgium. CG 4-C-12/17
F/E. 1183567 Sgt H.Simpson Killed Heverlee, Belgium. CG 4-C-12/17
A/G. 987897 Sgt F.Dykes Killed Heverlee, Belgium. CG 4-C-12/17
A/G. R/95905 F/Sgt W.M.Ellis Killed Heverlee, Belgium. CG 4-C-12/17

158 Squadron 4 Group Halifax HR840 NP/R
Aircraft crashed at Swalmen, 4 miles N.N.E of Roermond, Holland.
Pilot. 1388224 Sgt C.K.Surgey Killed Jonkerbos, Holland. 8-H-6
Nav. 145733 P/O C.Strand Killed Jonkerbos, Holland. 12-H-1
B/A. 659040 Sgt E.S.Coster Killed Jonkerbos, Holland. 8-H-9
W/OP. 1272556 Sgt K.G.Cottrell PoW. Stalag Luft 3, Sagan. 42772
F/E. 145673 F/O G.T.Ayton PoW. Stalag Luft 6, Heydekrug. 59
A/G. 1349772 Sgt W.George Killed Jonkerbos, Holland. 8-H-8
A/G. R/93458 W/O S.J.Marugg Killed Jonkerbos, Holland. 8-H-7

431 Squadron 4 Group Wellington HE203 SE/H
Pilot. NZ/415204 F/Sgt A.H.Smith Killed Jonkerbos, Holland. 12-H-4
Nav. 1432654 Sgt J.H.Bloxwich Killed Jonkerbos, Holland. 12-H-2
B/A. 1076957 Sgt A.Spence Killed Jonkerbos, Holland. 12-H-3
W/OP. 1376608 Sgt B.King Killed Jonkerbos, Holland. 7-H-4
A/G. 1199580 Sgt M.L.Buxton Killed Jonkerbos, Holland. 7-H-3

466 Squadron 4 Group Wellington HE212 HD/ ⸜
Crashed near Vollezeel, Ninove, Belgium at 04.00 hrs (30/5/43). Victim of Oblt
Fritz Engau, 5/NJG1, who was badly wounded by bomber's return fire and
crash landed.
Pilot. 147904 P/O H.S.R.Lloyd Killed Brussels, Belgium. X-17-27
Nav. 146015 P/O W.R.Hendon Killed Brussels, Belgium. X-17-28
B/A. 145811 P/O A.V.Harper Killed Brussels, Belgium. X-17-25
W/OP. 1380482 Sgt S.C.Luke Killed Brussels, Belgium. X-17-26
A/G. 1380227 Sgt W.J.Blundell Killed Brussels, Belgium. X-17-24

466 Squadron 4 Group Wellington MS494 HD/
Pilot. A/411972 W/O L.O.H.Upjohn PoW. Stalag 357, Kopernikus. 43
Nav. 1344018 W/O J.R.Paterson PoW. Stalag 357, Kopernikus. 223
B/A. 1318021 Sgt W.V.Garfield PoW. Stalag 4B, Muhlberg(Elbe). 222512
W/OP. 1080105 Sgt R.A.Napier PoW. Stalag 357, Kopernikus. 40
A/G. 1023216 F/Sgt F.Hay DFM Killed Jonkerbos, Holland. 24-B-8

466 Squadron 4 Group Wellington HZ269 HD/
Pilot. 160037 F/O J.C.Launder PoW. Stalag Luft 4, Sagan. 1448
Nav. 145729 F/O R.Hutton PoW. Stalag Luft 6, Heydekrug. 47
B/A. 1337450 F/Sgt R.Wills PoW. Stalag 357, Kopernikus. 52
W/OP. 1311799 F/Sgt F.L.J.Hall PoW. Stalag 357, Kopernikus. 48
A/G. 710102 W/O I.Farquahar PoW. Stalag 357, Kopernikus. 46

44 Squadron 5 Group Lancaster W4838 KM/B
Aircraft attacked by fighter on way to target between Cologne and Dussel-
dorf.Target bombed but attacked again on homeward flight, caught fire and
crashed at Peer, Belgium at 00.40 hrs (30/5/43).
Pilot. 160059 P/O D.W.Erickson Killed Heverlee, Belgium. 4-C-1
Nav. 1095961 F/Sgt L.Davies PoW. Stalag Luft 6, Heydekrug. 114
Evaded for 2 months, captured in Paris by Gestapo (18/7/43).
B/A. 653013 W/O C.Rees PoW. Stalag Luft 6, Heydekrug. 222633
W/OP. 1483582 Sgt G.E.Chadfield Killed Heverlee, Belgium. 4-C-3
F/E. 616692 W/O J.Grant PoW. Stalag 357, Kopernikus. 1310
A/G. 1214018 Sgt E.A.Thompson Killed Heverlee, Belgium. 4-C-2
A/G. NZ/411964 Sgt R.A.F.Woods Killed Heverlee, Belgium. 4-C-4

44 Squadron 5 Group Lancaster EE123 KM/K
Pilot. J/12470 F/O P.G.Holt Killed Jonkerbos, Holland. 7-H-1
Nav. 1316521 W/O D.E.D.Kimpton PoW. Stalag 357, Kopernikus. 404
B/A. 1552700 Sgt D.McColl Killed Jonkerbos, Holland. 12-H-5
W/OP. 1383984 Sgt W.Young Killed Jonkerbos, Holland. 24-B-4
F/E. 577958 Sgt I.Tucker Killed Jonkerbos, Holland. 24-B-7
A/G. 1576239 Sgt H.Robinson Killed Jonkerbos, Holland. 24-B-8
A/G. 1351487 Sgt R.T.Stoddart Killed Jonkerbos, Holland. 24-B-3

106 Squadron 5 Group Lancaster R5677 ZN/B
Pilot. 1314530 Sgt H.R.B.Whyatt Killed Reichswald Forest, Germany. 5-F-4
Nav. 1324110 Sgt R.F.Coverdale Killed Reichswald Forest, Germany. 5-E-18
B/A. 1575352 Sgt E.W.Cosnett Killed Reichswald Forest, Germany. 5-F-1
W/OP. 1042799 Sgt M.W.Moore Killed Reichswald Forest, Germany. 5-F-3
F/E. R/70694 Sgt L.T.Delorme Killed Reichswald Forest, Germany. 5-E-7
A/G. 1160856 Sgt A.W.Chapman Killed Reichswald Forest, Germany. 5-F-5
A/G. 1237320 Sgt J.Leadbetter Killed Reichswald Forest, Germany. 5-F-2

419 Squadron 6 Group Halifax JB805 VR/
Shot down and crashed near Binche, Belgium. Victim of Oblt Altendorf and Fw
Arndt, 2/NJG4, their 20th victory.
Pilot. R/102710 W/O P.S.Johnson Killed Charleroi, Belgium. CG V-24/26
Nav. 656658 F/Sgt R.S.Metcalf Killed Charleroi, Belgium. CG V-24/26
B/A. R/144487 F/Sgt T.W.Peets Killed Peronnes-lez-Binche, Belgium. MP 2-26
W/OP. 1164578 F/Sgt G.F.Humphreys Killed Charleroi, Belgium. CG V-24/26
F/E. 576634 Sgt C.P.Baker Killed Charleroi, Belgium. CG V-24/26
A/G. R/147012 F/Sgt D.J.Shtitz Killed Charleroi, Belgium. CG V-24/26
A/G. R/54363 F/Sgt E.L.Armstrong Killed Charleroi, Belgium. CG V-24/26

419 Squadron 6 Group Halifax JB793 VR/
Pilot. R/109935 F/Sgt F.E.Winegarden Killed Hotton, Namur. VII-C-9
Nav. R/137063 Sgt R.M.Mingay PoW. Stalag 4B, Muhlberg(Elbe). 270067
B/A. J/21463 F/Lt F.H.Hubbs PoW. Stalag Luft 3, Sagan. 3310
W/OP. R/101923 F/Sgt S.G.Ward PoW. Stalag 4B, Muhlberg(Elbe). 270099
F/E. 1527080 Sgt E.Hall Killed Hotton, Namur, Belgium. IV-C-9
A/G. R/158735 Sgt L.R.Lamoure Killed Hotton, Namur, Belgium. CG V-C-1/5
A/G. R/153603 F/Sgt R.M.Ricketts Killed Hotton, Namur, Belgium. CG V-C-1/5

428 Squadron 6 Group Wellington HE319 NA/Y
Pilot. R/102895 W/O F.L.Shellnut Missing, Runnymede Memorial 180
Nav. 1559352 Sgt D.C.Smith Missing, Runnymede Memorial 165
B/A. R/129522 F/Sgt J.G.A.Marshall Missing, Runnymede Memorial 185
W/OP. 1080691 Sgt J.F.Langley Missing, Runnymede Memorial 156
A/G. R/121431 Sgt H.Macmillan Missing, Runnymede Memorial 184

428 Squadron 6 Group Wellington LN424 NA/E
Pilot. J/17623 F/O J.A.Ferguson PoW. Stalag Luft 3, Sagan. 42776
2/Pilot. R/84487 F/Sgt J.Dywan PoW. Stalag 357, Kopernikus. 126
Nav. J/10712 F/Lt G.F.Tallman PoW. Stalag Luft 3, Sagan. 1507
B/A. J/17576 P/O J.H.Edwards PoW. Stalag 357, Kopernikus. 452
W/OP. 755176 W/O D.C.Smith PoW. Stalag 357, Kopernikus. 251
A/G. R/108414 W/O J.G.Sylvester PoW. Stalag Luft 4, Sagan. 260

429 Squadron 6 Group Wellington HZ471 AL/
Pilot. J/21221 F/O B.A.Richmond Missing, Runnymede Memorial 174
Nav. R/135017 F/Sgt I.S.Levitt Missing, Runnymede Memorial 183
B/A. R/113926 F/Sgt R.G.Bailey Missing, Runnymede Memorial 181
W/OP. 1384547 Sgt E.G.Collman Missing, Runnymede Memorial 145
A/G. R/95701 W/O W.S.Anglin Missing, Runnymede Memorial 179

432 Squadron 6 Group Wellington LN435 QO/X
Pilot. R/126558 W/O W.H.Grigg PoW. Stalag 357, Kopernikus. 154
Nav. 1383878 F/Sgt K.M.Jordan PoW. Stalag 357, Kopernikus. 1481
B/A. 658296 F/Sgt J.J.H.Barter PoW. Stalag 357, Kopernikus. 63
W/OP. 1272168 Sgt L.G.Hardy Killed Numansdorp, Holland. JG E-1
A/G. R/115765 F/Sgt G.W.Thompson Killed Rotterdam, Holland. LL-2-42

90 Squadron 3 Group Stirling EF397 WP/K
Crashed 8 miles south east of Newmarket after returning from operations.
Pilot. 129558 P/O E.A.Norton Killed East Portsmouth. A-3-6
Nav. NZ/42298 Sgt K.F.F.Johns Killed Haverhill, Suffolk. U-248
B/A. NZ/422656 Sgt J.F.Gustofson Killed Haverhill, Suffolk. U-146
W/OP. 1128694 Sgt W.C.Beck Killed South Shields (Harton). T-7431
F/E. 1340748 Sgt E.G.Brooke Killed Cadder, Lanarkshire. B-92C
A/G. 1485790 Sgt G.A.F.Johnston Killed Haverhill, Suffolk. U-197
A/G. 131352 Sgt G.O.Bradshaw Injured.

432 Squadron 6 Group Wellington HE553 QO/S
Crashed at Reeth near Richmond, Yorkshire after returning from operations.
Pilot. J/17798 P/O F.T.Dingwall Killed Ripon, Yorkshire. H-397 2/
Pilot. J/3989 F/Lt L.E.Blight Killed Ripon, Yorkshire. H-398
Nav. Sgt D.Harmon Injured.
B/A. Sgt F.J.Taylor Injured.
W/OP. Sgt K.E.LaChappelle Injured.
A/G. Sgt W.Leadley Injured.

Minelaying

30th/31st, 1943
27 aircraft, 12 Wellingtons from 1 Group, 10 Stirlings from 3 Group and 5 Lancasters from 5 Group dropped 80 mines in the Bay of Biscay area. There were no losses.

June, 1943

Moonlight Gives Germany Temporary Relief

On June 1st, 105 and 139 Squadrons were transferred from 2 Group to 8 Pathfinder Group. Both squadrons were equipped with Mosquito aircraft which already had a good record of low level attacks against German targets. Their fine record was maintained in 8 Group, 105 becoming the second *Oboe* equipped Mosquito squadron and 139 Squadron becoming leaders of the newly formed Light Night Striking Force (LNSF). These transfers were significant events in Bomber Command's battle against Germany, for both squadrons' brilliant achievements added a new dimension to the bomber offensive. At first, 139 Squadron raids were more of a nuisance value, but after six months they established a reputation for adaptability and reliability which finally made them the pathfinding leaders of the new LNSF.

New Moon For Minelaying Only

June 1st/2nd, 1943
During the first ten days of June, Bomber Command curtailed its operations because of the full moon phase. Minor minelaying were the only ones that were carried out during this period. The opening raid for the month of June was a minelaying operation by a force of 30 aircraft, 10 Stirlings and 20 Wellingtons, who went without loss to Texel, the Frisians and the Biscay areas laying 80 mines.

Casualties June 1st/2nd 1943. Target Minelaying

---

196 Squadron 4 Group Wellington HE163 ZO/
Aircraft over shot runway and crashed a quarter of mile west of Arram Grange Farm, Leconfield, E.Yorkshire after minelaying.
Pilot. 127926 F/O J.L.Dean Safe.
Nav. 133 470 P/O A.E.Bothwell Safe.
B/A. 131980 P/O J.R.Vickers Safe.
W/OP. 642824 F/Sgt S.A.Hurrell Safe.
A/G. R/88361 Sgt N.Butts Safe.

June 2nd - 6th, 1943
Another 13 Stirlings and 18 Wellingtons continued laying 88 mines in the Biscay area, again without losing any aircraft. The same area was visited on the following night, 3rd/4th June, when 15 Stirlings and 24 Wellingtons dropped 77 more mines without loss. The last minelaying operation during this moon period was on the night of 5th/6th June when a mixed force of 12 aircraft, 11 Stirlings and 1 Lancaster from 3 Group, dropped a further 64 mines along the Frisians. They too were fortunate and suffered no losses.

Düsseldorf

June 11th/12th, 1943
It was back again to Happy Valley for the bomber crews, with the red tapes on the briefing room wall maps leading to the city of Düsseldorf. 783 aircraft consisting of 326 Lancasters, 202 Halifaxes, 143 Wellingtons, 99 Stirlings and 13 Mosquitoes winged their way to where the initial Pathfinding marking had been carried out, exactly as planned. 86 of the bombers had however already aborted their missions for various reasons before reaching the target. Shortly after the raid commenced, an *Oboe* equipped Mosquito accidentally dropped its load of target markers 14 miles north east of the main aiming point and for a short period in the raid many main force bombers dropped their bomb loads on these markers. Cloud conditions varied from 5/10th to nil cloud over the target with good visibility, although a cross wind, much stronger than forecast, accounted for some of the inaccurate bombing. The wind however was a two edged sword for it helped to spread the fire through the town centre. The Pathfinder backers up quickly corrected the marking fault, but not before the open countryside north of Düsseldorf had received more than its fair share of that night's 1065.8 tons of high explosive and 351,235 incendiary bombs. German reports, which are lengthy for this raid, stated that much devastation was caused in the city centre, 130 acres of which was laid waste and another 1,000 acres very seriously damaged. There was also heavy damage in the industrial suburbs. With the increased

number of incendiaries in the bomb loads, much fire damage was caused and 1,292 people lost their lives in this raid. 38 aircraft failed to return from this operation, the Halifax squadrons of 4 Group bearing the brunt of the casualties. Aircrew losses were 145 killed, 55 missing, 52 made prisoners and 3 evaded capture.

Halifax Shot Down by British Convoy

One Halifax DT742 from 51 Squadron, 4 Group, piloted by Flight Sergeant J. H. Collins developed engine failure in the port outer engine shortly after take off and it had to be feathered. After flying down along the Norfolk coast the captain could not get his fully laden Halifax to climb at all on his remaining three engines, so he decided to abandon the sortie and headed out into the North Sea to safely jettison his bombs. In the area around Sheringham, flying at 3,000 feet and about 10 miles from the coast, unexpectedly the bomber met light and heavy *Flak*. Down below the crew saw a convoy with a British naval escort. The crew had not been warned about this convoy in their raid briefing, so the appearance of the convoy came as quite a surprise. Normally Naval liaison officers were based on bomber stations and usually gave out warnings about any expected naval activity before or after operational times. The pilot ordered his bomb aimer not to drop the bombs in case any of the ships below would be damaged and he also told the flight engineer to use the Verey pistol and fire off the colours of the day, which they had been given at briefing, to show that they were a friendly aircraft. Unfortunately the firing of the colours of the day seemed to act as a signal for all the ships in the convoy to open up with their guns. Further correct colours of the day were fired and the plane's navigation lights were switched on, but to no avail, in fact the ferocity of the gunfire increased. By this time the Halifax was badly hit, the starboard tanks had been holed and the leaking petrol caught fire as it spread on to the engine exhaust manifold, leaving a long trail of flames from the edge of the starboard wing. In seconds the aircraft was rapidly losing height and the captain in desperation tried to restart his feathered port outer engine, but this too caught fire. Flying in between the convoy barrage balloons, the bombs were reluctantly jettisoned and although the aircraft was now only about 50 feet above the waves and obviously going to ditch, the convoy ships persisted with their rapid gunfire. A direct hit by a shell was made in the middle of the fuselage, near the rest position, where the crew had been ordered to go in preparation for ditching and the wireless operator, Sergeant P. G. Spreckley, was killed instantly. The bomb aimer, Sergeant H. H. Parker, was seriously wounded in the stomach.

Ditching was successfully carried out, but the dinghy failed to release and was only extricated with great difficulty by the mid upper gunner, Sergeant B. S. Uppington. The other members of the crew managed to get the body of their wireless operator out of the aircraft and it wasn't until everybody was safely in the dinghy, that the bomb aimer admitted to his skipper that he had been wounded. A boat from a nearby trawler picked them all up about three quarters of an hour later, the Halifax being still afloat and burning furiously. The crew were later transferred to a destroyer which landed them at Harwich. It was later learned that the destroyer convoy escort had seen and identified the bomber in the light of its own firing, realised that it was friendly, but was unable to stop the remaining ships from continuing their attack. No explanation was forthcoming as to why the colours of the day were not recognised or as to why the bomber station had not been warned about the convoy movement that night. As a result of their courage and devotion to duty, the pilot and bomb aimer were both awarded immediate Distinguished Flying Medals.

Halifax Caught in a Master Blue Searchlight

Another of the missing aircraft was Halifax JD143, A-Able from 419 Squadron, captained by Flying Officer W. J. Boyce. It was one of the earlier aircraft over the target, bombing at 01.40 hours. According to post war PoW de-briefing records, the survivors of this bomber recount their experience of being shot down. Apparently after dropping their bomb load the pilot changed course for the turn off point some 10 miles from the city. On this short leg, the bomber had been caught by the dreaded master blue searchlight and then by another dozen lights. The crew had expected a follow up attack and the pilot corkscrewed the Halifax in an attempt to get away. The plane was illuminated in lights for about three minutes, still twisting and turning like a moth caught in a candle flame, but still no fighter or *Flak* attack was made until, suddenly a single shell exploded under the bomber's nose. The three crew in the forward compartment were wounded. The wireless operator, Sergeant D. E. Chambers, received the most serious injuries.

As if the *Flak* gunners had sensed that the bomber had been badly hit, more *Flak* came pouring up hitting the port wing. Both engines caught fire and the port outer finally exploded. The Halifax went into an uncontrollable dive and as there was a danger the wing would break off, the captain gave the bale out order. One of the survivors last out of the plane was Flying Officer G. L. Buck, the bomb aimer, who reports that he went out at about 2,000 feet after unsuccessfully trying to push out the badly wounded wireless operator who refused to jump. It can only be surmised that he was so badly wounded that he hoped his chances of survival were greater by a crash landing. All surviving crew members reported that it was obvious that the pilot realised the danger, but he would not leave his controls until all the crew were safely out. What happened to Warrant Officer H. A. Tripp, the second pilot, is something of a mystery, for according to crew survivors he did bale out because two of the survivors saw him go out from the back door and not from the front hatch which was jammed. Whether his 'chute failed to open or that he was killed on the ground is still a matter for conjecture, for he along with the pilot and wireless operator was killed.

Two Successful Evasions

From the crews which did not return from the Düsseldorf raid, two pilots were successful in evading capture. They were Flight Lieutenant C. O. Taylor, captain of Lancaster ED798 from 619 Squadron, and Canadian Pilot Officer R. F. Conroy, captain of Wellington HE593 from 429 Squadron, who relates the sequence of events from his aircraft being hit to his final return to the UK.

"My aircraft was hit by *Flak* south east of Eindhoven and I gave the order to bale out as the aircraft became out of control. The intercom was u/s and I got no response to the order. I baled out at 01.15 hours on June 12th, coming down in a field. I buried my 'chute in the mud of the field and continued to wear my Mae West until I found an opportunity of hiding it in a ditch. I then started walking north-west away from the aircraft, which was burning about 2 Kms away. I walked until dawn and hid up for the rest of the day in the centre of a field of very tall wheat.

I left the field about an hour before dark and walked until I got to the neighbourhood of a small village, where I hid in another field for the night of June 12th/13th. In the morning at 10.00 hours I started walking again, but after about an hour I reached a road on which there was a considerable amount of traffic. I realised that I could not cross without being seen and as I was still in uniform I hid in a ditch on the edge of the highway. Up to this stage I had eaten some of the chocolate from my escape box and milked a cow, putting the milk in my rubber water bottle. Leaving the ditch at about 22.00 hours, I crossed the road and walked all night still going north-west across country. I continued walking all the following day, June 14th, as well. About 14.00 hours I stopped at an isolated farmhouse. I watched the house for almost an hour and saw only a woman and two children during that time. I also observed that there were telephone wires or electric wires going into the house. As it was now raining and I was cold and hungry I decided to go to the house where I obtained some food from the woman after making her understand who I was. She was quite friendly, but obviously did not want to keep me. Finally she told me that there were some policemen nearby, but I think this was probably just an excuse to get rid of me.

I continued walking after leaving the house until around 22.00 hours, when I stopped at another isolated farmhouse. The only people I saw about the house were a woman and a small girl. But when I went to the house I found two men there as well. Without telling them who I was, I asked for some food. They did not appear to recognise my uniform, from which I had removed all badges. I then spoke to one of the men and pointed out a reference to the British in a newspaper which I had found in the fields two days before. When they discovered that I was a member of the Royal Air Force, they gave me a proper meal.

After an hour, the two men went out and returned with a man from the neighbouring village of Oirschot, which is about ten miles south east of Tilberg. When I told this man I wanted to get to Spain, he said it was impossible and suggested that I should remain there for the rest of the war or try to get to Switzerland. When I insisted that I wanted to get to Spain, he took me to another house in the same village and I spent the night in a barn.

The next day, Tuesday June 15th, the man from Oirschot brought me some civilian clothes and took me to his home. In the afternoon we both went by car to Esbeek on the Belgian frontier, about 12 miles north-east of Tilburg, where he left me at a restaurant. About 20.00 hours, a Dutch policeman took away one of the escape photographs I had in order to get me a Belgian identity card. The escape photographs of aircrew in civilian clothes had been issued to everyone on our squadron. That night I stayed at the home of the restaurant owner. Then at 20.00 hours on the 16th, the policeman took me to a dug out in a forest, south of Esbeek, where four Dutch students were hiding to escape German labour service. I stayed with them until the morning of the June 18th when another policeman took me by bicycle to a point in the woods about 2 kilometres from the frontier. From that point we walked to the border post, where the first policeman I had met was on duty. He gave me a Belgian Identity card and handed me over to a smuggler and his son. The son, who was a student, spoke English. They took me over the border to a village, from where we went by train to Turnhout. We then travelled by train on to Antwerp, where we changed trains for Brussels, arriving in the city around noon. From that point my journey was arranged for me by the underground organisation.

One of the Dutch policemen told me that all RAF personnel stopped by the police in Holland should identify themselves immediately. He said that he knew of a case where an RAF evader was picked up by a policeman, but did not disclose his identity and was taken to police HQ, where the policeman later was unable to do anything to prevent the evader from being handed over to the Germans. Had the RAF evader identified himself at once, the policeman would have taken him across the border to Belgium. After being taken by the organisation to the frontier of Andorra on 13th August, I was put in a party of thirteen which included Flying Officer Simpson, a Canadian air gunner from 405 Squadron Halifax HR854, who came down in France on the Montbeliard raid of July 15th/16th. Being in such a large party to make the night crossing into Spain, we were making very slow progress. So Flying Officer Simpson and I thought the party was too large and broke away from it on August 15th. That day we walked to a town, which was probably Berga, and continued south. At the outskirts of a village we stopped a man and asked for cigarettes. We also asked for directions to Barcelona and enquired if there were police in the next village. The man went ahead of us and when we arrived at this next village the police were waiting for us. They took us to their police station and they were quite friendly. After giving us lunch, a police escort took us to the Police HQ at Barcelona, where we remained in a cell until the 19th. We were then moved to a gaol at Barcelona, where the British Consul visited us. On September 8th we were escorted from the gaol by a Spanish Air Force officer and taken to the office of the Consulate General. That day we were taken to Alhama de Aragon, where we were interned in an hotel for a week. On release I was sent to Madrid arriving there on September 17th, leaving there on the 19th for Gibraltar, before I finally got back to the UK on October 2nd, 1943."

Another Düsseldorf Raider Evades

1392374 Sergeant W. G. Bailey was the navigator on Wellington HZ355, one of the three aircraft lost on this raid from 429 Squadron, based at East Moor, Yorkshire. It was captained by Pilot Officer R. C. Ellison. His plane was shot down by night fighters over Maeseyck near Hasselt, Belgium. He was fortunate that with the help of the underground organisation he made a relatively easy evasion back to the UK. The wireless operator 1378793 Edward Nicholson was not so lucky when he baled out. Landing in cornfield and unsure of his bearings he made for a glimmer of light which he saw about a mile away. It was chink of light from a bad piece of blackout in a farm building. After knocking, the door was opened by a young man who asked Nicholson if he was a British airmen. After replying in the affirmative and that his uniform confirmed this, he was invited in and given a meal and then changed into the civilian clothes which he had been given. The young man then left but soon returned with an elderly man who said that Nicholson should be moved immediately as there was a German Post nearby. He took Nicholson through some fields and carried the RAF uniform in a sack which he said he would dispose of later.

After reaching another farm house where Nicholson stayed for about one and half hours until it was nearly dawn, the man, who spoke fairly good English asked where the parachute had been left so that he could go and recover it. Then he told Nicholson to follow him to the village of Maeseyck, the man walking about 100 yards ahead. During the night Nicholson had witnessed at least three planes being shot down and as he walked to the village he saw many people being stopped by German Military personnel. It was obvious they were checking the area for the missing airmen. Both he and the man were fortunate enough to pass through four such groups without being stopped. He was taken to another farmhouse on the other side of the village, whose occupants were a widower, his son aged about 30 years and a daughter about 17 yrs, both of whom spoke good English. After two days, a car called at the farm and took the son and Nicholson to a farm about 10 miles away, between Measeyck and

Hasselt. The driver was armed and insisted that Nicholson carried a loaded revolver as well.

At this farm the family consisted of a man and his wife, their son and daughter-in-law and one farm labourer. Nicholson stayed there only one night before being taken on by bicycle accompanied by the son and the labourer. They cycled along the Albert Canal tow path towards Hasselt, where yet another man met them and took over responsibility for Nicholson. This man was a corn merchant living in Hasselt and was the head of the local escape organisation. After taking down full details and confiscating all escape kit material, except the money, Nicholson was introduced to the man's wife and his children, a boy of about seven and a girl of about nine. His new helper showed Nicholson the names of about 20 other airmen who had recently helped, including much to Nicholson's delight, one of his own crew Sergeant Mullaney, who was later made a prisoner of war.

After a week's stay Nicholson sensed that the family were getting anxious for him to be moved as one member of the organisation had recently been caught by the Germans. Two young ladies called at the house but they were unable to help as their father was also getting very worried about being caught. The Passport photographs that Nicholson carried and which were issued at his squadron back in the UK were found to be too large for the false identity papers, so a photographer had to be called in to take new ones. At the end of the week at about seven o'clock in the morning, the house was raided. There was heavy knocking at the door and when the owner looked through the window he saw that his home was surrounded by German soldiers. Nicholson was quickly warned of the danger and he climbed up through a fan light in the attic to try and get away through the roof, but the house was detached and the Germans were all around. The owner then called Nicholson to come down and said that it was useless to risk his life. Still hoping to evade capture Nicholson hid under some corn sacks which were left on the floor of the attic, but he was quickly discovered and cross examined by Gestapo men who were not convinced that he was an escaping airman and insisted that he was some sort of an agent. On being taken downstairs he saw that the owner was already chained hand and foot. Both Nicholson and the owner's wife were handcuffed separately and taken to Hasselt prison, where Nicholson spent a week in solitary confinement. He never saw the owner or his wife again. After this he was allowed a quarter of an hour exercise period in the prison yard and every day he saw a new face of someone who had helped or called to see him at the various farms. It was obvious that the whole local escape organisation had been uncovered.

Nicholson was finally sent to Stalag Luft 6, Heydekrug, Germany from where he was liberated by the King's Own Yorkshire Light Infantry, when the whole camp was being transferred on a forced route march between camps in May, 1945.

Casualties June 11th/12th, 1943. Target Düsseldorf

405 Squadron 8 Group Halifax HR797 LQ/A
Pilot. J/16995 F/Lt J.C.Harty PoW. Stalag Luft 4, Sagan. 1495
2/Pilot. R/67665 W/O J.Sommerville PoW. Repatriated.
Nav. J/17436 P/O B.L.Miller PoW. Stalag Luft 4, Sagan. 1613
B/A. 143129 F/O J.E.Patterson PoW. Stalag Luft 3, Sagan. 1614
W/OP. J/9635 F/O T.A.Fillingham Missing, Runnymede Memorial 173
F/E. R/70700 Sgt W.N.Tatham PoW. Stalag 357, Kopernikus. 18
A/G. R/84381 W/O N.H.Taylor Missing, Runnymede Memorial 179
A/G. J/17437 F/O F.E.Mackay PoW. Stalag Luft 3, Sagan. 1612

12 Squadron 1 Group Lancaster ED357 PH/S
Pilot, B/A, W/OP and F/E. baled out over the Zuider Zee and drowned.
Pilot. A/409256 F/Sgt D.M.Thompson Killed Amsterdam, Holland. JG 69-C-20
Nav. 1098656 Sgt K.Bowes Missing, Runnymede Memorial 143
B/A. 1553630 Sgt W.M.Ward Killed Amsterdam, Holland. JG 69-C-20
W/OP. 1345600 Sgt D.N.Campbell Killed Amsterdam, Holland. CG 69-C-19
F/E. 1172557 Sgt J.L.Osbourne Killed Amsterdam, Holland. JG 69-C-20
A/G. R/146605 W/O W.T.Pingle PoW. Stalag 357, Kopernikus. 227
A/G. R/51866 W/O C.W.A.Sparling PoW. Stalag 4, Sagan. 254

12 Squadron 1 Group Lancaster W4373 PH/F
Pilot. A/414132 F/Lt P.R.Ford Killed Reichswald Forest, Germany. 5-G-14
Nav. 657839 Sgt J.A.Osborn Killed Reichswald Forest, Germany. 5-G-10
B/A. 1235304 Sgt G.W.Twitty Killed Reichswald Forest, Germany. 5-H-14
W/OP. 953174 Sgt M.Harris Killed Reichswald Forest, Germany. 5-G-13
F/E. 1336681 Sgt R.A.C.Avery Killed Reichswald Forest, Germany. 5-G-9
A/G. 626653 Sgt F.Anderson Killed Reichswald Forest, Germany. 5-G-12

A/G. 1308435 Sgt M.W.Stone Killed Reichswald Forest, Germany. 5-G-11

12 Squadron 1 Group Lancaster ED522 PH/U
Pilot. 1048176 Sgt R.Highet Killed Reichswald Forest, Germany. 5-H-12
Nav. 1511671 Sgt W.A.Gillanders Killed Reichswald Forest, Germany. 5-H-13
B/A. 1332966 Sgt K.J.Tagg Killed Reichswald Forest, Germany. 5-G-16
W/OP. 1330672 Sgt S.L.Ford Killed Reichswald Forest. JG 5-G-17/18
F/E. 636547 Sgt J.E.Constable Killed Reichswald Forest, Germany. 5-G-15
A/G. 1577745 Sgt L.R.Evans Killed Reichswald Forest. JG 5-G-17/18
A/G. 961573 Sgt A.W.Lee Killed Reichswald Forest, Germany. 5-H-11

12 Squadron 1 Group Lancaster DV157 PH/Z
Aircraft ditched in North Sea.
Pilot. NZ/39907 F/Lt A.W.Doel Missing, Runnymede Memorial 197
Nav. 937812 W/O R.Durham DFM Missing, Runnymede Memorial 134
B/A. NZ/413294 F/Sgt O.K.Whyman Killed Amsterdam, Holland. CG 69-C-18
W/OP. 798684 W/O D.L Templeman PoW. Stalag 357, Kopernikus. 264
F/E. 569401 Sgt W.F.Biggs Killed Flushing, Holland. 2-D-11
A/G. NZ/40921 F/O O.K.Jones Killed Amsterdam, Holland. CG 69-C-18
A/G. 1140287 Sgt T.R.Pagett Missing, Runnymede Memorial 161

12 Squadron 1 Group Lancaster W4791 PH/
Pilot. 620520 F/Sgt L.Shepherd Killed Bevermijk, Holland. CG 683/688
Nav. 1453475 Sgt W.E.Cunliffe Killed Bevermijk, Holland. CG 683/688
B/A. 1452106 Sgt A.A.Gill Killed Bevermijk, Holland. CG 683/688
W/OP. 620520 Sgt L.Stephenson Killed Bevermijk, Holland. CG 683/688
F/E. 1284001 Sgt F.N.Pink Killed Bevermijk, Holland. CG 683/688
A/G. R/115668 Sgt K.B.Davidson Killed Bevermijk, Holland. CG 683/688
A/G. A/33396 F/Sgt W.R.Berry Killed Bevermijk, Holland. 689

12 Squadron 1 Group Lancaster W/4994 PH/
Pilot. F/Sgt W.F.Mizon
B/A. 1317420 Sgt T.G.Smale Killed Illogan, Redruth, Cornwall. 1-24
Bomb aimer killed by *Flak* over target.

100 Squadron 1 Group Lancaster ED786 HW/P
Pilot. 41443 S/Ldr J.R.Manahan DFC Missing, Runnymede Memorial 289
2/Pilot. 36029 W/Cdr R.A.I.Harrison Killed Bergen-op-Zoom, Holland. 4-C-10
Nav. 129356 F/O L.J.Collins Killed Bergen-op-Zoom, Holland. 4-C-9
B/A. 131165 P/O G.McVitty Killed Bergen-op-Zoom, Holland. 4-C-12
W/OP. 1210334 Sgt J.H.Mitchell Killed Bergen-op-Zoom, Holland. 4-C-8
F/E. 546539 Sgt R.E.Longster Missing, Runnymede Memorial 157
A/G. 1260942 Sgt W.G.Watts Killed Bergen-op-Zoom, Holland. 20-A-8
A/G. 1577953 Sgt F.H.Martin Killed Bergen-op-Zoom, Holland. 4-C-11

100 Squadron 1 Group Lancaster ED976 HW/S
Aircraft shot down at Voorst, Holland.
Pilot. 1384719 Sgt A.B.Magill Killed Voorst (Terwolde), Holland. 8A-1-6
Nav. 132773 F/O C.B.Fleming Killed Voorst (Terwolde), Holland. 8A-1-2
B/A. 658341 Sgt W.F.Bradley Killed Voorst (Terwolde), Holland. 8A-1-4
W/OP. 1385248 Sgt G.Glover Killed Voorst (Terwolde), Holland. 8A-1-3
F/E. 971807 Sgt E.N.Cummings Killed Voorst (Terwolde), Holland. 8A-1-5
A/G. R/134599 F/Sgt J.W.Lake Killed Voorst (Terwolde), Holland. 8A-1-1

A/G. R/139994 F/Sgt L.A.Stephenson PoW. Stalag 357, Kopernikus. 256

103 Squadron 1 Group Lancaster ED/914 PM/
Pilot. 1437956 W/O P.J.Scholes PoW. Stalag 357, Kopernikus. 19
Nav. 133330 F/O W.J.Harding-Haydon Killed Raalte, Holland. 20
B/A. 1234835 F/Sgt K.W.Woodcock PoW. Stalag 357, Kopernikus. 22
W/OP. 1333776 Sgt R.Watkinson Killed Raalte, Holland. 27
F/E. R/157058 F/Sgt A.Cook Killed Raalte, Holland. 21
A/G. 936200 F/Sgt G.Price PoW. Stalag 357, Kopernikus. 454
A/G. 1317088 Sgt E.Russell Killed Raalte, Holland. 19

460 Squadron 1 Group Lancaster W4960 UV/
Pilot. A/416324 F/Sgt R.S.Christie Killed Jonkerbos, Holland. 20-J-3
Nav. A/408309 F/Sgt J.Heath Killed Jonkerbos, Holland. 20-J-2
B/A. A/414352 F/Sgt J.H.Horwood Killed Jonkerbos, Holland. 20-J-6
W/OP. 1380317 Sgt R.L.Lewis Killed Jonkerbos, Holland. 20-J-1
F/E. 777739 Sgt R.S.Kerwin Killed Jonkerbos, Holland. 20-J-3
A/G. A/420637 F/O B.W.Bennett Killed Jonkerbos, Holland. 20-J-4
A/G. A/413866 F/Sgt P.J.Hogan Killed Jonkerbos, Holland. 20-J-7

199 Squadron 1 Group Wellington HE277 EX/Q
Pilot. R/108563 F/Sgt C.R.Andrews Missing Runnymede Memorial. 181
Nav. 1439058 Sgt W.H.Bellhouse Missing, Runnymede Memorial 142
B/A. 1338421 Sgt P.E.K.D.Merry Missing, Runnymede Memorial 159
W/OP. 1219223 Sgt W.E.Jackson Missing, Runnymede Memorial 154
A/G. 132447 Sgt L.R.Barrow Missing, Runnymede Memorial 141

15 Squadron 3 Group Stirling BF571 LS/U
Aircraft crashed into Waddenzee, off Ameland, Holland.
Pilot. 146982 P/O R.E.Allen Killed Bergen-op-Zoom, Holland. D-13-7
Nav. 1396120 Sgt A.C.Lake Missing, Runnymede Memorial 156
B/A. R/147410 Sgt L.W.J.Dawson Missing, Runnymede Memorial 186
W/OP. 861885 Sgt H.C.Relph Missing, Runnymede Memorial 163
F/E. 1534380 Sgt S.Wright Missing, Runnymede Memorial 170
A/G. 1294119 Sgt W.S.Champ Missing, Runnymede Memorial 145
A/G. 1558029 Sgt T.K.Fowler Missing, Runnymede Memorial 149

75 Squadron 3 Group Stirling BK817 AA/B
Aircraft crashed at Froidthier, near Liege at 01.35 hours (12/6/43).Victim of
Oblt Telge and Fw Telanig Stab II/NJG1 (19th Victory).
Pilot. 40625 S/Ldr R.H.Laud Killed Ostend, Belgium. 9-D-1
2/Pilot. 1338131 Sgt J.H.Russell Killed Ostend, Belgium. CG 9-D-2/7
Nav. 1349542 Sgt H.S.McQuader Killed Ostend, Belgium. CG 9-D-2/7
B/A. 1332768 Sgt H.S.Mulholland Killed Ostend, Belgium. CG 9-D-2/7
W/OP. 1059932 F/Sgt T.Whatmough Killed Ostend, Belgium. CG 9-D-2/7
F/E. 575638 Sgt A.R.Waite Killed Ostend, Belgium. CG 9-D-2/7
A/G. 1299618 Sgt F.J.Hawkins Killed Ostend, Belgium. CG 9-D-2/7

A/G. 848364 Sgt M.K.Matthews PoW. Stalag 357, Kopernikus. 211

115 Squadron 3 Group Lancaster DS647 KO/
Aircraft crashed near Udem, Holland.
Pilot. 61479 S/Ldr D.P.Fox DFC Killed Flushing, Holland. CG 5-H-5/8
Nav. R/102127 W/O K.L.Spring Killed Flushing, Holland. 5-F-10
B/A. 1380243 F/Sgt P.A.Chapman Killed Flushing, Holland. CG 5-H-5/8
W/OP. 1380770 F/Sgt A.M.Johnson Killed Flushing, Holland. CG 5-H-5/8
F/E. 957106 Sgt P.F.Nixon Killed Flushing, Holland. 5-H-10
A/G. 1334618 Sgt A.D.Bulmer Killed Flushing, Holland. 5-H-9
A/G. 975262 F/Sgt A.S.Spires Killed Flushing, Holland. CG 5-H-5/8

51 Squadron 4 Group Halifax HR788 MH/
Pilot. 656484 F/Sgt J.J.Anderson Killed Bergen-op-Zoom, Holland. 3-C-10
Nav. 1098278 Sgt A.R.Helliwell Killed Flushing, Holland. F-8
B/A. 658031 Sgt A.E.Brodie Killed Bergen-op-Zoom, Holland. 3-B-4
W/OP. 1382321 Sgt D.Glassman Missing, Runnymede Memorial 150
F/E. 632404 Sgt G.Luff Missing, Runnymede Memorial 157
A/G. 1266090 Sgt F.J.Biddle Killed Flushing, Holland. F-26
A/G. 1473151 Sgt G.E.Evans Killed Bergen-op-Zoom (Can), Holland. 6-G-1

51 Squadron 4 Group Halifax HR852 MH/
Pilot. 146866 F/O K.J.S.Harvey PoW. Stalag 4B, Muhlberg(Elbe). 250732
2/Pilot. USAAF Flt/Off D.S.Roberts PoW. Camp not known
Nav. 1387935 Sgt G.A.Galliers PoW. Stalag 357, Kopernikus. 32
B/A. 1315821 F/Sgt G.L.Dunn PoW. Stalag Luft 6, Heydekrug. 125
W/OP. R/82936 W/O H.L.Levere PoW. Stalag Luft 4, Sagan. 37
F/E. R/82304 W/O K.McEachern PoW. Stalag 357, Kopernikus. 38
A/G. 1167995 F/Sgt R.Linnett PoW. Stalag Luft 6, Heydekrug. 36
A/G. R/70890 W/O R.W.Featherstone PoW. Stalag 357, Kopernikus. 31

51 Squadron 4 Group Halifax DT742 MH/
Aircraft fired on by British convoy and had to ditch NE of Sheringham, Norfolk.(5306N 0010E)
Pilot. 1200598 F/Sgt J.H.Collins Rescued.
Nav. Sgt L.Green Rescued.
B/A. 1234389 Sgt H.H.Parker Rescued.(Seriously wounded)
W/OP. 1271792 Sgt P.G.Spreckley Killed Peterborough. E 3-9-42
F/E. Sgt E.Toole Rescued.
A/G. Sgt B.S.Uppington Rescued.
A/G. F/Sgt K.R.Brook Rescued.

76 Squadron 4 Group Halifax DK170 MP/C
Aircraft crashed 4 kilometres south of Bladel, Holland. Victim of Oblt Barte, II/NJG1.
Pilot. 1501266 Sgt A.J.N.Wilson Killed Flushing, Holland. CG JJB-82/85
Nav. 1131592 F/Sgt J.A.Lobban PoW. Stalag 357, Kopernikus. 651
B/A. 657952 Sgt J.Domnitz Killed Flushing, Holland. CG JJB-82/85
W/OP. 928713 Sgt J.J.Pawsey Killed Flushing, Holland. CG JJB-82/85
F/E. 1314108 Sgt C.K.Burton Killed Flushing, Holland. CG JJB-82/85
A/G. 1600509 Sgt D.B.Tibble Killed Flushing, Holland. JJB-80
A/G. R/147471 F/Sgt K.W.Lawson Killed Flushing, Holland. JJB-81

76 Squadron 4 Group Halifax DK200 MP/L
Aircraft crashed at Scherlebeek, Germany.
Pilot. 1313912 F/Sgt D.S.Phillips Killed Reichswald Forest, Germany. 18-B-7
Nav. 1337214 W/O J.Hills PoW. Stalag 357, Kopernikus. 33
B/A. 1511062 F/Sgt G.A.Burdett PoW. Stalag 357, Kopernikus. 85
W/OP. 1293199 Sgt N.W.S.Clack Killed Reichswald Forest, Germany. 18-B-6
F/E. 946155 Sgt C.G.Bird PoW. Stalag 357, Kopernikus. 26
A/G. 1331075 Sgt E.Cadmore Killed Reichswald Forest, Germany. 18-B-8
A/G. 1225545 Sgt E.W.A.Brice PoW. Stalag 357, Kopernikus. 27

77 Squadron 4 Group Halifax JD168 KN/T
Crashed at Oupeye, near Liege, Belgium. Victim of Hptm Von Bonin and Ofw
Johrden, 6/NJG1.
Pilot. 1387306 Sgt A.G.Endicott PoW. Stalag Luft 6, Heydekrug. 29
Nav. 1281607 Sgt R.G.Goodenough PoW. Stalag Luft 6, Heydekrug. 1309
B/A. 1430207 W/O L.S.Blanchard PoW. Stalag 357, Kopernikus. 1285
W/OP. 1332399 Sgt P.F.Wright PoW. Stalag 357, Kopernikus. 1352
F/E. 1455294 F/Sgt J.W.Walsh PoW. Stalag 357, Kopernikus. 277
A/G. 1602835 F/Sgt D.E.Burrows PoW. Stalag Luft 6, Heydekrug. 1291
A/G. 1809320 Sgt S.F.Hammond Killed Ostend, Belgium. 4-E-12 (Died of
wounds in aircraft)

78 Squadron 4 Group Halifax W7932 EY/
Pilot. 1334168 W/O F.Hemmings Killed Flushing, Holland. CG JJB-76/79
Nav. 993803 Sgt J.Stone Killed Flushing, Holland. JJB-74
B/A. 145699 P/O W.C.R.Foale Killed Flushing, Holland. CG JJB-76/79
W/OP. 1127874 Sgt A.Shaw Killed Flushing, Holland. CG JJB-76/79
F/E. 982053 Sgt J.Muir Killed Flushing, Holland. CG JJB-76/79
A/G. 1315951 Sgt T.W.R.Daniel Killed Flushing, Holland. JJB-75
A/G. 1119211 Sgt D.Montgomery Killed Flushing, Holland. JJB-73

78 Squadron 4 Group Halifax HR684 EY/
Pilot. 1265877 F/Sgt J.M.Gavagan Killed Reichswald Forest, Germany. 5-G-5
Nav. 658612 F/Sgt J.J.Jeal Killed Reichswald Forest, Germany. 5-G-4
B/A. 129640 F/O J.B.Binns Killed Reichswald Forest, Germany. 5-G-3
W/OP. 546698 Sgt T.A.Davies Killed Reichswald Forest, Germany. 5-G-6
F/E. 1277063 Sgt A.E.Hayes Killed Reichswald Forest, Germany. 5-G-8
A/G. R/156906 Sgt P.Hollyer Killed Reichswald Forest, Germany. 5-G-7
A/G. 1107264 W/O L.Booth PoW. Stalag 357, Kopernikus. 9641

158 Squadron 4 Group Halifax JD117 NP/U
Pilot. 1313650 Sgt R.G.Pope Killed Flushing, Holland. 5-H-13
Nav. 1586102 Sgt T.F.Potter Killed Flushing, Holland. 5-G-1
B/A. 1321156 Sgt R.A.C.Showler Killed Flushing, Holland. JG 5-G-3/4
W/OP. 1132146 Sgt F.Lee Killed Flushing, Holland. JG 5-G-3/4
F/E. 1370858 Sgt A.Glenn Killed Flushing, Holland. 5-H-12
A/G. 613142 Sgt F.G.Lay-Flurrie Killed Flushing, Holland. 5-G-2
A/G. 1467551 Sgt G.A.F.Green Killed Amsterdam. 69-B-21 Died 18/6/43

158 Squadron 4 Group Halifax HR719 NP/M
Aircraft crashed near Mook, Holland.
Pilot. 142579 F/Lt E.A.J.Laver Killed Rheinberg, Germany. CG 4-E-13/18
Nav. 142890 P/O E.J.Plumridge Killed Rheinberg, Germany. CG 4-E-13/18
B/A. 146022 P/O H.J.Clelland Killed Rheinberg, Germany. CG 4-E-13/18
W/OP. 146606 P/O F.R.Johnson Killed Rheinberg, Germany. CG 4-E-13/18
F/E. 143806 P/O W.S.Smith Killed Rheinberg, Germany. CG 4-E-13/18
A/G. 1336525 Sgt F.T.Adams Killed Rheinberg, Germany. CG 4-E-13/18
A/G. 127164 F/Lt W.T.Dean Killed Rheinberg, Germany. 4-E-12

431 Squadron 4 Group Wellington HE184 SE/M
Pilot. 148443 P/O W.D.Eaglesham Killed Flushing, Holland. E-32
Nav. 126471 F/O L.C.Long Killed Blankenburghe, Belgium. A-13
B/A. 147496 P/O H.T.McAusland Missing, Runnymede Memorial 132
W/OP. 147470 P/O J.H.Burrow Missing, Runnymede Memorial 131
A/G. 1190561 Sgt B.H.Stephenson Killed Ostend, Belgium. 9-5-27

431 Squadron 4 Group Wellington HE392 SE/L
Pilot. 37202 S/Ldr W.E.Mulford Missing, Runnymede Memorial 118
Nav. J/22548 F/O C.A.McDougall Missing, Runnymede Memorial 174
B/A. R/108675 W/O J.G.Breen Missing, Runnymede Memorial 179
W/OP. 1127149 Sgt J.R.Bell Missing, Runnymede Memorial 142
A/G. R/111159 F/Sgt E.S.Rheaume Killed Bergen-op-Zoom, Holland. 28-B-12

466 Squadron 4 Group Wellington HE154 HD/
Pilot. A/408829 F/Sgt F.W.R.Green Killed Amsterdam, Holland. CG 69-C-16
Nav. A/414782 F/Sgt K.E.Fletcher Killed Amsterdam, Holland. CG 69-C-16
B/A. 1388330 Sgt A.S.Jones Killed Amsterdam, Holland. CG 69-C-16
W/OP. A/420333 F/Sgt E.D.Milliken Killed Amsterdam, Holland. 69-C-17
A/G. A/413631 F/Sgt J.F.Mell Killed Amsterdam, Holland. 69-C-15

466 Squadron 4 Group Wellington HE150 HD/
Pilot. 125698 F/O F.Mackelden Killed Rheinberg, Germany. 3-A-12
2/Pilot. A/413315 F/Sgt R.W.Maroney Killed Rheinberg, Germany. 3-A-13
Nav. 125572 F/O S.Roxburgh Killed Rheinberg, Germany. 3-A-14
B/A. 1575212 Sgt T.C.Herbert Missing, Runnymede Memorial 153
W/OP. 146830 P/O E.M.Gold Killed Rheinberg, Germany. 3-A-15
A/G. 1219018 Sgt A.G.Rawlins Killed Rheinberg, Germany. 3-A-16

207 Squadron 5 Group Lancaster ED537 EM/O
Pilot. 657205 F/Sgt J.H.Elliott Missing, Runnymede Memorial 136
Nav. 1817407 Sgt R.A.Stringer Missing, Runnymede Memorial 166
B/A. 132142 F/O I.L.McDonnell Missing, Runnymede Memorial 125
W/OP. 1384157 Sgt H.J.Lygo Missing, Runnymede Memorial 157
F/E. 1556121 Sgt G.J.Morrice Missing, Runnymede Memorial 159
A/G. 1333157 Sgt D.J.Kingsnorth Missing, Runnymede Memorial 156
A/G. NZ/415737 F/Sgt L.E.G.Bishop Missing, Runnymede Memorial 198

467 Squadron 5 Group Lancaster W4983 PO/
Pilot. NZ/43706 S/Ldr D.C.Mackenzie DFC Killed Rheinberg. CG 3-A-3/7
2/Pilot. 40040 S/Ldr B.S.Ambrose Killed Rheinberg, Germany. CG 3-A-3/7
Nav. 145177 P/O D.C.Bovis Killed Rheinberg, Germany. CG 3-A-3/7
B/A. 657599 Sgt A.D.Moore Killed Rheinberg, Germany. 5-D-22
W/OP. A/408779 F/O L.Pietsch Killed Rheinberg, Germany. 3-A-2
F/E. 990173 Sgt J.F.McLuskey Killed Rheinberg, Germany. CG 3-A-3/7
A/G. 115097 F/Lt L.R.Betts Killed Rheinberg, Germany. CG 3-A-3/7
A/G. A/420614 F/Sgt J.B.Donohoe Killed Rheinberg, Germany. CG 3-A-3/7

467 Squadron 5 Group Lancaster ED304 PO/
Pilot. A/401083 F/Sgt B.F.Wilmot Missing, Runnymede Memorial 194
Nav. 1388792 F/Sgt T.W.Hill Missing, Runnymede Memorial 137
B/A. 1390403 Sgt K.T.White Missing, Runnymede Memorial 169
W/OP. A/412114 Sgt W.N.Cross Missing, Runnymede Memorial 195
F/E. 980916 Sgt A.McDonald Missing, Runnymede Memorial 157
A/G. 1345138 Sgt W.J.Fraser Missing, Runnymede Memorial 150
A/G. 1349352 Sgt W.Calvert Missing, Runnymede Memorial 144

619 Squadron 5 Group Lancaster ED978 PG/
Aircraft attacked by fighter crossing Dutch coast and crashed at 00.50 hours at
Tongres.
Pilot. 120030 F/Lt C.O.Taylor Evaded capture.
Nav. 122710 F/O S.E Harris PoW. Repatriated (2/2/45)
B/A. 1391363 W/O R.Evans PoW. Stalag 4B, Muhlberg(Elbe). 250721
W/OP. 1266966 W/O D.E.Inggs PoW. Stalag 357, Kopernikus. 12
F/E. R/70818 Sgt W.C.Anderson PoW. Stalag 4B, Muhlberg(Elbe). 259845
A/G. 1065575 Sgt J.H.Henderson PoW. Camp not known.
A/G. R/110251 W/O R.Chisholm PoW. Stalag 357, Kopernikus. 94

408 Squadron 6 Group Halifax JB972 EQ/Q
Pilot. J/17223 P/O A.G.Grant Killed Rheinberg, Germany. 3-A-8
Nav. J/17002 F/Lt R.E.Carter PoW. Stalag Luft 3, Sagan. 1490
B/A. J/11804 F/Lt T.B.Moore PoW. Stalag Luft 4, Sagan. 1504
W/OP. J/18027 P/O M.R.Laloge PoW. Stalag Luft 3, Sagan. 195
F/E. 906479 W/O K.R.Stentiford PoW. Stalag Luft 6 Heydekrug. 96593
A/G. R/91889 W/O A.E.Fowell Killed Rheinberg, Germany. 3-A-9
A/G. R/119753 F/Sgt J.M.R.Lang Killed Rheinberg, Germany. 3-A-10

419 Squadron 6 Group Halifax JD143 VR/A
W/OP (seriously wounded) refused to leave a/c resisting any attempt to get him
to bale out. Pilot sacrificed his life by trying to keep a/c under control to crash
land.
Pilot. J/12480 F/O W.J.Boyce Killed Rheinberg, Germany. 3-A-11
2/Pilot. R/68179 W/O H.A.Tripp Killed Reichswald Forest, Germany. 4-F-15
Nav. 124923 F/O D.I.Black PoW. Stalag Luft 3, Sagan. 1488
B/A. 127101 F/O G.L.Buck PoW. Stalag Luft 3, Sagan. 1611
W/OP. 1330903 Sgt D.E.C.Chambers Killed Reichswald Forest, . 1-G-7
F/E. 974746 F/Sgt D.N.Stewart PoW. Stalag 357, Kopernikus. 21
A/G. R/105379 F/Sgt R.M.Hall PoW. Stalag Luft 7, Bankau. 156
A/G. R/141114 W/O J.D.Gray PoW. Stalag 357, Kopernikus, Germany. 10

429 Squadron 6 Group Wellington HE593 AL/
Aircraft crashed South east of Eindhoven, Holland.
Pilot. R/55965 F/Sgt R.F.Conroy Evaded capture
Nav. R/63913 W/O G.A.Leitch Killed Eindhoven (Woensel). JG JJB-71/72
B/A. J/17486 P/O G.R.Densmore Killed Eindhoven (Woensel), Holland. JJB-70
W/OP. R/105521 W/O G.A.Nelson Killed Eindhoven (Woensel). JG JJB-71/72
A/G. R/144158 W/O J.Burns Killed Groesbeek (Can), Holland. XVI-F-11

429 Squadron 6 Group Wellington HF542 AL/
Aircraft shot down at Westendorp, Holland at 01.10 hours (12/6/43). Victim of
Lt.Baake, 1/NJG1.
Pilot. J/212939 F/O R.P.Davies Killed Wisch (Varssveld), Holland. A-8
Nav. R/128774 F/Sgt D.E.Campbell Killed Wisch (Varssveld), Holland. A-7
B/A. R/148402 Sgt R.Zeidel Missing, Runnymede Memorial 186
W/OP. R/108469 W/O L.P.R.Taillefer Missing, Runnymede Memorial 180
A/G. R/128077 F/Sgt A.J.McLachlan Killed Wisch (Varssveld), Holland. A-9

429 Squadron 6 Group Wellington HZ355 AL/
Aircraft shot down by fighter over Maesedyck near Hasselt, Belgium.
Pilot. 147969 P/O R.C.Ellison Missing, Runnymede Memorial 131
Nav. 1392374 Sgt W.G.Bailey Evaded capture
B/A. 1187663 W/O H.E.J.Horton PoW. Stalag 357, Kopernikus. 398
W/OP. 1378793 W/O E.C.Nicholson PoW. Stalag Luft 6, Heydekrug. 417
A/G. R/129105 W/O W.J.Mullaney PoW. Stalag 4B, Muhlberg(Elbe). 259891

426 Squadron 6 Group Wellington HZ261 OW/
Pilot. J/17659 P/O N.D.Hayes Missing, Runnymede Memorial. 175
Nav. J/20373 F/O J.L.Rawson Missing, Runnymede Memorial 174
B/A. R/146946 F/Sgt D.G.Richardson Missing, Runnymede Memorial 185
W/OP. R/119136 F/Sgt C.E.Schamehorn Missing, Runnymede Memorial 185
A/G. R/143462 F/Sgt D.A.Mackenzie Missing, Runnymede Memorial 184

432 Squadron 6 Group Wellington HE792 QO/U
Pilot. C/5577 F/Lt L.A.Bourgeois Missing, Runnymede Memorial 172
Nav. R/88414 Sgt J.A.M.Philpott Missing, Runnymede Memorial 185
B/A. J/21036 F/O G.A.McClintock Missing, Runnymede Memorial 174
W/OP. J/18605 P/O H.D.Warner Missing, Runnymede Memorial 178
A/G. R/153528 F/Sgt D.S.McRae Missing, Runnymede Memorial 185

196 Squadron 4 Group Wellington MS496 ZO/
Aircraft crashed at Stanhoe near Bircham Newton, Norfolk after operations to
Düsseldorf.
Pilot. 130647 F/O K.W.Jackson Killed Hunstanton.(New) Pilot.-55
Nav. 129599 F/O R.P.Lea Killed Gt Bircham.(St Marys) 1-3-1
B/A. 1481862 Sgt J.S.Atherton Injured.
W/OP. 1199954 Sgt S.H.Mortimer Injured.
A/G. 1314510 Sgt I.P.Prothero Injured.

428 Squadron 6 Group Wellington HE322 NA/J
Aircraft crashed on take off at Dalton Yorks. for operations to Düsseldorf.
Pilot. R/121729 Sgt W.Lachman Seriously Injured.
Nav. R/135170 F/Sgt J.C.Jette Killed Darlington.(West) W-7L-370
B/A. 1535621 Sgt R.Askew Killed Grimsargh, Lancashire. 6-13
W/OP. R/96762 F/Sgt J.E.R.Marchand Killed Darlington.(West) W-7L-369
A/G. R/66593 Sgt M.P.Scullion Killed Darlington.(West) W-7L-371

Pathfinder Training Exercise Bombs Münster

On the same night as the Düsseldorf raid, 8 Group Pathfinders carried out a training exercise with their bombers, which were all equipped with H^2S. The town of Münster was used as a target for seventy two aircraft comprising 29 Lancasters, 22 Halifaxes and 21 Stirlings, but only 33 of this force carried target indicators as well as bombs, the rest had only the normal bomb load. It appears that Bomber Command was not going to waste an opportunity of bombing Germany with skilled crews even when on an exercise. With such a small force the raid was over in ten minutes, but it must have been a terrible ten minutes for the town and its inhabitants. The aiming point, which was the railway station, was accurately marked and reconnaisance photos taken the following day confirmed the bomber crew reports that a great deal of damage had been caused. The town's records on this raid however are brief and state that railway installations suffered much damage and 132 buildings were destroyed and over 300 damaged with 52 people killed.

Bomber losses for these two raids were heavy, especially in the Pathfinder force exercise raid on Münster when 5 aircraft were lost, making a 6.9% loss for this comparatively small 8 Group force. Although Halifaxes from 35 Squadron were acting as Pathfinders, they were fortunate in not having any losses on this trip but one of their planes met very stiff opposition and was extremely lucky to make it back to their base at Graveley. Aircrew losses on the Pathfinder raid on Münster were 12 killed, 16 missing and 8 made prisoner.

Two German Fighters Shot Down

The Halifax piloted by Pilot Officer N. A. Cobb from 35 Squadron, was in serious trouble long before it had reached the target with its load of TIs. North of Aachen the plane was attacked by a fighter and both gunners were wounded. A small fire was started in the wing between the port engines and the rear turret was damaged, although reported serviceable by the rear gunner, Flight Sergeant N. T. Williams. A second attack was made by a single engined fighter which was spotted by the flight engineer, but as it passed below the twisting and turning Halifax, the rear gunner reported a further attack by a twin engined fighter, this time attacking from the rear. Williams quickly got a rapid burst in with his four Browning machine guns and the fighter broke off its attack and in seconds exploded only yards away from the rear turret. The flash temporarily blinded the gunner, but as he was slowly regaining his night vision, the first single engined fighter was seen preparing for another attack from the port quarter. The rear gunner quickly had him in his sights and opened fire when the enemy was about 400 yards away. Pieces began to break off the fighter, but it still continued its attack as if intent to ram the bomber if it could not shoot it down. Luckily only a few yards away from the bomber it started to disintegrate and nose dived down into the clouds below, obviously out of control.

The pilot then quickly ascertained the damage and the crew's injuries. The mid upper gunner, Flight Sergeant T. H. Smith, had been grazed in the head by a bullet and was quite dazed and the rear gunner had several bullet wounds in his legs and stomach. Not only was the bomber badly damaged but it now had little defence from any further attack, so the pilot decided that it would be wise to jettison the bomb load, but retain his important TIs and return to base with the best speed he could coax from his plane. Fortunately the Halifax returned safely to base. Flight Sergeant Williams, already the holder of the Distinguished Flying Medal and Bar whilst serving with 10 Squadron, received on his return an immediate award of the Conspicuous Gallantry Medal for his skill, tenacity and devotion to duty during this flight.

Casualties June 11th/12th, 1943. Target Münster

83 Squadron 8 Group Lancaster R5686 OL/G
Pilot. 104764 S/Ldr J.E.Swift DFC Killed Bergen-op-Zoom, Holland. 32-B-9
Nav. 44485 F/Lt C.V.J.Geary Missing, Runnymede Memorial 119
B/A. J/10662 F/O C.G.Miller Missing, Runnymede Memorial 174
W/OP. 124699 F/O D.O.Thomas Missing, Runnymede Memorial 129
F/E. 544783 Sgt N.Greenwood Missing, Runnymede Memorial 151
A/G. 1203309 Sgt J.J.Anderton Killed Bergen, Holland. 2-C-22
A/G. R/90884 W/O C.A.Nash Missing, Runnymede Memorial 180

156 Squadron 8 Group Lancaster ED935 GT/
Pilot. A/408724 F/Sgt K.L.W.Lay Missing, Runnymede Memorial 193
2/Pilot. 120216 F/O J.A.Cowley DFM Killed Amsterdam, Holland. CG 69-C-20
Nav. A411748 F/O J.J.Bryant Killed Amsterdam, Holland. CG 69-C-20
B/A. 743397 Sgt R.E.Ratcliff Missing, Runnymede Memorial 162
W/OP. 1320428 Sgt D.C.Bauman Missing, Runnymede Memorial 142
F/E. 1380012 Sgt W.J.Drake Killed Lemsterland(Lemmer), Holland. C-8-235
A/G. 1483600 Sgt J.R.Curtis Killed Lemsterland(Lemmer), Holland. C-8-234
A/G. 1533997 Sgt W.Forster Missing, Runnymede Memorial 149

7 Squadron 8 Group Stirling R9286 MG/C
Aircraft shot down by *Flak* off Den Helder. Last fix obtained at 03.58 hours (12/6/43). Position 5248N 0213E.
Pilot. 114251 F/O E.P.DeVille Missing, Runnymede Memorial 124
Nav. 116418 F/Lt W.M.Theobald Missing, Runnymede Memorial 121
B/A. 1128900 F/Sgt J.L.Wilson Missing, Runnymede Memorial 140
W/OP. 1283912 F/Sgt J.M.Davies Missing, Runnymede Memorial 136
F/E. 651014 F/Sgt T.J.Bainbridge Missing, Runnymede Memorial 135
A/G. 533882 F/Sgt H.Humphreys DFM Missing, Runnymede Memorial 137
A/G. R/128052 W/O J.Harrington Missing, Runnymede Memorial 180

35 Squadron 8 Group Halifax DT805 TL/Y
Aircraft shot down Zelhem, Holland at 01.43 hours (12/6/43). Victim of Hpt.Von Bonin, 6/NJG1.
Pilot. 132816 F/Lt S.G.Howe Killed Zelhem, Holland. E-2-11
Baled out but parachute not seen to open.
Nav. 137318 F/O W.H.Burgess PoW. Stalag Luft 3, Sagan. 1489
B/A. 48819 F/Lt G.P.Watts PoW. Stalag Luft 3, Sagan. 1510
W/OP. NZ/404712 F/O H.A.Jamieson PoW. Stalag Luft 3, Sagan. 1500
F/E. 149099 F/O A.H.Mundy PoW. Stalag Luft 3, Sagan. 39
A/G. 1118935 W/O G.M.Buchan PoW. Stalag Luft 6, Heydekrug. 42774
A/G. R/132193 F/Sgt F.W.Batty PoW. Stalag 4B, Muhlberg(Elbe). 735

35 Squadron 8 Group Halifax JB785 TL/Q

Pilot. 142149 P/O G.R.Herbert DFM Killed Rotterdam, Holland. LL-2-44

Nav. 1335457 F/Sgt E.Cassingham Killed Rotterdam, Holland. LL-1-43

B/A. 1453320 W/O R.H.Makin PoW. Stalag Luft 4, Sagan. 207

W/OP. 1059993 F/Sgt F.J.Greenwood Killed Rotterdam, Holland. JG LL-41/42

F/E. 566943 F/Sgt F.Stewart Killed Rotterdam, Holland. LL-2-43

A/G. 1331310 Sgt R.H.Boone Killed Rotterdam, Holland. JG LL-41/42

A/G. 49831 F/Lt A.V.Wallace PoW. Stalag Luft 3, Sagan. 1729

Mosquito Nuisance Raids

Five Mosquitoes went on nuisance raids on the same night as the major raids, two of them went to Duisburg and the other three went to Cologne, dropping a total of eleven 500lbs bombs. There were no losses.

Bochum

June 12th/13th, 1943

There was to be no respite for the Ruhr, for another heavy force of 501 planes, 323 Lancasters, 167 Halifaxes and 11 Mosquitoes took off for Bochum. From this force 52 aircraft had to make an early return to their bases again for a variety of technical reasons.

Small amounts of medium cloud were found en route with 7/10ths strato cumulus with tops around 8,000 to 10,000 feet over the target area. The exact centre of the town was the aiming point for the 107 sky markers dropped by the *Oboe* equipped Mosquitoes and the all Lancaster and Halifax main force caused severe damage with their 874.2 tons of high explosive bombs and 244,000 incendiaries which were dropped. PFF target indicators were generally accurate, except for a technical error by one aircraft which dropped its marker about 12 miles north of the aiming point and attracted some of the bombing. The raid lasted from 01.16 to 02.07 hours and *Flak* was moderate, chiefly of the barrage type. Searchlights were extremely active in large cones with enemy fighters flying around them. At debriefing one aircraft crew reported seeing five Ju88's over the target, in a five minute period. Daylight photographs, taken the next day, showed over 130 acres of the town centre destroyed. 24 aircraft failed to return from this mission, a loss rate of 4.8%, with the following crew losses, 89 killed, 36 missing, 43 made prisoners and there was one successful evasion.

Sergeant Stewart's Lucky Survival

Lancaster ED429 from 50 Squadron, captained by Pilot Officer J. M. McCrossan DFM, was one of the aircraft which did not return from this raid. Only a fortnight before Sergeant McCrossan, as he was then, along with his flight engineer were awarded the DFM for their efforts on the Wuppertal raid. There was only one lucky survivor from Lancaster ED429 on this Bochum operation and he was the bomb aimer, Sergeant George Stewart, who relates his miraculous escape.

"From the start of the operation we appeared to be dogged by unfortunate events, which to me did not augur well for our 12th operation. As we took off, the skipper had a lot of trouble in getting the heavily laden Lanc unstuck from the runway, as if it didn't want to go on this op. By bumping it a couple of times we managed to get airborne, clearing the boundary fence at the end of the runway by only a few feet. The gremlins also took a hand that night for we found that the gyro compass had been switched off and again as we reached oxygen height, the oxygen bottles in the aircraft had been turned off. We also had trouble with an engine overheating and as we continued on the flight I had a sense of foreboding, for we were getting behind in our schedule time. As we approached Bochum from the north I could see the red TIs go down and I knew at least we were bang on course. Flak was quite heavy by this time and getting quite accurate. On our bombing run we started to get hit. I thought to myself, 'Not another Wuppertal,' so I clipped on my chest 'chute and lay down on it in my bomb aimer's position and started to set up my bomb sight.

"Suddenly it happened. The aircraft blew up with a direct hit and I was blown out alive but unconscious. My first recollection on coming to my senses was to hear a noise in the distance, which became increasingly louder and then explode in my ears. I felt a severe pain in my head and shoulders and my feet felt extremely cold. It dawned on me slowly that I was no longer in the aircraft, but in mid air and that I was hanging from my 'chute, how it opened I don't know. I kept thinking of the crew and wondered whether the skipper and the rest of the crew had also got out like me. With these troubled thoughts and still feeling very dazed, I crashed into the ground face downwards. I must have lain on the ground for sometime for I can recall dawn was breaking when I was discovered by some *Luftwaffe* personnel. I was roughly searched and later placed on a stretcher and carried to a nearby hospital. I found out later that I had landed in a cemetery and was lucky to have missed crashing into the grave head stones.

"I remained in hospital for about 6 to 7 weeks and was kept under guard for most of that time. I experienced and endured our own bombing there and knew what it was like to watch through the hospital windows and see the red TIs go down. I was not allowed to go into a shelter, because I was classed as a "Terror Flieger". As I grew stronger from my injuries, I planned and attempted an escape but was unsuccessful. This episode must have prompted the *Luftwaffe* to remove me from the hospital because I was taken by an open truck through the Ruhr, where I saw the unbelievable destruction and havoc caused by the RAF bombings. I was then taken to Dulag Luft near Frankfurt, where I received a lengthy interrogation before being registered as a prisoner of war and sent to a camp near Stettin. After a short spell there all the prisoners were moved by railway trucks to another camp, Stalag Luft VI near Heydekrug, East Prussia and while there I passed a Medical Board for Repatriation. I was lucky again for I left by train as the camp was being evacuated and I missed the forced marches which I later heard about. I came home by way of Sweden and arrived in Liverpool on a Red Cross Hospital ship on 1st November, 1944."

158 Squadron Halifax Shot Down by an Ace

Another survivor of the Bochum raid was Sergeant Harry Leary, who was a mid upper gunner on Halifax HR740 'K for King', captained by New Zealand Sergeant S. C. Brown. It was the crew's 16th operation from 158 Squadron based at Lissett, and their aircraft was part of the squadron's 21 strong contribution to the bomber force that night. The Halifax had bombed the target and was on its return flight when it was intercepted by a Ju88 night fighter approximately 17 minutes flying time from the Dutch coast. It was a sudden attack in which the bomber was raked with cannon and machine gun fire, in spite of the returning fire from the two gunners. The aircraft was badly damaged and the starboard wing petrol tanks caught fire immediately, leaving a trail of flames issuing from it. The pilot realised it would only be a matter of time before the whole wing would explode and break off, so he gave the order for a quick bale out. Unknown to the pilot the intercom was out of commission and the first intimation that Harry had of the order to bale out was the flight engineer, Sergeant L. Martin, pulling at his legs, which were in the stirrup foot straps below the mid upper turret. At first Harry only felt an odd sensation in one leg and thought that he might have been hit by a piece of shrapnel, but the engineers' hand signs with his pulling and pushing to get Harry down and back to the rear exit door was sufficent to convince him that there was an emergency situation.

German records show that Halifax K for King had been shot down by an ace German night fighter pilot, *Oberleutnant* Hans Heinz Augenstein, who had 47 British bombers to his credit. He was killed before the war was over, by a Mosquito fighter on December 6th 1944 over Münster.

Harry's recollection of his bale out is hazy, the only thing he recalls with clarity is when he left the aircraft door, both his flying boots fell off and how cold his feet felt as he swayed down in his parachute from 20,000 feet. He landed luckily uninjured although very heavily in a small wood, which consisted of sapling trees. Before discarding and hiding his 'chute, he ripped long strips from it and after removing his socks, bound his feet with the silk before replacing his socks, for he realised that without adequate footwear his chances of evasion were slim. In the distance he could see a minor road with a few houses nearby, so he decided to hide up for the rest of the night in a neighbouring wood, from where he also spent the next day considering his next course of action. Fortunately he had in his battle dress top pocket a non issue compass, which he always carried, so on the evening of the next day he set off due west.

Harry, however, must have been spotted during the night, for at about 08.00 hours he was apprehended by three men wearing German type tunics and who were armed with revolvers. He was taken by them and walked down to a waiting car, which had a driver and a Dutch boy, aged about 12 years, who spoke reasonable English and interpreted the questions for the men. They were anxious to know Harry's squadron, the type of aircraft he flew and the place where he had bombed. Harry's non commital name, rank and number reply did not impress them. He was taken to what appeared to be a teacher's room in a village school and locked in. Shortly afterwards he was taken by car to a Burgomaster's office in a neighbouring village. The Burgomaster was obviously sympathetic to the German cause, for he shouted out questions in a very aggressive manner. In the absence of the Dutch boy interpreter, the questions did not mean much to Harry, who was quite indifferent to them. It was also at this office that he later met his pilot and flight engineer, who had been captured earlier. They did not admit any knowledge of knowing each other, for Harry was given the slight shake of head from the pilot, although in his heart Harry was very relieved to find that at least two more of his crew had escaped from the bomber.

From the office the three crew members, along with some other captured aircrew, were taken to the infamous Dulag Luft, a camp where all downed aircrew were first interrogated. After a further six days of questions and waiting, the three were transferred to a newly built NCO prisoner of war camp at Heydekrug, Stalag Luft 6 in Upper Silesia.

The *Insterburg* Incident

The early days in the prison camp were far from pleasant, but as Harry admits, bearable. It was when the Russian advance was made in July 1944 and also when the rapid strides eastwards were made by the British Eighth Army that the Germans took a tougher attitude. They began moving the prisoners away from the ever nearing front line. It was at this period that the prisoners began to suffer great privations. First they were taken by cattle truck, packed together in groups of 60 in trucks which really had only space for 40 men. Their initial journey took nearly four days, during which time they were given no food, very little water and had no sanitation, except for one old oil drum per truck. Many of the men were in a distressed condition, all were hungry, filthy and tired. All came without footwear, for the Germans had taken away all shoes and boots to prevent the men from escaping. Even so a few men managed to escape from those dreadful conditions. The cattle trucks finally arrived at the Baltic coast port of Memel, Lithuania, where the now bedraggled collection of men were herded on to a small old coal ship *The Insterburg*. Once on board, they were packed into the filthy dirty coal holds, which were awash with bilge water. There they were kept again without food and sanitation until they reached the port of Swinemünde. During the voyage many of the airmen were seasick, which certainly did not help the conditions on board. On one occasion an airman, who had been allowed on deck, was so distressed that he suddenly jumped overboard. It was obvious that there was no chance of escaping, yet he was shot at by the guards as he tried to swim away. On arrival at Swinemünde, it was a case of from the frying pan into the fire, for the town was being bombed at that moment by Allied bombers and for much of the time the airmen and their German guards were sheltering from the bombs under railway trucks and carriages. Harry recalls that it was an absolute shambles and there was total confusion, with the airmen manacled in pairs seeking any shelter they could find. Sadly some of the prisoners were killed in the raid.

The Run Up The Road

From the docks the prisoners were then forced to run still handcuffed in pairs, carrying their meagre possessions, to the next camp at Gross Tychow, Kiefheide, 4.5 Kilometres away. Now in a very weakened condition and in the full heat of a hot July day, the column of about 800 men staggered along. Loud threats by the officer in charge, Hauptmann Pickhardt, who insisted that the prisoners run faster, incited the guards to stab the airmen with their fixed bayonets, club them over the head with the rifle butts and fire recklessly over their heads, while along the flank of the column, guards with Alsatians allowed the dogs to savage any airmen who did not keep up with the column.

At last on arrival at the camp, the airmen were herded through the gate in single file, between rows of guards who clubbed and stabbed them as they went through. Of the 800 men who had made it this far, 160 had bayonet wounds, 90 had dog bites and many others had head wounds from being clubbed. On entry all the airmen were forced to lie face down, with no moving or talking and under threat of being shot. After all the horrors of the 4.5 kilometre run, which became known as 'The Run up the Road', Harry and his fellow prisoners later went on a 600 mile forced march westwards from February to May 1945, when the Gross Tychow camp again came under threat from the advancing Russian forces.

The column of sick and now undernourished men covered about 30 miles each day, sleeping rough in fields and forests, in rain and snow, with sometimes only tree branches as cover. It was considered a luxury to spend a night in a barn, with straw as a blanket or even better still to sleep in a pig sty, where the dung and straw made such a warm bed. The column unfortunately lost many men killed by British aircraft which strafed the column with machine guns and cannon when the column was incorrectly identified as a German troop column. More died of malnutrition, starvation and disease. It was not an uncommon sight, with such a serious scarcity of food, to see a horse which had dropped down dead by the roadside, being carved up for meat, and grass and rotting cabbage stalks being boiled and eaten. The dispirited guards were now lax and they were often supplemented by young German boys just into their teens, whose fixed bayonets often were taller than themselves. There were some escapes, but the majority of men were in no fit condition to make a run for it. Gradually the column of airmen was dispersed into various camps. Harry was put into a British Army prisoner of war camp, which was poorly guarded and had little food. Here men existed on dustbins of kitchen waste, old cabbage leaves and potato peelings brought to the camp by Germans who lived round about.

Harry's ordeal was at last over on May 2nd, 1945, when the British Eighth Army overran the camp and he and his liberated fellow prisoners were brought back to England to be demobbed and to go their separate ways, endeavouring to try to forget the nightmares of the past.

From the seven crew of the Halifax which had set off from Lissett, East Yorkshire, six were captured and made prisoners of war, but the seventh 1194036 Sergeant Syd Holroyd, the wireless operator, who evaded capture recounts his adventures before finally making it back to England.

"I baled out at Denekamp, Holland and my first move as soon as I landed was to bury my 'chute and flying kit. I then approached a nearby farmhouse. I was fortunate, for the farmer was prepared to help me and he sheltered me for two weeks, during which time I hid out in the fields surrounding the farm most of the time. On 28th June the farmer put me in touch with two English speaking men who took me to Hengelo. My helpers there were already sheltering an escaped French PoW named Paul Geham. Accompanied by a guide we were both sent on to Maastricht on 30th June. From there we made our way on foot towards the Belgian frontier, which we crossed at Fouron-le-Comte. We had started out from Maastricht with a guide, but he fell ill on the way and we had to go on alone. It was fortunate that we each had been given a map of the surrounding area which we had been advised to learn off by heart.

"At Fouron-le-Comte Geham spoke to some French girls and asked them to help us and one of them took us to the home of a hairdresser. Next day she turned up giving us some identity cards. The same morning one of the girls guided us to a nearby station, where we again met up with the hairdresser. This woman took us by train to Liege and after searching around the streets for several hours she found the address which I had been given at Hengelo. The people at this address passed us on to a poor family living in a suburb of Liege. We spent one night there before moving on to Tavigny. Here as instructed we got in touch with a railway worker, who passed us on to a civilian official at

Muno. This man arranged accommodation and also supplied us with French travel papers. He must have had some influence for not only did he advise us to make for Carignan but also arranged with the Frontier Police that we should be allowed free passage across the border. At Carignan, Geham and I met two priests who told us that it would be unwise to travel to Paris and that we should therefore travel with them to Reims. However at Reims, Geham decided that his chances would be better in Paris and he left on his own. The priests took me to stay overnight in a house of one of their friends living in the town. The next morning the priests and I left for Dijon, where I knew of another address which had been given to me. Unfortunately the owner of the house refused to help. Sensing that he could possibly betray us, we all left the town immediately and went on to Andelot-en-Montagne where the priests knew another priest, who might be prepared to help. I remained at the priest's home for about two days, while' further arrangements were made to go on to Les Fourges. Very early on the morning of July 9th, I set off for the Swiss border in the back of a woodman's cart. On the way the woodman lost his nerve and was quite scared, so I had to get out of the cart and walk on alone. I crossed the border about 09.30 hours. During the time I walked on alone, I encountered a German patrol of two soldiers, who fortunately did not see me as I hid for over half an hour under a fir tree, only a few yards from them. I was completely exhausted when I got over the border so I went to the nearest farmhouse in Switzerland and asked them to telephone the police. Shortly afterwards a gendarme arrived and I was taken to the local police station. Here I was searched, but by that time I had only my indentity card on me. That afternoon I was taken to the military headquarters at Neufchatel and four days later I was taken to Berne where I reported to the Swiss military authorities for further interrogations before being handed over to the British Legation.

"Early in September 1944, after spending over a year in an internment camp, Flight Lieutenant Ken Lee, Sergeant Noel Morley, both from the RNZAF, and I decided that we had enough of internment. As we had signed no papers that we would not try to leave the country we decided to make our own way out of Switzerland and make for southern France where we had heard on the radio that the American forces had invaded. I had previously been to Lausanne to contact a friend who I knew would help me. However when I returned there I found that he had left Switzerland, but his wife put me in touch with another man who arranged my journey to Annecy. Two days later Flight Lieutenant Lee and Sergeant Morley arrived as arranged at the house at which I was staying. We were given FFI passes and on September 8th 1944, two food control officers took us in a van to Chambery. The next day we were taken by car to Grenoble and from there we boarded a goods train to Sisterton. On the way we saw an American motor convoy going south. We smartly got off the train and we were taken by the Americans to their camp just south of Sisterton.

"From there the Americans arranged the rest of my journey via St Raphael and Toulon to Marseilles and then by air to Corsica then on to Naples. Here I reported to the Repatriation Camp and on September 15th, I was sent to Casablanca and then on to the UK where I arrived on Monday, September 18th 1944."

Casualties June 12th/13th. Target Bochum

83 Squadron 8 Group Lancaster ED603 OL/
Pilot. 127147 F/Lt E.A.Tilbury Killed Stavoren, Holland. I-29
Nav. 146295 P/O H.E.Howsam Killed Eindhoven(Woensel), Holland. D-1-9
B/A. J/17802 P/O A.G.Fletcher Killed Eindhoven(Woensel), Holland. D-1-8
W/OP. 127055 F/O G.R.Sugar Killed Hindeloopen, Holland. D-1-8
F/E. 51914 P/O A.B.Smart DFM Missing, Runnymede Memorial 133
A/G. 52074 F/Sgt R.E.Moore DFM Missing, Runnymede Memorial 132
A/G. 51543 P/O C.F.J.Sprack DFM Missing, Runnymede Memorial 133

97 Squadron 8 Group Lancaster ED816 OF/W
Pilot. 1457118 F/Sgt J.Thomas PoW. Stalag Luft 1, Barth Vogelsang. 266
Nav. 1252445 W/O M.C.J.Robertson PoW. Stalag 357, Kopernikus. 237
B/A. 1094825 F/Sgt E.Bloomfield PoW. Stalag 357, Kopernikus. 74
W/OP. 1088094 Sgt W.E.Doyle Missing, Runnymede Memorial 148
F/E. 1195291 Sgt C.J.Hanrahan PoW. Stalag 357.Kopernikus. 161
A/G. 629129 Sgt R.Bromley Killed Rotterdam, Holland. 424
A/G. 1438808 Sgt L.T.Beard Missing, Runnymede Memorial 142

100 Squadron 1 Group Lancaster W4989 HW/F
Pilot. 741554 W/O E.Dainty DFM Killed Reichswald Forest, Germany. 6-B-18
Nav. 1132279 Sgt R.L.Howarth Killed Reichswald Forest, Germany. 5-F-15
B/A. 1577781 Sgt R.B.Butler Killed Reichswald Forest, Germany. 5-F-18
W/OP. 129002 F/O G.May Killed Reichswald Forest, Germany. 5-F-17
F/E. 946017 Sgt J.A.Kinnear Killed Reichswald Forest, Germany. 5-G-2
A/G. 1577810 Sgt A.L.Payne Killed Reichswald Forest, Germany. 5-F-16
A/G. 1188499 Sgt D.W.Bartholomew Killed Reichswald Forest. 5-G-1

101 Squadron 1 Group Lancaster ED987 SR/
Pilot. 1315110 Sgt R.G.Claydon Missing, Runnymede Memorial 145
Nav. 131493 F/O D.C.Goodwin Missing, Runnymede Memorial 124
B/A. NZ/403582 W/O N.H.Lavin Missing, Runnymede Memorial 198
W/OP. 1383094 Sgt R.V.Fielding Missing, Runnymede Memorial 149
F/E. 626292 Sgt A.McLaw Missing, Runnymede Memorial 156
A/G. R/116366 F/Sgt W.D.McMurachy Missing, Runnymede Memorial 184
A/G. R/7817 F/Sgt E.J.St Germain Missing, Runnymede Memorial 185

103 Squadron 1 Group Lancaster ED916 PM/
Pilot. 144648 P/O G.D.J.King PoW. Stalag Luft 3, Sagan. 1501
Nav. 120477 F/O R.Hemingway PoW. Stalag Luft 3, Sagan. 1499
B/A. 1319877 Sgt F.N.Jay Killed Westerbrok, Holland. 33-1
W/OP. 1375609 F/Sgt G.W.Backhurst PoW. Stalag 357, Kopernikus. 23

F/E. 575917 F/Sgt C.S.King PoW. Stalag Luft 6, Heydekrug. 49
A/G. J/10210 F/Lt G.B.Milner Killed Westerbrok, Holland. 33-2
A/G. R/99277 W/O B.M.Godden PoW. Stalag 357, Kopernikus. 147

460 Squadron 1 Group Lancaster W4329 UV/
Pilot. A/404704 P/O L.H.M.Hadley DFC Killed Reichswald Forest. 3-E-9
Nav. A/400470 F/O U.D.H.Horne Killed Reichswald Forest, Germany. 3-E-7
B/A. A/412739 F/Sgt J.V.Stanley Killed Reichswald Forest, Germany. 3-D-16
W/OP. 149049 P/O E.H.Bond Killed Reichswald Forest, Germany. 3-E-8
F/E. A/22230 F/Sgt E.A.Baldwin Killed Reichswald Forest. CG 3-E-1/6
A/G. A/405504 F/Sgt N.R.Simpson Killed Reichswald Forest. CG 3-E-1/6
A/G. 911845 Sgt L.N.Connor Killed Reichswald Forest, Germany. CG 3-E-1/6

460 Squadron 1 Group Lancaster W4316 UV/Q
Pilot. 1388329 Sgt R.O.Vaughan Killed Ijsselmuiden(Grafhorst). B-47
Nav. A/412986 F/Sgt D.C.P.Lundie Killed Ijsselmuiden(Grafhorst). B-45
B/A. 132851 F/O C.W.R.Young Killed Ijsselmuiden(Grafhorst), Holland. A-48
W/OP. 1336716 Sgt D.A.Thomas Killed Ijsselmuiden(Grafhorst). A-46
F/E. 1433929 Sgt L.F.C.Day Killed Ijsselmuiden(Grafhorst), Holland. A-44
A/G. R/156778 Sgt J.C.Cornish PoW. Stalag Luft 6, Heydekrug. 304
A/G. A/409404 F/Sgt A.Gordon Killed Ijsselmuiden(Grafhorst), Holland. B-43

115 Squadron 3 Group Lancaster DS652 KO/
Aircraft crashed near Udem, Holland.
Pilot. NZ/411046 F/Sgt I.R.V.Ruff Killed Ameland (Nes), Holland. D-13-9
Nav. 1320356 Sgt N.W.Procter Missing, Runnymede Memorial 162
B/A. 1394588 Sgt P.D.Deck Missing, Runnymede Memorial 147
W/OP. 1367274 Sgt J.R.Glendenning Killed Ameland (Nes), Holland. D-13-10
F/E. 578264 Sgt J.F.Mustchen Missing, Runnymede Memorial 160
A/G. 1697335 Sgt A.A.Rush Missing, Runnymede Memorial 163
A/G. 1386752 F/Sgt F.Cuffey Killed Wonseradeel(Makkum), Holland. M-42

10 Squadron 4 Group Halifax W7909 ZA/
Pilot. 1503644 Sgt G.M.Inness Killed Reichswald Forest, Germany. 15-F-4
Nav. 1380739 Sgt K.A.Jenkins Killed Reichswald Forest. CG 15-D-16/17
B/A. 1392938 Sgt J.E.Senger Killed Reichswald Forest. CG 15-D-16/17
W/OP. 138672 Sgt F.C.W.Michell Killed Reichswald Forest, Germany. 15-F-2
F/E. 1435229 Sgt W.Sharp Killed Reichswald Forest, Germany. 15-D-18
A/G. 1133208 Sgt E.Smith Killed Reichswald Forest, Germany. 15-F-3
A/G. 1397923 Sgt R.G.Lepetit Killed Reichswald Forest. CG 15-D-16/17

51 Squadron 4 Group Halifax DT568 MH/
Aircraft crashed at Weerseld, Holland.
Pilot. NZ/416213 Sgt C.A.Chambers PoW. Stalag 357, Kopernikus. 42771
Nav. 129360 F/O A.Trott Killed Reichswald Forest, Germany. 24-A-14
B/A. 127005 F/O E.R.Midgeley Killed Weerselo(Rossum), Holland 8
W/OP. 1294625 Sgt A.W.Stevens Killed Weerselo(Rossum), Holland. 12
F/E. 578238 Sgt S.Wood Killed Weerselo(Rossum), Holland. 11
A/G. R/144839 Sgt M.L.Hutchings Killed Weerselo(Rossum), Holland. 10
A/G. 2213691 Sgt A.Roberts Killed Weerselo(Rossum), Holland. 9

76 Squadron 4 Group Halifax DK177 MP/H
Aircraft crashed 6 kilometres north of Neinborg, Germany.
Pilot. NZ/416163 P/O A.A.H.Pullan Killed Reichswald Forest. CG 23-D-12/15
Nav. 129348 F/O J.Kay Killed Reichswald Forest, Germany. CG 23-D-12/15
B/A. 1432404 Sgt J.G.Brown Killed Reichswald Forest. CG 23-D-12/15
W/OP. 1295163 Sgt L.C.Gearing Killed Reichswald Forest, Germany. 23-F-1
F/E. 1374808 Sgt I.B.Nicol Killed Reichswald Forest, Germany. CG 23-D-12/15
A/G. 1699340 Sgt H.Baker Killed Reichswald Forest, Germany. CG 23-D-12/15
A/G. 529409 W/O J.E.Buxton Killed Reichswald Forest, Germany. 23-D-11

78 Squadron 4 Group Halifax JD145 EY/
Pilot. 1266661 F/Sgt M.Baxter Missing, Runnymede Memorial 135
Nav. 1398262 Sgt W.H.Jordan Missing, Runnymede Memorial 155
B/A. 1387376 Sgt J.Angus Missing, Runnymede Memorial 140
W/OP. 1426357 Sgt C.W.Payne Killed Schiermonnikoog(Vrednhof). 103
F/E. 1443591 Sgt A.M.Young Missing, Runnymede Memorial 171
A/G. 1473923 Sgt E.Wright Killed Terschelling, Holland. 100
A/G. 1314467 Sgt E.Westall Missing, Runnymede Memorial 169

102 Squadron 4 Group Halifax JB868 DY/T
Pilot. 145835 P/O R.R.Hale Missing, Runnymede Memorial 131
2/Pilot. 1335010 Sgt A.C.Woodley Killed Sage, Germany. 7-B-12
Nav. 1479869 Sgt A.E.Muir Missing, Runnymede Memorial 160
B/A. 128624 F/O E.D.Wilcock Missing, Runnymede Memorial 130
W/OP. 1204788 Sgt W.A.Hobbis Missing, Runnymede Memorial 153
F/E. 1200710 Sgt A.E.J.Gibbs Killed Sage, Germany. 7-B-6
A/G. 858236 Sgt W.Hallows Missing, Runnymede Memorial 152
A/G. J/17768 P/O R.Quevillon Missing, Runnymede Memorial 177

158 Squadron 4 Group Halifax HR740 NP/K
Pilot. NZ/414583 F/O S.C.Brown PoW. Stalag 357, Kopernikus. 83
Nav. 966856 W/O D.H.Bernard PoW. Stalag Luft 3, Sagan. 481
B/A. 49577 F/O J.G.Fyfe PoW. Stalag Luft 3, Sagan. 1496
W/OP. 1194036 Sgt S.G.Holroyd Evaded Capture.
F/E. 985335 Sgt V.L.Martin PoW. Stalag Luft 6, Heydekrug. 209
A/G. 1816714 F/Sgt H.Leary PoW. Stalag Luft 6, Heydekrug. 198
A/G. 710107 W/O R.W.Robinson PoW. Stalag 357, Kopernikus. 238

158 Squadron 4 Group Halifax HR724 NP/W
Aircraft crashed near Ulft, Holland at 02.30 hours (13/6/43).
Distress call sent at 02.20 hours.
Pilot. 778821 W/O B.C.Wordsworth PoW. Stalag 357, Kopernikus. 289
Nav. 135415 P/O F.Oliver Killed Gendringen, Holland. B-30
B/A. 1320616 Sgt E.Thurlow Killed Gendringen, Holland. B-29
W/OP. 146938 P/O H.T.Woolridge Killed Gendringen, Holland. B-28
F/E. 903125 Sgt R.V.Pallant PoW. Stalag 357, Kopernikus. 42785
(Changed identity with Cpl W.Lea.)
A/G. 538725 Sgt R.J.Cook Killed Amsterdam, Holland. CG 69-B-21
Died in hospital.
A/G. 1691369 Sgt E.R.McConnel PoW. Stalag 357, Kopernikus. 203

9 Squadron 5 Group Lancaster ED558 WS/N
Aircraft shot down at Braamt, Holland at 01.30 hours (13/6/43). Victim of
Ofw.Kollak, 1/NJG1.
Pilot. 742752 W/O H.E.Wood Killed Bergh (Zeddam), Holland. 1
Nav. 129410 F/O L.C.Arthur PoW. Stalag Luft 3, Sagan. 756
B/A. 131978 F/O T.Mellard PoW. Stalag Luft 3, Sagan. 1503
W/OP. 1360429 F/Sgt J.L.Crawford PoW. Stalag 357, Kopernikus. 6
F/E. 967136 F/Sgt C.E.Clayton PoW. Stalag Luft 6, Heydekrug. 99
A/G. R/140083 W/O H.G.Watson Killed Bergh (Zeddam), Holland. 2
A/G. 1033161 F/Sgt W.R.Barker PoW. Stalag 357, Kopernikus. 61

49 Squadron 5 Group Lancaster ED584 EA/U
Pilot. 52151 P/O J.Hutchinson Missing, Runnymede Memorial 132
Nav. 147766 P/O C.S.Olson Killed Raalte, Holland. 23
B/A. 1577601 Sgt E.W.H.Johnson Killed Raalte, Holland. 25
W/OP. 1383133 Sgt B.R.Cripps Killed Raalte, Holland. 22
F/E. 1236721 Sgt C.W.Dudley Killed Raalte, Holland. 24
A/G. NZ/414536 F/Sgt L.E.Workman Killed Raalte, Holland. 26
A/G. 1628361 Sgt E.H.Pearson Missing, Runnymede Memorial 161

50 Squadron 5 Group Lancaster ED429 VN/
Aircraft crashed at Bovinghausen, Germany.
Pilot. 146317 P/O J.M.McCrossan DFM Killed Reichswald Forest. 3-D-15
Nav. 1345053 Sgt D.M.Buchan Killed Reichswald Forest, Germany. 3-D-14
B/A. 1023131 Sgt G.Stewart PoW. Stalag Luft 6, Heydekrug.
Repatriated November 1944.
W/OP. 1333266 Sgt J.K.Morgan Killed Reichswald Forest. CG 3-E-16
F/E. 935356 Sgt J.T.Wilkinson DFM Killed Reichswald Forest, Germany. 3-F-4
A/G. 933382 Sgt H.R.Stone Killed Reichswald Forest, Germany. CG 3-E-16
A/G. 1110660 Sgt J.Aitken Killed Reichswald Forest, Germany. CG 3-E-16

50 Squadron 5 Group Lancaster ED472 VN/
Pilot. 1169330 F/Sgt A.J.Weber Killed Reichswald Forest. CG 23-A-10/13
Nav. J/17260 P/O M.R.Felsen Killed Reichswald Forest, Germany. 23-A-14
B/A. 921667 F/Sgt R.Goldstraw Killed Reichswald Forest. CG 23-A-10/13
W/OP. 999350 F/Sgt F.Norman Killed Reichswald Forest. CG 23-A-10/13
F/E. 146404 P/O M.C.Carter Killed Reichswald Forest. CG 23-A-10/13
A/G. NZ/401823 F/O V.W.Ferguson Killed Reichswald Forest. 23-A-15
A/G. 1333840 Sgt R.C.Kerley Killed Reichswald Forest. CG 23-A-10/13

50 Squadron 5 Group Lancaster ED828 VN/
Pilot. 66031 F/Lt P.J.Stone DFC Killed Tubbergen (Reutem), Holland. U-3
Nav. 50746 F/Lt W.J.Glenn PoW. Stalag Luft 3, Sagan. 3010
B/A. 143468 F/O W.T.Batson DFM PoW. Stalag Luft 3, Sagan. 2255
W/OP. 553832 F/Sgt A.J.Mills Killed Tubbergen (Reutem), Holland. U-2
F/E. 571223 Sgt A.Hunter Killed Tubbergen (Reutem), Holland. U-4
A/G. J/10024 F/O M.D.S.Hicks Killed Tubbergen (Reutem), Holland. U-1
A/G. J/15771 F/O A.Smith Killed Tubbergen (Reutem), Holland. U-5

57 Squadron 5 Group Lancaster ED668 DX/
Pilot. 145672 P/O K.B.Dowding Missing, Runnymede Memorial 131
Nav. 1389310 Sgt T.M.A.Burgess Missing, Runnymede Memorial 144
B/A. 917340 Sgt W.G.Redman Missing, Runnymede Memorial 141
W/OP. 1271580 Sgt J.L.Hyam Missing, Runnymede Memorial 154
F/E. 1334489 Sgt G.A.Ayres Missing, Runnymede Memorial 162
A/G. 657050 Sgt S.E.Tuck Missing, Runnymede Memorial 167
A/G. J/18123 P/O C.J.Challenger Missing, Runnymede Memorial 175

408 Squadron 6 Group Halifax JB790 EQ/V
Pilot. J/9688 F/Lt G.R.Large PoW. Stalag Luft 3, Sagan. 1502
Nav. R/121901 W/O A.F.Rayment PoW. Stalag 357, Kopernikus. 230
B/A. J/20816 F/O F.L.Milburn Killed Reichswald Forest, Germany. 24-D-15
W/OP. R/133514 Sgt N.Bainblatt PoW. Stalag 357, Kopernikus. 25
F/E. 1487121 Sgt T.Leigh-Ross Killed Reichswald Forest, Germany. 24-D-16
A/G. R/96860 F/Sgt J.R.Forest PoW. Stalag Luft 3, Sagan. 30
A/G. R/137936 W/O D.H.Hutchinson PoW. Stalag 357, Kopernikus. 174

419 Squadron 6 Group Halifax DT616 VR/
Aircraft shot down by Bf110 nightfighter at 02.10 hours (13/6/43).
Pilot. R/114702 W/O B.D.Kirkham PoW. Stalag 357, Kopernikus. 15
Nav. R/127992 F/Sgt H.A.Taylor PoW. Stalag 357, Kopernikus. 262
B/A. 1488629 W/O D.B.Whittaker PoW. Stalag 357, Kopernikus. 285
W/OP. 1080364 F/Sgt F.J.Callaghan PoW. Stalag 357, Kopernikus. 5
F/E. R/71213 Sgt R.J.Hamilton PoW. Stalag 357, Kopernikus. 158
A/G. J/92947 P/O J.A.Mills PoW. Stalag 357, Kopernikus. 17
A/G. R/110555 W/O D.L.Gray PoW. Stalag 357, Kopernikus. 9

427 Squadron 6 Group Halifax DK183 ZL/
Pilot. J/16714 P/O A.M.Fellner PoW. Camp not known.
Nav. J/17164 P/O G.W.R.Dalton Killed Texel, Holland. K-3-54
B/A. J/17163 P/O W.A.Thurston PoW. Stalag Luft 3, Sagan. 1509
W/OP. J/17609 P/O B.L.Tedford Killed Texel, Holland. K-3-52
F/E. 640842 Sgt J.Imms Killed Flushing, Holland. 2-D-10
A/G. R/176201 Sgt A.Dixon Killed Sage, Germany. 7-A-10
A/G. J/17316 P/O G.S.Huston PoW. Stalag Luft 4, Sagan. 1699

Minor Operations

Minelaying was continued on the same night as the Bochum raid, when without suffering any loss, 34 Wellingtons from 1, 4 and 6 Groups laid 59 mines around the areas of St. Nazaire, Lorient and the Frisians.

June 13th/14th, 1943
Thirteen Mosquitoes continued to harass the German defences by raids on Berlin, Düsseldorf and Cologne. All planes returned

safely to their bases after dropping 8.5 tons of high explosive bombs from 28,000 feet through 10/10ths cloud which shrouded all three target areas. On the same night 18 Wellingtons from 1 and 6 Group and 12 Stirlings from 3 Group were sent minelaying around the Bay of Biscay ports dropping 65 mines. One aircraft was lost on the minelaying operation from which there were no survivors.

Casualties June 13th/14th, 1943. Minelaying

199 Squadron 1 Group Wellington HE597 EX/Y
Pilot. 123355 F/O W.E.Sawdy Killed Guidel, Lorient, France. 6-2
Nav. 1576202 Sgt E.Burton Killed Guidel, Lorient, France. JG 5-45/46
B/A. 124758 F/O S.Q.Robinson Killed Guidel, Lorient, France. 6-1
W/OP. 1270241 Sgt C.S.Bell Killed Guidel, Lorient, France. JG 5-45/46
A/G. 1397811 Sgt J.W.Stevens Killed Guidel, Lorient, France. 5-44

Oberhausen

June 14th/15th, 1943

Oberhausen was the target for a force of 197 Lancaster bombers led by six *Oboe* Mosquitoes. A high number of 40 bombers returned early on this operation. The target was 5 to 7/10ths cloud covered and sky marking was used once again, but this time very accurately, for very many buildings were destroyed and damaged. The PFF force was well timed, both in dropping the tracking and release flares. There was, however, a tendency for the spread of fires to go eastwards of the target centre. A large explosion was observed by some crews at 01.25 hours. Photo reconnaissance the next day showed that the centre of the town was virtually levelled. 85 people lost their lives and 258 were injured. The price paid for this was heavy, 17 Lancasters failed to return, a 8.4% loss rate. From the aircrew manning these planes 108 were killed, six were missing and nine became prisoners.

Casualties June 14th/15th, 1943. Target Oberhausen

12 Squadron 1 Group Lancaster W4992 PH/A
Pilot. A/416633 F/Sgt W.J.Tucker Killed Rheinberg, Germany. 3-A-17
Nav. 131896 F/Lt K.Truelove PoW. Stalag Luft 3, Sagan. 1508
B/A. 1045724 Sgt J.J.Simpson Killed Rheinberg, Germany. 3-A-18
W/OP. 1313708 Sgt B.O.Davies Killed Rheinberg, Germany. 3-A-22
F/E. 1088071 Sgt R.Fletcher Killed Rheinberg, Germany. 3-A-19
A/G. 1300587 Sgt T.Carter Killed Rheinberg, Germany. 3-A-21
A/G. NZ/39570 F/Sgt F.G.McKay Killed Rheinberg, Germany. 3-A-20

100 Squadron 1 Group Lancaster ED973 HW/D
First Operation for crew.
Pilot. 1385532 Sgt R.E.S.Weddell Killed Jonkerbos, Holland. 16-A-9
Nav. 1516659 Sgt A.R.Veitch Killed Jonkerbos, Holland. CG 16-A-5/7
B/A. 1533234 Sgt W.Cram Killed Jonkerbos, Holland. CG 16-A-5/7
W/OP. 1385000 Sgt G.A.Mason Killed Jonkerbos, Holland. CG 16-A-5/7
F/E. 1486601 Sgt A.Boydell Killed Jonkerbos, Holland. 16-A-8
A/G. 1457209 Sgt D.G.M.Ofield Killed Jonkerbos, Holland. CG 16-A-5/7
A/G. R/129380 F/Sgt E.B.Stevenson Killed Jonkerbos, Holland. 16-B-9

103 Squadron 1 Group Lancaster ED612 PM/
Pilot. 61007 F/Lt A.M.Brown Killed Rheinberg, Germany. 3-B-1
Nav. 130701 F/O H.F.Lewis Killed Rheinberg, Germany. 3-A-24
B/A. 1550613 Sgt J.Greenway Killed Rheinberg, Germany. 3-A-25

W/OP. 1379816 Sgt J.Cliffe Killed Rheinberg, Germany. 3-A-23
F/E. 1186852 Sgt E.H.Morley Killed Reichswald Forest, Germany. 30-E-17
A/G. R/97362 F/Sgt W.O'Connelly Killed Rheinberg, Germany. 3-B-2
A/G. 1253947 Sgt J.H.Saville Killed Rheinberg, Germany. 3-B-3

103 Squadron 1 Group Lancaster ED396 PM/
Pilot. 1530099 Sgt G.Whitehead Killed Reichswald Forest, Germany. 5-H-8
Nav. 1533201 Sgt J.Renwick Killed Reichswald Forest, Germany. 5-H-9
B/A. 130879 F/O S.H.Yates Killed Reichswald Forest, Germany. 5-H-7
W/OP. 624836 F/Sgt E.Shaw DFM Missing, Runnymede Memorial 139
F/E. 644429 Sgt J.J.Kerevan Missing, Runnymede Memorial 155
A/G. 636153 Sgt R.J.Bailes Killed Reichswald Forest, Germany. 5-H-11
A/G. 1565261 Sgt D.A.Ferguson Killed Reichswald Forest, Germany. 5-H-10

460 Squadron 1 Group Lancaster EE167 UV/
Pilot. A/411680 F/Sgt G.R.Cope Killed Jonkerbos, Holland. 7-H-5
Nav. A/409472 F/O H.L.Gordon Killed Jonkerbos, Holland. 11-H-6
B/A. A/405842 F/Sgt D.Douds Killed Jonkerbos, Holland. 11-H-5
W/OP. A/415021 F/Sgt D.H.Crouch Killed Jonkerbos, Holland. 11-H-3
F/E. 1135352 Sgt E.Booth PoW. Stalag Luft 6, Heydekrug. 75
A/G. R/144124 Sgt W.R.Matheson PoW. Camp not known.
A/G. A/408907 F/Sgt D.G.Finlason Killed Jonkerbos, Holland. 11-H-4

460 Squadron 1 Group Lancaster DV160 UV/
Pilot. 1320902 Sgt R.E.Crook Killed Flushing, Holland. CG 69-C-17
Nav. A/420697 F/Sgt S.J.Marriage Killed Flushing, Holland. 9-C-18
B/A. A/414196 F/Sgt C.R.Buckeridge Killed Flushing, Holland. CG 69-B-11
W/OP. 1127071 Sgt C.E.Grimshaw Killed Flushing, Holland. CG 69-C-17
F/E. A/14824 Sgt J.R.Morrison PoW. Stalag Luft 4, Sagan. 42783
A/G. 1334452 Sgt G.W.G.Fletcher Killed Flushing, Holland. CG 69-C-17
A/G. A/413307 F/Sgt D.R.Grant Killed Flushing, Holland. CG 69-C-18

460 Squadron 1 Group Lancaster LM324 UV/
Pilot. A/413178 F/O W.J.Dennett Killed Heverlee, Belgium. 4-E-3
Nav. A/413079 F/O A.C.R.Flashman Killed Heverlee, Belgium. 4-E-5
B/A. A/412785 F/Sgt T.Williams Killed Heverlee, Belgium. 4-E-6
W/OP. 1127216 Sgt E.A.Bogle Killed Heverlee, Belgium. 4-E-4
F/E. 1336115 Sgt R.E.Watson Killed Heverlee, Belgium. 4-E-2
A/G. A/410593 F/O W.E.Emery Killed Heverlee, Belgium. 4-E-7
A/G. A/14228 F/Sgt D.P.Birk Killed Heverlee, Belgium. 4-E-1

9 Squadron 5 Group Lancaster LM329 WS/
Pilot. 145515 P/O J.Evans Killed Flushing, Holland. 5-G-5
2/Pilot. 1383325 Sgt V.J.Tarr Killed Flushing, Holland. 5-H-11
Nav. 1437293 Sgt R.Borthwick Killed Flushing, Holland. 5-G-8
B/A. 1481843 Sgt A.W.Waite Killed Flushing, Holland. 5-G-7
W/OP. 1257583 F/Sgt W.J.Chapple Killed Flushing, Holland. 5-F-9
F/E. 1178195 Sgt V.G.L.Smith Killed Flushing, Holland. 5-G-6
A/G. 1316463 Sgt H.I.Ashdown Killed Flushing, Holland. 5-G-9
A/G. 1339242 Sgt D.W.Brough Killed Flushing, Holland. 5-G-10

44 Squadron 5 Group Lancaster W4936 KM/W
Pilot. 41408 S/Ldr G.B.Haywood Killed Eindhoven(Woensel), Holland. JJB-92
Nav. 121510 F/O R.Kirby Killed Eindhoven(Woensel), Holland. JJB-96
B/A. 1438273 Sgt R.Boardman Killed Eindhoven(Woensel), Holland. JJB-94
W/OP. 1295092 Sgt R.W.Rivers Killed Eindhoven(Woensel), Holland. JJB-95
F/E. 1212342 Sgt R.G.Foot Killed Eindhoven(Woensel), Holland. JJB-93
A/G. 1355955 Sgt R.C.H.Brand Killed Eindhoven(Woensel), Holland. JJB-97
A/G. 1380542 Sgt J.H.Armstrong Killed Eindhoven(Woensel), Holland. JJB-98

44 Squadron 5 Group Lancaster W4949 KM/E
Pilot. 146112 P/O P.J.Sherrman Missing, Runnymede Memorial 133
Nav. 148012 P/O N.L.Ballamy Missing, Runnymede Memorial 130
B/A. 124113 F/O F.M.Richards Killed Jonkerbos, Holland. 16-E-8
W/OP. 1331878 Sgt B.W.Card Missing, Runnymede Memorial 144
F/E. 618980 F/Sgt E.L.Pugh Missing, Runnymede Memorial 138
A/G. 1007571 Sgt C.W.Akeister Killed Jonkerbos, Holland. 16-E-7
A/G. 908724 Sgt G.C.A.Zedy Killed Jonkerbos, Holland. 16-E-9

49 Squadron 5 Group Lancaster ED453 EA/
Pilot. 1232054 W/O N.Nixon Killed Reichswald Forest, Germany. 12-H-4
2/Pilot. 1027306 Sgt E.Dangerfield Killed Reichswald Forest. 12-H-8
Nav. R/115874 F/Sgt S.D.Bird Killed Reichswald Forest, Germany. 12-H-3
B/A. 1551806 Sgt N.W.Fyfe Killed Reichswald Forest, Germany. 12-H-7
W/OP. 1199640 Sgt R.T.Moore Killed Reichswald Forest, Germany. 12-H-10
F/E. 1004224 Sgt C.Wilde Killed Reichswald Forest, Germany. 12-H-5
A/G. 1127204 Sgt R.K.B.Muir Killed Reichswald Forest, Germany. 12-H-9
A/G. 1324047 Sgt F.R.Fowler Killed Reichswald Forest, Germany. 12-H-6

49 Squadron 5 Group Lancaster ED434 EA/
Pilot. 1147365 W/O R.Frost PoW. Stalag 357, Kopernikus. 140
Nav. 127067 F/O A.E.Whittaker Killed Flushing, Holland. 5-F-2
B/A. 658990 Sgt V.Horsley Killed Flushing, Holland. 5-G-13
W/OP. 1050302 Sgt J.R.Coulsey Killed Flushing, Holland. 5-F-1
F/E. 1332226 F/Sgt N.C.Hitchcock PoW. Stalag 357, Kopernikus. 396
A/G. 1317569 Sgt P.A.Toms Killed Flushing, Holland. 5-G-12
A/G. R/99842 F/Sgt W.L.Chatfield Killed Flushing, Holland. 5-G-11

49 Squadron 5 Group Lancaster ED432 EA/
Pilot. 1388306 Sgt G.S.Cole Killed Renkum (Oosterbeek), Holland. 9
Nav. 1319045 Sgt C.A.S.Barnett Killed Renkum (Oosterbeek), Holland. CG 5/7
2/Nav. 143015 Sgt H.Biggin Killed Renkum (Oosterbeek), Holland. CG 5/7
B/A. 1535807 Sgt J.W.Deacon Killed Renkum (Oosterbeek), Holland. CG 5/7
W/OP. 1331734 F/Sgt J.F.Arnold PoW. Stalag Luft 1, Barth Vogelsang. 57
F/E. 572648 Sgt J.P.Harper Killed Renkum (Oosterbeek), Holland. 4
A/G. 1387914 F/Sgt J.H.D.Bryan PoW. Stalag 357, Kopernikus. 84
A/G. 1038105 Sgt H.R.Rhodes Killed Renkum (Oosterbeek), Holland. 8

50 Squadron 5 Group Lancaster ED810 VN/Z
Aircraft crashed at Meeuwen, Belgium. Possible victim of Oblt Telge, Stab II/NJG1.
Pilot. 127903 F/O A.V.Crawford Killed Schoonselhoof, Belgium. JG II-F-26/27
Nav. 1389014 Sgt A.E.Davey Killed Schoonselhoof, Belgium. II-F-23
B/A. 1388490 Sgt W.G.Reed Killed Schoonselhoof, Belgium. II-F-24
W/OP. 1133853 Sgt J.B.McHendry Killed Schoonselhoof, Belgium. II-F-21
F/E. 525494 Sgt L.Toal Killed Schoonselhoof, Belgium. II-F-25
A/G. 1602905 Sgt K.I.Bowerman Killed Schoonselhoof, Belgium. JG II-F-26/27
A/G. 1120118 Sgt C.J.Buckle Killed Schoonselhoof, Belgium. II-F-22

106 Squadron 5 Group Lancaster ED649 ZN/
Pilot. 127353 F/O H.D.Oates Killed Reichswald Forest, Germany. CG 5-H-3/4
Nav. 133463 F/O R.H.Parr Killed Reichswald Forest, Germany. 5-H-6
B/A. 131126 F/O D.L.Stevenson Killed Reichswald Forest, Germany. 5-H-2
W/OP. 1334936 Sgt R.A.Martin Killed Reichswald Forest. CG 5-H-3/4
F/E. 1277651 Sgt J.Hindley Killed Reichswald Forest, Germany. CG 5-H-3/4
A/G. 1627841 Sgt R.E.Bell Killed Reichswald Forest, Germany. CG 5-H-3/4
A/G. R/90888 F/Sgt J.V.Sweeney Killed Reichswald Forest, Germany. 5-H-15

106 Squadron 5 Group Lancaster R5551 ZN/
Pilot. J/17621 P/O D.S.Brown Killed Groesbeek (Can), Holland. XV-C-12
Nav. 1385801 Sgt R.A.Beaton Killed Arnhem (Moscawa), Holland. 18
B/A. R/85414 W/O R.S.Pegg PoW. Stalag Luft 4, Sagan. 224 2/
B/A. 131979 F/O E.G.Seall Killed Arnhem (Moscawa), Holland. 15
W/OP. 1209732 Sgt F.J.Stoker Killed Arnhem (Moscawa), Holland. 14
F/E. 1345984 Sgt E.C.McMillan Killed Arnhem (Moscawa), Holland. 16
A/G. 639777 Sgt A.G.Ballantyne Killed Arnhem (Moscawa), Holland. 12
A/G. 985040 Sgt K.Wilcock Killed Arnhem (Moscawa), Holland. 13

619 Squadron 5 Group Lancaster ED980 PG/
Pilot. 145513 P/O K.McCulloch Killed Eindhoven (Woensel), Holland. JJB-88
Nav. 127976 F/O H.Forshaw Killed Eindhoven (Woensel), Holland. JJB-86
B/A. 1395771 Sgt N.C.Richards Killed Eindhoven (Woensel), Holland. JJB-90
W/OP. 1312358 Sgt L.Timms Killed Eindhoven (Woensel), Holland. EE-90
F/E. 1122560 Sgt R.E.Tofts Killed Eindhoven (Woensel), Holland. JJB-87
A/G. 546586 Sgt P.J.Ruane Killed Eindhoven (Woensel), Holland. JJB-91
A/G. R/134679 F/Sgt R.H.Van-Camp Killed Groesbeek (Can), Holland. XVI-E-7

Cologne's Nuisance Raid

On the same night two Mosquitoes kept the sirens blowing in Cologne dropping 1.3 tons of bombs in their nuisance raids. They met fairly intensive *Flak* and even at the height the Mosquitoes were operating, there were many searchlights in operation. One Mosquito crew reported being coned for 30 seconds.

Minelaying

June 14th/15th, 1943

29 aircraft, 17 Wellingtons from 4 and 6 Groups and 12 Stirlings from 3 Group set out on a minelaying operation on the same night as the Oberhausen raid. Three aircraft, two Stirlings and one Wellington, returned early with equipment failures. The remainder dropped 59 mines in areas off Brittany and in the mouth of the River Gironde. One aircraft, Stirling BK646 from 75 Squadron captained by 130636 Flying Officer J. L. Edwards, failed to return from the minelaying operation. The aircraft after being damaged by anti aircraft fire was attacked by a fighter and crashed at Moulins, 15 miles south east of Rennes, France. Two of the crew, bomb aimer 134555 Pilot Officer R. G. Kirby and Canadian flight engineer R/66963 Sergeant J. G. F. Sansoucy managed with the help of the underground movement to evade capture and return to the UK. Four crew members became prisoners, but the pilot was killed.

Due to the nature of minelaying operations, which were mainly over the sea, the number of aircrew who were shot down on minelaying and who were fortunate to evade capture after baling out, was very small compared to crews on bombing raids over land.

Casualties June 14th/15th, 1943 Minelaying

75 Squadron 3 Group Stirling BK646 AA/N
Aircraft crashed at Moulins, 15 miles SE of Rennes, France.
Pilot. 130636 F/O J.L.Edwards Killed Bretteville-sur-Laize. XXVIII-G-7
Nav. NZ/42380 W/O E.G.Dunnett PoW. Stalag 4B, Muhlberg(Elbe). 83697
B/A. 134555 P/O R.G.Kirby Evaded capture.
W/OP. NZ/415558 W/O B.W.Rawlinson PoW. Stalag 357, Kopernikus. 426
F/E. R/66953 Sgt J.G.F.Sansoucy Evaded capture.
A/G. 1498348 Sgt E.F.Jones PoW. Stalag 357, Kopernikus. 403
A/G. 1698372 Sgt T.Maxwell PoW. Stalag 357, Kopernikus. 411

Nuisance Raid

June 15th/16th, 1943

A nuisance raid by six Mosquitoes was made on Berlin, lasting from 01.44 to 01.53 hours, when 3.7 tons of high explosive bombs were dropped. There was one early returner, but no losses were incurred.

Cologne

June 16th/17th, 1943

Although Cologne was the target for the Lancaster and Halifax force consisting of 156 Lancasters from 1 and 5 Groups plus 46 Lancasters and 10 Halifaxes from PFF. *Oboe* equipped Mosquitoes were not used. Again there was a high number of early returners, six of the PFF Lancasters returned early with faulty H^2S sets and 27 of the main force aircraft also returned early with various technical faults. Marking of the target was done by the remaining 16 Pathfinder heavy bombers which were equipped with H^2S. They used the sky marking technique, because there was 7/10ths to 10/10ths cloud up to 10,000 feet over the target with some nimbus up to 20,000 feet. Timing however was bad, the attack opening late and sky marking was sporadic and flares reported 8 miles apart, with the consequential scattered bombing. Many of the main force crews bombed on ETA (estimated time of arrival). Although damage was caused to the housing areas of the city, 401 houses being destroyed and 13,000 with varying amounts of damage, there was some industrial damage caused especially to the large Kalk Chemical works which was burnt out. 147 people lost their lives with a further 213 injured. 456 tons of high explosive bombs and 91,086 incendiaries were dropped but the cost was high, 14 aircraft being lost, a high loss rate of 6.3% for the main force and an even higher loss rate of 9.5% for the Pathfinders. Aircrew losses were 75 killed, 10 missing and 16 made prisoners of war.

Casualties June 16th/17th, 1943. Target Cologne

83 Squadron 8 Group Lancaster ED907 OL/H
Pilot. J/17498 P/O C.Murray Killed Rheinberg, Germany. 1-G-24
Nav. 980860 Sgt J.Holt PoW. Stalag 357, Kopernikus. 170
B/A. 1292358 Sgt F.W.Brown PoW. Stalag Luft 7, Banaku. 82
W/OP. 47896 F/O K.F.East PoW. Stalag Luft 3, Sagan. 2189
F/E. 980860 F/Sgt D.Chapman PoW. Stalag 357, Kopernikus. 93
A/G. 911921 F/Sgt R.D.Prichard PoW. Stalag 4B, Muhlberg(Elbe). 10585
A/G. J/10211 F/O J.G.Mackay Killed Rheinberg, Germany. 1-G-25

156 Squadron 8 Group Lancaster ED863 GT/
Pilot. 147211 P/O D.C.C.Busby C.G.M Killed Rheinberg, Germany. 4-E-19
Nav. 580706 W/O D.H.Orchard Killed Rheinberg, Germany. CG 4-E-20/23
B/A. 1231989 Sgt R.C.Balsdon Killed Rheinberg, Germany. 4-E-24
W/OP. 105177 F/O E.S.Hayes DFC Killed Rheinberg, Germany. CG 4-E-20/23
F/E. 646710 Sgt J.G.Lumley Killed Rheinberg, Germany. CG 4-E-20/23
A/G. 1369391 Sgt A.B.Kerrigan Killed Rheinberg, Germany. CG 4-E-20/23
A/G. 1340096 Sgt G.M.Murray Killed Rheinberg, Germany. 4-E-25

156 Squadron 8 Group Lancaster ED840 GT/
Aircraft crashed near Antwerp, Belgium.
Pilot. 40727 S/Ldr J.C.Mackintosh Killed Schoonselhoof, Belgium. II-F-29
Nav. 1331638 F/Sgt R.F.A.Elliott Killed Schoonselhoof, Belgium. II-F-30
B/A. 1194485 W/O E.E.Weare PoW. Stalag 4B, Muhlberg(Elbe). 222540
W/OP. 997011 F/Sgt P.Woodcock Killed Schoonselhoof, Belgium. II-F-28
F/E. 546108 F/Sgt R.C.Drinkwater PoW. Stalag Luft 6, Heydekrug. 122
A/G. 1391227 F/Sgt L.G.Ledamun PoW. Stalag 357, Kopernikus. 328
A/G. J/18012 P/O E.J.Monk Killed Schoonselhoof, Belgium. IVA-A-4

156 Squadron 8 Group Lancaster ED122 GT/
Pilot. 147190 P/O R.B.Miller Killed Rheinberg, Germany. CG 3-B-6/14
Nav. J/17943 P/O J.R.Wright Killed Rheinberg, Germany. CG 3-B-6/14
B/A. 1552158 F/Sgt H.Love Killed Rheinberg, Germany. CG 3-B-6/14
W/OP. 1067394 Sgt J.Tweedie Killed Rheinberg, Germany. CG 3-B-6/14
F/E. 577950 Sgt H.F.Sheppard Killed Rheinberg, Germany. CG 3-B-6/14
A/G. 1335335 Sgt J.A.G.Dawe Killed Rheinberg, Germany. CG 3-B-6/14
A/G. 1060108 Sgt E.G.G.Fisher Killed Rheinberg, Germany. CG 3-B-6/14

12 Squadron 1 Group Lancaster ED629 PH/K
Aircraft crashed at Lier, Belgium.
Pilot. 657684 Sgt A.C.Aylard Killed Heverlee, Belgium. 4-E-13
Nav. 1340990 Sgt T.Alexander Killed Heverlee, Belgium. 4-E-17
B/A. 1388418 Sgt M.R.Williams Killed Heverlee, Belgium. 4-E-14
W/OP. 1272458 Sgt H.J.P.Lackey Killed Heverlee, Belgium. 4-E-19
F/E. 1094144 Sgt J.Scott Killed Heverlee, Belgium. 4-E-16
A/G. 1389005 Sgt R.Swain Killed Heverlee, Belgium. 4-E-18
A/G. 1206109 Sgt J.W.N.Westlake Killed Heverlee, Belgium. 4-E-15

100 Squadron 1 Group Lancaster ED553 HW/R
Aircraft crashed in the Antwerp area, Belgium.
Pilot. 1339109 Sgt C.Boughton Killed Schoonselhoof, Belgium. II-F-13
Nav. 996958 Sgt D.H.N.Slinger Killed Schoonselhoof, Belgium. II-F-9
B/A. 1430565 Sgt G.Taylor Killed Schoonselhoof, Belgium. II-F-12
W/OP. 1330174 Sgt C.C.Dabson Killed Schoonselhoof, Belgium. II-F-10
F/E. 567344 Sgt A.J.Banfield Killed Schoonselhoof, Belgium. II-F-11
A/G. 1125516 Sgt W.E.Barley Killed Schoonselhoof, Belgium. II-F-8
A/G. 533846 Sgt J.Walker Killed Schoonselhoof, Belgium. II-F-7

103 Squadron 1 Group Lancaster ED945 PM/
Pilot. 127249 F/O K.I.Dexter Killed Eindhoven(Woensel), Holland. JJB-106
Nav. 1390821 Sgt W.T.Shepherd Killed Eindhoven(Woensel). JJB-105
B/A. 1335963 Sgt H.G.Thomas Killed Eindhoven(Woensel), Holland. JJB-109
W/OP. 1291030 Sgt H.Staples Killed Eindhoven(Woensel), Holland. JJB-107
F/E. 540625 Sgt R.C.Ridgway Killed Eindhoven(Woensel), Holland. JJB-111
A/G. 936076 Sgt J.M.Carroll Killed Eindhoven(Woensel), Holland. JJB-110
A/G. 1144359 Sgt R.A.Heslop Killed Eindhoven(Woensel), Holland. JJB-108

103 Squadron 1 Group Lancaster W4901 PM/
Pilot. 1333599 Sgt R.G.Winchester Killed Flushing, Holland. 5-F-6
Nav. 131492 F/O G.G.Tebble Killed Flushing, Holland. 5-F-5
B/A. 131774 P/O C.P.St Leger Killed Flushing, Holland. 5-F-3
W/OP. 1067882 Sgt A.M.Park Killed Flushing, Holland. 5-F-7
F/E. 520821 Sgt H.Rocknean Killed Flushing, Holland. 5-F-4
A/G. 1084438 Sgt J.A.Keighley Killed Flushing, Holland. 5-E-10
A/G. 1049404 Sgt D.E.McGill Killed Flushing, Holland. 5-F-8

460 Squadron 1 Group Lancaster W4332 UV/
Pilot. A/412338 F/Sgt F.G.Phillips Missing, Runnymede Memorial. 193
Nav. 127314 F/O E.F.Davey Missing, Runnymede Memorial 124
B/A. 1217983 Sgt G.D.Prince Killed Bergen-op-Zoom, Holland. 4-C-5
W/OP. 1358312 Sgt J.W.Ousley Killed Bergen-op-Zoom, Holland. 4-C-8
F/E. 1259229 Sgt J.H.Emmett Missing, Runnymede Memorial 148
A/G. A/420762 F/Sgt L.T.Little Killed Ostend, Belgium. 9-5-23
A/G. 1454835 Sgt F.Smith Killed Flushing, Holland. F-22

9 Squadron 5 Group Lancaster ED487 WS/D
Aircraft crashed at Vorst, Antwerp, Belgium
Pilot. 146971 F/O J.A.Aldersley PoW. Stalag Luft 3, Sagan. 291
Nav. 1320777 Sgt D.Webster Killed Schoonselhoof, Belgium. II-F-5
B/A. 1239366 F/Sgt H.Popplestone PoW. Stalag 4B, Muhlberg(Elbe). 250749
W/OP. 1334582 F/Sgt C.J.Sinclair PoW. Stalag 357, Kopernikus. 431
F/E. 539562 Sgt P.Hall Killed Schoonselhof, Belgium. II-F-3
A/G. 1809127 Sgt H.F.Poynter Killed Schoonselhoof, Belgium. II-F-6
A/G. R/123752 F/Sgt D.G.Tremblay Killed Schoonselhoof, Belgium. II-F-4

49 Squadron 5 Group Lancaster ED785 EA/
Pilot. 37615 S/Ldr G.G.Storey Killed Flushing, Holland. E-25
2/Pilot. 1148682 Sgt J.Burnside Killed Flushing, Holland. E-21
Nav. 133459 F/O R.C.Blythe Killed Flushing, Holland. F-25
B/A. 1348637 Sgt W.H.Waring Missing, Runnymede Memorial 168
W/OP. R/101741 Sgt M.G.Webb PoW. Stalag 357, Kopernikus. 283
F/E. 1271149 Sgt G.S.Underlin Killed Flushing, Holland. E-24
A/G. 991263 Sgt H.Buttrey Killed Flushing, Holland. E-23
A/G. R/102867 F/Sgt M.E.Bunn Killed Flushing, Holland. E-22

49 Squadron 5 Group Lancaster ED497 EA/
Pilot. 85661 F/Lt C.W.Dunnett Killed Eindhoven(Woensel), Holland. EE-69
Nav. 1339131 Sgt R.G.Smith Killed Eindhoven(Woensel). JG JJB-101/102
B/A. 1239969 Sgt W.A.Dutton Killed Eindhoven(Woensel), Holland. JJB-99
W/OP. 1313051 Sgt M.F.Haley Killed Eindhoven(Woensel). JG JJB-101/102

F/E. 1079596 Sgt R.F.Middlebrook Killed Eindhoven(Woensel). JJB-100
A/G. 1585667 Sgt R.M.W.Selby-Lowndes Killed Eindhoven. JJB-104
A/G. 138891 P/O C.A.Edwards Killed Eindhoven(Woensel). JJB-103

61 Squadron 5 Group Lancaster W4789 QR/
Pilot. 145859 P/O A.W.Pullan Missing Runnymede Memorial. 133
Nav. 569983 Sgt C.T.O.Dudley Killed Rheinberg, Germany 1-B-25
2/Nav. J/22363 F/O J.P.Laurin Missing, Runnymede Memorial 174
B/A. 131959 F/O J.R.H.Bell Missing, Runnymede Memorial 123
W/OP. 1132714 Sgt J.Nuttall Missing, Runnymede Memorial 160
F/E. 570570 Sgt B.S.Bridge Missing, Runnymede Memorial 143
A/G. 1381859 Sgt P.F.Cottle PoW. Stalag Luft 6, Heydekrug. 260472
A/G. R/136408 Sgt R.S.Morley Missing, Runnymede Memorial 185

467 Squadron 5 Group Lancaster ED737 PO/F
Pilot. A/414290 F/O J.E.Binnie PoW. Stalag Luft 4, Sagan. 71
2/Pilot. 120058 F/O A.Smith Killed Rheinberg, Germany. 3-B-4
Nav. 658613 Sgt R.L.Godden Killed Rheinberg, Germany. CG 3-B-6/14
B/A. 1237051 Sgt K.M.Taylor Killed Rheinberg, Germany. 3-B-5
W/OP. A/400415 F/O G.H.Joseph Killed Rheinberg, Germany. CG 3-B-6/14
F/E. 649185 Sgt N.M.Turnbull Killed Rheinberg, Germany. CG 3-B-6/14
A/G. R/137269 F/Sgt E.V.Doan PoW. Stalag Luft 6, Heydekrug. 120
A/G. 69116 W/O E.Lancake PoW. Stalag 357, Kopernikus. 196

460 Squadron 1 Group Lancaster W5007 UV/
Aircraft crashed at Elsham Wolds, Lincolnshire after operations to
Cologne.
Pilot. 155143 Sgt D.J.Straith Killed Banchory, Scotland 1254
Nav. A/420050 F/Sgt J.C.Plummer Killed Brigg, Lincolnshire. B - 23
B/A. A/414255 F/Sgt L.M.McDonnell Killed Brigg, Lincolnshire. B - 2
W/OP. 1334520 Sgt D.S.Gent Killed Brigg, Lincolnshire. B - 183
F/E. 975077 Sgt R.T.Harman Killed Twickenham.(Teddington) A-B-106
A/G. R/132570 Sgt W.Brodie Killed Brigg, Lincolnshire. C - 465
A/G. A/414549 F/Sgt N.O.B.Flintcroft Killed Brigg, Lincolnshire. C - 371

Mosquitoes Keep the Sirens Going

Berlin was visited on the same night by three Mosquitoes
with their harassing raids. 2.3 tons of bombs were dropped
from 25,000 feet on Dead Reckoning, due to the fact that the
city was completely cloud covered, although one aircraft did
manage to get a pin point through a gap in the cloud just

south of Lake Muritz. The defences showed no opposition and no aircraft were lost.

June 17th/18th, 1943
Three towns in the Ruhr, Cologne, Duisburg and Düsseldorf were each visited by a single Mosquito. Düsseldorf was the only town to escape any bombs being dropped as the Mosquito which visited that town had technical problems and was unable to drop its load. The other two towns had 0.8 tons of bombs dropped on each. Berlin was also scheduled for a visit by four Mosquitoes but only two dropped 1.6 tons of bombs on Germany's capital city that night.

Le Creusot

June 19th/20th, 1943
Pathfinders resorted to an old method of lighting up a target by dropping 546 flares instead of target indicators on the town of Le Creusot, where the Schneider Armaments Factory and the Breuil Steelworks were situated. 285 aircraft, composed of 181 Halifaxes, and 104 Stirlings from 3, 4, 6 and 8 (PFF) Groups, were despatched with orders to identify the target by the light of the flares dropped by the Pathfinders. Because the planners believed that the target was so small, crews were then instructed to make two runs over the target area and drop a short stick of bombs on each run, at altitudes ranging from 5,000 to 10,000 feet. Twelve aircraft were early returners and one Halifax, JB863 captained by 1331061 Flight Sergeant Norman Holledge from 77 Squadron based at Elvington, East Yorkshire crashed and blew up on take off with a full bomb load. All the crew were killed.

There was excellent illumination from the Pathfinder flares early in the raid and the first wave of bombers were able to identify their target visually and drop their bombs accurately. The unusual operational plan was bedevilled later in the raid by unpredicted smoke from the very great number of flares dropped, which lingered over the target area, so making identification very difficult for later crews. Coupled with this the raid planners at Bomber Command HQ had not anticipated the difficulties that many of the main force crews would encounter. Having for many previous operations bombed only on target indicators of one kind or another, they had very little or no practice in visual identification. 696.2 tons of HE bombs and 16,420 incendiaries were dropped. The result, however, from the many bombing photographs taken showed that the majority of these bombs had fallen at least three to four miles away from the factory targets and had fallen in the French residential area. Defences were only negligible and only two aircraft were lost on this raid. Twelve of the airmen were killed and two were made prisoners of war.

Flight Engineer Crawls Inside Wing

Stirling EH880 of 75 Squadron, captained by Flight Lieutenant J. Joll, was the lucky aircraft on this raid for it only returned safely to base due to the untiring efforts of the flight engineer, Sergeant G. Fallon. The plane had received a direct hit by an anti aircraft-shell which burst inside the main fuselage and shrapnel severed the petrol cock cables and an oil pipe line, which caused a very large quantity of oil to flow inside the fuselage. At first the engineer was unable to ascertain the point of the oil leak and in spite of the aircraft being over the target area, he decided to cut a hole in the side of the fuselage with a fire axe so that he could crawl into the wing. Having made a two foot square hole, he crawled inside the wing and turned on the petrol cocks by hand and also found the cause of the oil leak. It came from a punctured gun turret oil pipe lead, which he isolated. For this praiseworthy and courageous act in very adverse conditions, Sergeant Fallon received the immediate award of the Distinguished Flying Medal.

Casualties June 19th/20th, 1943. Target Le Creusot

10 Squadron 4 Group Halifax JD109 ZA/
Pilot. 1239046 Sgt J.Watson Killed Bretteville-sur-Laize. CG XXIV-D-1/4
Nav. 1377535 Sgt H.C.W.Nash Killed Bretteville-sur-Laize, France. XXIV-C-1
B/A. 1391576 Sgt W.J.McKay Killed Bretteville-sur-Laize, France. XXIV-E-6
W/OP. 1384984 Sgt W.G.Brown Killed Bretteville-sur-Laize. CG XXIV-D-1/4

F/E. 339812 Sgt G.W.Rockwood Killed Bretteville-sur-Laize. XXIV-D-5
A/G. 1324374 Sgt J.Sutcliffe Killed Bretteville-sur-Laize. CG XXIV-D-1/4
A/G. R/139045 F/Sgt E.J.Lewis Killed Bretteville-sur-Laize. CG XXIV-D-1/4

408 Squadron 6 Group Halifax JD107 EQ/Y.
Aircraft shot down by night fighter near Caen, France.
Pilot. 141129 F/Lt R.A.Symes B.E.M PoW. Stalag Luft 3, Sagan. 1823
Nav. 157440 P/O J.Denholm Killed Bretteville-sur-Laize, France. XX-B-10
B/A. J/17087 F/Lt M.Samuels Killed Bretteville-sur-Laize, France. XX-B-11
W/OP. A/411378 F/O P.R.Quance Killed Bretteville-sur-Laize, France. XX-B-7
F/E. J/17468 P/O D.C.Horner Killed Bretteville-sur-Laize, France. XX-B-12
A/G. R/120948 Sgt H.A.Brown Killed (Died November 1943)
A/G. J/12326 F/Lt R.J.J.Ball PoW. Stalag Luft 3, Sagan. 1691

77 Squadron 4 Group Halifax JB863 KN/V
Aircraft crashed one quarter of mile S of Heslington, Yorkshire after take off
for operations to Le Creusot.
Pilot. 1331061 F/Sgt N.R.Hollege Killed Hornchurch. A-178
Nav. 1339096 F/Sgt W.Cooke Killed Windsor.(New) GN-24
B/A. 130565 F/O A.W.S.Young Killed Wembley.(Alparton) FF-53
W/OP. 1310902 Sgt F.Danby Killed Liverpool.(Anfield) 12-1370
F/E. 1284804 Sgt A.H.Gurry Killed Ilford. No number
A/G. 1352806 Sgt D.H.Clinch Killed Caerphilly.(Penyrheol) H-135
A/G. R/131442 Sgt R.E.Macdonald Killed Pocklington, Yorkshire. X-46-3284

Station Bomb Dump Explosion

On Saturday, 19th June, there was a bomb disaster at Snaith airfield, East Yorkshire, the home base of 51 Squadron. Twenty aircraft had been ordered for the Le Creusot raid by 4 Group HQ and all the bombers were waiting to be bombed up when, at 13.30 hours, a tremendous explosion occurred in the Station Bomb Dump. It is believed to have originated in the Fusing Shed. A large quantity of incendiaries caught fire. All personnel on the station were forced to take cover in the air raid shelters until 17.00 hours, during which time a considerable number of heavy calibre bombs blew up. It was subsequently found that 18 airmen and NCOs had been killed or were missing. Fortunately the squadron aircraft which were widely dispersed on their hard standings were not damaged and with typical press on spirit, 14 of the 20 aircraft were bombed up, the bombs being transported by road from the neighbouring station at Holme on Spalding Moor. Later the same day thirteen aircraft from 51 Squadron took off on the raid and all returned safely.

Small Bombing Force to Montchanin

June 19th/20th, 1943
On the same night as the Le Creusot raid, the Pathfinder Force
had another target, an electrical transformer power station at
Montchanin, 5 miles south east of Le Creusot. It was planned
that 31 Pathfinder aircraft, 28 Lancasters and 3 Stirlings, some
equipped with H^2S, would fly on from the Le Creusot raid and
provide a further 160 TIs and 48 flares to mark the target for
the remainder of this small force of Lancaster bombers to attack.
The raid was a complete failure for the crews mistook another
factory, the Henri Paul iron and bronze works for the power
station and dropped 109 tons of high explosive bombs, but
without much success. No aircraft were lost from this secondary
raid.

Minor Operations

Six Mosquitoes visited Cologne, Duisburg and Düsseldorf on the
same night, dropping a total of 1.6 tons of high explosive bombs.
One Mosquito returned early and there were no aircraft losses.

Minelaying

June 19th/20th, 1943
Twelve Lancasters from 3 Group went minelaying in the River
Gironde estuary, where 55 mines were laid. One aircraft,
Lancaster DS668 from 115 Squadron, failed to return. It was
captained by 124415 Flying Officer D. F. Brown and the bomber
crashed at Champtoce, France, after being attacked by a night
fighter. Two members of the crew, with the aid of the
underground movement, managed to evade capture. They were
the wireless operator, 537866 Sergeant A. H. Shepphard, and
flight engineer, 577112 Sergeant C. F. Trott. According to their
reports the navigator, Pilot Officer Pitchford, and bomb aimer,
Sergeant Davidson, were wounded in the attack. These last two
airmen were made prisoners of war, spending the early part of

their period as prisoners in hospital. The remaining uninjured crew members were also captured. The pilot was extremely unfortunate to bale out and land in the River Loire wher he was drowned.

Casualties June 19th/20th, 1943. Minelaying

115 Squadron 1 Group Lancaster DS668 KO/
Aircraft crashed at Champtoce, France
Pilot. 124415 F/O D.F.Brown Killed Ingrandes-sur-Loire, France 1
Nav. 137108 F/O C.N.Pitchford PoW. Stalag Luft 3, Sagan. 1164
B/A. R/134223 W/O A.S.Davidson PoW. Stalag 4B, Muhlberg(Elbe). 250716
W/OP. 537866 Sgt A.H.Shepphard Evaded capture.
F/E. 577112 Sgt C.F.Trott Evaded capture.
A/G. 1028246 Sgt R.Gould PoW. Camp not known.
A/G. 928303 F/Sgt L.F.King PoW. Stalag 357, Kopernikus. 326

Friedrichshafen

June 20th/21st, 1943
Friedrichshafen, on the shores of Lake Constance, was where a factory, the old Zeppelin works, was situated making the *Würzburg* radar sets. This was the target for a small force of 56 Lancasters from 5 Group and four Lancasters from 97 Squadron, 8 Group. This was an extremely important target, for these *Würzburg* sets were a key part of the air defence system of Germany. They controlled the German fighter interception boxes which were strategically positioned across the western bomber approaches. The Bombing Plan (Operation *Bellicose*) developed by 5 Group HQ was a departure from operations undertaken up to this time, as the raid was to be controlled by a pilot from just one Lancaster. This was a new innovation and in the bombing campaign it would be later known as the Master Bomber.

The attack was started in bright moonlight by four Lancasters from 97 Squadron (PFF), dropping target indicators for the first wave to drop their bombs. Early in the raid the controlling pilot, Group Captain Slee DSO's, Lancaster (ED702) developed engine trouble and he was forced to hand over control to his deputy, Wing Commander Gomm DSO of 467 Squadron. He had to amend the height of the attack from the planned 5,000 to 10,000 feet by ordering the bomber force to a new altitude of 15,000 feet due to the ferocity of the *Flak* and searchlight defences. This meant that no one had a correct target wind and this may have accounted for some of the inaccurate bombing. The second wave of aircraft planned to do a time and distance bombing run from a point on Lake Constance's shore line to the radar factory. This bombing technique was being actively developed by 5 Group at the time and would be used by them later in the bombing campaign. The target aiming point was quite small and later a photographic flight showed that only about 10% of the 158.5 tons of HE and 5,456 incendiary bombs had fallen on to the small factory buildings, but these had caused considerable damage. The German night fighters did not have their expected field day in the bright moonlight conditions on the homeward leg because the whole force waited until everyone had bombed, then flew on to airfields at Maison Blanche, Algiers, and Blida in North Africa, completely deceiving the waiting fighters on the homeward route. This raid became the first Shuttle Raid, although some damaged bombers had done this previously after the La Spezia raid on 13th/14th April. No aircraft were lost on this raid, but some of the Pathfinder aircraft had taken a lot of *Flak* over the target area and had to remain for some time for repair at the North African bases. The only casualty on this operation was bomb aimer 1335225 Sergeant B. L. May, who was killed by a *Flak* shrapnel in Lancaster EE116 from 619 Squadron, captained by Flight Sergeant W. McLeod. Sergeant May was buried in El Alio War Cemetery, Algiers, North Africa.

Casualties June 20th/21st, 1943. Target Friedrichshafen

619 Squadron 5 Group Lancaster EE116 PG/
Pilot. 1053159 F/Sgt W.Mcleod.
B/A. 1335225 Sgt B.L.May Killed El Alio, Algiers, N.Africa 12-G-4 Bomb aimer killed by *Flak* over target.

Minor Operations

June 20th/21st, 1943
The continuing nuisance raids by the Mosquitoes were kept up

when four of them went to Berlin, dropping 3.1 tons of bombs while another went to Düsseldorf to drop its load of 0.8 tons of bombs. No losses were sustained by these fast flying bombers.

Minelaying

On the same night 12 Lancasters from 1 Group and three Stirlings from 3 Group kept up their never ending minelaying operations, laying 69 mines on this occasion, in the Baltic sea area. Two Lancasters returned with their mines as they were unable to get an accurate fix for dropping. There were no aircraft losses.

Krefeld

June 21st/22nd, 1943

It was back to the Ruhr once more on the night of 21st/22nd June, when a large force of 705 aircraft - 262 Lancasters, 209 Halifaxes, 117 Stirlings, 105 Wellingtons and 12 Mosquitoes were scheduled to attack the town of Krefeld. Three of the Mosquito Pathfinders returned early with defective equipment and 39 main force bombers were forced to return with engine and technical problems. The moonlight period was not quite over and the night fighters took full advantage of this phase of moon. For a change, the Ruhr area had very good visibility with just a thin layer of cloud over the target area. The Pathfinder Mosquitoes dropped perfect target indicators starting at 01.30 hours and at six minute intervals until 02.19 hours. These were accurately backed up by the heavy bombers of the Pathfinders, 31 H^2S equipped Pathfinders were detailed to drop yellow TIs if no red indicators were showing and 37 backers up dropped green on yellow or red TIs. The main force dropped 1,031.6 tons of high explosives and 364,324 incendiaries in an area two to three miles radius from the aiming point. Large fires were started, a particularly large explosion was seen at 01.40 hours and by 02.10 hours the whole town appeared to be a raging inferno with smoke rising up to 15,000 feet. Krefeld town records show that an immense amount of damage was done, 50% of the town centre was completely gutted and 1,056 people lost their lives with a further 4,550 injured in this terrible attack. Nearly 100,000 people lost their homes, either through them being completely destroyed or very badly damaged and unfit for habitation. There was a heavy cost to be paid for this raid and many of the aircraft were claimed by the night fighters which were very active. 42 aircraft were reported missing from this operation a loss rate of 6.8% of the attacking force. The aircrew losses were 150 killed, 67 missing, 62 became prisoners and two airmen made successful evasions.

Ditching Saves Two Crews

On this Krefeld raid one Halifax crew from 35 Squadron escaped with their lives although their plane was lost. It was Halifax BB368 which had encountered heavy *Flak* on the outward flight, just south of Rotterdam, and as a result the starboard engine was put out of action. The pilot, Sergeant D. H. Milne, pressed on with his flight towards the target, flying on three engines. He bombed from a lower altitude of 19,000 feet as his damaged aircraft was unable to get any higher.

From the target area the Halifax began to lose height and by the time the Dutch coast was in sight the plane was down to 14,000 feet, but still with sufficient height to keep away from any *Flak*. Immediately they had crossed the coastline, the port inner engine cut out, but the Halifax still flew along on its two remaining engines, though now it began rapidly losing height. As a precaution the wireless operator sent out a distress signal and it was fortunate that this was done, for as soon as the English coast came into sight a third engine, the starboard inner, cut out. There was no alternative for the pilot but to order ditching positions for the crew and he successfully ditched the bomber in a relatively calm sea at 03.00 hours, about 30 miles north of Cross Sands lighthouse, near Cromer. All the crew safely scrambled into their dinghy and they soon saw two Mustang fighters circling them, obviously in response to their earlier and timely distress call. The crew fired the colours of the day from their Verey Pistol to show their exact position. The fighters quickly flew off in the direction of the coastline and shortly afterwards two Walrus Air Sea Rescue planes from 287 Squadron alighted on the water near to the dinghy and the battle weary crew were safely rescued. They were soon back on operations, but unfortunately all the crew were killed on the Cologne raid of July 3rd/4th, 1943.

Another Halifax, JD206 T for Tommy from 102 Squadron 4 Group, had to ditch in the English Channel 18 miles off Le Havre. The aircraft had been hit by *Flak* near Overflakee on the way to the target and had lost an engine. The pilot, Sergeant G. S. Honey, had to jettison his bombs before ditching as the plane was unable to maintain height. All the crew took to the dinghy and put out the sea drogue to stop their easterly drift to the French coast. They were first spotted by a passing Mustang and then by a Typhoon at 15.30 hours. Two Walrus aircraft from 277 Squadron were soon on the scene as they had been attracted by the red Verey cartridge fired from the dinghy. The pilot was taken aboard one Walrus and flown back to Martlesham and the remainder of the crew taken aboard the second Walrus which taxied to a waiting Motor Gunboat. The crew were taken aboard and landed at Felixstowe. These Air Sea Rescues illustrated the very efficient service which operated and was always on the alert when bombers were going and returning from their raids.

431 Squadron Commander Lost

Wellington HF518, J for Johnny from 431 Squadron, was one of the 42 missing aircraft from this Krefeld raid. It was captained by Wing Commander J. Coverdale, the squadron commander, and crewed by two recently decorated officers, navigator Pilot Officer G. C. Parslow DFM and Flying Officer J. B. G. Bailey DFC, who had been awarded their decorations for their actions on the night of 23rd/24th May.

Two Aircrew Successfully Evade

There were two aircrew who managed to evade capture after the Krefeld raid. One was the Polish navigator from Wellington HE347 of 305 Squadron, P/2115 Pilot Officer. J. Gasecki, and the other was bomb aimer 135880 Pilot Officer. A. Hagan DFC. Hagan was from Halifax JD205 of 77 Squadron, which was attacked by an Me210 and set on fire. The intercom was also put out of action in the course of the attack and the bomb aimer received word from the navigator to bale out at 02.30 hours at 14,000 feet over Esch, near Boxtel, Holland. The rest of the crew, except for the two gunners who were killed, were made prisoners of war. The navigator, Sergeant F. G. Hawthorne, who evaded until August 11th 1943, was captured and made prisoner when he, along with some other evaders, were led into a German trap in Brussels when the infamous 'Captain' was involved in the evasion plans. Hawthorne had suffered a bad internal haemorrhage due to his heavy parachute landing and he had been looked after by a Swiss nurse and doctor during his evasion period.

After Pilot Officer Jozef Gasecki's return to the UK in October, 1943, he was posted as a navigator to 307 Squadron, based at Church Fenton, Yorkshire. The squadron was equipped with Mosquito aircraft and flew intruder sorties. On Sept 17th, 1944, the squadron was detailed to fly six patrols in support of Operation *Market Garden*, the operation in which a large force of airborne troops were landed over a stretch of country covering Eindhoven, Nijmegen and Arnhem in Holland. Unfortunately thick haze and fog interfered with their support mission, although one Mosquito was missing the remainder had to return to Coltishall airfield. It was at this airfield on the following day when flying back to their home base that Flying Officer Gasecki and his pilot Flight Lieutenant S. Madej collided with another Mosquito crewed by Flight Lieutenant W. J. Griffiths and Flight Lieutenant G. J. Lane. Both aircraft were badly damaged, but Gasecki's Mosquito burst into flames and crashed, killing the Polish crew. The other Mosquito crew made a forced landing on one engine and managed to safely extricate themselves from the aircraft before it burst into flames.

Pathfinder Squadrons Pay a Heavy Price

Thirty per cent of the aircraft missing from the Krefeld raid were from 8 Group Pathfinder Force. 35 Squadron and 7 Squadron particularly had high losses of five Halifaxes and four

Stirlings respectively. Stirling EF387 MG/D, captained by Squadron Leader C. A. Hughes from 7 Squadron, had on board that night a second pilot, Wing Commander C. O. Bastian DFC. The bomber was attacked by a night fighter at about 00.50 hours over Holland only ten minutes flying time from the target, when two engines caught fire. A bale out order was given and all the crew got out safely except for the rear gunner who was killed in the attack.

'The Captain'

Wing Commander Bastian's post war interrogation makes interesting reading because he was on the loose for over two months and he recounts how he met up with the infamous 'captain' who was so instrumental in betraying to the Germans many aircrew who were attempting to evade and who no doubt was ultimately responsible for Bastian's capture as well. His post war interrogation report reads as follows -

"I landed in a field of standing rye near Vanrais, Holland. As it was nearly one in the morning I thought it best after hiding my parachute to lay up where I was for the rest of the night. I stayed there until dusk the next night. I then contacted a farmer who was passing by and he later brought a local schoolmaster to me who spoke English and from whom I obtained a pair of overalls and a cloth cap. In this disguise I made my way south to the Belgian border, walking mostly by night, though I did venture forth in the day occassionally. I lay up in whatever cover I could find, sometimes in the open and sometimes in barns or outbuildings. I experienced little difficulty in obtaining both food and advice from the farming folk en route. My progress was fairly slow as I was careful to keep my day's march within the limits of the area about which I had already obtained fairly accurate accounts regarding the locations of German troops, etc.

"I crossed the frontier in the neighbourhood of Roermond and was aided in doing so by the kindly and helpful advice of a Dutch farmer I had contacted. He took me to the border himself and showed me where to cross to avoid the control point.

"About 3rd July I reached the outskirts of the village called Haelen, about 10 miles north-east of Louvain, after having spent an unpleasant 48 hours negotiating the Bourg Leopold area where a considerable force of German soldiers were located. Towards the evening of 3rd July I contacted a farmer who passed near where I was resting in a field of grain. He was friendly and told me to stay where I was and that he would bring a friend to see me. He left, but very soon he returned along with several people, amongst whom was a man who spoke excellent English. This man said he could help me and after bringing food, shaving tackle and water, took me after dark to his house in Haelen. Apparently it was not safe for me to stay there, so later that night I was escorted to another village about 4 miles away where I was lodged overnight in an estaminet and next day a guide arrived and took me to Louvain.

"He took me to the home of a family where I remained for over six weeks. I was well fed and comfortably lodged with this family who also provided me with some civilian clothes, purchased with the organisation funds. With my host I moved about Louvain quite freely, going to cinemas, cafés, etc and also made some reconnoitring of possible targets, including the local Phillips Electric Works. During my stay I had no Belgian identity card.

"About 15th August the local Resistance carried out a train wrecking operation near Louvain and immediately German patrols became very active in the town checking up on suspects etc. When a patrol came to the street in which I lived and appeared to be heading for the house, my host and I made a hasty exit via the roof and then hid in a back tool shed. The patrol did in fact call at my host's home and made some enquiries, though I believe nothing further came of it. However for my greater safety I stayed that night at the home of a next door neighbour. Here I met an English woman who said she was a member of an escape organisation. Living with her was another evader, Flying Officer Sneyder from 83 Squadron, and arrangements were made for Sneyder and myself to leave the next day for Brussels. So the following morning we both left by train escorted by an elderly Belgian lady. She was a charming maiden lady of about 60 years of age. She wore Belgian war ribbons of the last war during which I understood she had been engaged in Intelligence work for the Allies. Upon arrival in Brussels we were taken to a furnished flat situated in the shopping district not far from the Guildhall. There was I recall, a shop of some sort on the street level of the building in which the flat was situated. The flat was unoccupied, but we met here an officer from the Belgian Salvation Army. He was a man of about 35 years of age, well built, height about 5'9", dark hair and moustache and brown eyes. He was a married man with one small child and he and his wife kept a restaurant nearby from which he brought us two hot meals daily.

"We remained in this flat four or five days, during which time we were visited several times by two young Belgian girls, one of them, I do not know which, was called Yvonne. They both spoke good English and were about 25 years of age. Both were brunettes and were attractive looking girls. One was rather quiet and reserved while the other was somewhat flamboyant and assertive, considerably made up and rather Jewish looking. The day before we left the flat, the Jewish looking girl came to visit us accompanied by a man she referred to as the 'Captain'. He was a man of about 40/45 years of age, height 5'8" and powerfully built. He had dark greying hair and a close cropped moustache of the same colour. His complexion can best be described as weather beaten and across one cheek, I believe the left, he had a scar. One finger was missing from one hand. He spoke very good English with a marked Canadian accent.'

Many other aircrew who attempted evasions refer to their dealings with the 'captain', who sometimes went under the name of Captain Jackson, but he was really called De Litter and was born in Belgium. He is reported to have been employed by Dr. Schipert, a known German agent.

"The same day one of the girls brought to the flat five more evading aircrew, two Americans, one a Warrant Officer and the other a Sergeant of a Fortress crew and three RAF Sergeants all members of a Boston crew. Next day the 'Captain' arrived and took us all in a petrol driven car to what he called his Depot. This was a fairly substantial house of three storeys situated near a large block of flats, in the neighbourhood of 218 Tervuren Avenue. In charge of it was a caretaker aged about 30 years of age and his wife, their family consisting of a boy about 14 years of age. Many people visited the 'Depot' which the 'Captain' said was once the Swiss Legation. There was a telephone installed in the house on which the 'Captain' held many conversations in French. We stayed here for a few more days during which time we were joined by nine more evaders a mixed party of Australian, Canadian and American personnel.

"The night before we left as the original party of seven, the 'Captain' briefed us about the train journey to Paris, which he said was the next stop on our journey home and very plausibly explained that it was both necessary and advisable to leave with him any papers or letters which we might have in our possession and also any money, maps, identity cards or discs etc. This we all did.

"Before setting out on our journey we were taken individually by the two guides, who were to escort us to Paris, to have our photographs taken for the purpose of preparing Belgian identity cards for the journey. After this had been done we left next day by train, the seven of us occupying one carriage while the two guides sat outside in the corridor. I thought this a very odd arrangement and not very good for security. These guides I took to be Belgian, they were both middle aged men, one of whom was stout with thinning hair, small moustache, dark complexion and wearing spectacles, the other a quiet slim man with grey hair, thin faced and clean shaven. They were both about 50 years of age.

"At the French frontier a German military control boarded the train and the guides then collected all our identity cards which they showed to the control. What they said to them I do not know as the German patrol did not enter the compartment. Although we must have looked a suspicious lot, seven young men in motley attire, the German guards paid little attention to us. All this made me quite concerned about the whole setup.

"About midday we arrived at Charleville, where we were told we had to change trains. Here we were handed over to two other guides, French I presumed, and we were told that we would have a meal at a nearby hotel. One of the guides led the way while I followed with the rest of the party straggling behind. We had not far to walk to the hotel, where a guide led us up a flight of stairs into a bedroom. There was a wash basin there and I had just commenced to wash my hands when I saw from the window several cars pull up outside the hotel. A party of fully armed German military personnel got out and without any hesitation walked straight up the stairs and into the room where we were all congregated. An officer was in charge of the party and he immediately told us to get our hands up. I looked up from my ablutions and then turned back and continued washing up, hoping that our guide would be equal to the occasion and say something as he did in the railway train. The tone of the German officer's command, however, brooked no disobedience and I made haste to obey. The guide by this time also had his hands up in the air. We were then bundled into the waiting cars and taken to the nearby *Luftwaffe* barracks and placed in confinement. By this time the guide had disappeared but later in the day two of our party maintained that from the window of their room they had seen him walk through the barrack gates and receive a salute from the German sentry on duty as he passed. I was eventually taken to Dulag Luft, where I spent three days before being transferred to Stalag Luft III, where I spent the rest of the war before being liberated at Trendhorst on Thursday, 3rd May, 1945."

Corroboration of the 'Captain's' method of betraying aircrew evaders comes from 148840 Flying Officer P. N. Croft, another Pathfinder who was a bomb aimer on Halifax HR 799 captained by New Zealander Flying Officer Hickson, also shot down on the Krefeld raid. According to Croft's post war interrogation report they had bombed the target and were on their route home when, at 01.00 hours, just north of Venlo they were attacked either by a German operated Halifax bomber or one of the attacking bombers had fired on them by mistake. Two of the crew were killed instantly, but the remainder managed to obey the bale out order when the bomber caught fire. The navigator, Pilot Officer A. F. Hutchinson, and Croft landed quite close to each other and were quickly helped by a schoolteacher who took them to his father's farm where they stayed for four days. They were provided with civilian clothes and then taken on to Grubben-vorst where they stayed another two nights before moving on to stop at a butcher's shop for two nights then finally moving to an empty house. That night a Lancaster bomber was shot down and crashed in the village main street, burning down most of the village. The Germans came quickly to the scene and to avoid being captured the schoolteacher moved the two evaders to another house belonging to a miller in a neighbouring village where they stayed for a further 8 days. On July 16th, both were taken on to Roermond where they stayed at a farm for five days, when a lady who said she was a member of the Fiat Libertas Organisation came to see them. She took away their escape kits and told the two airmen that she was going to arrange their return to the UK.

Pilot Officer Hutchinson left on a bicycle on 23rd July, escorted by a young man. (Croft later found out that Hutchinson was captured the day before him). Croft left on 30th July, similarly escorted by the same young man on a bike. They rode to Weert and were joined there by Squadron Leader Carpenter and Warrant Officer Brazil before going on to Bree. There they met the 'Captain' for the first time. He organised the rest of the journey for them. He took them to Brussels by car and they arrived there at about 18.00 hours. The three airmen were taken to a flat where they met up with quite a number of evaders including Flying Officer Giddey a 467 Squadron Australian pilot shot down on the Düsseldorf raid of 25th June, Flight Sergeant A. Guy, a wireless operator from 78 Squadron who was shot down on the Gelsenkirchen raid of 25th/26th June and who was later repatriated, Sergeant E. L. McVittie, a Warrant Officer from 76 Squadron shot down on the Mulheim raid of 22nd June and Sergeant F. G. Hawthorne, navigator from 77 Squadron shot down on the Krefeld raid of 21st/22nd. They all stayed at the flat until 7th August, when a party of nine were taken by the 'Captain' and one of his men by train to Paris.

A similar incident which Wing Commander Bastian had experienced happened to the evaders. On the train as they crossed the French/Belgian border all other passengers were made to get off the train for a security check whereas the German guards paid no attention to the party, who must have looked highly suspicious all in one compartment. They reached Paris at 16.00 hours and were taken to an hotel. They had not been there for more than 10 minutes when the Gestapo arrived and arrested them. Croft spent a month in Fresnes Prsion before finally being sent to Stalag 4B at Muhlberg. He was liberated by the Russians on 23rd April, 1945.

Krefeld Raid Victim Finally Escapes

1575535 Sergeant W. A. Poulton was the bomb aimer of Halifax JD244 from 51 Squadron based at Snaith, East Yorkshire. The aircraft was captained by Warrant Officer F. J. Heathfield. After bombing the target at Krefeld and while turning on to the homeward leg the Halifax was hit by *Flak* which disabled two engines. The pilot struggled to fly the damaged bomber as far away from the target as possible, but shortly afterwards a third engine went u/s and the pilot was forced to give the bale out order. He countermanded this order after some of the crew had already baled out, as he realised that the aircraft was now too low for them to bale out safely. He decided to crash land the aircraft at Baelen, 2 to 3 miles south-east of Mol, Belgium. Sergeant R. H. Masters, an American in the RCAF, and an air gunner in the crew was one of those who had baled out and he landed 5 kms from Postel, Belgium. He was helped by the underground movement, but was captured when he reached Bescanon, en route to Switzerland in December, 1943.

Sergeant Poulton's post war interrogation reveals what happened to him.

"After landing from the bale out I met up with the rear gunner, Sergeant Cooper, who was badly wounded in his left arm. We went to a café in the town and knocked at the door. Fortunately the owner let us enter and I was allowed to bandage up the gunner's arm. We both then went to the local railway station with a view to catching a train to Brussels. At the station I met a Belgian who had been a sergeant in the Belgian Army and I spoke to him in French explaining our position. He told me that there was little chance of our getting away that day as there were too many Germans about. When I asked him to get a doctor for the gunner, he said that if he did the gunner would certainly be handed over to the Germans, but on looking at the wound he thought maybe it would be wiser to see a doctor as without medical treatment the gunner could possibly lose the arm. We had some discussion about this and finally concluded that the gunner should surrender himself by going for medical help. I later heard that he had in fact been taken prisoner. I spent the rest of the night in the woods nearby where I changed into civilian clothes which the friendly Belgian ex sergeant had provided. The next day I caught a train to Brussels via Antwerp accompanied by the Belgian and a friend. I stayed in the Belgian's house for a week after which I was taken on to the house of an English woman who was a member of an underground organisation. For the next six months I remained in Brussels staying at various addresses in the city, where I was being continously assured that I was just about to leave and would be back in the UK shortly.

"In February, 1944, I was sent to Charleroi where again I received the same vague assurance that I would be moving on presently. By this time I was getting frustrated of being fobbed off so on July 1st, 1944, I returned to Brussels on my own and stayed with the woman who had previously sheltered me. About 10th August I was told that at last I was starting my journey home and I left for Antwerp accompanied by two members of the organisation. We stayed in a house in Antwerp until 16th August when a young woman arrived and told me that from now on she was arranging the rest of my journey and I was to go with her. She eventually handed me over to two other men, who said that they were members of the financial control committee set up by the Belgian Government to distribute awards to helpers of evaders and to make sure that the helpers were genuine. They demanded to know the names and addresses of the people with whom I had been staying. I thought this line of inquiry by a questionable Government official at this time of the war seemed very suspicious indeed and so I refused to tell them anything, whereupon I was marched off to the Gestapo HQ. My fears and doubts as to their claims had been justified.

"I was placed in a civilian gaol for two weeks during which time I was constantly threatened with being shot as a spy. After this time I was transferred to Dulag Luft and then on to Stalag Luft 7 at Bankau. On January 19th, 1945, all the prisoners in the camp were force marched towards Central Germany to get away from the advancing Russian forces. Nearly all the prisoners were in a very weak state and later in the march twenty of us decided that we could not carry on for another day. We were ably assisted by our Medical Officer, Captain H. O. Watson, who reported that we were unfit for the march. The next morning we were given transport to the SS Hospital at Lossen near Schurgast. When we arrived we were told that there was no room for us and that we were to carry on to Brieg am Oder. Instead of this we hid up in a local castle. We were visited by the local village priest who took us to his home and gave us food and shelter. On January 25th he was forced to flee as the SS troops were due to arrive in the village, but he made sure that we were provided with food before he went. We were looked after by a kindly Austrian guard in charge of a French camp nearby.

"A few days later we were visited by the SS to whom we feigned severe sickness. They left but said that they would return. This prompted us to make a quick decison as to our next move. We thought that the best hiding place would be in the French camp as we hoped that the SS would not think of looking for us there. We accordingly arranged with our Austrian guard to take us in. After some days of shelling and strafing the French camp was taken over by the Russians on 4th February, 1945. We were sent on to Oppeln and from there we walked to Gleiwitz. We reached Odessa by the end of February, 1945."

Caught, But Still Persistant in Escape Bids

137306 Flight Lieutenant M. P. Ellis was the tail gunner in Stirling R9272, MG/W captained by Flight Lieutenant J. S. Watt DSO DFC from 7 Squadron Pathfinder Group, which was hit by *Flak* and shortly afterwards attacked by an enemy fighter over Holland on the way to Krefeld. The oxygen bottles amidships caught fire and then exploded. An immediate bale out order was given and Flight Lieutenant Ellis and the Wireless Operator 137667 Flight Lieutenant J. H. Ross were the only crew members to escape from the doomed bomber. Both Became prisoners. After the war, Ellis reported the subsequent events in his interrogation report

"I landed in a small copse between Tilburg and Eindhoven slightly injuring my back in the process. My hand had already been injured by *Flak* in the aircraft. I buried my Mae West, parachute and harness in a ditch and walked west. After I had gone about five miles, I hid in a cornfield and went to sleep. I woke up early next morning and heard some labourers speaking Dutch, I approached them and asked for some water. They indicated the direction of the Belgian border and after I had filled my rubber water bottle, I set off walking towards it.

"After walking for about eight hours I reached the Belgian frontier, but just as I was crossing over the border I was observed by a member of the Wehrmacht. He yelled at me to stop, so I made off as fast as I could towards a cornfield. I hid myself as well as I could, but within a few minutes I was discovered and arrested.

"I was taken down to the frontier post and later taken by bus to the Field Security Centre in Antwerp. I was briefly interrogated and then moved to a guard room in another part of the town, where I was kept for two days. On the second day I was joined by my wirelss operator Flight Lieutenant H. Ross. The next day we were taken by lorry to Brussels, where we were placed in St Gilles Prison. We stayed there for three weeks after which we were taken by train to Dulag Luft arriving there on July 1st. We were kept in solitary confinement for six days before being moved to Stalag Luft III at Sagan & Belaria.

*On March 27th, 1944, I escaped from Stalag Luft III by hiding in the tarpaulin of a lorry which was sent into the camp with a load of stones. I had noticed the lorry in the morning and decided to prepare myself to get out of the camp on it in the afternoon if an opportunity should occur. I had saved 14 bars of chocolate and I had in my possession a map and compass. My intention was to get to Stettin and pick up a boat there. I had decided that when I reached the River Elbe I would stow away on a barge, also I had in mind to steal some dungarees or working clothes if I saw any on washing lines etc.

*At 17.00 hours on March 27th, I saw my chance and whilst somebody else was talking to the driver to distract his attention, I rolled myself up in the tarpaulin used for covering the vehicle. We drove out of the camp stopping for a few minutes at each gate. After about 15 minutes we drove into the Transport Lager near to the camp and went into a garage. As soon as the driver had gone, I ran straight to the barbed wire and climbed over, as there were no sentry boxes in this lager and no guards.

*I found myself in a field on the other side of the wire and walked as fast as I could in a northerly direction. At dusk I had to stop walking as I had lost my compass and did not wish to enter the forest which confronted me on such a dark night for fear I should get lost, also the ground was thickly covered with snow and the going was difficult. I therefore hid in a barn and went to sleep.

At first light the next morning I set off walking again. At 14.00 hours I reached the neighbourhood of Christianstadt, and whilst I was crossing a main road into a wood I was spotted by a policeman. To avoid him I ran through the wood and down to a stream which ran alongside it. I thought it was a shallow stream so I ran into it and found that the water came up to my neck. Just then a shot was fired over my head. I could see a Home Guard waiting for me on the other bank so deciding the game was up I swam back to the otherside and gave myself up to the policeman. He took me down to the police station at Christianstadt, where I was kept for two hours. I was then taken by two SS men by car to Sagan Police Station. On arrival there I was questioned by an SS captain and then placed in a cell. Later that evening I was joined by Flight Lieutenant Long (later shot) and Flight Lieutenant R. A.

---

*On March 24th 1944, 76 RAF Officers had succeeded in making a mass escape from Stalag Luft III. Most of them were recaptured following the greatest internal 'hue and cry' ever mounted in Germany. Hitler ordered that all were to be shot as an example to others, but Goering, under whose ultimate command the the Air Force camps fell, argued that similar treatment might be meted out to Luftwaffe aircrew held by the Allies. Hitler then relented a little by ordering that more than half of the recaptured aircrew were to be shot. Thus fifty RAF officers lost their lives. Officially 'shot whilst escaping' they were actually murdered by the SS.

Bethell. The next morning, March 29th, Flight Lieutenant Kolnowski (Later shot) was put in my cell and in the afternoon Flight Lieutenant Pohe and Flight Lieutenant Hake, both of whom were also shot. That evening we were all taken to the Hauptmann's office and told we were going away. Shortly afterwards we were taken in a heavily armed car with a police patrol to Gorlitz Prison. I was put in a cell with Flight Lieutenants Long, Bethell and Kolnowski, while Flight Lieutenants Pohe and Hake were placed in a separate cell.

*On the morning of March 30th, Flight Lieutenants Kolnowski and Long were taken away and in the afternoon Flight Lieutenant Bethell was taken away and later myself. I was taken to an office where I was interrogated by two elderly civilian men and a good looking young girl. I was asked my name number and rank and my age, all of which I answered. Then I was asked my father's and my mother's Christian names which I refused to answer and told the two men that I was from the Belaria camp and not from the North Compound at Sagan. As far as I could tell it was purely a routine interrogation at the end of which I was asked to sign a paper. I refused, but they signed it with their own names. The whole interview lasted about 30 minutes. I was then taken back into a cell with Flight Lieutenant Bethell. On Friday, 31st March, we were joined by Flight Lieutenants Armstrong and Nelson. Every day the people in my cell were changed, I did not know most of them, the only one I can recall is Flight Lieutenant H. C. Marshall. Every two days I was moved to the next cell going progressively further down the line towards the last cell. Frequently I heard the sound of a lorry driving up and the occupants of the end cell being put into it. Whether this was a game of nerves being played by the Germans with the air of uncertainty I don't know. By April 6th Flight Lieutenant Long and I had reached the cell next to the end one and the next morning I heard the guard call out Long's name and then mine, after which we were placed in the end cell. The guard told us that we would be going away in the morning. What he meant by going away was still very much of a mystery.

*On the morning of 7th April for some unknown reason we were moved back to our old cell and we remained there until April 11th. On that day whilst Flight Lieutenant Long had left the cell to go to the lavatory. I was taken out and put in a solitary confinement cell. Later in the day I saw Flight Lieutenant Long being escorted down the corridor past my cell so I shouted out to him, asking him if he was alright and whether I could still borrow his comb as I had done each day. The next day the comb was brought to my cell and after using it I returned it to the guard. On April 13th the comb did not arrive, so I presumed that Long had forgotten to send it. Later that day a civilian came to my cell and asked if I was Flight Lieutenant Long. When I told him my name, he quickly left. Later that day I heard a lorry drive up and Flight Lieutenant Long was taken away.

*I remained in Gorlitz in solitary confinement until April 25th, when I was taken back to Stalag Luft 3 Sagan & Belaria by two plain clothes men. I was again sentenced to 21 days solitary. During the remainder of my imprisonment I did not have much opportunity of escaping but I did act as a watcher for three tunnel operations, all of which were discovered before completion. I was liberated from Stalag IIIA, Luckenwalde on April 27th, 1945, by the Russian forces and I was taken by lorry to Halle from where I was flown back to the UK via Brussels arriving on May 8th, 1945."

Casualties June 21st/22nd, 1943. Target Krefeld

7 Squadron 8 Group Stirling EF387 MG/D
Aircraft shot down by fighter at Oploo, Holland.
Pilot. 63428 S/Ldr C.A.Hughes PoW. Stalag Luft 3, Sagan. 1654
2/Pilot. 77925 W/Cdr C.O.Bastian PoW. Stalag Luft 3, Sagan. 2254
B/A. NZ/39664 F/O C.F.P.Brown PoW. Oflag 7B, Eichstatt. 222489
W/OP. NZ/412879 W/O W.J.Hasen PoW. Stalag Luft 3, Sagan. 222516
F/E. 1039006 W/O A.T.H.Perkins PoW. Stalag 357, Kopernikus. 225
A/G. 1383830 F/Sgt R.T.Cox Killed Eindhoven (Woensel), Holland. EE-12
A/G. NZ/404346 F/O T.J.Elliot PoW. Stalag Luft 3, Sagan. 1651

7 Squadron 8 Group Stirling EF366 MG/L
Aircraft crashed near Achel, Belgium at 01.40 hours. (22/6/43). Victim of Hpt. Wandam 1/NJG5.
Pilot. A/413222 F/O R.B.Meiklejohn Killed Heverlee, Belgium. 8-Killed-1
Nav. NZ/414679 P/O C.H.G.Redwood Killed Heverlee, Belgium. 8-Killed-2
B/A. 1339839 F/Sgt F.Hugo PoW. Stalag 4B Muhlberg(Elbe). 222518
W/OP. 1331718 F/Sgt L.E.Ellingham PoW. Stalag 4B Muhlberg(Elbe). 222508
F/E. 929448 Sgt F.W.Coles PoW. Stalag 357, Kopernikus. 23619
A/G. 1456893 F/Sgt J.Kilfoyle PoW. Stalag 357, Kopernikus. 43262
A/G. 751798 W/O E.A.Brown PoW. Stalag 357, Kopernikus. 320

7 Squadron 8 Group Stirling R9266 MG/J
Aircraft crashed at Krefeld, Germany.
Pilot. 110952 F/Lt C.D.Ince DFC * Missing, Runnymede Memorial 119
Nav. 120538 F/Lt H.A.Winfield PoW. Stalag Luft 3, Sagan. 1511
B/A. 1237998 F/Sgt E.Davenport PoW. Stalag Luft 1, Barth Vogelsang. 109
W/OP. 50736 F/O J.W.Roch PoW. Stalag Luft 3, Sagan. 1727
F/E. 568506 W/O F.C.Fray PoW. Stalag 357, Kopernikus. 137
A/G. 137117 F/Lt A.C.Collings PoW. Stalag Luft 3, Sagan. 1492
A/G. 1059878 F/Sgt T.Allcock PoW. Stalag 357, Kopernikus. 55

7 Squadron 8 Group Stirling R9272 MG/W
Aircraft crashed at Gilze Rijen, Holland.
Pilot. 110643 F/Lt J.S.Watt DSO, DFC Missing, Runnymede Memorial 122
Nav. 137665 F/Lt F.A.G.Tompkins Missing, Runnymede Memorial 121
B/A. 1434193 Sgt A.J.Sutton Missing, Runnymede Memorial 166
W/OP. 137667 F/O J.H.Ross PoW. Stalag Luft 3, Sagan 1704
F/E. 1127694 Sgt D.S.Donaldson Missing, Runnymede Memorial 147
A/G. 1090679 Sgt F.J.B.Dukes Killed Bergen-op-Zoom, Holland. 27-A-7
A/G. 137306 F/Lt M.P.Ellis PoW. Stalag Luft 3, Sagan. 1696

35 Squadron 8 Group Halifax BB361 TL/U
Pilot. J/15834 F/Lt T.H.Lane PoW. Stalag Luft 3, Sagan. 1659
Nav. 130105 F/Lt P.M.Jackson PoW. Stalag Luft 3, Sagan. 1655
B/A. 148058 P/O G.W.Darling PoW. Stalag 357, Kopernikus. 108
W/OP. A/403977 W/O A.P.Balson PoW. Stalag 357, Kopernikus. 43240
F/E. 570456 F/Sgt F.J.Rogers PoW. Stalag 357, Kopernikus. 239
A/G. 652721 W/O R.F.McDonald PoW. Stalag 357, Kopernikus. 205
A/G. 120076 F/Lt D.R.Alexander PoW. Stalag Luft 3, Sagan. 1648

35 Squadron 8 Group Halifax W7878 TL/J
Pilot. 127957 F/O M.W.P.Clarke Killed Bergen-op-Zoom, Holland. 32-B-10
Nav. 1078821 Sgt B.J.Dowse Missing, Runnymede Memorial 148
B/A. 1600686 Sgt F.M.Mazin Missing, Runnymede Memorial 158
W/OP. 1331566 Sgt H.R.Fink Killed Bergen, Holland. 2-C-6
F/E. 577177 Sgt C.M.Harcombe Killed Bergen, Holland. 2-C-7
A/G. R/81607 F/Sgt J.Richer Missing, Runnymede Memorial 185
A/G. 950711 Sgt A.C.Mcleod Missing, Runnymede Memorial 158

35 Squadron 8 Group Halifax HR848 TL/
Pilot. 147363 F/O R.J.Quigly PoW. Stalag Luft 6, Heydekrug. 4251
Nav. 126886 F/O J.H.R.St John Killed Uden, Holland. 5-E-5
B/A. 1321990 Sgt F.R.Carpenter PoW. Stalag 357, Kopernikus. 91
W/OP. 1204190 Sgt F.J.Williams PoW. Stalag 4B Muhleburg(Elbe). 250740
F/E. 1010564 Sgt J.I.Barrie Killed Uden, Holland. 5-E-4
A/G. 941955 Sgt J.White Killed Uden, Holland. 5-E-7
A/G. 126833 F.O R.B.Capon Killed Uden, Holland. 5-E-6

35 Squadron 8 Group Halifax HR685 TL/V
Pilot. J/18204 P/O J.W.Andrews Missing, Runnymede Memorial 175
Nav. 1392675 Sgt F.V.Barnard Missing, Runnymede Memorial 141
B/A. 1338696 Sgt D.J.Jones Missing, Runnymede Memorial 155
W/OP. 1382671 Sgt R.A.Muldoon Missing, Runnymede Memorial 160
F/E. R/121633 W/O N.T.MacAulay Killed Texel, Holland. Killed-5-100
A/G. 1306838 Sgt W.D.Robertson Missing, Runnymede Memorial 163
A/G. 575419 Sgt R.M.Scott Missing, Runnymede Memorial 164

35 Squadron 8 Group Halifax HR799 TL/R
Aircraft hit by *Flak* over Holland.
Pilot. NZ/412231 F/O W.H.Hickson PoW. Stalag Luft 3, Sagan. 2190
2/Pilot. A/34017 F/Sgt H.J.Krohn Killed Jonkerbos, Holland 7-I-1
Believed shot on landing or during parachute descent.
Nav. 1576732 F/Sgt A.F.Hutchinson PoW. Stalag 357, Kopernikus. 323
B/A. 148840 F/O P.N.Croft PoW. Stalag 4B, Muhleberg(Elbe). 222672
W/OP. R/92579 Sgt J.H.Graham PoW. Stalag 4B, Muhlenerg(Elbe). 222423
F/E. 1033029 F/Sgt F.S.Maltas PoW. Stalag 357, Kopernikus. 331
A/G. 1268822 Sgt J.F.Dowsing PoW. Stalag Luft 6, Heydekrug. 121
A/G. 155006 P/O W.G.L.Brown Killed Jonkerbos, Nijmegen, Holland. 7-H-8

35 Squadron 8 Group Halifax BB368 TL/H
Aircraft ditched 30 miles east of Cromer, Norfolk.
Pilot. A/416596 Sgt D.H.Milne Rescued
Nav. 1385054 Sgt P.R.Lissener Rescued
B/A. 1384312 Sgt A.G.Cox Rescued
W/OP. 1129588 Sgt J.Jolly Rescued
F/E. 1045872 Sgt T.B.M.Smith Rescued
A/G. 1333462 Sgt R.A.M.Bowring Rescued
A/G. 1117841 Sgt K.Wolstencroft Rescued

83 Squadron 8 Group Lancaster EE121 OL/K
Pilot. 124457 F/O H.Mappin Missing Runnymede Memorial. 126
Nav. 1390587 Sgt A.J.Boar Killed Bergen-op-Zoom, Holland. 97
B/A. 1330159 Sgt G.A.Livett Killed Bergen-op-Zoom, Holland. 94
W/OP. 1210039 Sgt A.A.Crank Missing, Runnymede Memorial 146
F/E. 536786 Sgt C.E.Wigett Missing, Runnymede Memorial 169
A/G. 966497 Sgt W.Anderson Missing, Runnymede Memorial 140
A/G. 1335872 Sgt F.W.Turner Killed Bergen-op-Zoom, Holland. 101

83 Squadron 8 Group Lancaster ED997 OL/R
Pilot. 1389587 F/Sgt D.W.C.Fletcher Killed Jonkerbos, Holland. 7-I-7
Nav. 148401 F/Sgt L.A.C.Angell Killed Jonkerbos, Holland. 7-I-4
B/A. 630736 Sgt A.E.McWilliam Killed Jonkerbos, Holland. 7-I-5
W/OP. 1312384 Sgt L.V.Tanner Killed Jonkerbos, Holland. 7-I-8
F/E. 1025185 Sgt E.Lidster Killed Jonkerbos, Holland. 7-I-3
A/G. 1698546 Sgt R.Metcalfe Killed Jonkerbos, Holland. 7-I-2
A/G. R/97867 F/Sgt G.C.Wicken Killed Jonkerbos, Holland. 7-I-6

156 Squadron 8 Group Lancaster ED885 GT/
Pilot. NZ/416136 P/O J.A.Marson Missing Runnymede Memorial. 198
Nav. 1386296 Sgt G.A.P.Edwards Missing, Runnymede Memorial 148
B/A. 1118735 Sgt J.A.Ottey Missing, Runnymede Memorial 160
W/OP. 1395762 Sgt E.A.Bowman Missing, Runnymede Memorial 143
F/E. 1322553 Sgt F.J.Willett Missing, Runnymede Memorial 169
A/G. 1267833 Sgt A.Shacklady Missing, Runnymede Memorial 164
A/G. 1578580 Sgt G.W.Brown Missing, Runnymede Memorial 143

405 Squadron 8 Group Halifax JD124 LQ/
Pilot. J/16203 F/Lt S.L.Murrell DFC Killed Rheinberg, Germany. 3-B-22
Nav. J/16996 P/O F.W.Hodge Killed Rheinberg, Germany. 3-C-1
B/A. J/16796 P/O J.H.T.J.Lemieux Killed Rheinberg, Germany. 3-B-23
W/OP. J/17110 P/O R.A.Livingston DFC Killed Rheinberg, Germany. 3-C-2
F/E. J/17634 P/O A.W.Nichols BEM Killed Rheinberg, Germany. 15-F-12
A/G. J/18505 P/O E.D.Rowe Killed Rheinberg, Germany. 3-B-25
A/G. C/8142A F/Sgt R.l.Robinson Killed Rheinberg, Germany. 3-B-24

100 Squadron 1 Group Lancaster ED556 HW/B
Pilot. J/17471 P/O J.R.Thurlow Killed Bergen-op-Zoom (Can), Holland. 11-F-9
Nav. 148761 P/O C.E.Thompson Killed Bergen-op-Zoom, Holland. 24-B-2
B/A. 1579168 Sgt K.E.Walters Killed Bergen-op-Zoom, Holland. 23-C-3

W/OP. 1017022 Sgt A.Jarman Killed Bergen-op-Zoom, Holland. 23-C-3
F/E. 1213196 Sgt R.H.Pyle Killed Bergen-op-Zoom, Holland. JG 24-B-3/4
A/G. 999158 Sgt S.Maisner Killed Bergen-op-Zoom, Holland. 24-B-1
A/G. 1441506 Sgt G.C.W.Norton Killed Bergen-op-Zoom, Holland. JG 24-B-3/4

101 Squadron 1 Group Lancaster ED650 SR/L
Pilot. 148571 P/O D.H.Brook Killed Rheinberg, Germany. 3-B-15
Nav. 1392079 Sgt G.Hopkin Killed Rheinberg, Germany. 3-B-16
B/A. 1396732 Sgt T.E.W.Latter Killed Rheinberg, Germany. 3-B-17
W/OP. J/15700 F/Lt W.J.Sibbald DFC Killed Rheinberg, Germany. 3-B-19
F/E. 1078101 Sgt A.C.Keightley Killed Rheinberg, Germany. 3-B-18
A/G. 1454670 Sgt N.Ellis Killed Rheinberg, Germany. 3-B-20
A/G. 1578815 Sgt K.Henson Killed Rheinberg, Germany. 3-B-21

460 Squadron 1 Group Lancaster W4939 UV/
Pilot. A/414436 F/Sgt A.W.Teerman Killed Rheinberg, Germany. 3-C-14
Nav. 865141 Sgt A.L.T.Hoskins Killed Rheinberg, Germany. 3-C-16
B/A. 1230178 Sgt H.Thomson PoW. Stalag Luft 6, Heydekrug. 269
W/OP. 1312636 Sgt J.E.O Cassell Killed Rheinberg, Germany. 3-C-15
F/E. 144884 P/O H.J.Trafford Killed Rheinberg, Germany. 3-C-17
A/G. 1683293 Sgt J.Hetherington Killed Rheinberg, Germany. 3-C-18
A/G. 659011 Sgt B.D.O'Neill Killed Rheinberg, Germany. 3-C-19

166 Squadron 1 Group Wellington HE924 AS/C
Pilot. 1382415 F/Sgt A.Burgess Killed Jonkerbos, Holland. 7-H-7
Nav. 148758 P/O G.R.Wright Killed Jonkerbos, Holland. 3-H-2
B/A. 1150780 F/Sgt W.F.Payne Missing, Runnymede Memorial 138
W/OP. A/411398 P/O J.K.Somers Killed Jonkerbos, Holland. 16-C-8
A/G. 1303397 Sgt E.Jeffs Killed Jonkerbos, Holland. 7-H-6

300 Squadron 1 Group Wellington HE327 BH/S
Pilot. P/780940 Sgt M.Bronicki Missing, Northolt Memorial
Nav. P/794632 Sgt M.Glass Killed Castricum, Holland. J-5
B/A. P/784506 Sgt S.Nogacki Missing, Northolt Memorial
W/OP. P/794546 Sgt S.Jama Missing, Northolt Memorial
A/G. P/704315 Sgt J.Lezuch Missing, Northolt Memorial

300 Squadron 1 Group Wellington HE985 BH/W
Pilot. P/782554 F/Sgt M.Bialobrowka Missing, Northolt Memorial
Nav. P/2014 P/O T.Blajda Missing, Northolt Memorial
B/A. P/781076 Sgt T.Ciuchcinski Missing, Northolt Memorial
W/OP. P/794311 Sgt F.Trzebuchowski Missing, Northolt Memorial
A/G. P/703492 Sgt R.Jacenik Missing, Northolt Memorial

305 Squadron 1 Group Wellington HE347 SM/F
Aircraft crashed near Antwerp, Belgium at 01.35 hours (22/6/43).
Pilot. P/782788 Sgt S.Szpalinski Killed Schoonselhoof, Belgium. F-1
Nav. P/2115 P/O J.Gasecki Evaded capture
B/A. P/794590 F/Sgt A.Fried PoW. Stalag Luft 6, Heydekrug. 139
W/OP. P/794724 F/Sgt R.Raczkowski PoW. Stalag 4B, Muhlberg(Elbe). 1279
A/G. P/780898 Sgt L.Makarski Killed Schoonselhoof, Belgium. H-15

15 Squadron 3 Group Stirling BK815 LS/V
Aircraft crashed Kallo/Melsele, near Antwerp, Belgium at 01.00 hours.
Pilot. 142853 P/O E.F.Curtis Killed Schoonselhooof, Belgium. II-E-20
2/Pilot. 591584 F/Sgt F.D.McQuillan Killed Schoonselhoof, Belgium. II-E-19
Nav. 1576447 Sgt A.F.Stephens Killed Schoonselhoof, Belgium. JG II-F-2
B/A. 131956 F/O E.N.Billington Killed Schoonselhoof, Belgium. II-E-21
W/OP. J/16516 F/O R.J.Hunter Killed Schoonselhoof, Belgium. JG II-F-2
F/E. 574589 Sgt R.T.Davis Killed Schoonselhoof, Belgium. IVA-A-1
A/G. 1479054 Sgt J.P.Martin Killed Schoonselhoof, Belgium. II-E-18
A/G. 1042277 W/O G.A.Waugh PoW. Stalag 357, Kopernikus. 3439

90 Squadron 3 Group Stirling EE887 WP/T
Aircraft shot down at Hoogwoud, Holland.
Pilot. A/414077 P/O H.N.Peters Killed Bergen, Holland. 2-D-13
Nav. 1330671 Sgt D.J.Davies Killed Bergen, Holland. 2-D-15
B/A. 1336188 Sgt B.A.Abraham Killed Bergen, Holland. 2-D-17
W/OP. 1332841 Sgt A.S.Andrews Killed Bergen, Holland. 2-D-14
F/E. 1083274 Sgt E.Bradshaw Killed Bergen, Holland. 2-D-20
A/G. 1025077 Sgt D.Gillis Killed Bergen, Holland. 2-D-19
A/G. R/109583 Sgt R.R.Law Killed Bergen, Holland. 2-D-16

149 Squadron 3 Group Stirling BK799 OJ/O
Aircraft crashed near Makkum in the Zuider Zee, Holland.
Pilot. 148179 P/O J.Lowrie Killed Eindhoven, (Woensel), Holland. CG M-40/41
Nav. 125540 F/O D.H.Lyne Killed Eindhoven, (Woensel), Holland. CG M-40/41
B/A. 1559064 Sgt A.Coull Killed Eindhoven, (Woensel), Holland. CG M-40/41
W/OP. 1312340 Sgt D.C.Fudge Killed Eindhoven, (Woensel). CG M-40/41
F/E. 1017417 Sgt J.Atkinson Killed Eindhoven, (Woensel). CG M-40/41
A/G. 1319154 Sgt E.G.Hird Killed Eindhoven, (Woensel), Holland. M-38
A/G. 1279016 Sgt E.C.Waite Killed Eindhoven, (Woensel), Holland. M-39

218 Squadron 3 Group Stirling BK722 HA/G
Aircraft crashed at Maarheze, Holland after fighter attack.
Pilot. A/414083 P/O D.R.Rich Killed Eindhoven, (Woensel), Holland. EE-73
Nav. 1318687 F/Sgt F.Fawcett PoW. Stalag 357, Kopernikus. 133
B/A. 657663 Sgt B.Kermode Killed Eindhoven, (Woensel), Holland. EE-10
W/OP. 929453 Sgt H.Burrows Killed Eindhoven, (Woensel), Holland. EE-32
F/E. 636587 F/Sgt H.Hill PoW. Stalag 357, Kopernikus. 168
A/G. 1315676 F/Sgt A.J.Small PoW. Stalag 357, Kopernikus. 249
A/G. R/145804 W/O J.S.McDonald PoW. Stalag 357, Kopernikus. 204

218 Squadron 3 Group Stirling BK712 HA/G
Aircraft crashed at Langdorp, Belgium at 02.00 hours (22/6/43). Victim of
Lt.Schnaufer and Lt. Baro, Stab II/NJG1 (13th Victory).
Pilot. A/412846 P/O W.G.Shillinglaw Killed Langdorp, Belgium. CG 4/5
2/Pilot. 128521 F/O A.R.Helvard Killed Langdorp, Belgium. 3
Nav. 1214848 Sgt P.D.McArdle Killed Langdorp, Belgium. CG 4/5
B/A. 1167033 Sgt T.R.Lunn Killed Langdorp, Belgium. 2
W/OP. NZ/404092 F/Sgt D.J.Ashby-Peckham Killed Langdorp. CG 4/5
F/E. 1258721 Sgt R.P.Goward Killed Langdorp, Belgium. CG 4/5
A/G. 1581644 Sgt A.E.Gurney Killed Langdorp, Belgium. CG 4/5

A/G. 1314586 Sgt E.D.Hart Killed Langdorp, Belgium. 1

51 Squadron 4 Group Halifax JD244 MH/
Pilot. 1235550 W/O F.J.Heathfield PoW. Stalag 4B, Muhlberg(Elbe). 222714
Nav. 121248 F/O H.J.Dothie PoW. Stalag Luft 3, Sagan. 1650
B/A. 1575535 W/O W.A.Poulton PoW. Stalag Luft 7, Bankau.
W/OP. 1382175 F/Sgt W.C.Beresford PoW. Stalag Luft 6, Heydekrug. 69
F/E. 1231135 Sgt D.G.Keane PoW. Stalag 357, Kopernikus. 184
A/G. R/138344 W/O R.H.Masters PoW. Stalag Luft 4, Sagan. 1473
A/G. 1384226 F/Sgt R.Cooper PoW. Stalag 357, Kopernikus. 100

77 Squadron 4 Group Halifax W1157 KN/U
Pilot. 1337889 Sgt M.J.Fitzgerald Missing, Runnymede Memorial 149
Nav. 1099748 Sgt G.Wood Missing, Runnymede Memorial 170
B/A. 130572 F/O R.C.Bishop Missing, Runnymede Memorial 123
W/OP. R/106197 W/O F.O.Turner Missing, Runnymede Memorial 180
F/E. 644295 Sgt R.Forster Missing, Runnymede Memorial 149
A/G. 1800945 Sgt J.M.Dalton Missing, Runnymede Memorial 147
A/G. 1346461 Sgt J.J.McPherson Missing, Runnymede Memorial 158

77 Squadron 4 Group Halifax JD205 KN/Y
Pilot. 1452977 F/Sgt J.Gardner PoW. Stalag 357, Kopernikus. 3470
Nav. 1548758 Sgt F.G.Hawthorne PoW. Stalag 4B, Muhlberg(Elbe). 22271
B/A. 135880 P/O A.Hagan DFC Evaded capture
W/OP. 1331341 W/O D.A.Clark PoW. Stalag Luft 3, Sagan. 226555
F/E. 1213238 F/Sgt S.H.A.Nicholson PoW. Stalag 357, Kopernikus. 219
A/G. R/109695 W/O R.H.King Killed Arnhem (Moscawa), Holland. XV-F-6
A/G. R/113684 F/Sgt A.R.Currie Killed Arnhem (Moscawa), Holland. XV-F-7

77 Squadron 4 Group Halifax JB852 KN/G
Pilot. 1042116 Sgt S.Hirsch Killed Ede, Holland. CG H-7/11
Nav. 1681266 Sgt C.W.Falckh Killed Ede, Holland. CG H-7/11
B/A. 658993 Sgt R.G.Kingsland Killed Ede, Holland. CG H-7/11
W/OP. 1272101 Sgt N.V.Hickling Killed Ede, Holland. CG H-7/11
F/E. 643976 Sgt J.Phillips Killed Ede, Holland. CG H-7/11
A/G. 1144424 Sgt W.G.Garratt Killed Durnbach, Germany. (11-7-43) 5-K-18
A/G. 1322722 Sgt E.Dawson Killed Ede, Holland. H-6

102 Squadron 4 Group Halifax JD206 DY/T
Aircraft hit by *Flak* at Overflakee and ditched 18 miles off Le Havre, France.
Pilot. Sgt G.S.Honey Rescued.
Nav. Sgt R.Ward Rescued.
B/A. Sgt R.O.Tudberry Rescued.
W/OP. Sgt J.Brennan Rescued.
F/E. Sgt A.J.Dick Rescued.
A/G. Sgt F.R.Hayward Rescued.
A/G. Sgt D.A.Wagar Rescued.

158 Squadron 4 Group Halifax HR735 NP/N
Aircraft crashed near Bericulm, Holland.
Pilot. NZ/415786 P/O C.H.Robinson DFC Killed Bergen-op-Zoom. 25-B-2
2/Pilot. 1332036 Sgt E.B.Fisher Killed Bergen-op-Zoom, Holland. 25-B-4
Nav. 1526249 Sgt G.A.Hill Missing, Runnymede Memorial 153
B/A. 1435856 Sgt W.T.Dunning Missing, Runnymede Memorial 148
W/OP. 1270788 Sgt H.F.Barham Missing, Runnymede Memorial 141
F/E. 1269598 Sgt S.G.B.Hayes Killed Uden, Holland. 5-E-8
A/G. 1573827 Sgt D.D.Cuthbert Killed Bergen-op-Zoom, Holland. 25-B-1
A/G. 1078078 Sgt G.B.Mycock Killed Bergen-op-Zoom, Holland. 25-B-3

431 Squadron 4 Group Wellington HF518 SE/J
Pilot. 27048 W/Cdr J.Coverdale Missing, Runnymede Memorial 118
Nav. 146687 P/O G.C.Parslow DFM Missing, Runnymede Memorial 132
B/A. R/93489 W/O H.S.Fawns Missing, Runnymede Memorial 180
W/OP. 48551 F/O J.B.G.Bailey DFC Missing, Runnymede Memorial 123
A/G. J/17663 F/O B.S.Fudge Missing, Runnymede Memorial 173

44 Squadron 5 Group Lancaster LM330 WM/Q
Pilot. 52755 P/O H.C.Thompson Missing, Runnymede Memorial 133
2/Pilot. 149518 P/O L.S.Welsh Missing, Runnymede Memorial 134
Nav. 914451 Sgt S.D.Mindel Missing, Runnymede Memorial 115
B/A. 1386784 Sgt L.A.Harrison Missing, Runnymede Memorial 152
W/OP. 1130657 Sgt N.N.England Missing, Runnymede Memorial 148
F/E. 1130425 Sgt L.R.McGrath Missing, Runnymede Memorial 157
A/G. 1477557 Sgt N.Metcalfe Missing, Runnymede Memorial 159
A/G. 624543 Sgt J.H.Arlow Missing, Runnymede Memorial 140

57 Squadron 5 Group Lancaster W4377 DX/
Pilot. 946806 Sgt G.G.Kitson Killed Eindhoven, (Woensel), Holland. EE-6
Nav. 1394734 Sgt A.D.Pain Killed Eindhoven, (Woensel), Holland. EE-2
B/A. 1284770 Sgt M.H.Burston Killed Eindhoven, (Woensel), Holland. EE-4
W/OP. 1212711 Sgt L.J.Ray Missing, Runnymede Memorial 162
F/E. 1541699 Sgt G.Hull Killed Eindhoven, (Woensel), Holland. EE-1
A/G. 1361331 Sgt H.Alexander Killed Eindhoven, (Woensel), Holland. EE-3
A/G. 1699156 Sgt G.A.Robinson Killed Eindhoven, (Woensel), Holland. EE-5

619 Squadron 5 Group Lancaster EE198 PG/
Pilot. 901880 Sgt D.V.Jordan Killed Jonkerbos, Holland. 3-G-3
Nav. 127972 F/O W.M.Girdwood Killed Jonkerbos, Holland. 3-G-4
B/A. 1387764 Sgt E.Stanley Killed Jonkerbos, Holland. 3-G-5
W/OP. 1313057 Sgt B.Howes Killed Jonkerbos, Holland. 3-G-2
F/E. 1160814 Sgt W.A.Davies Killed Jonkerbos, Holland. 3-G-1
A/G. 1300347 Sgt F.Burton Killed Jonkerbos, Holland. 12-H-7
A/G. 1600874 Sgt W.J.Parkes Killed Jonkerbos, Holland. 4-H-1

408 Squadron 6 Group Halifax BB375 EQ/T
Aircraft attacked by enemy fighter and exploded before remaining crew could bale out.
Pilot. J/18083 P/O C.C.Reichert Missing, Runnymede Memorial 177
Nav. J/22511 F/Lt J.C.B.Russell PoW. Stalag Luft 3, Sagan. 1705
B/A. J/16554 P/O J.E.Monohan Missing, Runnymede Memorial 176

W/OP. J/18226 P/O J.P.Dockerill Missing, Runnymede Memorial 175
F/E. R/54088 Sgt G.M.McLean Missing, Runnymede Memorial 186
A/G. R/108583 Sgt G.I.Pridham PoW. Camp not known.
A/G. J/18245 P/O W.Searle Missing, Runnymede Memorial 177

408 Squadron 6 Group Halifax DT772 EQ/E
Pilot. 148798 P/O D.Brooke Killed Amersfoort, Holland. JG 13-7-145
Nav. J/18162 P/O G.E.Bisheff Killed Amersfoort, Holland. 13-7-141
B/A. R/138932 F/Sgt J.C.Macdonald Killed Amersfoort, Holland. 13-7-142
W/OP. 1386247 Sgt M.D.Shakespeare Killed Amersfoort, Holland. 13-7-144
F/E. R/94570 F/Sgt C.L.Sebelius Killed Amersfoort, Holland. 13-7-146
A/G. R/76467 F/Sgt W.D.Walsh Killed Amersfoort, Holland. JG 13-7-145
A/G. R/108014 F/Sgt J.R.Archambault Killed Amersfoort, Holland. 13-7-143

408 Squadron 6 Group Halifax JD209 EQ/B
Pilot. J/17175 P/O J.G.A.Patry Killed Reichswald Forest. CG 25-E-8/9
Nav. J/18252 P/O N.Kellner Killed Reichswald Forest, Germany. CG 25-E-8/9
B/A. 1319221 Sgt D.Rudge Killed Reichswald Forest, Germany. CG 25-E-8/9
W/OP. 1382402 F/Sgt G.A.Freeman PoW. Stalag Luft 6, Heydekrug. 138
F/E. R/69969 Sgt J.H.W.Bishop PoW. Stalag Luft 1, Barth Vogelsang. 72
A/G. J/18112 F/O E.Moorcroft PoW. Stalag 357, Kopernikus. 415
A/G. R/106451 W/O A.B.Lewis Killed Reichswald Forest. CG 25-E-8/9

419 Squadron 6 Group Halifax W1271 VR/P
Crew on attachment from 428 Squadron.
Pilot. NZ/414671 P/O C.R.Pearce Killed Bergen-op-Zoom, Holland. 27-A-3
Nav. NZ/413703 P/O W.T.Ellis Killed Bergen-op-Zoom, Holland. 25-C-8
B/A. 1385555 Sgt G.J.D.Thompson Killed Bergen-op-Zoom, Holland. 23-B-1
W/OP. 1202224 Sgt W.J.Randall Killed Bergen-op-Zoom, Holland. 18-B-2
F/E. R/53029 Sgt J.J.F.Holland Killed Bergen-op-Zoom, Holland. 11-F-4
A/G. 651974 Sgt J.Galloway Killed Bergen-op-Zoom, Holland. 25-C-7
A/G. NZ/412903 P/O E.L.Robson Killed Bergen-op-Zoom, Holland. 25-A-1

429 Squadron 6 Group Wellington HZ520 AL/
Pilot. 1380201 W/O E.A.Eames PoW. Stalag Luft 6, Heydekrug. 311
Nav. 130258 F/O E.F.Lapham PoW. Stalag Luft 3, Sagan. 1700
B/A. 656099 F/Sgt H.V.Holmes Killed Eindhoven, (Woensel), Holland. EE-11
W/OP. 1385666 Sgt W.H.Wright PoW. Stalag 357, Kopernikus. 365
A/G. J/13068 F/O D.S.Milne Killed Eindhoven, (Woensel), Holland. EE-72

429 Squadron 6 Group Wellington HE981 AL/
Pilot. J/13992 F/O J.L.F.Lown Killed Bergen-op-Zoom, Holland. CG 25-C-1/2
Nav. R/119786 F/Sgt A.J.Sieffert Killed Bergen-op-Zoom. CG 25-C-1/2
B/A. R/82786 W/O J.K.Wood Killed Bergen-op-Zoom, Holland. CG 25-C-1/2
W/OP. R/131818 F/Sgt A.S.Rhodes Killed Bergen-op-Zoom. CG 25-C-1/2
A/G. R/116334 Sgt W.H.Calder Killed Bergen-op-Zoom, Holland. CG 25-C-1/2

429 Squadron 6 Group Wellington HZ517 AL/
Pilot. J/17554 P/O G DeBussac Killed Jonkerbos, Holland. 15-H-1
Nav. J/17487 P/O M.B.Spence Killed Jonkerbos, Holland. 11-I-8
B/A. J/12302 F/O W.A.Fellows Killed Jonkerbos, Holland. 15-H-2
W/OP. R/109811 F/Sgt G.D.Cole Killed Jonkerbos, Holland. 11-I-7
A/G. R/116471 W/O D.E.Palamtier Killed Jonkerbos, Holland. 11-I-6

429 Squadron 6 Group Wellington HZ519 AL/
Pilot. R/131714 F/Sgt E.A.Star Missing, Runnymede Memorial 185
Nav. R/132169 F/Sgt J.Kopchuk Killed Flushing, Holland. F-3
B/A. R/157098 F/Sgt J.P.G.O'Reilly Killed Flushing, Holland. F-1
W/OP. R/143317 F/Sgt C.F.Orlinski Killed Flushing, Holland. F-10
A/G. R/105126 F/Sgt W.G.Parkinson Missing, Runnymede Memorial 185

158 Squadron 4 Group Halifax HR785 NP/G
Aircraft crashed at Bran Road, Lincoln on route for operations to Krefeld.
Pilot. 1318312 Sgt K.C.Smart Killed Kingston on Thames. A-1260
Nav. 1392262 Sgt W.C.T.Dempsey Killed London, (Manor Park). 7
B/A. 134156 F/O R.N.Freeman Killed Thurlby, (St Germains). B-4
W/OP. 1377043 Sgt R.P.Hansford Killed Thurlby, (St Germains). B-3
F/E. 961265 Sgt K.E.G.White Killed Crayford, Kent 14-22
A/G. 1350043 Sgt A.W.Reffles Killed Portsmouth.(Eastney). G-12-2
A/G. F/Sgt C.K.Rowe Killed

A Single Mosquito Sortie to Hamborn

A lone Mosquito made a raid on Hamborn on the same night as
the main force went to Krefeld. After dropping its 0.8 ton bomb
load on the target, it returned safely to base.

Mulheim

June 22nd/23rd, 1943

557 aircraft, - 242 Lancasters, 155 Halifaxes, 93 Stirlings, 55 Wellingtons and 12 Mosquitoes flew through fine and clear skies to Mulheim. 58 bombers did not arrive at the target having at various stages returned to their bases with technical and engine problems. Although there was slight, thin cloud masking the target area, the initial Pathfinders marked accurately and were well timed. The now familiar pattern followed, with the main force coming in to saturate the target with their bombs. The attack was well concentrated, apart from a slight spread to the north of the aiming point. Large explosions were seen at 01.22, 01.26, 01.35 and 01.46 hours. Both ground and air defences were very active with enemy fighters being airborne in large numbers.

One hundred and forty seven 250 lbs target indicators marked the target during the course of the attack, when 754.7 tons of high explosive bombs and 266,664 incendiaries were dropped. The rescue and fire services on the ground were hampered by the ferocity of the attack and fire storm areas raged out of hand. Bombing photographs taken during the raid showed that the neighbouring town of Oberhausen was also badly hit. German records note that 578 people were killed and 1,174 injured. Damage to public buildings and housing was widespread and over half of the town was destroyed. The bomber force continued to suffer its high losses, 35 aircraft did not return from this raid, a 6.3% loss rate. Aircrew losses were 165 killed, 38 missing, 33 made prisoners of war and there were three evaders.

Three More Aircrew are Helped to Evade Capture

Three aircrew reported as failing to return from this Mulheim operation were lucky to have the help of an escape organisation to evade capture and made it back to the UK. One of these was 1384785 Sergeant George Duffee, who was acting as a second pilot on board Halifax JB855 from 78 Squadron which was captained by Flight Lieutenant L. Knight. The other two fortunate airmen to evade were navigator 133580 Pilot Officer

D. I. Turner and bomb aimer 1258269 Sergeant A. F. Kellett, who were in Stirling EF348 from 15 Squadron captained by Flight Sergeant J. W. Newport. The Stirling crashed at Kessinich, Belgium and was the second victory for Oblt. Autenreith of 6/NJG1.

According to Kellett, the bomber did not reach the target because of insufficient fuel and was on its homeward flight after jettisoning its bombs, when it was attacked by a fighter, which made three passes altogether. It was only on the last attack that the engines and wing tanks were hit and caught fire. The aircraft then went out of control and the pilot gave the bale out order.

Kellett landed in a hayfield, which he later found out was somewhere west of the Wessen Canal. He was caught on his parachute descent in a searchlight beam, so as soon as he landed he wasted no time in trying to collect and hide his 'chute and starting to run in a northerly direction. He continued for what appeared to be about three miles and then using his compass he started off westwards. For the next four nights he walked and during the daytime hid and rested in barns. During this period he had no food because he had forgotten to take his escape pack with him on this operation. He met no one during his four days and he was only able to quench his thirst by drinking some rather dirty water. All this time he thought that he was in Germany, for on one occasion he overheard some people talking in what appeared to be German. In fact they were speaking Flemish, which Kellett did not recognise.

At about 06.30 hours on June 28th, when he was about half a mile from Tongerloo, he saw what appeared to be a deserted house and intended using it for some shelter, but a dog suddenly came out of a side building and started barking. A man then emerged and after Kellett had mentioned to him the names of various countries he found that he was in Belgium. The man asked if he was German, but when Kellett replied that he that he was an RAF airman the man took out a matchbox from his pocket and motioned that Kellett should do the same. Fortunately Kellett had a matchbox with him and when the man saw the British markings, he seemed satisfied. The man said that there were many German soldiers about and pointed out a house where Kellett should go for help. Kellett took his advice and on knocking at the door of the house he was met by a man and woman with their two daughters. They took him inside and gave him some bread and milk, his first food for four days. They also gave him some old civilian clothes and allowed him to sleep in their barn. At 17.00 hours that same day, a young girl of about 12 years of age came to see him and asked him some personal details. The next day Kellett was visited by the girl's mother who spoke good English. He was moved to another address, where he stayed for three days before being moved two miles away to a farm owned by two men, staying there for about 15 days. During this time he hid in the haystack all day and slept in the house during the night, as his helpers thought it would not be safe for any of the farm labourers to see him.

He was frequently visited by the mother of the girl, but it appeared that she did not know how to help any further. Kellett suggested that if she could help get him into France, he would try to make his own way from there. Finally the woman brought some more civilian clothes and arranged for him to go by bicycle to Maeseyck, from which point he was met by members of an underground organisation and the rest of the journey back to the UK was arranged for him.

Back with Empty Petrol Tanks

Halifax JD110, KN/P captained by Australian Flight Sergeant F. E. Mathers from 77 Squadron based at Elvington, Yorkshire, was one of the bombers which was extremely lucky to make it back to England after the Mulheim raid. The bomber had a fairly uneventful flight to the target, which was bombed at 01.48 hours from 19,000 feet, but as soon as the bombs had been dropped the aircraft was hit by heavy anti-aircraft fire and the starboard outer engine burst into flames. The pilot quickly feathered the engine and the flames were extinguished, but more trouble followed three minutes later when another *Flak* burst caused the port inner engine to catch fire. The damaged Halifax was now in a critical position, with damaged aileron controls, holed petrol tanks and flying only on two engines.

The pilot bravely decided to head for home but as the homeward flight continued the aircraft steadily lost height until it was down to 3,000 feet by the time the North Sea was reached. Realising that it was going to be touch and go to reach the English coast, the captain ordered all movable equipment and the mid upper guns and ammunition to be jettisoned in an effort to maintain height.

Now down to 2,000 feet the bomber was spotted by an Me110 pilot, who was obviously on the look out for damaged stragglers in the homeward bomber stream. He made three determined attacks. The first attack damaged the important radio intercom link between rear gunner and pilot. In the next attack, unable to get response from the rear gunner, the pilot turned into the fighter attack which fortunately allowed the gunner, Sergeant Speedie, to get in two short bursts before his guns jammed. As the fighter came into the last attack firing at the bomber from 400 yards, Sergeant Speedie was quickly back in action with his guns, having cleared the stoppage, and returned fire at 200 yards before seeing the enemy dive down into the sea.

By now the altimeter was showing 1,000 feet and was quickly down to 500 feet when the English coast came into view. The wireless operator, Sergeant G. French obtained an accurate MF/DF fix from his faulty radio set which he had repaired after the damage caused in the first fighter attack. This enabled the pilot to fly the bomber to Martlesham Heath, a fighter airfield. However, with the wheels unable to be put down, there was no alternative but to make a belly landing which Flight Sergeant Mathers did without causing very much additional damage to the aircraft or any injury to his crew. For the last quarter of an hour of the flight the petrol tank gauges in the Halifax had all been registering zero!

For his valiant efforts Flight Sergeant F. E. Mathers was awarded the Conspicious Gallantry Award, a medal given to non commissioned airmen and which is equivalent to the Distinguished Service Order awarded to commissioned officers. Sergeants French and Speedie each received the Distinguished Flying Medal.

Unfortunately three months later, on September 5th, the now commissioned Pilot Officer Mathers CGM and his crew in

Halifax JB889 KN/K failed to return from a bombing operation against Mannheim. Pilot Officer Mathers, Sergeant Speedie and Sergeant French were killed and are buried in the Durnbach Military Cemetery, Germany.

Identical Twins Lost in Bomber

One of the four Stirling bombers from 75 Squadron lost on this Mulheim raid was EH889, AA/Z for Zebra captained by Flight Lieutenant T. F. McCrorie. The remains of this Stirling were found in the Zuider Zee, Holland after the war. In the crew were two Canadian aircrew, both wireless operators and identical twins, Warrant Officer R. D. Tod and Warrant Officer R. E. Tod DFM. For two brothers to be in the same crew was quite exceptional and to be identical twins was unique. The Canadian Air Force authorities had allowed these brothers to train together in Canada and also to be posted to the same squadron and on to the same crew when they went overseas. As both were trained wireless operators they alternated duties. On one operation one took up his duties on the radio while the other manned one of the gun turrets. On the following trip they would change places and duties in the crew. According to a surviving elder brother, who was a gunner on flying boats, the twins were as alike as two peas in a pod and people found it extremely difficult to know who was who. Fellow aircrew on 75 Squadron could only distinguish one from the other by the striped blue and white ribbon of the DFM. This was awarded to Sergeant R. Ernest Tod for his part as a wireless operator in relaying the position of his very badly damaged bomber which successfully ditched in the English Channel after evading German fighters when returning from the Frankfurt raid on April 10th/11th 1943. The brothers are buried in adjoining graves in Medemblik Cemetery, Holland.

Minor Operations

June 23rd/24th, 1943
Berlin and Cologne were raided on the same night when four Mosquitoes dropped 3.1 tons of bombs on each without suffering any loss.

Minelaying

Minelaying by seventeen Stirlings and three Lancasters from 3 Group, ten Halifaxes from 6 Group, twelve Wellingtons from 1 Group and ten Wellingtons from 4 Group also took place. These aircraft laid 173 mines without suffering any losses.

Casualties June 22nd/23rd, 1943. Target Mulheim

83 Squadron 8 Group Lancaster W4982 OL/O
Pilot. 146988 P/O M.E.Rust Killed Reichswald Forest, Germany. 6-A-8
Nav. 1384018 Sgt J.M.Hurson Killed Reichswald Forest, Germany. 6-A-13
B/A. 13381181 Sgt S.Williams Killed Reichswald Forest, Germany. 6-A-12
W/OP. 1383228 Sgt E.C.Stally Killed Reichswald Forest, Germany. 6-A-11
F/E. 533104 Sgt L.Ashworth Killed Reichswald Forest, Germany. 6-A-9
A/G. 1395829 Sgt G.C.Chapman Killed Reichswald Forest, Germany. 6-A-14
A/G. 1454500 Sgt F.F.Foden Killed Reichswald Forest, Germany. 6-A-10

97 Squadron 8 Group Lancaster ED928 OF/B
Pilot. J/17547 P/O G.W.Armstrong Killed Utrecht(Soestbergen). 12D-1-5
Nav. 1385811 F/Sgt J.J.Mansfield Killed Utrecht(Soestbergen). 12D-1-3
B/A. R/79102 W/O J.B.S.P.H.David Killed Utrecht(Soestbergen). 12D-1-4
W/OP. 1380623 Sgt D.E.Williams Killed Utrecht(Soestbergen). 12D-1-2
F/E. 985543 Sgt E.Bellis PoW. Stalag 357, Kopernikus. 66
A/G. 134081 F/O S.Blackhurst Killed Utrecht(Soestbergen), Holland. 12D-1-6
A/G. 1042275 W/O A.R.Laing PoW. Stalag 357, Kopernikus. 194

156 Squadron 8 Group Lancaster ED599 GT/
Aircraft crashed near Maarn, Holland.
Pilot. A/413469 F/Sgt J.T.Winterbon Killed Amersfoort, Holland. 13-8-156
Nav. 127318 F/O E.G.Grove Killed Amersfoort, Holland. CG 13-7-139/140
B/A. 971675 Sgt W.H.Gordon Killed Amersfoort, Holland. CG 13-7-139/140
W/OP. 1332098 F/Sgt J.W.Bembridge Killed Amersfoort, Holland. 13-8-152
F/E. 572670 Sgt E.A.Duchene Killed Amersfoort, Holland. CG 13-7-139/140
A/G. 542456 F/Sgt J.S.F.V.Crawley Killed Amersfoort, Holland. 13-7-138
A/G. 936175 Sgt W.P.Smith Killed Amersfoort, Holland. 13-8-150

101 Squadron 1 Group Lancaster LM325 SR/J
Pilot. 1338722 Sgt R.A.Waterhouse Killed Uden, Holland. 5-E-2
Nav. 131897 F/O T.B.Tomkins Killed Uden, Holland. 5-F-12
B/A. 1529904 F/Sgt E.A.Williams PoW. Stalag 357, Kopernikus. 364
W/OP. 1312690 Sgt E.Smith Killed Uden, Holland. 5-F-13
F/E. 1539830 Sgt J.Osbourne Killed Uden, Holland. 5-F-11
A/G. 1335912 Sgt R.B.Cooper Killed Uden, Holland. 5-E-3
A/G. 1481508 Sgt V.Sugden Killed Uden, Holland. 5-E-1

103 Squadron 1 Group Lancaster ED773 PM/
Pilot. C/1201 F/Lt A.E.Spurr Killed Dunkirk, France. 2-4-10
Nav. 138591 P/O E.Griffiths Killed Dunkirk, France. 2-4-8
B/A. 135659 F/O W.H.Wood Killed Dunkirk, France. 2-4-9
W/OP. 127969 F/O D.M.Grant Killed Dunkirk, France. 2-4-5
F/E. 1062633 Sgt J.W.M.Jones Missing, Runnymede Memorial 155
A/G. 1586779 Sgt A.E.Ponsford Killed Dunkirk, France. 2-4-6
A/G. R/98422 F/Sgt W.L.Moran Killed Dunkirk, France. 2-4-7

460 Squadron 1 Group Lancaster EE166 UV/
Pilot. A/416669 F/O L.E.Harrison Killed Reichswald Forest, Germany. 6-B-8
Nav. 1525488 F/Sgt W.H.Bartlett Killed Reichswald Forest, Germany. 6-B-4
B/A. A/409544 F/O R.J.Hefferman Missing, Runnymede Memorial 188
W/OP. 1199948 Sgt S.K.Brown Killed Reichswald Forest, Germany. JG 6-B-5/6
F/E. 517656 Sgt J.S.Callcut Killed Reichswald Forest, Germany. 6-B-7
A/G. 1376525 Sgt K.A.C.Cotton Killed Reichswald Forest. JG 6-B-5/6
A/G. A/412553 F/Sgt R.J.Lockrey Killed Reichswald Forest, Germany. 6-B-3

15 Squadron 3 Group Stirling EF348 LS/N
Aircraft crashed at Kessenich, Belgium. Victim of Oblt Autenreith, 6/NJG1.
(2nd Victory).
Pilot. 1383342 F/Sgt J.W.Newport Killed Heverlee, Belgium. 8-K-3
Nav. 133580 P/O D.I.Turner Evaded capture.
B/A. 1258269 Sgt A.F.Kellett Evaded capture.
W/OP. 990901 W/O T.Mosedale PoW. Stalag Luft 4, Sagan. 43349
F/E. 1431427 F/Sgt D.S.P.Roberts PoW. Stalag 357, Kopernikus. 234
A/G. 1340793 Sgt W.C.Macaulay Killed Heverlee, Belgium. 8-K-4
A/G. R/119393 W/O J.J.G.Damboise PoW. Stalag 357, Kopernikus. 577

15 Squadron 3 Group Stirling BK656 LS/A
Aircraft shot down near Deelen, Holland by fighter from II/NJG1.
Pilot. NZ/16111 F/O J.V.Hawkins Killed Ede, Holland. CG H-14
Nav. NZ/416183 F/Sgt D.J.Tickle Killed Ede, Holland. CG H-14
B/A. NZ/421149 F/O L.J.Gwynne Killed Ede, Holland. CG H-14
W/OP. NZ/415519 F/Sgt A.W.Crozier Killed Ede, Holland. H-13
F/E. 952308 Sgt F.H.Williams Killed Ede, Holland. CG H-14
A/G. 1028048 Sgt G.C.Hutton Killed Ede, Holland. CG H-14
A/G. 1699504 Sgt M.Webster Killed Ede, Holland. H-12

75 Squadron 3 Group Stirling BK810 AA/G
Aircraft crashed at Oostum, Holland.
Pilot. NZ/41344 P/O F.M.McKenzie Killed Jonkerbos, Holland. 11-H-7
Nav. NZ/412947 W/O A.E.West PoW. Stalag 357, Kopernikus. 475
B/A. NZ/422175 F/Sgt J.F.Blank Killed Reichswald Forest, Germany. 31-D-10
W/OP. NZ/415986 W/O B.H.Broadhead PoW. Stalag 4B Muhlberg(Elbe).
F/E. 1323983 F/Sgt R.A.W.Triptree PoW. Stalag 357, Kopernikus. 359
A/G. 520340 F/Sgt J.R.G.Chrystal PoW. Stalag Luft 6, Heydekrug. 95
A/G. NZ/421329 W/O E.W.McGonigal PoW. Stalag 357, Kopernikus. 334

75 Squadron 3 Group Stirling EH889 AA/Z
Aircraft crashed in the Zuider Zee, Holland.
Pilot. 68770 F/Lt T.F.McCrorie Killed Bergen-op-Zoom (Can), Holland. 190
Nav. 51042 P/O W.Stuckey Killed Eindhoven (Woensel), Holland. 0-31
B/A. NZ/404946 F/Sgt J.L.Richards Missing, Runnymede Memorial 199
W/OP. R/91741 W/O R.D.Tod Killed Medemblik, Holland. 250
F/E. 625045 Sgt E.Grainger Missing, Runnymede Memorial 151
A/G. R/91742 W/O R.E.Tod DFM Killed Medemblik, Holland. 249
A/G. 1003148 Sgt R.A.Kennedy Killed Wieringermeer(Middenmeer), Holland.

75 Squadron 3 Group Stirling EF/408 AA/P
Aircraft crashed in the Zuider Zee, off Oosterland, Holland,
Pilot. 656588 F/Sgt B.B.Wood Killed Reichswald Forest. CG 19-G-4/6
Nav. NZ/402563 F/Sgt G.K.Samson Killed Reichswald Forest. CG 19-G-4/6
B/A. NZ/415738 F/Sgt S.R.Bissett Killed Reichswald Forest. CG 19-G-4/6
W/OP. 1331432 Sgt E.Reader Killed Reichswald Forest, Germany. 19-G-3
F/E. 1266998 Sgt S.L.Webb Killed Reichswald Forest, Germany. 19-G-1
A/G. 1609558 Sgt F.J.Hobbs Killed Reichswald Forest, Germany. 19-G-2
A/G. 1235070 Sgt C.B.Hemmings Killed Reichswald Forest, Germany. 19-G-7

75 Squadron 3 Group Stirling EF399 AA/O
Aircraft crashed at Markelo, Holland after fighter attack.
Pilot. NZ/412200 F/Sgt K.A.Burbridge Killed Markelo, Holland. 4-C-13
Nav. NZ/42314 F/Sgt W.F.Wilcockson Killed Markelo, Holland. 4-C-17
B/A. NZ/417077 F/Sgt A.J.McEwin Killed Markelo, Holland. 4-C-14
W/OP. NZ/413872 F/Sgt D.E.Martin Killed Markelo, Holland. 4-C-16
F/E. 1142645 Sgt G.Lockey Killed Markelo, Holland. 4-C-15
A/G. 1304742 Sgt G.Cameron Killed Markelo, Holland. JG 4-C-11/12
A/G. 1132866 Sgt K.F.Shaw Killed Markelo, Holland. JG 4-C-11/12

90 Squadron 3 Group Stirling BK804 WP/J
Aircraft crashed at Duisberg/Beek, Germany.
Pilot. 1044114 F/Sgt J.A.Robson Missing, Runnymede Memorial 139
Nav. 657159 Sgt G.Kipling Missing, Runnymede Memorial 156
B/A. 658095 Sgt J.Picton Missing, Runnymede Memorial 161
W/OP. 1196410 Sgt D.Sanders Killed Reichswald Forest, Germany. 5-H-17
F/E. 1289237 Sgt N.Graham Killed Reichswald Forest, Germany. 6-A-1
A/G. 522339 Sgt C.R.Fenwick Missing, Runnymede Memorial 149
A/G. 1335044 Sgt R.Hammond Killed Reichswald Forest, Germany. 5-H-18

90 Squadron 3 Group Stirling BK665 WP/D
Aircraft crashed at Kehrum, Germany.
Pilot. 147780 P/O P.C.McNair Killed Rheinberg, Germany. CG 9-B-12/14
Nav. 1349394 Sgt J.S.Porter Killed Rheinberg, Germany. CG 9-B-12/14
B/A. 1097549 Sgt A.Thompson Killed Rheinberg, Germany. CG 9-B-12/14
W/OP. 1117247 F/Sgt F.A.Hamer PoW. Stalag Luft 6, Heydekrug. 394
F/E. 1011861 Sgt G.W.Lawson Killed Rheinberg, Germany. 9-B-11
A/G. 1384797 Sgt D.C.Davids PoW. Stalag Luft 6, Heydekrug. 110
A/G. 517825 F/Sgt B.T.Smy PoW. Stalag Luft 6, Heydekrug. 252

214 Squadron 3 Group Stirling EH882 BU/O
Aircraft crashed at Essen, Germany.
Pilot. 118668 F/Lt W.J.Hein Killed Reichswald Forest, Germany. CG 20-E-1/3
Nav. 1365085 F/Sgt G.S.Graveson PoW. Stalag 357, Kopernikus. 151
B/A. 1389946 F/Sgt P.E.Goldsmid PoW. Stalag Luft 6, Heydekrug. 155
W/OP. 1382995 F/Sgt S.G.Morrison PoW. Stalag 357, Kopernikus. 216
F/E. 577156 Sgt G.M.Phillips Killed Reichswald Forest, Germany 6-E-17
A/G. 751698 Sgt K.S.Gillard Killed Reichswald Forest, Germany. CG 20-E-1/3
A/G. R/88342 W/O R.McNeil Killed Reichswald Forest, Germany. CG 20-E-1/3

218 Squadron 3 Group Stirling BF572 HA/K
Aircraft crashed in the North Sea off Amsterdam, Holland.
Pilot. A/4166320 F/Sgt J.B.H.Smith Killed Castricum, Holland. CG J-5
Nav. 798741 Sgt R.H.Cramm Missing, Runnymede Memorial 146
B/A. 1425083 Sgt W.H.Davies Killed Bergen-op-Zoom (Can), Holland. 1-H-5
W/OP. 1270648 Sgt C.R.Minns Missing, Runnymede Memorial 159
F/E. 1318644 Sgt G.E.Rose Missing, Runnymede Memorial 163
A/G. R/182511 F/Sgt G.Labuik Killed Amsterdam, Holland. 69-B-11
A/G. 518394 F/Sgt P.W.Farr PoW. Stalag 357, Kopernikus. 314

620 Squadron 3 Group Stirling EE875 QS/A
Aircraft crashed off Bergen, Holland in the North Sea.
Pilot. 658284 Sgt T.Nicholson Missing, Runnymede Memorial 160
Nav. 1394386 Sgt K.W.Read Missing, Runnymede Memorial 162
B/A. 134161 F/O T.H.Boundy Missing, Runnymede Memorial 123
W/OP. 1384980 Sgt A.A.T.Woodward Missing, Runnymede Memorial 170
F/E. 1316326 Sgt R.O.Jasper Missing, Runnymede Memorial 155
A/G. 1304641 Sgt H.J.Wells Killed Bergen-op-Zoom, Holland. 28-A-9
A/G. 109856 Sgt R.Jackson Missing, Runnymede Memorial 154

10 Squadron 4 Group Halifax BB324 ZA/X
Pilot. 1345595 Sgt R.M.Pinkerton Missing, Runnymede Memorial 161
Nav. 1600601 Sgt F.T.Nuttall Killed Amsterdam, Holland. 69-B-10
B/A. 1438563 Sgt W.Waring Missing, Runnymede Memorial 168
W/OP. 1127145 Sgt J.Conway Killed Amsterdam, Holland. CG 69-B-13
F/E. 1139371 Sgt F.Holmes Killed Amsterdam, Holland. CG 69-B-13
A/G. R/85550 F/Sgt J.F.K.Crowe Killed Noordwijk, Holland. 5-3
A/G. R/104425 F/Sgt T.L.Macaskill Missing, Runnymede Memorial 183

51 Squadron 4 Group Halifax JD251 MH/
Pilot. 1218608 Sgt R.H.Elliott Missing, Runnymede Memorial 148
Nav. 1386459 Sgt T.Bennett Missing, Runnymede Memorial 142
B/A. 1388302 Sgt W.R.Newton Missing, Runnymede Memorial 160
W/OP. 1386521 Sgt F.Hawes Killed Rheinberg, Germany. 4-F-6
F/E. 531867 Sgt J.E.Davidson PoW. Repatriated 6/2/45.
A/G. 1260526 Sgt S.W.Kennedy Killed Rheinberg, Germany. 4-F-7
A/G. 1809779 Sgt C.J.Matthews Missing, Runnymede Memorial 158

76 Squadron 4 Group Halifax DK224 MP/Q
Aircraft crashed near Zuilen, N.W.of Utrecht, Holland.
Victim of Oblt Baake., 1/NJG1
Pilot. 145478 F/O J.Carrie PoW. Stalag Luft 3, Sagan. 2187
2/Pilot. A/16 G/Cpt D.E.L.Wilson PoW. Stalag Luft 3, Sagan. 2293
Nav. 1320704 F/Sgt R.W.Hibbs PoW. Stalag 357, Kopernikus. 167
B/A. 1572977 Sgt G.B.Thomason PoW. Stalag Luft 7, Bankau. 870
W/OP. 1122691 W/O E.L.McVittie PoW. Stalag 4B, Muhlberg(Elbe). 222736
F/E. 1384738 Sgt R.Huke Killed Utrecht (Soestbergen), Holland. 12D-1-1
A/G. R/90427 W/O R.H.Hammett PoW. Stalag 357, Kopernikus. 159
A/G. 649143 F/Sgt S.M.Davies PoW. Stalag Luft 6, Heydekrug. 115

77 Squadron 4 Group Halifax JD213 KN/V
Aircraft crashed in North Sea.
Pilot. A/413676 F/Sgt E.A.Sims Killed Wendune, Belgium. B-10
Nav. 701907 F/Sgt D.H.R.Kelly Killed Bergen, Holland. 2-C-12
B/A. 1338934 Sgt T.W.C.Luther Missing, Runnymede Memorial 157
W/OP. 1140418 Sgt T.Ogle Killed Rotterdam, Holland. LL-2-48
F/E. 1455546 Sgt J.Westbarn Missing, Runnymede Memorial 169
A/G. 1699809 Sgt J.Fitzsimmons Missing, Runnymede Memorial 149
A/G. R/149306 F/Sgt O.D.Thompson Missing, Runnymede Memorial 186

77 Squadron 4 Group Halifax DT700 KN/U
Pilot. 111112 F/Lt C.C.Marshall Missing, Runnymede Memorial 120
Nav. 1488238 Sgt P.M.Thornycroft Missing, Runnymede Memorial 167
B/A. 1575532 Sgt G.R.Hill Killed Bergen, Holland. 2-C-11
W/OP. 916677 Sgt W.E.Hughes Missing, Runnymede Memorial 154
F/E. 1123826 Sgt W.F.Eades Killed Amsterdam, Holland. CG 69-B-10
A/G. 1586956 Sgt G.R.Hazell Missing, Runnymede Memorial 152
A/G. 1490344 Sgt W.C.Lewis Missing, Runnymede Memorial 156

78 Squadron 4 Group Halifax JB855 EY/
Pilot. 128902 F/Lt L.Knight Killed Eindhoven(Woensel), Holland. EE-16
2/Pilot. 1384785 Sgt G.Duffee Evaded capture
Nav. 133466 F/O H.J.Standfast PoW. Stalag Luft 3, Sagan. 1665
B/A. 131594 F/O R.D.Caldecourt Killed Eindhoven(Woensel), Holland. EE-14
W/OP. 133560 F/O S.A.C.Cutler Killed Eindhoven(Woensel), Holland. EE-13
F/E. 1380680 Sgt F.C.Simons Killed Eindhoven(Woensel), Holland. EE-17
A/G. 1347034 Sgt F.J.R.Bain Killed Eindhoven(Woensel), Holland. EE-15
A/G. 1603525 F/Sgt J.H.Lee PoW. Stalag 357, Kopernikus. 199

78 Squadron 4 Group Halifax W7930 EY/
Pilot. 656206 F/Sgt E.Tipler Killed Amersfoort, Holland. CG 13-8-147/149
Nav. 1333246 Sgt J.E.Woodward Killed Amersfoort, Holland. CG 13-8-147/149
B/A. 1219022 Sgt W.Anderson Killed Amersfoort, Holland. CG 13-8-147/149
W/OP. 1332379 Sgt C.P.Johns Killed Amersfoort, Holland. CG 13-8-147/149
F/E. 573996 Sgt L.D.Lingwood Killed Amersfoort, Holland. CG 13-8-147/149
A/G. 1163588 Sgt T.H.Bell Killed Amersfoort, Holland. CG 13-8-147/149
A/G. 1398791 Sgt D.E.Tuddenham Killed Amersfoort, Holland. 13-8-151

158 Squadron 4 Group Halifax JD259 NP/R
Aircraft crashed at Leest, Belgium at 02.30 hours. Possible victim of II/NJG1.
Pilot. A/415377 F/Sgt L.E.Cavanagh Killed Schoonselhoof, Belgium. II-E-27
Nav. 1411102 Sgt T.R.Forster Killed Schoonselhoof, Belgium. II-E-26
B/A. 135633 F/O D.V.Elliott Killed Schoonselhoof, Belgium. II-E-23
W/OP. 1217286 Sgt W.R.Green Killed Schoonselhoof, Belgium. II-E-24
F/E. 572568 Sgt R.J.Sage Killed Schoonselhoof, Belgium. II-E-22
A/G. 151179 P/O R.A.C.Maund Killed Schoonselhoof, Belgium. II-E-28
A/G. R/657647 F/Sgt O.W.Todd Killed Schoonselhoof, Belgium. II-E-25

431 Squadron 4 Group Wellington HE394 SE/V
Pilot. 118483 F/Lt D.A.Hine Killed Rheinberg, Germany. 3-C-4
Nav. 48947 F/O H.D.Quilter Killed Rheinberg, Germany. 3-C-5
B/A. 148054 P/O R.E.Mercer Killed Rheinberg, Germany. 3-C-6
W/OP. 1111947 Sgt E.Batty Killed Rheinberg, Germany. 3-C-7
A/G. 1575740 Sgt A.E.Wilke Killed Rheinberg, Germany. 3-C-8

466 Squadron 4 Group Wellington HE326 HD/
Pilot. 142518 P/O A.L.Ford Killed Reichswald Forest, Germany. 6-A-7
Nav. 146023 P/O C.W.Hewitt Killed Reichswald Forest, Germany. 6-A-5
B/A. 145522 P/O R.L.Amesbury Killed Reichswald Forest, Germany. 6-A-6
W/OP. 1265390 W/O R.W.Fox PoW. Stalag 357, Kopernikus. 134
A/G. 615979 Sgt A.H.Richardson Killed Reichswald Forest, Germany. 6-A-4

9 Squadron 5 Group Lancaster ED699 WS/L
Pilot. 147533 P/O K.Denness Killed Reichswald Forest, Germany. 6-C-5
Nav. 1389594 Sgt A.G.Bryan Killed Rheinberg, Germany. 3-C-10
B/A. 132698 F/O R.W.Winfield Killed Rheinberg, Germany. 3-C-9
W/OP. 1330448 Sgt A.F.S.Day Killed Rheinberg, Germany. CG 3-C-11/13
F/E. 911975 Sgt C.Hunt Killed Rheinberg, Germany. CG 3-C-11/13
A/G. 1256384 Sgt E.W.Geraghty Killed Rheinberg, Germany. CG 3-C-11/13
A/G. 1270585 Sgt G.F.Kilsby Killed Reichswald Forest, Germany. 30-F-4

207 Squadron 5 Group Lancaster ED692 EM/
Pilot. 1254719 F/O P.G.Herrin Missing, Runnymede Memorial 125
Nav. J/13419 F/O W.H.Flatt Missing, Runnymede Memorial 173
B/A. 130501 F/O G.W.Kleinberg Missing, Runnymede Memorial 125
W/OP. 1272044 Sgt S.Payton Killed Rheinberg, Germany. 4-F-8
F/E. 572504 Sgt P.Mills Missing, Runnymede Memorial 159
A/G. 1480790 Sgt R.Bradshaw Missing, Runnymede Memorial 143
A/G. 1315318 Sgt G.A.H.Male Killed Rheinberg, Germany. 4-F-9

427 Squadron 6 Group Halifax DK141 ZL/
Pilot. R/102390 F/Sgt J.D.Hamilton Killed Bergen-op-Zoom (Can). 11-F-8
Nav. R/90121 W/O J.J.Rensbury Killed Bergen-op-Zoom (Can). 11-F-10
B/A. 629132 Sgt G.D.Sharp Killed Bergen-op-Zoom (Can), Holland. 25-A-4
W/OP. 1199977 Sgt N.G.Whiting Killed Bergen-op-Zoom (Can). 27-A-11
F/E. R/60309 W/O J.A.Spencer PoW. Stalag 357, Kopernikus. 255
A/G. R/151903 F/Sgt P.J.A.Dennis Killed Bergen-op-Zoom (Can). 11-F-12
A/G. R/147160 F/Sgt G.L.Tyrone Killed Bergen-op-Zoom (Can). 25-A-3

427 Squadron 6 Group Halifax DK225 ZL/
Pilot. 110633 F/Lt K.Webster Killed Bergen, Holland. 2-D-33
Nav. 1476382 F/Sgt T.Mitchell PoW. Stalag 357, Kopernikus. 338
B/A. NZ/413718 P/O E.R.Strang Killed Bergen, Holland. 2-D-24
W/OP. 147911 P/O A.E.Humphreys Killed Bergen, Holland. 2-D-21
F/E. 1459749 Sgt C.Sampson Killed Bergen, Holland. 2-D-22
A/G. R/122089 Sgt G.L.Tucker Killed Bergen, Holland. 2-D-25
A/G. NZ/413773 F/Sgt D.H.Northcoat Killed Bergen, Holland. 2-D-26

427 Squadron 6 Group Halifax DK139 ZL/
Pilot. J/16783 P/O G.A.Cadmus Killed Reichswald Forest, Germany. 6-B-17
Nav. J/15727 F/O G.T.Vicary Killed Reichswald Forest, Germany. 6-B-16
B/A. 126960 F/O A.J.Manning Killed Reichswald Forest, Germany. 30-F-1
W/OP. R/98396 Sgt A.D.Deane Killed Reichswald Forest, Germany. 2-F-6
F/E. 649831 Sgt S.T.Booth Killed Reichswald Forest, Germany. 5-H-15
A/G. R/86923 W/O C.P.Bearisto Killed Reichswald Forest, Germany. 6-C-4
A/G. J/17344 P/O M.M.Meyer Killed Reichswald Forest, Germany. 5-H-16

427 Squadron 6 Group Halifax DK191 ZL/
Aircraft crashed at Warnsveld, Holland at 01.35 hours (23/6/43).
Pilot. J/10353 F/O N.D.Reid Killed Warnsveld(Wichmon), Holland. CG E-14/17
Nav. J/14193 P/O A.A.Pariseau Killed Warnsveld(Wichmon). CG E-14/17
B/A. 1394512 Sgt P.B.Robinson Killed Warnsveld(Wichmon), Holland. E-18
W/OP. J/21403 F/O B.M.Gracie Killed Warnsveld(Wichmon), Holland. E-13
F/E. 1437312 Sgt D.Mann Killed Warnsveld(Wichmon), Holland. CG E-14/17
A/G. R/131460 F/Sgt H.P.Heximer Killed Warnsveld(Wichmon), Holland. E-12
A/G. R/103340 F/Sgt N.F.Notley Killed Warnsveld(Wichmon). CG E-14/17

429 Squadron 6 Group Wellington HF457 AL/
Aircraft shot down at Houthalen, 12 kilometres NNE of Hasselt, Belgium.
Victim of Oblt Hans Autenreith, 6/NJG4 based at Dijon, France, who came
back at Major Walter Ehle's request to assist II/NJG1 at St Trond, Belgium.
Pilot. J/17777 P/O W.A.Sneath Killed Heverlee, Belgium. 8-K-6
Nav. J/21825 F/Lt R.G.Clarke PoW. Stalag Luft 4, Sagan. 1491
B/A. J/21465 F/Lt A.B.Drummond-Hay PoW. Stalag Luft 3, Sagan. 1493
W/OP. 1058762 Sgt J.T.Hindley Killed Heverlee, Belgium. 8-K-7
A/G. R/176395 F/Sgt J.O.Hills Killed Heverlee, Belgium. 8-K-5

429 Squadron 6 Group Wellington HZ312 AL/
Pilot. C/1664 W/Cdr J.L.Savard DFC Killed Reichswald Forest. 6-A-16
Nav. J/10050 F/O J.S.McIntyre Killed Reichswald Forest, Germany. 6-A-15
B/A. R/79494 W/O J.C.A.Laberge Killed Reichswald Forest, Germany. 6-A-17
W/OP. 971456 W/O J.Allen Killed Reichswald Forest, Germany. 6-B-1
A/G. J/17396 P/O J.O.R.Bonenfant Killed Reichswald Forest, Germany. 6-A-18

Shuttle Raid from North Africa

June 23rd/24th, 1943
The Ruhr had one night's respite when 53 Lancasters - 51 from 5 Group and two from 8 Group - which had three nights previously bombed Friedrichshafen and had flown on to North Africa, made a raid on La Spezia on their return flight to England. Four of them had to return to North Africa with technical problems before reaching the target. Only minor damage was caused to an oil depot, which was the target. No aircraft were lost from this operation. The other eight Lancasters from the original 61 strong force were not serviceable for this return raid.

Nuisance and Minelaying Raids

June 23rd/24th, 1943
Six Mosquitoes paid visits to Duisberg and Cologne, three to each city, dropping 2.3 tons of bombs on each. No aircraft were lost. Minelaying was also continued with 11 Stirlings and two Lancasters from 3 Group, 14 Wellingtons from 1 Group and three Wellingtons from 6 Group dropping 79 mines in their respective mining areas.

Wuppertal

June 24th/25th, 1943

It was Wuppertal again on the target maps of 630 aircraft, a force consisting of 251 Lancasters, 171 Halifaxes, 101 Wellingtons, 98 Stirlings and 9 Mosquitoes

Again there was a high number of early returners, the force being depleted by 79 aircraft. The aiming point was on the Elberfeld half of Wuppertal, for the Barmen area of the town had been practically obliterated in the attack of 29th/30th May. The position of the town in the Ruhr was such that location by night was almost impossible by visual means. Its shape was long and narrow, demanding a high degree of bombing accuracy to attain effective concentration. Its size, estimated by population, was slightly greater than that of Coventry, where the Germans in a devastatingly successful attack on the night of 14th/15th November, 1940, destroyed approximately 100 acres in the centre of the town in a raid lasting two hours. Wuppertal was a town of 929 acres and after 20 minutes of this raid 870 acres were in ruins. The Pathfinders started the raid at 01.01 hours and were again accurate and punctual with their main marking and backing up. Again the usual creep-back occurred, this time perhaps more pronounced, although it did not greatly affect the outcome of the raid. If anything Elberfeld suffered more damage than its neighbouring half of Barmen, a large industrial area which was completely wiped out with the 815.7 tons of HE bombs and 331,748 incendiaries that were dropped. The number of houses completely destroyed rose to 3,000 and approximately 1,800 people were killed with 2,400 injured. A large explosion in the centre of the target area was seen at 01.16 hours. Searchlights were very active between Cologne and Düsseldorf where many bombers encountered enemy fighters. *Flak* also was more intense than in the previous Wuppertal/Barmen raids. 35 aircraft and their crews were lost. The persistent high casualties were beginning to have a demoralising effect on some squadrons who seemed to suffer an above average loss rate and these nightly forays to the Ruhr with the seemingly ever mounting losses caused added strain and tension in the crews. Aircrew casualties on this raid were 116 killed, 63 missing, 44 made prisoners of war and one made a successful evasion.

7 Squadron Commander Lost, But One Man Evades

One of the missing aircraft was a Stirling from 7 Squadron, Pathfinder Force captained by a very experienced Squadron Commander, Wing Commander R. G. Barrell DSO, DFC. who was killed on this his 60th operation. On the outward flight the Stirling was attacked by a German night fighter and set on fire. The pilot ordered the crew to bale out at about midnight. One of the four bale out survivors was flight engineer Pilot Officer J. Hudson DFC, who came down about a kilometre from the south coast of a neck of land which joins Zuid Beveland to the Dutch mainland. He landed close to a dyke where some Dutch fortifications had been blown up by the Germans, the nearest village being Bath. After hiding his 'chute, harness and Mae West in some swampy ground beside the dyke, Pilot Officer Hudson started to walk eastwards. He soon found that walking was extremely painful, as he had twisted his left ankle badly in a heavy landing. Unable to continue, he hid in a nearby field of beans and after purifying some dyke water with his Halazone tablets, he made a meal of the beans and drank his water. He remained in the field until the next morning, when he was found by a local farmer. Asking him for some food, Pilot Officer Hudson told him his identity. The farmer, who was unable to speak English, went away and returned with an English speaking Dutchman who took the limping flight engineer to a farmer's barn just north of Bath, where he remained for the next three days until the hue and cry of the German search parties had died down. Later he was taken into the farmhouse itself where he was sheltered for six weeks until mid August, when arrangements had been completed by the underground escape organisation for his journey back to England.

'The Captain' Claims Three More Victims

Lancaster W4320 from 460 Squadron, captained by Australian Warrant Officer G. Stooke, was hit by *Flak* on the way to the target. Two engines were rendered useless and although the bomber flew on for a further hour on the remaining two engines, the bale out order had to be eventually given and all the crew got out safely about 25 miles north-west of Liege , Belgium at 01.50 hours. Three of the crew were helped by the underground movement. The pilot in the course of his evasion met up with the bogus 'Captain' in Brussels and suffered the same betrayal as so many other aircrew for he was arrested in Paris on June 29th. Two other members of the crew, the wireless operator Flight Sergeant D. T. Toohig and the Australian navigator Warrant Officer C. R. Craven, met up with each other shortly after landing. They too received help but from a different underground group from that which had helped their pilot. However, their ultimate fate was the same, for they also were passed into the 'Captain's' hands in Brussels and they were arrested in a Paris hotel on the 14th July, 1943.

Casualties June 24th/25th, 1943. Target Wuppertal

7 Squadron 8 Group Lancaster ED595 MG/Q
Pilot. 78524 W/Cdr R.G.Barrell DSO, DFC Killed Bergen-op-Zoom. 3-B-3
Parachute failed to open, died of injuries.
Nav. NZ/41330 F/Lt F.Hilton DFC Killed Bergen-op-Zoom (Can). 6-F-10
B/A. J/15421 F/Lt J.A.Emery PoW. Stalag Luft 3, Sagan. 1772
W/OP. 142839 F/O S.G.Keatley PoW. Stalag Luft 3, Sagan. 719
F/E. 143810 P/O H.J.Hudson DFC E Evaded capture
A/G. 647914 W/O E.G.Pointer DFM Killed Bergen-op-Zoom, Holland. 3-B-10
Failed to bale out, reasons not known.
A/G. 906682 W/O J.A.Pearson DFM PoW. Stalag 357, Kopernikus. 344

7 Squadron 8 Group Stirling R9281 MG/V
Aircraft crashed into North Sea.
Pilot. 120803 F/O A.J.Davis Missing, Runnymede Memorial 124
Nav. 655452 F/Sgt F.Fazackerley Missing, Runnymede Memorial 149
B/A. 1335742 Sgt H.R.Glover Killed Castricum, Holland. CG J-6
W/OP. 1375694 Sgt A.R.J.Hunt Killed Ostend, Belgium. 9-3-43
F/E. 1063345 Sgt G.Thompson Missing, Runnymede Memorial 167
A/G. 49951 F/O J.F.Hanrahan Missing, Runnymede Memorial 124
A/G. 1331481 Sgt S.C.Carter Killed Bergen, Holland. 2-C-21

7 Squadron 8 Group Stirling EF392 MG/N
Aircraft crashed off Castricum, Holland into the North Sea.
Pilot. A/402882 S/Ldr J.R.Savage Missing, Runnymede Memorial 187
2/Pilot. 149607 P/O F.J.Haines Missing, Runnymede Memorial 131
Nav. 656215 F/Sgt S.J.Barnes Killed Bergen-op-Zoom (Can), Holland. 2-C-9

B/A. 1507631 Sgt S.A.Errington Missing, Runnymede Memorial 148
W/OP. 1377873 Sgt A.A.Caley Missing, Runnymede Memorial 144
F/E. 569405 F/Sgt G.H.Cox Missing, Runnymede Memorial 135
A/G. R/14004 F/Sgt N.R.Morrison Missing, Runnymede Memorial 185
A/G. 1323191 Sgt D.R.Spanton Missing, Runnymede Memorial 165

97 Squadron 8 Group Lancaster LM327 OF/Y
Pilot. 42071 F/Lt J.L.Moore DFC Missing, Runnymede Memorial 120
Nav. J/8437 S/Ldr J.P.McMillin Missing, Runnymede Memorial 172
B/A. 51895 P/O W.J.Stephen DFM Missing, Runnymede Memorial 133
W/OP. 630845 F/Sgt A.Tomlinson Missing, Runnymede Memorial 139
F/E. 572001 F/Sgt R.A.Kerckhove Missing, Runnymede Memorial 137
A/G. 1392050 Sgt J.W.Darroch Missing, Runnymede Memorial 147
A/G. 1809975 Sgt L.L.Davis Missing, Runnymede Memorial 147

156 Squadron 8 Group Lancaster ED858 GT/
Pilot. A/403742 P/O R.J.Hudson Missing, Runnymede Memorial 191
Nav. 1213064 Sgt R.Brown Killed Rheinberg, Germany. 4-F-10
B/A. 1193006 Sgt W.S.Brooks Missing, Runnymede Memorial 143
W/OP. 629048 Sgt H.Jones Missing, Runnymede Memorial 155
F/E. 1314768 Sgt A.T.Barlow Missing, Runnymede Memorial 141
A/G. 1356283 Sgt K.Richards Killed Rheinberg, Germany. 4-F-11
A/G. 1222832 Sgt K.C.C.Adams Killed Rheinberg, Germany. 4-F-12

156 Squadron 8 Group Lancaster EE127 GT/
Pilot. A/416018 P/O L.F.Brown Missing, Runnymede Memorial 190
Nav. 1391936 F/Sgt A.V.Newall Missing, Runnymede Memorial 138
B/A. 1207245 Sgt J.Malpass Missing, Runnymede Memorial 158
W/OP. 569239 Sgt I.H.Bradley Missing, Runnymede Memorial 143
F/E. J/17985 Sgt R.F.Worthington Missing, Runnymede Memorial 178
A/G. 1330123 Sgt C.Easton Missing, Runnymede Memorial 148
A/G. 1264739 Sgt R.Gilbert Missing, Runnymede Memorial 150

405 Squadron 8 Group Halifax HR816 LQ/C
Pilot. 1316904 W/O P.C.Andrews PoW. Stalag Luft 3, Sagan. 6471
Broke both ankles after bale out.
Nav. 1023994 W/O G.Jones PoW. Stalag 357, Kopernikus. 181
B/A. R/102920 W/O W.Kingsley PoW. Stalag 357, Kopernikus. 189
W/OP. 1079868 F/Sgt F.Bowker PoW. Stalag 357, Kopernikus. 76
F/E. R/60745 Sgt C.W.Price Killed Rheinberg, Germany. 3-D-1
Died of wounds after bale out.
A/G. 1300168 W/O G.C.Tisbury PoW. Stalag 357, Kopernikus. 270
A/G. R/141400 F/Sgt J.W.Kucinsky Killed Rheinberg, Germany. 5-D-23
Killed in aircraft.

101 Squadron 1 Group Lancaster W4311 SR/O
Pilot. 1390339 Sgt J.E.W.Lane Killed Jonkerbos, Holland. 11-I-4
Nav. 658849 Sgt T.W.Connor Killed Jonkerbos, Holland. 11-I-1
B/A. 1338327 Sgt S.F.Barber Killed Jonkerbos, Holland. 11-I-3
W/OP. 1386325 Sgt S.E.Williams Missing, Runnymede Memorial 170
F/E. 1320885 Sgt R.W.Ridgley Killed Jonkerbos, Holland. 11-H-8
A/G. 1560291 Sgt N.Fotheringham Killed Jonkerbos, Holland. 11-I-5

A/G. 702593 Sgt A.Twohy Killed Jonkerbos, Holland. 11-I-2

460 Squadron 1 Group Lancaster W4320 UV/
Nav. and W/OP. captured by Gestapo in Paris attempting to evade.
Pilot. A/409332 W/O G.Stooke PoW. Stalag 4B, Muhlberg(Elbe). 222556
Nav. A/412915 W/O C.R.Craven PoW. Stalag 4B, Muhlberg(Elbe). 222498
B/A. A/413169 Sgt N.F.Conklin PoW. Stalag 4B, Muhlberg(Elbe). 222496
W/OP. 1385973 W/O D.T.Toohig PoW. Stalag Luft 6, Heydekrug. 1343
F/E. 626263 F/Sgt C.W.Broadbent PoW. Stalag 357, Kopernikus. 297
A/G. A/409603 W/O F.B.Shaw PoW. Stalag 357, Kopernikus. 351
A/G. A/414258 Sgt S.R.Nowlan PoW. Stalag 357, Kopernikus. 342

166 Squadron 1 Group Wellington HF594 AS/Q
Pilot. J/17355 P/O R.E.Currie Killed Brussels, Belgium. X-17-22
Nav. 146093 P/O N.B.Touzel Killed Brussels, Belgium. JG X-17-19/20
B/A. 1096561 Sgt N.A.M.Cawthra Killed Brussels, Belgium. JG X-17-19/20
W/OP. 1379610 Sgt G.H.Williams Killed Brussels, Belgium. X-17-21
A/G. 1580879 Sgt F.Needham Killed Brussels, Belgium. X-17-23

300 Squadron 1 Group Wellington HF606 BH/C
Pilot. P/784058 Sgt J.Jawoszek Killed Reichswald Forest, Germany.
Nav. P/0916 F/Lt J.Obrycki Killed Reichswald Forest, Germany.
B/A. P/781725 Sgt E.Bartosiak Killed Reichswald Forest, Germany.
W/OP. P/781577 Sgt F.Skoskiewicz Killed Reichswald Forest, Germany.
A/G. P/784500 Sgt S.Jacewicz Killed Reichswald Forest, Germany.

300 Squadron 1 Group Wellington HE376 BH/G
Pilot. P/01500 F/Lt W.Turecki PoW. Stalag Luft 3, Sagan. 2289
Nav. P/794235 Sgt A.Bielski Killed Rheinberg, Germany. CG D-III-3/4
B/A. P/781203 Sgt J.Bijowski Killed Rheinberg, Germany. CG D-III-3/4
W/OP. P/794425 Sgt K.Zarniewski Killed Rheinberg, Germany. CG D-II-3/4
A/G. P/704311 F/Sgt R.Kosiarski PoW. Stalag 357, Kopernikus. 1278

15 Squadron 3 Group Stirling EH890 LS/U
Aircraft ditched 15 miles off Orfordness.
Pilot and W/OP. awarded DFM.
Pilot. 1316716 Sgt W.Towse Rescued.
Nav. Sgt J.Barass Rescued.
B/A. 742176 W/O T.Martin PoW. Stalag 357, Kopernikus. 392998
W/OP. 651401 Sgt N.Pawley Rescued.
F/E. Sgt H.Brodie Rescued.
A/G. Sgt W.Duval Rescued.
A/G. Sgt J.Baldwin Rescued.

75 Squadron 3 Group Stirling EH902 AA/K
Aircraft crashed near Wissenkerke, Holland.
Pilot. NZ/40364 P/O N.Bluck Killed Flushing, Holland. F-12
Nav. NZ/416460 F/Sgt J.B.Cooksey Killed Bergen-op-Zoom, Holland. 14-C-1
B/A. NZ/413905 F/Sgt G.W.Strong Killed Flushing, Holland. F-13
W/OP. 1072258 Sgt M.Kendlaw Killed Bergen-op-Zoom (Can), Holland. 7-AA-6
F/E. 938834 Sgt J.W.Gillard Killed Bergen-op-Zoom, Holland. 4-C-7
A/G. 1434609 Sgt D.Armitage Killed Flushing, Holland. F-14
A/G. 1397680 Sgt L.R.Cant Killed Flushing, Holland. F-7

90 Squadron 3 Group Stirling BK813 WP/O
Aircraft crashed at Haasrode, Belgium. Victim of Ofw Kollak & Fw Hermann 7/NJG4.
Pilot. A/16774 F/Sgt W.H.Teede Killed Haasrode, Leuven, Belgium. 5
Nav. 658831 Sgt H.Levine Killed Haasrode, Leuven, Belgium. 8
B/A. 1319009 Sgt A.C.Harris Killed Haasrode, Leuven, Belgium. 3
W/OP. NZ/403611 F/Sgt L.Petersen Killed Haasrode, Leuven, Belgium. 4
F/E. 1178476 F/Sgt E.H.Stanton PoW. Stalag 357, Kopernikus. 353
A/G. 1346152 Sgt P.J.Taylor Killed Haasrode, Leuven, Belgium. 6
A/G. NZ/42327 F/Sgt G.Henderson Killed Haasrode, Leuven, Belgium. 7

90 Squadron 3 Group Stirling BK628 WP/G
Pilot. 1374039 F/Sgt J.M.Steel Missing, Runnymede Memorial 139
Nav. 1455215 Sgt A.N.Cooper Missing, Runnymede Memorial 146
B/A. 1532521 Sgt W.A.Taylor Missing, Runnymede Memorial 166
W/OP. 1292832 Sgt H.Taylorson Missing, Runnymede Memorial 166
F/E. 1348699 Sgt W.N.Nisbett Missing, Runnymede Memorial 160
A/G. 1800277 Sgt C.W.Dixon Missing, Runnymede Memorial 147
A/G. 1108687 Sgt J.C.Gardner Missing, Runnymede Memorial 150

214 Squadron 3 Group Stirling EE883 BU/T
Aircraft crashed into North Sea near Noordwijk, Holland.
Pilot. 1497411 Sgt C.K.Miller Missing, Runnymede Memorial 159
Nav. 1396511 Sgt P.D.Straton Missing, Runnymede Memorial 166
B/A. 1536320 Sgt R.G.Akers Missing, Runnymede Memorial 140
W/OP. 1333413 Sgt R.A.H.Smith Missing, Runnymede Memorial 165
F/E. 1323326 Sgt J.A.Hitchins Missing, Runnymede Memorial 153
A/G. 1356712 Sgt S.Seward Killed Bergen, Holland. 2-C-13
A/G. 1622196 Sgt T.Jones Killed Noordwijk, Holland. 6-2

218 Squadron 3 Group Stirling BF501 HA/N
Crashed Kaggevinne, 1.5 kilometres SW of Diest, Belgium at 01.59 hours (25/6/43). Victim of Staffelkapitän Oblt Hans Autenreith, 6/NJG1.
Pilot. R/107769 W/O J.W.Hoey Killed Kaggevinne, Diest, Belgium. JG 5
2/Pilot. 1433512 Sgt P.E.Collingwood Killed Kaggevinne, Diest, Belgium. JG 5
Nav. 701975 F/Sgt L.DeBotte Killed Kaggevinne, Diest, Belgium. JG 6
B/A. 1452815 Sgt L.Edgoose Killed Kaggevinne, Diest, Belgium. JG 6
W/OP. 1204724 Sgt A.W.Erne Killed Kaggevinne, Diest, Belgium. 8
F/E. 1052427 Sgt J.Thompson Killed Kaggevinne, Diest, Belgium. 4
A/G. 979965 Sgt T.E.Lloyd Killed Kaggevinne, Diest, Belgium. 7
A/G. 1331174 F/Sgt R.F.Garrod Killed Kaggevinne, Diest, Belgium. JG 5

218 Squadron 3 Group Stirling EH892 HA/U
Aircraft crashed after fighter attack at Neustadt, Germany.
Pilot. 37538 S/Ldr A.Beck Killed Rheinberg, Germany. CG 9-F-13/16
2/Pilot. 127914 F/O R.J.Johnson Killed Rheinberg, Germany. CG 9-F-13/16
Nav. 143425 P/O H.B.Barrett Killed Rheinberg, Germany. CG 9-F-13/16
B/A. NZ/411899 P/O R.V.Phelps-Hopkins Killed Rheinberg. CG 9-F-13/16
W/OP. 128613 F/O L.G.Flynn Killed Rheinberg, Germany. CG 9-F-13/16
F/E. 622172 W/O S.G.Garbett PoW. Stalag 357, Kopernikus. 142

A/G. 1149134 F/Sgt E.Quigley PoW. Stalag Luft 7, Bankau. 943
A/G. 138204 F/Lt R.H.Nuttall PoW. Stalag Luft 3, Sagan. 1663

620 Squadron 3 Group Stirling BK800 QS/Z
Aircraft crashed at Hasslinghausen, Germany.
Pilot. 1132708 F/Sgt R.P.Reynolds Killed Reichswald Forest. CG 31-C-8/12
Nav. NZ/42304 F/O J.F.Needham PoW. Stalag Luft 3, Sagan. 1724
B/A. 1081660 Sgt J.Garbutt Killed Reichswald Forest, Germany. CG 31-C-8/12
W/OP. 1261280 Sgt J.Lindley Killed Reichswald Forest, Germany. 3-E-10
F/E. 572760 Sgt J.D.Cresswell Killed Reichswald Forest. CG 31-C-8/12
A/G. 1046519 Sgt P.J.Court Killed Reichswald Forest, Germany. CG 31-C-8/12
A/G. J/14554 F/O R.J.Burke Killed Reichswald Forest, Germany. CG 31-C-8/12

431 Squadron 4 Group Wellington HF604 SE/B
Pilot. 31183 P/O J.Valentine
W/OP. 976215 W/O W.H.Jewels PoW. Stalag 4B, Muhlberg(Elbe). 222527
Aircraft was shot up by enemy fighter.Rear gunner was wounded in the attack
and the wireless operator baled out over France. Pilot brought aircraft back
and landed at Manston, Kent.

51 Squadron 4 Group Halifax JD250 MH/
Pilot. 119333 F/O J.N.Mackenzie Killed Amsterdam, Holland. 69-B-9
Nav. 138391 P/O A.J.Fitchett Killed Castricum, Holland. CG J-6
B/A. 135112 F/O C.A.Johnson Missing, Runnymede Memorial 125
W/OP. 1024896 Sgt R.W.Stevenson Missing, Runnymede Memorial 165
F/E. 802586 Sgt W.Blackie Missing, Runnymede Memorial 142
A/G. R/104347 F/Sgt W.Andrews Missing, Runnymede Memorial 181
A/G. R/100833 F/Sgt R.E.Murdock Killed Flushing, Holland. F-249

76 Squadron 4 Group Halifax DK166 MP/D
Aircraft shot down at Lovenich, NW of Cologne, Germany.
Pilot. J/3491 F/Lt G.H.Cheetham Killed Rheinberg, Germany. 4-F-19
Nav. 132866 F/Lt J.D.Danks PoW. Stalag Luft 3, Sagan. 1349
B/A. 1321760 Sgt G.I.Simpkin Killed Rheinberg, Germany. 4-F-20
W/OP. 1238296 F/Sgt K.R.Newton PoW. Stalag 357, Kopernikus. 218
F/E. 1136458 F/Sgt R.H.Evans PoW. Stalag Luft 6, Heydekrug. 129
A/G. 1076507 F/Sgt J.M.Sweeney PoW. Stalag 357, Kopernikus. 354
A/G. 1816632 Sgt E.Harper Missing, Runnymede Memorial 152

78 Squadron 4 Group Halifax JB962 EY/
Pilot. NZ/417092 F/Sgt K.F.Morrison Killed Rheinberg, Germany. 4-F-14
Nav. 1389031 Sgt P.A.Kennedy Killed Rheinberg, Germany. 4-F-15
B/A. 1553551 Sgt I.Macrae Killed Rheinberg, Germany. 4-F-18
W/OP. 1370416 Sgt W.Cox Killed Rheinberg, Germany. 4-F-16
F/E. 950236 Sgt W.Barry Killed Rheinberg, Germany. 4-F-17
A/G. NZ/413738 F/Sgt E.W.J.Collingwood Missing, Runnymede Memorial 198
A/G. 1304123 Sgt T.S.Payne Missing, Runnymede Memorial 161

102 Squadron 4 Group Halifax JD144 DY/Q
Pilot. 1332395 F/Sgt K.R.W.Sheppard Killed Leopoldsburg, Belgium. VIII-A-1
Nav. 657647 Sgt A.G.Tovey Killed Schoonselhoof, Belgium. IVA-D-19

B/A. 1261272 F/Sgt W.R.Cole PoW. Stalag Luft 6, Heydekrug. 303
W/OP. 1082024 Sgt F.Gettings Killed Florennes, Belgium. 3-29
F/E. 1506856 F/Sgt C.Rushton PoW. Stalag 357, Kopernikus. 349
A/G. 1365713 Sgt J.J.Macdonald Killed Florennes, Belgium. 3-31
A/G. 910303 Sgt M.H.Clack Killed Florennes, Belgium. 3-30

102 Squadron 4 Group Halifax JB834 DY/C
Pilot. 1218435 F/Sgt J.A.Marsden Missing, Runnymede Memorial 138
Nav. 129357 F/O J.E.Lewis Missing, Runnymede Memorial 125
B/A. 130511 F/O J.A.Perkins Missing, Runnymede Memorial 128
W/OP. 1311751 Sgt R.H.Barnes Missing, Runnymede Memorial 141
F/E. 1461188 Sgt J.S.R.Ablett Missing, Runnymede Memorial 140
A/G. 1451908 Sgt T.A.Hicks Missing, Runnymede Memorial 153
A/G. 1293070 Sgt P.A.G.Warwick Killed Rheinberg, Germany. 4-F-13

50 Squadron 5 Group Lancaster ED712 VN/
Pilot. A/409287 F/Sgt J.A.Brock Killed Rheinberg, Germany. 3-C-20
Nav. 658137 Sgt R.H.Cookson Killed Rheinberg, Germany. 3-C-21
B/A. A/26228 Sgt T.W.Page Killed Rheinberg, Germany. 3-C-23
W/OP. 1123748 Sgt T.G.Wilkinson Missing, Runnymede Memorial 169
F/E. 1079916 Sgt B.Veal Missing, Runnymede Memorial 168
A/G. 658294 Sgt L.L.Seal Missing, Runnymede Memorial 164
A/G. R/123129 W/O W.Pearson Killed Rheinberg, Germany. 3-C-24

57 Squadron 5 Group Lancaster ED781 DX/
Pilot. 1239601 Sgt S.Fallows Killed Heverlee, Belgium. 8-H-5
Nav. 1385433 Sgt H.Naiman Killed Heverlee, Belgium. 8-H-1
B/A. 1338290 Sgt I.H.Lambdin PoW. Stalag 357, Kopernikus. 406
W/OP. 1385312 Sgt W.G.T.Day Killed Heverlee, Belgium. 8-H-3
F/E. 1078563 Sgt J.W.Sykes Killed Heverlee, Belgium. 8-H-6
A/G. 1101417 Sgt R.B.Simpson Killed Heverlee, Belgium. 8-H-2
A/G. 624670 Sgt F.J.M.Steer Killed Heverlee, Belgium. 8-H-4

419 Squadron 6 Group Halifax JD214 VR/U
Shot down by FW 190 fighter at 01.00 hours (25/6/43) and crashed
Wageningen, Arnhem, Holland.
Pilot. R/122559 F/Sgt G.V.Neale PoW. Stalag 357, Kopernikus. 340
Nav. R/143359 F/Sgt R.S.McLachlan PoW. Stalag 357, Kopernikus. 335
B/A. R/114232 W/O W.N.Jaffray PoW. Stalag 357, Kopernikus. 324
W/OP. 1179550 F/Sgt P.J.Griffiths PoW. Stalag 357, Kopernikus. 320
F/E. 1500989 F/Sgt R.A.Cleaver PoW. Stalag 357, Kopernikus. 302
A/G. R/91128 F/Sgt D.E.Kenwell PoW. Stalag 357, Kopernikus. 325
A/G. R/142459 W/O W.P.McLeod PoW. Stalag 357, Kopernikus. 336

419 Squadron 6 Group Halifax JD147 VR/C
Aircraft shot down by enemy fighter.
Pilot. J/7433 S/Ldr B.N.Jost DFC Killed Jonkerbos, Holland. 8-G-6
Nav. 1069568 W/O E.B.Pope PoW. Stalag 357, Kopernikus. 346
B/A. NZ/412786 W/O A.W.A.Bruce PoW. Stalag 357, Kopernikus. 647
W/OP. J/15706 F/O R.O.E.Goodwin Killed Flushing, Holland. 23-1
F/E. R/71026 Sgt J.B.Johnson Killed Jonkerbos, Holland. 8-G-7

A/G. 1379386 W/O L.Barker PoW. Stalag Luft 6, Heydekrug. 11027
A/G. 545864 F/Sgt R.E.Austin PoW. Stalag 357, Kopernikus. 293

419 Squadron 6 Group Halifax JD258 VR/K
Crew on attachment from 428 Squadron.
Pilot. 1496432 Sgt R.Whitfield Killed Eindhoven(Woensel), Holland. EE-26
Nav. J/22529 F/O R.J.L.Fowler Killed Groesbeek, Holland. XVI-D-3
B/A. 129159 F/O W.A.Donnelly Killed Eindhoven(Woensel), Holland. EE-25
W/OP. 1134562 Sgt C.Gorton Killed Eindhoven(Woensel), Holland. EE-31
F/E. 1684544 Sgt P.Stephenson Killed Eindhoven(Woensel), Holland. EE-30
A/G. 2216248 Sgt J.Dean Killed Eindhoven(Woensel), Holland. EE-28
A/G. R/98960 F/Sgt M.P.Kimber Killed Groesbeek, Holland. XVI-D-4

427 Squadron 6 Group Halifax DK135 ZL/
Aircraft found in Rozenberg Polder, Holland in August 1967.
Pilot. J/8219 F/O L.W.Somers Missing, Runnymede Memorial 174
Nav. J/22206 F/O M.Shvemar Killed Rotterdam, Holland. LL-1-45
B/A. J/22537 F/O V.M.White PoW. Stalag Luft 3, Sagan. 1707
W/OP. 1027401 Sgt L.A.Bone PoW. Stalag Luft 6, Heydekrug. 296
F/E. 1371842 Sgt W.G.Arthur Killed Rotterdam, Holland. LL-1-46
A/G. R/137620 F/Sgt J.N.Walton Missing, Runnymede Memorial 186
A/G. 1313797 Sgt F.C.Ashby Missing, Runnymede Memorial 140

429 Squadron 6 Group Wellington HZ521 AL/
Pilot. R/90360 W/O L.F.O'Leary Killed Heverlee, Belgium. 2-F-4
Nav. R/133222 F/Sgt E.B.Peart Killed Heverlee, Belgium. 2-F-1
B/A. R/150902 F/Sgt C.W.Keay Killed Heverlee, Belgium. 2-F-5
W/OP. 1191334 Sgt J.M.Meech Killed Heverlee, Belgium. 2-F-2
A/G. R/155731 F/Sgt H.S.Hicks Killed Heverlee, Belgium. 2-F-3

432 Squadron 6 Group Wellington HF572 QO/J
Pilot. 1216316 Sgt N.Goldie Killed Bergen-op-Zoom, Holland. 25-C-5
Nav. 1390957 Sgt G.Liddle Killed Bergen-op-Zoom, Holland. 25-C-3
B/A. 658650 Sgt F.W.N.Trowbridge Killed Bergen-op-Zoom, Holland. 25-C-4
W/OP. 1331007 Sgt C.K.Killick Killed Bergen-op-Zoom, Holland. 25-C-6
A/G. R/80605 F/Sgt W.A.Sparrow Killed Bergen-op-Zoom, Holland. 25-C-9

432 Squadron 6 Group Wellington HZ518 QO/A
Pilot. R/135156 F/Sgt J.J.C.Mercier Missing, Runnymede Memorial 185
Nav. J/22212 F/O J.R.G.Gingras Killed Bergen, Holland. 2-C-26
B/A. R/158749 F/Sgt M.R.Deverell Killed Bergen-op-Zoom (Can). 8-F-2
W/OP. 1312182 Sgt M.P.Tobin Missing, Runnymede Memorial 167
A/G. R/55654 F/Sgt M.Lagace Killed The Hague, Holland. AP-4-69

Minor Operations

June 24th/25th, 1943
Four Mosquitoes set out to raid Duisburg but only two actually reached the target area and dropped 1.6 tons of bombs.

Four Stirlings from 3 Group also set out minelaying, but only two dropped their six mines at the mouth of the River Gironde. There were no losses from the Mosquito operations, but one Stirling from 15 Squadron ditched 15 miles off Orfordness on its return from minelaying. Six of the crew were rescued, the seventh crew member, the bomb aimer, 742176 Sergeant T. Martin, had already baled out over the French coast was captured and spent the rest of the war as a prisoner.

Gelsenkirchen

June 25th/26th, 1943

Gelsenkirchen, a town in the middle of the Ruhr, was the target for a large force of 473 aircraft, made up of 214 Lancasters, 134 Halifaxes, 73 Stirlings, 40 Wellingtons and 12 Mosquitoes from 8 Group, Pathfinders. This nightly show of strength by Bomber Command reflects the superb work put in by the ground staff who maintained such a high rate of serviceable aircraft every night despite the engine trouble and airframe damage sustained by many bombers on their nightly attacks on the Fatherland.

Gelsenkirchen was noted for its oil refineries and although it had not received the full attention of a complete raid for a long time, it had been hit by bombs when neighbouring towns had been attacked. On this night there was 3/10ths cloud over the North Sea thickening to 10/10ths from the Dutch coast to the Ruhr, where cloud tops were 8,000 to 10,000 feet. The initial *Oboe* Mosquitoes found the target aiming point completely cloud covered and although some marking took place, four of the nine *Oboe* Mosquitoes had unserviceable sets and were unable to continue marking. The other three Mosquitoes were not *Oboe* equipped and carried only nine 500 pound bombs as their load. Only minor damage was done to the town, more bombs falling on other Ruhr towns than Gelsenkirchen. Still a high rate of losses continued, 30 aircraft failing to return to their bases with 118 aircrew killed, 50 missing and 36 becoming prisoners. Because of the afterglow in the northern sky, aircraft operated in almost daylight conditions. The glow from the ground fires reflected on the cloud covered target also made the bombers more easily spotted by the night fighters. The loss rate was 6.3% and it was getting dangerously near to the point that continued losses of this size were far too high a price to pay for the damage that was being caused to the German industry and also any effect it would have on the morale of the German people.

Gunner Fails to Bale Out

A returning Lancaster, W4830 from 61 Squadron, had a port outer engine catch fire on its return flight in the vicinity of

Sheringham and, as the plane was at 3,000 feet, the pilot ordered a bale out. All the crew baled out safely except for some unexplicable reason the mid upper gunner, 1816030 Sergeant K. Lloyd failed to do so and was killed when the aircraft crashed near Spalding, Lincolnshire.

Last Trip of a Tour

The attack on Gelsenkirchen was to be the 30th and last of their first tour of operations for Warrant Officer Peter Stead and his crew, who were flying a Wellington from 196 Squadron. Obviously the crew's nerves were taut on this their final trip, all hoping that they would make it back to base. This is shown in the pilot's first hand account of the operation.

"The weather was expected to be bad over the target, but over this country the weather was broken cloud, quite high, about 6,000 feet. We took off at dusk and climbed up to the bottom of the cloud level and setting course up through it headed off towards Germany. We crossed Holland over 10/10ths cloud and onward into Germany. The cloud showed no sign of breaking up and Jerry was not disposed to shoot at us so we had a quiet run in. The cloud still remained quite thick, so we stayed high above it. We could see quite a few fires beneath it, each indicating a success to enemy fighters. Soon the *Flak* began to rise in the Ruhr, barrage stuff, heavy, very intense *Flak*.

"PFF put down several flares, but they were not very helpful at first. However they had the job weighed up by the time we got there and we soon had the position of the target as we turned in. By this time the barrage was really terrific, shells were bursting in a corridor area from 14,000 to 23,000 feet about half a mile either side of the target and about eight miles long. A tremendous and highly concentrated barrage, it surpassed anything I had ever seen before. Below there was nothing to see except cloud, with fires and bomb bursts shining through.

"As soon as the bombs had gone we turned tightly to starboard and ran for home. The *Flak* remained terrific, but we were lucky enough to come through unscathed. On the way home I spotted an aircraft in front. It was no more than a speck, but I mentioned it to the crew. No sooner had I done so than it turned sharply to port and climbed up very rapidly on to our port beam. I kept up a running commentary and as he came towards us I turned towards him climbing steeply. He passed underneath and I identified him as a Lancaster, no doubt he thought we were a twin engined German fighter. Two friends, each evading the other, in case we might be the enemy. Just a pointer to the constant vigilance and precautions that had to be taken when any aircraft was sighted. The remainder of the trip was quiet and we had no excitement and landed at base about dawn. We were all glad to take the opportunity of standing down and getting some rest."

Casualties June 25th/26th, 1943. Target Gelsenkirchen

100 Squadron 1 Group Lancaster ED988 HW/J
Pilot. A/415174 F/Sgt L.J.Naile Missing Runnymede Memorial. 193
Nav. 1387214 Sgt R.W.Mepstead Killed Amsterdam, Holland. CG 69-B-19
B/A. 132095 F/O C.P.Reynolds Missing, Runnymede Memorial 129
W/OP. 1126212 Sgt J.Dillon Missing, Runnymede Memorial 147
F/E. 1005899 Sgt C.Connah Missing, Runnymede Memorial 145
A/G. 650926 Sgt L.Bennett Killed Amsterdam, Holland. CG 69-B-19
A/G. NZ/416016 Sgt L.G.Porritt Killed Amsterdam, Holland. CG 69-B-19

101 Squadron 1 Group Lancaster ED373 SR/K
Aircraft attacked by night fighter off Dutch coast.
B/A. baled out first and his 'chute blown back over land. Bodies of remaining crew washed ashore at Zandvoort, Holland.
Pilot. A/405803 F/Sgt I.W.Banks Killed Amsterdam, Holland. CG 69-B-18
Nav. 1218772 Sgt H.J.Toze Killed Amsterdam, Holland. CG 69-B-18
B/A. 658112 F/Sgt T.G.Brook PoW. Stalag 357, Kopernikus. 374
W/OP. 1037458 Sgt H.W.Snowdon Killed Amsterdam, Holland. CG 69-B-18
F/E. 1297129 Sgt N.S.Mould Killed Amsterdam, Holland. CG 69-B-18
A/G. 1607031 Sgt G.V.Branson Killed Amsterdam, Holland. CG 69-B-18
A/G. 1317561 Sgt R.Pugh Missing, Runnymede Memorial 162

101 Squadron 1 Group Lancaster LM318 SR/Y
Pilot. 778764 F/Sgt G.Hay Killed Reichswald Forest, Germany. 3-E-15
Nav. 1558645 Sgt F.Macleay Killed Reichswald Forest, Germany. 3-E-14
B/A. A/409241 F/Sgt H.K.Smith Killed Reichswald Forest, Germany. 3-E-13
W/OP. 1386189 Sgt B.L.Scott Killed Reichswald Forest, Germany. 3-E-17
F/E. 521148 Sgt W.A.Bush Killed Reichswald Forest, Germany. 3-E-16
A/G. A/416674 F/Sgt F.L.I.Hill Killed Reichswald Forest, Germany. 3-E-12
A/G. 1038740 Sgt T.D.Millns Killed Reichswald Forest, Germany. 3-E-11

103 Squadron 1 Group Lancaster ED528 PM/
Pilot. A/411886 F/O A.E.Egan PoW. Stalag Luft 3, Sagan. 42781
Nav. A/412501 P/O S.B.Elliott Killed Reichswald Forest, Germany. 3-F-2
B/A. A/412467 W/O W.Miller PoW. Stalag 357, Kopernikus. 413
W/OP. 1187561 Sgt J.Brown Killed Reichswald Forest, Germany. 3-F-3
F/E. 569265 W/O J.S.Johnston PoW. Stalag 357, Kopernikus. 179
A/G. 1352833 Sgt H.A.Horrell Killed Reichswald Forest, Germany. 3-E-18
A/G. 1431391 Sgt C.A.Britton Killed Reichswald Forest, Germany. 3-F-1

103 Squadron 1 Group Lancaster W4901 PM/
Shot down over Holland
Pilot. J/8221 F/Lt A.H.Languille PoW. Stalag Luft 4, Sagan. 1777
Nav. 138338 F/lt C.E.L.Grant PoW. Stalag Luft 3, Sagan. 1693
B/A. 136894 F/Lt C.B.Reynolds PoW. Stalag Luft 3, Sagan. 1821

W/OP. 127968 F/Lt D.Towers PoW. Stalag Luft 3, Sagan. 1729
F/E. 1383322 Sgt R.L.Hollywood Killed Naarlemmermeer(Hoofddorp). I-3
A/G. 1454465 F/Sgt G.J.Wallis PoW. Stalag 357, Kopernikus. 360
A/G. C/16683 Sgt J.H.Addison Killed Amsterdam, Holland. CG 69-C-8
Died in hospital 30/6/43.

166 Squadron 1 Group Wellington HF589 AS/W
Pilot. A/415108 W/O M.J.Arthur PoW. Stalag 357, Kopernikus. 292
Nav. 1389163 F/Sgt L.A.Butterworth PoW. Stalag Luft 6, Heydekrug. 300
B/A. 1431774 Sgt J.Bailey Killed Utrecht(Soestbergen), Holland. JG 12D-1-7
W/OP. 1132242 Sgt J.Orr Killed Utrecht(Soestbergen), Holland. 12D-1-8
A/G. 15007792 Sgt S.Gaskin Killed Utrecht(Soestbergen). JG 12D-1-7

166 Squadron 1 Group Wellington HE346 AS/M
Pilot. A/402531 W/O C.A.Matthews Missing, Runnymede Memorial 191
Nav. 1499905 Sgt A.Mortimer Missing, Runnymede Memorial 159
B/A. 1517817 Sgt J.P.Priestley Missing, Runnymede Memorial 162
W/OP. 1383146 Sgt N.R.Parry Missing, Runnymede Memorial 161
A/G. 1620011 Sgt T.Ball Missing, Runnymede Memorial 141

15 Squadron 3 Group Stirling BK699 LS/E
Aircraft crashed near Harlingen, Holland.
Pilot. 134746 F/O M.A.Chapman Missing, Runnymede Memorial 123
Nav. 50509 P/O R.F.Pavely DFM Missing, Runnymede Memorial 133
B/A. 131966 F/O A.Woodward Missing, Runnymede Memorial 130
W/OP. 1023509 Sgt J.Condron Missing, Runnymede Memorial 145
F/E. 1212244 Sgt T.E.Warbey Missing, Runnymede Memorial 168
A/G. 954610 Sgt A.K.Smith Missing, Runnymede Memorial 165
A/G. R/142311 F/Sgt D.E.Campbell Killed Bergen-op-Zoom, Holland. E-4-12

75 Squadron 3 Group Stirling BK768 AA/L
Aircraft crashed in the Zuider Zee, Holland.
Pilot. NZ/416155 F/O W.R.Perrott Killed Amsterdam, Holland. 69-B-15
Nav. NZ/42317 F/Sgt G.D.Thompson Killed Harderwijk, Holland. 2-12
B/A. NZ/416188 F/Sgt C.J.Whitelaw Missing, Runnymede Memorial 199
W/OP. 1314162 Sgt C.C.Mould Missing, Runnymede Memorial 153
F/E. 611325 Sgt W.Hilditch Missing, Runnymede Memorial 153
A/G. 1809432 Sgt G.W.Colyer Killed Amsterdam, Holland. CG 69-B-14
A/G. 1302829 Sgt H.Squire Killed Amsterdam, Holland. CG 69-B-14

90 Squadron 3 Group Stirling EH900 WP/Y
Aircraft crashed at Legden, Germany.
Pilot. A/415087 F/Lt F.C.McKenzie Killed Reichswald Forest. 23-E-18
Nav. 130588 F/O A.V.I.Cook Killed Reichswald Forest, Germany. 23-E-5
B/A. 1385752 Sgt W.E.Walter Killed Reichswald Forest. CG 23-E-6/8
W/OP. 1333017 Sgt C.D.H.Campbell Killed Reichswald Forest. CG 23-E-6/8
F/E. 995196 Sgt E.Wilson Killed Reichswald Forest, Germany. 23-E-10
A/G. 984107 Sgt J.C.Davidson Killed Reichswald Forest, Germany. 23-E-9
A/G. 1397129 Sgt F.W.Ealden Killed Reichswald Forest. CG 23-E-6/8

214 Squadron 3 Group Stirling BK767 BU/L
Aircraft shot down Ijerlo, Holland at 01.23 hours (26/6/43).Victim of Oblt.
Meister, 1/NJG4.
Pilot. 148123 P/O B.H.Church Killed Aalten(Berkenhove), Holland. 591-1
Nav. 1600154 F/Sgt E.G.Taylor PoW. Stalag Luft 6, Heydekrug. 261
B/A. 133803 F/O J.F.Tritton Killed Aalten(Berkenhove), Holland. 590-2
W/OP. NZ/411092 F/Lt K.A.Neilson PoW. Stalag Luft 3, Sagan. 1661
F/E. 1476771 Sgt W.H.Thompson Killed Aalten(Berkenhove), Holland. 589-1
A/G. 1384993 Sgt W.T.Davis Killed Aalten(Berkenhove), Holland. 590-1
A/G. 1048627 Sgt F.Mills Killed Aalten(Berkenhove), Holland. 589-2

218 Squadron 3 Group Stirling EH898 HA/G
Aircraft shot down at Lichtenvoorde, Holland at 01.17 hours (26/6/43).
Pilot. 146707 P/O E.C.Hughes Killed Lichtenvoorde, Holland. 17
Nav. NZ/391573 F/Lt A.E.Boulton PoW. Stalag Luft 4, Sagan. 1768
B/A. 1575014 Sgt C.R.Jacques Killed Lichtenvoorde, Holland. 9
W/OP. 1332167 Sgt B.A.W.Jennings Killed Lichtenvoorde, Holland. 8
F/E. 624385 Sgt D.O'Sullivan Killed Lichtenvoorde, Holland. 7
A/G. 553608 Sgt E.Towe Killed Lichtenvoorde, Holland. 16
A/G. 1809479 Sgt H.S.Pagett Killed Lichtenvoorde, Holland. 18

218 Squadron 3 Group Stirling EF430 HA/W
Aircraft crashed after fighter attack at Empe, Holland.
Pilot. 70456 S/Ldr D.M.Maw PoW. Stalag Luft 3, Sagan. 1702
Nav. 1549392 F/Sgt R.Baker PoW. Stalag 357, Kopernikus. 294
B/A. 1354375 F/Sgt J.S.Foster PoW. Stalag 357, Kopernikus. 315
W/OP. 1134385 Sgt K.W.Durnell PoW. Stalag Luft 6, Heydekrug. 309
F/E. 1480774 F/Sgt D.Holden PoW. Stalag Luft 3, Sagan. 321
A/G. 1301802 F/Sgt W.I.Thomas PoW. Stalag 357, Kopernikus. 356
A/G. 1087881 F/Sgt S.C.Cummins PoW. Stalag 357, Kopernikus. 305

115 Squadron 3 Group Lancaster DS666 KO/
Pilot. 1336977 Sgt R.Rashley Missing Runnymede Memorial. 162
Nav. 1049563 Sgt C.M.Sibbald Missing, Runnymede Memorial 164
B/A. J/20818 F/O G.Davidson Missing, Runnymede Memorial 173
W/OP. 1131924 Sgt A.Corns Missing, Runnymede Memorial 146
F/E. 1425681 Sgt F.L.Beeston Missing, Runnymede Memorial 142
A/G. 1581444 Sgt E.Green Missing, Runnymede Memorial 151
A/G. 1577574 Sgt A.Worsdale Missing, Runnymede Memorial 170

51 Squadron 4 Group Halifax JD261 MH/
Pilot. 127541 F/O D.H.V.Davis Killed Eindhoven(Woensel), Holland. EE-19
Nav. 1578211 Sgt A.H.Hawes Killed Eindhoven(Woensel), Holland. EE-23
B/A. 133877 F/O D.G.Howse Killed Eindhoven(Woensel), Holland. EE-20
W/OP. 1242821 Sgt A.D.McFarlane Killed Eindhoven(Woensel). EE-24
F/E. 108845 Sgt J.Roberts Killed Eindhoven(Woensel), Holland. EE-33
A/G. 1602476 Sgt A.W.Fairmaner Killed Eindhoven(Woensel), Holland. EE-21
A/G. R/91595 F/Sgt K.R.Wood Killed Groesbeek (Can), Holland. XV-F-5

51 Squadron 4 Group Halifax HR731 MH/
Pilot. 1390052 Sgt A.Osmond Missing, Runnymede Memorial 160
Nav. 1576506 Sgt G.C.Mortimer Killed Harderwijk, Holland. 2-6
B/A. 1585435 Sgt T.G.Barton Missing, Runnymede Memorial 141
W/OP. 1027741 Sgt P.Blundell Killed Amersfoort, Holland. 13-8-167
F/E. 573249 Sgt B.Huggan Missing, Runnymede Memorial 154
A/G. 1300003 Sgt J.Emerson Missing, Runnymede Memorial 148
A/G. 1358058 Sgt J.Rorison Killed Harderwijk, Holland. 2-10

78 Squadron 4 Group Halifax JB928 EY/
Pilot. 111418 F/O M.H.Oddie Killed Bergen, Holland. 2-C-5
Nav. 1576732 F/Sgt A.J.Hutchinson PoW. Stalag 357, Kopernikus. 323
B/A. 135109 F/O P.Daulby PoW. Stalag Luft 3, Sagan. 1695
W/OP. 1310249 F/Sgt A.J.Guy PoW. Repatriated 6/2/45.
F/E. 646303 F/Sgt A.D.Gillespie PoW. Stalag Luft 6, Heydekrug. 317
A/G. R/140303 F/Sgt T.L.Roberts PoW. Stalag 357, Kopernikus. 348
A/G. 140905 F/O D.W.Lusty PoW. Stalag Luft 3, Sagan. 1701

102 Squadron 4 Group Halifax JB843 DY/F
Pilot. 1431059 Sgt K.Gore Killed Bergen, Holland. CG 2-C-1/3
Nav. 1388972 Sgt J.H.Wright Killed Bergen, Holland. 2-C-4
B/A. 1233573 Sgt T.E.Judd Killed Bergen-op-Zoom, Holland. 30-A-6
W/OP. 1079029 Sgt F.H.Mitchell Killed Bergen, Holland. CG 2-C-1/3
F/E. 1119079 Sgt T.M.Sugden Killed Bergen, Holland. CG 2-C-1/3
A/G. 1337461 Sgt J.B.Foskett Killed Bergen, Holland. CG 2-C-1/3
A/G. 1575135 Sgt D.A.H.Gough Killed Bergen-op-Zoom, Holland 28-B-10

196 Squadron 4 Group Wellington HE412 ZO/
Pilot. 143667 P/O N.B.Smythe Killed Amersfoort, Holland. 13-8-153
Nav. 143577 P/O G.W.Pollard Killed Amersfoort, Holland. 13-8-157
B/A. A/413469 F/Sgt J.T.Winterborn Killed Amersfoort, Holland. 13-8-154
W/OP. 1379768 Sgt G.H.W.Peach Killed Amersfoort, Holland. 13-8-156
A/G. 1318256 Sgt R.A.Barlow Killed Amersfoort, Holland. 13-8-155

466 Squadron 4 Group Wellington HF544 HD/
Pilot. A/406634 F/Sgt A.B.R.Airy Missing, Runnymede Memorial 191
Nav. A/414960 F/O W.E.Riley Killed Amsterdam, Holland. 69-B-16
B/A. 1255176 Sgt G.C.Green Missing, Runnymede Memorial 151
W/OP. 1266030 Sgt T.M.Atkinson Missing, Runnymede Memorial 141
A/G. 1435337 Sgt G.R.Johnson Missing, Runnymede Memorial 155

9 Squadron 5 Group Lancaster ED831 WS/H
Pilot. NZ/40230 S/Ldr A.M.Hobbs DFC Killed Amsterdam. CG 69-B-15
Nav. 106546 F/O J.H.Sams Killed Amsterdam, Holland. CG 69-B-15
B/A. 148375 P/O K.G.Mott Killed Schellinkhout(Hoorn), Holland. 26
W/OP. 1200299 Sgt E.C.Bishop Killed Amsterdam, Holland. CG 69-B-15
F/E. 573844 Sgt F.W.Sanderson Killed Amsterdam, Holland. CG 69-B-17
A/G. 1575968 Sgt W.C.Rowlands Killed Amsterdam, Holland. CG 69-B-17
A/G. 1575183 F/Sgt W.Slater Killed Amersfoort, Holland. 13-8-165

44 Squadron 5 Group Lancaster R5740 KM/O
Pilot. 145476 P/O D.M.Sharp Missing, Runnymede Memorial 133
Nav. 1316701 Sgt R.J.Dash Missing, Runnymede Memorial 147
B/A. 1385570 Sgt R.H.W.Thompson Missing, Runnymede Memorial 167
W/OP. 1271185 Sgt N.H.Morris Missing, Runnymede Memorial 159
F/E. 530175 F/Sgt T.Johnstone Missing, Runnymede Memorial 137
A/G. 1399828 Sgt E.R.H.Griffiths Missing, Runnymede Memorial 151
A/G. 1455580 Sgt K.W.Langstaffe Missing, Runnymede Memorial 156

57 Squadron 5 Group Lancaster ED943 DX/
Pilot. 118486 F/Lt D.H.Reid DFC Killed Texel, Holland. CG K-5-102
2/Pilot. 132788 F/O W.J.Wheeler Killed Texel, Holland. CG K-5-102
Nav. 149139 P/O J.C.Evans DFM Killed Texel, Holland. CG K-5-102
B/A. 656180 Sgt A.M.Sandars Killed Texel, Holland. CG K-5-102
W/OP. 155842 P/O J.W.Palmer Killed Texel, Holland. CG K-5-102
F/E. 630317 Sgt G.S.Hodges Killed Texel, Holland. CG K-5-102
A/G. 1586042 Sgt D.Telfer Killed Texel, Holland. CG K-5-102
A/G. 124740 F/O E.H.Patrick Killed Texel, Holland. CG K-5-102

106 Squadron 5 Group Lancaster W4367 ZN/
Pilot. 143377 P/O P.J.Page Killed Harderwijk, Holland. 2-16
Nav. 1032799 F/Sgt J.Hancock Killed Harderwijk, Holland. 2-18
B/A. 995660 W/O J.Macmillan PoW. Stalag 344, Lamsdorf. 25636
W/OP. 990571 F/Sgt J.Pass DFM Killed Harderwijk, Holland. 2-8
F/E. 576427 Sgt E.E.Tyler Killed Harderwijk, Holland. 2-7
A/G. 1317697 F/Sgt H.E.Davies Missing, Runnymede Memorial 136
A/G. 1251211 F/Sgt J.C.Welch Missing, Runnymede Memorial 139

106 Squadron 5 Group Lancaster R5572 ZN/
Aircraft crashed at Baak, Holland at 03.45 hours (26/6/43).
Pilot. J/17733 F/O E.W.Davidson PoW. Stalag 4B, Muhlberg (Elbe). 222404
Nav. 1316732 Sgt J.G.V.Williams Killed Steenderen(Zutphen), Holland. JG 9
B/A. 1323595 Sgt E.W.H.Browne Killed Steenderen(Zutphen), Holland. JG 9
W/OP. 1212997 Sgt J.A.Francis Killed Steenderen(Zutphen), Holland. 6
F/E. 1134233 Sgt S.Cowgill Killed Steenderen(Zutphen), Holland. 8
A/G. R/128162 W/O L.F.Sparling Killed Steenderen(Zutphen), Holland. 5
A/G. R/153561 F/Sgt C.H.Sinclair Killed Steenderen(Zutphen), Holland. 7

106 Squadron 5 Group Lancaster W4256 ZN/V
Aircraft shot down at Hippolytushoef, Wieringen Holland
Pilot. 1318824 Sgt S.G.White Killed Hippolytushoef. CG C-12-370/372
Nav. 147316 P/O G.W.B.Enright Killed Hippolytushoe). CG C-12-370/372
B/A. J/22535 F/O J.E.D.Craigie Killed Hippolytushoef. CG C-12-370/372
W/OP. 1294682 Sgt J.F.Bates Killed Hippolytushoef.. CG C-12-370/372
F/E. 14477856 Sgt E.C.Crook Killed Hippolytushoef. CG C-12-370/372
A/G. 1531330 Sgt E.T.Harding Killed Hippolytushoef, . CG C-12-370/372
A/G. A/415456 F/Sgt M.B.Watt Killed Hippolytushoef, Holland. CG C-12-367

106 Squadron 5 Group Lancaster EE125 ZN/
Pilot. 36135 S/Ldr A.M.Young Missing, Runnymede Memorial 119
Nav. 146345 P/O P.E.Bevis Missing, Runnymede Memorial 130
B/A. R/141249 Sgt A.Dickison Missing, Runnymede Memorial 181
W/OP. 652146 F/Sgt C.L.Mallett DFM Missing, Runnymede Memorial 138
F/E. 1153818 Sgt J.R.Hayle Missing, Runnymede Memorial 152
A/G. 1392710 Sgt G.H.Peel Missing, Runnymede Memorial 161
A/G. 126807 F/O J.Bell DFM Missing, Runnymede Memorial 123

408 Squadron 6 Group Halifax JB858 EQ/S
Pilot. J/18184 P/O B.R.Milligan Killed Reichswald Forest. JG 12-D-1/2
2/Pilot. R/131168 F/Sgt J.F.Male Killed Reichswald Forest. 12-D-6
Nav. J/13839 F/O F.C.Culbert Killed Reichswald Forest. JG 12-D-1/2
B/A. 155095 P/O J.H.McNess Killed Reichswald Forest, Germany. 12-D-7
W/OP. J/18207 P/O D.Aiken Killed Reichswald Forest, Germany. 12-D-3
F/E. 52814 F/O R.B.Wright PoW. Stalag Luft 3, Sagan. 290
A/G. J/18041 P/O J.D.B.Hunter Killed Reichswald Forest, Germany. 12-D-3
A/G. J/18289 P/O G.N.Acton Killed Reichswald Forest, Germany. 12-D-4

427 Squadron 6 Group Halifax DK190 ZL/
Crashed Gorssel, Holland at 01.13 hours (26/6/43). Victim of Hptm.Dormann,
III/NJG1.
Pilot. R/98109 W/O F.J.Higgins DFM Killed Gorssel, Zutphen, Holland. A-10
Nav. J/13072 F/O G.T.Matynia Killed Gorssel, Zutphen, Holland. A-6
B/A. R/102677 W/O A.K.Young Killed Gorssel, Zutphen, Holland. A-8
W/OP. R/103778 W/O R.R.Stickney Killed Gorssel, Zutphen, Holland. A-9
F/E. 1345736 Sgt F.J.Hunter Killed Gorssel, Zutphen, Holland. A-11
A/G. R/119924 W/O W.Kashamar Killed Gorssel, Zutphen, Holland. A-12
A/G. J/18454 P/O H.G.Froude Killed Gorssel, Zutphen, Holland. A-7

427 Squadron 6 Group Halifax DK180 ZL/
Pilot. J/17025 P/O G.A.Gagnon Killed Bergen, Holland. 2-D-28
Nav. J/13420 F/O R.J.Frost PoW. Stalag Luft 4, Sagan. 1697
B/A. R/114415 W/O C.R.Page PoW. Stalag 357, Kopernikus. 343
W/OP. R/108426 Sgt J.R.Hooley PoW. Stalag Luft 4, Sagan. 322
F/E. 623715 Sgt K.A.Shannon PoW. Stalag 357, Kopernikus. 1612
A/G. R/104179 Sgt A.A.McKinnon PoW. Stalag 357, Kopernikus. 329
A/G. R/116469 W/O C.R.Munson PoW. Stalag Luft 7, Bankau. 43239

61 Squadron 5 Group Lancaster W4830 QR/
Aircraft crashed near Spalding, Lincolnshire after operations.
Pilot. 1434780 Sgt D.H.Pearce Baled out.
Nav. 846474 Sgt H.W.Beasley Baled out.
B/A. 133829 Sgt R.C.Everitt Baled out.
W/OP. 102404 Sgt J.Robson Baled out.
F/E. 778204 Sgt A.B.Woodvine Baled out.
A/G. 1816030 Sgt K.Lloyd Killed Aberdare, Wales. X-7-16
A/G. 1407780 Sgt J. Penswick Baled out.

Minor Operations

June 25th/26th, 1943

A mixed force of 33 aircraft - 24 Wellingtons, seven Stirlings and two Lancasters went to two mining areas, the Frisians and around the French Ports. One Lancaster from 115 Squadron did not return from these missions. There were no survivors.

Casualties June 25th/26th, 1943. Minelaying

115 Squadron 3 Group Lancaster DS663 KO/
Pilot. 1317727 Sgt F.A.Whitehead Killed Nantes(Pont-du-Cens). CG L-C-26
Nav. 1321791 Sgt P.E.Glover Killed Nantes(Pont-du-Cens). CG L-C-26
B/A. 131560 F/O F.Parry Killed Nantes(Pont-du-Cens), France. CG L-C-26
W/OP. 1387194 Sgt E.R.Richardson Killed Nantes(Pont-du-Cens). CG L-C-26
F/E. 1454385 Sgt L.F.Price Killed Nantes(Pont-du-Cens), France. CG L-C-26
A/G. 1177976 Sgt E.G.Baker Killed Nantes(Pont-du-Cens), France. CG L-C-26
A/G. 1551754 Sgt W.M.McGowan Killed Nantes(Pont-du-Cens). CG L-C-26

June 26th/27th, 1943

16 Wellingtons, eight each from 4 and 6 Groups, went minelaying around Lorient and Brest. One 432 Squadron Wellington, HF568, failed to return. No trace of the crew was found. Mosquitoes also continued with their nuisance raids when four went to Hamburg and three went to Duisburg droppimg a total 5.4 tons of bombs without losses.

Casualties June 26th/27th, 1943. Minelaying

432 Squadron 6 Group Wellington HF568 QO/Y
Pilot. R/95448 W/O W.W.Horn Missing, Runnymede Memorial 179
Nav. R/120845 F/Sgt F.H.Schull Missing, Runnymede Memorial 185
B/A. R/146302 F/Sgt G.D.W.Tate Missing, Runnymede Memorial 185
W/OP. R/104824 W/O L.J.Davidson Missing, Runnymede Memorial 179
A/G. R/92054 Sgt L.G.McKenzie Missing, Runnymede Memorial 186

June 27th/28th, 1943

Minelaying was continued at La Pallice and the River Gironde, when 30 aircraft, consisting of 15 Lancasters from 1 Group and 15 Stirlings from 3 Group laid 149 mines. One Lancaster, ED377 captained by J/20349 Flying Officer F. S. Buck from 101 Squadron, failed to return. Apparently about one mile east of

Cande, France, the skipper had given a bale out order and after two crew members, the wireless operator 0076266 Sergeant K. B. Coulter and the bomb aimer 1534177 Sergeant J. N. Sparkes, had baled out the aircraft exploded in mid air. Sergeant Coulter was captured and died later from burns. Sergeant Sparkes was luckier for he received support from an underground organisation, which helped him evade capture and he returned to the UK.

Casualties June 27th/28th, 1943. Minelaying

101 Squadron 1 Group Lancaster ED377 SR/Q
Aircraft exploded after bomb aimer and wireless operator baled out and crashed 1 mile east of Cande, France.
Pilot. J/20349 F/O F.S.Buck Killed Nantes(Pont-du-Cens), France. L-C-10
Nav. 1321959 Sgt G.W.Fuller Killed Nantes(Pont-du-Cens), France. L-C-9
B/A. 1534177 Sgt J.N.Sparkes Evaded capture
W/OP. 1076266 Sgt K.B.Coulter Killed Nantes(Pont-du-Cens), France. L-C-12
F/E. 1411197 Sgt K.D.S.Mordecai Killed Nantes(Pont-du-Cens), France. L-C-8
A/G. 1206892 Sgt H.T.Clarke Killed Nantes(Pont-du-Cens), France. L-C-7
A/G. 1803966 Sgt K.W.Gadson Killed Nantes(Pont-du-Cens), France. L-C-11 .

Cologne

June 28th/29th, 1943
After a gap of two nights without a major attack Bomber Command was back on the warpath to the Ruhr, this time the target being the city of Cologne on the banks of the River Rhine. 608 aircraft were despatched and the force was made up of 267 Lancasters, 169 Halifaxes, 85 Wellingtons, 75 Stirlings and 12 Mosquitoes. A turn back number of 74 aircraft was again high.

The meteorologists were unsure about their weather forecasts for the target area. They anticipated cloud over the area, but thought this would probably break up. This forecast necessitated the Pathfinders to have a double plan to cover this air of uncertainty, their aircraft had to carry both ground and air markers. Whether this caused the resultant problems is not clear, but five of the twelve *Oboe* Mosquitoes did not reach the target and of the remaining seven, only six were able to drop their sky markers. These went into the 10/10ths cloud where they disappeared and the backers up were not able to see them, the cloud was so thick that even the glare was not visible.

The *Oboe* Mosquitoes were very late in opening the attack, seven minutes elapsed with bombers milling around Cologne waiting for the first markers to be dropped at 01.47 hours, seven minutes after zero hour. It resembled Piccadilly Circus at a very busy rush hour and many of the bombers lost on this attack could have been the result of mid air collisions or being bombed by other aircraft.

Halifax HR837, NP/F piloted by Flight Sergeant Doug Cameron stationed at 158 Squadron Lissett, Yorkshire, was one of the lucky crews who lived to tell the tale of being bombed by a friendly aircraft. Shortly after they had released their bombs over the target, their aircraft was struck simultaneously by cannon shells from an attacking Ju88 and a 1,000 lb bomb dropped by an aircraft overhead. The bomb passed through the fuselage a few feet behind the mid upper turret, leaving a gaping hole about four feet square and a very shocked mid upper gunner who fortunately escaped physical injury. The cannon shells had ripped holes in the port wing. For his airmanship in bringing the damaged bomber safely back to base, Flight Sergeant Cameron was awarded the DFM. Such was the skill of this pilot that he later finished his tour of operations ending up as a Flight Lieutenant and also the holder of the DFC.

The poor showing by the *Oboe* Primary markers would have normally resulted in very sporadic and poor bombing, but in spite of these setbacks on this night the main force of bombers excelled themselves, for they gave Cologne its worst air raid of the war. Occasional gaps in the dense clouds enabled some crews to observe fires and explosions in the southern part of the city. There was one terrific explosion which turned the sky scarlet and lasted for some seconds. Searchights were ineffective because of the cloud, but barrage *Flak* was intense and fighters were very active. 18 flares were dropped by PFF and a total of 839.3 tons of high explosive bombs and 317,805 incendiaries rained down on Cologne. Considerable damage was caused to both industrial premises and housing and the casualty figures were exceptionally high, 4,377 people killed and 10,000 injured. It was on this occasion that the Dom (Cologne Cathedral), was damaged by high explosive bombs but fortunately without any incendiaries causing any fire damage. Some public statements circulating after the war claimed that bomber crews had been instructed to keep their bomb loads clear of the Cathedral and use it only as a reference point for bombing, but these statements were completely without foundation. 25 aircraft did not return from this operation, a 4.1% loss rate, and from their crews 133 were killed, 20 missing, 19 made prisoners and two airmen made succesful evasions.

Two Wellingtons crashed in the UK. The first from 166 Squadron, captained by Pilot Officer W. B. McGinn, had only reached the East Coast on the outward flight when both engines cut out. All the crew abandoned the bomber 3 miles north of Skegness, except for the bomb aimer, 1080547 Sergeant J. R. Whittaker, who was killed in the bale out.

The second Wellington, DK183 from 427 Squadron captained by Flight Lieutenant V. F. Ganderton, was attacked by an enemy fighter 20 miles east of Bruges, Belgium, while on its way to the target. As the bomber was very badly damaged after being raked by cannon shells, the pilot decided to jettison the bombs and return to base. A landing was found to be impossible and the crew had to bale out at Isleham, Suffolk. Two crew members suffered slight injuries. Flight Lieutenant Ganderton was promoted to a Squadron Leader and awarded an immediate DFC for his efforts and skill in bringing his very badly damaged bomber back to friendly skies where his crew could bale out in comparative safety.

Sergeant Dolby's Last Operation

Australian Flight Sergeant Bob Gates and his crew in Lancaster ED563 from 467 Squadron based at Bottesford, Lincolnshire were not flying in their normal aircraft Q-Queenie on this raid. Much to their regret it was unserviceable and their stand by aircraft brought them no luck at all, for they were among the aircrew listed as missing after the Cologne raid. There were only two survivors from the crew, the bomb aimer Sergeant H. G. Pyke and the wireless operator, Sergeant Bernard Dolby, who in 1990 lives in Peterborough, and who relates the tragic events of the crew's last operation.

*We were on our way to the target at 00.15 hours and were flying at

21,000 feet over south-west Holland when we were suddenly attacked by an enemy night fighter. Our aircraft sustained quite extensive damage. The port wing became a sheet of flame and the pilot's flying controls were all rendered useless. With still a full bomb load aboard and unable to release it, the captain had no choice but to order all the crew to make a quick exit and bale out. Things happened too quickly for any panic and I walked back to the rear hatch and spoke to the mid upper gunner, Sergeant T. W. J. Copeland, who was busy taking off his fur lined flying boots and replacing them with ordinary shoes, which he said would give him a better chance to escape once he was down on the ground. I noticed that the rear turret was swung round to the side, so I presumed that Blondie, our nickname for Sergeant Hole the rear gunner, had already baled out. It was a pitch black night and I don't remember much about going out or dropping down that 21,000 feet or even landing. The first thing I remembered was being picked up by two young girls from the branches of a tree. I learned later that they were called Trees and Lenie. They took me to a doctor's house, for I had injured my ankle, but the doctor was not at home. Like many Dutch doctors he had refused to work for the Germans and was in hiding at a nearby farmhouse, but was still treating the local inhabitants and helping Allied airmen who needed treatment and who were trying to evade capture. He normally worked in the cellar of his garage, operating often without anaesthetics.
"

Since the war this Doctor, named Harry Staperts, has related what happened to Bernard Dolby in a book he has written about his wartime experiences as a doctor in Holland, in which he writes :-

"I found my house full of excited villagers surrounding a very handsome young man, whose nationality I easily identified straight away by the penetrating aroma of an English cigarette. Five minutes later the village constable arrived to say that the Germans would soon be there. I treated the young man's foot which had been injured on landing and then even more people began to arrive. There was a festive mood, some Dutch patriots started to sing the National Anthem. Our last bottle of brandy was brought out of hiding and placed on the table. The drawback was that nobody could talk with the English airman. The conversation consisted of looking friendly at him, nodding and gently patting his shoulder. I started to recite an English poem I had to learn as punishment at school. 'Under the spreading chestnut tree -------'. To our astonishment our injured airman added, 'His hair is crisp and black and long. . . . ' Unbelievably we knew the same English poem."

Sergeant Dolby was given a hearty breakfast by the two girls and before the Germans arrived to take him away to captivity, he gave his watch and cigarette case to them rather than let the Germans have them. For the next 18 months Sergeant Dolby was moved from camp to camp as the British and Americans advanced from the west and the Russians from the east. It was while they were being moved from Stalag 357 across the River Elbe that he and two pals made an escape break, the day before RAF fighters mistakenly strafed the prisoner of war marching column, killing 70 of the men. The three escapees lived in a wood for a week before meeting up with the advancing American Army. Sergeant Dolby and his pals were soon back in Blighty and he was shortly reunited with his parents in their village bakery at Great Gidding, Bedfordshire.

After the war many efforts by Doctor Staperts to trace Sergeant Dolby, finally resulted in a wonderful reunion which took place in 1987 when Bernard and his wife were the doctor's guests at his home in Holland. The doctor's first remarks being, "How nice of you to come back after 44 years to let me see how your foot is getting on."

Sergeant Dolby's damaged Lancaster crashed at St. Oldilienburg, Holland a few miles from the German/Dutch border. How the remainder of the crew met their deaths is not known, but four of them are buried at the Jonkerbos War Cemetery, Nijmegen. The pilot's body was never found. His name is commemorated on the Runnymede Memorial for those airmen with no known grave.

Two More Evaders

There were two evaders who made it back to the UK after the Cologne operation. One was 1334644 Sergeant D. R. G. Eldridge who was attached to 51 Squadron from 1663 Heavy Conversion Unit to enable him to get battle experience. He acted as a second pilot on board Halifax HR839 captained by Pilot Officer J. P. Tay. The aircraft was attacked by an enemy fighter and set on fire. A bale out order was given at 02.00 hours and Sergeant Eldridge was the only survivor of the bomber which crashed at Mol, twenty miles north of Hasselt, Belgium. The other evader, flight engineer 1490330 Sergeant D. C. Foster, was a member of the crew in Stirling EE880 from 149 Squadron, captained by Flying Officer A. R. Porter.

Pilot Blinded by Perspex

Lancaster ED753 from 50 Squadron based at Skellingthorpe, Lincolnshire, on this Cologne raid was piloted by 22 year old Sergeant C. J. M. Wilkie who was making his 16th operation. Over Cologne on the bomb run, his aircraft was coned at 19,500 feet by a group of searchlights and while trapped in their glare the bomber attracted very heavy *Flak*. In the *Flak* bursts the large Lancaster perspex cockpit cover was shattered and the resultant splinters caught the pilot full in the face, temporarily blinding him. The same *Flak* burst also wounded the bomb aimer, Pilot Officer Hearn, and the navigator, Sergeant Heath, who in spite of his wounds which he did not report to the rest of the crew, guided the half blind pilot over the target and released the bombs.

After turning on the homeward leg, the aircraft was still under accurate heavy ack ack fire, but by now Sergeant Wilkie had managed to remove the splinters from his left eye and he was able to evade the still probing searchlights and ensuing *Flak*. Damage assessment was made and it was found that the nose of the Lancaster had been riddled with shell splinters and the crew in this section had all been wounded, Pilot Officer Hearn having three wounds in his left arm, Sergeant Heath wounded in the right shoulder and Sergeant Forts, a second navigator on the crew for this trip, was also cut about the face by the flying perspex.

Sergeant Wilkie had great difficulty in piloting his bomber back to base, but was successful in making a good landing at 03.58 hours. For his valiant efforts he was awarded the CGM, Pilot Officer Hearn the DFC and Sergeant Heath the DFM. Sergeant Wilkie was subsequently commissioned but was fated to die in action later in his tour.

Conspicuous Gallantry Medal Awarded

Another of the rarely awarded Conspicious Gallantry Medals was given on this Cologne operation. It was awarded to Sergeant

E. T. G. Hall, a mid upper gunner on 115 Squadron. He was in the crew of Lancaster DS669 captained by Sergeant Jolly. The aircraft was on the homeward flight after successfully bombing the target when at 02.42 hours. Sergeant White, the rear gunner, reported two yellow fighter flares being dropped at their own height. He then reported two single engined FW190 fighters closing in on the port quarter below. The pilot responded by going into a corkscrew evasive action and both mid upper and rear gunners opened fire when the enemy fighter was at 250 yards. One of the fighters broke away without firing and the second fighter fired a short burst of cannon and machine gun fire which went below the twisting Lancaster. The rear gunner managed to get in another return burst as the second fighter broke away and was not seen again, but the first enemy fighter then returned. It attacked from 200 yards dead astern. The bomber's gunners opened up, but simultaneously so did the FW190 pilot who sprayed the rear turret, killing the gunner, Sergeant White, and starting a fire in the rear of the fuselage. Still intent on inflicting more lethal damage the enemy fighter came in to about 50 yards. Sergeant Hall, the mid upper gunner, although now sitting above the burning fuselage kept up with the return fire and the fighter finally broke off to starboard and was last seen by the bomb aimer on fire and going down in a steep dive. Because of the intense heat and acrid smoke Sergeant Hall was forced to leave the mid upper turret, the bomber's last remaining means of defence. He then armed himself with a fire extinguisher and, helped by the wireless operator Sergeant Crowther, they both tackled the fire and eventually managed to extinguish it. Only later did they find to their horror that the rear turret had been completely shot away taking with it the body of Sergeant White.

Without an oxygen supply both airmen were now exhausted, but they managed to crawl back to their respective crew positions and plug into their normal oxygen supply. Sergeant Jolly managed to fly the badly damaged bomber back to base, where he landed without tail trim, with propellers on the port engines badly damaged by cannon fire and lacking intercom with the rest of the crew. For his outstanding bravery Sergeant

Hall was awarded the CGM and Sergeants Jolly and Crowther the DFM.

PoW Navigator Awarded the Military Cross

1332785 Flight Sergeant Stanley Kiran Gordon-Powell was the navigator in Halifax HR812, TL/F captained by 146337 Pilot Officer G. T. Beveridge, one of two aircraft lost on the Cologne operation from 35 Squadron, Pathfinder Force.

The aircraft was shot down by a fighter and crashed at Liege, Belgium with only three of the crew surviving a bale out and eventually ending up as prisoners of war after landing. Flight Sergeant Gordon-Powell took steps to evade capture and joined up with some members of an underground movement, who attempted to take him to Bordeaux. Whilst passing through Paris the party of evaders was ambushed and the Flight Sergeant was arrested by the Gestapo and sent to Stalag 4B at Muhlberg (Elbe). During his captivity which covered a period of two years, he made several attempts to escape.

On the first occasion he changed identity with Private Charles Lieper of the Durham Light Infantry in order to get out on a working party at Bitterfeld and from there it was relatively easy to walk away. He was joined on this first attempt by Flight Sergeant Simpson of 51 Squadron and a Private Pace of the SAA. In September 1943 they walked to Würzen, which is east of Liepzig, then to Delitzch, north of Liepzig. They walked by night and slept in haystacks by day. Their food consisted of Red Cross chocolate and raisins. On their fifth day of freedom they were recaptured in a small village, 5 kilometres south of Wurzen. All were taken back to the working party and each received seven days solitary confinement as punishment.

Undeterred by the lack of success, Pace and Gordon-Powell escaped again in the same way in May 1944 and followed the same route. Again they were picked up, but this time on their third day out, and they were taken back to the working party with an increased punishment of 14 days in the cooler.

His third attempt was made in August, 1944, in the company of three soldiers, Private Baron RE, Private Smurrenberg SAA and Guardsman Barclay, Scots Guards. This time Gordon-

Powell stole a key of their hut door and all walked out of their hut after the last roll call of the day. In company of Baron, Gordon-Powell went to the railway siding at Bitterfeld and stowed away on a goods train. They changed goods train at Halle and moved on via Hanover to Hamm and Dortmund. Jumping off the train near Dortmund they approached a Pole for help and he took them to a hiding place, but then he betrayed them to the Germans. They were arrested and taken back to Muhleberg, where they heard that Smurrenberg and Barclay, had been picked up on the first day at Bitterfeld Station without even boarding a train. After completing his now regular escape punishment, Gordon-Powell attempted his fourth escape on September 19th. In the company this time of Private A. M. Kuhn he again escaped from a fatigue party. He had obtained civilian clothes from some Italian workers and both escapers made their way as far as Eisterwerda, 15 kilometres from Muhleberg, before they were again captured by some German civilians and returned again to Stalag 4B for the usual solitary punishment.

Undaunted he made a fifth escape attempt on January 3rd, 1945, when again in company of Private Kuhn he left a fatigue party by walking away when the guards were not looking. This time both had put on civilian clothes under their uniform and had stocked up with chocolates and cigarettes, which they hoped to trade for food coupons. They walked as far as Neuburgdof which was only 3 kilometres from the camp and bought railway tickets to Riesa and from there travelled to Dresden and then on to Berlin. In the capital city they were stopped for questioning but successfully got away by pretending that they were French forced labour workers. They continued by train via Hamburg to Neumunster, where they managed to get shelter in a workers' canteen. Next day they continued by train to Flensburg, where they waited until nightfall before attempting to cross the Danish border. There was a severe blizzard that night and in the storm they experienced very bad luck when they bumped into a patrolling German Customs guard, who arrested them. They were returned to Stalag 4B once again and this time were told by the Germans that if they were caught attempting to escape once again they would be shot.

Even the most ardent escaper would by now have been put off not only by the German threat but with the bad luck which seemed to dog each attempt. But not Gordon-Powell. On March 21st, 1945, with the same companion who had accompanied him on his previous attempt, he again reached Berlin. Here the two escapers made contact with a Dutch doctor, who fed and hid them for two days. Both subsequently travelled by train to the Danish frontier, they crossed by wading through a swamp, which almost enveloped them and then they waded shoulder high in water across a river. They were helped at the frontier by Frank Stitz of Flensburg who was an active anti-Nazi and who had helped many German Army deserters to escape. After walking some miles into Denmark they approached a milkman who told them where to avoid the Germans who were living in about six local farms but where they would get some friendly help. The first farmer they approached gave them food and that evening moved them by bicycle to another farm 20 kilometres away. There they soon found that they were safely in the hands of a Resistance movement, and on the morning of April 17th, 1945, they were taken to a local doctor's house, then to the harbour and placed aboard a trawler which took both the escapers to Helsingborg, Sweden. Here they were met by the Danish Vice Consul who arranged for their journey to Stockholm in April, 1945.

For his determination and success in escaping Flight Sergeant Gordon Powell found on his return to the UK that he had been promoted to Warrant Officer rank and awarded the Military Cross, a rare distinction for a member of the Royal Air Force to receive.

Casualties June 28th/29th, 1943. Target Cologne

97 Squadron 8 Group Lancaster LM323 OF/U
Pilot. 86637 F/Lt F.P.Seward Killed Heverlee, Belgium. 3-A-7
Nav. 102108 F/Lt E.Sanderson Killed Heverlee, Belgium. 3-A-9
B/A. 133097 F/O E.E.Lawton Killed Heverlee, Belgium. 3-A-10
W/OP. 932945 F/Sgt K.I.Smith Killed Heverlee, Belgium. 3-A-11
F/E. 969331 Sgt B.E.Lewis Killed Heverlee, Belgium. 3-A-8
A/G. 988537 F/Sgt M.D.Horner Killed Heverlee, Belgium. 3-A-13
A/G. 1043869 Sgt A.Monaghan Killed Heverlee, Belgium. 3-A-12

35 Squadron 8 Group Halifax HR850 T/S
Pilot. J/16276 F/Lt N.Cobb DFC Killed Rheinberg, Germany 11-B-11
2/Pilot. 1816702 F/Sgt D.G.Ireland PoW. Camp not known.
Nav. 126984 F/Lt L.Whiteley PoW. Stalag Luft 3, Sagan. 1703
B/A. J/89257 P/O W.P.Trask PoW. Stalag 357, Kopernikus. 358
W/OP. 120037 F/Lt D.A.Codd PoW. Stalag Luft 3, Sagan. 1893
F/E. J/17395 F/O C.H.Bullock PoW. Stalag Luft 3, Sagan. 1692
A/G. 46796 F/Lt M.A.Sachs PoW. Stalag Luft 3, Sagan. 1706
A/G. 162523 F/O J.E.Matthews PoW. Stalag 357, Kopernikus. 333

35 Squadron 8 Group Halifax HR812 TL/F
Aircraft shot down over Liege, Belgium.
Pilot. 146337 P/O G.T.Beveridge Killed Heverlee, Belgium. 9-F-7
Nav. 1318497 Sgt H.C.Billett PoW. Stalag 357, Kopernikus. 648
B/A. 1332875 W/O S.K.Gordon-Powell MC PoW. Stalag 4B, Muhlberg(Elbe).
222596 Escaped April 17th 1945.
W/OP. 1203417 W/O R.J.Taylor PoW. Stalag 357, Kopernikus. 355
F/E. R/125005 Sgt L.E.Carey Killed Heverlee, Belgium. CG 6-D-1/20
A/G. 1494700 Sgt W.Hughes Killed Heverlee, Belgium. CG 6-D-1/20
A/G. 1322681 Sgt F.C.Compton Killed Heverlee, Belgium. CG 6-D-1/20

12 Squadron 1 Group Lancaster EE195 PH/
Pilot. 40304 S/Ldr F.J.Knight Killed Bergen-op-Zoom, Holland. 28-B-8
Nav. J/16069 F/O H.C.Treherne Killed Bevermijk, Holland. 690
B/A. 777884 F/Sgt M.P.Noble Killed Castricum, Holland. JG J-7
W/OP. 1377776 Sgt F.D.Ayerst Killed Castricum, Holland. J-4
F/E. 1387360 Sgt J.R.Boxall Missing, Runnymede Memorial 143
A/G. 621280 F/Sgt F.Birkin Missing, Runnymede Memorial 135
A/G. 1237208 Sgt E.F.Lawrence Missing, Runnymede Memorial 156

100 Squadron 1 Group Lancaster ED609 HW/O
Pilot. 1236390 W/O A.J.Thomas Killed Eindhoven(Woensel), Holland. EE-63
Nav. 1538446 Sgt M.Riley Killed Eindhoven(Woensel), Holland. EE-64
B/A. 1537404 Sgt E.W.Evans PoW. Stalag 4B, Muhlberg(Elbe). 222510
W/OP. 1080262 Sgt R.Winn Killed Eindhoven(Woensel), Holland. EE-67
F/E. 757997 Sgt H.W.G.Vickers Killed Eindhoven(Woensel), Holland. EE-68
A/G. 1315508 Sgt J.H.Davies Killed Eindhoven(Woensel), Holland. EE-65
A/G. 1412570 Sgt W.W.Hill Killed Eindhoven(Woensel), Holland. EE-66

100 Squadron 1 Group Lancaster ED362 HW/C
Aircraft shot down at Rijsoord, Holland. Victim of Hptm Hans-Dieter
Frank, 2/NJG1.
Pilot. J/14569 F/O P.J.Pascoe Killed Rotterdam, Holland. CG LL-1-47/48
Nav. 1396922 Sgt H.H.Gentle Killed Rotterdam, Holland. CG LL-1-47/48
B/A. 135657 P/O C.B.Wood Killed Rotterdam, Holland. CG LL-1-47/48
W/OP. 1118706 Sgt J.Reffin Killed Rotterdam, Holland. CG LL-1-47/48
F/E. 1489514 Sgt F.Wheeldon Killed Rotterdam, Holland. CG LL-1-47/48
A/G. R/135983 F/Sgt R.D.W.Moulton Killed Rotterdam. CG LL-1-47/48
A/G. 1303434 F/Sgt R.G.Storr PoW. Stalag 4B, Muhlberg(Elbe). 222422

300 Squadron 1 Group Wellington HZ438 BH/
Crashed at Rhode St Pierre, Belgium at 04.00 hours (29/6/43). Victim of
Lt.Schnaufer and Lt.Baro, II/NJG1.
Pilot. P/782266 F/Sgt M.Kleinshmidt Killed St Peters, Rode, Belgium.
Nav. P/1976 F/O S.Boguslawski Killed St Peters, Rode, Belgium.
B/A. P/794544 Sgt P.Mazgaj Killed St Peters, Rode, Belgium.
W/OP. P/781965 Sgt M.Cieslik Killed St Peters, Rode, Belgium.
A/G. P/793149 Sgt T.Knebloch Killed St Peters, Rode, Belgium.

149 Squadron 3 Group Stirling BK703 OJ/K
Aircraft crashed after fighter attack at Netersel, Holland.
Pilot. 126945 F/O W.R.Booker Killed Eindhoven(Woensel). CG EE-47/49
Nav. 1197641 Sgt D.W.B.Channing Killed Eindhoven(Woensel). CG EE-47/49
B/A. 1438154 Sgt C.D.Herbert Killed Eindhoven(Woensel). CG EE-47/49
W/OP. 1132427 Sgt K.Broadhurst Killed Eindhoven(Woensel). CG EE-47/49
F/E. 524705 Sgt R.Franklin Killed Eindhoven(Woensel). CG EE-47/49
A/G. 957304 Sgt A.D.Hall Killed Eindhoven(Woensel), Holland. CG EE-47/49
A/G. R/81305 F/Sgt C.V.Howden Killed Eindhoven(Woensel). CG EE-47/49

149 Squadron 3 Group Stirling EE880 OJ/O
Aircraft crashed between Teilt and Houwaart, Belgium.
Pilot. 124823 F/O A.R.Porter Missing, Runnymede Memorial 128
Nav. 656801 Sgt P.Butterworth Killed Houwaart, Belgium. CG 4/6
B/A. 422663 F/Sgt L.B.McCallum Missing, Runnymede Memorial 199
W/OP. NZ/412392 W/O I.A.Mears PoW. Stalag 357, Kopernikus. 337
F/E. 1490330 Sgt D.C.Foster Evaded capture
A/G. 1086924 Sgt A.Derbys Killed Houwaart, Belgium. CG 4/6
A/G. 1699589 Sgt B.S.Swainston Killed Houwaart, Belgium. CG 4/6

149 Squadron 3 Group Stirling BF483 OJ/C
Pilot. 1439048 Sgt R.K.Scott Missing, Runnymede Memorial 164
Nav. NZ/416150 Sgt A.B.Parton Missing, Runnymede Memorial 199
B/A. NZ/421940 F/O R.J.Peattie Missing, Runnymede Memorial 198
W/OP. NZ/41514 F/Sgt T.T.R.H.Tomoana Missing, Runnymede Memorial 199
F/E. 1163110 Sgt R.J.Cockshott Missing, Runnymede Memorial 145
A/G. 1699772 Sgt R.A.Cooper Missing, Runnymede Memorial 146
A/G. 1076330 Sgt J.Douglas Missing, Runnymede Memorial 147

15 Squadron 3 Group Stirling BK694 LS/C
Aircraft crashed at Lommel, Belgium. Victim of Hptm.Hoffman & Ofw.Hofler
4/NJG5.
Pilot. 149998 P/O J.B.Keen Killed Heverlee, Belgium. CG 6-D-1/20
Nav. 1576901 Sgt P.F.P.Venton Killed Heverlee, Belgium. CG 6-D-1/20
B/A. N/Z 413827 W/O J.Duckett PoW. Stalag 357, Kopernikus. 308
W/OP. 1383413 Sgt A.A.Walrond Killed Heverlee, Belgium. CG 6-D-1/20
F/E. 648137 Sgt G.A.Pryke Killed Heverlee, Belgium. CG 6-D-1/20
A/G. 1316302 Sgt W.G.Johnson Killed Heverlee, Belgium. CG 6-D-1/20
A/G. 1217614 Sgt D.Thomas Killed Heverlee, Belgium. CG 6-D-1/20

15 Squadron 3 Group Stirling EH888 LS/Z
Aircraft crashed at Heeschwijk, Holland.
Pilot. 149206 P/O A.F.Saunders Killed Amersfoort, Holland. 13-8-161
Nav. 958658 Sgt H.Mallen PoW. Stalag 357, Kopernikus. 330
B/A. 1333334 Sgt G.E.Matthews Killed Amersfoort, Holland. 13-8-159
W/OP. 1224414 Sgt S.J.Devereux Killed Amersfoort, Holland. 13-8-160
F/E. 993649 Sgt J.L.Garfit Killed Amersfoort, Holland. 13-8-158
A/G. 953242 Sgt F.W.Davis Killed Amersfoort, Holland. 13-8-164
A/G. 965752 Sgt F.S.Kennedy Killed Amersfoort, Holland. 13-8-163

115 Squadron 3 Group Lancaster DS669 HS/
Pilot. 1346616 Sgt W.Jolly DFM
A/G. 1308157 Sgt G.White Missing, Runnymede Memorial 169
Rear gunner missing after fighter attack.

10 Squadron 4 Group Halifax HR697 ZA/F
Pilot. A/401939 F/Sgt R.H.Geddes Killed Jonkerbos, Holland. 3-G-8
Nav. 1386316 Sgt D.Brown Killed Jonkerbos, Holland. 3-G-6
B/A. 148755 P/O R.E.Bradshaw Killed Jonkerbos, Holland. 4-G-8
W/OP. 1113359 F/Sgt C.Entwhistle Killed Jonkerbos, Holland. 4-G-2
F/E. 143801 P/O H.E.Cross Killed Jonkerbos, Holland. 3-G-7
A/G. A/411231 W/O R.Shannon PoW. Stalag 357, Kopernikus. 350
A/G. 1424526 Sgt A.W.Booth Killed Jonkerbos, Holland. 4-G-4

10 Squadron 4 Group Halifax DT783 ZA/
Pilot. 117424 F/O S.Peate Killed Eindhoven(Woensel), Holland. EE-70
Nav. R/137366 F/Sgt P.L.Rakoczy Killed Eindhoven(Woensel), Holland. EE-60
B/A. 134671 F/O H.H.Pearson Killed Eindhoven(Woensel), Holland. EE-61
W/OP. 1081675 Sgt A.Bailey Killed Eindhoven(Woensel), Holland. EE-57
F/E. 547328 Sgt H.Pape Killed Eindhoven(Woensel), Holland. EE-62
A/G. R/116318 F/Sgt H.Erikson Killed Eindhoven(Woensel), Holland. EE-59
A/G. R/90889 F/Sgt J.G.Sweeney Killed Eindhoven(Woensel), Holland. EE-58

51 Squadron 4 Group Halifax DT513 MH/
Pilot. 1332421 F/Sgt D.W.Sigournay Killed Bergen, Holland. 2-C-14
Nav. 133331 F/O F.R.Haines Missing, Runnymede Memorial 124
B/A. 1086890 Sgt M.Wood Missing, Runnymede Memorial 170
W/OP. 1333026 Sgt E.W.W.Pierce Missing, Runnymede Memorial 161
F/E. 1333800 Sgt E.Kent Missing, Runnymede Memorial 155
A/G. 1622347 Sgt S.Bonner Missing, Runnymede Memorial 143
A/G. 1308219 Sgt R.V.Boyd Missing, Runnymede Memorial 143

51 Squadron 4 Group Halifax HR839 MH/
Shot down at Mol, 20 miles north of Hasselt, Belgium.Possible victim of
II/NJG1 fighter.
Pilot. 145472 P/O J.P.Tay Killed Schoonselhoof, Belgium. IVA-A-10
2/Pilot. 1334644 Sgt D.R.G.Eldridge Evaded capture
Nav. 126884 F/O T.H.Popley PoW. Stalag Luft 3, Sagan. 1703
B/A. 1451970 Sgt A.C.Redshaw Killed Schoonselhoof, Belgium. IVA-A-9
W/OP. 52068 P/O J.L.R.Houlston DFM Killed Schoonselhoof. IVA-B-42

F/E. 653815 Sgt A.Smith Killed Schoonselhoof, Belgium. IVA-A-7
A/G. 1554168 Sgt W.C.Butler Killed Schoonselhoof, Belgium. IVA-A-6
A/G. R/92411 W/O A.E.Vidal Killed Schoonselhoof, Belgium. IVA-A-8

76 Squadron 4 Group Halifax DK137 MP/R
Aircraft crashed at Vottem, 18 kilometres north of Liege, Belgium.
Pilot. 1313333 Sgt G.C.Parritt Killed Heverlee, Belgium. 4-B-6
Nav. 1335461 F/Sgt L.Harris Killed Heverlee, Belgium. CG 6-D-1/20
B/A. 658131 Sgt B.L.Howard Killed Heverlee, Belgium. CG 6-D-1/20
W/OP. 1382654 Sgt R.E.Archer Killed Heverlee, Belgium. CG 6-D-1/20
F/E. 1039031 Sgt J.L.Burnside Killed Heverlee, Belgium. CG 6-D-1/20
A/G. 517088 Sgt C.G.L.Vallance Killed Heverlee, Belgium. CG 6-D-1/20
A/G. 1321293 Sgt R.J.Coggins Killed Heverlee, Belgium. CG 6-D-1/20

76 Squadron 4 Group Halifax DK150 MP/E
Aircraft crashed at Angermund, Germany.
Pilot. 1229472 Sgt D.Coles Killed Reichswald Forest, Germany. 6-B-14
Nav. 50039 F/O K.E.Moon Killed Reichswald Forest, Germany. 6-B-13
B/A. 50232 F/O H.W.Chester Killed Reichswald Forest, Germany. 6-B-15
W/OP. R/56096 Sgt J.C.R.James Killed Reichswald Forest, Germany. 6-B-10
F/E. 1349571 Sgt R.J.McAulay Killed Reichswald Forest, Germany. 6-B-12
A/G. 1652528 Sgt L.Glover-Price Killed Reichswald Forest, Germany. 6-B-11
A/G. 1810044 Sgt R.B.Twitchen Killed Reichswald Forest, Germany. 6-B-9

78 Squadron 4 Group Halifax JB907 EY/
Pilot. A/420055 F/Sgt P.W.J.Rendle Killed Maastricht, Belgium. 4-157
Nav. 591204 Sgt G.J.Samuel Killed Maastricht, Belgium. 4-162
B/A. 1337838 Sgt C.A.Morris Killed Maastricht, Belgium. JG 4-159/160
W/OP. 1035453 Sgt T.I.L.Dagg Killed Maastricht, Belgium. JG 4-159/160
F/E. 1146906 Sgt L.Howarth Killed Maastricht, Belgium. 4-163
A/G. 1699994 Sgt F.Hill Killed Maastricht, Belgium. 4-161
A/G. R/92330 F/Sgt W.R.Townsend Killed Maastricht, Belgium. 4-158

431 Squadron 4 Group Wellington HE443 SE/O
Pilot. 1042441 F/Sgt J.Parker Killed Rheinberg, Germany. CG 7-B-19-23
Nav. 1319315 Sgt G.Hacker Killed Rheinberg, Germany. CG 7-B-19/23
B/A. 124708 F/O C.H.Ashworth Killed Rheinberg, Germany. CG 7-B-19/23
W/OP. 1268645 Sgt R.H.Willshire Killed Rheinberg, Germany. CG 7-B-19/23
A/G. 1312800 Sgt D.P.Kelly Killed Rheinberg, Germany. CG 7-B-19/23

44 Squadron 5 Group Lancaster ED307 KM/
Pilot. 1334066 Sgt C.V.L.R.Hulbert Killed Eindhoven(Woensel). EE-52
Nav. 657255 Sgt J.A.Sykes Killed Eindhoven(Woensel), Holland. CG EE-54/56
B/A. 1438888 Sgt A.Tooth Killed Eindhoven(Woensel), Holland. EE-50
W/OP. 1379595 Sgt T.R.Jones Killed Eindhoven(Woensel). CG EE-54/56
F/E. 1581747 Sgt D.M.Lewis Killed Eindhoven(Woensel), Holland. EE-53
A/G. 756167 Sgt G.A.Denney Killed Eindhoven(Woensel), Holland. EE-51
A/G. A/425298 F/Sgt P.J.Galligan Killed Eindhoven(Woensel). CG EE-54/56

619 Squadron 5 Group Lancaster ED979 PG/
Pilot. 1246721 F/Sgt T.P.Murphy Killed Eindhoven(Woensel), Holland. EE-45
Nav. 134213 F/O E.Harper Killed Eindhoven(Woensel), Holland. EE-42
B/A. 131976 F/O A.Mackay Killed Eindhoven(Woensel), Holland. EE-40
W/OP. 1330344 Sgt N.E.Rivers Killed Eindhoven(Woensel), Holland. EE-43
F/E. 531481 Sgt J.Adsetts Killed Eindhoven(Woensel), Holland. EE-39
A/G. R/64856 F/Sgt J.H.W.Walker Killed Groesbeek (Can), Holland. XV-F-4
A/G. 614065 Sgt R.A.Grace Killed Eindhoven(Woensel), Holland. EE-41

207 Squadron 5 Group Lancaster ED569 EM/B
Pilot. J/12826 F/O P.C.D.Russell Killed Wognum, Hoorn, Holland. CG 13-A
Nav. 132145 F/O F.E.Fielding Killed Wognum, Hoorn, Holland. CG 13-A
B/A. 1315873 Sgt A.W.Richardson Killed Wognum, Hoorn, Holland. CG 13-A
W/OP. 1081067 Sgt D.Scragg Killed Wognum, Hoorn, Holland. CG 13-A
F/E. 536785 Sgt V.H.J.Watkins Killed Wognum, Hoorn, Holland. CG 13-A
A/G. 1174531 Sgt W.W.R.Cook Killed Wognum, Hoorn, Holland. CG 13-A
A/G. 1586374 Sgt J.T.Lloyd Killed Wognum, Hoorn, Holland. CG 13-A

467 Squadron 5 Group Lancaster ED363 PO/
Aircraft shot down over Vlodrop, Holland by Me 109 fighter.
Pilot. A/415132 F/Sgt R.I.Gates Missing, Runnymede Memorial 192
Nav. 655855 Sgt H.H.Mooney Killed Jonkerbos, Holland. 16-A-4
B/A. 1314734 W/O H.G.Pike PoW. Stalag 357, Kopernikus. 520
W/OP. 1213545 W/O B.H.Dolby PoW. Stalag Luft 6, Heydekrug. 306
F/E. 1456974 Sgt G.R.Cayless Killed Jonkerbos, Holland. 16-A-2
A/G. R/129552 W/O T.W.J.Copeland Killed Jonkerbos, Holland. 16-A-3
A/G. 1337529 Sgt J.G.Hole Killed Jonkerbos, Holland. 16-A-1

419 Squadron 6 Group Halifax JD215 VR/
Pilot. C/14078 F/O H.W.Fowler AFM Killed Mierlo, Holland. VII-B-1
Nav. J/14770 F/O W.B.Mayes Killed Groesbeek(Can), Holland. XV-F-2
B/A. J/21038 F/O D.R.Agnew Killed Groesbeek(Can), Holland. XV-F-3
W/OP. J/5901 F/Lt A.C.Raine Killed Eindhoven(Woensel). JG EE-74/75
F/E. 1368890 Sgt J.E.Dickson Killed Eindhoven(Woensel). JG EE-74/75
A/G. R/113091 F/Sgt W.G.Otterholme Killed Groesbeek(Can). XVI-B-15
A/G. R/104231 F/Sgt W.A.Hood Killed Eindhoven(Woensel), Holland. EE-36

166 Squadron 1 Group Wellington HE922 AS/
Aircraft crashed north of Skegness, Lincolnshire on way to operations to
Cologne. Bomb aimer released 'chute prematurely.
Pilot. 128888 P/O W.B.McGinn Baled out.
Nav. 658149 Sgt R.Hadley Baled out.
B/A. 1080547 Sgt J.R.Whittaker Killed Widnes. 50-1885
W/OP. 1131177 Sgt G.I.Turnbull Baled out.
A/G. 1311513 Sgt R.Henshaw Baled out.

427 Squadron 6 Group Halifax EB148 ZL/
Aircraft crashed at Isleham, Suffolk after operations to Cologne.
Pilot. J/10133 F/Lt V.F.Ganderton Baled out.
Nav. J/133272 P/O E.F.Soeder Baled out.

B/A. 1530231 Sgt K.Hignett Baled out.
W/OP. 1269696 Sgt F.J.Thompson Baled out.
F/E. 1261283 Sgt J.Morrison Baled out.
A/G. R/97038 Sgt F.B.Carleton Baled out.
A/G. R/106513 F/Sgt W.Newcombe Baled out.

Nuisance Raid

June 28th/29th, 1943
Four Mosquitoes were over Hamburg on the same evening, when
they visually identified their aiming point, the densely builtup
area north of the Docks, where 3.1 tons of HE were dropped
without suffering any loss.

Final Operation for June

June 29th/30th, 1943
16 Wellingtons, eight each from 1 and 4 Groups, were
despatched for minelaying around Lorient and St Nazaire.
Thirty mines were laid and one of the Wellingtons, HF481,
captained by Flight Sergeant G. S. Colless from 466 Squadron,
failed to return. No trace of the crew was ever found.

Casualties June 29th/30th, 1943. Minelaying

466 Squadron 4 Group Wellington HF481 HD/
Pilot. A/413826 F/Sgt G.S.Colless Missing, Runnymede Memorial 192
Nav. NZ/39307 F/Sgt R.T.Smit Missing, Runnymede Memorial 199
B/A. A/401503 Sgt E.O.Gregory Missing, Runnymede Memorial 195
W/OP. A/420152 Sgt B.K.Conroy Missing, Runnymede Memorial 192
A/G. A/413555 F/Sgt D.A.Dunn Missing, Runnymede Memorial 192

July 1943
The End of the Battle

Three nights stand down were given to many of the battle weary bomber crews, although minor operations still took place, the first on the night of July 1st/2nd, when 12 Lancasters went minelaying to the Frisians without suffering any loss.

July 2nd/3rd, 1943

32 Wellingtons laden with mines set off to two minelaying areas, the Frisians and around the Brittany ports. Mosquito aircraft still harassed the Ruhr towns. Three aircraft dropped bombs on Cologne and two bombed Duisburg again without suffering any loss.

Cologne

July 3rd/4th, 1943

Main force and Pathfinder crews heard their Station Commanders announce at briefing that Cologne was again to be the target. 653 aircraft left their bases, 293 Lancasters, 182 Halifaxes, 89 Wellingtons, 76 Stirlings and 13 Mosquitoes droned across the summer evening skies of England, all struggling with their heavy bomb loads to gain altitude before reaching the enemy coast and their first taste of the German defences. Little did they realise that on this raid they would encounter a new form of defence over the target itself, for this was the opening night of the single engined fighter *Wilde Sau* (Wild Boar) technique.

The aiming point for this Cologne raid was on the eastern bank of the River Rhine, where most of the industrial plants were situated. This was accurately marked by the *Oboe* Mosquitoes and continually supported throughout the period of the raid by the Pathfinder backers up. The main force carried out a successful attack although many crews encountered fighters over the target area and 12 bombers were claimed shot down by them. This number was disputed by the *Flak* defences who claimed the bombers as their victories. Crews who returned after encountering these single engined fighters had much doubt cast on their sightings and claims when reporting to the station intelligence officers at debriefing.

At Binbrook, the home base for 460 Squadron, there was a serious mishap before the planes took off on this Cologne raid. In the early part of the evening two aircraft which were being bombed up caught fire and were completely destroyed. As a result of this three other aircraft were damaged. For the space of half an hour there was much concern as the aircraft involved carried 4,000 lb bombs, although fortunately some were not fused. After several terrific explosions which caused considerable damage, obliterating several huts in the vicinity and smashing hangar windows, the fires were extinguished but an area of about 500 square yards was littered with pieces of aircraft. Luckily no one was hurt, although several of the ground crew were in the first aircraft when it caught fire and all had to make a run for it. With the usual press on spirit the squadron managed to get 17 of their aircraft airborne for Cologne.

Damaged Halifax Makes it Back

Halifax NA179, LQ/B Beer, from 405 RCAF Squadron, captained by 1339011 Sergeant Al Phillips based at Gransden Lodge, was a PFF backer up on this raid. It was one of the aircraft which encountered an Me109 on its bomb run to the target. In spite of the rear gunner Sergeant Lloyd Kohnke's warning to the pilot to dive to port, the fighter caught the bomber with a hail of fire. Luckily because of the immediate response by the pilot it caught only the tail end of the aircraft, but the damage was sufficient to make the huge bomber plunge into a headlong dive towards the roaring inferno below. Due to the strenuous efforts of the pilot and his flight engineer, Sergeant Bert Maclean, who were hanging on for dear life to heave back the control column, the Halifax slowly regained more or less an even keel. The rear gunner in the meantime had spotted the same fighter coming around again for a further attack and the whole crew braced themselves as the mid upper gunner, Sergeant Joe King, reported that he had a sight of the incoming fighter. The bomb aimer, Sergeant Vernon Knight, lay prone in the nose and was still endeavouring to drop his high explosive load of three

1,000lb and eight 500lb bombs which the bomber carried as well as its green target indicators. He was trying to keep the pilot on a steady bomb run, but because of the situation it was decided not to drop the green back up markers as there was no guarantee of complete accuracy which was essential for the following main force. The main bomb doors were found to be jammed and although the flight engineer tried to pump them open by hand, they would not budge an inch. One 1,000 lb bomb was hand released and fell through the doors. The rear gunner reported that he was firing his four Brownings. He must have waited very patiently for the enemy to come into his sights and amid the chattering clatter of about 800 rounds from the four Browning machine guns the rear gunner's voice came over the intercom with a report that he had hit the fighter which was breaking off its attack and diving away. Unsure whether this was a German ruse, the gunners kept open an eagle eye for its return but luckily there were no further sightings.

By now the bomber was becoming unmanageable and it was obvious that serious damage had been done to the elevators and rudders for they were not responding to the controls. The four Merlin engines were still running sweetly and there was enough fuel in the tanks to get back to base. The only way the control column could be held back was by four of the crew, Sergeant Ron Andrews the wireless operator, Sergeant Bill Mainprize the navigator, the flight engineer and the bomb aimer hanging on to a dinghy line rope that had been tied around the control column so helping the pilot in his efforts to control the bomber, which was inclined to go into a steep dive all the time. On the homeward leg the bomber was unable to take any evasive action and when an assessment of the damage was made it was found that as well as rudder and elevator damage, the astro dome had been shattered, the mid upper gunner wounded and damage caused to the main fuselage. With the exception of the TIs the remaining bombs were finally hand released and jettisoned. When base was reached and priority landing instructions given, the pilot decided that an attempt to land should be made as soon as he had checked that the undercarriage was safely down. The bomber's approach was long and low with the four crew members pulling with all their strength on the control column and listening to the pilot's commands when to strengthen or when to release the tension on the rope. A landing was sucessfully carried out, but with tremendous difficulty. On inspection in the dispersal bay afterwards, a considerable amount of the tail and rudder surface had been shot away. A cannon shell had passed through the starboard wing causing internal damage to the spar and the remaining bomb doors were peppered with shell holes. The rear gunner had a remarkable escape because he received only a few cuts from pieces of metal, from the considerable damage around him. He could only claim a fighter probably shot down, because he was unable to see it hit the ground. The pilot was awarded an immediate Distinguished Flying Medal for his airmanship in bringing his bomber and crew back safely to base.

31 aircraft went missing as a result of this raid, a 4.6% loss rate. Many men were not as fortunate as Sergeant Phillips and his crew for 124 aircrew were killed. 37 missing, 35 made prisoners and four managed to evade capture.

Three Crew Killed in Fighter Attack

One of the missing bombers was Halifax JD159 from 419 RCAF Squadron, captained by Canadian Pilot Officer A. H. Bell. The navigator, Flight Sergeant A. O. Simpson, recalls that on the way to the target there had been no problems until they were well into Belgium and approaching Brussels. The hammer blows of cannon fire from a fighter disturbed the quiet talk of the crew. There was no panic and the crew did not appear to be unduly concerned at being jumped on unawares by a night fighter. Their complacency was however suddenly changed when further hammer blows heralded a second attack and then the situation changed dramatically inside the bomber. The second attack had instantly killed the flight engineer, Pilot Officer W. B. Taylor, and the pilot was mortally wounded. The navigator recalls somebody shouting in the intercom, 'Get the hell out of here - bale out,' and then another voice asking, 'Is that right Skipper, is it a bale out?' The answer from the dying skipper was, 'Yes, get the hell out of it.' Needing no second invitation the bomb aimer, Flight Sergeant R. O. Williston, and the navigator opened the front hatch and baled out quickly from an altitude of between 15,000 to 17,000 feet. The navigator, apart from badly wrenching his knee and receiving cuts from landing on a barbed wire fence at Boordmeerbeck, near Malines, was quite safe. He was quickly rounded up by a German patrol and taken to Brussels Prison before being transferred to Dulag Luft for interrogation and then spending the rest of the war as a prisoner at Stalag 357 at Kopernikus. The pilot and the second pilot, Flight Sergeant J. A. Andrews, who flew with them on this operation were killed and are buried with the flight engineer at Schoonselhoof Cemetery, Belgium. The remainder of the crew became prisoners of war in various camps in Germany.

Bomb Aimer Joins a Resistance Group

From the aircrew who did not return after this Cologne operation, some were lucky enough to evade capture, but not all of them made it back to England. One man stayed hidden in Belgium until the Allied forces liberated that country. He was Flying Officer H. Nock, a bomb aimer from Halifax JD262, captained by Sergeant J. S. Garnham. He was shot down at Rance, Belgium, at 02.40 hours on July 4th by a German pilot, Ofw. Ludwig Meister from 1/NJG4. Only one other member of the crew, the navigator, Warrant Officer A. Gibson escaped alive from the plane and he fractured his shoulder on landing and was captured.

Flying Officer Harry Nock recounts the events during his 14 months in Belgium.

"After bombing Cologne we were on our return journey when we were attacked by a German fighter and our aircraft burst into flames. Three of the crew were able to get out but one was killed as his 'chute got tangled up with one of the engines which fell off the plane. I landed near Rance in Belgium at about 02.00 hours on July 4th. My 'chute caught up in a tree and I was suspended in mid air, but after a considerable time I managed to reach the ground and later met up with Sergeant Gibson, our navigator, who had been injured in his landing, fracturing a shoulder. Some civilians who had been watching our parachute descent eventually picked us up and took us to a farmhouse nearby, where Gibson's shoulder was attended to and I was was moved on to a house in

Rance. The civilians assured me that our 'chutes had been destroyed. At the house to which I had been taken, I was made to feel very welcome being supplied with food, shelter and clothing. I was later told that the woman at the farm where I had left Gibson had telephoned the German Authorities, because she thought he needed further medical help and the Germans had arrived and taken him as a PoW. All the folk in the neighbouring countryside were in an uproar over this incident. The woman had been suspected for some time as a collaborator and her farm had been burned down some time previously by some patriots. It was said that she had taken the personal property of different airmen who had parachuted down in the farm area.

"I went back to her farm next day and questioned her, finding that she was in possession of a watch belonging to Gibson, which was an RAF issue to navigators. She was rather frightened and gave up the watch reluctantly after stating that Gibson had given it to her. This watch is now in my possession. Before I finally left this part of the country I was told that the woman was under arrest by L'Armee Blanche, pending trial for her collaboration with the Germans.

"I had to stay for one night in the woods in a small hut belonging to one of my helpers and was brought to a house in Rance on July 5th, where I remained until September. During this time for security reasons I was moved off and on to other farms as the Germans were still hunting for me. In September I moved to La Fagne, but during my stay in Rance I had contacted a Belgian, a patriot who remained with me all the time I was in Belgium.

"The two of us while in La Fagne organised a local group of patriots in a nearby wood. Fourteen Russians and one Belgian who had escaped from a German labour camp joined us. With the help of the local gendarme we were supplied with rifles, machine guns and pistols, which had been hidden since 1940. Most of them were of French or Belgian origin. We continually made raids on local organisations which co-operated with the Germans. Shortly before February 26th, 1944, we were denounced by a member of the Rexist's party, who gave away our exact location and we were attacked by about 300 Germans. Three of the Russians got slightly wounded in the skirmish, but all of us were able to get away after inflicting casualties on the Germans, who had to withdraw. The Belgian and I went to hide in a house in Rance. The next day, February 27th, the Germans, about 150 strong, mainly SS troops and Gestapo, arrived again and surrounded the area in which the Belgian and I were hiding. Four of the houses were searched, after which the German soldiers seemingly got discouraged and luckily for us did not search the fifth house in which we were hiding. During the search the Germans arrested my friend's wife and kept her prisoner for four months. They tried to get information from her, but she refused to talk.

"We realised that we had to curtail our activities for some time to come. We contacted the Russians again and dug fox holes in a wood nearby. The whole area was searched periodically, but we were never discovered. The local patriots supplied us with food and other necessities. By then we had contacted a member of the regular Armee Blanche and we were put under their command. They had told us to remain quiet and await orders for a general uprising. We remained hidden in the woods until September 1944.

*During the nights we often listened to a radio at a local farm, but here again we were denounced. On July 17th, 1944, six Rexists appeared unexpectedly and entered the house where we were sitting around the radio but we were able to get away through a rear window, the Rexists still firing at us. After we had left, the Rexists went on the rampage through the place, searching everything and causing a lot of damage. They took with them anything of value, including 15,000 francs which belonged to the 73 year old sister of the owner of the house and 8,000 francs and two 20 franc gold pieces belonging to the owner. They were practically all the wordly wealth of these people and they were left destitute. The farmer was an extremely good and fervent patriot who supplied the Armee Blanche with much food and other needs.

*On August 29th, 1944, we were told by the leader of the Armee Blanche to stand by, as the Allies were to drop paratroopers behind the German lines in Belgium. However this action never took place. On September 1st we captured a party of Germans, who were retreating from the advancing Allied armies. As we could not guard or keep prisoners we simply shot them after taking away all their equipment. On September 2nd, 1944, the Americans arrived and I contacted them and asked them what I should do with all the captured equipment. I was told to keep it and distribute it to my party of patriots to clean up pockets of local German resistance.

I made several attempts to get back to the UK, but was unsuccessful as everybody was extremely busy and did not want to be bothered with me. On September 14th, I managed to reach Florennes, where I contacted an American officer Lieutenant Colonel R. P. Carr, who kindly arranged to have me flown back to the UK.

Reports published after the war mention the Mouvement National Belge, an underground organisation which normally passed on aircrew to 'Comete', another organisation for further transportation to Gibraltar. It was this MNB which picked up Flying Officer Nock and they contacted a Belgian secret agent code named Mill, who had been dropped in Belgium in August 1941, with a wireless operator code named Millstone. They sent a signal to London (MI9) and Nock was mentioned in a message dated August 12th, 1943. A translation of the message which was in French is as follows :-

'NOCK Harry Arthur serial number 125420 Flying Officer, 51 Squadron Bomber Command, whose Halifax was shot down returning from Cologne on July 4th 1943 at 2 in the morning is in good health.'

Two of the other evaders came from Halifax JB913 of 408 Squadron. They were the pilot R/108567 Sergeant E. B. Dungey and air gunner R/124853 Sergeant A. T. Bowlby. The rest of the crew had been captured and made prisoners. The Halifax was shot down north of Diest, Belgium at 00.35 hours by a fighter piloted by a German Fighter pilot, Hauptmann Millius of II/NJG1 and was his 10th bomber victory.

The fourth evader was New Zealander 413756 Flight Sergeant R. A. Hodge, a wireless operator on Stirling BF530 from 149 Squadron, piloted by Pilot Officer G. A. Cozens DFM. The aircraft was shot down at 00.58 hours near Geetbets-Beetz, Belgium, by a German fighter pilot, Oblt. Schnaufer, of II/NJG1, it being claimed as his 19th victory. Except for the bomb aimer, Flying Officer J. J. Needham, who spent the rest of the war as a prisoner, the rest of the crew failed to bale out and were killed.

Bomb Aimer Beaten Up By Gestapo

One of the three missing Pathfinder aircraft was Halifax HR813 from 405 RCAF Squadron, captained by 135400 Flight Lieutenant R. B. Smith DFC. The bomber was on the way back from the target when it was attacked by a night fighter over Wavre, Belgium, and the aircraft became a mass of flames. The bale out order was given and all the crew successfully baled out except for the rear gunner, Pilot Officer J. Rankin, who had been killed in the fighter attack. Four of the crew managed to evade capture for some time through the help of an underground movement, but the pilot, flight engineer (Flying Officer H. A. M. Clee) and the wireless operator (Flight Lieutenant J. J. Anderson) were arrested on July 14th. Like so many aircrew before them they were betrayed by the so called 'Captain' in Brussels.

The fourth crew member, also named Anderson, was Flight Lieutenant L. M.Anderson, the bomb aimer. He was not arrested until April 1944. His post war interrogation reveals his story from the time he baled out.

"On landing I hid my flying kit and parachute, put my sweater over my battle dress and proceeded on foot towards Namur. After I had covered a short distance and because it was nearly dawn, I entered some woods, where I remained hidden for two days. On April 5th I continued on foot toward Namur which I reached the next day. I spoke to a few people along the way, but they could not understand me. I then continued on to Charleroi which I reached on April 7th. After I had gone a short way in the town I noticed that four German soldiers seemed to be following me. I finally evaded them by ducking into a doorway and hiding while they passed. I was unable to get help in Charleroi, so I set out for Chimay. On the way I took a wrong road leading to Rance, which I reached on April 11th. During all this time I had nothing to eat and I was very hungry indeed. Just outside Rance I approached a man to whom I declared myself, he took me to his home where I was given a meal and remained for two days. While I was there I was supplied with civilian clothes, maps and information on how to cross the frontier into France, which I crossed on April 13th near Forges Phillips.

"I reached a small railway town north east of Vervins, where a woman gave me some sandwiches and I then continued towards Vervins which I reached that evening. I spent the night in a wheat field on the outskirts of the town and continued through Laon, where I was given a meal by some kind people, then I carried on towards Soissons. From there I continued on foot in the direction of Paris. On the way I plucked up enough courage to go to a wayside railway staion and purchased a ticket for Paris, which I reached about noon. That evening I slept in a gravel pit on the outskirts of the city.

"The next morning I hitch hiked in a laundry van to Etampes. Here the driver bought me a ticket for Orleans, from where I continued on foot to Vierzon. Between Vierzon and Romorantin I approached a farmhouse where I was given food and I sheltered there for a week. While I was resting in the farmhouse a doctor called and attended to my badly blistered feet. He then took me to his home in Charost where I stayed for another two weeks until my feet healed. Then the doctor took me by car and train to a point about 25 miles due east of Tours, where I was handed over to the Maquis about the middle of August 1943. I remained with these Resistance fighters until late September when I went to stay with a man at La Varenne. Whilst there I met a French Count who could speak English, and who was later arrested with me. On December 24th, 1943, the Count called for me and took me to the home of his friends somewhere between Loches and Blere. From here I went to stay with a Countess in a castle near Loches. She was blind and spoke perfect English. About the middle of February, 1944, I returned to stay with my former host at La Varenne, where I stayed until April 17th, 1944, when I was captured by the Gestapo.

"On the evening of my capture I was sitting alone in the front room of the house when I noticed two cars coming down the road at a fast rate. I immediately got suspicious and ran out of the back of the house into the fields. I turned and saw a car stop on each side of the house and saw four Germans stepping out of each car. They started firing at me with revolvers, but I kept on running. One of them then opened up with a machine gun, so I had to flatten myself on the ground. I was captured immediately, searched and handcuffed. My French identity cards were taken from me and also my escape maps. As I approached the house with a revolver stuck in my back, I saw the English speaking Count seated in one of the cars with a guard, he had apparently been captured earlier in the afternoon. Just then my host and hostess arrived at the house and were immediately arrested and beaten up by the guards. I was then badly beaten outside the house and then dragged in and made to drink a glass of vinegar, before being beaten again about the head with a rubber truncheon.

"The four of us were taken to Tours, where we were put in solitary confinement. I was frequently interrogated concerning my movements and beaten up. I eventually made a fictitious story naming a different route from the one I had taken but I did not attempt to name any fictious persons. From Tours I was sent to Angers, where I remained again for 18 days in solitary confinement and interrogated many times with bad beatings. At last I was taken to Fresnes Prison in Paris, where I remained for a month, with only minor interrogations compared with my previous ones, before I was finally sent to Stalag Luft 3 at Sagan to stay until I was liberated en route to Lubeck by British Forces in May 1945."

Casualties July 3rd/4th, 1943. Target Cologne

97 Squadron 8 Group Lancaster ED917 OF/Q
Pilot. 47411 F/O L.G.Rembridge Missing, Runnymede Memorial. 129
Nav. 133704 F/O H.W.Parry Killed Rheinberg, Germany. 4-F-25
B/A. 50475 F/O W.J.Hills Missing, Runnymede Memorial 125
W/OP. 751063 W/O G.R.Cobby Missing, Runnymede Memorial 134
F/E. 517511 Sgt R.C.S.Golding Missing, Runnymede Memorial 150
A/G. 936947 Sgt F.M.Lamb Missing, Runnymede Memorial 156
A/G. 1297209 Sgt A.Jones Missing, Runnymede Memorial 155

35 Squadron 8 Group Halifax HR673 TL/B
Pilot. A/416596 F/Sgt D.H.Milne Killed Heverlee, Belgium. 5-A-1
Nav. 1385054 Sgt P.R.Lissner Killed Heverlee, Belgium. CG 6-D-1/20
B/A. 1384312 Sgt A.G.Cox Killed Heverlee, Belgium. CG 6-D-1/20
W/OP. 1129588 Sgt J.Jolly Killed Heverlee, Belgium. CG 6-D-1/20
F/E. 1045872 Sgt T.R.M.Smith Killed Heverlee, Belgium. 5-A-4
A/G. 1333462 Sgt R.A.H.Bowring Killed Heverlee, Belgium. 5-A-3
A/G. 1117841 Sgt K.Wolstencroft Killed Heverlee, Belgium. 5-A-2

405 Squadron 8 Group Halifax HR813 LQ/
Pilot. 135400 F/Lt R.B.Smith DFC PoW. Stalag Luft 3, Sagan. 2087

Nav. J/16774 F/Lt F.W.Frudd PoW. Stalag Luft 3, Sagan. 2086

B/A. J/16829 F/Lt L.M.Anderson PoW. Stalag Luft 3, Sagan. 6293

W/OP. J/17006 F/O J.I.Anderson PoW. Stalag Luft 4, Sagan. 2079

F/E. C/18157 P/O H.A.M.Clee PoW. Stalag Luft 4, Sagan. 1298

A/G. R/114997 W/O G.K.Harrison PoW. Stalag 357, Kopernikus. 395

A/G. J/17005 P/O J.Rankin Killed Heverlee, Belgium. 2-F-10

12 Squadron 1 Group Lancaster ED820 PH/A
Aircraft crashed at Ernage, near Namur, Belgium.

Pilot. J/8380 F/O A.R.Herron Killed Heverlee, Belgium. CG 2-F-7/8

Nav. 1600016 Sgt D.R.Baird Killed Heverlee, Belgium. CG 2-F-7/8

B/A. 1535229 Sgt H.Williams PoW. Stalag Luft 1, Barth Vogelsang. 1351

W/OP. 1026801 Sgt T.E.Edmundson Killed Heverlee, Belgium. CG 2-F-7/8

F/E. 627752 Sgt M.L.Green Killed Heverlee, Belgium. CG 2-F-7/8

A/G. 654128 Sgt A.L.Baseley Killed Heverlee, Belgium. 2-F-6

A/G. R/147647 F/Sgt M.E.Combres Killed Heverlee, Belgium. 2-F-9

12 Squadron 1 Group Lancaster W4958 PH/B
Pilot. 148446 P/O N.E.Hill Missing, Runnymede Memorial 132

2/Pilot. 1391687 W/O C.W.Young PoW. Stalag 357, Kopernikus. 366

Nav. 1350937 Sgt L.S.Capp Killed Rheinberg, Germany. 4-F-21

B/A. 1382323 Sgt S.Whitelock Missing, Runnymede Memorial 169

W/OP. 1127161 Sgt S.Barham Missing, Runnymede Memorial 141

F/E. 1230508 Sgt J.E.Foy Missing, Runnymede Memorial 149

A/G. 1119284 Sgt L.H.Everton Missing, Runnymede Memorial 149

A/G. R/54015 F/Sgt S.E.Eversfield Missing, Runnymede Memorial 181

103 Squadron 1 Group Lancaster W5012 PM/O
Aircraft crashed near Assesse, Belgium.

Pilot. 126832 F/O L.P.Oldham Killed Florennes, Dinant, Belgium. CG 3-35/38

Nav. 130389 F/O R.K.Lamb Killed Florennes, Dinant, Belgium. CG 3-35/38

B/A. 1231499 Sgt P.E.Wilkins Killed Florennes, Dinant, Belgium. 3-34

W/OP. 1144201 Sgt S.Foster Killed Florennes, Dinant, Belgium. CG 3-35/38

F/E. 642091 Sgt E.Betts Killed Florennes, Dinant, Belgium. CG 3-35/38

A/G. 1607348 Sgt R.H.Ingram Killed Florennes, Dinant, Belgium. 3-32

A/G. 1210564 Sgt R.W.Freeman Killed Florennes, Dinant, Belgium. 3-33

103 Squadron 1 Group Lancaster JA672 PM/
Pilot. 115108 F/O D.C.Bradshaw Missing, Runnymede Memorial 123

Nav. 1072872 Sgt R.W.Baybut Missing, Runnymede Memorial 142

B/A. 136889 F/O W.T.Shannon Missing, Runnymede Memorial 129

W/OP. 1084519 Sgt G.R.White Missing, Runnymede Memorial 169

F/E. 144215 P/O A.F.J.Perrott Missing, Runnymede Memorial 133

A/G. 139114 Sgt J.T.Vodden Missing, Runnymede Memorial 168

A/G. 1352452 Sgt A.McKechan Missing, Runnymede Memorial 158

460 Squadron 1 Group Lancaster W4844 UV/
Pilot. A/411885 P/O C.Edwards Missing, Runnymede Memorial 191
Nav. A/421093 F/O W.F.Spier Missing, Runnymede Memorial 189
B/A. A/22378 F/Sgt C.F.J.Truscott Missing, Runnymede Memorial 194
W/OP. 1074494 Sgt C.Young Missing, Runnymede Memorial 171
F/E. 1623946 Sgt A.E.Tytherleigh Missing, Runnymede Memorial 167
A/G. 1317610 Sgt W.J.Rees Missing, Runnymede Memorial 289
A/G. A/420653 F/Sgt L.J.Frazer Missing, Runnymede Memorial 192

166 Squadron 1 Group Wellington HF595 AS/Y
Pilot. 40894 S/Ldr A.A.Cookson Killed Heverlee, Belgium. 4-B-1
Nav. 1343392 F/Sgt J.C.Clark DFM Killed Heverlee, Belgium. CG 6-D-1/20
B/A. 1027850 F/Sgt W.Scarlett DFM Killed Heverlee, Belgium. 4-B-4
W/OP. 139952 P/O R.S.Rich Killed Heverlee, Belgium. 4-B-2
A/G. R/99568 W/O W.H.Pym Killed Heverlee, Belgium. 4-B-3

15 Squadron 3 Group Stirling BK648 LS/J
Aircraft crashed at Menden, Germany.
Pilot. J/17251 F/Lt L.W.Hunt Killed Rheinberg, Germany. CG 14-A-2/7
2/Pilot. 1386599 Sgt G.W.Barber Killed Rheinberg, Germany. CG 14-A-2/7
Nav. 155545 P/O H.C.Dillingham Killed Rheinberg, Germany. CG 14-A-2/7
B/A. 1389976 Sgt D.O.Humphries Killed Rheinberg, Germany. CG 14-A-2/7
W/OP. 1291689 Sgt C.l.Warrell Killed Rheinberg, Germany. CG 14-A-2/7
F/E. 574277 Sgt C.L.Chalker Killed Rheinberg, Germany. 14-A-8
A/G. 1377224 Sgt M.L.C.Criswick Killed Rheinberg, Germany. CG 14-A-2/7
A/G. 610306 Sgt S.W.Munn Killed Rheinberg, Germany. 14-A-9

90 Squadron 3 Group Stirling EH907 WP/O
Aircraft crashed at Moorsele, Belgium.
Pilot. 1333473 F/Sgt M.L.B.Morrison Killed Ghent, Belgium. 18-6-12
Nav. 1337039 Sgt A.P.McGinley Killed Ghent, Belgium. 18-6-16
B/A. 1811706 Sgt A.F.Leonard Killed Ghent, Belgium. 18-6-11
W/OP. 1125722 Sgt W.McQuire Killed Ghent, Belgium. 18-6-15
F/E. 1268317 Sgt M.Scheddle Killed Ghent, Belgium. 18-6-14
A/G. 1425265 Sgt C.Reddell Killed Ghent, Belgium. 18-6-13
A/G. 1304421 Sgt C.H.Fenton Killed Ghent, Belgium. 18-6-10

90 Squadron 3 Group Stirling BK718 WP/M
Aircraft crashed at Mehlem, Germany.
Pilot. 139424 F/Lt R.C.Platt Killed Overloon, Holland. III-A-6
Nav. 148843 F/Sgt A.Gilmour Killed Overloon, Holland. III-A-5
B/A. 1553565 Sgt R.Freeland Killed Overloon, Holland. III-A-2
W/OP. 1379617 Sgt O.Beard Killed Overloon, Holland. III-A-4
F/E. 632757 Sgt H.Murray Killed Overloon, Holland. III-A-1
A/G. 155192 Sgt G.O.Smith Killed Overloon, Holland. III-A-3
A/G. 1315147 Sgt I.H.Norris PoW. Stalag 357, Kopernikus. 341

149 Squadron 3 Group Stirling BF530 OJ/B
Crashed at 00.58 hours (4/7/43) at Geetbets/Beetz, Belgium.Victim of
Oblt.Schnaufer, II/NJG1.
Pilot. 148793 P/O G.A.Cozens DFM Killed Heverlee, Belgium. 3-A-1
2/Pilot. 1334032 Sgt R.F.Hathaway Killed Heverlee, Belgium. 3-A-2
Nav. 125567 F/O E.G.Redman DFC Killed Heverlee, Belgium. CG 6-D-1/20
B/A. J/13275 F/Lt J.J.Needham PoW. Stalag Luft 4, Sagan. 1784
W/OP. NZ/413756 F/Sgt R.A.Hodge Evaded capture
F/E. 577048 Sgt P.Hodgkinson Killed Heverlee, Belgium. 3-A-3
A/G. 637252 Sgt W.J.Williams Killed Heverlee, Belgium. 3-A-4
A/G. 149063 P/O L.W.Curtis Killed Heverlee, Belgium. CG 6-D-1/20

214 Squadron 3 Group Stirling BK717 BU/U
Aircraft crashed at Zaamslag, Holland.
Pilot. 1385945 Sgt R.E.Thallon Killed Flushing, Holland. F-19
Nav. 127471 F/O J.K.Paterson Killed Flushing, Holland. F-17
B/A. 1320541 Sgt F.Field Killed Flushing, Holland. F-18
W/OP. 1216471 Sgt G.E.Patrick Killed Flushing, Holland. F-16
F/E. 1529258 Sgt J.Sellers Killed Flushing, Holland. F-20
A/G. 1405182 Sgt P.D.White Killed Flushing, Holland. F-15
A/G. 1319590 W/O L.L.Kelley PoW. Stalag Luft 6, Heydekrug. 650

115 Squadron 3 Group Lancaster DS662 HS/
Pilot. 1239665 Sgt B.Stokes-Roberts Missing, Runnymede Memorial 166
Nav. 132034 P/O R.L.Donovan Missing, Runnymede Memorial 124
B/A. 1493760 Sgt T.Shevels PoW. Stalag 357, Kopernikus. 429
W/OP. 1319268 Sgt D.Crowsley Missing, Runnymede Memorial 146
F/E. 567872 Sgt D.Wilcox Missing, Runnymede Memorial 169
A/G. 1562966 Sgt G.Thompson Missing, Runnymede Memorial 167
A/G. 1413665 Sgt S.Finch Killed Rheinberg, Germany. 4-F-24

10 Squadron 4 Group Halifax DT784 ZA/M
Pilot. A/411593 F/Sgt A.Morley Killed Hotton, Belgium. VIII-C-4
Nav. 658633 F/Sgt R.L.Watson PoW. Stalag 357, Kopernikus. 362
B/A. 1314899 F/Sgt R.J.West PoW. Stalag 357, Kopernikus. 363
W/OP. 1324626 F/Sgt R.C.Samways PoW. Stalag Luft 7, Bankau. 678
F/E. 1150484 F/Sgt W.R.Readhead PoW. Stalag 357, Kopernikus. 347
A/G. 1186870 Sgt F.Sadler Killed Hotton, Belgium. VIII-C-5
A/G. 1065014 Sgt J.R.Barlow PoW. Stalag 357, Kopernikus. 369

51 Squadron 4 Group Halifax JD262 MH/E
Aircraft crashed 02.40 hours (4/7/43) at Rance, Belgium.Victim of Oblt Ludwig
Meister, 1/NJG4.
Pilot. 1036702 Sgt J.S.Garnham Killed Gosselies, Charleroi, Belgium. 1-46
Nav. 914683 W/O J.N.Gibson PoW. Stalag 357, Kopernikus. 118
B/A. 125420 F/O H.A.Nock Evaded capture
W/OP. 1386398 Sgt A.T.Bishop Killed Gosselies, Charleroi, Belgium. 2-4
F/E. 938121 Sgt R.F.Knight Killed Gosselies, Charleroi, Belgium. 1-48
A/G. 1671282 Sgt J.J.Costello Killed Gosselies, Charleroi, Belgium. 1-47
A/G. 1609880 Sgt R.E.Debben Killed Gosselies, Charleroi, Belgium. 1-49

102 Squadron 4 Group Halifax BB428 DY/Q
Pilot. 1187305 F/Sgt R.G.Jenkins Killed Rheinberg, Germany. 11-E-23
Nav. J/14676 F/O R.Hodgson Killed Rheinberg, Germany. 11-E-19
B/A. 1387309 Sgt A.E.Garlick Killed Rheinberg, Germany. CG 11-E-20/22
W/OP. 1212563 Sgt J.Peck Killed Rheinberg, Germany. CG 11-E-20/22
F/E. 1057140 Sgt J.Galloway PoW. Stalag Luft 1, Barth Vogelsang. 316
A/G. 1563789 Sgt W.McConnell Killed Rheinberg, Germany. CG 11-E-20/22
A/G. 626680 F/Sgt L.C.Watson PoW. Stalag Luft 1, Barth Vogelsang. 361

158 Squadron 4 Group Halifax HR734 NP/P
Aircraft crashed at St Trond, Belgium. Victim of Ofw.Kollak 7/NJG4.
Pilot. R/119661 F/Sgt C.W.Preston Killed Heverlee, Belgium. 10-D-1
Nav. 1397711 Sgt C.E.H.Carey PoW. Stalag Luft 6, Heydekrug. 382
B/A. 1335930 W/O J.Redman PoW. Camp not known
W/OP. 1192755 W/O V.G.A.Moss PoW. Stalag 357, Kopernikus. 416
F/E. 1391917 Sgt E.D.C.Mackintosh Killed Heverlee, Belgium. 10-D-4
A/G. 1801878 Sgt D.Lock Killed Heverlee, Belgium. 10-D-3
A/G. 651948 Sgt F.H.Walton Killed Heverlee, Belgium. 10-D-2

196 Squadron 4 Group Wellington HZ478 ZO/
Aircraft crashed 02.23 hours (4/7/43) at Solre-sur-Sambre, Belgium. Victim of
Hptm Wilhelm Herget, I/NJG1
Pilot. 120442 F/O E.D.Eastwood Killed Gosslies, Charleroi, Belgium. 1-40
2/Pilot. 131071 F/O J.H.Stewart Killed Gosslies, Charleroi. JG 1-44/45
Nav. 117361 F/O H.C.Wheal Killed Gosslies, Charleroi, Belgium. 1-43
B/A. 1043901 F/Sgt H.Langlands Killed Gosslies, Charleroi, Belgium. 1-42
W/OP. 1270148 Sgt A.R.Stone Killed Gosslies, Charleroi, Belgium. JG 1-44/45
A/G. 1085416 Sgt M.Dixon Killed Gosslies, Charleroi, Belgium. 1-41

196 Squadron 4 Group Wellington HE980 ZO/
Pilot. 1332441 F/Sgt P.Gee Killed Heverlee, Belgium. CG 6-D-1/20
Nav. 1316535 Sgt R.S.Naile Killed Heverlee, Belgium. 10-D-5
B/A. 1431243 Sgt A.H.Taylor Killed Heverlee, Belgium. CG 6-D-1/20
W/OP. 1027411 Sgt G.N.Downing Killed Heverlee, Belgium. CG 6-D-1/20
A/G. 1586200 Sgt A.J.Horne Killed Heverlee, Belgium. 10-D-6

431 Squadron 4 Group Wellington LN284 SE/Q
Pilot. 1337474 Sgt N.H.Apperley Killed Rheinberg, Germany. JG 3-D-7/8
Nav. J/14571 F/Lt R.C.Sutherland PoW. Stalag Luft 3, Sagan. 1728
B/A. 136396 F/O A.M.Penman Killed Rheinberg, Germany. JG 3-D-7/8
W/OP. 1381877 Sgt V.G.Trew Killed Rheinberg, Germany. 3-D-5
A/G. 1477306 Sgt G.A.Lilley Killed Rheinberg, Germany. 3-D-6

466 Squadron 4 Group Wellington HF569 HD/
Pilot. 142522 P/O J.W.Edmonds DFC Killed Heverlee, Belgium. 4-D-1 *
Nav. 146010 P/O C.Halliday Killed Heverlee, Belgium. 4-D-3
B/A. 1322755 Sgt P.V.Cook Killed Heverlee, Belgium. 4-D-2
W/OP. 142513 P/O F.H.Levi Killed Heverlee, Belgium. 4-D-4
A/G. 142835 P/O P.P.G.O'Brien Killed Heverlee, Belgium. 4-D-5
* Last Operation of the Tour.(30th)

9 Squadron 5 Group Lancaster ED689 WS/K
Pilot. 101565 F/Lt J.A.Wakeford DFC Missing, Runnymede Memorial 121
2/Pilot. 1078562 Sgt T.G.Porter Missing, Runnymede Memorial 162
Nav. J/13362 F/O J.B.Reeves Missing, Runnymede Memorial 174
B/A. R/84638 W/O G.F.Dohaney Killed Rheinberg, Germany. 4-F-23
W/OP. 1029538 Sgt A.F.Backler Killed Rheinberg, Germany. 4-F-22
F/E. 1068297 Sgt J.E.Owen Missing, Runnymede Memorial 160
A/G. 909231 Sgt H.L.Wilson Missing, Runnymede Memorial 170
A/G. 1432434 Sgt H.J.Hawkridge Missing, Runnymede Memorial 152

408 Squadron 6 Group Halifax JB796 EQ/C
Pilot. 156318 P/O J.C.M.Taylor Killed Poix-de-la-Somme, Amiens, France. E-7
Nav. J/22793 F/O A.B.Foster Killed Poix-de-la-Somme, Amiens, France. E-9
B/A. R/82956 F/Sgt R.M.Hicks Killed Poix-de-la-Somme, Amiens, France. E-8
W/OP. 1032154 Sgt T.Riley Killed Poix-de-la-Somme, Amiens, France. E-4
F/E. R/89237 Sgt A.R.Warwick Killed Poix-de-la-Somme, Amiens, France. E-5
A/G. J/18190 P/O P.E.Cote PoW. Stalag Luft 3, Sagan. 579
A/G. J/18199 P/O A.E.Kelly Killed Poix-de-la-Somme, Amiens, France. E-6

408 Squadron 6 Group Halifax JB913 EQ/F
Aircraft shot down north of Diest, Belgium at 00.35 hours (4/7/43).Victim of
Hptm Millius, II/NJG1.(10th Victory).
Pilot. R/108567 Sgt E.B.Dungey Evaded capture
Nav. 127065 F/Lt V.W.Foster PoW. Stalag Luft 3, Sagan. 1712
B/A. 128519 F/O T.Lowry PoW. Stalag Luft 3, Sagan. 1722
W/OP. 1313341 Sgt R.Evans PoW. Stalag Luft 6, Heydekrug. 313
F/E. C/87177 P/O T.N.Brown PoW. Stalag 357, Kopernikus. 299
A/G. R/124853 F/Sgt A.T.Bowlby Evaded capture
A/G. J/18183 F/O R.H.Speller PoW. Stalag Luft 3, Sagan. 352

419 Squadron 6 Group Halifax JD159 VR/Y
Aircraft crashed at Muizeno, north of Mechelen, Belgium at 01.00 hours.
Pilot. J/17340 P/O A.H.Bell Killed Schoonselohof, Belgium. IVA-A-2
2/Pilot. R/99890 F/Sgt J.A.Anderson Killed Schoonselhoof, Belgium. IVA-A-5 *
Nav. 1335324 F/Sgt A.O.Simpson PoW. Stalag Luft 6, Heydekrug. 430
B/A. R/76596 F/Sgt R.O.Williston PoW. Stalag 4B, Muhlberg(Elbe). 261494
W/OP. R/73263 W/O J.D.H.Arseneaut PoW. Stalag Luft 3, Sagan. 261413
F/E. C/18110 P/O W.B.Taylor Killed Schoonselhoof, Belgium. IVA-A-3
A/G. 543228 F/Sgt J.F.Graham PoW. Stalag Luft 6, Heydekrug. 390
A/G. R/85492 F/Sgt G.E.Aitken PoW. Stalag 357, Kopernikus. 367
* 1st operation

429 Squadron 6 Group Wellington LN296 AL/
Pilot. 85935 F/Lt R.H.Brinton Killed Bergen-op-Zoom (Can), Holland. 11-H-11
Nav. R/133344 F/Sgt J.P.Bishop Killed Bergen-op-Zoom (Can). 11-H-12
B/A. 1387043 F/Sgt P.G.Rothera Killed Bergen-op-Zoom (Can. 12-H-2
W/OP. J/9637 F/Lt F.A.Reynolds Killed Bergen-op-Zoom (Can). 11-H-10
A/G. 921967 F/Sgt E.C.Blackman Killed Bergen-op-Zoom (Can). 12-H-1

432 Squadron 6 Group Wellington LN285 QO/K
Pilot. J/17662 P/O W.H.Taylor Killed Maubeuge, France. A-14
Nav. J/22810 P/O G.R.Bousefield Killed Maubeuge, France. A-13
B/A. R/131602 F/Sgt W.E.Armstrong Killed Maubeuge, France. A-11
W/OP. 1577059 Sgt F.B.Jackson Killed Maubeuge, France. A-10
A/G. R/141441 F/Sgt D.A.Hogg Killed Maubeuge, France. A-12

432 Squadron 6 Group Wellington HZ481 QO/W
Pilot. R/96292 W/O P.K.Chambers Killed Heverlee, Belgium. 8-E-1
Nav. J/17804 P/O R.F.Moore Killed Heverlee, Belgium. 8-E-2
B/A. R/90400 W/O B.L.Owen Killed Heverlee, Belgium. 8-E-3
W/OP. R/98027 W/O L.H.A.McCormick Killed Heverlee, Belgium. 8-E-4
A/G. R/122401 W/O B.H.Garoutte Killed Heverlee, Belgium. CG 6-D-1/20

76 Squadron 4 Group Halifax DK174 MP/W
Aircraft crash landed at Hartfordbridge after operations to Cologne.
Pilot. Sgt G.C.G.Greenacre Safe.
Nav. Sgt A.S.Arneil Safe.
B/A. P/O A.Thorpe Safe.
W/OP. Sgt J.A.Henthorn Safe.
F/E. P/O A.D.Maw Safe.
A/G. P/O A.Monk Safe
A/G. Sgt L.T.Brown Wounded.

78 Squadron 4 Group Halifax JD203 EY/
Aircraft crash landed near Ashtead, Surrey after operations to Cologne.
Pilot. S/Ldr P.Bunclark Safe
Nav. 973782 Sgt J.Moore Baled out.
B/A. 1320698 Sgt R.Dixon Baled out.
W/OP. 119340 F/Lt D.Bradford Baled out.
F/E. F/Sgt E.Matthews Safe
A/G. R/94772 F/Sgt L.Mallory Baled out.
A/G. J/17653 P/O J.Castle Baled out.

432 Squadron 6 Group Wellington HE630 QO/B
Aircraft crashed into a house at Gravesend, Kent after operations to Cologne.
Pilot. R/125250 Sgt J.W.Baker Killed Brookwood, Woking. 40-I-7
Nav. P/O E.W.Bovard Seriously injured
B/A. R/133341 Sgt G.E.Lewis Killed
W/OP. 1091687 Sgt J.Holmes Killed Brookwood, Woking. 25-C-3
A/G. Sgt D.K.Ryan Safe

432 Squadron 6 Group Wellington HF493 QO/C
Aircraft crashed at Cobham, Kent after operations to Cologne.
Pilot. R/133334 Sgt R.C.Burgess Baled out (Injured)
Nav. Sgt J.B.Bell Killed
B/A. R/141458 W/O A.Dubois PoW. Stalag 357, Kopernikus. 384 (Baled out over Continent).
W/OP. 1344774 Sgt W.Calderwood Baled out (Injured)
A/G. R/162928 Sgt J.D.Mufford Baled out (Injured)

Nuisance and Minelaying Raids

July 3rd/4th, 1943
On the same night as the Cologne raid four Mosquitoes made diversionary raids on Duisburg and another four went to Hamborn without any loss. A force of 14 Stirlings also went minelaying to the Frisians, where two were shot down. There were no survivors.

Casualties July 3rd/4th, 1943. Mining (Frisians)

15 Squadron 3 Group Stirling BF579 LS/V
Pilot. 1432645 Sgt J.Hall Missing, Runnymede Memorial 152
Nav. 1459710 Sgt J.Close Missing, Runnymede Memorial 145
B/A. R/99460 F/Sgt V.Shea Missing, Runnymede Memorial 185
W/OP. 1295229 Sgt F.A.Dalton Missing, Runnymede Memorial 146
F/E. 1042163 Sgt J.Eccles Missing, Runnymede Memorial 148
A/G. 1331953 Sgt W.H.Dickinson Missing, Runnymede Memorial 157
A/G. R/180070 F/Sgt J.A.Davie Missing, Runnymede Memorial 181

214 Squadron 3 Group Stirling EE882 BU/J
Pilot. 1390997 Sgt R.G.Armsworth Missing, Runnymede Memorial 140
Nav. 1474216 Sgt F.E.Pilkington Missing, Runnymede Memorial 161
B/A. 1045726 Sgt R.Mailey Missing, Runnymede Memorial 158
W/OP. 1093765 Sgt H.A.Clark Missing, Runnymede Memorial 145
F/E. 1385391 Sgt A.L.Warren Missing, Runnymede Memorial 168
A/G. 1750577 Sgt F.W.Morrell Missing, Runnymede Memorial 159
A/G. R/181570 Sgt A.R.Dixon Missing, Runnymede Memorial 181

A Brief Respite for Bomber Crews

Many bomber crews had a four day stand down from operations, although they kept up their rigorous training flights, bombing practice and fighter affiliation exercises. Some crews however were kept busy on minor operations of minelaying and nuisance raids during this period. Minor was the term used for the number of aircraft involved and not of the type of opposition which would be encountered.

July 4th/5th, 1943
Thirteen Stirlings went minelaying in the River Gironde area, a favourite spot, to keep the number of mines well stocked up. They suffered no losses.

July 5th/6th, 1943

A mixed force of 34 bombers kept up the minelaying in the Frisians and around the French west ports, while four Mosquitoes went to Cologne and four went to Hamburg. Two aircraft were lost, Stirling EF436 from 75 Squadron, captained by NZ/40586 Flight Sergeant Ray Thomas, and Wellington HF601 of 466 Squadron captained by 26062 Wing Commander John Owen. Owen was on attachment to the squadron from 4 Group Headquarters. There were no survivors from these aircraft.

Casualties July 5th/6th, 1943. Minelaying (Frisians)

75 Squadron 3 Group Stirling EF436 AA/A
Pilot. NZ/40586 F/Sgt R.Thomas Missing, Runnymede Memorial 72
Nav. 658070 Sgt W.E.Stobbs Missing, Runnymede Memorial 166
B/A. 1321755 Sgt D.A.A.Tayler Missing, Runnymede Memorial 94
W/OP. 1262086 Sgt J.B.McLoughlin Missing, Runnymede Memorial 158
F/E. 941667 Sgt A.Lackenby Missing, Runnymede Memorial 156
A/G. A/410555 Sgt C.J.Moore Missing, Runnymede Memorial 196
A/G. 1153956 Sgt L.O.Lewington Missing, Runnymede Memorial 156

466 Squadron 4 Group Wellington HF601 HD/
Pilot. 26062 W/Cdr J.J.Owen Killed Le Conquet, Brest, France. 4 *
Nav. 119477 F/O E.H.Swain Killed Le Conquet, Brest, France. CG 1-3
B/A. 126819 F/O F.Darbyshire Missing, Runnymede Memorial 124
W/OP. J/17237 P/O A.M.Long Killed Le Conquet, Brest, France. CG 1-3
A/G. 145801 P/O J.F.Ray Killed Le Conquet, Brest, France. CG 1-3
* On attachment from 4 Group HQ, the remainder of crew came from 196 Squadron.

July 6th/7th, 1943

Thirty seven aircraft continued minelaying around the Bay of Biscay ports and again three Mosquitoes made a nuisance raid on Düsseldorf, while four Mosquitoes continued to keep the air raid sirens going for a second night at Cologne. One aircraft, Lancaster W4363 piloted by A/409649 Flight Sergeant D.I.S.Barr, was lost minelaying and the crew was never found. There were no minelaying operations on July 7th/9th, but the Mosquitoes continued their relentless air raids on cities in the Ruhr. Four of them went to Cologne for the third consecutive night and four went to Düsseldorf for its second night of air raids.

Casualties July 6th/7th, 1943. Minelaying

103 Squadron 1 Group Lancaster W4363 PM/
Pilot. A/409649 F/Sgt D.l.S.Barr Missing, Runnymede Memorial 192
Nav. 1125865 Sgt R.F.Garside Missing, Runnymede Memorial 150
B/A. 1029631 Sgt H.Gardinder Missing, Runnymede Memorial 150
W/OP. A/409550 F/Sgt G.H.Isaacs Missing, Runnymede Memorial 193
F/E. 1719973 Sgt P.Maynard Missing, Runnymede Memorial 158
A/G. 1606517 Sgt D.F.O Turner Missing, Runnymede Memorial 167
A/G. 1493771 Sgt R.Hollas Missing Runnymede Memorial. 153

Cologne

July 8th/9th, 1943

The four day stand down from major operations for bomber crews came to an end when again Cologne was the target for a Lancaster force of 282 bombers, mainly from 1 and 5 Groups, led by six Mosquitoes from 8 Group which performed the sky marking for the Lancasters. It was a very successful attack on the north western and south western areas of the city. Much damage was caused to some areas which had escaped in previous raids. 500 people were killed and a further 48,000 people were made homeless, making the staggering total of 350,000 people losing their homes as a result of the last three raids on the city. Seven Lancasters were lost, a loss rate of 2.5% and from their crews 33 were killed, seven were missing and nine made prisoner.

There was a single evader. From Lancaster W4275 of 101 Squadron captained by 141975 Pilot Officer W. G. A. Ager, the bomb aimer, 1384517 Sergeant F. B. G. Delorie, evaded capture. Of the remainder of the crew, who were all on their second tour of operations, four were killed and two made prisoners of war.

Casualtiers July 8th/9th, 1943. Target Cologne

97 Squadron 8 Group Lancaster ED923 OF/V
Pilot. 131597 F/O R.B.Palmer Killed Heverlee, Belgium. CG 9-C-4/7
Nav. 130517 F/O R.C.Datta Killed Heverlee, Belgium. CG 9-C-4/7
B/A. 1437794 Sgt W.Stephens Killed Heverlee, Belgium. 9-C-2
W/OP. 1210390 Sgt A.R.Harris Killed Heverlee, Belgium. CG 9-C-4/7
F/E. 1544099 Sgt C.V.King Killed Heverlee, Belgium. CG 9-C-4/7
A/G. 591992 Sgt D.Cameron Killed Heverlee, Belgium. 9-C-3
A/G. 1810435 Sgt D.C.H.Holding Killed Heverlee, Belgium. 9-C-1

101 Squadron 1 Group Lancaster ED697 SR/V
Fix requested at 00.45 hours - 5040N 0045E - Height 18,000 ft. Nothing further heard due to radio interference.
Pilot. A/413113 F/Lt R.C.Fleming Missing, Runnymede Memorial. 187
Nav. 1391524 Sgt F.W.A.Powell Missing, Runnymede Memorial 162
B/A. 932772 Sgt J.G.Barrett Missing, Runnymede Memorial 141
W/OP. 1085201 Sgt S.R.Conneff Missing, Runnymede Memorial 145
F/E. 1329764 Sgt A.A.Sharman Missing, Runnymede Memorial 164
A/G. 929350 Sgt D.A.Stevenson Missing, Runnymede Memorial 165
A/G. R/117549 W/O J.W.Johnson Missing, Runnymede Memorial 180

101 Squadron 1 Group Lancaster W4275 SR/C
2nd Tour of operations for crew.
Pilot. 141975 P/O W.G.A.Ager PoW. Stalag Luft 3, Sagan. 3234
Nav. 1454411 Sgt A.Griffiths Killed Marly Gomont, St.Quentin, France. 1
B/A. 1384517 Sgt F.B.G.Delorie Evaded Capture
W/OP. 1382585 Sgt S.Jenkins Killed Marly Gomont, St.Quentin, France. 4
F/E. 1716135 Sgt G.W.Lloyd Killed Marly Gomont, St.Quentin, France. 3
A/G. 140882 P/O G.C.Parker Killed Marly Gomont, St.Quentin, France. 2
A/G. 1575404 F/Sgt J.A.Borton PoW. Stalag 357, Kopernikus. 372

49 Squadron 5 Group Lancaster ED663 EA/
Crashed 02.53 hours (9/7/43) at Grobendonk, Belgium.Victim of Oblt
Schnaufer II/NJG1.
Pilot. 146972 P/O S.C.Eyles Killed Schoonselhoof, Belgium. IVA-B-49
Nav. 155994 P/O D.R.Fullager Killed Schoonselhoof, Belgium. IVA-B-48
B/A. 156554 P/O W.S.Ashworth Killed Schoonselhoof, Belgium. IVA-B-45
W/OP. 1330349 Sgt G.G.Shepherd Killed Schoonselhoof, Belgium. IVA-B-44
F/E. 920484 Sgt D.W.Neal Killed Schoonselhoof, Belgium. IVA-B-46
A/G. R/135579 F/Sgt M.Barrett Killed Schoonselhoof, Belgium. IVA-B-50
A/G. R/178430 F/Sgt R.E.Labrie Killed Schoonselhoof, Belgium. IVA-B-47

57 Squadron 5 Group Lancaster ED947 DX/G
Aircraft crashed at Evergem near Ghent, Belgium on the outward flight to
target.
Pilot. 149527 F/O H.C.Lewis PoW. Stalag Luft 6, Heydekrug. 407
Nav. 1579174 F/Sgt J.R.Twiggs PoW. Stalag 357, Kopernikus. 442
B/A. 1506934 F/Sgt W.N.Bailey PoW. Stalag 357, Kopernikus. 368
W/OP. 1330052 F/Sgt J.A.Hodgson PoW. Stalag 357, Kopernikus. 397
F/E. 1803891 F/Sgt J.S.Yeeles PoW. Stalag Luft 1, Barth Vogelsang. 451
A/G. 1560248 F/Sgt J.G.Stevenson PoW. Stalag 357, Kopernikus. 438
A/G. R/108804 W/O H.Dewar PoW. Stalag 357, Kopernikus. 385

106 Squadron 5 Group Lancaster R5573 ZN/
Pilot. R/109281 F/Sgt K.H.McLean Killed Heverlee, Belgium. CG 5-A-19/21
Nav. R/128853 Sgt D.H.McLeod Killed Heverlee, Belgium. CG 5-A-19/21
B/A. 1388470 Sgt R.W.L.Muir Killed Heverlee, Belgium. CG 5-A-19/21
W/OP. 1164248 Sgt R.C.Barrett Killed Heverlee, Belgium. 5-A-16
F/E. 616090 Sgt S.Leigh Killed Heverlee, Belgium. 5-A-15
A/G. A/412967 F/Sgt L.R.Johnson Killed Heverlee, Belgium. 5-A-17
A/G. 1388875 Sgt E.Hannell Killed Heverlee, Belgium. 5-A-18

106 Squadron 5 Group Lancaster ED720 ZN/
Crashed near Cambrai, France.
Pilot. USAAF 1st Lt E.L.Roaner Killed Grave not known.
2/Pilot. 149510 P/O G.F.Disbury Killed Cambrai 1-B-10/11
Nav. 1440585 Sgt W.Bailey Killed Cambrai(Routes-de-Solesme) 1-B-13
B/A. 1048639 W/O F.H.Smooker PoW. Stalag Luft 3, Sagan. 263424
W/OP. 1271588 Sgt J.Houghan Killed Cambrai(Routes-de-Solesmes) 1-B-10/11

F/E. 752196 Sgt E.W.J.Amor Killed Cambrai(Routes-de-Solesmes) 1-B-12
A/G. R/99456 F/Sgt J.R.Calder Killed Cambrai(Routes-de-Solesmes) 1-B-9
A/G. R/111837 F/Sgt D.A.Turner Killed Cambrai(Routes-de-Solesmes)1-B-14

Minor Operations

July 8th/9th, 1943
While the Cologne raid was in progress eight Mosquitoes went on a raid to Duisburg and a force of 46 aircraft went minelaying in the areas of Texel, Brittany and Biscay ports. One minelaying bomber failed to return from which there were no survivors.

Casualties July 8th/9th, 1943. Minelaying

166 Squadron 1 Group Wellington HF453 AS/
Pilot. NZ/416173 F/Sgt D.F.Scott Missing, Runnymede Memorial. 199
Nav. 1338184 Sgt F.H.Shaw Missing, Runnymede Memorial 164
B/A. 1578977 Sgt A.N.Taylor Missing, Runnymede Memorial 166
W/OP. 1314016 Sgt G.W.D.Dean Missing, Runnymede Memorial 147
A/G. 1233887 Sgt D.W.Ellis Missing, Runnymede Memorial 148

Gelsenkirchen

July 9th/10th, 1943
Gelsenkirchen was the target for 418 aircraft, 218 Lancasters and 190 Halifaxes led by 10 *Oboe* Mosquitoes. It was a night best forgotten by the PFF Mosquito force, for five of their aircraft had defective equipment and one of the remaining five dropped its initial sky marker 10 miles away from the aiming point. It too must have had an unserviceable *Oboe* set, but the mistake had been made and the following main force bombing was very scattered as a result. The raid could only be classed as a failure with minimal damage caused for the loss of twelve aircraft, a 2.95% loss rate with 39 aircrew killed, one missing, 27 made prisoners and six evaders. Additionally a Halifax, DK176 of 76 Squadron, crashed on landing back at its base of Holme on Spalding Moor. Fortunately all the crew survived with only minor injuries. From the six evaders, five came from Lancaster ED480 of 9 Squadron. These were the pilot, R/119731 Sergeant J. D. Duncan, navigator, 1262465 Flight Sergeant H. T. Brown, bomb aimer, 1499890 Sergeant G. Bartley, wireless operator,

1127645 Sergeant S. Hughes, and gunner R/84436 Sergeant D. B. Macmillan. The other two members of the crew, flight engineer Flight Sergeant S. Blunden and air gunner Sergeant L. Warner, were quickly captured and made prisoners. Sergeant Macmillan relates the circumstances of the loss of the plane and his subsequent evasion.

"After bombing the target our aircraft was hit by *Flak* and as we had lost a lot of petrol from our wing tanks, the skipper decided to head for France knowing we had no chance of getting back to base. The bale out order was given about 03.00 hours on 10th July near Le Cateau, France. I was the last but one to leave the aircraft.

"I came down in a large grain field about a mile south west of the town, badly spraining both ankles on landing. After hiding my flying gear under some brushwood I had to sit a while because my legs were quite numb from the shock sustained on the landing. When I could feel and move them more freely, I decided to walk in the direction of the sound of some clock chimes, thinking that the sounds came from a church, where I would try to get some help. I knew that the aircraft crashed not far away and thinking that if I walked too far I would come up against a cordon which would be drawn round it by the Germans, I decided to hide somewhere quite near.

"While passing through the outskirts of the town I heard someone whistling and scaled a low wall to get out of sight, but in so doing I made some noise and found myself covered by a rifle held by a young German soldier. There was no way I could get away. He marched me with hands above my head to a guardroom nearby, where I was searched by a Sergeant. He handed back my escape box, purse and pencil, but confiscated my cigarettes, watch, matches and a ten shilling note. He failed to find my escape compass button on my battle dress. After making me write down my name rank and number on a piece of paper he telephoned someone. I believe it was for some form of transport, but apparently none was available. After he had consulted with two other German soldiers, I was marched off in the charge of what appeared to be a German Private.

"My ankles were swollen and they were giving me a lot of pain so after walking a little way, I sat down on a low stone wall and took off my flying boots, showing the soldier my swollen ankles and started to rub them. After a time the soldier showed signs of impatience and wanted me to get my boots on and continue walking. In turning around on the wall to reach one of my boots, I accidentally knocked it over the back of the wall. Feeling over for it in the darkness, my hand came in contact with a large stone. I pretended by gestures and grunting to be in considerable pain and held out my left hand for the German to pull me up, which he did, offering me his left hand. As he did so, I pulled him towards me and then crashed the stone, which I had kept all the time in my right hand, against the left side of his head. He went down with a clatter. I tried to get the bayonet off from his fallen rifle, but failed to do so. I hurriedly searched him and recovered my watch and cigarettes, but found nothing else of much use on him. He was quite senseless, bleeding a little from his nose, so I bundled him over the side of the wall. By now I was feeling quite shaken and my only thought was to hurriedly get out of the town, although I was tempted to go back to get the German's boots. I got on to a main road, which according to my compass went south. As I walked along I had to quickly get into a ditch to avoid a German motor cyclist. I started out at 04.30 hours and by 09.00 hours had reached the village of Busigny on the Le Cateau to Cambrai road. Here I went to the local railway station to see if I could catch a train out of the place, as my ankles were not strong enough for any length of walk. At the booking office, there was an elderly French clerk. I asked him for, 'Un Paris' and put down four of the 50 Franc notes from my escape box. He gave me a ticket without any comment and handed me back two of the notes with some small change as well as a ticket. I asked, 'Train quelle heure?' and he wrote 4-30 on the back of my ticket.

"I then left the station with the intention of passing the intervening time hiding somewhere, but just outside the station I passed a farm cart with three young Frenchmen in it. They called out to me at first in French but when I did not reply, one called out in English. I declared who I was to them and they took me to a small field outside the village, before they went off to get me some food. After an hour, two of them returned, accompanied by a middle aged Frenchman, who spoke English. This man advised against providing me with civilian clothes, on the grounds that I would be shot as a spy if I was caught. I was left hiding in the field for the rest of the day but towards evening I was taken by car to Catillon, from where the rest of my journey was arranged for me by an escape organisation. During this journey I met up with a Flight Sergeant Lee from 620 Squadron and we travelled some part of the way together back to the UK."

The sixth evader was wireless operator 1106437 Sergeant A. H. Reynolds from Halifax DK229 of 428 Squadron, captained by Squadron Leader F. H. Bowden DFC and Bar. The rest of the Halifax crew, except for the pilot who was killed, were captured after their bale out and were made prisoners. Sergeant Reynolds' evasion was unusual in that he that he baled out over Germany, where the chances of getting away were very much slimmer than from occupied countries. He recalls:.

"On the return flight from the target, while I believe we were still flying over Germany, I saw the navigator, Sergeant N. Rowe, reach for his 'chute. I switched over to intercom and asked him what was wrong. He replied that an engine had caught fire and another had cut out and could not be restarted. Soon after we received a bale out order from the skipper. I followed the navigator and bomb aimer, Pilot Officer J.

Gritten, out of the plane at about 3,000 feet. I landed in the middle of a small field and immediately hid my flying gear in a haystack and put on a pair of RAF issue black shoes I had brought with me before going into the corner of the field to decide my next course of action. However, dogs started to bark as I got near the corner so I retraced my steps. I attempted to leave the field several times but each time the dogs started to bark, so I decided to wait until daybreak when I saw a small wood nearby, where I was able to sleep.

*Early next morning, 10th July, I ate some Horlicks tablets before starting to walk in a south-westerly direction. I followed the outskirts of a small copse, avoiding two farm labourers working in a field. I reached what looked like a minor road and continued along it, keeping to the hedgerow and carefully avoiding making any contacts as I was still unsure of what country I was in. After a couple of hours I came to a main road and decided to hide in a hedge until dark.

*That evening I walked up the main road, dodging into the ditch by the roadside whenever traffic or people approached. I walked for some time until I came near to a small village which I dared not pass, so I hid in some woods until daybreak. At dawn on the 11th, I walked through the woods and fed on some loganberries. It was raining heavily by now, so I entered a deserted hut and sheltered there for the rest of the day. At dusk I set off again, having filled my water bottle from puddles I found in cart tracks. As I passed through the village, one or two people passed me in the darkness, but took no notice. I contined walking until I came to a fork in the road and decided to take the road going in a south-westerly direction. There was a sign post there, with the name Asbach on it, so I guessed from that I was still somewhere in Germany. While walking on this stretch of road I passed two women and also a car which shone its headlights on me for a few seconds. Luckily neither the women nor the car stopped. Thankfully as I was unable to avoid them, there being no ditch or hedgerow to scramble into. I continued walking, passing through two small villages until I came to a wood, where I hid and slept until daybreak. On July 12th, I went through the wood, refilled my water bottle from a small stream and fed on some wild raspberries. There were some deer in the woods and I startled one which attracted the attention of a peasant who was doing some work in a clearing. I dived into some undergrowth and lay still for some time hoping that he would not discover me. My luck was in, so I decided to return to the main road again and made my way to the edge of the wood. Here I saw a man and a woman scything some grass and I was forced to retreat further back into the undergrowth. While I lay hidden I tore off my epaulettes and pulled my blue sweater over my tunic and camouflaged my water bottle with a large blue handerchief which I had taken previously from a scarecrow. At dusk on July 13th I walked for about an hour and then got off the road as it appeared to be leading to an autobahn. I went into a small copse and ate some bird's eggs and raspberries. As I was coming out of the woods I saw three children, so I was forced to hide for a while in a barn. I decided to return to the road which I now could see led over the autobahn. On the road I passed two peasant women, but they took no notice of me. I left the road when it swung left and made my way across open country. I was seen by a labourer working in a field, so I made a quick exit into a nearby wood and lay low until dark. That night I walked until I came to a town, which appeared to have some kind of smelting works. There were a large number of people about, so I thought it would be wise to wait until daylight before attempting to bypass it.

"At dawn on the following morning, July 14th, I by passed the town and as there were very few people about decided to continue my journey by day. I passed over the crest of a hill and came upon an agricultural district. Several people in the fields saw me, but took no notice. When it was dark I went into a cherry orchard I had seen and made a meal of cherries, filling my pockets with them as well.

"The next day I made my way to the top of a nearby hill from which I could see a very large river, which I guessed must have been the Rhine. I think at that time I was somewhere between Honnef and Neuwied just below Linz. I hid in some bushes until it was dark. To the right of me I could see a bridge and decided to make for it. I went through a small village and reached a footpath running along a river bank. I followed this path until I came to the bridge, which only led to a small island, so I was forced to retrace my steps and then continue towards Honnef. That night I slept under some trees and at dawn I climbed up another nearby hill to see if I could find some other bridges, but the trees obscured my view. As I was still uncertain whether the town I was near was Honnef and wanted to make sure, I thought a visit to the railway station would give me the exact position. I missed my way and found myself in the yard of some kind of metal works, where I was able to see the people working. I retraced my way and finally reached the station confirming the name of the town. I felt there was no hope of getting across the river there, so decided to make my way towards Koblenz. I could see Bonn from Honnef, but at that time I thought it was Cologne.

"That night I rested in a barley stook and at dawn on the 17th continued walking along the footpath. Along the way a German asked me for a light for his cigarette. I was under the impression at the time that he asked me in English, but I cannot be sure of this. I replied 'Nein Nein' and continued walking on and fortunately he took no further notice of me. I was a little unsettled by this encounter, so I went into a large bed of nettles and waited until darkness fell. At dusk I started out again and passed through several small towns but when it started getting light I hid in some bushes. Early on the next morning I set off walking once again and I dug up some potatoes in a field and as it was very misty, I took a chance and lit a small fire to cook them. At this point in my travels I made the decision that it was better policy to walk by day and rest by night, as I was getting very little sleep whilst hiding during the day.

"I followed a path for some distance and it eventually led me into a yard which looked like some sort of barge repair shop, with railway lines running through it. There were many people about all dressed in some type of green uniform, which was not the German army type of uniform. Finding myself unexpectedly in the yard I could not turn back, so I took a gamble and walked for a big iron gate in the opposite side wall of the yard. No one took the slightest bit of notice and I walked safely through the gate and out to the other side.

"I went through the town and swung right back on to the river side, continuing on the path once again. I even paddled in the river, as my feet were getting sore by this time. That afternoon I reached the outskirts of Neuweid and I lay down in a small park for a while. Two policemen passed but completely ignored me. After a short rest I continued through the middle of the town until I finally saw a bridge over the river, which was being used by pedestrians.

"I noticed a German officer going up some steps to the bridge, so I followed him. When he got to the top he turned right. I was about to follow him, when I noticed that he was approaching a sentry, so I immediately turned left and found myself back in a small park on the same side of the river. I sat down a while to consider my next step and decided to try my luck and risk walking past the sentry. There was a small booth near the sentry, which looked like a toll booth for pedestrains, as I had observed all the people stopping there. I walked past the booth and the sentry without being stopped and as I crossed the bridge I saw yet another sentry positioned on the opposite side. It appeared that if anyone loitered on the bridge the sentries would call out and move them on. I thought my troubles were over, but there was yet a third sentry to pass, but I needn't have worried for he took no more notice of me than the other two.

"Now safely across the river I turned right to get on to a main road to what I believed to be Miesenheim. As I was walking along a party of civilian cyclists armed with rifles passed me going in the same direction. Two of them turned round and stared at me, but fortunately did not stop. That night I slept in a small hollow near to a stream. At dawn I stole some more potatoes and went further down a narrow gully to cook them. In doing so I stumbled across a tramp, who came over to me and started to speak. I simply shrugged my shoulders and went away.

"I walked all day and slept in the open that night. The next day, July 20th, came a piece of good fortune for I was able to steal a bicycle which I saw leaning against a tree on the outskirts of a wood. I quickly cycled off on it. I kept to the main roads always trying to keep in a south-westerly direction, hoping that eventually I would reach France and get some help. On the evening of July 21st, I reached the village of Prum. By now I was feeling very weak. I was fortunate, however, in being able to steal some fresh milk from some cans standing on the side of the road, which certainly helped me along and put new spirit into me. On the further side of Prum I hid my bike and sheltered in the loft of a cowshed. The next morning I set off once more. I ate anything I could find by the wayside. After about 17kms the road forked and I had to make a decision which road to take, for I realised by now I was getting rather weak and wondered whether I would have enough strength to make it into France. I opted for the northerly fork which looked as if it might take me into Belgium. I think I had reached Lunebach and then turned in the direction of St Vith. Once on this road while I was resting, a German officer passed me on a motor cycle, he slowed down and turned round and looked at me, but again my luck was still in, for he quickly picked up speed and passed on.

"After a short while I cycled through a strange area where there were a lot of dug outs and a line of anti tank traps strung along the countryside. Fortunately the area was completely deserted and I was never challenged. From St Vith, I went on to Malmedy and then swung left for Trois Ponts. As I was riding along this road I saw a large notice with the word Wehrmacht on it and after going a short distance realised that it was meant for use of the Army only. I doubled back rather smartly and got on to what looked to be the civilian road parallel to the one I had just left. Before I reached Stavelot I saw a small collection of houses and a barrier slung across the road with an armed guard and a police dog standing beside it. It was obviously some sort of frontier post. I had no option but to go through and I knew that if I got off my cycle I would be challenged, so I mounted the pavement and rode straight through, repeating the same thing on another barrier some yards away. I was not challenged and breathed a sigh of relief once I was through. I arrived in Stavelot on July 22nd, at about 17.00 hours. By this time I was really starving and felt extremely weak. I decided to approach some likely person and ask for assistance. I rode through the town until I came to some isolated houses, where I saw an old man near one of the cottages. Seizing the opportunity when no one appeared to be about I went round to the back door to speak to him. He could not understand me at all, so I went round to the front door and just as I was about to knock, another man came out. I asked if he was Belgian and he said that he was. I then declared myself to him, showing him my identity discs and flying badge. He kept me talking outside for a while, but when the road was clear he whisked me in rather smartly, and introduced me to his wife.

"At first they were very suspicious, but at least they gave me some food. The man left the house and returned with a much younger man who questioned me closely in French, which I did not understand very well. I showed him my escape kit and he examined my clothing very carefully. I told him that I intended going on alone to Trois Ponts, after I had rested, but he said that there were a lot of Germans around there and many controls and advised me not to go. I was allowed to wash and shave and rested in this house for some considerable time, for by now my nerves had completely gone to pieces. From this point on I was fortunate in that an escape organisation took care of me and planned the rest of my journey. I arrived in Gibraltar in March, 1944."

Casualties July 9th/10th, 1943. Target Gelsenkirchen

405 Squadron 8 Group Halifax LQ/P
Pilot. J/14059 F/O B.A.St.Louis
B/A. J/20168 P/O A.C.Law Killed Cambridge. 14539
Piece of *Flak* penetrated nose of aircraft. Bomb aimer was hit in the head and killed instantly.

12 Squadron 1 Group Lancaster DV164 PH/W
Pilot. 1386466 Sgt L.F.Jeffries Killed Reichswald Forest, Germany. 3-F-11
Nav. R/58798 F/Sgt C.N.Roy Killed Reichswald Forest, Germany. 3-F-9
B/A. 135035 F/O E.B.Oldham Killed Reichswald Forest, Germany. 3-F-5
W/OP. 1313855 Sgt L.R.Vincent Killed Reichswald Forest, Germany. 3-F-8
F/E. 1221258 Sgt J.Irwin Killed Reichswald Forest, Germany. 3-F-10
A/G. 923584 Sgt C.J.P.Meyer Killed Reichswald Forest, Germany. 3-F-7
A/G. A/410586 F/Sgt G.W.Addinsall Killed Reichswald Forest, Germany. 3-F-6

77 Squadron 4 Group Halifax JD126 KN/C
Pilot. 22395 F/Sgt K.W.Morrison Killed Jonkerbos, Holland. CG 20-H-1/7
Nav. 656329 Sgt E.F.Fare Killed Jonkerbos, Holland. CG 20-H-1/7
B/A. 1551466 Sgt A Thompson Killed Jonkerbos, Holland. CG 20-H-1/7
W/OP. 1313492 Sgt G.J.Greening Killed Jonkerbos, Holland. CG 20-H-1/7
F/E. 535709 Sgt W.McElroy Killed Jonkerbos, Holland. CG 20-H-1/7
A/G. 531347 Sgt H.Williams Killed Jonkerbos, Holland. CG 20-H-1/7
A/G. 1455838 Sgt K.Foster Killed Jonkerbos, Holland. CG 20-H-1/7

102 Squadron 4 Group Halifax BB249 DY/Z
Aircraft shot down at 02.40 hours (10/7/43) near Rochefort-Eprave, Belgium.
Victim of Hpt.Geiger III/NJG1.
Pilot. A/416561 F/Sgt A.T.Fraser Killed Florennes, Dinant, Belgium. 3-39
Nav. 656840 F/Sgt T.E.Stockton PoW. Stalag 344, Lamsdorf. 222473
B/A. 1391823 Sgt R.Brand PoW. Stalag 357, Kopernikus. 373
W/OP. 1190925 F/Sgt J.G.H.Mansell Killed Florennes, Dinant, Belgium. 3-40
F/E. 622725 Sgt W.Morse Killed Florennes, Dinant, Belgium. 3-42
A/G. R/180332 F/Sgt R.F.Glass Killed Florennes, Dinant, Belgium. 3-41
A/G. 618706 F/Sgt H.Edwards PoW. Stalag 4B, Muhlberg(Elbe). 222507

158 Squadron 4 Group Halifax HR933 NP/P
Pilot. 103516 F/Lt J.C.Bridger DFC PoW. Stalag Luft 3, Sagan. 1709
Nav. 145173 P/O W.P.Banks PoW. Stalag Luft 3, Sagan. 1637
B/A. 1388852 F/Sgt B.R.Elden PoW. Stalag 4B, Muhlberg(Elbe). 83677
W/OP. 1221385 F/Sgt J.G.Scudamore PoW. Stalag 4B, Muhlberg(Elbe). 83673
F/E. 1447545 Sgt E.W.Groom PoW. Stalag 357, Kopernikus. 602
A/G. 1312795 F/Sgt R.Rake PoW. Stalag 4B, Muhlberg(Elbe). 222458
A/G. 1184154 Sgt G.E.Kendrick PoW. Repatriated Sept 1944.

9 Squadron 5 Group Lancaster ED480 WS/
Aircraft crashed at Troisvilles and crew baled out near Le Cateau, France.
Pilot. R/119731 Sgt J.D.Duncan Evaded capture.
Nav. 1262465 F/Sgt H.T.Brown Evaded capture.
B/A. 1499890 Sgt G.Bartley Evaded capture.
W/OP. 1127645 Sgt S.Hughes Evaded capture.
F/E. 913554 F/Sgt S.Blunden PoW. Stalag 357, Kopernikus. 371
A/G. 1267098 Sgt L.G.Warner PoW. Stalag 357, Kopernikus. 444
A/G. R/84436 Sgt D.B.Macmillan Evaded capture.

50 Squadron 5 Group Lancaster ED617 VN/
Crashed near Amiens, France.
Pilot. 145508 P/O R.L.Hendry Killed Poix-de-la-Somme, France. CG D-33/36
Nav. 130269 F/O K.Toner Killed Poix-de-la-Somme, France. CG D-33/36
B/A. 1348093 Sgt A.McDowall Killed Poix-de-la-Somme, France. CG D-33/36
W/OP. 1315271 Sgt A.Baldwin Killed Poix-de-la-Somme, France. CG D-33/36
F/E. 1126993 Sgt D.D.Rhynd Killed Poix-de-la-Somme, France. CG D-33/36
A/G. 1861645 Sgt P.A.Chapman Killed Poix-de-la-Somme. France. E-3
A/G. 1050802 Sgt A.S.Cousins Killed Poix-de-la-Somme, Amiens, France. E-1

61 Squadron 5 Group Lancaster W4763 QR/
Pilot. 527257 F/Sgt J.O.Ingram Killed Losser, Enschede, Holland. 1
Nav. 1433908 W/O J.D.Skinner PoW. Stalag 357, Kopernikus. 432
B/A. 130291 F/O R.E.Ryder PoW. Stalag Luft 3, Sagan. 1786
W/OP. 1036180 F/Sgt J.T.Sharp PoW. Stalag Luft 3, Sagan. 269878
F/E. 1624227 F/Sgt J.E.Wood PoW. Stalag 4B, Muhlberg(Elbe). 83714
A/G. A/420709 W/O J.R.Patching PoW. Stalag 357, Kopernikus. 419
A/G. 1318726 F/Sgt R.J.Westcott PoW. Stalag 4B, Muhlberg(Elbe). 83698

50 Squadron 5 Group Lancaster ED475 VN/
Aircraft ditched 4 miles off Hastings, Sussex, on return flight. Spotted by
Observer Corps 90 minutes after ditching and rescued by Air Sea Rescue
Launch at 05.30 hours (10/7/43).
Pilot. Sgt J.Clifford Rescued.
Nav. F/O J.A.Brett Rescued.
B/A. Sgt J.Short Rescued.
W/OP. Sgt S.J.King Rescued.
F/E. Sgt T.McKenna Rescued.
A/G. 650588 Sgt G.Batey Missing Runnymede Memorial. 142
Baled out over Channel.
A/G. Sgt K.A.Wargent Rescued.

78 Squadron 4 Group Halifax JD157 EY/
Aircraft ditched 150 yards from Seaford, Sussex, on return flight.One crew
member picked up by Air Sea Rescue launch, the remainder waded ashore.
Pilot. F/Sgt S.Liggett Rescued.
Nav. Sgt L.Trowbridge Rescued.
B/A. Sgt S.Watt Rescued.
W/OP. Sgt J.Birrell Rescued.
F/E. Sgt E.Goaling Rescued.
A/G. Sgt D.Hughes Rescued.
A/G. Sgt K.Smith Rescued.

408 Squadron 6 Group Halifax JB922 EQ/H
Pilot. J/14308 F/O T.R.Mellish Killed Reichswald Forest, Germany. 6-C-2
Nav. R/127844 W/O W.H.Plewman PoW. Stalag 357, Kopernikus. 424
B/A. 135886 F/O E.Crouch Killed Reichswald Forest, Germany. 6-C-3
W/OP. R/125451 W/O A.N.Pixley PoW. Stalag 357, Kopernikus. 423
F/E. 1545630 Sgt J.S.Pickering PoW. Stalag 357, Kopernikus. 421
A/G. R/91398 F/Sgt W.R.Prentice Killed Reichswald Forest, Germany. 6-C-1
A/G. R/157014 W/O W.G.Willis PoW. Stalag Luft 6, Heydekrug. 447

408 Squadron 6 Group Halifax JD216 EQ/P
Pilot. J/15308 F/O H.B.Lancaster Killed Reichswald Forest, Germany. 15-G-3
2/Pilot. C/20348 F/O J.W.Richardson Killed Reichswald Forest. 15-G-7
Nav. R/58757 F/Sgt J.J.Stefanchuk Killed Reichswald Forest. 15-G-6
B/A. R/92645 F/Sgt G.V.Reid Killed Reichswald Forest, Germany. 15-A-7
W/OP. 1199028 Sgt J.M.Macdonald Killed Reichswald Forest. 15-G-5
F/E. 1063523 Sgt W.R.Bryans Killed Reichswald Forest, Germany. 15-A-6
A/G. R/69464 Sgt J.H.C.McLung Killed Reichswald Forest, Germany. 15-G-2
A/G. 1316753 Sgt J.W.Sturgess Killed Reichswald Forest, Germany. 15-G-4

428 Squadron 6 Group Halifax DK229 NA/W
Pilot. 89593 S/Ldr F.H.Bowden DFC * Killed Rheinberg, Germany. 11-E-24 *
Nav. 1427177 W/O H.N.F.Rowe PoW. Stalag Luft 6, Heydekrug. 83684
B/A. 129061 F/Lt R.J.Gritten PoW. Stalag Luft 3, Sagan. 1714
W/OP. 1196437 Sgt A.H.Reynolds Evaded capture
F/E. R/68465 W/O H.McGeach PoW. Stalag 357, Kopernikus. 412
A/G. 2216252 F/Sgt J.W.N.Hurst PoW. Stalag 357, Kopernikus. 400
A/G. J/16773 F/Lt B.M.Fitzgerald PoW. Stalag Luft 4, Sagan. 1711
* At the end of a second tour of operations.

10 Squadron 4 Group Halifax HR843 ZA/
Aircraft crash landed at Staplefield, near Gatwick after operations to
Gelsenkirchen. Navigator and flight engineer baled out over target.
Pilot. Sgt J.Foulston Safe
Nav. R/124747 W/O J.G.McDonald PoW. Stalag 357, Kopernikus. 408
B/A. Sgt J.S.Moore Safe
W/OP. Sgt H.Spalding Safe
F/E. 576754 F/Sgt C.G.Street PoW. Stalag 357, Kopernikus. 440
A/G. Sgt N.A.Chappell Safe
A/G. Sgt B.B.Collings Safe

Minelaying

July 9th/10th, 1943
There were no losses from the minor operations carried out when
18 aircraft were minelaying around the Frisians and Texel and
four Mosquitoes raided Nordstern.

Turin

July 12th/13th, 1943

After these series of raids on Germany, Italy's turn came again when an all Lancaster force of 295 bombers from 1, 5 and 8 Groups made Turin their target. This was intended to hasten the surrender of Italy now that the Allied Forces were advancing north from the toe of Italy. This raid followed almost immediately after Mussolini was deposed as Italy's Dictator. Cloud over France was a welcome cover on the outward leg, but many crews experienced severe icing and sixteen aircraft turned back before they crossed the Alps. Once over, the route was clear to the target and the turning point at Lake Annecy was well marked by the Pathfinders. The main weight of the attack started south west of the aiming point and fell just short of the centre of the city, but this was by far Turin's worst attack and was carried out in clear weather conditions. Some Pathfinder crews were late in marking, but it did not matter a great deal, for over half the main force were so late that the last TIs had burnt out before they arrived. Much material damage was caused to the Fiat Works, and there was also a high cost in lives, 792 people were killed and 914 were injured. Photo reconnaissance the next day reported over 50 fires still burning in the city. Thirteen aircraft failed to return from this mission and from these missing bombers 28 aircrew were killed and 54 were missing.

The bombers' route on this operation was exceptionally long, over 1,600 miles, for it was routed on the return leg along the west coast of France, skirting the Brest Peninsula, this was due to the very few hours of darkness available on this July night.

A fighter attack sealed the fate of Lancaster DV181 from 106 Squadron. The pilot, Flying Officer C. Hayley, radioed back to base at 06.30 hours the following message, 'We are being attacked by fighter. . . . ' the sound then went indistinct before cutting off and no trace of the aircraft and its crew has ever been found.

VC Holder Lost

One of the missing aircraft, Lancaster ED331, was piloted by Squadron Leader J.D.Nettleton of 44 (Rhodesia) Squadron. Nettleton was awarded the Victoria Cross for his bravery on the low level daylight Augsburg raid on April 17th, 1942. His Lancaster went down and was lost in the English Channel after an attack by a German night fighter.

Bomber Attacks U-Boat

Another homeward bound PFF bomber, piloted by Flying Officer M. R. Chick, sighted two U-boats on the surface of the sea off St Nazaire. From his low altitude of 2,000 feet he dived down to let his gunners have a few bursts at them. The wireless operator managed to send a message back to base with this information and Coastal Command were quickly alerted. A Beaufort aircraft was despatched to intercept the submarines and sank one of them.

Casualties July 12th/13th, 1943. Target Turin

156 Squadron 8 Group Lancaster ED919 GT/
Pilot. A/414137 P/O J.J.Hardcastle Missing, Runnymede Memorial. 191
Nav. 1318874 Sgt L.W.Dallimore Missing, Runnymede Memorial 146
B/A. 1330446 Sgt J.F.W.Cullum Missing, Runnymede Memorial 146
W/OP. 626974 Sgt T.E.Dickins Missing, Runnymede Memorial 147
F/E. 748494 Sgt J.A.Walker Missing, Runnymede Memorial 168
A/G. 1586893 Sgt H.H.G.Sticklemore Missing, Runnymede Memorial 164
A/G. 1551096 Sgt J.Archibald Missing, Runnymede Memorial 140

12 Squadron 1 Group Lancaster LM328 PH/F
Pilot. 148437 P/O T.B.Forbes Missing, Runnymede Memorial. 131
Nav. 148817 F/O L.A.Matthews PoW. Stalag 357, Kopernikus. 410
B/A. 1217408 Sgt W.F.Thomas Missing, Runnymede Memorial 167
W/OP. 1366131 F/Sgt L.D.Mitchell PoW. Stalag Luft 6, Heydekrug. 414
F/E. 937612 Sgt A.Hales Missing, Runnymede Memorial 151
A/G. 1622030 F/Sgt E.Southon PoW. Stalag 357, Kopernikus. 435
A/G. 1321244 Sgt G.L.A.Deasley Missing, Runnymede Memorial 147

100 Squadron 1 Group Lancaster ED561 HW/F
Pilot. 655402 F/Sgt W.R.Caldwell Killed St.Oulph, Troyes, France. CG 1
Nav. 1052254 Sgt F.Barnes Killed St.Oulph, Troyes, France. CG 1
B/A. 128586 F/O W.E.Leddiman Killed St.Oulph, Troyes, France. CG 1
W/OP. 157281 P/O F.W.Holmes Killed St.Oulph, Troyes, France. CG 1

F/E. 1267471 Sgt G.T.Causer Killed St.Oulph, Troyes, France. CG 1
A/G. 1528101 Sgt C.H.Glover Killed St.Oulph, Troyes, France. CG 1
A/G. R/97647 W/O J.A.Firth Killed St.Oulph, Troyes, France. CG 1

100 Squadron 1 Group Lancaster EE183 HW/P
Pilot. 148132 F/O A.G.Sadler PoW. Stalag Luft 3, Sagan. 1335
Nav. 1031746 F/Sgt M.J.Maloney PoW. Stalag 357, Kopernikus. 409
B/A. 657440 Sgt W.E.Broxup PoW. Stalag 357, Kopernikus. 378
W/OP. 1294029 F/Sgt R.A.A.Howe PoW. Stalag 357, Kopernikus. 402
F/E. 1487782 F/Sgt J.Egelston PoW. Stalag 4B, Muhlberg(Elbe). 83711
A/G. 1585987 F/Sgt R.R.W.Parker PoW. Stalag 357, Kopernikus. 418
A/G. A/413537 Sgt A.Burton PoW. Stalag 4B, Muhlberg(Elbe). 22673

103 Squadron 1 Group Lancaster ED769 PM/
Pilot. R/91900 W/O H.R.Graham Missing, Runnymede Memorial 179
Nav. R/138602 Sgt B.W.Walls Missing, Runnymede Memorial 186
B/A. 135658 F/O E.H.Hawkins Missing, Runnymede Memorial 125
W/OP. 1132042 Sgt G.E.Trowsdale Missing, Runnymede Memorial 167
F/E. 1623574 Sgt L.Cervi Missing, Runnymede Memorial 145
A/G. 1803626 Sgt N.G.Tippin Missing, Runnymede Memorial 167
A/G. R/122699 Sgt R.McWatts Missing, Runnymede Memorial 186

44 Squadron 5 Group Lancaster ED331 KM/Z
Pilot. 41452 W/Cdr J.D.Nettleton V.C. Missing, Runnymede Memorial 118
2/Pilot. 128653 F/O A.R.Ludlow Missing, Runnymede Memorial 125
Nav. 119301 F/O K.S.Juniper Missing, Runnymede Memorial 125
B/A. 113332 F/Lt D.Cramp Missing, Runnymede Memorial 119
W/OP. 525539 P/O J.E.Money Missing, Runnymede Memorial 132
F/E. 1254727 F/Sgt D.E.A.Seager Missing, Runnymede Memorial 139
A/G. A/403704 F/Lt I.M.Wood Missing, Runnymede Memorial 187
A/G. 50437 F/O F.I.Calcutt Missing, Runnymede Memorial 123

49 Squadron 5 Group Lancaster ED726 EA/
Pilot. 126710 F/O J.G.Miller AFM Missing, Runnymede Memorial. 126
Nav. R/89875 W/O J.W.Gillin Missing, Runnymede Memorial 180
B/A. 13020 F/O G.Lockie Missing, Runnymede Memorial 125
W/OP. 1335292 Sgt H.G.J.H.Read Missing, Runnymede Memorial 162
F/E. 957450 Sgt P.A.U.Goodyear Missing, Runnymede Memorial 151
A/G. 1235499 Sgt D.W.Bettinson Missing, Runnymede Memorial 142
A/G. 1550975 Sgt R.Burnett Missing, Runnymede Memorial. 144

50 Squadron 5 Group Lancaster DV156 VN/
Pilot. 145469 P/O E.J.Burnett Missing, Runnymede Memorial 131
2/Pilot. 650588 Sgt G.Batey Missing, Runnymede Memorial 142
Nav. 52767 P/O F.O'Carroll Missing, Runnymede Memorial 132
B/A. 1202331 Sgt S.H.Rayner Missing, Runnymede Memorial 162
W/OP. 149484 P/O J.E.Manning Missing, Runnymede Memorial 132
F/E. 52311 P/O T.Stenhouse Missing, Runnymede Memorial 133
A/G. 146695 P/O A.J.Holloway Missing, Runnymede Memorial 132
A/G. 1336604 Sgt J.T.Wilson Missing, Runnymede Memorial 170

57 Squadron 5 Group Lancaster ED861 DX/
Pilot. NZ/414673 F/Sgt J.Pickett Missing, Runnymede Memorial 199
Nav. 1230512 Sgt G.C.Grew Missing, Runnymede Memorial 151
B/A. 1345599 F/Sgt W.H.C.Doran Missing, Runnymede Memorial 136
W/OP. 1209070 Sgt G.Haywood Missing, Runnymede Memorial 152
F/E. 1234599 Sgt C.E.P.Still Missing, Runnymede Memorial 166
A/G. 1323063 Sgt J.A.Carpenter Missing, Runnymede Memorial 144
A/G. 1021749 Sgt E.E.Goldstraw Missing, Runnymede Memorial 150

106 Squadron 5 Group Lancaster DV181 ZN/
Message received at base at 06.30 hrs (13/7/43) - 'We are being attacked by
fighter....' transmission then became indistinct before being cut off.
Pilot. 130637 F/O C.Hayley Missing, Runnymede Memorial 125
Nav. J/14171 F/O M.O.Hovinen Missing, Runnymede Memorial 173
B/A. 1553503 Sgt H.W.Millar Missing, Runnymede Memorial 159
W/OP. 1235764 Sgt K.G.Rathbone Missing, Runnymede Memorial 162
F/E. 1575213 Sgt E.Horton Missing, Runnymede Memorial 154
A/G. 1580260 Sgt R.W.Ball Missing, Runnymede Memorial 141
A/G. 1389996 Sgt H.C.Hambling Missing, Runnymede Memorial 152

207 Squadron 5 Group Lancaster ED412 EM/Q
Pilot. 155766 P/O H.Badge Killed Vevey, Switzerland. 89
Nav. 45724 F/Lt A.C.Jepps Killed Vevey, Switzerland. 90
B/A. 1149750 Sgt A.C.Wright Killed Vevey, Switzerland. 91
W/OP. 950684 Sgt E.Higgins Killed Vevey, Switzerland. 87
F/E. 991246 Sgt R.Wood Killed Vevey, Switzerland. 88
A/G. 1230748 Sgt J.A.Spence Killed Vevey, Switzerland. 85
A/G. A/410446 F/Sgt R.O.C.Brett Killed Vevey, Switzerland. 86

467 Squadron 5 Group Lancaster JA676 PO/
Pilot. 40468 F/Lt R.W.A.Gibbs Missing, Runnymede Memorial. 119
Nav. 132148 F/O S.G.Norris Missing, Runnymede Memorial 127
B/A. 130290 F/O J.E.Pearce Missing, Runnymede Memorial 174
W/OP. 1153128 Sgt D.J.Banks Missing, Runnymede Memorial 141
F/E. 1623211 Sgt E.A.Roper Missing, Runnymede Memorial 163
A/G. 138889 P/O S.O.Tate Missing, Runnymede Memorial 133
A/G. 1052247 Sgt D.A.Chisholm Missing, Runnymede Memorial 145

467 Squadron 5 Group Lancaster ED531 PO/
Pilot. A/416693 F/O G.D.Mitchell Killed Vevey, Switzerland. 104
Nav. A/414737 F/O H.R.St-George Killed Vevey, Switzerland. 99
B/A. 134667 F/O W.H.Morgan Killed Vevey, Switzerland. 103
W/OP. A/409844 F/Sgt J.M.Maher Killed Vevey, Switzerland. 98
F/E. 1031846 Sgt B.K.H.Evans Killed Vevey, Switzerland. 100
A/G. A/414193 F/Sgt H.B.Bolger Killed Vevey, Switzerland. 102
A/G. A/19117 F/Sgt A.D.Terry Killed Vevey, Switzerland. 101

467 Squadron 5 Group Lancaster LM311 PO/
Aircraft crashed on landing at Bottesford, Lincolnshire after operations.
Pilot. A/415117 P/O C.A.Chapman Killed North Hinksey, Oxford. I-2-7
Nav. 1551320 Sgt A.E.Michaels Killed St.Kentigens, Glasgow. 11-2
B/A. 1349535 Sgt N.C.Smith Killed Newington, Edinburgh. RI-224
W/OP. 1369188 Sgt P.Donlevy Killed Dalkeith B-215
F/E. 980381 Sgt J.Greenwood Killed Mankinholes, Todmorden. 596
A/G. 967187 F/Sgt W.Bruce Killed Falkirk 7-192
A/G. 1372826 Sgt W.S.Buchanan Killed Cardonne, Glasgow. F-835

Minelaying

July 9th/10th, 1943
On the same night 22 Wellingtons went minelaying in the Brest,
Lorient and St Nazaire areas, they did not suffer any loss.

Aachen

July 13th/14th, 1943
As staff in the Headquarters of Bomber Command were
preparing their plans for the onslaught on Hamburg, the Ruhr
raids continued with the town of Aachen being singled out as the
penultimate target in the Battle of the Ruhr. 374 aircraft, a
force made up of 18 Lancasters, 214 Halifaxes, 76 Wellingtons,
55 Stirlings and 11 Mosquitoes, went in on the attack. A strong
tail wind which was not forecast to the main force of bombers
caused them to arrive very early over the target area and by the
time the Pathfinders accurately marked the aiming point, there
was an above average number of bombers circling the target. All
decided to make bomb runs at practically the same time and
apart from the town of Aachen receiving an exceptionally large
number of bombs, with high explosive and incendiaries falling
within a few minutes, some bomber crews themselves had hair
raising tales to tell on their return. Some saw bomb loads falling
from bombers above them in the very clear visibility there was
that night. No doubt some of the bomber losses must have been
caused by mid air collisions or damage caused by falling bombs.
Aachen town records report a terror attack on their town that
night because of the ferocity of the initial bombing and the
resultant damage caused. Large industrial buildings were

severely damaged. 294 people were killed and 745 injured. Some panic amongst people in certain areas of town was also reported. Twenty aircraft were lost, a loss rate of 5.3%. From their valuable crews 83 lost their lives, nine were never found, 37 were made prisoners and nine managed, with the help of the underground organisations, to make it safely back to the UK.

158 Squadron Flight Engineer Evades

One of the missing aircraft was Halifax HR720 of 158 Squadron based at Lissett, East Yorkshire. It was captained by Flight Sergeant G. R. J. Duthie. Five of the crew were made prisoners of war, the pilot was killed and the flight engineer, Sergeant J. N. Hempstead, evaded capture and relates his story.

"On the outward flight to Aachen our aircraft was attacked at 01.45 hours by an enemy fighter and immediately caught fire. The pilot gave the order to bale out and I came down in a field in the neighbourhood of Vorstenbosch about 5 kilometres south of Uden. I managed temporarily to bury my 'chute, harness and Mae West in a ditch and as I could see our aircraft burning about a mile away I began to walk towards it. After going only about 50 yards I heard some voices and saw four or five Dutch lads cycling past hurrying towards the burning aircraft. I decided to take a chance and stopped the last one cycling by. He realised that I was a member of the crew from the aircraft and brought back two of his comrades. They quickly cut up my 'chute and destroyed the harness and Mae West. One of them took me on the back of his bicycle through the village of Vorsten-Bosch and we stopped outside a farm, where I was given some food and also some shoes and a long overcoat. I had lost my boots in the bale out. I was then taken into the middle of a cornfield and told to lie low until the following morning. At about 10.00 hours on the 14th one of the Dutch lads returned and brought some food with him. He told me that my pilot had been killed in the crash, but had no news about the rest of my crew. He then left me promising to return later in the evening with some friends. They arrived as promised at about 23.00 hours and took me to the village where a discussion took place in the home of the father of one of the boys. It was obvious to me they were considering how to help me. They thought that they knew of someone in Amsterdam who could help, but in the meantime it was wiser if I stayed hidden in the field. For the next five days I lay in the middle of the cornfield, being fed in the daytime by the family of one of the boys. During this time I also got the news from my helpers that they had seen four of my crew being taken away by the Germans.

"On 19th July one of the boys brought some civilian clothes and told me to be ready to leave the field at 13.00 hours. I did as I was instructed and walked down the road where I met a boy who was cycling with another man. We were soon joined by a small dark man who wore glasses. From this point my journey was arranged for me.

"On October 9th, I met up in Amsterdam with 1213143 Sergeant R. A. Smith, who was a wireless operator from 10 Squadron and had been shot down on 26th July on a raid to Essen. He had left the Hague by train with three Dutchmen and had recently arrived in Amsterdam. At the railway station we were both hidden by the Station Master who appeared to be a friend of my helper. At 05.00 hours we all went over to a platform where the Paris train was waiting. We got underneath the train and lay on an iron platform under a carriage. The train left at 07.30 hours and arrived at Gare Du Nord, Paris, at about 21.30 hours. Feeling very stiff we got out from our hiding place under the train carriage and from the shelter of an adjacent stationary train we took off our overalls which were thickly covered with dirt and grime. We then walked to the station toilet where we had a wash and made ourselves look a little more presentable. On the station we had our first set back, for we lost one of the Dutchmen who was travelling with us and who unfortunately had the address in his suitcase where we had been told to go. My helper, however, found another place for us to stay, an address which I cannot remember. The next day my helper managed to find our lost friend who had also obtained some travelling papers for us, which stated that we were Dutchmen travelling to Bordeaux with permission to break our journey in Paris. On 11th October we met up with our "lost" Dutchman again and went with him to stay at an hotel where he was registered.

"At 22.00 hours on Thursday, October 14th, we caught a train to Bordeaux, which arrived there at about 07.00 hours on the 15th. We stayed in the station waiting room until 09.00 hours and then caught another train for Bayonne. At midday we got off the train at Dax, for my helper had been told that there was a control check point between Dax and Bayonne. We spent the rest of that day in an hotel room and that night we went to catch the 21.30 hours train to Irun. My helper, who always went first, came back and told us that the train was full of troops, so we therefore went over to the other side of the station, jumped down on to the railway line, dodged underneath a stationary train and got underneath the Irun train. I lay flat on the brake bar and clung with my hands and feet on to the cross girders. It was extremely difficult to hang on when the train was in motion and when the brake bar was moved. The train got into Hendaye about two and half hours later. My helper got off and went to check, coming back with the news that some of the carriages were to be dropped off and that we would have to move to a position further up the train. We scrambled out and ran up the track and again got underneath another carriage.

"By the time our train reached Irun it was considerably overdue and we found that the Lisbon train which we had intended to catch had already left. To stay hidden we all made a dash for the goods yard and sat underneath a goods wagon, where we stayed all day. By this time we were very hungry, as we had nothing to eat since we left Dax. At night the line of wagons under which we were hiding began to move, so we had to hurriedly scramble out before being pinned under the wagon. We moved to a line of nearby wagons and once again sat down under the wagon girders. After a short time a railway worker came along tapping the wheels. My helper lost his balance and fell off his perch. Realising that we would all be found we ran away, but got separated. Luckily I found Smith later and we went over to the other side of the station where the Spanish trains were standing and slipped into an empty compartment, now without any of our helpers. We slept that night in the empty train and in the early morning a railway cleaner who came into the carriage told us that the train was due to go to San Sebastian.

"The train left Irun at 17.00 hours on October 16th and arrived at San Sebastian half an hour later. Smith and I found that we were unable to leave the station without a ticket so went over to the other side of the station and went out through the goods yard still wearing our overalls and berets. Outside in a street we stopped a man and asked him the way to the British Consulate. Our luck was in, for he even took us there and we waited outside until 10.00 hours when an official arrived to open up. The next day we were taken by car to Madrid and later on to Gibraltar, leaving there by air and arriving back in Portreath, UK on October 28th, 1943."

Pilot in Persistent Escape Bids

Canadian Warrant Officer M. E. Sobkowicz was the pilot of Halifax DK142, from 427 Squadron based at Leeming, Yorkshire. His aircraft was attacked by two enemy fighters just after crossing the Dutch coast on the way to the target. In the ensuing encounter the mid upper turret was found to be unserviceable and the rear gunner was only able to give a short burst in reply to the enemy attack. It was left to the pilot to take as much evasive action as he could but the cards were stacked against the bomber as the fighters made four co-ordinated attacks. One of the bomber's engines was put out of action and without any further defence the captain had no option but to signal to his crew, who were not all on intercom because that too was knocked out, that they should bale out. Unable to ascertain whether the two gunners had received the order to abandon the aircraft, the pilot decided to crash land about 25 kilometres south west of Utrecht. His post war interrogation discloses what happened

after this.

"I was quite shaken after the crash landing of the plane, but after I checked that there were no members of my crew left in the aircraft (they must have all baled out when I gave the order), I set fire to it. I lit a fire inside the fuselage, leaving my parachute and harness inside. This was about 01.45 hours on July 14th, 1943.

"I then walked towards some bushes about 600 yards away, crossing two small ditches on the way. Before reaching a wood I came to a haystack, so I burrowed deep into it to hide as I had seen some Germans arrive and then leave the site of the burning aircraft. I remained there until about 04.00 hours when it started getting light then moved into the wood where I remained all day until 17.00 hours. As I left I took off my black tie and carried my tunic across my arm. I walked westwards along a railway track passing a small country station on the way, which I bypassed by a small road which led to a village. I attempted to skirt this but came to a very large river, there was a large bridge which I could see in the distance, but I guessed that it would be heavily guarded so I did not attempt to cross there. Instead I used a smaller bridge and walked across some fields until I came to yet another smaller river which was fast flowing. I crossed this by means of an inverted 'U' bridge. This brought me into a farm yard where a farmer shouted at me, but I kept on walking and only waved back at him. The farmer's son then came out of the house and shouted 'Englander', so I turned back to meet them. They took me into the farm, where the old woman there gave me some food.

"The farmer and his son then left the house and returned soon afterwards accompanied by about ten men. One of these was an ex Dutch Army Reserve Officer. He did not speak very good English, but as he was the only one who could speak some of my language he did all the talking, consulting the others from time to time. He advised me that I was surrounded on three sides and that the only way out was to go south and then north-west, he said that because I had no knowledge of the language and was injured, there was little chance of my trying to evade. I told him that I would make my own way to the best of my ability. The whole crowd seemed to be very much afraid, but they were friendly. The farmer in whose house I had the meal told me through the ex officer that he had another son who was being held in Germany on forced labour and that he believed that his son would be returned home if he were to hand me over to the Germans. I insisted that I would continue on my own and the crowd dispersed. The old lady gave me some sandwiches and tomatoes and then showed me a picture of Queen Wilhelmina and began to cry. I tried to pay for the food with money from my escape box, but she would not accept anything.

"Just as I was about to leave the house, the farmer came back accompanied by a Dutch policeman, who saluted me and shook hands, but I understood from his gestures that he had no choice but to take me with him. He took me to his home which was the Police Depot for the area and telephoned the Germans. I had given my escape kit, except for the maps, compass and file to the old woman at the farm before I left.

"About 40 German soldiers and three officers arrived in two lorries and they tried to get me to tell them what kind of aircraft I had been in and how many men had been in the crew with me. They took me to a gaol in Utrecht, where I was searched, but I managed to retain my file, compass and maps. I was again questioned, but I pretended not to understand. On the following day I was taken to Amsterdam where I was kept in solitary confinement for three days. During the time I was at Amsterdam I managed to see Sergeant Green, the bomb aimer in my crew and we were able to exchange a few words. He told me that Sergeant J. H. Brown, the mid upper gunner, and Sergeant J. F. Hutchings the wireless operator were safe and Sergeant R. T. Hayes my navigator had been brought to the gaol all bloody and beaten up. About July 18th I was taken from Amsterdam to Dulag Luft, where I tried my first attempt at escaping. Using my file I tried to cut through the cell window bars, but a guard detected me and for my efforts I got knocked around a bit by him. I then went on to Stalag Luft 6 at Heydekrug.

"My second attempt to escape came on the spur of the moment in November 1943, when the lights of the perimeter fence at the camp failed for about 10 minutes during a storm. A Canadian Sergeant, whose name I don't recall, quickly decided to make a ladder out of some bed boards to get over the fence. By the time he had knocked the ladder together the lights had come on again, we thought that was the end of our attempt, but the lights went off again and this time we took the ladder and quickly climbed over the fence. We got to the outskirts of Memel by the following morning, having obtained food at a farmhouse, where we were not asked any questions. We both then went into a wood and slept. On waking we found that both of us had a type of dysentery, probably contracted through drinking polluted water from some streams we had come across. We waited until the next morning to see if we would be any better but by then we were so weak we could hardly stand or help ourselves so we gave ourselves up to the nearest civilian we came across. We were taken back to Stalag Luft 6 and were admitted into hospital. At a later date when recovered we were sentenced to seven days in the cooler.

"My third attempt was from the same camp in February 1944. This attempt was better prepared, in that I had maps, compass, chocolate, iron rations and some ready money. I also had the names and addresses of two contacts. On the selected day when I got a signal from one of the prisoners who was acting as a watcher that I was not being observed, I dived into the garbage wagon which was being loaded in the compound. Laying in the wagon I was quickly covered with other garbage that was being thrown in. About half an hour later the wagon was driven out of the camp and on the way to the dump one of the two men jumped off, leaving only the driver to tip the wagon. As soon as the wagon stopped I stood up from the mountain of rubbish and jumped off. Unluckily the driver had got out of his cab rather smartly and started screaming as I ran away up the hill back to the camp. However, my legs were so cramped after laying in the garbage that they went dead and I tried to crawl to the nearby river bank. Two guards arrived and one of them beat me with a whip. I was able to get up and tried to defend myself by sliding down the river bank. I tried to dash across the frozen river but the two guards gave chase. One of them went through the ice and up to his waist in water. By this time I had managed to get up the bank on the other side and ran along the side of a small adjoining brook towards a wood about 300 yards away. After running some distance, my foot slipped and I rolled down the bank. Within seconds one of my pursuers caught up with me. I was severely beaten and then taken back to camp. Both of the guards were Obergefreiters in the *Luftwaffe*. One was a short man of slight build with a very big nose. The other guard who fell through the ice was a bigger man, with a scar running from his nose to his lip. He was promoted the day following my capture. At the moment of my capture he was violent with rage and kept on hitting me with the butt of his bayonet. I think if I had shown any resistance at all, he would have gladly sunk the bayonet into me. He simply didn't look as if he was sane at the time. I was given nine days in the cooler, but I told the Camp Commandant in no uncertain terms what I thought of the treatment I had received when I was captured.

"I was evacuated from Stalag Luft 6 in July, 1944, and in company of the rest of the prisoners from the camp sent by ship from Memel to Stettin under the most objectionable conditions. On arrival at Stettin the 700 of us were put aboard a train and we were chained. At Keifhilde we were taken off the train and marched towards Stalag Luft IV at Gross Tychow. On the way we were forced marched too quickly and finally were made to run as we were pursued by dogs and bayonets were used by the guards. I was struck twice with a bayonet and in order to maintain the peace it was necessary to drop our kit and any items of value which were never returned to us. I was finally liberated by the Allied Forces at Oflag XIB, Fallingbostel on the 16th April, 1945."

One of Warrant Officer Sobkowicz's gunners, R/169774 Sergeant J. H. Brown, did evade capture with the help of an underground organisation and returned to England. The remainder of the crew became prisoners of war.

Casualties July 13th/14th, 1943. Target Aachen

35 Squadron 8 Group Halifax HR819 TL/K
Pilot. NZ/415372 F/Sgt E.W.Saywell Missing, Runnymede Memorial. 199
Nav. 1231515 F/Sgt F.W.Whittaker Missing, Runnymede Memorial 139
B/A. 1379660 Sgt E.R.Moore Missing, Runnymede Memorial 159
W/OP. 1267837 F/Sgt R.W.Wilson PoW. Stalag 357, Kopernikus. 450
F/E. 1021591 Sgt S.F.Hughes Missing, Runnymede Memorial 154
A/G. 1321748 Sgt F.F.Ward Missing, Runnymede Memorial 168
A/G. 1080667 Sgt J.Marsh Missing, Runnymede Memorial 158

405 Squadron 8 Group Halifax HR905 LQ/
Pilot. 39805 S/Ldr D.L.Wolfe DFC Killed Jonkerbos, Holland. 16-E-6
2/Pilot. NZ/413997 F/O D.J.Smith PoW. Stalag Luft 3, Sagan. 1629
Nav. J/9764 F/Lt R.G.Morrison DFC Killed Jonkerbos, Holland. 16-E-1
B/A. J/17710 P/O E.M.Witt Killed Jonkerbos, Holland. 16-E-2
W/OP. J/6843 F/O G.G.McGladrey DFC Killed Jonkerbos, Holland. 16-E-3
F/E. R/68061 Sgt D.Bebensee DFM Killed Jonkerbos, Holland. 16-E-5
A/G. J/12952 F/Lt D.M.Clarke PoW. Stalag Luft 4, Sagan. 6474
A/G. J/18062 P/O T.H.N.Emerson DFM Killed Jonkerbos, Holland. 10-E-4

90 Squadron 3 Group Stirling EE873 WP/D
Aircraft crashed at Rothem, Belgium at 01.45 hrs (14/7/43) after being shot down by fighter.
Pilot. 144181 F/Lt C.E.Coombs Killed Heverlee, Belgium. 5-A-8
2/Pilot. 149523 P/O E.Candy Killed Heverlee, Belgium. 5-A-9
Nav. 127306 F/O P.D.Swallow Killed Heverlee, Belgium. 5-A-10
B/A. 1501167 Sgt W.G.Dawson Killed Heverlee, Belgium. 5-A-11
W/OP. 1332091 Sgt C.A.Long Killed Heverlee, Belgium. 5-A-12
F/E. 1474536 Sgt J.C.Bradshaw Killed Heverlee, Belgium. 5-A-14
A/G. 1002829 Sgt R.Clarke Evaded capture
A/G. 1585887 Sgt E.B.Potter Killed Heverlee, Belgium. 5-A-13

115 Squadron 3 Group Lancaster DS690 KO/
Crashed at Les Hayons, nr Bouillon, Belgium at 02.10 hours (14/7/43).Victim of Hptm.August Geiger.
Pilot. 70789 S/Ldr The Hon R.A.Baird Killed Les Hayons, Bouillon. CG
Nav. 127974 F/O W.J.Moorcroft Killed Les Hayons, Bouillon, Belgium. CG
B/A. 1235107 F/Sgt R.A.Walker Killed Les Hayons, Bouillon, Belgium. CG
W/OP. A/406795 F/Sgt N.Robinson Killed Les Hayons, Bouillon, Belgium. CG
F/E. 1330882 Sgt E.Smith Killed Les Hayons, Bouillon, Belgium. CG
A/G. 1318179 Sgt H.Matthews Killed Les Hayons, Bouillon, Belgium. CG
A/G. 777926 W/O J.E.C.Odendaal PoW. Stalag 4B, Muhlberg(Elbe). 83699

115 Squadron 3 Group Lancaster DS660 KO/P
Pilot. J/5829 F/Lt R.B.Larson PoW. Stalag Luft 3, Sagan. 1778
Nav. 138396 P/O C.Armstrong Killed Grevillers (Brit), Arras. 18-E-26
B/A. 131977 F/O F.L.Yates Killed Grevillers (Brit), Arras. 18-E-24
W/OP. 1077619 Sgt P.Williams Killed Grevillers (Brit), Arras. JG 18-E-21/22
F/E. 1653104 Sgt M.Jones Killed Grevillers (Brit), Arras, France. 18-E-25
A/G. 1044231 Sgt D.Murphy Killed Grevillers (Brit), Arras. JG 18-E-21/22
A/G. 1601296 Sgt J.A.T.Newton Killed Grevillers (Brit), Arras. 18-E-23

78 Squadron 4 Group Halifax JB801 EY/
Pilot. 1233316 W/O P.Horrocks Killed Rotterdam, Holland. LL-2-49
Nav. J/21895 F/O C.D.Hosken Killed Rotterdam, Holland. LL-2-52
B/A. 1575981 Sgt A.S.Jelfs Killed Rotterdam, Holland. LL-2-50
W/OP. 1007496 Sgt J.Chaplin Killed Rotterdam, Holland. LL-1-50
F/E. 951610 Sgt W.H.Harrles Killed Rotterdam, Holland. LL-1-49
A/G. 1528496 Sgt G.Bowden Killed Rotterdam, Holland. LL-2-51
A/G. 1810021 Sgt R.W.Rouse Killed Rotterdam, Holland. LL-2-53

78 Squadron 4 Group Halifax JD108 EY/
Shot down 02.36 hours (14/7/43) at Froidchapelle, Belgium.Victim of
Oblt.Rudolf Altendorf, II/NJG4
Pilot. NZ/415206 W/O K.A.Toon Killed Gosselies, Charleroi, Belgium. CG 1/3
Nav. 1315850 Sgt D.Cowell Evaded capture
B/A. 1479074 Sgt R.Falcus Evaded capture
W/OP. 1217692 F/Sgt S.Burridge Killed Gosselies, Charleroi, Belgium. CG 1/3
F/E. 1280330 Sgt L.G.Donaldson Evaded capture
A/G. 1071995 F/Sgt G.M.Campbell PoW. Stalag Luft 1, Barth Vogelsang. 380
A/G. 133519 F/Lt J.D.Nesbit Killed Gosselies, Charleroi, Belgium. CG 1/3

78 Squadron 4 Group Halifax JD175 EY/
Pilot. 1239391 W/O C.M.Colbourn Killed Rheinberg, Germany. 4-G-1
Nav. R/99088 W/O A.R.Lutes Killed Rheinberg, Germany. 4-G-2
B/A. R/91899 W/O Z.Yonker Missing, Runnymede Memorial 179
W/OP. 1029601 Sgt A.Slack Killed Rheinberg, Germany. 4-G-3
F/E. 1130826 Sgt F.Oakley Killed Rheinberg, Germany. 4-G-4
A/G. 1394459 Sgt W.V.Gerrard Killed Rheinberg, Germany. 4-G-6
A/G. 1602056 Sgt W.Robinson Killed Rheinberg, Germany. 4-G-5

102 Squadron 4 Group Halifax JD297 DY/Q
Pilot. 33133 W/Cdr H.R.Coventry DFC Killed Maubeuge, France. A-4
Nav. 119303 F/Lt F.E.King DFC Killed Maubeuge, France. A-7
B/A. 127125 F/O C.F.Read Killed Maubeuge, France. A-9
W/OP. 990520 Sgt W.Brown Killed Maubeuge, France. A-6
F/E. 568487 Sgt G.T.Pine-Coffin Killed Maubeuge, France. A-5
A/G. 1738601 Sgt W.Hardy Killed Maubeuge, France. A-8
A/G. 76910 F/Lt G.F.Hogg Killed Maubeuge, France. A-3

102 Squadron 4 Group Halifax JB894 DY/X
Pilot. 1550957 Sgt R.G.Amos Killed Rheinberg, Germany. CG 3-D-11/13
Nav. 1397808 Sgt B.P.Dowthwaite Killed Rheinberg, Germany. 3-D-9
B/A. 1319671 Sgt W.H.J.Smith Killed Rheinberg, Germany. 3-D-10
W/OP. 1540341 Sgt J.R.Fradley Killed Rheinberg, Germany. CG 3-D-11/13
F/E. 649887 Sgt J.R.G.Smith Killed Rheinberg, Germany. CG 3-D-11/13
A/G. 1530814 F/Sgt D.H.Brown PoW. Stalag 357, Kopernikus. 376
A/G. 1491394 Sgt J.Raw Killed Maastricht, Holland. 2-113

158 Squadron 4 Group Halifax JD116 NP/A
Pilot. 45374 S/Ldr R.S.Williams DFC Killed Rheinberg, Germany. 3-D-14
Nav. 129446 F/Lt D.R.Bigg PoW. Stalag Luft 3, Sagan. 1767
B/A. 1501100 Sgt J.Quayle Killed Rheinberg, Germany. 3-C-5
W/OP. 146097 F/O A.S.Gosling PoW. Stalag Luft 3, Sagan. 1775
F/E. 52700 P/O S.H.C.Watts Killed Rheinberg, Germany. 5-B-4
A/G. 145800 P/O W.Edmond Killed Rheinberg, Germany. 3-D-17
A/G. 145717 P/O W.R.Binnington Killed Rheinberg, Germany. 3-D-16

158 Squadron 4 Group Halifax HR720 NP/B
Aircraft crashed at Vorstenbosch, Holland.
Pilot. NZ/415298 F/Sgt G.R.J.Duthie Killed Uden, Holland. 5-E-9
Nav. R/133108 W/O F.D.Granger PoW. Stalag 357, Kopernikus. 391
B/A. 1335861 F/Sgt T.E.F.Carr PoW. Stalag 4B, Muhlberg(Elbe). 222490
W/OP. 1211259 F/Sgt G.H.King PoW. Stalag 357, Kopernikus. 405
F/E. 540151 Sgt J.N.Hempstead Evaded capture
A/G. A/415646 W/O J.R.Grey PoW. Stalag 357, Kopernikus. 393
A/G. 545380 W/O T.Pinkney PoW. Stalag 357, Kopernikus. 422

466 Squadron 4 Group Wellington LN288 HD/
Aircraft shot down by Chievres Flak at 02.15 hours (14/7/43) and crashed at
Badour, Belgium.
Pilot. A/413856 F/Sgt W.A.Gunning Killed Chievres, Belgium. CG 14/15
Nav. R/135639 F/Sgt H.C.Jordan Killed Chievres, Belgium. CG 14/15
B/A. A/422157 Sgt R.Feakes Killed Chievres, Belgium. CG 14/15
W/OP. 1336969 Sgt D.W.Covell Killed Chievres, Belgium. CG 14/15
A/G. 1192627 Sgt T.F.Cummins Killed Chievres, Belgium. CG 14/15

408 Squadron 6 Group Halifax DT769 EQ/J
Aircraft shot down over Holland.
Pilot. J/15677 F/O A.O.Smuck Killed Tilburg (Gilzerbaan). CG A-1-20/30
Nav. 1342347 W/O B.Domigan PoW. Stalag Luft 3, Sagan. 1476
B/A. 127961 F/Lt J.J.Kelly PoW. Stalag Luft 3, Sagan. 1776
W/OP. 13332114 Sgt R.Barneveld Killed Tilburg (Gilzerbaan). CG A-1-20/30
F/E. 577754 Sgt J.Foggon Killed Tilburg (Gilzerbaan), Holland. CG A-1-20/30
A/G. R/124347 F/Sgt D.G.McKay Killed Tilburg (Gilzerbaan). CG A-1-20/30
A/G. R/109630 W/O D.L.G.Brown Killed Bergen-op-Zoom (Can, Holland. 5-G-8

419 Squadron 6 Group Halifax BB323 VR/
Aircraft shot down by two Ju88 fighters.
Pilot. 0885971 2/Lt(USAF) B.J.J.Furey PoW. Camp not known
Nav. R/138762 F/Sgt M.Cottenden PoW. Stalag Luft 4, Sagan. 381
B/A. 1339611 F/Sgt G.C.Perrett PoW. Stalag 357, Kopernikus. 420
W/OP. R/113329 W/O J.C.Gilchrist PoW. Stalag Luft 4, Sagan. 388
F/E. 616950 Sgt J.S.Carmichael PoW. Stalag 357, Kopernikus. 383
A/G. R/117446 W/O K.LaSalle PoW. Stalag Luft 4, Sagan. 1320
A/G. 656918 F/Sgt W.C.Batkin Killed Jonkerbos, Holland. 12-H-6

427 Squadron 6 Group Halifax DK142 ZL/
Pilot. R/82529 W/O M.E.Sobkowicz PoW. Stalag Luft 4, Sagan. 434
Nav. R/225060 Sgt R.T.Hayes PoW. Stalag 4B, Muhlberg(Elbe). 83678
B/A. R/157241 W/O W.H.Green PoW. Stalag 357, Kopernikus. 392
W/OP. R/131774 W/O J.F.Hutchings PoW. Stalag 357, Kopernikus. 399
F/E. R.86659 W/O S.W.Bryant PoW. Stalag Luft 4, Sagan. 649
A/G. R/169774 Sgt J.H.Brown Evaded Capture
A/G. R/62743 W/O J.R.R.Poudrier PoW. Stalag Luft 3, Sagan. 222537

428 Squadron 6 Group Halifax EB209 NA/C
Aircraft crashed at 02.30 hours (14/7/43) at Sinsin, S.W.of Marche, Belgium.
Pilot. J/23524 F/O W.D.F.Ross PoW. Stalag Luft 4, Sagan. 1785 *
Nav. R/117638 F/Sgt W.B.Webber PoW. Stalag 357, Kopernikus. 455
B/A. R/130363 W/O T.Chliszczyk PoW. Stalag 357, Kopernikus. 588
W/OP. R/110357 Sgt D.J.Webb Evaded capture
F/E. R/656117 F/Sgt A.M.Winter PoW. Stalag 4B, Muhlberg(Elbe) 83656
A/G. J/96449 P/O J.C.A.Hayes PoW. Stalag Luft 3, Sagan. 222712
A/G. R/130220 Sgt E.A.Bridge Evaded capture
* On second tour of operations.

428 Squadron 6 Group Halifax DK228 NA/D
Aircraft crashed at Mesnil/St Blaise, Belgium, shot down by fighter.
Pilot. J/15548 F/Lt W.G.Weeks Killed Medemblik, Holland. 4-48 *
Nav. J/10178 F/O E.D.Robertson Killed Medemblik, Holland. 4-52
B/A. J/16779 F/O W.F.Stewart Killed Medemblik, Holland. 4-53
W/OP. R/90240 W/O J.R.Goodfellow Killed Medemblik, Holland. 4-54
F/E. R/56703 Sgt S.Zayets Killed Medemblik, Holland. 4-51
A/G. 1813538 Sgt A.D.Dawson Killed Medemblik, Holland. 4-50
A/G. J/11359 F/O H.B.Ward Killed Medemblik, Holland. 4-49
* On second tour of operations.

428 Squadron 6 Group Halifax DK257 NA/Q
Aircraft shot down by night fighter near Eindhoven, Holland.
Pilot. J/8213 F/Lt D.S.Morgan PoW. Stalag Luft 3, Sagan. 1782
Nav. J/11226 F/O F.H.Ditchburn PoW. Stalag Luft 4, Sagan. 1771
B/A. R/114680 Sgt J.P.O'Leary Evaded capture
W/OP. J/18039 F/O B.L.Gillis PoW. Stalag Luft 3, Sagan. 389
F/E. 1582632 F/Sgt D.Brown PoW. Stalag 357, Kopernikus. 375
A/G. 1230791 Sgt T.H.Pritchard Missing, Runnymede Memorial 162
A/G. 1384142 Sgt M.Edwards Missing, Runnymede Memorial 148

432 Squadron 6 Group Wellington HE353 QO/R
Pilot. R/122956 F/Sgt C.L.Dyson Killed Medemblik, Holland. 4-44
Nav. R/133336 F/Sgt R.Stewart Killed Medemblik, Holland. JG 4-46/47
B/A. R/142160 F/Sgt H.O.Lee Killed Medemblik, Holland. JG 4-46/47
W/OP. J/18331 P/O W.C.Campbell Killed Medemblik, Holland. 4-45
A/G. R/131923 F/Sgt J.W.McKendry Killed Medemblik, Holland. 4-43

Small Diversionary Raids

July 13th/14th, 1943
A diversionary raid on Cologne was made by two Mosquitoes, both returned safely to their base.

July 14th/15th, 1943
On a similar raid to Berlin by eight Mosquitoes, one aircraft, DZ515 crewed by 102139 Flying Officer R. Clarke and 850080 Flight Sergeant E. J. Thorne from 139 squadron, failed to return. Their bodies were never found.

Casualties July 14th/15th, 1943. Target Berlin

139 Squadron 8 Group Mosquito DZ515 XD/
Pilot. 102139 F/O R.Clarke Missing, Runnymede Memorial 123
Nav. 850080 F/Sgt E.J.Thorne Missing, Runnymede Memorial 139

Peugeot Factory

July 15th/16th, 1943

The concluding raids of the Ruhr offensive began with a force of 165 Halifaxes, 134 from 4 Group in Yorkshire and the remaining 31 from 405 and 35 Squadrons from 8 Group (Pathfinders). They attacked the Peugeot motor factory in the Montbeliard suburb of Souchaux, a French town near to the Swiss border.

The target was quite small and the Pathfinder bombers dropped their target indicators about half a mile south-east and beyond the planned aiming point. It was a relatively clear moonlit night with comparatively little opposition from *Flak* or fighters over the target area itself, although fighters were reported on the tracks in and out. From photographic reconnaissance reports the following day, the target itself remained relatively unscathed with most of the bomb damage in the French town centre. From underground reports the factory production was not halted at all. The pall of smoke which blotted out the whole of the target area did not make bombing easy for the later crews and this undoubtedly caused some of the bombs to be spread out, a large proportion of them being wasted. This type of raid to targets in the occupied countries illustrated the problems of accurate marking of small targets and the devastating results to the friendly civilian population if the raid was not successful. Photographs taken by the French after the raid show the mass funeral of 123 civilians who perished, their coffins being transported on the backs of the newly completed Peugot trucks made at the factory.

One Halifax from 405 Squadron, piloted by Flying Officer M. Sattler was attacked by a night fighter shortly after leaving the target area. Both gunners identified it as a Dornier Do217, but were puzzled because they could clearly see in the bright moonlight, RAF roundels on its wings and it had typical British type camouflage. The pilot put his Halifax into some very violent corkscrew manoeuvres in an effort to escape, but the fighter still managed to hit the bomber with its firing. Seven attacks were made by the fighter and each time the pilot put his Halifax into a very steep and tight turn in order to let his gunners have the opportunity to return fire. On the eighth attack the Dornier broke away with one of its engines in flames. It spiralled into a dive and hit the ground where it quickly caught fire. The mid upper gunner, Flying Officer W. R. W. Anderson, who had kept up the bomber's return fire was wounded in the attack sustaining four wounds in his left arm. In the running battle the Halifax had been severely damaged. The right aileron had been damaged, the DR and P4 compasses had been put out of action and the petrol tanks pierced, but fortunately without a resultant fire. The pilot and his crew nursed the bomber, with its depleted petrol supply back to the UK, but were unable to make home base and landed safely at Middle Wallop.

Five bombers were lost on this raid and from their crews 13 were killed, seven were never found, five made prisoners and a relatively large number of ten managed to evade capture.

One of the missing bombers was a PFF Halifax B Mark II HR864, LQ-A for Apple of 405 RCAF Squadron based at Gransden Lodge, captained by Flight Lieutenant Foy DFC. Fortunately all the crew escaped by baling out, succeessfully evaded capture and returned to the UK. One of the crew, Flying Officer Hughie Huston from Vancouver, Canada, the navigator, recounts his story of being shot down and his subsequent evasion to get back to the UK.

"The night of the 15th July turned out to be a beautiful clear and moonlit night and according to the briefing beforehand, the target was supposed to be, "a piece of cake". The run up into the target was routine, turning points were marked with markers at precisely the right moment from exactly the correct altitude of 5,000 feet, but then things began to fall apart. After the confirmation signal of, 'Bomb Doors closed' had been given by the skipper, the mid upper gunner informed him that the photo flash was still jammed in the chute and consequently no photo of the aiming point had been taken. On hearing this the pilot switched on the aircraft navigation lights, turned the Halifax around and flew back against the main bomber stream in an attempt to get a picture. This was a manouevre not normally recommended especially with an illuminated aircraft, but it was successfully completed and the photo flash was duly pushed out and the photo taken. After clearing the target for the second time, the navigator suggested to the pilot that in view of the 75 knot tailwind forecast at around 20,000 feet, it might be judicious to climb and get full benefit of this wind on the return leg to base. The pilot, however, was quite content to stay at his existing height. It was suggested that in such clear moonlight, if he was not going to climb, it might be less conducive to detection by enemy night fighters to descend to a much lower altitude. Shortly after this the rear gunner reported that a Wellington was closing in from the port quarter, the navigator interrupted this report by pointing out the fact that no Wellingtons were included in the force that night and it was no doubt a twin engined enemy fighter. No confirmation of this was needed, for the placid night erupted with the chattering of the Halifax's 303 calibre machine guns and then six very much larger bangs, with the bomb aimer confirming that an aircraft had cut below the plane in a sharp port turn. The fighter came in once again, but this time only the rear gunner was able to offer any opposition for the mid upper gunner had reported a gun stoppage. Once again the chattering of the machine guns was mixed with six loud bangs and to add to the first damage of the starboard inner propeller being completely shattered, the starboard outer engine had now cut out. This left the Halifax very vulnerable against a further attack and it was also doubtful whether it would be able to fly and sustain sufficient height on two port engines. Fortunately the fighter did not persist with the attack and the pilot was left to struggle as best he could in the losing battle to maintain height. After thirty minutes of steadily losing altitude the skipper was told that there was only 700 feet of air below the plane and the terrain ahead on the way back was well above this height. On hearing this the pilot, realising the hopeless situation, ordered all the crew to bale out as quickly as possible.

Hughie Huston always made a practice of carrying a 'diversion kit' with him on operations. It consisted of a small piece of webbing kit and contained soap, towel, shaving cream, razor, one blank cheque, 3 packs of cigarettes and half a dozen chocolate bars. Little did he realise that he would need to use it in France in a bale out situation. On hearing the bale out order, the navigator hung this bag around his neck with the straps between the parachute hooks on his harness, but unfortunately when he bent down from his navigator's table position to release the escape hatch beneath him, the bag swung in front, so he had to place it on the table. As soon as he had snapped the parachute pack on, he jumped through the hatch just catching himself in time to snatch the bag with one hand. Not counting, as soon as he saw the Halifax tail wheel whizz by, he pulled the ripcord and felt a terrible jerk as the 'chute opened. Before he had time to realise that the damn thing at least worked, he landed heavily with a thud and was dragged backwards down a grassy knoll, entangled in the 'chute shroud lines. There was utter silence after the hectic last few minutes. Quickly untangling himself he dug a hole in the side of a nearby ditch into which he buried the parachute and Mae West. Then putting the

Pole Star behind him, he started off due south and quickly came to a paved road. Realising that he could walk much better and quicker if he got rid of the over-size flying boots which were over his shoes, he took them off and buried them behind a tree on the roadside. After crossing that first road he found himself in a much larger field where he spotted someone coming towards him. Immediately he flattened himself as best hě could between two big furrows and eased out the .38 revolver from the inside of his battle dress. The figure still came forward and then he heard a shout, "Hughie is that you?" It was the bomb aimer, Squadron Leader Lambert DFC. who was in the same crew.

On his reckoning it was a wiser course of action to start walking due south, for Hughie guessed after the bale out that the aircraft would have veered to starboard and therefore due south was the quickest way to clear the area. After further walking at a brisk pace both airmen arrived in a small patch of woods where they decided to lay concealed. In the background they could hear the faint sounds of exploding ammunition from the burning Halifax and the roar of the *Luftwaffe* planes flying back and forth, obviously searching for survivors.

After dark they set off again and soon came to a wide canal. They followed this in a south-westerly direction until they came to a narrow unguarded bridge which they crossed and once more headed south. Seeing a narrow track in a wood which ran like an arrow due north and south, it was obvious that it was little used so off they went and followed this track for days, or more correctly for nights, for during daylight they hid up all the time until finally coming near to the edge of a small village. The weather by now had turned bad, raining quite heavily and as they both felt that they had come a long way from the crashed aircraft's position, it seemed opportune to try and get some help. Squadron Leader Lambert suggested the first house in view, but Huston was not too keen for although it was well apart from the rest of the village, he noticed that it had some telephone or electric wires running towards its roof and thought it would be wiser to give it a miss in case the owner was not too willing to help and could then call for assistance. Finally spotting a small holding with a nearby barn they closely watched it for a while and saw a young French girl making a trip to the outside loo in

527

her nightie. After her return to the house they both made a mad dash to the barn where they surprised an elderly woman collecting eggs. After reassuring her that they were Canadian airmen in the RAF they were fortunately made welcome into the house, fed and given old clothing to replace their uniforms.

Towards evening they left after being told to cross a bridge over the River Loire before dusk as the bridge was guarded from dusk to dawn. Madame at the smallholding also asked them why they had not gone into the first house at the edge of the village. On hearing their explanation they were told how lucky they had been for six Germans lived there with one French woman to keep them amused. It was obvious that this was their first lucky escape and both hoped that their luck would hold.

After leaving the small holding with grateful thanks to their helpers and now dressed in civilian clothes they soon came to the bridge, just as the guards were forming up for inspection before assuming their nightly sentry duties. Crossing boldly and luckily without being questioned or asked for a pass, both now plodded southwards in broad daylight, being welcomed and fed on the way by the French peasants who were unable to offer any other form of assistance. One Sunday, however, when they did not realise that even the poorest peasant would not demean themselves wearing clothes such as theirs, they met a middle aged woman on the road, who looked them up and down and asked whether they spoke English. When they replied yes and enquired whether she did, her reply was, "No, No, only kiss me, beefsteak, that's all." It was their good fortune to have met Madame Martin, the widowed mother of a captain in the French Medical Corps in Africa, who was prepared to hide them in a rock quarry nearby while she went to enlist the aid of a notary in the village of Chatelus Malvaleix, who had a working knowledge of English. Their stay there slipped from days into weeks, and their confidence in help coming was put to the test. Fortunately the weather was fine which helped considerably. After two and a half months Madame Martin had at last contacted the underground movement and after false identity cards were produced both airmen were briefed as to their new identities and whisked off to Paris, where they joined up with three Americans of the USAAF and five Frenchmen heading for

North Africa. They were all put on a train to Toulouse by members of the underground movement, then from Toulouse by a bus on a rail track to a mountain resort. Afterwards they travelled in a charcoal burning Peugeot car to a goatherd's hut on the slopes of the Pyrenees. The irony of being transported in this type of car was not lost on them. They were the last group to be escorted over the mountains from France to Spain that year, crossing near the border of Andorra. It was a tough five days and nights before they finally arrived in Spain and were taken by truck to the British Embassy in Barcelona on November 21st, just over four months after their bale out. From Barcelona it was by car to Madrid then to La Linea and a short bus ride to Gibraltar, from where they flew back to the UK in a DC3 aircraft.

On the Run for Nearly a Year

1338225 Warrant Officer B. A. Lee was the rear gunner of Halifax DT768 from 78 Squadron, one of the four aircraft lost on the Montbeliard raid from 4 Group. The aircraft had a lot of engine trouble and at 00.20 hours it suddenly lost flying speed and went into a steep dive. The pilot, Pilot Officer O. P. Marshall, was unable to control the aircraft so he ordered an immediate bale out. Five of the crew were able to get out of the hurtling aircraft but the remaining two, the pilot and bomb aimer, Flying Officer N. S. M. Reid, were killed when the plane crashed. All the survivors baled out north-east of Nogent-le-Rotrou, and from the post war interrogation report Warrant Officer Lee relates his experiences.

"My 'chute got entangled in a tree so I never bothered about it and left all my flying gear at the bottom of the tree and started walking in a southerly direction until I came to a road. I continued to walk until 05.00 hours when I was surprised to see a young woman coming along on a cycle so early in the morning. She stopped and made me to understand that I was to go into the hedge and hide and that she would be back to bring me some food and clothing. After an hour she returned with some bread and meat and a blue blouse. She told me to keep hidden and that she would return after a short time, but as I considered that I was too close to where my plane had crashed and I now had a blouse as some sort of disguise I decided to push on a little further.

"I walked for several days and nights, resting for a few hours in the early mornings. One day as I was walking along a country lane and feeling rather tired and very foot sore, I decided around noon to rest in a hedge. Just as I was about to lay down two men on cycles overtook me so I waited until they were well past before I scrambled into the hedge. However one of the men came back, sat beside me, and asked in French if I was English. At the same time he pulled up my trouser leg and revealed my flying boot.

"We talked in a sort of sign language and I made him understand that I had come down by parachute. He told me to carry on walking to within a kilometre of Mondoubleau, where he would meet me with some clothes and food. By now the thought of food was tantalising as I had lived for several days on Horlicks tablets and apples I had taken from orchard. I walked for about half an hour before the second cyclist returned and brought me clothes and food. I changed into the civilian clothes, and the man walked along the road and allowed me to ride his bike to a farm. Here I was told to go to bed which I thankfully did. When I got up it was getting dark and the man then served me a meal. The cyclist returned at 22.00 hours and we walked into Mondoubleau, where I was taken into a house. I was there for about two days when a man and his married daughter came to visit. She could speak English and it was obvious that her visit was to check and prove that I was English.

"These people came to visit a few days later and this time they brought some maps. I suggested that I should leave and get away to Spain, but they told me to stay where I was as they expected an invasion soon. I listened to their advice and just helped around the house to keep myself occupied. Owing to the frequent comings and goings to and from the house, and my looking in drawers and finding many different kinds of maps, I thought this might be the meeting place of a Resistance Group. I asked the lady of the house if this was so and with great reluctance she admitted that it was a Resistance Group Headquarters.

"One day a cyclist arrived and asked me if I would like to send a radio message to my people in England. I took up the offer and I gave him a brief message. He went away with it and when he returned he confirmed the message had been sent. Another man turned up during this period who told me he was the head of a resistance movement in another area. He spent most of his time typing and looking at maps, but no one was allowed to see what he had written He occasionally went off to visit Paris.

"Another day he said he was meeting a girl at the station. She would be wearing feathers in her hat so that she could be recognised. She duly arrived and was brought to the house and she told me that I could write a letter to my people in England and she would take it and see that it went over by plane, which would be leaving from somewhere in the Paris area. I wrote this letter saying that I was alright, but I did not not mention my location. I found when I did return to England neither the radio message nor letter ever got through. This same girl told me that if I liked to go to St Nazaire that I could go on a fishing boat with two or three intelligence officers and be picked up by submarine and taken to England. When I asked how I could get to St Nazaire, which I knew was a highly protected U-Boat base, she just shrugged her shoulders. The people who I was staying with had no confidence in the man who did the typing or the girl. The man was always very frightened that the Gestapo was coming and spent quite a lot of his time watching people arriving by bus. They were very strange people.

"One day he came in and said that there were Gestapo people in the town and he just went off and I didn't see him again. The cyclist also heard about this rumour of Gestapo in the area and as a precaution I was taken to another farm somewhere east of the town. As there were several scares in Mondoubleau about Gestapo in the area I went to this farm each time for a few days.

"In October, 1943, the cyclist told me that he was expecting some arms to be dropped by the RAF and showed me some batteries and coloured glass. He asked if this would do for signalling to the aircraft. As it was all he had I agreed that it would do, but nothing happened as the code word had been discovered.

"In the middle of November, I was awakened in the early morning by the lady of the house as she had heard cars coming into the town. At about 08.00 hours I saw German troops and was told that they were looking for a parachutist, which I presumed was me. I went to hide in the garage and although the house was searched three times and the garage once I was not discovered. In the evening a man arrived and took me to another house and I stayed there for two nights and returned to the first house during the day. On December 15th I was taken by car to a chateau near Lunay, but I stayed there for only ten days as the owner of the chateau received information that the Gestapo were coming to the area on Christmas night. To get me away he took me on the pillion of a motorcycle to Mazange, where we met a priest who supplied me with identity papers and ration cards and took me to a house. Here I met a man called Harry Gregory, a soldier from the Loyals who had been there since the time of Dunkirk. I stayed at the house until June 1944, and nothing of any great importance happened until just before the invasion when the owner of the chateau said that there might be a chance of getting me away by plane. During my long stay at this house I also met another Dunkirk soldier named Brierley, also from the Loyals, who was not particularly friendly with his Army colleague Gregory. One morning both Brierley and I were warned to be at a certain place to be picked up by car. We travelled about three hours in the car, being told that we were going to get on a plane. En route we stopped at another chateau and went in but the owner said he knew nothing about us or our plane and would have nothing to do with us. The driver of our car left us after giving us 1,000 Francs.

"Not knowing where we were and the chateau owner being very

unhelpful in not giving us our position except that we should cross over a river and go to a village, we set off as instructed. On the way we were stopped by some Frenchmen and asked for our identity cards. While the cards were being examined more Frenchmen turned up and we were taken to a local cafe and searched. We declared ourselves as we thought that they were members of the Maquis. We were given pistols and put in a car and driven to a lodge where for some unknown reason our pistols were taken from us. At the lodge we met with an English woman who told us that she had been dropped by parachute a little time before. Both of us were a little unhappy at the situation we were now in as the Maquis were a very careless lot, shooting off their pistols at odd times. The day after we arrived we were taken to see a German prisoner who the Maquis had captured and who was kept prisoner in the chateau attic. We also met up with two other English airmen and an American at this chateau.

"We were awakened the next morning, Sunday, to the sound of rifles and grenades. The five of us, who were all evaders, took to the woods at the back of the chateau, but a German patrol quickly rounded us up. We were taken to Romorantin and as we alighted from the lorry we were beaten up with the rifle butts of the German guards. They also tried to smash our faces against a wall. Our wrists were tied up with wire and then we were all tied up to each other and knocked down and beaten with a whip. I was eventually cut loose and kicked into a room where I was interrogated by two German Army officers. I was beaten up so badly that I can hardly remember what I said to them. We were all then taken to Orleans where we suffered another interview, by the Gestapo this time. I was finally sent to Stalag Luft VII at Bankau on July 11th, 1944, and was liberated by the Russians in April 1945, at Luckenwalde. Since my return to this country I have heard that some of my helpers in France were put into concentration camps."

The flight engineer, Flying Officer P. D. Ablett, from Lee's crew also had bad luck in his evasion attempt for he was captured crossing the Pyrenees on 29th August, 1943. He fell ill in the mountains of Andorra, where he had been taken by a guide. He lost his way and was captured. Then he spent about six weeks in Fresnes Prison, Paris, before being transferred to a prison camp in Germany.

The wireless operator, Sergeant. I. J. Sansum, was the only one of the crew to successfully escape back to the UK, and his interrogation report shows how this was achieved.

"On landing I badly sprained my ankle and after getting rid of my flying gear I started to hobble in the hope of finding some other members of my crew. After about two hours and having no success I lay down in a straw stack in a farmyard and went to sleep around 02.30 hours. The following morning I was discovered by a young boy. As I speak only a few French words I had difficulty in explaining who I was, but I finally managed to make myself understood. He went to his mother who brought me some milk and then told me I must move as the gendarmes would soon be arriving. I took her advice and painfully hobbled An. as my ankle, by now was badly swollen, was giving me a great deal of pain I had no alternative but to lay down in a field. While I lay there a woman brought some cows into the field and saw me, she did not offer any help but told me to shut the gate when I left. About half an hour later a man came and he told me that it was important that I should be hidden as there were a lot of Germans about. He then carried me across his shoulders into a nearby wood and later returned with some food and wine.

"Then he went away and returned later with a note written in bad English, but which asked me if I had any means of getting away or if I had any friends or any other means of helping myself. I wrote on the back of the note stating that I had 2,000 francs and a map. A reply came back saying that this was not much and that I had better give myself up.

"I explained to my helper the contents of the last note and he went away returning with a horse and cart. Carrying me into the cart he covered me with straw and drove into Nogent-le-Rotrou where he drove into the back yard of a house. He carried me inside and gave me some food and introduced me to the author of the notes. She was a young girl who spoke a little English. After I had eaten she left the house and came back with a man who spoke good English who told me that it would not be safe to remain as there was a German garrison in the town.

"I was given an old mackintosh to cover my uniform and again put on to a horse drawn cart and this time driven by another man to his farm about two kilometres out of town, where I remained for three weeks while my ankle improved. During my time at this farm I was constantly visited by the young girl who had written the notes. She brought me English books to read and told me that she was trying to get in touch with someone else who would maybe help me. After two weeks she managed to contact an organisation in Paris, who arranged the rest of my journey for me. I finally reached Gibraltar on Wednesday, November 10th, 1943, and was flown back to the UK the following day."

Casualties July 15th/16th, 1943. Target Montbeliard

405 Squadron 8 Group Halifax HR854 LQ/A
Pilot. J/15609 F/Lt J.H.Foy DFC Evaded capture.
Nav. J/15071 F/O H.T.Huston Evaded capture.
B/A. J/1326 S/Ldr A.Lambert DFC Evaded capture.
W/OP. 1377432 Sgt G.Macgregor Evaded capture.
F/E. R/58807 Sgt J.B.McDougall E Evaded capture.
A/G. J/12681 F/O P.W.Simpson Evaded capture.
A/G. R/85446 F/Sgt A.D.Prior Evaded capture.

10 Squadron 4 Group Halifax JD211 ZA/Y
Pilot. 1312130 F/Sgt W.F.Pyle Missing, Runnymede Memorial. 138
Nav. 1386848 Sgt H.Stockley Missing, Runnymede Memorial 166
B/A. 1392530 Sgt R.A.Burrell Missing, Runnymede Memorial 144
W/OP. 1366787 Sgt F.J.Richardson Missing, Runnymede Memorial 163
F/E. 572721 Sgt E.T.Cooke Missing, Runnymede Memorial 146
A/G. 635420 Sgt D.Enoch Missing, Runnymede Memorial 148
A/G. 1356741 Sgt W.H.R.Clark Missing, Runnymede Memorial 145

10 Squadron 4 Group Halifax JB961 ZA/R
Pilot. 658718 Sgt H.B.Mellor Killed Recey-ur-Ource, Dijon, France. 1-3
Nav. 1501434 Sgt J.D.G.Bunker Killed Recey-ur-Ource, Dijon, France. 1-1
B/A. 149906 P/O H.M.Smith Killed Recey-ur-Ource, Dijon, France. 1-2
W/OP. 1129034 Sgt B.G.A.Cooper Killed Recey-ur-Ource, Dijon, France. 1-4
F/E. 1297114 Sgt R.A.W.Morse Killed Recey-ur-Ource, Dijon, France. 1-7
A/G. 1551651 Sgt S.Arthur Killed Recey-ur-Ource, Dijon, France. 1-5
A/G. 1620745 Sgt R.D.McKeown Killed Recey-ur-Ource, Dijon, France. 1-6

78 Squadron 4 Group Halifax DT768 EY/
Pilot. 147956 P/O O.P.Marshall Killed Nogent-le-Rotrou, Chartres. 33-1
Nav. 129582 F/Lt D.J.Gibson PoW. Stalag Luft 3, Sagan. 2912
B/A. 125422 F/O N.S.M.Reid Killed Nogent-le-Rotrou, Chartres, France, 33-2
W/OP. 1311760 Sgt I.J.Sansum Evaded capture
F/E. 149064 F/O P.D.Ablett PoW. Stalag Luft 3, Sagan. 261408
A/G. 1473756 F/Sgt A.J.Stevenson PoW. Stalag 357, Kopernikus. 230
A/G. 1338225 W/O B.A.Lee PoW. Stalag Luft 7, Bankau. 80

158 Squadron 4 Group Halifax HR752 NP/T
Pilot. 1343832 F/Sgt R.Deans Killed Sacquinay, Dijon, France. 1
Nav. 658501 Sgt J.Little Evaded capture
B/A. 1417057 Sgt G.G.Arnold Evaded capture
W/OP. 1211327 Sgt D.G.Bingley Killed Sacquinay, Dijon, France. CG 2
F/E. 635257 W/O V.C.Wainwright PoW. Stalag Luft 6, Heydekrug. 443
A/G. 638104 Sgt I.R.L.Acton-Hill Killed Sacquinay, Dijon, France. CG 2
A/G. 1318280 Sgt D.S.Loveland Killed Sacquinay, Dijon France. CG 2

76 Squadron 4 Group Halifax DK179 MP/S
Outer two engines cut due to lack of fuel, aircraft crashed in a potato field near
Goole, Lincolnshire after operation to Montbeliard.
Pilot. 34251 W/Cdr D.Smith Safe.
Nav. 144318 P/O P.M.J.Harris Baled out.
B/A. 1316204 Sgt D.K.Williams Baled out.
W/OP. 1191179 Sgt S.W.Palmer Baled out.
F/E. 778852 Sgt G.H.Cranswick Baled out
A/G. F/Lt H.M.Ashton Safe.
A/G. Sgt H.B.Thompson Safe.

Bologna and Genoa

July 15th/16th, 1943

The second raid of the night was made by 24 Lancasters from 5 Group on two targets in Italy, the first at Bologna and the second at Genoa, both with fairly important electrical sub stations as aiming points. The purpose of these raids was to disrupt as much as possible the passage of German troop reinforcements arriving by an electrified railway at the battle front in Sicily. Detailed results from this attack are not known. The whole force flew on to bases in North Africa after the attack. Two Lancasters were lost on this raid when they collided over the target. The crew from one aircraft, Lancaster DV167 captained by Flight Lieutenant C. H. Head from 50 Squadron, were all killed but the second crew were more fortunate as all survived except the flight engineer, 948474 Sergeant J. W. Edwards.

Escape from a Train

The pilot of Lancaster JA679 was NZ/413414 Flying Officer Malcom Head, from 9 Squadron. His aircraft was one of the Lancasters which collided over the target sustaining very serious damage. After attempting to continue flying for a further 20 minutes the pilot was compelled to order a bale out at 05.00 hours. All the crew managed to bale out, but the flight engineer's parachute failed to open and he was killed. Four of the crew became prisoners of war. The wireless operator, Flight Sergeant J. F. Merchant, succeeded in evading capture and the pilot, although initially captured, managed to escape and relates how he succeeded in doing this.

"After coming down in my parachute I landed in a field about four kilometres from Mirandola in northern Italy. My aircraft had crashed not too far away and was burning furiously so I ran as far as I could away from it. However, I was quickly caught by a patrol and taken to what appeared to be the city hall in Miranadola and locked in a small upstairs room where I was interrogated first by some Italian officers and then by some civilian Italians in the presence of a German. When I refused to speak I was threatened by the German as to the dire consequences of not answering his questions, but no force was used and the interrogation did not carry on when I continued to remain silent.

"I was joined by some other of my crew members who had been captured and together we were taken in a large car to Bologna aerodrome where we remained in custody for two nights. On 19th July we were all taken by train to Poggio where at first we were all placed in solitary confinement before being placed in pairs in cells. I strongly suspected that these cells were wired with hidden microphones to record any loose talk we had between ourselves. Our captors must have been disappointed with their results, for on August 1st we were moved again by train to Rome. Here we were placed in a very large house, which appeared to be some sort of private residence. It housed mostly RAF officers, but there were some so called Army officers whom we suspected of being stool pigeons. After only four days, on August 5th, we were all moved to a prisoner of war camp at Chieti Campo 21.

"When the Italians signed the Armistice all prisoners received orders from the Camp Senior British Officer to remain in camp and not to attempt to escape. All prisoners obeyed these orders and on September 18th the Germans arrived and took over guarding the camp. Five days later we were moved to Sulmona, where the Germans were making plans to move prisoners to Germany. Whilst at the camp at Sulmona, I teamed up with an Army officer, Lieutenant Ward from the 11th Sikhs, and we attempted to escape by climbing through the window of a latrine. From there we had only to penetrate the outside wire to get away, but the German guards had spotted us and after seeing their tommy guns trained on us we quickly gave up the attempt. We were put into punishment cells for three days, during which time the first draft of prisoners were moved out en route for Germany.

"When the last draft of prisoners were about to go on October 3rd, Lieutenant Ward and I along with one other prisoner in the cells at that time hid behind the doors of the three cells we were occupying, hoping that the Germans would not search them. Unfortunately as the guards opened the cell doors we were seen when some guards moved in with some kit that they were going to store and they quickly put us in with the last draft on the train, which the German guards said was proceeding to Austria.

"As we had no intention of being guests of the Reich for the remainder of the war we inspected our temporary travelling prison for any way of getting out. We had been on the train only two hours when a group of five (Captains King, Cheer and Wood, Lieutenant Ward and myself) discovered a loose ventilator and when the train stopped just before Goriano Sicoli we all got through the aperture, although by the time that Ward got out the train was passing through the station and doing about 20 mph. Ward was quickly surrounded by an excitable group of Italians who were very helpful and took all five of us to a deserted railway hut just east of Gariano Sicoli, the idea being that we should remain hidden there until our advancing troops arrived. While there we were joined by two Sicilian ex-officers who wanted to get down to our lines and fight with the British. We stayed in this hut until October

16th, Italian railway officials providing us with some food, but on that date they told us that they did not think it was safe to remain in Goriano any longer. We all then decided to start walking along the railway line out of the town area. We didn't get very far before we were called upon to halt by a German sentry outside a house along the track and we found ourselves facing a German patrol with an Officer in charge. We were rounded up and taken back into Goriano and locked up in a barn in a traffic maintenance unit. On October 19th we were all taken by truck to Roccaraso where we were interrogated, chiefly with a view of discovering the names of those who had helped us. As we were in no mood to give them any names, the interrogation was not pressed and on 21st October we were again moved by truck to Castel di Sangro, where we were put in an improvised prisoner of war camp for three nights. Lieutenant Ward made an escape from here but was quickly recaptured. The rest of us commenced to dig a tunnel, but this was discovered.

"On October 24th we were put on a train moving north. We had been on it for about two hours confined in a sort of sub compartment of a guards van with a German Feldwebel and six guards accommodated in the main compartment. As the train was passing through a tunnel, we were able to lower the window and managed to feel for the latch outside which we released. Half an hour later when it was dark enough and the train was moving slowly enough, the seven of us jumped out. The German guards started to take pot shots at us, but we all got away, although in the confusion I lost the others. I soon picked up Ward and one of the Sicilian officers and we three moved off together. Later we picked up Captain Cheer. We stayed about eight days in the mountains near to where we had jumped the train and then moved south with a guide who took us across the Sangro river. From here we moved via Montalto and Forli del Sannio, where we were shot at by German troops. I was hit in the left arm, which was broken and Captain Cheer had been hit in the arm and leg and as he could not run he was recaptured. The rest of us finally reached Isernia where we made contact with forward British troops on about November 8th. Leiutenant Ward by this time had a bad septic foot, so both he and I were taken to hospital at Sevro. Then I was moved to a hospital at Bari before finally getting to Cairo on November 10th. I left Cairo on February 8th, arriving in the UK on February 9th, 1944."

Casualties July 15th/16th, 1943. Targets Bologna/Genoa

50 Squadron 5 Group Lancaster DV167 VN/
Pilot. 49307 F/Lt C.H.Hunt Missing Runnymede Memorial. 119
Nav. 130194 F/O A.D.S.Snell Missing, Runnymede Memorial 129
B/A. 1383547 Sgt W.J.Hood Missing, Runnymede Memorial 153

W/OP. 1454431 Sgt R.G.Goff Killed Milan, Italy. V-A-2
F/E. 1192341 Sgt W.C.Trowbridge Killed Milan, Italy. JG V-A-1
A/G. 149985 P/O K.A.Barr Missing, Runnymede Memorial 130
A/G. 1192341 Sgt R.A.Wilkinson Killed Milan, Italy. JG V-A-1

9 Squadron 5 Group Lancaster JA679 EA/
Pilot. NZ/413414 F/O M.R.Head Escaped after capture.
Nav. 149689 F/O D.R.Walter PoW. Stalag IIA, Altengrabow. 140381
B/A. 125646 F/Lt R.S.Shaw PoW. Stalag Luft 3, Sagan. 2599
W/OP. R/107847 F/Sgt J.F.Merchant Evaded capture.
F/E. 948474 Sgt J.W.Edwards Killed Ravenna, Italy. 1-G-24
A/G. R/88234 F/Sgt W.J.McCoombes PoW. Camp not known.
A/G. R/66618 Sgt F.S.Findlay PoW. Stalag IIA, Altengrabow. 140694

Nuisance Raid on Berlin

July 15th/16th, 1943
Six Mosquitoes also made a raid on Germany's capital city of
Berlin, without any loss.

Minor Operations

July 16th/17th, 1943
There was a minor raid again on power stations at Cislago and
Reggio in northern Italy by 5 Group when 18 Lancasters made
the long trip to and from their UK bases losing one Lancaster,
DV183 from 207 Squadron captained by 145679 Pilot Officer L.
E. Stubbs. All the crew except for the wireless operator, 982855
Sergeant E. Morris, were killed and are buried in Milan, Italy.
Morris was lucky, for after baling out he managed to evade
capture and eventually returned to the UK.

Another Lancaster from 467 Squadron, captained by Australian Flight Lieutenant R. Carmichael on the same raid was
attacked by a night fighter over the target. In the course of the
attack the navigator, 1320579 Sergeant A. E. Murray, was killed
and the bomber so badly damaged that the pilot realised that he
would never be able to make the crippled aircraft climb back
over the Alps. He decided to head for an airfield in North Africa,
where he made a safe landing, The body of Sergeant Murray is
buried at Blida, North Africa.

Munich was the target for six Mosquitoes on the same night. They suffered no loss.

Casualties July 16th/17th, 1943. Targets Cislago/ Brugherio

207 Squadron 5 Group Lancaster DV183 EM/W
Pilot. 145679 P/O L.E.Stubbs Killed Milan, Italy. VI-A-12
Nav. 146344 P/O A.H.Coas Killed Milan, Italy. VI-A-8
B/A. 124200 F/O E.Mawson Killed Milan, Italy. VI-A-13
W/OP. 982855 Sgt E.Morris Evaded capture
F/E. 1960145 Sgt R.C.Mitchell Killed Milan, Italy. VI-A-11
A/G. R/98047 Sgt R.M.Furman Killed Milan, Italy. VI-A-10
A/G. 1436222 Sgt W.O'Brien Killed Milan, Italy. VI-A-9

467 Squadron 5 Group Lancaster PO/
Pilot. A/412391 F/Lt R.Carmichael
Nav. 1320579 Sgt A.E.Murray Killed El Alia, Algiers, N.Africa. 12-F-18
Navigator killed in fighter attack over target. Aircraft landed at Blida, North Africa.

Minelaying

July 18th/19th, 1943
Apart from minelaying in the St Nazaire area by 16 Wellingtons from No. 1 Group, from which all aircraft returned safely to base, Bomber Command stood down from the Battle of the Ruhr ready to make a much bigger and heavier assault on one of Germany's biggest cities, Hamburg. This campaign started on the night of July 24th/25th, 1943.

Statistics

In the 141 days and nights of the Battle of the Ruhr period from 5th/6th March to 24th July 1943, Bomber Command operated on 61 nights (bombing operations) and 69 nights (minelaying operations) dropping approximately 47,657.7 tons of bombs during 20,837 night sorties.

The Battle of the Ruhr was the start of the RAF's intensive bombing campaign against Germany and during this comparatively short period of the war the cost of battle was extremely high. 981 aircraft of different types were lost on bombing missions and 64 aircraft on minelaying sorties. Aircrew losses were 4,171 killed, 1,347 Missing, 1,183 prisoners of war, 133 evaded capture and 14 men were interned.

Little Friends - The Fighter Intruders.

While the heavy bomber crews were conducting their campaign against the German industrial heartland, the long-range fighter crews of Fighter Command were playing their part by harrying the *Luftwaffe* on take-off and hunting the German fighters down as they sought the bomber stream. A new radar device code-named *Serrate* had been fitted to the Beaufighters of 141 Squadron, Commanded by Wing Commander J.R.D.Braham DSO, DFC. This equipment was designed to seek out the radar used by the German fighters and proved to be exceedingly effective. This was the beginning of what the German crews would come to call *'The Mosquito Scourge'* during 1944-45. Indeed, within months the *Luftwaffe* airfield *Flak* crews would receive standing orders that, if two aircraft were seen to cross the airfield boundary in quick succession, they were to open fire on the second one without prior identification for it would certainly be a British fighter. Additionally, Defiants of 515 Squadron were fitted with a radar-jamming device code-named *Mandrel*, to confuse the *Luftwaffe* defences. These aircraft patrolled over the Channel to provide a screen through which the bombers could pass, thus allowing the German fighter controllers little time to dispose their forces.

During the Battle of the Ruhr, Fighter Command aircrew made the following claims whilst on *Intruder* or *Ranger* sorties over enemy occupied territory:

Claims for enemy aircraft destroyed

4/5.5.43
605 Sqn Mosquito. F/O B.Williams - Do217 destroyed at Eindhoven.

7/8.5.43
418 Sqn Mosquito. P/O Craft - Ju88 destroyed near Bretigny.

12/13.5.43
418 Sqn Mosquito F/Lt Beveridge - Ju88 damaged at Orleans/Bricy.
418 Sqn Mosquito F/Lt Beveridge - Ju87 damaged at Orleans/Bricy.
418 Sqn Mosquito F/Lt Beveridge - Enemy aircraft damaged at Orleans/Bricy.

13/14.5.43
605 Sqn Mosquito. F/O A.G.Woods - He111 damaged at Laon.

14/15.5.43
157 Sqn Mosquito F/Lt Tappin - FW190 destroyed at Evreux.
609 Sqn Typhoon F/O Van Lierde - He111 destroyed near Blankenburghe.

20/21.5.43
418 Sqn Mosquito S/Ldr Bennell - Enemy aircraft dam Melun.
29 Sqn Mosquito F/O Crome - He111 destroyed at Dijon.

25/26.5.43
418 Sqn Mosquito. Sgt James - Enemy aircraft damaged at Dreux.

29/30.5.43
605 Sqn Mosquito Sgt Linn - Do217 destroyed at St Trond.

11/12.6.43
605 Sqn Mosquito P/O D.S.Wood - Enemy aircraft destroyed at Gilze-Rijn.

12/13.6.43
605 Sqn Mosquito F/O Smart - Enemy aircraft damaged at Twente.

14/15.6.43
141 Sqn Beaufighter W/Cdr J.R.D.Braham - Bf110 destroyed near Stavoren.

15/16.6.43
605 Sqn Mosquito F/O Smart - He177 destroyed at Aalborg.

16/17.6.43
141 Sqn Beaufighter F/O MacAndrew Bf110 damaged near Eindhoven.
141 Sqn Beaufighter W/Cdr J.R.D.Braham Ju88 damaged near Schouwen.
605 Sqn Mosquito F/Sgt Irving - Enemy aircraft destroyed at Venlo.
605 Sqn Mosquito F/Sgt Irving - Enemy aircraft damaged at Venlo.

19/20.6.43
605 Sqn Mosquito F/O Dacre - Do217 destroyed at Compeigne.
605 Sqn Mosquito F/O Dacre - Bf110 destroyed at St Dizier.

20/21.6.43
418 Sqn Mosquito F/Lt Beveridge - Do217 probably destroyed at St Dizier.

21/22.6.43
141 Sqn Beaufighter S/Ldr Winn - Ju88 destroyed at Weert.

22/23.6.43
605 Sqn Mosquito Sgt Linn - Me210 destroyed at Venlo.
141 Sqn Beaufighter F/O Kelsey - Bf110 destroyed at Rijssen.

24.25.6.42
141 Sqn Beaufighter W/Cdr J.R.D.Braham - Bf110 destroyed near Gilze-Rijn.
418 Sqn Mosquito F/Sgt Kingsbury - Enemy aircraft damaged at Nantes.

25/26.6.43
141 Sqn Beaufighter F/O Kelsey - Bf110 dest NW Rheine.

26/27.6.43
418 Sqn Mosquito S/Ldr Moran - He111 destroyed at Avord.
418 Sqn Mosquito S/Ldr Moran - Ju88 destroyed at Avord.

28/29.6.43
418 Sqn Mosquito F/Sgt Kingsbury - FW190 damaged at St Trond.

3/4.7.43
157 Sqn Mosquito F/Lt Benson Do217 dest St Trond.
141 Sqn Beaufighter F/O White Bf110 dam Aachen.
418 Sqn Mosquito F/Lt Spencer Enemy aircraft dam Melun.

12/13.7.43
605 Sqn Mosquito S/Ldr Mack Do217 dam Eindhoven.

13/14.7.43
605 Sqn Mosquito F/O Smart Do217 dest Eindhoven.
141 Sqn Beaufighter F/Sgt Frost Bf110 dam E Schouwen.

15/16.7.43
141 Sqn Beaufighter F/O White Bf110 dest SE Rheine.

CASUALTIES

16/17.5.43
96 Sqn Beaufighter missing. F/O Hunt and F/Sgt Fermer lost at Rambouillet.

17/18.5.43
151 Sqn Mosquito missing. W/Cdr Ivins and F/Sgt Daly lost at Dinard.
410 Sqn Mosquito missing. NW Guernsey. F/O Boucher and Sgt Fyfe lost.
410 Sqn Mosquito Crashed West Malling. P/O Green wounded by Flak.

18/19.5.43
307 Sqn Mosquito missing. F/O Dziegiclewski and F/O Wiegel lost.

20/21.5.43
605 Sqn Mosquito missing. Sgt Adams and Sgt Wright lost Grandcourt.

21/22.5.43
515 Sqn Defiant lost S Portsmouth on *Mandrel* Patrol. F/Sgt Macauley and Sgt Wager lost.

25/26.5.43
605 Sqn Mosquito missing. Sgt Smith and Sgt Chilton lost Loosduinen.

27/28.5.43
307 Sqn Mosquito missing. F/O Fusinski and F/O Tabaczinski lost from Vechta.

17/18.7.43
410 Sqn Mosquito missing. P/O Wood and F/O Slaughter lost Dieppe.
515 Sqn Defiant missing to fighter over Channel on *Mandrel* patrol. F/O Walters and F/Sgt Neil lost. Enemy fighter subsequently shot down by a 256 Squadron Mosquito crew.

25/26.6.43
515 Sqn Defiant missing off Amsterdam on *Mandrel* patro F/O Sinton and gunner lost.

22/23.6.43
418 Sqn Mosquito missing. F/Sgt Finlay and navigator lost near Bretteville-sur-Laize.

21/22.6.43
400 Sqn Mustang missing. F/O Watlington lost from Tours.

16/17.5.43
141 Sqn Beaufighter missing. F/O Sawyer and F/Sgt Smith lost off Renesse.

17/18.6.43
3 Sqn Typhoon missing. P/O W.H.Moore lost at Brugge.

Armstrong, P/O C. 115 Sqn. 519
Armstrong, F/Sgt E.L. 419 Sqn. 354
Armstrong, F/Sgt G.E. 166 Sqn. 264
Armstrong, P/O G.W. 97 Sqn. 434
Armstrong, Sgt J.D. 76 Sqn. 166
Armstrong, Sgt J.H. 44 Sqn. 393
Armstrong, F/O J.R. 77 Sqn. 137
Armstrong, P/O T. 57 Sqn. 267
Armstrong, F/Sgt W.E. 432 Sqn. 492
Armstrong, F/Lt. Unit unknown. 419
Armsworth, Sgt R.G. 214 Sqn. 493
Arneil, Sgt A.S. 76 Sqn. 492
Arnold, Sgt G.G. 158 Sqn. 534
Arnold, Sgt J.F. 49 Sqn. 393
Arnott, Sgt P. 15 Sqn. 336
Arsenaut, W/O J.D.H. 419 Sqn. 491
Arthur, P/O D.I. 100 Sqn. 111
Arthur, Sgt J.L. 617 Sqn. 313
Arthur, F/O L.C. 9 Sqn. 388
Arthur, W/O M.J. 166 Sqn. 455
Arthur, Sgt W.G. 427 Sqn. 450
Arthur, Sgt S. 10 Sqn. 534
Asbury, Sgt R.A. 44 Sqn. 167
Ashcroft, Sgt B.P. 156 Sqn. 244
Ashcroft, F/O E.R.V. 103 Sqn. 144
Ashdown, Sgt H.I. 9 Sqn. 392
Ashdown, Sgt L.E. 158 Sqn. 101
Ashley, F/Sgt W. 78 Sqn. 266
Ashton, F/Lt H.M. 76 Sqn. 534
Askew, Sgt R. 428 Sqn. 341, 345, 373
Aspden, Sgt E.J. 431 Sqn. 142
Aston, Sgt J.C. 83 Sqn. 151
Ashby-Peckham, F/Sgt D.J. 218 Sqn. 424
Ashton, Sgt H.G. 10 Sqn. 326
Ashton, F/Lt R.H. 12 Sqn. 249
Ashworth, Sgt L. 83 Sqn. 434
Ashworth, P/O W.S. 49 Sqn. 497
Askham, Sgt C. 156 Sqn. 281
Allison, W/O S.H. 57 Sqn. 308
Arthur, Sgt J.L. 617 Sqn. 313
Ashworth, F/O C.H. 431 Sqn. 474
Astell, F/Lt W. DFC, 617 Sqn. 314
Astell, F/Lt W. DFC, 617 Sqn. 314
Atha, Sgt J.L. 158 Sqn. 344
Atherton, Sgt J.S. 196 Sqn. 372
Atkins, Sgt J.F. 196 Sqn. 251
Atkinson, Sgt A.E. 429 Sqn. 298
Atkinson, Sgt D.K. 100 Sqn. 207
Atkinson, F/Lt H.P. 405 Sqn. 256
Atkinson, Sgt J. 149 Sqn. 424
Atkinson, Sgt R. 102 Sqn. 68, 69
Atkinson, Sgt T.M. 466 Sqn. 457
Atter, F/Lt D.W. 77 Sqn. 245
Aumand, F/Sgt M.J.A.J. 425 Sqn. 104, 115
Austin, Sgt F.W. 51 Sqn. 159
Austin, Sgt H.W. 199 Sqn. 325
Austin, F/Sgt R.E. 419 Sqn. 450
Avann, F/Sgt R.J. 467 Sqn. 338
Avent, Sgt J.W. 10 Sqn. 295
Avery, Sgt J. 7 Sqn. 263
Avery, Sgt J.V. 431 Sqn. 197
Avery, Sgt R.A.C. 12 Sqn. 365
Awad, F/Lt C.M.S. 429 Sqn. 247
Axtell, F/Sgt T. DFM, 51 Sqn. 209
Ayerst, Sgt F.D. 12 Sqn. 471
Aylard, Sgt A.C. 12 Sqn. 397
Ayres, Sgt G.A. 57 Sqn. 389
Ayres, F/Sgt R.J. 35 Sqn. 342
Ayton, F/O G.T. 158 Sqn. 352
Babbington-Browne, P/O K.D. 61 Sqn. 69
Backhurst, Sgt G.W. 103 Sqn. 385
Bacon, Sgt B.A. 90 Sqn. 282

Backler, Sgt A.F. 9 Sqn. 491
Badge, P/O H. 207 Sqn. 511
Bagg, F/Sgt A.J., 15 Sqn. 69
Baggaley, Sgt R.F.F. 10 Sqn. 326
Bagley, Sgt A.E. 57 Sqn. 145
Bailey, Sgt A. 10 Sqn. 473
Bailey, W/O A.G. 432 Sqn. 345
Bailey, Sgt J. 166 Sqn. 455
Bailey, Sgt J.A. 426 Sqn. 143
Bailey, F/O J.B.G. DFC, 431 Sqn. 320, 330,
  408, 425
Bailey, F/Sgt R.G. 429 Sqn. 354
Bailey, Sgt S.A.J. 12 Sqn. 334
Bailey, Sgt W. 106 Sqn. 497
Bailey, Sgt W.G. 429 Sqn. 363, 372
Bailey, F/Sgt W.M. 57 Sqn. 497
Bailes, Sgt R.J. 103 Sqn. 392
Bain, W/O D.L. 429 Sqn. 141, 142
Bain, Sgt F.J.R. 78 Sqn. 438
Bainblatt, Sgt N. 408 Sqn. 389
Bainbridge, F/Sgt T.J. 7 Sqn. 375
Baird, Sgt D.R. 12 Sqn. 487
Baird, S/Ldr The Hon R.A. 115 Sqn. 519
Bakeman, F/Sgt E.H. 12 Sqn. 189
Baker, Sgt A.R. 156 Sqn. 157
Baker, Sgt C.P. 419 Sqn. 354
Baker, Sgt E.G. 115 Sqn. 460
Baker, Sgt E.G.F.B. 115 Sqn. 343
Baker, P/O F.G. 428 Sqn. 339
Baker, Sgt H. 76 Sqn. 386
Baker, P/O G.R. 426 Sqn. 82
Baker, Sgt G.W.F. 106 Sqn. 139
Baker, Sgt J.W. 432 Sqn. 492
Baker, F/Sgt R. 218 Sqn. 456
Baker, Sgt R.D. 466 Sqn. 58
Baker, F/Sgt R.H. 460 Sqn. 208
Baker, F/Lt T.B. 10 Sqn. 235
Bakewell, F/Lt L. 419 Sqn. 50. 51, 59
Balcer, P/O C.R. 428 Sqn. 252
Baldock, Sgt H. 214 Sqn. 57
Baldwin, Sgt A. 50 Sqn. 506
Baldwin, Sgt E.A. 460 Sqn. 386
Baldwin, Sgt J. 15 Sqn. 446
Balfour, Sgt R.D. 101 Sqn. 247
Ball, Sgt E.F. 97 Sqn. 131
Ball, Sgt J.H. 460 Sqn. 165
Ball, Sgt R.W. 106 Sqn. 511
Ball, Sgt T. 166 Sqn. 455
Ball, S/Ldr W.A.C. DFC. 156 Sqn. 80
Ballamy, P/O N.L. 44 Sqn. 393
Ballantyne, Sgt A.G. 106 Sqn. 394
Balley, F/Lt J.W.N. 77 Sqn. 166
Balsdon, Sgt R.C. 156 Sqn. 397
Balson, W/O A.P. 35 Sqn. 421
Bamford, Sgt C.G. 49 Sqn. 210
Bandeen, Sgt F.A. 57 Sqn. 138
Bandy, Sgt F.A. 75 Sqn. 351
Banescu, W/O G. 405 Sqn. 323
Banfield, Sgt A.J. 100 Sqn. 397
Banks, Sgt D.F.R. 158 Sqn. 236
Banks, F/Sgt I.W. 101 Sqn. 454
Banks, F/Sgt E.W. DFM, 156 Sqn. 281
Banks, Sgt D.J. 467 Sqn. 511
Bannatyne, Sgt W.W. 467 Sqn. 212
Banyer, F/Sgt J. 15 Sqn. 264
Barber, Sgt A.L. 106 Sqn. 258
Barber, Sgt D.R. 9 Sqn. 257
Barber, Sgt G.W. 15 Sqn. 488
Barber, Sgt S.F. 101 Sqn. 445
Barber, Sgt W.J. DFM, 158 Sqn. 223
Barclay, F/Sgt G. 49 Sqn. 237
Barclay, W/O G.S. 166 Sqn. 166

Bell, Sgt E. 35 Sqn. 349
Bell, F/Sgt E.M. 429 Sqn. 48, 59
Bell, Sgt G. 7 Sqn. 69
Bell, F/O J. DFM, 106 Sqn. 459
Bell, Sgt J.A. 78 Sqn. 210
Bell, Sgt J.B. 432 Sqn. 492
Bell, Sgt J.C. 460 Sqn. 208
Bell, F/Lt J.I.M. 76 Sqn. 265
Bell, Sgt J.R. 431 Sqn. 370
Bell, F/O J.R.H. 49 Sqn. 399
Bell, Sgt K.F. 196 Sqn. 284
Bell, Sgt R. 10 Sqn. 235
Bell, Sgt R. 12 Sqn. 281
Bell, Sgt R. 75 Sqn. 325
Bell, Sgt R.E. 106 Sqn. 394
Bell, Sgt T.H. 78 Sqn. 438
Bell, Sgt W. 101 Sqn. 129
Bellhouse, Sgt W.H. 199 Sqn. 367
Bellis, Sgt E. 97 Sqn. 434
Bembridge, F/Sgt J.W. 156 Sqn. 434
Bemi, W/O F. 420 Sqn. 168
Beney, Sgt E.T. 7 Sqn. 69
Benjamin, Sgt K. 428 Sqn. 143
Bennell, S/Ldr. 418 Sqn. 542
Bennett, F/O B.W. 460 Sqn. 367
Bennett, Air Com D.C. AOC No 8 (PFF)
 Group, Bomber Command. 12, 18, 19
Bennett, P/O D.E. 420 Sqn. 59
Bennett, Sgt E.W.J. 158 Sqn. 246
Bennett, Sgt H.W. 214 Sqn. 140
Bennett, W/O J.A. 419 Sqn. 59
Bennett, Sgt L. 100 Sqn. 454
Bennett, P/O R.F. 75 Sqn. 351
Bennett, Sgt T. 51 Sqn. 437
Bennett, Sgt W.J. 57 Sqn. 329
Bennetton, Sgt F.S. 75 Sqn. 270
Benson, Sgt A. 166 Sqn. 324
Benson, Sgt G.E. 78 Sqn. 113
Benson, F/Lt. 157 Sqn. 543
Bentley, Sgt H. 78 Sqn. 113
Bentley, P/O R.H.W. 75 Sqn. 270
Bentley, W/O T.L. 405 Sqn. 244
Beresford, F/Sgt W.C. 51 Sqn. 425
Berkeley, F/Sgt F.R. 158 Sqn. 216, 217,
 223
Bernard, W/O D.H. 158 Sqn. 387
Berresford, Sgt D.L. 101 Sqn. 335
Berridge, F/Lt G.F. 218 Sqn. 251
Berry, Sgt A.W. 50 Sqn. 211
Berry, Sgt H.A.J. 149 Sqn. 294
Berry, Sgt K.G. 115 Sqn. 352
Berry, F/Sgt W.R. 12 Sqn. 366
Berry, F/Sgt W.S. 7 Sqn. 111
Bertera, F/O D. 158 Sqn. 215, 223
Berthiaume, P/O J.F.E.G. 7 Sqn. 334
Bertram, S/Ldr F.C. 77 Sqn. 257
Bertram, P/O N. 10 Sqn. 158
Bertrand, Sgt L. 428 Sqn. 162, 163, 168
Bessette, F/Sgt B.J.A. 15 Sqn. 221
Bestwick, Sgt F. 61 Sqn. 81
Bestwick, Sgt W.H. 57 Sqn. 329
Bethell, F/Lt R.A. Unit unknown. 418-9
Betteridge, W/O R.S.J. 57 Sqn. 308
Bettinson, Sgt D.W. 49 Sqn. 510
Betts, Sgt E. 103 Sqn. 487
Betts, Sgt E.W. 426 Sqn. 286
Betts, F/Lt L.R. 467 Sqn. 371
Beveridge, Sgt C. 10 Sqn. 295
Beveridge, P/O G.T. 35 Sqn. 468, 471
Beveridge, F/Lt. 418 Sqn. 541, 542
Bevis, P/O P.E. 106 Sqn. 459
Bialobrowka, F/Sgt M. 300 Sqn. 423

Bickham. F/O C.J. 75 Sqn. 250
Biddle, Sgt F.J. 51 Sqn. 368
Bidduph, Sgt S. 149 Sqn. 315
Bidmead, W/O W.E. 431 Sqn. 185
Bielski, Sgt A. 300 Sqn. 446
Biffen, F/Sgt J.S. 460 Sqn. 324
Bigg, F/Lt D.R. 158 Sqn. 520
Biggin, Sgt H. 49 Sqn. 393
Biggs, Sgt E.A. 408 Sqn. 139
Biggs, Sgt S. 103 Sqn. 207
Biggs, Sgt W.F. 12 Sqn. 366
Bijowski, Sgt J. 300 Sqn. 446
Bilham, Sgt R.P. 149 Sqn. 158
Billett, Sgt H.C. 35 Sqn. 471
Billington, Sgt C.L. 83 Sqn. 151
Billington, F/O E.N. 15 Sqn. 424
Billington, Sgt W. 83 Sqn. 151
Bingley, Sgt D.G. 158 Sqn. 534
Binnie, F/O J.E. 467 Sqn. 399
Binning, P/O L.H.R. 149 Sqn. 112
Binnington, P/O W.R. 158 Sqn. 520
Binns, F/O J.B. 78 Sqn. 369
Birbeck, F/Sgt A.F. 467 Sqn. 338
Birchall, W/O R. 408 Sqn. 212
Bird, Sgt C.G. 76 Sqn. 369
Bird, F/O K.S. 218 Sqn. 223
Bird, Sgt S.D. 49 Sqn. 393
Birk, F/Sgt D.P. 460 Sqn. 392
Birkhead, Sgt D. 10 Sqn. 326
Birkin, F/Sgt F. 12 Sqn. 471
Birkland, Flt Lt. 192
Birrell, Sgt J. 78 Sqn. 506
Birrell, Sgt J.W.S. 10 Sqn. 352
Birtles, Sgt C. 50 Sqn. 186
Birtwhistle, Sgt F.R. 97 Sqn. 140
Bisheff, P/O G.E. 408 Sqn. 427
Bishell, Sgt H.S.F. 106 Sqn. 114
Bishop, Sgt A.T. 51 Sqn. 489
Bishop, Sgt B.H. 158 Sqn. 101
Bishop, Sgt E.C. 9 Sqn. 457
Bishop, Sgt J.H.W. 408 Sqn. 427
Bishop, Sgt J.P. 420 Sqn. 247
Bishop, F/Sgt J.P. 429 Sqn. 491
Bishop, F/Sgt L.E.G. 207 Sqn. 370
Bishop, Sgt M.W. 419 Sqn. 127, 130
Bishop, F/O R.C. 77 Sqn. 425
Bishop, F/O S.A. 100 Sqn. 342
Bishop, Sgt T.D. 35 Sqn. 269
Bissett, F/Sgt S.R. 75 Sqn. 436
Bissett, F/Sgt W.M. 427 Sqn. 143
Bisson, P/O G.E. 405 Sqn. 161. 167
Black, Sgt A.M.H. 51 Sqn. 327
Black, P/O C.N. 408 Sqn. 154
Black, F/O D.I. 419 Sqn. 371
Black, F/O G.J. 156 Sqn. 151
Black, Sgt G.R. 44 Sqn. 84
Blackborrow, Sgt E.B. 10 Sqn. 343
Blackburn, Sgt J.S. 15 Sqn. 222
Blackford, W/O C.L. 149 Sqn. 136
Blackhall, P/O R.O. 408 Sqn. 261, 267
Blackhurst, F/O S. 97 Sqn. 434
Blackie, Sgt W. 51 Sqn. 448
Blackman, F/Sgt E.C. 429 Sqn. 491
Blackweall, F/Sgt E.K. 78 Sqn. 266
Blackwell, F/Sgt A.E. 78 Sqn. 58
Blackwell, Sgt W.A. 460 Sqn. 342
Blair, Sgt F.C. DFM, 466 Sqn. 289
Blair, P/O J.L. 149 Sqn. 260
Blajda, P/O T. 300 Sqn. 423
Blake, W/O F.H. 158 Sqn. 153
Blake, Sgt P.R.J. 51 Sqn. 283
Blake, W/O R.B. 90 Sqn. 196

Bratt, Sgt D.S. 49 Sqn. 58
Bray, Sgt L.R. 51 Sqn. 208
Braybrook, Sgt S. 76 Sqn. 209
Brazil, W/O. Unit u/k. 414
Breen, W/O J.G. 431 Sqn. 370
Brennan, Sgt C. 617 Sqn. 314
Brennan, Sgt J. 102 Sqn. 425
Brennen, Sgt D. 83 Sqn. 151
Brett, Sgt B.T. 51 Sqn. 235
Brett, F/O J.A. 50 Sqn. 506
Brett, F/Sgt R.O.C. 207 Sqn. 511
Brian, F/Sgt W.L.F. 75 Sqn. 249
Brice, Sgt E.W.A. 76 Sqn. 369
Brice, Sgt K.O. 408 Sqn. 154
Brick, Sgt G. 101 Sqn. 263
Bridge, Sgt B.S. 49 Sqn. 399
Bridge, Sgt E.A. 428 Sqn. 522
Bridger, F/Lt J.C. DFC, 158 Sqn. 505
Bridger, P/O L.M. 77 Sqn. 80
Briffett, Sgt S.J. 51 Sqn. 208
Brigden, F/Sgt C.M. 51 Sqn. 245
Briggs, Sgt A. 61 Sqn. 81
Briggs, Sgt H.A. 51 Sqn. 256
Brinton, F/Lt R.H. 429 Sqn. 491
Brisbane, F/O W.C. 51 Sqn. 208
Britton, Sgt A.J. 57 Sqn. 237
Britton, Sgt C.A. 103 Sqn. 454
Britton, Sgt F.J. 7 Sqn. 195
Broadbent, F/Sgt C.W. 460 Sqn. 446
Broadbent, P/O H. 214 Sqn. 282
Broadhead, W/O B.H. 75 Sqn. 435
Broadhead, Sgt E. 7 Sqn. 334
Broadhurst, Sgt K. 149 Sqn. 471
Brock, Sgt H. 100 Sqn. 80
Brock, F/Sgt J.A. 50 Sqn. 449
Brockway, Sgt A.J. 419 Sqn. 330
Broderick, Sgt J. 214 Sqn. 158
Brodie, Sgt A.E. 51 Sqn. 368
Brodie, Sgt H. 15 Sqn. 446
Brodie, P/O I.J.D. 75 Sqn. 69
Brodie, Sgt W. 460 Sqn. 399
Brodrick, F/Lt L.C.J. 106 Sqn. 191, 192, 193, 197
Brok, P/O D.H. 101 Sqn. 423
Bromfield, Sgt L.S. 90 Sqn. 265
Bromley, Sgt R. 97 Sqn. 385
Bromley, Sgt T.L. 15 Sqn. 222
Bromwich, Sgt A.T.C. 44 Sqn. 307
Bronicki, Sgt M. 300 Sqn. 423
Brook, F/Sgt K.R. 51 Sqn. 368
Brook, F/Sgt T.G. 101 Sqn. 454
Brooke, P/O D. 408 Sqn. 427
Brooke, Sgt E.G. 90 Sqn. 355
Brookes, AVM G.E. AOC No 6 (RCAF) Group, Bomber Command. 12
Brookes, Sgt M.J.H. 77 Sqn. 295
Brooks, Sgt W.S. 156 Sqn. 445
Brotherton, Sgt A. 7 Sqn. 334
Brough, Sgt D.W. 9 Sqn. 392
Brough, F/Sgt R. 77 Sqn. 137
Brougham-Faddy, Sgt P.L. 156 Sqn. 206
Broughton, F/Sgt D.O. 429 Sqn. 286
Brown, Sgt A. 51 Sqn. 337
Brown, F/Lt A.M. 103 Sqn. 391
Brown, W/O A.W. 425 Sqn. 104, 115
Brown, W/O B. 51 Sqn. 283
Brown, F/O C.F.P. 7 Sqn. 420
Brown, Sgt C.V. 44 Sqn. 84
Brown, Sgt D. 10 Sqn. 473
Brown, Sgt D. 106 Sqn. 139, 258
Brown, F/Sgt D. 428 Sqn. 522
Brown, F/Sgt D.B. 76 Sqn. 265

Brown, F/O D.F. 115 Sqn. 403, 404
Brown, F/Sgt D.H. 102 Sqn. 520
Brown, P/O D.J. 218 Sqn. 250
Brown, W/O D.L.G. 408 Sqn. 467
Brown, Sgt D.N. 78 Sqn. 266
Brown, Sgt D.R. 35 Sqn. 349
Brown, P/O D.S. 106 Sqn. 394
Brown, W/O E.A. 7 Sqn. 420
Brown, F/Sgt E.G. 35 Sqn. 269
Brown, Sgt E.G. 51 Sqn. 283
Brown, Sgt F.W. 83 Sqn. 396
Brown, F/Sgt G. 76 Sqn. 209
Brown, Sgt G.W. 156 Sqn. 422
Brown, Sgt H.D. 460 Sqn. 123
Brown, Sgt H.G. 15 Sqn. 264
Brown, F/Sgt H.T. 9 Sqn. 498, 506
Brown, F/Sgt I.S. 100 Sqn. 207
Brown, Sgt J. 103 Sqn. 454
Brown, Sgt J.A. 214 Sqn. 282
Brown, Sgt J.G. 76 Sqn. 386
Brown, F/O J.H. 35 Sqn. 66, 67, 68
Brown, Sgt J.H. 427 Sqn. 517-8, 521
Brown, P/O L.F. 156 Sqn. 445
Brown, Sgt L.T. 76 Sqn. 492
Brown, Sgt M.P. 429 Sqn. 247
Brown, F/Lt N.S.H. 166 Sqn. 160
Brown, Sgt R. 156 Sqn. 445
Brown, P/O R. 166 Sqn. 184
Brown, Sgt R, 207 Sqn. 77, 79, 81
Brown, Sgt R.W. 49 Sqn. 138
Brown, Sgt S. 102 Sqn. 296
Brown, F/O S. 420 Sqn. 198
Brown, Sgt S.C. 156 Sqn. 244
Brown, F/O S.C. 158 Sqn. 379, 387
Brown, Sgt S.H.C. 76 Sqn. 209
Brown, Sgt S.K. 460 Sqn. 435
Brown, F/O T. 419 Sqn. 286
Brown, F/O T.D. 166 Sqn. 342
Brown, P/O T.H. 7 Sqn. 129
Brown, W/O T.L. 35 Sqn. 194
Brown, P/O T.N. 408 Sqn. 491
Brown, F/Sgt W. 51 Sqn. 327
Brown, Sgt W. 102 Sqn. 520
Brown, Sgt W.G. 10 Sqn. 401
Brown, P/O W.G.L. 35 Sqn. 421
Browne, Sgt E.W.H. 106 Sqn. 458
Browne, Sgt J.B. 44 Sqn. 258
Brownlee, Sgt J.P.H. 77 Sqn. 257
Brownlow, Sgt F.C. 158 Sqn. 246
Brownhill, Sgt G. 207 Sqn. 77, 81
Browning, Sgt J.R. 101 Sqn. 269
Brownlie, F/Sgt J. 102 Sqn. 266
Broxup, Sgt W.E. 100 Sqn. 510
Bruce, W/O A.W.A. 419 Sqn. 449
Bruce, Sgt N. 196 Sqn. 223
Bruce, F/Sgt W. 467 Sqn. 512
Bryan, Sgt A.G. 9 Sqn. 439
Bryan, P/O C.E.T. 103 Sqn. 189
Bryan, F/Sgt J.H.D. 49 Sqn. 393
Bryans, P/O R.J. 218 Sqn. 283
Bryans, Sgt W.R. 408 Sqn. 507
Bryant, Sgt C.E. 218 Sqn. 326
Bryant, Sgt L.D. 35 Sqn. 334
Bryant, Sgt J. 57 Sqn. 237
Bryant, F/O J.J. 156 Sqn. 375
Bryant, W/O S.W. 427 Sqn. 521
Bryant, Sgt W.H. 90 Sqn. 336
Buchan, Sgt D. 50 Sqn. 348
Buchan, Sgt D.M. 50 Sqn. 388
Buchan, W/O G.M. 35 Sqn. 375
Buchanan, Sgt T.A.S. 166 Sqn. 264
Buchanon, Sgt W.S. 467 Sqn. 512

Campbell, F/O J.M. 218 Sqn. 136
Campbell, Sgt K.M. 218 Sqn. 352
Campbell, F/O P. 419 Sqn. 330
Campbell, P/O W.C. 432 Sqn. 522
Camps, Sgt A. 149 Sqn. 316
Candish, Sgt E.J. 460 Sqn. 264
Candy, P/O E. 90 Sqn. 519
Canning, Sgt L.W. 218 Sqn. 223
Cant, Sgt L.R. 75 Sqn. 446
Canter, Sgt W.L. 408 Sqn. 197
Cantley, Sgt A.C. 408 Sqn. 212
Capon, F/O R.B. 35 Sqn. 421
Capon, Sgt M.G.W. 460 Sqn. 207
Capp, Sgt L.S. 12 Sqn. 487
Capron, F/O R.A. 467 Sqn. 258
Cardoo, Sgt A.R. 75 Sqn. 351
Carey, Sgt J.H.R. 75 Sqn. 350
Card, Sgt B.W. 44 Sqn. 393
Carey, Sgt C.E.H. 158 Sqn. 490
Carey, Sgt L.E. 35 Sqn. 471
Carleton, Sgt F.B. 427 Sqn. 476
Carley, F/Sgt J.W. 419 Sqn. 252
Carlon, F/O T.E. 405 Sqn. 102
Carlton, F/Sgt J.M. 419 Sqn. 237
Carmichael, Sgt J.S. 419 Sqn. 467
Carmichael, F/Lt R. 467 Sqn. 538, 539
Carne, Sgt R.D. 466 Sqn. 314
Carnell, F/Sgt B. 214 Sqn. 100
Carney, Sgt W.C. 218 Sqn. 298
Carpenter, Sgt F.R. 35 Sqn. 421
Carpenter, Sgt J.A. 57 Sqn. 511
Carpenter, W/O L.C. 106 Sqn. 344
Carpenter, S/Ldr. Unit unknown. 414
Carr, AVM C.R. AOC No 4 Group, Bomber
    Command. 11
Carr, Sgt E, 61 Sqn. 69
Carr, F/O R.H. 44 Sqn. 84
Carr, F/Sgt R.S. DFM, 207 Sqn. 114
Carr, F/Sgt T.E.F. 158 Sqn. 521
Carr, Sgt W. 49 Sqn. 138
Carrie, F/O J. 76 Sqn. 438
Carroll, Sgt J.M. 103 Sqn. 398
Carruthers, P/O A. 214 Sqn. 100
Carter, Sgt E. 77 Sqn. 236
Carter, F/Sgt G.C. 214 Sqn. 239
Carter, F/Sgt G.C. 428 Sqn. 268
Carter, P/O M.C. 50 Sqn. 388
Carter, F/Lt R.E. 408 Sqn. 371
Carter, Sgt S.C. 7 Sqn. 444
Carter, Sgt T. 12 Sqn. 391
Carter, Sgt T. 100 Sqn. 234
Carter, Sgt W. 166 Sqn. 155
Cartier, P/O J.L.R.F. 428 Sqn. 143
Cartmell, Sgt J.L. 101 Sqn. 195
Carty, Sgt H.D.G. 429 Sqn. 141, 142
Cartwright, F/O D.L. 429 Sqn. 82
Cartwright, Sgt P.F. 431 Sqn. 223
Carvajal, F/Sgt E.R. 425 Sqn. 188
Casey, Sgt J. 35 Sqn. 269
Cash, Sgt G.H.J. 214 Sqn. 158
Cash, F/Sgt J.C. 431 Sqn. 197
Cassell, Sgt J.E.O. 460 Sqn. 423
Cassingham, F/Sgt E. 35 Sqn. 376
Castellari, F/Sgt R.L. 166 Sqn. 184
Castle, W/O G.R. 467 Sqn. 101
Castle, P/O J. 78 Sqn. 492
Catch, P/O H. 214 Sqn. 282
Caulton, Sgt I. 166 Sqn. 160
Causer, Sgt G.T. 100 Sqn. 510
Cavanagh, F/O F.N.S. 408 Sqn. 139
Cavanagh, F/Sgt L.E. 158 Sqn. 439
Cavill, Sgt E. 35 Sqn. 342

Cawthra, Sgt N.A.M. 166 Sqn. 446
Cayless, Sgt D.R. 207 Sqn. 475
Cazaly, F/O C.K. 467 Sqn. 344
Cervi, Sgt L. 103 Sqn. 510
Chadfield, Sgt G.E. 44 Sqn. 353
Chadwick, Sgt A. 90 Sqn. 239
Chaffey, Sgt F.M. 78 Sqn. 328
Chalker, Sgt C.L. 15 Sqn. 488
Challenger, P/O C.J. 57 Sqn. 389
Challis, P/O E. 214 Sqn. 129
Chalmers, Sgt J.G. 466 Sqn. 167
Chalmers, Sgt T. 467 Sqn. 338
Chamberlain, Sgt W.E. 100 Sqn. 111
Chambers, Sgt C.A. 51 Sqn. 386
Chambers, Sgt D.E.C. 419 Sqn. 360, 371
Chambers, W/O P.K. 432 Sqn. 492
Chambers, Sgt R. 50 Sqn. 211
Chambers, Sgt W.J. 51 Sqn. 337
Champ, Sgt W.S. 15 Sqn. 367
Chandler, Sgt F.J. 76 Sqn. 257
Chandler, Sgt J.J. 75 Sqn. 351
Channing, Sgt D.W.B. 149 Sqn. 471
Chaplin, Sgt J. 78 Sqn. 519
Chapman, F/Sgt A.E. 100 Sqn. 342
Chapman, Sgt A.W. 106 Sqn. 354
Chapman, P/O C.A. 467 Sqn. 512
Chapman, F/O C.E. 426 Sqn. 59
Chapman, F/Sgt D. 83 Sqn. 396
Chapman, Sgt G.C. 83 Sqn. 434
Chapman, F/O M.A. 15 Sqn. 455
Chapman, Sgt P.A. 50 Sqn. 506
Chapman, F/Sgt P.A. 115 Sqn. 368
Chapman, Sgt R.J. 460 Sqn. 235
Chapman, Sgt W.P.D. 460 Sqn. 136
Chappell, Sgt N.A. 10 Sqn. 507
Chappell, Sgt S.F. 100 Sqn. 165
Chapple, S/Ldr J.H.B. 78 Sqn. 266
Chapple, F/Sgt W.J. 9 Sqn. 392
Charlick, F/Sgt D.H.V. 460 Sqn. 136
Charlesbois, Sgt E.W.L. 102 Sqn. 113
Charlton, Sgt J.T. 218 Sqn. 58
Charlton, P/O W.R.K. 460 Sqn. 208
Chatfield, F/Sgt W.L. 49 Sqn. 393
Chatterton, Sgt H. 49 Sqn. 167
Cheetham, F/O A. 50 Sqn. 186
Cheetham, F/Lt G.H. 76 Sqn. 448
Cherry, Sgt F.J. 408 Sqn. 139
Chester, F/O H.W. 76 Sqn. 474
Chesterman, S/Ldr H.W.A. AFC, 7 Sqn. 183
Chick, F/O M.R. PFF. 509
Child, F/Sgt R. 214 Sqn. 325
Chilton, Sgt. 605 Sqn. 543
Chilvers, Sgt K.G. 428 Sqn. 345
Chipchase, Sgt K.W. 83 Sqn. 100
Chisholm, Sgt D.A. 467 Sqn. 511
Chisholm, W/O R. 619 Sqn. 371
Chisholm W/O (RCAF) Unit unknown. 333
Chisnall, Sgt L.M. 166 Sqn. 335
Chiswell, W/O D.R. 78 Sqn. 58
Chittock, F/Sgt W.V. 51 Sqn. 245
Chitty, F/O D.J.D. 77 Sqn. 236
Chivers, F/O E.K. 57 Sqn. 329
Chivers, F/O M.E. 61 Sqn. 188, 189
Chiverton, P/O H.G.R. 102 Sqn. 267
Chliszczyk, W/O T. 428 Sqn. 522
Chretien, F/Lt G.T. 405 Sqn. 102
Christie, F/Sgt R.S. 460 Sqn. 367
Christy, P/O R. 49 Sqn. 329
Chrysler, F/Sgt C.K. 109 Sqn. 341
Chrystal, F/Sgt J.R.G. 75 Sqn. 435
Church, P/O B.H. 214 Sqn. 456
Church, Sgt D. 75 Sqn. 250

Conwell, Sgt P.G. 196 Sqn. 189
Cook, F/Sgt A. 103 Sqn. 367
Cook, F/O A.V.I. 90 Sqn. 455
Cook, Sgt C.H.D. 44 Sqn. 84
Cook, Sgt E.D. 75 Sqn. 195
Cook, Sgt E.W. 9 Sqn. 153
Cook, Sgt G.T. 149 Sqn. 316
Cook, Sgt P.V. 466 Sqn. 490
Cook, F/O R.H.D. 199 Sqn. 282
Cook, F/O R.G. 425 Sqn. 168
Cook, Sgt R.J. 158 Sqn. 387
Cook, Sgt S.A.J. 207 Sqn. 338
Cook, Sgt W.A. 49 Sqn. 237
Cook, Sgt W.R. 101 Sqn. 324
Cook, Sgt W.W.R. 207 Sqn. 475
Cooke, Sgt E.T. 10 Sqn. 534
Cooke, W/O G.H. 420 Sqn. 114
Cooke, Sgt K.B. 420 Sqn. 246
Cooksey, F/Sgt J.B. 75 Sqn. 446
Cooksey, F/Sgt R.F. 460 Sqn. 158
Cookson, S/Ldr A.A. 166 Sqn. 488
Cookson, F/O J. 51 Sqn. 327
Cookson, Sgt R.H. 50 Sqn. 449
Coombes, Sgt H.J. 57 Sqn. 186
Coombs, F/Lt C.E. 90 Sqn. 519
Coons, F/Sgt D.B. 426 Sqn. 82
Cooper, F/O A.N. 76 Sqn. 209
Cooper, Sgt A.N. 90 Sqn. 447
Cooper, F/O B. Unit unknown. 333
Cooper, F/Lt B.E. 15 Sqn. 336
Cooper, Sgt B.G.A. 10 Sqn. 534
Cooper, Sgt B.W.D. 100 Sqn. 234
Cooper, F/S E.N. 460 Sqn. 136
Cooper, Sgt G. 57 Sqn. 237
Cooper, Sgt G.S. 156 Sqn. 226
Cooper, F/O G.W. 115 Sqn. 343
Cooper, Sgt H.C. 15 Sqn. 294
Cooper, Sgt J. 103 Sqn. 234
Cooper, W/O J. 158 Sqn. 352
Cooper, Sgt J.D. 460 Sqn. 123
Cooper, Sgt R. 51 Sqn. 425
Cooper, Sgt R.A. 149 Sqn. 471
Cooper, Sgt R.B. 101 Sqn. 434
Cooper, F/O W.G. 214 Sqn. 133, 139
Cope, F/Sgt G.R. 460 Sqn. 392
Cope, Sgt H.C. 76 Sqn. 58
Cope, Sgt R. 49 Sqn. 211
Copeland, Sgt T.W.J. 467 Sqn. 464, 475
Copley, F/Sgt L. 214 Sqn. 188
Corbett, F/Sgt J.A. 420 Sqn. 116
Corbett, Sgt J.B. 9 Sqn. 337
Cordery, Sgt S. 106 Sqn. 167
Cordingley, Sgt R. 460 Sqn. 136
Corey, F/O J.G. 424 Sqn. 114
Corley, Sgt L.E. 156 Sqn. 206
Cornish, Sgt J.C. 460 Sqn. 386
Cornish, F/O O.M. 83 Sqn. 262
Corns, Sgt A. 115 Sqn. 456
Corrin, Sgt H.G. 75 Sqn. 250
Cosgrove, Sgt P.M. 100 Sqn. 342
Cosnett, Sgt E.W. 106 Sqn. 354
Costello, Sgt J.J. 51 Sqn. 489
Costello, W/O R.M. 199 Sqn. 325
Coster, Sgt E.S. 158 Sqn. 352
Cote, P/O P.E. 408 Sqn. 491
Cottam, Sgt A.P. 617 Sqn. 312
Cottenden, Sgt M. 419 Sqn. 467
Cotter, P/O P.C. 50 Sqn. 199, 211
Cottle, Sgt P.F. 49 Sqn. 399
Cotton, F/Sgt E.J. 51 Sqn. 343
Cotton, Sgt K.A.C. 460 Sqn. 435
Cottrell, Sgt K.G. 158 Sqn. 352

Coughlin, Sgt J.A. 102 Sqn. 296
Coulam, 35 Sqn. 68F/Sgt A.G.M.
Coull, Sgt A. 149 Sqn. 424
Coulsey, Sgt J.R. 49 Sqn. 393
Coulson, Sgt K. 156 Sqn. 226
Coulson, Sgt R. 50 Sqn. 186
Coulter, Sgt K.B. 101 Sqn. 461
Coupe, F/Sgt H. 199 Sqn. 342
Couper, F/Sgt J.R. 419 Sqn. 51, 59
Coupland, Sgt T.J. 408 Sqn. 197
Court, Sgt H.F. 51 Sqn. 343
Court, Sgt P.J. 620 Sqn. 448
Courtney, P/O J.B. 90 Sqn. 57
Courtney, Sgt J.J. 408 Sqn. 197
Cousins, Sgt A.J. 460 Sqn. 235
Cousins, Sgt A.S. 50 Sqn. 506
Cousins, W/O C.H. 76 Sqn. 327
Coutts, F/Sgt L.R. 428 Sqn. 246
Covell, Sgt D.W. 466 Sqn. 521
Coverdale, Sgt R.F. 106 Sqn. 354
Cowgill, Sgt S. 106 Sqn. 458
Cowham, Sgt S.W. 207 Sqn. 252
Cowie, Sgt D. 9 Sqn. 114
Cowley, F/O J.A. 156 Sqn. 375
Coventry, W/Cdr H.R. DFC, 102 Sqn. 520
Coventry, F/Lt S.W.J. 100 Sqn. 332
Coverdale, W/Cdr J. 431 Sqn. 408, 426
Cowell, Sgt D. 78 Sqn. 520
Cox, F/Sgt A. DFM, 405 Sqn. 161, 162, 167
Cox, Sgt A.G. 35 Sqn. 422, 486
Cox, Sgt D.M. 7 Sqn. 76, 80
Cox, Sgt E.W. 51 Sqn. 208
Cox, F/Sgt G.H. 7 Sqn. 445
Cox, F/Sgt R.T. 7 Sqn. 420
Cox, Sgt T. 10 Sqn. 270
Cox, Sgt W. 78 Sqn. 448
Cozens, P/O G.A. DFM, 149 Sqn. 484, 489
Cozens, W/O P.J. 420 Sqn. 198
Crabtree, Sgt M. 77 Sqn. 71, 81
Craft, P/O. 418 Sqn. 541
Craggs, F/O J.B. 15 Sqn. 294
Craigie, F/O J.E.D. 106 Sqn. 458
Craigie, F/Lt R.A. 467 Sqn. 258
Cram, Sgt D. 44 Sqn. 307
Cram, Sgt W. 100 Sqn. 391
Cramer, F/Sgt P.J. 103 Sqn. 234
Cramm, Sgt R.H. 218 Sqn. 437
Cramp, F/Lt D. 44 Sqn. 510
Crandell, Sgt T.M. 419 Sqn. 237
Cranham, Sgt J.R. 10 Sqn. 352
Crank, Sgt A.A. 83 Sqn. 422
Cranswick, Sgt G.H. 76 Sqn. 534
Craven, W/O C.R. 460 Sqn. 444, 446
Crawford, F/O A.V. 50 Sqn. 394
Crawford, Sgt F.P. 10 Sqn. 112
Crawford, Sgt I.D. 77 Sqn. 257
Crawford, F/Sgt J.L. 9 Sqn. 388
Crawley, F/Sgt J.S.F.V. 156 Sqn. 434
Crawley, W/O T.S.J. 158 Sqn. 329
Crebbin, F/O J.P. DFC, 83 Sqn. 233
Creevy, Sgt D.W. 12 Sqn. 334
Cresswell, Sgt A. 196 Sqn. 284
Cresswell, Sgt J.D. 620 Sqn. 448
Crew, Sgt G.C. 57 Sqn. 511
Cribb, Sgt R.J. 51 Sqn. 339
Cribbin, P/O G. 467 Sqn. 344
Crimmins, W/O R.T. 429 Sqn. 286
Cripps, Sgt B.R. 49 Sqn. 388
Criswick, Sgt M.L.C. 15 Sqn. 488
Crockatt, P/O D.E. 405 Sqn. 244
Croft, F/O P.N. 35 Sqn. 413, 414, 415
Crome, F/O. 29 Sqn. 542

Edmundson, Sgt T.E. 12 Sqn. 487
Edwards, Sgt A.V. 90 Sqn. 282
Edwards, P/O C. 460 Sqn. 488
Edwards, P/O C.A. 49 Sqn. 399
Edwards, Sgt D.R. 156 Sqn. 226
Edwards, Sgt E.D. 149 Sqn. 136
Edwards, F/Sgt E.K. 428 Sqn. 317
Edwards, Sgt F.G.G. 100 Sqn. 80
Edwards, Sgt G.A.P. 156 Sqn. 422
Edwards, Sgt G.H. 467 Sqn. 258
Edwards, Sgt H. 102 Sqn. 505
Edwards, Sgt H.W. 76 Sqn. 58
Edwards, P/O J.F. 61 Sqn. 211
Edwards, W/O J.G. 51 Sqn. 208
Edwards, F/O J.H. 405 Sqn. 160
Edwards, P/O J.H. 428 Sqn. 354
Edwards, Sgt J.L. 51 Sqn. 327
Edwards, F/O J.L. 75 Sqn. 395
Edwards, Sgt J.W. 9 Sqn. 538
Edwards, Sgt M. 428 Sqn. 522
Edwards, Sgt P.J. 101 Sqn. 129
Edwards, Sgt R.G. 166 Sqn. 184
Edwards, Sgt R.I. 199 Sqn. 112
Edwards, P/O T. 76 Sqn. 137
Edwards, Sgt T.E. 77 Sqn. 80
Edwards, Sgt T.L. 166 Sqn. 184
Egan, F/O A.E. 103 Sqn. 454
Egan, W/O G.A. 76 Sqn. 151
Egan, F/Sgt J.J. 214 Sqn. 326
Egan, W/O J.P. 467 Sqn. 331, 332, 338
Egelston, F/Sgt J. 100 Sqn. 510
Eggleton, Sgt D.L.N. 218 Sqn. 166
Eke, Sgt E.W. 90 Sqn. 282
Eld, W/O G.V. 207 Sqn. 139
Elden, F/Sgt B.R. 158 Sqn. 505
Elder, Sgt D.C. 103 Sqn. 189
Elderfield, F/O H. 50 Sqn. 199, 211
Eldridge, Sgt D.R.G. 51 Sqn. 465, 473
Eldridge, F/Lt J.G. DFC, 166 Sqn. 324
Eldridge. Sgt P.H. 158 Sqn. 153
Eley, Sgt A.K. 156 Sqn. 226
Elford, W/O N.R. 15 Sqn. 325
Elford, W/O R.O. 35 Sqn. 281
Elhorn, Sgt H.B. 420 Sqn. 187
Elkins, Sgt R.G. 103 Sqn. 234
Elkins, Sgt V.N. 102 Sqn. 113
Elford, W/O R.O. 35 Sqn. 281
Ellard, Sgt C.W. 408 Sqn. 267
Ellingham, F/Sgt L.E. 7 Sqn. 420
Ellingham, Sgt T.E. 207 Sqn. 252
Elliot, F/O T.J. 7 Sqn. 420
Elliot, F/O D.V. 158 Sqn. 439
Elliott, Sgt H. 166 Sqn. 184
Elliott, F/Sgt H.J. 207 Sqn. 370
Elliott, F/O G.W. 425 Sqn. 188
Elliott, F/O M.A.S. 76 Sqn. 166
Elliott, P/O R.F. 90 Sqn. 239
Elliott, F/Sgt R.F.A. 156 Sqn. 397
Elliott, Sgt R.H. 51 Sqn. 437
Elliott, P/O S.B. 103 Sqn. 454
Elliott, F/O W.G. 419 Sqn. 268
Ellis, Sgt D.W. 166 Sqn. 498
Ellis, Sgt H.C. 44 Sqn. 258
Ellis, F/Lt G.I. 149 Sqn. 239
Ellis, Sgt L. 7 Sqn. 183
Ellis, P/O L.J. 44 Sqn. 258
Ellis, F/Lt M.P. 7 Sqn. 417, 420
Ellis, Sgt N. 101 Sqn. 423
Ellis, F/St W.H. 75 Sqn. 238
Ellis, F/Sgt W.M. 158 Sqn. 352
Ellis, P/O W.T. 428 Sqn, attached to 419
Sqn. 427

Ellison, P/O R.C. 429 Sqn. 363, 372
Elmes, W/O R. 408 Sqn. 289, 297
Elsworthy, Sgt G. 12 Sqn. 248
Elt, Sgt K.W. DFM, 405 Sqn. 91, 92, 93, 94,
101
Elwell, Sgt B. 75 Sqn. 195
Emberson, P/O T.E. 15 Sqn. 264
Emerson, Sgt J. 51 Sqn. 457
Emerson, Sgt R.V. 57 Sqn. 237
Emerson, P/O T.H.N. DFM, 405 Sqn. 519
Emery, F/Lt A.A. DFM, 51 Sqn. 159
Emery, F/Lt J.A. 7 Sqn. 444
Emery, F/O W.E. 460 Sqn. 392
Emes, W/O D.J. 51 Sqn. 295
Emmett, Sgt J.H. 460 Sqn. 398
Emmons, Sgt K.E. 408 Sqn. 267
Emms, Sgt A.E. 7 Sqn. 259
Endicott, Sgt A.G. 77 Sqn. 369
Enever, F/Lt H. 419 Sqn. 285
England, Sgt N.N. 44 Sqn. 426
Enoch, Sgt D. 10 Sqn. 534
Enright, P/O G.W.B. 106 Sqn. 458
Enright, Sgt J.N. 78 Sqn. 174, 175, 176,
177, 180, 185
Entwhistle, F/Sgt C. 10 Sqn. 473
Entwhistle, F/O H. 102 Sqn. 344
Erdbeer, Sgt W.J. 158 Sqn. 344
Erickson, P/O D.W. 44 Sqn. 353
Erikson, F/Sgt H. 10 Sqn. 473
Erne, Sgt A.W. 218 Sqn. 447
Erne, Sgt K.F. 218 Sqn. 251
Errington, Sgt G. 466 Sqn. 224
Errington, Sgt S.A. 7 Sqn. 445
Erzinger, F/O J.D. 102 Sqn. 284
Espy, P/O H.J. 35 Sqn. 129
Estcourt, F/O K. 90 Sqn. 351
Ethier, Sgt J.P.O. 426 Sqn. 297
Etienne, F/O H.T. 214 Sqn. 57
Evans, Sgt A.R. 57 Sqn. 159
Evans, Sgt B.K.H. 467 Sqn. 511
Evans, F/O D.A. 35 Sqn. 323
Evans, W/O D.F. 420 Sqn. 168
Evans, F/O D.W.H. 207 Sqn. 285
Evans, Sgt E.W. 100 Sqn. 471
Evans, Sgt G.E. 51 Sqn. 368
Evans, Sgt G.H. 9 Sqn. 153
Evans, Sgt G.J. 49 Sqn. 237
Evans, Sgt G.R. 49 Sqn. 329
Evans, Sgt H. 101 Sqn. 207
Evans, P/O J. 9 Sqn. 392
Evans, P/O J.C. DFM, 57 Sqn. 458
Evans, P/O J.W. 214 Sqn. 325
Evans, Sgt J.W.C. 101 Sqn. 324
Evans, Sgt L.R. 12 Sqn. 366
Evans, F/Sgt N.I. 50 Sqn. 211
Evans, Sgt R. 408 Sqn. 491
Evans, W/O R. 619 Sqn. 371
Evans, Sgt R.D. 149 Sqn. 282
Evans, F/Sgt R.H. 76 Sqn. 448
Everitt, Sgt R.C. 61 Sqn. 459
Exton, Sgt L. 76 Sqn. 86, 102
Everden, Sgt L.L. 75 Sqn. 222
Everill, F/O J.M. 166 Sqn. 184
Everiss, F/O S.F. 90 Sqn. 222
Everitt, Sgt D.B. 10 Sqn. 196
Eversfield, F/Sgt S.E. 12 Sqn. 487
Everton, Sgt L.H. 12 Sqn. 487
Ewing, Sgt W.M. 57 Sqn. 308
Eyles, P/O S.C. 49 Sqn. 497
Fadden, W/O L.R. 426 Sqn. 320, 330
Fair, F/Sgt W.T. 467 Sqn. 258

Ford, P/O A.L. 466 Sqn. 439
Ford, F/Sgt C.J. 83 Sqn. 233
Ford, Sgt J.B. 90 Sqn. 222
Ford, P/O J.I.P. 196 Sqn. 251
Ford, F/Lt P.R. 12 Sqn. 365
Ford, Sgt S.L. 12 Sqn. 366
Forest, F/Sgt J.R. 408 Sqn. 389
Forland, F/Sgt O.W. 426 Sqn. 279, 286
Forrest, Sgt J. 218 Sqn. 166
Forshaw, F/O H. 619 Sqn. 394
Forster, W/O A. 76 Sqn. 265
Forster, Sgt R. 77 Sqn. 425
Forster, P/O T.N. 78 Sqn. 152
Forster, Sgt T.R. 158 Sqn. 439
Forster, Sgt W. 156 Sqn. 375
Forsyth, P/O H.E. 149 Sqn. 294
Forth, Sgt W.N. 218 Sqn. 265
Forts, Sgt. 50 Sqn. 466
Fortune, Sgt H. 15 Sqn. 222
Foskett, Sgt J.B. 102 Sqn. 457
Foster, F/O A.B. 408 Sqn. 491
Foster, P/O A.L. 7 Sqn. 195
Foster, F/Sgt C.S. 419 Sqn. 131
Foster, Sgt D.C. 149 Sqn. 465. 472
Foster, P/O E.A. 115 Sqn. 245
Foster, Sgt K. 12 Sqn. 293
Foster, F/Sgt J.S. 218 Sqn. 456
Foster, Sgt K. 77 Sqn. 505
Foster, Sgt R.N.P. 49 Sqn. 211
Foster, Sgt S. 103 Sqn. 487
Foster, F/Lt V.W. 408 Sqn. 491
Fotheringham, Sgt N. 101 Sqn. 445
Foulds, F/O L. 207 Sqn. 252
Foulston, Sgt J. 10 Sqn. 507
Fountain, F/Sgt G.L. 12 Sqn. 293
Fowell, W/O A.E. 408 Sqn. 371
Fowler, Sgt F.R. 49 Sqn. 393
Fowler, F/O H.W. 419 Sqn. 475
Fowler, Sgt T.K. 15 Sqn. 367
Fowler, F/O R.J.L. 419 Sqn (attached from
  428 Sqn). 450
Fowles, Sgt J.S.W. 102 Sqn. 296
Fowlie, F/O W.A. 90 Sqn. 57
Fox, S/Ldr D.P. DFC, 115 Sqn. 368
Fox, F/O G. 429 Sqn. 123
Fox, Sgt R.R. 7 Sqn. 195
Fox, W/O R.W. 466 Sqn. 439
Fox, W/O V.A. 7 Sqn. 80
Foy, Sgt J.E. 12 Sqn. 487
Foy, F/Lt J.H. DFC, 405 Sqn. 525, 533
Fradley, Sgt J.R. 102 Sqn. 520
Frampton, Sgt C.E. 460 Sqn. 165
Francis, P/O E.G. 196 Sqn. 246
Francis, F/O G.C. 97 Sqn. 140
Francis, Sgt I. 9 Sqn. 153
Francis, Sgt J.A. 106 Sqn. 458
Francis, Sgt J.T. 166 Sqn. 335
Francis, Sgt R.D. 9 Sqn. 153
Frank, Sgt N.H. 149 Sqn. 294
Frank, Sgt R. 97 Sqn. 140
Frankland, P/O E.V. 10 Sqn. 158
Franklin, F/Sgt K.D. 429 Sqn. 187
Franklin, Sgt R. 149 Sqn. 471
Franks, Sgt J.R. 158 Sqn. 155
Fraser, F/Sgt A.T. 102 Sqn. 505
Fraser, F/O D.G. 426 Sqn. 280, 286
Fraser, W/O J.D. 428 Sqn. 168
Fraser, Sgt J.H.M. 218 Sqn. 136
Fraser, P/O J.W. 617 Sqn. 314
Fraser, F/O K.E. 9 Sqn. 159
Fraser, F/Sgt R.D. 12 Sqn. 281
Fraser, Sgt W.J. 467 Sqn. 371

Fray, W/O F.C. 7 Sqn. 420
Frazer, F/Sgt L.J. 460 Sqn. 488
Freburg, F/O P.G. DFC, 7 Sqn. 183
Freel, Sgt J. 10 Sqn. 112
Freeland, Sgt R. 90 Sqn. 488
Freeland, W/O W.W. 7 Sqn. 69
Freeman, F/Sgt G.A. 408 Sqn. 427
Freeman, F/Sgt H.G. 51 Sqn. 327
Freeman, Sgt L.G. 214 Sqn. 325
Freeman, F/O R.N. 158 Sqn. 428
Freeman, Sgt R.W. 103 Sqn. 487
Freeman, F/Sgt W.E. 12 Sqn. 248
French, Sgt G. DFM, 77 Sqn. 432, 433
Freshwater, Sgt J.M. 83 Sqn. 57
Frewen, F/Sgt S.D. 428 Sqn. 317
Fried, F/Sgt A. 305 Sqn. 423
Frost, Sgt K.J. 207 Sqn. 338
Frost, W/O R. 49 Sqn. 393
Frost, F/O R.J. 427 Sqn. 459
Frost, F/Sgt. 141 Sqn. 543
Froud, Sgt L.P. 158 Sqn. 155
Froude, P/O H.G. 427 Sqn. 459
Frudd, F/Lt F.W. 405 Sqn. 487
Fry, Sgt A.H. 103 Sqn. 144
Fry, P/O E.J. 76 Sqn. 58
Fry, F/Lt J.R. 419 Sqn. 237
Fry, F/Sgt W. 51 Sqn. 327
Fudge, F/O B.S. 431 Sqn. 426
Fudge, Sgt D.C. 149 Sqn. 424
Fudge, F/Sgt H.P. 149 Sqn. 294
Fuge, W/O A.J. 158 Sqn. 217, 223
Fulcher, Sgt L.T. 467 Sqn. 153
Fullager, P/O D.R. 49 Sqn. 497
Fuller, F/Sgt M.D. 35 Sqn. 334
Fuller, P/O M.J.D. 617 Sqn. 312
Fulton, P/O J.T.S. 149 Sqn. 136
Fulton, Sgt R.O. 83 Sqn. 57
Funnell, Sgt D.E. 10 Sqn. 196
Funnell, Sgt R.E. 156 Sqn. 244
Furey, 2nd Lt B.J.J. USAAF. 419 Sqn. 467
Furman, Sgt R.M. 207 Sqn. 539
Fusinski, F/O. 307 Sqn. 543
Fyfe, F/O J.G. 158 Sqn. 387
Fyfe, Sgt N.W. 49 Sqn. 393
Fyfe, Sgt. 410 Sqn. 543
Fyffe, Sgt D.W. 49 Sqn. 138
Fyffe, Sgt. 466 Sqn. 289
Gage, Sgt D.F. 466 Sqn. 186
Gagnon, P/O G.A. 427 Sqn. 459
Gaisford, Sgt R.G. 90 Sqn. 222
Gait, Sgt L.J. 10 Sqn. 112
Galas, Sgt M. 300 Sqn. 282
Galbraith, Sgt D. 102 Sqn. 266
Gale, Sgt G.C. 7 Sqn. 165
Gallagher, F/Sgt G.B. 214 Sqn. 223
Gallantry, F/Sgt T. 76 Sqn. 85, 86, 87, 88,
  102
Galassman, Sgt D. 51 Sqn. 368
Galliers, Sgt G.A. 51 Sqn. 368
Galligan, F/Sgt P.J. 44 Sqn. 474
Galloway, Sgt J. 102 Sqn. 490
Galloway, Sgt J. 428 Sqn, attached to 419
  Sqn. 427
Galloway, F/Sgt M. 78 Sqn. 328
Galloway, Sgt M. 102 Sqn. 296
Gamble, W/O H. 78 Sqn. 266
Gamble, F/Lt R.H.P. 408 Sqn. 154
Ganderton, F/Lt V.F. 427 Sqn. 463, 475
Garai, F/O E.S. 218 Sqn. 351
Garbas, Sgt F.A. 617 Sqn. 314
Garbett, W/O S.G. 218 Sqn. 447
Garbutt, Sgt J. 620 Sqn. 448

Goldsmid, F/Sgt P.E. 214 Sqn. 437
Goldspink, Sgt J.J. 419 Sqn. 131
Goldstraw, Sgt E.E. 57 Sqn. 511
Goldstraw, F/Sgt R. 50 Sqn. 388
Goldthorpe, F/Sgt C. 460 Sqn. 324
Gomm, W/Cdr DSO, 467 Sqn. 404
Gonce, P/O H.B. 156 Sqn. 206
Good, Sgt G.J. 100 Sqn. 207
Goodchild, F/Sgt K.A. 51 Sqn. 283
Goode, Sgt H.F. 467 Sqn. 212
Goodenough, Sgt R.G. 77 Sqn. 369
Gooderham, F/O D.S. 431 Sqn. 296
Goodfellow, Sgt E.G. 158 Sqn. 246
Goodfellow, W/O J.R. 428 Sqn. 522
Goodhand, Sgt A. 12 Sqn. 249
Gooding, W/O R. 460 Sqn. 158
Goodley, F/Lt L.G. DFC. 156 Sqn. 80
Goodson, F/O J.C. DFM, 35 Sqn. 349
Goodwin, F/O D.C. 101 Sqn. 385
Goodwin, F/O R.O.E. 419 Sqn. 449
Goodwin, Sgt S.L. 207 Sqn. 285
Goodyear, Sgt P.A.U. 49 Sqn. 510
Goodyear, Sgt R.E. 78 Sqn. 328
Gordon, F/Sgt A. 460 Sqn. 386
Gordon, Sgt A.D. 405 Sqn. 160
Gordon, Sgt A.J. 214 Sqn. 158
Gordon, Sgt D.B. 460 Sqn. 350
Gordon, F/O H.L. 460 Sqn. 392
Gordon, Sgt J.R. 166 Sqn. 184
Gordon, Sgt W.H. 156 Sqn. 434
Gordon-Powell, F/Sgt S.K. MC, 35 Sqn.
  468-9, 471
Gore, Sgt K. 102 Sqn. 457
Gorton, Sgt C. 419 Sqn (attached from 428
  Sqn). 450
Gorton, F/Sgt J. 12 Sqn. 349
Gosling, F/O A.S. 158 Sqn. 520
Gosling, Sgt P.E.M. 51 Sqn. 339
Gosnell, Sgt W.H. 78 Sqn. 113
Gosper, P/O L.G. DFC, 7 Sqn. 68
Goudge, F/Lt I.P.C. 12 Sqn. 349
Gough, Sgt D.A.H. 102 Sqn. 457
Gould, Sgt J. 15 Sqn. 221
Gould, Sgt J.W. 466 Sqn. 58
Gould, Sgt R. 115 Sqn. 404
Gould, Sgt S.F. 90 Sqn. 196
Gould, F/O S.W. 83 Sqn. 307
Goulding, Sgt J. 12 Sqn. 234
Goulet, Sgt J.R.A. 425 Sqn. 104, 115
Gourde, F/Sgt R.R. 419 Sqn. 252
Gowan, W/O A.W. 35 Sqn. 349
Gowan, Sgt C.G. 102 Sqn. 284
Goward, Sgt R.P. 218 Sqn. 424
Gowing, Sgt R. 158 Sqn. 152
Gowling, F/Sgt G.R. 419 Sqn. 330
Grace, F/Sgt J.P.M. 156 Sqn. 165
Grace, Sgt M.J. 57 Sqn. 258
Grace, Sgt R.A. 619 Sqn. 475
Gracie, F/O B.M. 427 Sqn. 440
Graham, Sgt A. 75 Sqn. 250
Graham, Sgt H.E. 12 Sqn. 349
Graham, Sgt H.G. 196 Sqn. 267
Graham, W/O H.R. 103 Sqn. 510
Graham, F/Sgt J.F. 419 Sqn. 491
Graham, Sgt J.H. 35 Sqn. 421
Graham, F/Lt J.J.B. 405 Sqn. 263
Graham, Sgt N. 90 Sqn. 436
Graham, P/O R. 420 Sqn. 59
Grainger, Sgt E. 75 Sqn. 436
Grainger, W/O J.G. 102 Sqn. 246
Grainger, P/O J.K. 75 Sqn. 195
Graley, K. RAF. 110

Granbois, W/O A.B. 405 Sqn. 154
Granger, W/O F.D. 158 Sqn. 521
Grant, P/O A.G. 408 Sqn. 371
Grant, F/O B.A. 420 Sqn. 142
Grant, F/Lt C.E.L. 103 Sqn. 454
Grant, P/O D.E. 102 Sqn. 267
Grant, F/O D.M. 103 Sqn. 435
Grant, F/Sgt D.R. 460 Sqn. 392
Grant, Sgt F. 12 Sqn. 248
Grant, Sgt F.W. 408 Sqn. 130
Grant, Sgt G.A.A. 218 Sqn. 351
Grant, W/O J. 44 Sqn. 353
Grant, F/Sgt J. 49 Sqn. 329
Grant, F/Sgt J.A. 460 Sqn. 342
Grant, Sgt R.C. 12 Sqn. 248
Grant, F/O W.A. 408 Sqn. 267
Granville, Sgt. 101 Sqn. 269
Graveson, F/Sgt G.S. 214 Sqn. 437
Gray, W/O D.L. 419 Sqn. 389
Gray, Sgt D.M. 460 Sqn. 165
Gray, F/Lt E.N. 156 Sqn. 263
Gray, P/O H. 425 Sqn. 224
Gray, W/O J.D. 419 Sqn. 371
Gray, F/Sgt W.D. 35 Sqn. 349
Grayson, Sgt H.L. 7 Sqn. 125
Grayson, Sgt H.L. 408 Sqn. 130
Greasley, Sgt W.E. 101 Sqn. 111
Green, W/O A.S. 419 Sqn. 321, 330
Green, F/Sgt B.F.K. 51 Sqn. 245
Green, Sgt C. 90 Sqn. 282
Green, Sgt E. 115 Sqn. 456
Green, F/Sgt F.W.R. 466 Sqn. 370
Green, Sgt G.A.F. 158 Sqn. 369
Green, Sgt G.C. 466 Sqn. 457
Green, Sgt J.W. 199 Sqn. 169
Green, Sgt K.F. 97 Sqn. 131
Green, Sgt L. 51 Sqn. 368
Green, Sgt L 101 Sqn. 207
Green, Sgt M.L. 12 Sqn. 487
Green, Sgt T.C. 75 Sqn. 195
Green, F/O T.H. 51 Sqn. 327
Green, Sgt W.R. 158 Sqn. 439
Green, W.O W.H. 427 Sqn. 517, 521
Green, P/O. 410 Sqn. 543
Greenacre, Sgt G.C.G. 76 Sqn. 492
Greene, Sgt P.A. 77 Sqn. 166
Greenfield, Sgt J. 196 Sqn. 284
Greenhalgh, Sgt C. 76 Sqn. 328
Greenhalgh, Sgt E. 214 Sqn. 129
Greening, Sgt F.C. 50 Sqn. 284
Greening, Sgt G.J. 77 Sqn. 505
Greenway, Sgt J. 103 Sqn. 391
Greenwood, F/Sgt F.J. 35 Sqn. 376
Greenwood, Sgt J. 467 Sqn. 512
Greenwood, Sgt J.W. 15 Sqn. 222
Greenwood, Sgt N. 83 Sqn. 375
Greer, F/Sgt J.M. 420 Sqn. 143
Gregory, Sgt E.O. 466 Sqn. 476
Gregory, P/O G.H.F. DFM, 617 Sqn. 314
Gregory, Sgt T.J. 57 Sqn. 285
Greig, F/Sgt K.O. 408 Sqn. 345
Grenfell, F/Lt K.H. 460 Sqn. 136
Grenon, F/Sgt A.J. 428 Sqn. 317
Grey, Sgt D. 106 Sqn. 308
Grey, W/O J.R. 158 Sqn. 521
Grey, F/Lt R. 78 Sqn. 295
Griffin, F/Sgt C.A.F. 425 Sqn. 198
Griffin, W/O R.G. 57 Sqn. 186
Griffith, Sgt T. 83 Sqn. 262
Griffith, Sgt W.D. 51 Sqn. 245
Griffiths, Sgt A. 101 Sqn. 497
Griffiths, P/O E. 103 Sqn. 435

Hodge, F/Sgt R.A. 149 Sqn. 484, 489
Hodge, Sgt R.W. 35 Sqn. 349
Hodges, Sgt A.M. 100 Sqn. 234
Hodges, Sgt G.S. 57 Sqn. 458
Hodgkinson, F/O G.A.E. 50 Sqn. 211
Hodgkinson, Sgt P. 149 Sqn. 489
Hodgson, Sgt E. 100 Sqn. 111
Hodgson, Sgt J. 57 Sqn. 258
Hodgson, F/Sgt J.A. 57 Sqn. 497
Hodgson, P/O J.R.A. 166 Sqn. 140
Hodgson, F/O R. 102 Sqn. 490
Hodgson, Sgt R.L. 101 Sqn. 151
Hodgson, Sgt W.F. 78 Sqn. 152
Hoey, W/O J.W. 218 Sqn. 447
Hogan, F/Sgt P.J. 460 Sqn. 367
Hogan, W/O R.W.G. 101 Sqn. 129
Hogben, F/Sgt R.S. 460 Sqn. 235
Hogben, Sgt. 101 Sqn. 269
Hogg, F/Sgt D.A. 432 Sqn. 492
Hogg, F/Lt G.F. 102 Sqn. 520
Hogg, Sgt J. 35 Sqn. 334
Holbeach, Sgt K.A. 429 Sqn. 82
Holcombe, W/O H. 158 Sqn. 138
Holden, Sgt A. 431 Sqn. 185
Holden, F/Sgt D. 218 Sqn. 456
Holden, P/O W. 7 Sqn. 263
Holderness, Sgt J.A. 156 Sqn. 157
Holding, Sgt D.C.H. 97 Sqn. 496
Holding, Sgt W. 51 Sqn. 245
Holdsworth, P/O D.A. 61 Sqn. 211
Hole, Sgt J.G. 467 Sqn. 464, 475
Holland, P/O F. 405 Sqn. 101
Holland, F/O H.E. 50 Sqn. 211
Holland, Sgt J.J.F. 428 Sqn, attached to
  419 Sqn. 427
Hollas, Sgt R. 103 Sqn. 494
Holledge, F/Sgt N. 77 Sqn. 400
Hollett, Sgt W.A. 207 Sqn. 246
Holliman, F/O S.M. 218 Sqn. 250
Holloway, P/O A.J. 50 Sqn. 510
Holloway, P/O I.A.M. 149 Sqn. 239
Hollyer, Sgt P. 78 Sqn. 369
Hollywood, Sgt R.L. 103 Sqn. 455
Holm, W/O G.R. 57 Sqn. 186
Holman, Sgt W.J. 102 Sqn. 284
Holme, Sgt H.P. 75 Sqn. 249
Holmes, F/Lt A.L. 51 Sqn. 60
Holmes, Sgt F. 10 Sqn. 437
Holmes, S/Ldr F.A. DFC, 429 Sqn. 224
Holmes, Sgt F.B. 218 Sqn. 283
Holmes, F/Sgt F.E. 158 Sqn. 210
Holmes, P/O F.W. 100 Sqn. 509
Holmes, F/Sgt H.V. 429 Sqn. 427
Holmes, Sgt J. 405 Sqn. 342
Holmes, Sgt J. 432 Sqn. 492
Holmes, F/O L.H. 408 Sqn. 213
Holroyd, Sgt S.G. 158 Sqn. 383, 387
Holt, Sgt J. 83 Sqn. 396
Holt, F/O P.G. 44 Sqn. 353
Holtham, Sgt R.H. 408 Sqn. 139
Home, W/O A.L. 57 Sqn. 285
Hone, Sgt D.T. 101 Sqn. 269
Honey, Sgt G.S. 102 Sqn. 408, 425
Hood, F/Sgt J.R. 156 Sqn. 268
Hood, F/Sgt W.A. 419 Sqn. 475
Hood, Sgt W.J. 50 Sqn. 537
Hood-Morris, Sgt R.E.H. 207 Sqn. 338
Hook, Sgt J.B.J. 7 Sqn. 263
Hookway, W/C S.G. DFC. 156 Sqn. 57
Hooley, Sgt J.R. 427 Sqn. 459
Hooper, F/O C.B. 12 Sqn. 334
Hooper, Sgt F.G. 75 Sqn. 350

Hooper, Sgt H.C. 101 Sqn. 269
Hooper, Sgt J. 408 Sqn. 330
Hoos, F/O R. 35 Sqn. 349
Hope, F/Lt R.B. DFC, 83 Sqn. 151
Hopgood, F/Lt J.V. DFC, 617 Sqn. 314
Hopkin, Sgt G. 101 Sqn. 423
Hopkinson, F/O D. 617 Sqn. 314
Hopley, F/Sgt A.F. 426 Sqn. 297
Hopps, Sgt R.J. 97 Sqn. 268
Hopson, P/O G.E. 207 Sqn. 338
Hopwood, W/O N.C. 460 Sqn. 350
Horahan, F/Sgt L.M. 420 Sqn. 224
Horn, W/O B.W.T. 78 Sqn. 328
Horn, W/O C.L. 408 Sqn. 267
Horn, W/O W.W. 432 Sqn. 460
Horne, P/O A.E. DFM, 408 Sqn. 297
Horne, Sgt A.J. 196 Sqn. 490
Horne, W/O A.M. DFM. 49 Sqn. 58
Horne, W/O D.A.P. 102 Sqn. 113
Horne, Sgt K.G. 90 Sqn. 251
Horne, Sgt L.A. 97 Sqn. 268
Horne, F/O U.D.H. 460 Sqn. 386
Horner, F/Sgt E.T. 466 Sqn. 316
Horner, F/Sgt M.D. 97 Sqn. 470
Horrell, Sgt C.A. 103 Sqn. 454
Horrocks, W/O P. 78 Sqn. 519
Horsfall, Sgt D.T. 617 Sqn. 313
Horsley, Sgt V. 49 Sqn. 393
Horton, Sgt E. 106 Sqn. 511
Horton, W/O H.E.J. 429 Sqn. 372
Horton, Sgt R.C. 101 Sqn. 151
Horwood, F/Sgt A.J. 44 Sqn. 130
Horwood, F/Sgt D.R. 428 Sqn. 286
Horwood, F/Sgt J.H. 460 Sqn. 367
Hosken, F/O C.D. 78 Sqn. 519
Hoskins, Sgt A.L.T. 460 Sqn. 423
Hough, P/O E. 50 Sqn. 284
Hough, Sgt G. 101 Sqn. 269
Houghan, Sgt J. 106 Sqn. 497
Houlgrave, Sgt J.W. 149 Sqn. 136
Houliston, Sgt G.W. 103 Sqn. 189
Houston, F/O A.M. 76 Sqn. 166
Houlston, P/O J.L.R. DFM, 51 Sqn. 473
Houston, F/Sgt J.Y. 405 Sqn. 342
Houston, F/Lt R.G. 35 Sqn. 349
Houston, Sgt S.J. 100 Sqn. 234
Hovinen, F/O M.O. 106 Sqn. 511
How, F/Sgt T.F. 426 Sqn. 297
Howard, Sgt B.L. 76 Sqn. 474
Howard, W/O D.H. 78 Sqn. 152
Howard, Sgt E.J.C. 10 Sqn. 295
Howard, Sgt E.T. 218 Sqn. 136
Howard, Sgt G.R. 7 Sqn. 80
Howard, Sgt J.S. 218 Sqn. 298
Howard, F/O R.J. 425 Sqn. 188
Howarth, Sgt A. 51 Sqn. 151
Howarth, Sgt J. 10 Sqn. 343
Howarth, Sgt J.K. 76 Sqn. 151
Howarth, Sgt L. 78 Sqn. 474
Howarth, Sgt R.L. 100 Sqn. 385
Howden, Sgt C.V. 149 Sqn. 471
Howe, F/Sgt R.A.A. 100 Sqn. 510
Howe, F/Lt S.G. 35 Sqn. 375
Howell, Sgt A.C. 75 Sqn. 250
Howell, Sgt F.J. 106 Sqn. 308
Howell, F/Sgt R.T. 51 Sqn. 295
Howell, S/Ldr T.L. 149 Sqn. 239
Howell, W/O W.J. 419 Sqn. 285
Howes, Sgt A.J. 428 Sqn. 316, 317
Howes, Sgt B. 619 Sqn. 426
Howes, Sgt V.C. 75 Sqn. 250
Howes, Sgt W.R. 218 Sqn. 351

Linacre, Sgt J. 466 Sqn. 58
Lind, Sgt N.E. 12 Sqn. 248
Lindley, Sgt J. 620 Sqn. 448
Lindrea, Sgt J.D. 90 Sqn. 239
Lindsay, F/Sgt R.N. 106 Sqn. 106, 107, 108, 114
Lindsey, F/O L.E. 156 Sqn. 244
Ling, Sgt D.R. 100 Sqn. 234
Lingwood, Sgt L.D. 78 Sqn. 438
Link, Sgt R.C. 49 Sqn. 138
Linklater, P/O I.A.H. DFM, 207 Sqn. 114
Linn, Sgt. 605 Sqn. 542
Linnett, F/Sgt R. 51 Sqn. 368
Lishman, Sgt R.G. 207 Sqn. 77, 81
Lissener, Sgt P.R. 35 Sqn. 422
Lissner, Sgt P.R. 35 Sqn. 486
Lister, F/Sgt H.A. 156 Sqn. 341
Litchfield, Sgt E.G. 429 Sqn. 247
Litoloff, Sgt B.L. 207 Sqn. 114
Little, Sgt J. 158 Sqn. 534
Little, F/Sgt L.T. 460 Sqn. 398
Littlefair, Sgt R.W. 106 Sqn. 308
Littlewood, Sgt D. 214 Sqn. 336
Livermore, P/O T.R. 408 Sqn. 329
Livett, Sgt G.A. 83 Sqn. 422
Livingston, P/O R.A. DFC, 405 Sqn. 422
Llewellyn, Sgt I.W.L. 101 Sqn. 151
Lloyd, Sgt G.M. 51 Sqn. 339
Lloyd, Sgt G.W. 101 Sqn. 497
Lloyd, Sgt H. 149 Sqn. 351
Lloyd, F/Sgt H. 460 Sqn. 158
Lloyd, P/O H.S.R. 466 Sqn. 353
Lloyd, Sgt J.T. 207 Sqn. 475
Lloyd, Sgt K. 61 Sqn. 453, 459
Lloyd, Sgt T.E. 218 Sqn. 447
Lobban, F/Sgt J.A. 76 Sqn. 368
Lock, Sgt D. 158 Sqn. 490
Locke, F/Lt J.B. 76 Sqn. 113
Lockey, Sgt G. 75 Sqn. 436
Lockie, F/O G. 49 Sqn. 510
Lockrey, F/Sgt R.J. 460 Sqn. 435
Lockwood, P/O J.N. 467 Sqn. 344
Lockwood, F/Lt R. 15 Sqn. 238
Locksmith, P/O G.W. 51 Sqn. 283
Logan, Sgt C.R. 214 Sqn. 139
Logan, P/O R.F. 109 Sqn. 341
Logan, S/Ldr S.E. DFC, 405 Sqn. 94, 95, 96, 102
London, Sgt D. 419 Sqn. 127, 130
Long, Sgt A.M. 196 Sqn. 225
Long, P/O A.M. 466 Sqn. 494
Long, Sgt C.A. 90 Sqn. 519
Long, Sgt C.A. 617 Sqn. 313
Long, F/O L.C. 431 Sqn. 370
Long, Sgt N. 57 Sqn. 267
Long, F/Lt. Unit unknown. 418, 419
Longley, Sgt C.H. 51 Sqn. 256
Longstaff, F/Sgt E.J. 218 Sqn. 223
Longster, Sgt R.E. 100 Sqn. 366
Loose, Sgt R.V. 158 Sqn. 155
Lord, P/O M. 7 Sqn. 129
Lord, F/O R.A. 166 Sqn. 215, 221
Loudon, Sgt A. 15 Sqn. 184
Lough, Sgt W.R. 77 Sqn. 257
Love, F/Sgt H. 156 Sqn. 397
Love, Sgt G.S. 44 Sqn. 84
Lovegrave, Sgt F.T. 214 Sqn. 139
Loveland, F/O A.C. 78 Sqn. 58
Loveland, Sgt D.S. 158 Sqn. 534
Loveless, Sgt J.H. 102 Sqn. 266
Lovell, P/O D.G. 83 Sqn. 111
Loverseed, Sgt R.B. 57 Sqn. 284

Lowdell, Sgt J.S. 102 Sqn. 113
Lowe, Sgt R. 166 Sqn. 335
Lowery, F/Sgt W. 218 Sqn. 250
Lowings, Sgt J.L.S. 102 Sqn. 344
Lowis, Sgt C. 78 Sqn. 266
Lown, F/O J.L.F. 429 Sqn. 427
Lowrie, P/O J. 149 Sqn. 424
Lowry, F/Lt R.H. 419 Sqn. 297
Lowrey, F/O T. 408 Sqn. 491
Lowther, Sgt R.W. 75 Sqn. 184
Lucas, Sgt A. 196 Sqn. 140
Ludlow, F/O A.R. 44 Sqn. 510
Luff, F/O E. 156 Sqn. 57
Luff, Sgt G. 51 Sqn. 368
Luke, Sgt A. 77 Sqn. 236
Luke, Sgt S.C. 466 Sqn. 353
Lumley, Sgt J.G. 156 Sqn. 397
Lundie, F/Sgt D.C.P. 460 Sqn. 386
Lundy, Sgt E.E. 428 Sqn. 286
Lunn, F/Lt G.A. 429 Sqn. 224
Lunn, Sgt T.R. 218 Sqn. 424
Lunney, F/Lt R.H. 7 Sqn. 194
Lupton, Sgt S. 61 Sqn. 285
Lupton, F/O S.J. 166 Sqn. 214, 221
Luscombe, Sgt T.H. 166 Sqn. 155
Lusty, F/O D.W. 78 Sqn. 457
Lutes, W/O A.R. 78 Sqn. 520
Luther, Sgt T.W.C. 77 Sqn. 438
Luther, F/O W.C. 158 Sqn. 352
Luton, P/O L.R.S. DFC, 7 Sqn. 100
Lutton, Sgt R.L. 466 Sqn. 267
Lutwyche, Sgt P. 15 Sqn. 166
Luxford, F/Lt F.E. 405 Sqn. 154
Lygo, Sgt H.J. 207 Sqn. 370
Lynch, F/Sgt L.A. 83 Sqn. 100
Lyne, F/O D.H. 149 Sqn. 424
Lynn, Sgt R.W. 196 Sqn. 267
Lyon, Sgt A.J.L. 101 Sqn. 263
Lyon, P/O P.G. 158 Sqn. 101
Lyons, F/Lt C.S. 15 Sqn. 238
Lyons, F/O H.N. 15 Sqn. 325
Lyster, Sgt R.F. 51 Sqn. 235
Mabee, F/O G.F. 49 Sqn. 138
McAleese, Sgt P. 51 Sqn. 60
McAllister, F/O L.D. 196 Sqn. 142
McAlpine, W/O W.J. 405 Sqn. 149, 154
McArdle, Sgt P.D. 218 Sqn. 424
McArthur, W/O L.N. 83 Sqn. 151
McAulay, Sgt R.J. 76 Sqn. 474
McAusland, P/O H.T. 431 Sqn. 370
McBriar, P/O W.R. 51 Sqn. 209
McBride, F/O J.D. 408 Sqn. 154
McCall, Sgt W. 149 Sqn. 294
McCallum, Sgt G.L.K. 102 Sqn. 249
McCallum, F/Sgt L.B. 149 Sqn. 471
McCardle, W/O F.G. 51 Sqn. 208
McCarthy, S/Ldr R.W. 7 Sqn. 195
McCaskill, P/O D.G. 75 Sqn. 195
McCaughey, F/O P.S. 15 Sqn. 184
McCaw, F/Sgt J.F. 218 Sqn. 136
McCellan, Sgt S.S. 44 Sqn. 258
McClintock, F/O G.A. 432 Sqn. 372
McClure, F/O A. 76 Sqn. 87, 102
McClure, S/Ldr D.A.J. DFC, 83 Sqn. 111
McCoghill, W/O C.M. 83 Sqn. 149
McColl, Sgt D. 44 Sqn. 353
McColl, P/O K.S. 408 Sqn. 154
McConnel, Sgt E.R. 158 Sqn. 387
McConnell, Sgt W. 102 Sqn. 490
McCoombes, F/Sgt W.J. 9 Sqn. 538
McCormick, Sgt A.T. 426 Sqn. 320, 330
McCormick, Sgt J. 78 Sqn. 152

McQuillan, F/Sgt F.D. 15 Sqn. 424
McQuire, Sgt W. 90 Sqn. 488
McRae, F/Sgt D.S. 432 Sqn. 372
McRae, F/Sgt R. 405 Sqn. 323
McRorie, F/Lt T.F. 75 Sqn. 433, 436
McShane, Sgt T.H. 214 Sqn. 140
McStay, Sgt T.S. 77 Sqn. 166
McVicar, Sgt A. 75 Sqn. 195
McVittie, Sgt E.L. 76 Sqn. 414, 438
McVitty, P/O G. 100 Sqn. 366
McWatts, Sgt R. 103 Sqn. 510
McWilliam, Sgt A. 75 Sqn. 350
McWilliam, Sgt A.E. 83 Sqn. 422
Macadam, Sgt J.S. 10 Sqn. 295
MacAndrew, F/O. 141 Sqn. 542
Macaskill, F/Sgt T.L. 10 Sqn. 437
MacAulay, W/O N.T. 35 Sqn. 421
Macaulay, Sgt W.C. 15 Sqn. 435
Macauley, F/Sgt. 515 Sqn. 543
MacCausland, F/O V.S. 617 Sqn. 313
MacCullum, W/O G.L. 405 Sqn. 256
Macdonald, Sgt A.M. 420 Sqn. 187
Macdonald, P/O H.T. 419 Sqn. 154
Macdonald, F/Sgt I. 408 Sqn. 212
Macdonald, W/O I.R. 408 Sqn. 197
Macdonald, F/Sgt J.C. 408 Sqn. 427
Macdonald, Sgt J.J. 102 Sqn. 449
Macdonald, F/O J.K. 420 Sqn. 59
Macdonald, Sgt J.M. 408 Sqn. 507
Macdonald, Sgt R.G. 405 Sqn. 102
MacDonald, W/O W.A. 405 Sqn. 101
MacEachen, F/Sgt H.A. 166 Sqn. 249
Macfarlane, F/Sgt D.W. 77 Sqn. 337
MacFarlane, Sgt G.B. 83 Sqn. 135
MacFarlane, W/O G.S. 83 Sqn. 205
Macfarlane, Sgt J. 83 Sqn. 111
Macfarlane, F/O J.D. 420 Sqn. 116
Macfarlane, P/O W. 61 Sqn. 211
Macgregor, Sgt G. 405 Sqn. 533
Machell, Sgt H.G. 408 Sqn. 212
Mack, S/Ldr. 605 Sqn. 543
Mackintosh, Sgt E.D.C. 158 Sqn. 490
Mackay, F/O A. 619 Sqn. 475
Mackay, Sgt A.I. 103 Sqn. 234
Mackay, F/O F.E. 405 Sqn. 365
Mackay, P/O G. 83 Sqn. 151
Mackay, F/O J.G. 83 Sqn. 396
Mackelden, F/O F. 466 Sqn. 370
Mackelvie, Sgt C.D. 90 Sqn. 239
Mackenzie, Sgt A. 156 Sqn. 129
Mackenzie, F/Sgt D.A. 426 Sqn. 372
Mackenzie, S/Ldr D.C. DFC, 467 Sqn. 371
Mackenzie, P/O E.S. 156 Sqn. 281
Mackenzie, P/O I.C. 408 Sqn. 197
Mackenzie, F/O J.N. 51 Sqn. 448
Mackenzie, Sgt M.W. 405 Sqn. 101
Mackenzie, F/Sgt P.M. 460 Sqn. 235
Mackie, F/Sgt J.D.D. 158 Sqn. 251
Mackie, F/Lt N.A. DFC, 83 Sqn. 88, 89, 90, 91, 100
Mackintosh, Sgt J. 12 Sqn. 249
Mackintosh, S/Ldr J.C. 156 Sqn. 397
Macksimchuk, F/Sgt J.T. 166 Sqn. 264
Maclean, Sgt A. 405 Sqn. 478
Macleay, Sgt F. 101 Sqn. 454
Macleod, Sgt N. 149 Sqn. 158
Macmillan, Sgt D.B. 9 Sqn. 499, 506
Macmillan, Sgt H. 428 Sqn. 354
Macmillan, W/O J. 106 Sqn. 458
Macmillan, F/O J.D. 431 Sqn. 296
MacNeill, F/Sgt R.W. 76 Sqn. 137
Macpherson, F/Sgt J.C. 51 Sqn. 337

Macqueen, F/Lt A.F. DFC, 83 Sqn. 111
Macquire, F/O J.J. 405 Sqn. 101
Macrae, Sgt I. 78 Sqn. 448
Madej, F/Lt S. 307 Sqn. 409
Madge, F/O R.G. 428 Sqn. 339
Magill, Sgt A.B. 100 Sqn. 366
Maginnis, Sgt R. 12 Sqn. 293
Magnusson, F/Sgt C.N. 428 Sqn. 317
Maguire, Sgt A.G. 50 Sqn. 146
Maher, F/Sgt J.M. 467 Sqn. 511
Maher, W/O M.J.J. 51 Sqn. 327
Mahoney, P/O E.A. 460 Sqn. 235
Mahony, Sgt J.D. 77 Sqn. 284
Mailey, Sgt R. 214 Sqn. 493
Mainprize, Sgt W. 405 Sqn. 479
Mains, Sgt G.R. 156 Sqn. 151
Maisenbacher, F/Sgt W.M. 10 Sqn. 158
Maisner, Sgt S. 100 Sqn. 423
Makarski, Sgt L. 305 Sqn. 423
Makin, F/O D. 199 Sqn. 335
Makin, W/O R.H. 35 Sqn. 376
Malcolm, W/O T. 15 Sqn. 264
Male, Sgt G.A.H. 207 Sqn. 439
Male, F/Sgt J.F. 408 Sqn. 459
Malkin, F/Sgt J.E. 424 Sqn. 198
Mallen, Sgt H. 15 Sqn. 473
Mallett, F/Sgt C.L. DFM, 106 Sqn. 459
Mallory, F/Sgt L. 78 Sqn. 492
Maloney, F/Sgt M.J. 100 Sqn. 510
Malpass, Sgt J. 156 Sqn. 445
Maltas, F/Sgt F.S. 35 Sqn. 421
Maltby, Sgt C. 10 Sqn. 295
Manahan, S/Ldr J.R. DFC, 100 Sqn. 366
Mander, Sgt J.O. 78 Sqn. 328
Mank, P/O M. 7 Sqn. 195
Mann, Sgt D. 427 Sqn. 440
Mann, F/Sgt W.E. 428 Sqn. 286
Manning, F/O A.J. 427 Sqn. 440
Manning, P/O J.E. 50 Sqn. 510
Manning, Sgt W.A. 77 Sqn. 344
Mansell, F/Sgt J.G.H. 102 Sqn. 505
Mansfield, F/Sgt J.J. 97 Sqn. 434
Mansfield, F/Sgt P.L. 50 Sqn. 186
Mansford, Sgt A.R. 102 Sqn. 68, 69
Mansley, Sgt J.K. 57 Sqn. 258
Manson, Sgt W.M. 428 Sqn. 252
Mant, P/O G.S. 467 Sqn. 101
Mantha, Sgt R.R. 158 Sqn. 344
Mantle, P/O E.H. DFM*. 106 Sqn. 139
Mappin, F/O H. 83 Sqn. 422
Maracle, Sgt C. 405 Sqn. 342
Marchand, Sgt J.E.R. 428 Sqn. 341, 345, 373
Marczuk, Sgt W. 300 Sqn. 166
Marean, F/Sgt F.A. 78 Sqn. 113
Margerum, Sgt C.A. 101 Sqn. 247
Margetson, Sgt G.S. 207 Sqn. 81
Marion, P/O B.H. 166 Sqn. 163, 164, 166
Marlin, Sgt C.G.L. 44 Sqn. 138
Marlow, Sgt G. 77 Sqn. 287
Marlow, Sgt J.L. 75 Sqn. 222
Marnoch, F/O J.M. 100 Sqn. 335
Maroney, F/Sgt R.W. 466 Sqn. 370
Marriage, F/Sgt S.J. 460 Sqn. 392
Marriott, Sgt J. DFM, 617 Sqn. 312
Marriott, P/O J.R. 405 Sqn. 244
Marriott, F/Lt J.W. 51 Sqn. 208
Marriott, F/Sgt L.D.E. 78 Sqn. 296
Marsden, F/Sgt J.A. 102 Sqn. 449
Marsden, F/Sgt L.S. 408 Sqn. 102
Marsden, Sgt R. 617 Sqn. 313
Marsden, F/O W.A. 44 Sqn. 329

Miller, W/O D.H. 44 Sqn. 84
Miller, F/Lt E.V. DFC, 214 Sqn. 321
Miller, F/O G. 426 Sqn. 280, 286
Miller, W/O G.W. 149 Sqn. 112
Miller, F/Sgt I.G. 460 Sqn. 207
Miller, F/O J.G. AFM, 49 Sqn. 510
Miller, P/O R.B. 156 Sqn. 397
Miller, Sgt R.S.G. 12 Sqn. 323
Miller, W/O W. 103 Sqn. 454
Miller, F/Sgt. 214 Sqn. 50
Millett, F/Sgt G.H. 467 Sqn. 101
Milligan, P/O B.R. 408 Sqn. 459
Milliken, F/Lt R.E. 100 Sqn. 207
Milliken, F/Sgt E.D. 466 Sqn. 370
Millns, Sgt T.D. 101 Sqn. 454
Mills, F/Sgt A.J. 50 Sqn. 388
Mills, Sgt F. 214 Sqn. 456
Mills, P/O J.A. 419 Sqn. 389
Mills, Sgt J.F. 10 Sqn. 295
Mills, Sgt K.A. 10 Sqn. 112
Mills, Sgt P. 207 Sqn. 439
Mills, Sgt P.B. 149 Sqn. 239
Mills, F/Sgt W.D. 218 Sqn. 345
Millward, P/O J. 218 Sqn. 101
Milne, F/Sgt D.H. 35 Sqn. 407, 422, 486
Milne, F/O D.S. 429 Sqn. 427
Milne, Sgt E. 158 Sqn. 138
Milne, Sgt J. 429 Sqn. 224
Milner, F/Lt G.B. 103 Sqn. 386
Milt, P/O F.C. 83 Sqn. 206
Minchin, Sgt J.W. 617 Sqn. 314
Mindel, Sgt S.D. 44 Sqn. 426
Mingay, Sgt R.M. 419 Sqn. 354
Minnis, P/O H. DFC, 115 Sqn. 245
Minnitt, Sgt A.C.P. 78 Sqn. 290, 291, 296
Minns, Sgt C.R. 218 Sqn. 437
Minshaw, Sgt L.C. 78 Sqn. 210
Minton, F/Lt A.R. 214 Sqn. 294
Minton, Sgt J.D. 51 Sqn. 327
Misseldine, Sgt J. 149 Sqn. 112
Mitchell., Sgt F.H. 102 Sqn. 457
Mitchell, F/Sgt G. 61 Sqn. 69
Mitchell, Sgt G.D. 12 Sqn. 293
Mitchell, F/O G.D. 467 Sqn. 511
Mitchell, Sgt J.H. 100 Sqn. 366
Mitchell, Sgt J.I. 9 Sqn. 116
Mitchell, Sgt L.B. 76 Sqn. 209
Mitchell, F/Sgt L.D. 12 Sqn. 509
Mitchell, Sgt R.C. 207 Sqn. 539
Mitchell, F/Sgt T. 427 Sqn. 440
Mitchener, Sgt G.J. 166 Sqn. 335
Mitton, 76 Sqn. 137Sgt C.H.
Mix, P/O R.D. 61 Sqn. 252
Mizon, F/Sgt W.F. 12 Sqn. 203, 206, 366
Mobley, Sgt I. 196 Sqn. 284
Mock, Sgt H.R.H. 102 Sqn. 266
Mockford, P/O P.A.K. 207 Sqn. 252
Moffatt, W/O B.A. 75 Sqn. 168
Moffatt, Sgt C.M. 115 Sqn. 112
Moffatt, P/O M.Q. 102 Sqn. 284
Mollison, Sgt A.M. 90 Sqn. 57
Monaghan, Sgt A. 97 Sqn. 470
Monaghan, F/Sgt A.D. 57 Sqn. 308
Money, P/O J.E. 44 Sqn. 510
Money, Sgt K.G. 218 Sqn. 283
Money, F/Lt K.P.C. 405 Sqn. 101
Monk, P/O A. 76 Sqn. 492
Monk, P/O E.J. 156 Sqn. 397
Monk, P/O P.V. 100 Sqn. 207
Monk, P/O W.G. 90 Sqn. 251
Monks, Sgt J. 101 Sqn. 207
Monohan, P/O J.E. 408 Sqn. 426

Montgomery, Sgt D. 78 Sqn. 369
Montigue, Sgt R.J.B. 100 Sqn. 165
Moody, Sgt B. 405 Sqn. 263
Moody, Sgt V.C.G. 78 Sqn. 266
Moon, Sgt D.F. 102 Sqn. 284
Moon, Sgt J.W. 50 Sqn. 146
Moon, F/O K.E. 76 Sqn. 474
Mooney, Sgt H.H. 207 Sqn. 475
Mooney, P/O J.O.B. 103 Sqn. 207
Mooney, Sgt L. 101 Sqn. 269
Moorcroft, F/O E. 408 Sqn. 427
Moorcroft, F/O W.J. 115 Sqn. 519
Moore, Sgt A.D. 467 Sqn. 371
Moore, F/Sgt A.T.W. 100 Sqn. 332
Moore, Sgt B.A. 75 Sqn. 287
Moore, Sgt C.J. 75 Sqn. 494
Moore, F/Sgt E.N. 166 Sqn. 264
Moore, Sgt E.R. 35 Sqn. 518
Moore, Sgt F. 78 Sqn. 266
Moore, Sgt F.G. 61 Sqn. 252
Moore, Sgt G.E. 101 Sqn. 129 ·
Moore, Sgt H.W. 77 Sqn. 337
Moore, F/Lt J.L. DFC, 97 Sqn. 445
Moore, Sgt J.S. 10 Sqn. 507
Moore, F/O K. 460 Sqn. 158
Moore, Sgt M.W. 106 Sqn. 354
Moore, Sgt R. 78 Sqn. 492
Moore, Sgt R. 405 Sqn. 102
Moore, F/Sgt R.E. DFM, 83 Sqn. 385
Moore, P/O R.F. 432 Sqn. 492
Moore, Sgt R.T. 49 Sqn. 393
Moore, Sgt S. 218 Sqn. 346
Moore, Sgt S.J. 7 Sqn. 183
Moore, F/Lt T.B. 408 Sqn. 371
Moore, Sgt W. 7 Sqn. 183
Moore, P/O W.H. 3 Sqn. 544
Moore, F/Sgt W.H. 156 Sqn. 341
Moores, Sgt S.A. 35 Sqn. 281
Mora, Sgt C.M.W. 15 Sqn. 242, 244
Moran, W/O T.M. 77 Sqn. 283
Moran, Sgt W.L. 103 Sqn. 435
Moran, S/Ldr. 418 Sqn. 542
Mordecai, Sgt D.G. 460 Sqn. 165
Morey, F/Sgt W. 90 Sqn. 282
Morgan, F/Lt D.S. 428 Sqn. 522
Morgan, F/O D.W.H. 166 Sqn. 165
Morgan, F/Sgt F.W. 12 Sqn. 293
Morgan, P/O I.M. 196 Sqn. 223
Morgan, Sgt J. 100 Sqn. 80
Morgan, Sgt J.G. 466 Sqn. 186
Morgan, Sgt J.I.P. 77 Sqn. 295
Morgan, Sgt J.K. 50 Sqn. 388
Morgan, F/O W.H. 467 Sqn. 511
Morley, F/Sgt A. 10 Sqn. 489
Morley, Sgt E.H. 103 Sqn. 392
Morley, Sgt N. Unit unknown. 384
Morley, Sgt R.S. 49 Sqn. 399
Morley, W/O T. 7 Sqn. 194
Morrell, Sgt F.W. 214 Sqn. 493
Morrice, Sgt G.J. 207 Sqn. 370
Morris, Sgt C.A. 78 Sqn. 474
Morris, F/Sgt C.R.S. 460 Sqn. 342
Morris, W/O D.L. 77 Sqn. 71, 81
Morris, Sgt E. 207 Sqn. 538-9
Morris, Sgt E.S. 166 Sqn. 324
Morris, Sgt H.J. 15 Sqn. 335
Morris, F/Sgt J. 420 Sqn. 114
Morris, Sgt J.H. 419 Sqn. 164, 167
Morris, Sgt K. 57 Sqn. 237
Morris, Sgt N.H. 44 Sqn. 458
Morris, Sgt R.M. 9 Sqn. 307
Morris, Sgt T.B. 149 Sqn. 351

Percy, P/O G. 156 Sqn. 80
Perkins, W/O A.T.H. 7 Sqn. 420
Perkins, F/O J.A. 102 Sqn. 449
Perlman, F/Sgt E.H. 51 Sqn. 343
Perrett, F/Sgt G.C. 419 Sqn. 467
Perring, P/O C.B. 15 Sqn. 221
Perrot, P/O A.F.J. 103 Sqn. 487
Perrot, F/O W.R. 75 Sqn. 455
Perry, Sgt B.W.A. 425 Sqn. 188
Perry, W/O K.O. 405 Sqn. 154
Perry, Sgt P. 460 Sqn. 136
Perry, W/O W.J.H. 78 Sqn. 296
Peters, P/O H.N. 90 Sqn. 424
Peters, Sgt G.C. 51 Sqn. 245
Peters, Sgt M.D. 102 Sqn. 249
Petersen, F/Sgt L. 90 Sqn. 447
Pettigrew, P/O G.M. 103 Sqn. 234
Pettigrew, P/O J.B. 426 Sqn. 297
Petts, F/O H.N. 100 Sqn. 335
Pheloung, Sgt C.E. 51 Sqn. 155
Phelps-Hopkins, P/O R.V. 218 Sqn. 447
Phillips, Sgt A.J. 7 Sqn. 263
Phillips, F/Sgt D.S. 76 Sqn. 369
Phillips, F/Sgt E.J. 10 Sqn. 235
Phillips, F/Sgt F.G. 460 Sqn. 398
Phillips, Sgt G. 75 Sqn. 250
Phillips, F/O G.J. 467 Sqn. 258
Phillips, Sgt G.M. 214 Sqn. 437
Phillips, Sgt H.L. 15 Sqn. 244
Phillips, Sgt J. 77 Sqn. 425
Phillips, F/O J. 218 Sqn. 326
Phillips, Sgt J.A. DFM, 405 Sqn. 478-9
Phillips, P/O P.H. 12 Sqn. 293
Phillips, Sgt W.E. 90 Sqn. 222
Philpott, Sgt J.A.M. 432 Sqn. 372
Phin, Sgt K.C. 214 Sqn. 129
Phipps, W/O W.W. 405 Sqn. 154
Piatkowski, F/O H. 300 Sqn. 325
Piche, P/O K.M. 15 Sqn. 221
Picken, F/Lt W.J. DFC. 106 Sqn. 58
Pickens, A/O W.G. 50 Sqn. 307
Pickering, Sgt J.S. 408 Sqn. 507
Pickett, F/Sgt J. 57 Sqn. 511
Pickford, Sgt L. 196 Sqn. 223
Pickles, Sgt J.H. 10 Sqn. 352
Pickup, P/O R.L. 57 Sqn. 145
Picton, Sgt J. 90 Sqn. 436
Pierce, P/O E.G. 218 Sqn. 288, 298
Pierce, Sgt E.W.W. 51 Sqn. 473
Pierpoint, Sgt H. 12 Sqn. 324
Pierson, Sgt R.L 75 Sqn. 222
Pietsch, F/O L. 467 Sqn. 371
Piggott, Sgt J. 429 Sqn. 286
Pike, W/O G.H. 207 Sqn. 475
Pike, Sgt R.J. 78 Sqn. 258
Pilkington, Sgt F.E. 214 Sqn. 493
Pilon, F/Sgt F.R. 408 Sqn. 212
Pinchin, Sgt K.A. 199 Sqn. 169
Pine-Coffin, Sgt G.T. 102 Sqn. 520
Pink, Sgt F.N. 12 Sqn. 366
Pinkerton, Sgt F.W. 12 Sqn. 135
Pinkerton, Sgt R.M. 10 Sqn. 437
Pinckney, W/O T. 158 Sqn. 521
Pirie, F/Sgt J.A. 75 Sqn. 351
Pitchford, P/O C.N.. 115 Sqn. 403, 404
Pitman, Sgt D.A. 78 Sqn. 210
Pitt, Sgt W.C. 76 Sqn. 152
Pittard, Sgt R.W. 15 Sqn. 336
Pitts, W/O D.C. 431 Sqn. 60
Pixley, W/O A.N. 408 Sqn. 507
Plank, F/Sgt L.K. 420 Sqn. 224
Plant, F/Sgt H. 83 Sqn. 281

Plaskett, P/O S. 106 Sqn. 258
Platt, Sgt F.J. 76 Sqn. 137
Platt, F/Lt R.C. 90 Sqn. 488
Platt, Sgt V.S. 35 Sqn. 349
Plaunt, W/O D.C. 97 Sqn. 114
Playfair, F/Lt A. 408 Sqn. 197
Pleasance, P/O R.V.C. 9 Sqn. 186
Plenderleith, Sgt N.P. 10 Sqn. 326
Plewman, W/O W.H. 408 Sqn. 507
Plowright, Sgt P. 100 Sqn. 184
Plummer, F/Sgt J.C. 460 Sqn. 399
Plumridge, P/O E.J. 158 Sqn. 370
Plyley, Sgt D.G. 419 Sqn. 330
Podolsky, Sgt A. 83 Sqn. 206
Pohe, F/Lt. Unit unknown, 419
Pointer, W/O E.G. 7 Sqn. 444
Poland, Sgt R.G. 76 Sqn. 113
Pollard, P/O G.W. 102 Sqn. 457
Pollon, W/O E.S. 90 Sqn. 336
Polom, Sgt F. 300 Sqn. 115
Pomfret, Sgt J. 460 Sqn. 235
Pond, Sgt A.L.W. 51 Sqn. 245
Ponsford, F/Sgt A.E. 103 Sqn. 435
Poole, Sgt S. 156 Sqn. 129
Poole, Sgt S. 419 Sqn. 330
Pooley, Sgt F.H.E. 214 Sqn. 336
Pooley, Sgt J.T. 90 Sqn. 265
Pope, W/O E.B. 419 Sqn. 449
Pope, Sgt R.G. 158 Sqn. 369
Pople, F/Sgt J.W. 78 Sqn. 296
Popplestone, F/Sgt H. 9 Sqn. 398
Popley, F/O T.H. 51 Sqn. 473
Porritt, Sgt L.G. 100 Sqn. 454
Portch, P/O A.L.S. 156 Sqn. 158
Porter, F/Sgt A.H. 35 Sqn. 342
Porter, F/O A.R. 149 Sqn. 465, 472
Porter, F/O C.E. 419 Sqn. 126, 127, 130
Porter, Sgt J.S. 90 Sqn. 436
Porter, Sgt T.G. 9 Sqn. 491
Portrey, Sgt T.L. 218 Sqn. 351
Potter, P/O A.R. 196 Sqn. 251
Potter, Sgt E.B. 90 Sqn. 519
Potter, F/Sgt R.L. 460 Sqn. 136
Potter, Sgt T.F. 158 Sqn. 369
Potts, F/Lt J. 12 Sqn. 256
Poudrier, W/O J.R.R. 427 Sqn. 521
Poulter, F/Sgt J.L. 90 Sqn. 336
Poulton, W/O W.A. 51 Sqn. 415, 425
Powell, Sgt E.T. 12 Sqn. 334
Powell, Sgt F.W.A. 101 Sqn. 496
Powell, Sgt G.J. 106 Sqn. 58
Powell, P/O L. 214 Sqn. 196
Power, P/O. 426 Sqn. 243
Powers, F/Sgt H.F. 102 Sqn. 113
Powis, Sgt G.G. 460 Sqn. 350
Poynter, Sgt H.F. 9 Sqn. 398
Pozer, F/O S.M.N. 429 Sqn. 247
Pratt, Sgt F.T. 196 Sqn. 246
Prebble, Sgt S. 10 Sqn. 213
Precious, Sgt H. 9 Sqn. 153
Prentice, F/Sgt W.R. 408 Sqn. 507
Preston, F/Sgt C.W. 158 Sqn. 490
Price, F/S C.J. 78 Sqn. 176, 180, 185
Price, Sgt C.W. 405 Sqn. 445
Price, F/Sgt G. 103 Sqn. 367
Price, W/O H.W. 10 Sqn. 343
Price, Sgt L.F. 115 Sqn. 460
Prichard, F/Sgt R.D. 83 Sqn. 396
Pridden, W/O W.E.E.B. 158 Sqn. 251
Pridgeon, F/Sgt W.F. 460 Sqn. 235
Pridham, Sgt G.I. 408 Sqn. 427
Priestley, F/O G.D. 50 Sqn. 284

Reeves, F/O J.B. 9 Sqn. 491
Reffin, Sgt J. 100 Sqn. 471
Reffles, Sgt A.W. 158 Sqn. 428
Reichert, P/O C.C. 408 Sqn. 426
Reid, W/O A.M. 15 Sqn. 69
Reid, Sgt D.H. 51 Sqn. 209
Reid, F/Lt D.H. DFC, 57 Sqn. 458
Reid, F/Sgt G.V. 408 Sqn. 507
Reid, F/O N.D. 427 Sqn. 440
Reid, F/O N.S.M. 78 Sqn. 529, 534
Reid, F/O R.R. 115 Sqn. 343
Reid, W/O W.J. 61 Sqn. 285
Reid, F/Sgt W.J. 429 Sqn. 298
Reid, Sgt W.M. 419 Sqn. 297
Reilly, Sgt A. 97 Sqn. 268
Reilly, F/O R.M. 405 Sqn. 256
Relph, Sgt H.C. 15 Sqn. 367
Rembridge, F/O L.G. 97 Sqn. 486
Renaut, W/O M. 90 Sqn. 57
Rendle, F/Sgt P.W.J. 78 Sqn. 474
Rensbury, W/O J.J. 427 Sqn. 439
Renshaw, Sgt A.S. 83 Sqn. 307
Renwick, Sgt J. 103 Sqn. 392
Reynolds, Sgt A.H. 428 Sqn. 500, 507
Reynolds, F/Lt C.B. 103 Sqn. 454
Reynolds, F/O C.P. 100 Sqn. 454
Reynolds, F/Lt F.A. 429 Sqn. 491
Reynolds, Sgt G.W.F. 101 Sqn. 263
Reynolds, W/O H.G. 405 Sqn. 102
Reynolds, F/Sgt R.P. 620 Sqn. 448
Reynolds, F/O W.C. 207 Sqn. 338
Rheaume, F/Sgt E.S. 431 Sqn. 370
Rhodes, F/Sgt A.S. 429 Sqn. 427
Rhodes, Sgt H.F. 428 Sqn. 143
Rhodes, Sgt H.R. 49 Sqn. 393
Rhynd, Sgt D.D. 50 Sqn. 506
Riach, P/O G. 78 Sqn. 152
Rich, P/O D.R. 218 Sqn. 424
Rice, AM E.A.B. AOC No 1 Group, Bomber
    Command. 10
Rich, Sgt P.C.W. 51 Sqn. 283
Rich, P/O R.S. 166 Sqn. 488
Rich, Sgt T. 218 Sqn. 250
Richards, Sgt D.J. 35 Sqn. 281
Richards, F/O F. 61 Sqn. 69
Richards, P/O F.M. 44 Sqn. 393
Richards, Sgt H.N. 76 Sqn. 152
Richards, F/Sgt J. 51 Sqn. 151
Richards, Sgt J. 75 Sqn. 185
Richards, S/Ldr J.C. 12 Sqn. 234
Richards, F/Sgt J.L. 75 Sqn. 436
Richards, Sgt K. 156 Sqn. 268, 445
Richards, Sgt N.C. 619 Sqn. 394
Richardson, Sgt A.H. 466 Sqn. 439
Richardson, Sgt A.W. 207 Sqn. 475
Richardson, Sgt C.A. 51 Sqn. 337
Richardson, F/Sgt D.G. 426 Sqn. 372
Richardson, Sgt E.R. 115 Sqn. 460
Richardson, Sgt F.J. 10 Sqn. 534
Richardson, Sgt H. 57 Sqn. 138
Richardson, W/O J.G. 199 Sqn. 112
Richardson, Sgt J.W. 77 Sqn. 337
Richardson, F/O J.W. 408 Sqn. 507
Richardson, Sgt S. 44 Sqn. 167
Richardson, F/Sgt T.E. 166 Sqn. 184
Richardson, Sgt T.F. 214 Sqn. 188
Richardson, F/Lt T.H.O. 78 Sqn. 152
Richardson, Sgt W.G. 51 Sqn. 151
Richer, F/Sgt J. 35 Sqn. 421
Richmond, F/O B.A. 429 Sqn. 354
Richmond, W/O H. 408 Sqn. 213
Richmond, F/Sgt J.R. 12 Sqn. 293

Richmond, Sgt N.P. 460 Sqn. 207
Richmond, Sgt R.S. 12 Sqn. 349
Rickenson, F/Lt L.A. DFC, 83 Sqn. 281
Ricketts, F/Sgt R.M. 419 Sqn. 354
Ridd, Sgt J.H. 83 Sqn. 151
Ridd, Sgt T.J. 106 Sqn. 153
Riddle, F/O C.H. 75 Sqn. 351
Rider, W/O J.J. 467 Sqn. 101
Ridge, Sgt A. 218 Sqn. 166
Ridgeway, Sgt R.C. 103 Sqn. 398
Ridgley, Sgt R.W. 101 Sqn. 445
Ridings, F/Sgt D.G. 156 Sqn. 263
Rigby, F/O J.E. 51 Sqn. 327
Riley, Sgt H. 51 Sqn. 208, 217
Riley, Sgt M. 100 Sqn. 471
Riley, Sgt R.G. 156 Sqn. 80
Riley, Sgt T. 408 Sqn. 491
Riley, F/O W.E. 466 Sqn. 457
Rimmer, F/Sgt C.F. 100 Sqn. 184
Rimmer, Sgt V.A. 61 Sqn. 189
Riordan, Sgt J.M.P. 75 Sqn. 336
Ripley, P/O J.G. 15 Sqn. 69
Rishton, Sgt W. 101 Sqn. 120
Rispin, W/O R.G. 420 Sqn. 168
Ritchie, Sgt D.S. 429 Sqn. 224
Rivers, Sgt N.E. 619 Sqn. 475
Rivers, Sgt R.W. 44 Sqn. 393
Rivet, W/O L.A. 426 Sqn. 330
Rixon, F/Sgt R. 156 Sqn. 157
Roaner, 1st Lt E.L. USAAF, 106 Sqn. 497
Robb, Sgt D.A. 57 Sqn. 329
Robb, Sgt F.A. 76 Sqn. 209
Robbins, W/O E.A. 106 Sqn. 344
Roberts, Sgt A. 51 Sqn. 386
Roberts, Sgt A.E. 50 Sqn. 146
Roberts, Sgt A.R., 100 Sqn. 111
Roberts, Sgt C.W. 617 Sqn. 313
Roberts, F/Sgt D.E. 218 Sqn. 223
Roberts, Flt Off D.S. USAAF. 51 Sqn. 368
Roberts, F/Sgt D.S.P. 15 Sqn. 435
Roberts, Sgt F.D. 405 Sqn. 160
Roberts, F/Sgt F.V. 405 Sqn. 263
Roberts, Sgt G.E. 51 Sqn. 208
Roberts, F/Lt H.A.7 51 Sqn. 283
Roberts, Sgt J. 51 Sqn. 456
Roberts, F/Sgt J. 158 Sqn. 329
Roberts, W/O J.L. 75 Sqn. 350
Roberts, F/Sgt N.W. 408 Sqn. 139
Roberts, P/O R.D. DFM, 158 Sqn. 251
Roberts, Sgt R.H. 57 Sqn. 186
Roberts, F/Sgt T.L. 78 Sqn. 457
Roberts, Sgt W.A. 50 Sqn. 307
Robertson, Sgt D.C. 466 Sqn. 314
Robertson, Sgt D.L. 156 Sqn. 151
Robertson, F/O E.D. 428 Sqn. 522
Robertson, P/O I.D. 61 Sqn. 252
Robertson, Sgt J. 49 Sqn. 138
Robertson, W/O J.D. 57 Sqn. 308
Robertson, Sgt J.H. 35 Sqn. 269
Robertson, W/O M.C.J. 97 Sqn. 385
Robertson, F/Sgt R.L. 466 Sqn. 314
Robertson, Sgt W.D. 35 Sqn. 421
Robertson, Sgt W.M. 218 Sqn. 136
Robertson, Sgt T.C. 49 Sqn. 210
Robinson, Sgt C. 218 Sqn. 240
Robinson, Sgt D.H. 90 Sqn. 282
Robinson, Sgt D.J. 467 Sqn. 153
Robinson, Sgt F.N. 218 Sqn. 265
Robinson, Sgt G.A. 57 Sqn. 426
Robinson, Sgt H. 44 Sqn. 353
Robinson, F/Sgt N. 115 Sqn. 519
Robinson, Sgt N.O. 156 Sqn. 226

Smith, Sgt J. 103 Sqn. 80
Smith, Sgt J. 207 Sqn. 285
Smith, Sgt J.A. 214 Sqn. 222
Smith, F/Sgt J.A. 428 Sqn. 246
Smith, F/Sgt J.P.H. 218 Sqn. 437
Smith, Sgt J.C. 102 Sqn. 296, 328
Smith, Sgt J.E. 10 Sqn. 112
Smith, W/O J.F. 425 Sqn. 168
Smith, W/O J.M.T. 149 Sqn. 265
Smith, Sgt J.R.G. 102 Sqn. 520
Smith, Sgt J.T. 102 Sqn. 236
Smith, W/O J.W. 76 Sqn. 328
Smith, F/Sgt J.W.T. DFM, 408 Sqn. 159
Smith, Sgt K. 78 Sqn. 506
Smith, W/Cdr K.B. DSO, 9 Sqn. 186
Smith, F/Sgt K.I. 97 Sqn. 470
Smith, Sgt K.J. 102 Sqn. 344
Smith, Sgt L.C. 460 Sqn. 207
Smith, F/Sgt L.G. 101 Sqn. 324
Smith, Sgt L.R. 15 Sqn. 335
Smith, Sgt N.C. 467 Sqn. 512
Smith, Sgt P. 102 Sqn. 352
Smith, Sgt P.A. 425 Sqn. 168
Smith, Sgt P.R. 83 Sqn. 263
Smith, Sgt P.T. 61 Sqn. 237
Smith, Sgt R.A. 75 Sqn. 195
Smith, Sgt R.A.H. 214 Sqn. 447
Smith, F/Lt R.B. DFC, 405 Sqn. 484, 486
Smith, Sgt R.C. 35 Sqn. 129
Smith, Sgt R.E. 460 Sqn. 235
Smith, Sgt R.G. 49 Sqn. 398
Smith, Sgt S. 218 Sqn. 346
Smith, Sgt S.G. 101 Sqn. 111
Smith, Sgt T.B.M. 35 Sqn. 422
Smith, Sgt T. 149 Sqn. 315
Smith, F/Sgt T.H. 35 Sqn. 374
Smith, Sgt T.H. 431 Sqn. 284
Smith, Sgt T.R.M. 35 Sqn. 486
Smith, Sgt V.G.L. 9 Sqn. 392
Smith, Sgt W. 9 Sqn. 337
Smith, Sgt W.H.J. 102 Sqn. 520
Smith, Sgt W.P. 156 Sqn. 434
Smith, P/O W.S. 158 Sqn. 370
Smith, F/Sgt. 141 Sqn. 544
Smith, Sgt. 605 Sqn. 543
Smith-Jones, F/Sgt H.V. 428 Sqn. 252
Smithdale, Sgt A. 57 Sqn. 237
Smooker, W/O F.H. 106 Sqn. 497
Smuck, F/O A.O. 408 Sqn. 521
Smy, F/Sgt B.T. 90 Sqn. 436
Smythe, P/O N.B. 196 Sqn. 457
Sneath, P/O W.A. 429 Sqn. 440
Snell, F/O A.D.S. 50 Sqn. 537
Sneyder, F/O. 83 Sqn. 411
Snook, F/Sgt W.C. 115 Sqn. 245
Snowdon, Sgt H.W. 101 Sqn. 454
Sobkowicz, W/O M.E. 427 Sqn. 515, 518, 521
Sobell, F/Sgt H. 7 Sqn. 259
Soeder, P/O E.F. 427 Sqn. 475
Solly, Sgt F.A. 460 Sqn. 235
Somers, P/O J.K.F 166 Sqn. 423
Somers, F/O L.W. 427 Sqn. 450
Somerville, Sgt T.C. 44 Sqn. 138
Sommerville, W/O J. 405 Sqn. 365
Southern, F/O D.J.N. 49 Sqn. 167
Southon, F/Sgt E. 12 Sqn. 509
Southon, F/O F.A. 83 Sqn. 150
Sovereign, F/Sgt C.F. 405 Sqn. 342
Spalding, Sgt H. 10 Sqn. 507
Spanton, Sgt D.R. 7 Sqn. 65-6, 69, 445
Sparkes, Sgt J.N. 101 Sqn. 461

Sparkes, Sgt R.R. 101 Sqn. 269
Sparling, W/O C.W.A. 12 Sqn. 365
Sparling, W/O L.F. 106 Sqn. 458
Sparrow, F/Sgt W.A. 432 Sqn. 450
Speedie, Sgt. DFM, 77 Sqn. 432-3
Speller, F/O R.H. 408 Sqn. 491
Spenbourge, Sgt H.O. 12 Sqn. 206
Spence, Sgt A. 431 Sqn. 353
Spence, Sgt J.A. 207 Sqn. 511
Spence, P/O M.B. 429 Sqn. 427
Spencer, W/O A.E. 467 Sqn. 101
Spencer, Sgt A.R. 61 Sqn. 81
Spencer, Sgt B. 467 Sqn. 338
Spencer, F/O D.G. 51 Sqn. 208
Spencer, P/O G.L. 405 Sqn. 102
Spencer, F/Sgt H.P. 51 Sqn. 256
Spencer, W/O J.A. 427 Sqn. 439
Spencer, F/O J.F. 428 Sqn. 143
Spencer, Sgt W.A. 15 Sqn. 244
Spencer, F/Lt. 418 Sqn. 543
Spicer, Sgt B.E. 57 Sqn. 159
Spiece, W/O G.T. 12 Sqn. 293
Spier, F/O W.F. 460 Sqn. 488
Spiers, Sgt J. 50 Sqn. 211
Spires, F/Sgt A.S. 115 Sqn. 368
Spooner, P/O D. 15 Sqn. 264
Spoonsler, W/O H. 149 Sqn. 351
Sprack, P/O C.F.J. DFM, 83 Sqn. 385
Sprackling, F/O L.W. 83 Sqn. 57
Spreckley, Sgt P.G. 51 Sqn. 359, 368
Spring, W/O K.L. 115 Sqn. 368
Sproule, W/O E.A. 166 Sqn. 335
Spurr, F/Lt A.E. 103 Sqn. 435
Squire, Sgt H. 75 Sqn. 455
Squires, Sgt B.W. 101 Sqn. 263
Squires, Sgt M.C.C. 102 Sqn. 140
Stacey, Sgt W.H. 51 Sqn. 245
Stafford, W/O G.C. DFM, 156 Sqn. 158
Stafford, Sgt S. 103 Sqn. 144
Stally, Sgt E.C. 83 Sqn. 434
Stamp, P/O R.C. 158 Sqn. 152
Standfast, F/O H.J. 78 Sqn. 438
Standrigg, Sgt W. 97 Sqn. 140
Stanford, F/O N.J. 101 Sqn. 263
Staniforth, Sgt J. 196 Sqn. 267
Stanley, Sgt E. 619 Sqn. 426
Stanley, Sgt F.T. 419 Sqn. 268
Stanley, F/Sgt J.V. 460 Sqn. 386
Stanley, W/O R.W. 149 Sqn. 351
Stanley, Sgt T. 103 Sqn. 189
Stannard, Sgt F.D. 214 Sqn. 294
Stanners, Sgt F.W. 10 Sqn. 112
Stanton, F/Sgt E.H. 90 Sqn. 447
Staples, Sgt H. 103 Sqn. 398
Stapleton, F/Sgt F.G. 76 Sqn. 113
Star, F/Sgt E.A. 429 Sqn. 428
Stark, Sgt A.I. 166 Sqn. 264
Stark, F/Lt R.H. 51 Sqn. 295
Starthern, Sgt J.H. 214 Sqn. 158
Stas, Sgt L.L. 78 Sqn. 152
Stead, W/O P. 196 Sqn. 225, 454
Steed, Sgt E.A. 101 Sqn. 111
Steed, Sgt P.D. 101 Sqn. 195
Steel, Sgt A. 57 Sqn. 284
Steer, Sgt G. 51 Sqn. 295
Steel, F/Sgt J.M. 90 Sqn. 447
Steele, F/Sgt R.J. 12 Sqn. 334
Steer, Sgt F.J.M. 57 Sqn. 449
Stefanchuk, F/Sgt J.J. 408 Sqn. 507
Stenhouse, P/O T. 50 Sqn. 510
Stentiford, W/O K.R. 408 Sqn. 371
Stephen, F/Sgt W. 149 Sqn. 196

Sweetlove, Sgt R.S. 100 Sqn. 165
Swift, Sgt C.R. 156 Sqn. 68
Swift, S/Ldr J.E. 83 Sqn. 375
Swire, P/O W.H. 9 Sqn. 153
Sykes, Sgt J.A. 44 Sqn. 474
Sykes, Sgt J.W. 57 Sqn. 449
Sylvester, W/O J.G. 428 Sqn. 354
Symes, F/Lt R.A. BEM, 408 Sqn. 402
Symons, W/O A.T. 427 Sqn. 224
Syms, Sgt S.R. 50 Sqn. 211
Szpalinski, Sgt S. 305 Sqn. 423
Szeremeta, Sgt T. 300 Sqn. 241
Szymanowicz, Sgt H. 300 Sqn. 282
Tabaczynski, F/O R. 300 Sqn. 282
Tabaczinski, F/O. 307 Sqn. 543
Tacey, W/O A. 35 Sqn. 68
Tagg, Sgt K.J. 12 Sqn. 366
Tagg, Sgt L. 90 Sqn. 239
Taillefer, W/O L.P.R. 429 Sqn. 372
Tait, F/Sgt J.M. 78 Sqn. 123
Tait, Sgt J.R. 218 Sqn. 166
Tallman, F/Lt G.F. 428 Sqn. 354
Talman, Sgt R.E. 426 Sqn. 338
Tate, Sgt L.J. 106 Sqn. 167
Tanner, F/O H.E. 408 Sqn. 139
Tanner, Sgt L.V. 83 Sqn. 422
Tannock, Sgt A. 35 Sqn. 349
Tappin, F/Lt. 157 Sqn. 541
Tarr, Sgt V.J. 9 Sqn. 392
Tarrant, Sgt A.B. 75 Sqn. 69
Tassell, F/Sgt E.J. 77 Sqn. 245
Tate, F/O F.R.H. 57 Sqn. 237
Tate, F/Sgt G.D.W. 432 Sqn. 460
Tate, P/O S.O. 467 Sqn. 511
Tatham, Sgt W.N. 405 Sqn. 365
Tay, P/O J.P. 51 Sqn. 465, 473
Tayler, Sgt D.A.A. 75 Sqn. 494
Tayler, Sgt R.H. 196 Sqn. 251
Taylor, F/Sgt A. 106 Sqn. 344
Taylor, P/O A.E. 102 Sqn. 246
Taylor, Sgt A.H. 196 Sqn. 490
Taylor, W/O A.H. 419 Sqn. 127, 130
Taylor, Sgt A.J. 44 Sqn. 84
Taylor, Sgt A.J. 617 Sqn. 313
Taylor, Sgt A.M. 35 Sqn. 349
Taylor, Sgt A.N. 166 Sqn. 498
Taylor, Sgt A.R. 218 Sqn. 298
Taylor, Sgt A.W. 97 Sqn. 114
Taylor, Sgt B.E. 196 Sqn. 267
Taylor, Sgt C. 44 Sqn. 307
Taylor, Sgt C. 429 Sqn. 286
Taylor, F/Lt C.O. 619 Sqn. 360, 371
Taylor, W/O D.E. 10 Sqn. 235
Taylor, F/Sgt E.G. 214 Sqn. 456
Taylor, Sgt F.J. 432 Sqn. 355
Taylor, S/Ldr F.V. 420 Sqn. 193, 198
Taylor, Sgt G. 100 Sqn. 397
Taylor, Sgt G.A. 9 Sqn. 186
Taylor, F/Sgt H.A. 419 Sqn. 389
Taylor, Sgt H.S. 10 Sqn. 270
Taylor, W/O J. 76 Sqn. 137
Taylor, F/Sgt J. 426 Sqn. 143
Taylor, F/Sgt J.A.C. 405 Sqn. 159
Taylor, P/O J.C.M. 408 Sqn. 491
Taylor, W/O J.E. 207 Sqn. 139
Taylor, Sgt J.M. 51 Sqn. 137
Taylor, F/Sgt J.T. 57 Sqn. 267
Taylor, F/O J.T.R. DFC, 7 Sqn. 194
Taylor, Sgt K.M. 467 Sqn. 399
Taylor, Sgt K.W. 156 Sqn. 157
Taylor, P/O L.K. 424 Sqn. 187
Taylor, Sgt N.E. 44 Sqn. 307

Taylor, W/O N.H. 405 Sqn. 365
Taylor, Sgt P.J. 90 Sqn. 447
Taylor, P/O R.E. DFM, 432 Sqn. 345
Taylor, Sgt R.H.G. 57 Sqn. 138
Taylor, W/O R.J. 35 Sqn. 471
Taylor, F/Sgt T. 460 Sqn. 350
Taylor, F/O T.M. 101 Sqn. 207
Taylor, Sgt W.A. 90 Sqn. 447
Taylor, Sgt W. 214 Sqn. 57
Taylor, P/O W.B. 419 Sqn. 480
Taylor, P/O W.H. 432 Sqn. 492
Taylorson, Sgt H. 90 Sqn. 447
Tebble, F/O G.G. 103 Sqn. 398
Tedford, P/O B.L. 427 Sqn. 389
Teede, F/Sgt W.H. 90 Sqn. 447
Teerman, F/Sgt A.W. 460 Sqn. 423
Tees, Sgt F. 617 Sqn. 313
Telfer, Sgt A. 49 Sqn. 237
Telfer, Sgt D. 57 Sqn. 458
Telfer, W/O T.W. 9 Sqn. 159
Templeman, W/O D.L. 12 Sqn. 366
Tennis, P/O H.A. 429 Sqn. 286
Terry, F/Sgt A.D. 467 Sqn. 511
Terry, P/O F.A. 7 Sqn. 183
Testal, F/Sgt G.E. 76 Sqn. 257
Tester, Sgt K.A. 57 Sqn. 145
Tetley, F/Lt W.A. DFC, 35 Sqn. 349
Thallon, Sgt R.E. 214 Sqn. 489
Theobald, F/Lt W.M. 7 Sqn. 375
Thibaudeau, Sgt J.E.A. 428 Sqn. 268
Thick, F/O L.W.S. 76 Sqn. 328
Thom, Sgt J.M. 49 Sqn. 58
Thomas, Sgt A.B. 115 Sqn. 185
Thomas, F/Sgt B.W. 76 Sqn. 257
Thomas, W/O A.J. 100 Sqn. 471
Thomas, Sgt D. 15 Sqn. 472
Thomas, Sgt D.A. 460 Sqn. 386
Thomas, F/O D.O. 83 Sqn. 375
Thomas, E. 426 Sqn. 338
Thomas, Sgt E.G. 78 Sqn. 223
Thomas, Sgt H.G. 103 Sqn. 398
Thomas, Sgt H.G. 115 Sqn. 352
Thomas, F/Lt I.W. 44 Sqn. 329
Thomas, Sgt J. 61 Sqn. 285
Thomas, F/Sgt J. 97 Sqn. 385
Thomas, Sgt J.C. 218 Sqn. 352
Thomas, Sgt L.E. 10 Sqn. 112
Thomas, F/Sgt R. 75 Sqn. 494
Thomas, Sgt R.A. 35 Sqn. 129
Thomas, Sgt U. 156 Sqn. 129
Thomas, Sgt W.F. 12 Sqn. 509
Thomas, F/Sgt W.I. 218 Sqn. 456
Thomason, Sgt G.B. 76 Sqn. 438
Thompson, Sgt A. 12 Sqn. 505
Thompson, Sgt A. 90 Sqn. 436
Thompson, F/Lt A.W. 408 Sqn. 297
Thompson, Sgt B. 76 Sqn. 265
Thompson, P/O C.E. 100 Sqn. 422
Thompson, Sgt D.E. 428 Sqn. 268
Thompson, W/O D.H. 428 Sqn. 345
Thompson, P/O D.L. 75 Sqn. 250
Thompson, F/Sgt D.M. 12 Sqn. 365
Thompson, Sgt E.A. 44 Sqn. 353
Thompson, Sgt F. 408 Sqn. 329
Thompson, F/Lt F.D.J. 7 Sqn. 99
Thompson, Sgt F.J. 427 Sqn. 476
Thompson, P/O F.M. 51 Sqn. 209
Thompson, Sgt G. 7 Sqn. 444
Thompson, Sgt G. 115 Sqn. 489
Thompson, F/Sgt G.D. 75 Sqn. 455
Thompson, Sgt G.J.D. 419 Sqn. 427
Thompson, Sgt G.K. 429 Sqn. 247

Wood, Sgt P.J. 78 Sqn. 328
Wood, F/Lt R. 35 Sqn. 349
Wood, Sgt R. 207 Sqn. 511
Wood, F/O R.G. 426 Sqn. 224
Wood, Sgt S. 51 Sqn. 386
Wood, P/O S.M. 466 Sqn. 167
Wood, F/O W.H. 103 Sqn. 435
Wood, P/O. 410 Sqn. 543
Wood, P/O. 605 Sqn. 542
Woodall, Sgt R. 78 Sqn. 223
Woodcock, F/Sgt P. 156 Sqn. 397
Woodcock, F/Sgt K.W. 103 Sqn. 367
Woodfield, Sgt R.G. 149 Sqn. 158
Woodhouse, F/O H.W. 9 Sqn. 337
Woodland, Sgt W. 12 Sqn. 256
Woodley, Sgt A.C. 102 Sqn. 387
Woodley, Sgt J.W.R.H. 77 Sqn. 166
Woodroffe, F/O D.R. 158 Sqn. 352
Woodrow, Sgt S.A. 214 Sqn. 129
Woods, F/O A.G. 605 Sqn. 541
Woods, Sgt J.B. 214 Sqn. 188
Woods, Sgt R.A.F. 44 Sqn. 353
Woodvine, Sgt A.B. 61 Sqn. 459
Woodward, F/O A. 15 Sqn. 455
Woodward, Sgt A.A.T. 620 Sqn. 437
Woodward, Sgt J.E. 78 Sqn. 438
Woodward, Sgt T.J. 156 Sqn. 158
Woolnough, F/Sgt W.O. 156 Sqn. 206
Woolridge, P/O H.T. 158 Sqn. 387
Woonton, F/Sgt H.T. 35 Sqn. 227, 233
Woosnam, Sgt W. 51 Sqn. 159
Worden, F/Sgt A.C. 51 Sqn. 337
Wordsworth, W/O B.C. 158 Sqn. 387
Workman, F/Sgt L.E. 49 Sqn. 388
Worsdale, Sgt A. 115 Sqn. 456
Worsnop, Sgt F.A. 83 Sqn. 307
Worthington, Sgt J. 75 Sqn. 168
Worthington, Sgt R.F. 156 Sqn. 445
Wozniak, Sgt M. 300 Sqn. 57
Wragge, P/O G. 7 Sqn. 259
Wright, Sgt A. 78 Sqn. 152
Wright, Sgt A.C. 207 Sqn. 511
Wright, Sgt A.T.M. 101 Sqn. 335
Wright, F/Sgt C.S. 460 Sqn. 324
Wright, Sgt E. 78 Sqn. 387
Wright, Sgt E.A. 214 Sqn. 57
Wright, F/O F.J. 12 Sqn. 334
Wright, Sgt G.C. 76 Sqn. 209
Wright, P/O G.R. 166 Sqn. 423
Wright, Sgt J.H. 102 Sqn. 457
Wright, P/O J.R. 156 Sqn. 397
Wright, F/Sgt J.S. 49 Sqn. 497
Wright, Sgt J.W. 166 Sqn. 294
Wright, F/Sgt L.A. 51 Sqn. 327
Wright, Sgt P.F. 76 Sqn. 369
Wright, F/O R.B. 106 Sqn. 459
Wright, P/O R.G. 76 Sqn. 137
Wright, F/O R.J. 405 Sqn. 159
Wright, Sgt S. 15 Sqn. 367
Wright, Sgt W.H. 429 Sqn. 427
Wright, W/O W.S. 76 Sqn. 109, 113
Wright, Sgt. 605 Sqn. 543
Wurr, Sgt D. 218 Sqn. 298
Wyatt, Sgt W.H. 158 Sqn. 344
Wykes, Sgt J. 75 Sqn. 287
Wynn, P/O I.A. 100 Sqn. 335
Wynn, F/Sgt R.G. 156 Sqn. 281
Yates, F/O F.L. 115 Sqn. 519
Yates, F/O S.H. 103 Sqn. 392
Yeates, Sgt G.H. 35 Sqn. 129
Yelland, Sgt C.W. 49 Sqn. 211
Yellin, W/P P.F. 431 Sqn. 142

Yeo, Sgt G.A. 617 Sqn. 313
Yeo, Sgt L.J. 44 Sqn. 167
Yielder, F/Sgt A.C. 466 Sqn. 58
Yonker, W/O Z. 78 Sqn. 520
Young, W/O A.K. 427 Sqn. 459
Young, Sgt A.M. 78 Sqn. 387
Young, S/Ldr A.M. 106 Sqn. 459
Young, F/O A.W.S. 77 Sqn. 402
Young, Sgt C. 460 Sqn. 488
Young, W/O C.W. 12 Sqn. 487
Young, F/O C.W.R. 460 Sqn. 386
Young, P/O G.A. 61 Sqn. 81
Young, W/O G.K. 466 Sqn. 224
Young, P/O G.W. DFC, 90 Sqn. 336
Young, Sgt H.D. 158 Sqn. 352
Young, S/Ldr H.M. DFC, 617 Sqn. 313
Young, Sgt J. 35 Sqn. 206
Young, F/Sgt J.P. 51 Sqn. 137
Young, F/Lt J.O. DFC, 106 Sqn. 139
Young, Sgt K.R. 106 Sqn. 114
Young, F/O L. 166 Sqn. 141
Young, Sgt N. 7 Sqn. 129
Young, Sgt W. 44 Sqn. 353
Younger, F/Sgt R.G. 156 Sqn. 165
Zaleschuk, F/Sgt D. 408 Sqn. 212
Zambra, Sgt R. 149 Sqn. 260
Zapfe, F/Sgt M.E. 51 Sqn. 327
Zareikin, P/O S. 102 Sqn. 344
Zarniewski, Sgt K. 300 Sqn. 446
Zayets, Sgt S. 428 Sqn. 522
Zeavin F/Sgt M. 426 Sqn. 82
Zedy, Sgt G.C.A. 44 Sqn. 393
Zeidel, Sgt R. 429 Sqn. 371

Bomber Command Groups
1 Group. 10, 13, 49, 57, 80-2, 111-2, 115,
118, 120, 122-3, 129, 130, 132, 135-6,
141-2, 144-5, 151, 155, 158, 160, 165-6,
168-9, 184, 189, 195, 206-8, 214, 221,
234-5, 241, 247-9, 256, 260, 263-4, 269,
281-2, 293-4, 315, 323-5, 334-5, 342-3,
345, 349-50, 355, 365-7, 385-6, 389-92,
396-9, 406, 422, 434-5, 441, 445-6, 454-5,
460, 471-2, 475, 476, 487-8, 496, 498,
505 508-10, 538
2 Group. 10, 18, 190, 356
3 Group. 11, 13, 18, 57-8, 69, 81, 100-1,
112, 118, 129-30, 136-7, 139-40, 145,
158, 166, 168, 184-5, 187-8, 195-6, 221-3,
238-9, 240, 244-5, 249-51, 260, 264-5,
270, 282-3, 288, 294, 298, 308, 314-6,
345-6, 350-2, 355, 367-8, 386, 390, 395,
400, 406, 424, 434-7, 441, 446-8, 451,
455-6, 460, 472-3, 488-9, 493, 519
4 Group. 11, 13, 18, 49, 58, 60, 71, 80-1,
101-3, 112-3, 115, 121-3, 130, 137-8, 140,
142, 151-3, 155, 158-9, 166-8, 175, 185-6,
196-8, 200, 208-9, 210, 213, 215, 223-4,
235, 237, 245-6, 251, 256-8, 260, 265-7,
270, 280, 283-4, 290, 295-7, 314-7, 325-6,
335-7, 326-9, 337, 339, 343-4, 346, 352-3,
358, 368-70, 372, 386-7, 389, 395, 400-2,
408, 425-6, 428, 434, 437-9, 448-9, 456-7,
460, 473-4, 476, 489-90, 492, 505-7,
519-20, 521, 524, 529, 534
5 Group. 12, 13, 18, 49, 58, 69, 81, 84,
101, 114-6, 130-1, 138-9, 140, 145, 153,
159, 167-8, 186, 189, 197, 199, 210-2,
237, 241, 246, 252, 257-8, 267, 284-5,
299, 307-8, 312-4, 329, 337-8, 344, 353-5,
370-1, 388-9, 392-3, 394, 396, 398-9,
404-5, 426, 434, 437-9, 441, 449, 457-9,

218 Sqn. 11, 14, 58, 101, 136, 166, 223, 240, 250, 251, 265, 283, 288, 298, 326, 337, 345, 351, 424, 437, 447, 456
226 Sqn, 10
256 Sqn. 543
277 Sqn. 408
287 Sqn. 408
300 (Polish) Sqn. 10, 14, 57, 115, 166, 241, 282, 325, 423, 446, 472
301 (Polish) Sqn. 10, 14
305 (Polish) Sqn. 10, 14, 408, 423
307 Sqn. 409, 543
400 Sqn. 544
405 (RCAF) Sqn. 12, 14, 19, 91, 94, 101, 102, 149, 154, 159, 160, 161, 167, 241, 244, 263, 293, 323, 342, 346, 365, 422, 445, 478, 484, 487, 505, 519, 524-5, 533
408 (RCAF) Sqn. 12, 14, 98, 102, 130, 139, 154, 159, 197, 212, 213, 261, 267, 288, 297, 329, 345, 371, 389, 402, 426, 427, 459, 484, 491, 507, 521
410 Sqn. 543
418 Sqn. 541, 542, 543
419 (RCAF) Sqn. 12, 14, 50, 59, 126, 130, 131, 132, 149, 154, 164, 237, 252, 268, 272, 285, 286, 297, 322, 330, 354, 359, 371, 389, 427, 449, 450, 475, 480, 491, 521
420 (RCAF) Sqn. 12, 14, 59, 114, 116, 142, 143, 167, 168, 171, 183, 187, 193, 198, 224, 243, 246, 247
424 (RCAF) Sqn. 12, 14, 114, 171, 187, 198
425 (RCAF) Sqn. 12, 14, 104, 115, 168, 188, 198, 224
426 (RCAF) Sqn. 12, 14, 59, 82, 122, 123, 143, 156, 160, 186, 224, 243, 279, 286, 297, 320, 330, 338, 372
427 (RCAF) Sqn. 12, 14, 105, 143, 224, 389, 439, 440, 450, 459, 463, 475, 515, 521
428 (RCAF) Sqn. 12, 14, 141, 143, 160, 162, 168, 198, 246, 252, 286, 316, 317, 339, 340, 345, 354, 373, 500, 507, 522
429 (RCAF) Sqn. 11, 14, 48, 59, 82, 105, 123, 141, 142, 187, 224, 247, 286, 298, 354, 360, 363, 372, 427, 428, 440, 450, 491
431 (RCAF) Sqn. 11, 14, 60, 105, 113, 123, 142, 185, 197, 223, 284, 296, 316, 319, 330, 337, 353, 370, 408, 426, 439, 448, 474, 490
432 (RCAF) Sqn. 345, 347, 355, 372, 450, 459, 491, 521, 435. 443, 446, 478, 488
460 (RAAF) Sqn. 10, 122, 136, 158, 165, 207, 208, 235, 324, 342, 350, 367, 386, 392, 398, 399, 423
464 (RAAF) Sqn. 10, 264
466 Sqn (RAAF) Sqn. 11, 58, 167, 186, 224, 267, 280, 289, 297, 314, 316, 353, 370, 439, 457, 476, 490, 494, 521
467 Sqn. 101, 153, 212, 258, 331, 338, 344, 371, 399, 463, 475, 511, 512, 538-9
487 (RNZAF) Sqn. 10
515 Sqn. 541, 543
605 Sqn. 541, 542, 543
609 Sqn. 541
617 Sqn. 310, 312, 313, 314
619 Sqn. 360, 371, 394, 405, 426, 475
620 Sqn. 437, 448, 500
1658 HCU. 215
1663 HCU. 465

Royal Air Force Airfields
Bardney. 13
Binbrook. 15, 478
Bircham Newton. 372
Bottesford. 12, 15, 463, 512
Bourn. 11, 13, 19
Breighton. 10, 13, 15
Burn. 11, 14
Carnaby, 46
Chedburgh. 11, 14, 15, 133, 139, 140, 281, 298
Church Fenton. 409
Coltishall. 149, 409
Coningsby. 140
Cranwell. 320
Croft. 12, 14, 243
Dalton, 12, 14, 373
Dishforth. 12, 14, 82, 104, 156, 242
Docking. 258
Downham Market. 11, 14
Driffield. 287
Dunholm Lodge. 13
East Moor. 11, 14, 59
East Wretham. 11, 13, 105
Elsham Wolds, 10, 13, 399
Elvington. 11, 280, 400, 431
Feltwell. 10
Fiskerton. 12, 13
Ford. 204
Foulsham. 10
Gransden Lodge. 11, 14, 19, 478, 523
Graveley, 12, 13, 18, 269, 373
Great Massingham. 10
Grimsby (Waltham). 10, 13
Hemswell. 10, 14
Holme on Spalding Moor. 10, 13, 269, 402, 498
Ingham. 10, 14
Kirmington. 10, 14, 214
Lakenheath. 11, 14
Langar. 12, 14
Leconfield. 11, 14, 15, 280, 356
Leeming. 12, 14, 515
Leuchars. 233
Linton upon Ouse. 11, 13, 14, 85, 172, 175, 290
Lissett. 14, 148, 155, 215, 379, 383, 462, 513
Ludford Magna. 13
Manston. 46, 279, 448
Marham. 10, 13, 14, 19
Martlesham Heath. 320, 330, 408
Melbourne. 11, 13
Mepal. 13
Methwold. 10
Middleton St George. 12, 14, 171, 243, 330
Middle Wallop. 524
Mildenhall. 242
Mildenhall. 13, 242
Newmarket. 11, 13, 287, 347, 355
Oakington. 12, 13, 18
Oulton. 10
Pershore. 334
Pocklington. 11, 13, 133, 140, 280
Redhill. 87
Riccall. 215
Ridgewell. 11, 13
Rufforth. 11
Scampton. 12, 13, 15, 18, 116, 299
Skellingthorpe. 12, 13, 348, 466
Skipton on Swale. 15

Miscellaneous Personnel

Other titles from
Air Research Publications

The Whitley Boys
4 Group bomber operations 1939-1940.
A graffic and detailed account of offensive operations in the first year of WWII as experienced by a Whitley gunner. Includes detailed descriptions of raids and complete loss / casualty list.
224 pages ISBN 1 871187 11 7 Price £11.95

Blitzed! The Battle of France May-June 1940
The struggle to halt the German invasion of Europe. Includes RAF and Luftwaffe loss listings.
256 pages ISBN 1 871187 07 9 Price £15.95

Battle over the Third Reich
A photogragraphic account of the battle for air supremacy over Germany as seen by the Luftwaffe.
184 pages ISBN 1 871187 10 9 Price £17.95

Intruders over Britain
The most detailed history of the German night intruder offensive ever published. Includes extensive appendices of Luftwaffe and Allied aircraft / crew losses.
208 pages ISBN 1 871187 16 8 Price £11.95

Spitfire Squadron
No. 19 Squadron at war 1939-1941
Including a reprint of the classic book 'Spitfire!'
192 pages ISBN 1 871187 09 5 Price £14.95

It's Dicey Flying Wimpys (Around Italian Skies)
No. 205 Group operations 1944-1945
A gripping account of one of the little known aspects of the air war written by a Wimpy pilot.
224 pages ISBN 1 871187 15 X Price £14.95